Die nuclei waren fuer den Krieg	They
Und fuer den allgemeinen Sieg.	And t.
Und fragt man, wer ist Schuld daran,	*(refrain)*
So ist die Antwort: Otto Hahn.	

Wie ist das moeglich, fragt man sich,
The story seems wunderlich.
Und fragt man, wer ist Schuld daran
So ist die Antwort: Otto Hahn.

You ask, how's it possible;
The story seems wonderful.
(refrain)

Die Feldherrn, Staatschefs, Zeitungsknaben,
Ihn everyday im Munde haben.
Und fragt man, wer ist Schuld daran,
So ist die Antwort: Otto Hahn.

For generals, statesmen journalists,
Every day he's on their lips.
(refrain)

Even the sweethearts in the world (s)
Sie nennen sich jetzt: "Atom-girls."
Und fragt man, wer ist Schuld daran,
So ist die Antwort: Otto Hahn.

Even the sweethearts in the world(s)
Call themselves the atom girls.
(refrain)

Verliert man jetzt so seine Wetten,
So heisst's you didn't split the atom.
Und fragt man, wer ist Schuld daran,
So ist die Antwort: Otto Hahn.

Lagging when the race is run
Means you didn't split the atom.
(refrain)

Ein jeder weiss, das Unglueck kam
Infolge splitting von Uran,
Und fragt man, wer ist Schuld daran,
So ist die Antwort: Otto Hahn.

Oh, what misery has come
From splitting of uranium.
(refrain)

Die energy macht alles waermer.
Only die Schweden werden aermer.
Und fragt man, wer ist Schuld daran,
So ist die Antwort: Otto Hahn.

The energy removes the cold;
Only the Swedes have lost some gold.
(refrain)

Auf akademisches Geheiss
Kriegt Deutschland einen Nobel-Preis.
Und fragt man, wer ist Schuld daran,
So ist die Antwort: Otto Hahn.

The Academy's order is precise;
A German wins the Nobel Prize.
(refrain)

In Oxford Street, da lebt ein Wesen,
Die wird das heut' mit Thraenen lesen.
Und fragt man, wer ist Schuld daran,
So ist die Antwort: Otto Hahn.

In Oxford Steet someone resides
Reading now with tearful eyes.
(refrain)

Es fehlte damals nur ein atom,
Haett er gesagt: I marry you madam.
Und fragt man, wer ist Schuld daran,
So ist die Antwort: Otto Hahn.

Lacked a single, tiny atom
For him to say: I marry you madam.
(refrain)

Dies ist nur unsre-erste Feier,	We've begun to celebrate:
Ich glaub die Sache wird noch teuer,	Things will yet accelerate.
Und fragt man, wer ist Schuld daran,	*(refrain)*
So ist die Antwort: Otto Hahn.	
Und kommen wir aus diesem Bau,	We'll leave here sometime, somehow;
We hope, we'll be quite lucky now.	We hope, we'll be quite lucky now.
Und fragt man, wer ist Schuld daran,	If you ask who bears the blame,
Stets ist die Antwort: Otto Hahn.	Otto Hahn's the culprit's name.

Taken from a letter written by Werner Heisenberg to the British physicist Patrick M. S. Blackett from Farm Hall; dated September 18, 1945:[3]

> ...From the spring of 1941 onwards, I was practically in charge [of the nuclear energy project] and later also officially. Since that time, the bulk of our work was done on uranium and on nuclear physics in general (high tension apparatus), besides that, work was done on cosmic rays, as you will know from our book, and also work in the various departments (x-ray laboratory, low temperature laboratory and optics) was continued on a reduced scale. As the first aim of our scientific work we had intended to build a "Brenner" [reactor] with D_2O [deuterium oxide], graphite and uranium metal. This "burner" was to be a strong source of neutrons. In war-time, naturally, these results would have been followed by technical developments which would have aimed at a practical use of the energy. We had, however, hoped that the "burner" could in peace-time be used in the preparation of powerful radioactive substances for chemical research at Hahn's institute and also perhaps for experiments at my institute with neutron-beams of great intensity...

The following is from Farm Hall Report 4:

> **WEIZSÄCKER:** In our case even the scientists said it couldn't be done.
>
> **BAGGE:** That's not true. You were there yourself at that conference in Berlin. I think it was on 8 September that everyone was asked—Geiger, Bothe and you Harteck were there too—and everyone said it must be done at once. Someone said, "Of course it is an open question whether one ought to do a thing like that." Thereupon Bothe got up and said, "Gentlemen, it <u>must</u> be done." Then Geiger got up and said, "If there is the slightest chance that it is possible—it must be done." That was on 8 September '39.

---

[3] The letter is from the Farm Hall transcripts, Report 8.

HITLER'S URANIUM CLUB

THE SECRET RECORDINGS AT FARM HALL

HITLER'S URANIUM CLUB

THE SECRET RECORDINGS AT FARM HALL

Jeremy Bernstein

Aspen Center for Physics
Aspen, Colorado

Introduction by David Cassidy

American Institute of Physics   **Woodbury, New York**

Acknowledgments

Extracts from Erich Bagge's diary are from *Von der Uranspaltung bis Calder Hall* by Erich Bagge, Kurt Diebner, and Kenneth Jay, published in the series "Rowohlts Deutsche Enzyklopädie." Copyright © 1957 by Rowohlt Taschenbuch Verlag GmbH, Hamburg. Reprinted with permission.

Letters from Max von Laue to Paul Rosbaud reprinted with the permission of Theodore H. Von Laue.

Extract from poem from Walther Gerlach to his wife is from *Walther Gerlach–Physiker–Lehrer–Organisator*, page 122, Deutsches Museum, 1989. Reprinted with permission.

AIP Press
American Institute of Physics
500 Sunnyside Boulevard
Woodbury, NY 11797-2999

Library of Congress Cataloging-in-Publication Data
Berstein, Jeremy, 1929–
   Hitler's uranium club : the secret recordings at Farm Hall / by
Jeremy Bernstein : with introduction by David Cassidy.
      p. cm.
   Includes bibliographical references and index.
   ISBN 1-56396-258-6
   1. Atomic bomb--Germany--History. 2. Nuclear weapons--
Germany--History. 3. Scientists--Germany--Correspondence. I. Title.
QC773.3.G3B47 1995   95-609
355.8'25119'092243--dc20   CIP
[B]

10   9   8   7   6   5   4   3   2   1

CONTENTS

PREFACE

In practical terms, the Germans came nowhere near manufacturing an actual nuclear weapon during World War II. That being the case, why should the circumstances surrounding this non-event still arouse such passionate debate? I think that there are two reasons. On the one hand, many of the people who were involved in the successful development of the Allied nuclear weapons had serious moral misgivings, especially once they saw what the use of the weapon meant in terms of human misery. A sense of how these people felt was expressed by the Harvard nuclear physicist Kenneth Bainbridge, who immediately after the first successful test at Trinity, said to Oppenheimer, "Now we are all sons of bitches."[1] I mention these misgivings to show just how sensitive a subject this is for the people involved in the Allied program, a large number of whom are still alive and very articulate.

On the other hand—and this is where the debate begins—there is the version of this history promulgated by the German nuclear scientists after the war, some of whom are also still alive and also very articulate. Their version is built on the proposition that, unlike their American counterparts who actually constructed this "immoral" weapon, they, the Germans, took the moral high ground and "prevented" this weapon from falling into the hands of Hitler. In other words, they deliberately and consciously withheld their knowledge and expertise for the sake of some higher ethical purpose. If this were true, then these scientists, all of whom collaborated with the regime—some were members of the Nazi Party and some were not— could salvage something of their moral stature that had been irreparably tarnished by this collaboration. They could claim that they functioned morally in an immoral regime, while their Allied counterparts did just the opposite. It is this mixture of emotions—Allied and German—with their respective feelings of misgivings and guilt that is so combustible.

It is not suprising, then, that just about every decade since the war has produced a book that deals in one way or another, usually contradictory, with all of this. The first major work was Samuel Goudsmit's *Alsos*, published in 1947, which was by the physicist who had been in charge of collecting Allied intelligence on the German program during the war. Goudsmit attributed the failure of the German nuclear program to "certain failures on the part of German scientific organization, [and] certain stupidities on the part of German scientists and their government."[2] But

---

[1] "Now we are..." Bainbridge, who was the physics department chairman when I was a graduate student and a post-doctoral at Harvard, told me this story himself.

[2] The exact references to these books along with some commentary is given in the notes to the next section. The Goudsmit quote is from *Alsos*, p. 232.

two years later, the Swiss journalist Robert Jungk published the English edition of his best-selling book *Brighter Than a Thousand Suns*, which spelled out the claims of the German scientists in detail and thereby attempted to discredit Goudsmit. In 1968, British journalist David Irving, using newly available German documents, wrote a book entitled *The German Atomic Bomb*, which demonstrated, contrary to the German version that, at least for a time during the war, the Germans had seriously tried to work on nuclear weapons. Of the several more recent studies, in 1989 historian Mark Walker produced a book entitled *German National Socialism and the Quest for Nuclear Power*, which, using even a wider range of documents, argued that while the Germans after 1942 were not specifically trying to build a bomb, they were consciously developing bomb technology. In 1993 American journalist Thomas Powers wrote a book entitled *Heisenberg's War* in which he attempted to argue the case that Heisenberg actually sabotaged the embryonic German nuclear weapons program, implying that he, Heisenberg, had a deep and serious knowledge of how to build a bomb that he deliberately withheld from everyone.

At first sight, when confronted with such a maze of contradictory assertions and emotions, one might naively think that the way through would be to interview all the principals involved to see if one could not come to a consensus. As anyone who has tried to do this sort of thing soon discovers, however, memory often obscures fact instead of unveiling it. The German scientists involved have told the same story over and over again for so many years that one wonders if they themselves now know what part of it is literally true and what part is invention. What is needed in situations like this are the contemporary documents—what people really said and wrote at the time—and not some post-facto, often self-serving, reconstruction. Ideal would be a recording, or a transcript of a recording, that would bring such conversations back to life.

As explained in the Introduction by David Cassidy, it has been known since 1947 that some such documents must exist. But it was only recently after much campaigning by historians that the Farm Hall transcripts were declassified.[3]

When I first saw these transcripts soon after their release in February of 1992, I had something of the feeling that Champollion must have felt in August of 1808 when he saw a newly produced copy of the Rosetta stone—the key to the decipherment of the Egyptian hieroglyphics. Like Champollion with his knowledge of languages, I felt that if one knew enough about the subject matter, then by

---

[3] An authoritative description of the actual monitoring process can be found in Sir Charles Frank's introduction to the British Institute of Physics publication of the transcripts under the title *Operation Epsilon: The Farm Hall Transcripts*, Institute of Physics Publishing, Bristol and Philadelphia, 1993. This version of the reports is intended for readers who have a considerable technical background (since there are no notes or editorial commment), as is Sir Charles's introduction.

reading both the lines in the transcripts and what was between the lines, one could hope to reach into both the Germans' state of mind and their state of knowledge as it was in 1945. What seemed to be needed here—the equivalent of the Sanskrit, Arabic and Persian Champollion needed to decipher the hieroglyphics—was a certain familiarity with the physics of nuclear weapons. Although I was too young to have been at Los Alamos, I did get into physics in the late 1940s when nuclear weapons loomed very large. When I received my Ph.D. in 1955, jobs in universities were scarce, and I thought seriously of employment at one of the weapons laboratories. To this end, I spent the summer of 1957 as an intern at Los Alamos where I was exposed to some nuclear weapons technology and witnessed some actual testing in the Nevada desert. For the next two years or so I consulted at the Rand Corporation and at the General Atomic Company on problems that had a nuclear weapons component. Furthermore, most of my teachers, people like Bainbridge, Robert Marshak, Norman Ramsey, Victor Weisskopf and, later, people like Hans Bethe, I. I. Rabi, Robert Oppenheimer, Robert Wilson, Stanislaw Ulam and Robert Serber had been at Los Alamos. I talked to them extensively about their experiences and when I went to work at the Brookhaven National Laboratory I talked to Goudsmit on an almost daily basis. Indeed, when I started writing about science for the general public, a substantial part of what I wrote—profiles of people like Einstein, I. I. Rabi, John Wheeler, and Hans Bethe—reflected this experience. *Toute proportion garde*, just as Champollion, young as he was, felt that a lifetime of immersion in the relevant background made his decipherment of the Rosetta stone possible, I felt a lifetime of at least partial immersion in what I would call, for lack of a better term, the "culture" of nuclear weapons, had prepared me to read the Farm Hall reports.

As I read them, it became clear to me that they constitute a dramatic encounter analogous to a stage play, a documentary would be a better description, if only one understood enough of the technical material and historical background to make the content comprehensible. I tried my hand at a commentary on a part of the reports for *The New York Review of Books*,[4] enough to convince me that they could be understood by a larger audience if guided by some technical and historical comments. That is what this book is. I have gone through the entire group of archival reports, annotating it and explaining the physics and the historical context where necessary so that as much of it will be understandable to as many readers as possible.

In the transcripts of their conversations one finds the Germans' raw, unreconsidered reaction to Hiroshima and one sees that after the shock has worn off they begin to construct the *Lesart*[5]—the version of their own history that they were to repeat for the next several decades, and are still repeating.

---

[4] *The New York Review of Books*, August 13, 1992, p. 47.

[5] The term "Lesart," used in this context, was introduced by Max von Laue. There will be much more about this later.

One also relives the almost surreal series of events surrounding the award, while still in detention, of the Nobel Prize for Chemistry to Otto Hahn for the discovery of nuclear fission a few months after Hiroshima. It becomes painfully clear that Hahn, Heisenberg and the rest of the leading nuclear scientists knew very little about the physics of nuclear weapons and most of what they finally did understand they figured out at Farm Hall, after Hiroshima.

It is also clear from these reports that, in the beginning, by no means had they tried to avoid working on a bomb, nor had they thought it impossible to make one. Of the moral issues next to nothing is said, at least in these transcripts.

We get to know the detainees as individuals. None comes across as overtly evil. We are not overhearing here six months of conversation among Party functionaries. These are cultivated people and, indeed, men of exceptional ability including several Nobel Prize winners and in the case of one of them, Max von Laue, a courageous anti-Nazi. That is what makes the behavior of most of them so difficult to understand. What motivated them? Why did the ones who had the choice of leaving Germany choose not to leave and to serve such a vile and grotesque regime? While the transcripts may provide no final answers, as the reader will discover, there is much they do reveal.

To appreciate what one is reading I have made annotations, some of them fairly extensive, that I hope will help the reader. I have placed these annotations in the proximity of the material that they refer to rather than putting them into the introductory essay so that the reader will have them at hand. I have also modified some of the equations in the transcripts cosmetically. Nothing has been left out. I have chosen to use the American-held set of the reports, since it turns out that it is somewhat more complete than the British version. However, I have corrected some spelling mistakes in the names. Certain names are spelled in the original reports in several different ways. I have given one consistent, correct spelling for these names. Clearly the original transcripts were prepared in some haste so that they would be available on a timely basis. In addition, for some reason, some of the proper names have been given entirely in capital letters in the original. There does not seem to be any purpose in maintaining this style here, especially since it is distracting. The reader will also find two versions of Heisenberg's fascinating technical lecture of the 14th of August 1945. This is the lecture in which he reveals his limited knowledge of the physics of nuclear weapons. In the English version of this lecture I have cleaned up some of the notation, while in the German version, which is also given, I leave the notation as it was in the original. The idea is to make this material available to as wide a readership as possible.

I owe a debt to many people. Some of these debts have been acknowledged in the notes. Here I would like to thank Gerald Holton for his support and helpful criticism, and Arnold Kramish for supplying the American set of the reports and the two very important letters from von Laue to Rosbaud to be discussed. Elihu Abrahams, Lowell Brown, and Robert Serber made very valuable suggestions as did Mark Walker. David Cassidy's help has been invaluable both as a source for historical material and as a friendly critic. This is a much better book than it would have been without him. I would also like to thank Maria Taylor of the American Institute of Physics and Bill Sweet who expertly edited the final version, and Cynthia Blaut and Lisa Rutley for their efforts in the production of the book.

Jeremy Bernstein

INTRODUCTION

David Cassidy

This book contains new insights into one of the unanswered questions of recent world history. Why, with their head start in not only research in nuclear fission but in other technological feats, didn't the Germans succeed in building a nuclear bomb during World War II? Now, 50 years later, this book brings to the public, for the first time, expertly annotated transcripts of recently declassified intelligence reports from that time. These reports contain verbatim conversations among ten German atomic scientists before, during, and after the atomic bombing of Japan in August 1945. In terror of the consequences should German scientists succeed in constructing an atomic bomb and with Hitler promising the use of a new "superweapon," Allied scientists had worked feverishly to build the atomic bomb as quickly as possible. These secret reports from Farm Hall, the English country manor that housed the captured German scientists, now offer the world a unique insight into the mindset of the scientists on the other side, both before and after Hiroshima, and as they struggled to come to terms with their wartime work and to prepare for the postwar nuclear era in Germany.

During the waning weeks of World War II in Europe, as Allied armies swept across a chaotic Germany in defeat, two teams of the world's leading nuclear scientists strove to complete their work. One team, sequestered at Los Alamos in the New Mexico desert, hastened to assemble the first of three atomic bombs, two of which would startle the world that summer with the destruction of two Japanese cities. The other team, a group of German scientists and technicians that had recently fled the Allied bombing of Berlin for southern Germany, worked day and night to build what, unbeknownst to them, the Allies had managed to build more than two years earlier—a critical, self-sustaining nuclear reactor.

As they impatiently assembled what would be their last attempt at a reactor, the German scientists slowly realized that it would fail. If only a little more uranium and heavy water could be found, the reactor would surely become critical. Alas, it was too late. Within hours after French troops swept through the area at the end of April 1945, the Alsos Mission, a secret American science intelligence unit, halted the German nuclear effort and captured many of the German nuclear scientists, along with most of their equipment and technical papers. By VE Day, May 8, the Alsos Mission had confirmed the nonexistence of a German atom bomb and had singled out ten of the German scientists for extended internment under American and British control. After the scientists had languished at several locations in France and Belgium, on July 3, 1945 British authorities flew the ten scientists to England where they were held incommunicado for exactly six months at Farm Hall near Cambridge.

A little over a month after the scientists had settled into the comforts of Farm Hall, the news of Hiroshima astounded the German scientists, as it did the rest of the world. Believing themselves far ahead of the Allies in nuclear research, the German scientists suddenly realized that they were in fact far behind. How had the Allies done it? Why had they themselves made such little progress in comparison? How could they explain this to themselves, to their countrymen, to their former enemies?

"Where I really would like to have been, that night a stunned world first learned of the atom bomb," wrote Samuel A. Goudsmit, the scientific head of the Alsos Mission in his book *Alsos*, "was in England among the interned German physicists."[1] Fortunately British Intelligence provided him and us, if not the opportunity to be there, nearly the next best thing: their reports containing lengthy transcriptions of, and reports on, the scientists' conversations during their six-month stay at Farm Hall, including many of the conversations that occurred that night of August 6, 1945 and during the days and weeks thereafter. These reports constitute the core of this book.

The Farm Hall Reports

Farm Hall had long been used as a "safe house" by British foreign Intelligence, MI6. Before the German scientists arrived, physicist R. V. Jones, a leading figure in British scientific intelligence, had the rooms (and possibly the grounds) outfitted with hidden microphones. A team of bilingual British military personnel monitored all of the scientists' conversations and recorded those that appeared of intelligence value in the state-of-the-art medium of the day: reusable shellacked metal disks. From their selection of what to save, we can see that the eavesdroppers were primarily interested not in posterity, but in such immediate matters as morale, political orientation, loyalty to the western Allies and, after Hiroshima, the extent of German knowledge of nuclear fission.

The British agents transcribed only those recorded conversations that proved of special intelligence value and translated them into English. These conversations were then summarized and excerpted from the English in weekly or biweekly reports compiled and signed by the British officer in charge at Farm Hall, Major T. H. Rittner and, after Rittner fell ill, by his second-in-command, Captain P.L.C. Brodie. In some important instances, however, the reports contained transcriptions of the original German as appendixes. Rittner or Brodie forwarded several copies of the typed, top-secret reports from Farm Hall to the persons in charge of the operation, Michael Perrin, an official of the British atomic bomb program, and Lieutenant Commander Eric Welsh, a British naval intelligence officer in London. Copy number 1 went to the American consulate in London and from there it went directly to the

---

[1] Goudsmit, *Alsos*, p. 132.

head of the Manhattan Project in Washington, D.C., Major General Leslie R. Groves. Groves carefully studied each report, adding an occasional marginal line or comment.

Goudsmit excerpted several quotations from the Farm Hall transcriptions in his 1947 account of the Alsos Mission, the book *Alsos*, but for security reasons he was not permitted to reveal their source. The existence of these reports remained a secret until 1962, when Groves referred to them in his appropriately named memoir, *Now It Can Be Told,* in which he provided a number of further quotations. Since then historians, scientists and many others have clamored for the American and British governments to release the full reports. However, all of their requests met with stubborn refusal—in recent years apparently in part because of the complicated bureaucratic provenance of the reports and in part because of the objections of surviving former Farm Hall detainees.

Finally, after a concerted effort by leading scientists and historians of the Royal Society and the British Academy at the end of 1991, Lord Mackay announced in February 1992 the release of the British copies of the Farm Hall reports to the public.[2] Moved by the British action, ten days later the National Archives and Records Administration in Washington, D.C., declassified Groves's copies of the reports.[3] A completely unedited publication of the British version of the reports appeared as *Operation Epsilon: The Farm Hall Transcripts.*[4] The current edition, thoroughly edited and annotated by Jeremy Bernstein, is based upon the copy of the reports in American hands, which sometimes differ slightly in both wording and extent (as noted in the text) from their British counterparts.

It is important to keep in mind what these reports are and are not. These are *not* the complete original conversations of the German scientists during their six months of captivity at Farm Hall. One of the language technicians in the Farm Hall recording team later estimated that perhaps only 10% of the conversations finally found their way into these reports.[5] In several instances the German original (with some typographical errors) is also available, and a comparison with the English indicates that the translations, though rough in spots, were actually quite well done. Some of the conversations, such as those with British visitors, were originally in English. Except where the original German was included in the reports, the German transcriptions are not available in the British or American files and are apparently lost. The original recordings were re-shellacked at Farm Hall and the disks reused.

---

[2] Facsimile of letter in Charles Frank, *Operation Epsilon*, p. 16. The British copy of the reports is now available at the Public Record Office, Kew, Class WP 208, Piece Number 5019.

[3] The American copy of the reports is now held at the National Archives II, College Park, Maryland, in Record Group 77, Manhattan Engineer District.

[4] Institute of Physics, Bristol, UK, 1993; U.S. distribution through University of California Press, Los Angeles.

[5] Frank, *Operation Epsilon*, p. 12.

Despite such shortcomings, these reports are still of major historical significance. There are few, if any, other instances in recorded history where we have the conversations of leading figures as they complete one era, come to terms with it and prepare their strategy for the next. It is as though these men were lifted out of history at a crucial turning point—from the age of conventional weapons to the post-world-war nuclear era—placed within a timeless container and told to discuss their past and future as the recorders roll. Because of this we gain unequaled insights into the personalities of these scientists, into their knowledge of fission physics, into how they viewed themselves and their work, into how they came to terms with their past in Nazi Germany, both for themselves individually and for public consumption, and into how they prepared to influence the course of science in a future Germany. At the same time, these transcriptions and commentaries provide us with new information and perspectives regarding many of the heated controversies that have long surrounded the motives and aims, rationales and failures of German wartime research on the utilization of the awesome power unleashed by nuclear fission.

It should also be noted that these documents do not stand alone. Most of the scientists' top-secret reports to the German authorities on their fission research were captured in 1945 and long since declassified. A number were published in Heisenberg's *Collected Works*, and most, along with a treasure trove of other previously unpublished documents, are available on microfilm.[6] These further documents greatly facilitate comparison of the scientists' statements at Farm Hall with their actual wartime work. In addition, during the Farm Hall period, one of the detainees (Erich Bagge) maintained a diary that he later published and which is excerpted in the Coda to this book.[7] While held at Farm Hall, Max von Laue wrote extensive letters to his son at Princeton University on his impressions of events there,[8] and later he wrote of Farm Hall to Paul Rosbaud, two of these letters appearing in Appendix 2. Several other scientists wrote of their experiences soon after their release, and some began presenting their version of German war research. These can be compared with the wartime documents and the Farm Hall discussions. Some such comparisons are made here and in Jeremy Bernstein's commentaries accompanying the edited text, but others are left for interested readers.

The Detainees

By war's end the German nuclear effort employed hundreds of scientists, engineers, technicians, craftsmen and students. The main research group, located

---

[6] See Irving, *Third Reich Documents*.

[7] Erich Bagge, Kurt Diebner, and Kenneth Jay, *Von der Uranspaltung bis Calder Hall* (Rowohlt, Hamburg, 1957).

[8] *Nachlass* Max von Laue, *Handschriftenabteilung*, Deutsches Museum, Munich, 1976–20.

at the Kaiser-Wilhelm Institute for Physics in Berlin, alone employed 55 persons, of whom 19 were professional scientists and engineers.

As the Alsos Mission rolled into southern Germany, numerous German nuclear documents and researchers fell into Allied hands. Documents were brought to Alsos Headquarters in Heidelberg for study, where Samuel Goudsmit also personally interrogated most of the nuclear scientists. Goudsmit faced the difficult task of deciding who among them could be left safely at large in Germany and who should be held in military custody. Some of the ten he included were well-known scientists; others were not. This was a point of complaint for at least one status-conscious theoretician among them. "What kind of a selection is this?" he reportedly objected.[9] Several of those whom one might expect to have been included, because of their central roles in the fission project, were not detained.

One factor that Goudsmit evidently considered was the scientists' ability to continue forbidden fission research. As indicated by the comments and markings on his copy of the Farm Hall reports, Groves apparently regarded the detention of the German scientists as a means of keeping them out of Soviet and French hands. Groves seemed especially interested in talk among the German scientists about defecting to the Soviets or about returning to their main research institute, by then in the French zone of occupation.

As Goudsmit makes clear in *Alsos,* the principal factor in deciding to hold Max von Laue and Otto Hahn, who had not played significant roles in the wartime fission project, was his desire that these senior men should have an influence on the reconstruction of the scientific establishment in postwar Germany.[10] Von Laue, a highly respected physicist who had won the Nobel Prize in 1914, had courageously opposed the Nazi regime and had not engaged in any war-related research. Goudsmit included him in the Farm Hall group for those very reasons. His reports to Washington included strong recommendations (which went largely unheeded) that von Laue and Hahn, the co-discoverer of nuclear fission, be consulted during planning for the postwar treatment of German science. With no way of knowing this, von Laue repeatedly expressed bafflement about his detention at Farm Hall.

The ten scientists interned by the Alsos Mission were first taken to France, then transferred to Belgium, and finally brought to Farm Hall on July 3rd, 1945. Besides Hahn and von Laue, the group included Erich Bagge, who had worked on isotope separation; Kurt Diebner, a leader of nuclear research in the German Army Weapons Bureau; Walther Gerlach, a distinguished physicist and chief administrator of nuclear research from 1944 to 1945; Paul Harteck, a Hamburg professor and very effective member of the German nuclear program who had worked mainly on heavy water and reactor design; Werner Heisenberg, the most prestigious member

---

[9]*Alsos*, p. 104.

[10]*Ibid.*, pp. 101, 104–106.

of the nuclear program and the most influential scientist in it; Horst Korsching, who had worked on isotope separation under Diebner and Heisenberg; Carl Friedrich von Weizsäcker, an outstanding young physicist and protégé of Heisenberg, whose father had been the number-two man in Hitler's foreign ministry; and Karl Wirtz, an expert on heavy water and isotope separation. (See Appendix 4 for further details on the detainees.)

Missing from among the likely candidates for detention at Farm Hall were Walther Bothe, who had performed important moderator research and attempted to construct an accelerator in Heidelberg; Fritz Bopp, who worked on reactor theories at the Kaiser-Wilhelm Institute for Physics and was captured by the French; Manfred von Ardenne, who directed a reactor construction project in—of all places—the research bureau of the Reich Post Office and was captured by the Soviets; and Wilhelm Groth, who worked closely with Harteck.

The backgrounds of the ten scientists detained at Farm Hall hint at some of the alliances and conflicts that can be seen in the Farm Hall documents. The most obvious conflict is that between the Heisenberg and Diebner groups; but others occurred between members and nonmembers of the Nazi Party, along the lines of age and status, and along nationalistic lines. Max von Laue recalled some of these factional conflicts in one of his letters to Paul Rosbaud in 1959, which is published in an Appendix to this book.

German War Time Nuclear Research: A Short Synopsis

The discovery of nuclear fission occurred in Germany during the year immediately preceding the outbreak of World War II. Because of this coincidence, scientists on both sides of the coming war felt called upon to inform their respective governments of the military potential of nuclear energy. Like their Allied counterparts, German scientists immediately alerted government agencies, and when Hitler attacked Poland in September 1939 Germany was the only nation to have a military research effort already in place.

The Organization of German Research

An important alert to German officials was a letter dated April 24, 1939, in which Hamburg professors Harteck and Groth informed Erich Schumann, the head of weapons research in the German Army Weapons Bureau (*Heereswaffenamt*), of the possibility of a powerful new explosive. A skeptical Schumann handed the matter to his Army expert for nuclear physics and explosives, Kurt Diebner, who immediately established a military research effort. Diebner drafted Bagge to the cause.

With the outbreak of war in September 1939, Diebner and Bagge issued military orders to Germany's leading nuclear scientists to attend research planning sessions in Berlin. Among those in attendance were most of the later Farm Hall detainees. The assembled scientists, who called themselves the Uranium Club (*Uranverein*), concluded that much more research was required to determine the practical feasibility of nuclear weapons and reactor development. The club members scattered to their institutes with specific research tasks assigned by Diebner and Bagge under the authority of the Army's Weapons Bureau.

As the scientists headed for their labs, the Weapons Bureau took control of the government-sponsored Kaiser-Wilhelm Institute for Physics in the Berlin suburb of Dahlem, ousting its Dutch-born director, Peter Debye, who soon left for the United States. The Army established its main reactor research project at the institute. At the same time, Germany's leading nuclear theorist, Heisenberg, who had joined the Uranium Club soon after the outbreak of war, leapt to the challenge of nuclear fission. Aided in part by the publication by Bohr and Wheeler of their theory of nuclear fission, within three months Heisenberg produced the first of two secret comprehensive technical reports to the Army Weapons Bureau outlining the prospects and methods for the practical exploitation of fission. The conclusion of his first report, dated 6 December 1939, stated that a controlled fission reactor was technically feasible and that uranium vastly enriched in the rare isotope ^{235}U would constitute a powerful new explosive, "which surpasses the explosive power of the strongest explosive materials by several orders of magnitude."[11] These survey reports established Heisenberg as Germany's leading authority on nuclear fission, and his reports became the fundamental blueprint for German research throughout the war.

Heisenberg concentrated in his theoretically based surveys on the first step toward the utilization of nuclear energy, the construction of a working reactor. Hindered by only very preliminary data on nuclear constants, Heisenberg examined the use of different moderators with different amounts of natural uranium in two geometrical reactor arrangements, spherical and cylindrical configurations of uranium and moderator arranged in alternating layers. He predicted that graphite and "heavy water" (water in which the hydrogen atoms possess an extra neutron in the nucleus) would prove the best materials to slow the neutrons so that they could fission a ^{235}U nucleus rather than being captured by the more plentiful ^{238}U. In order to prevent the neutrons from escaping, Heisenberg estimated that the reactor should be about one cubic meter in volume and filled with large amounts of the extremely rare materials. He predicted that a chain reaction would occur in a layer configuration with at least 600 liters of encapsulated heavy water, alternating with one metric ton of graphite, and two to three metric tons of pure uranium oxide. But nowhere near these amounts were available at that time in Germany or its captured territories.

By enriching the ^{235}U content of natural uranium through isotope separation, Heisenberg also predicted that a smaller reactor could be built to run at a higher

---

[11] Heisenberg, "Die Möglichkeit der technischen Energiegewinnung aus der Uranspaltung," in *Heisenberg: Collected Works*, Vol. **A2**, p. 396. Dated 6 December 1939.

temperature. This, he later suggested, could be used to drive German ships and submarines around the world. If one could obtain enough nearly pure ^{235}U—he did not say how much—and compressed it into a ball, the effect of the chain reaction would be nearly instantaneous, producing an incredibly powerful explosion. In urging the Army to support isotope separation, Heisenberg pointed out that separation was the "surest method" to obtain a working reactor, and, most importantly, it was "the only method for producing explosives."[12]

Heisenberg's reports had set the German effort in the right direction, but he also made several important technical errors that ultimately hindered any progress. These he apparently fully realized only years later at Farm Hall, after hearing of the first atomic bombs. The first set of errors concerned what happened after the reactor went critical and how an explosive reaction occurs. This led Heisenberg to misunderstand the nature of a controlled reaction and to miscalculate the needed critical mass for an uncontrolled explosion. A further error concerned the use of graphite as a moderator.

As he would do later at Farm Hall, late in 1939 Heisenberg solved the diffusion equation for fission neutrons moving through a mixture of natural uranium and heavy water, but he reached the false conclusion that such a reactor would stabilize itself at an equilibrium temperature due to the absorption of fission neutrons by the abundant uranium isotope ^{238}U. He did not realize that with larger amounts of material a much higher absorption rate is required through the presence of a "control substance"; otherwise the chain reaction would increase without stopping, leading to a messy meltdown. If the reactor is fueled by uranium enriched in the rare, fissionable isotope ^{235}U, he believed that the reactor would stabilize at ever higher temperatures as the enrichment increased, until finally, if sufficient enriched uranium is present, a critical reactor radius is reached, above which the reaction would no longer stabilize itself but would increase instantaneously. In other words, wrote Heisenberg in 1939, "the entire radiation energy of all available uranium atoms would be set free all at once."[13] This critical radius would result in a critical mass of several tons for an exploding reactor, a figure that is cited at Farm Hall but which is far off from the actual critical mass of pure ^{235}U alone of about 50 kilograms. As these early errors indicate, Heisenberg had completely misunderstood the more subtle aspects of reactor and bomb physics. There is no clear indication in his research reports that he substantially revised these preliminary notions about reactor behavior. Only in the wake of Hiroshima does he state explicitly at Farm Hall that a slow-neutron reaction will not explode.

The graphite error was more immediately devastating to the project. Again using very imprecise data, Heisenberg predicted in his second report (dated 29 February 1940) that graphite, a form of carbon, would not serve as an adequate

---

[12] *Ibid.*

[13] *Ibid.*, p. 389.

moderator after all. Calculations by von Weizsäcker's assistants at the Kaiser-Wilhelm Institute for Physics supported this prediction. Subsequent measurements by Bothe and co-workers in Heidelberg on neutron absorption in graphite seemed to confirm the result and supported the fateful decision to ignore readily available graphite as a moderator and to look instead solely to precious heavy water for use in a reactor. Bothe and the other German researchers had not realized that even the purest industrial graphite still contained sufficient impurities to render it useless as a moderator. If they had used truly purified graphite—as the Allied scientists knew was needed—they would have achieved a much different result, freeing the German project from its dependence upon heavy water and thereby accelerating progress to the extent that the project would mostly likely have attracted greater state support.

Research Accelerates

Until more sources of uranium and heavy water became available through the conquests of the German Army, the Uranium Club concentrated on confirming Heisenberg's predictions and obtaining precise measurements of the properties of the reactor materials. These were necessary steps preliminary to the attempt to construct a working reactor. Three technical problems required resolution: the scientists had to develop suitable methods of isotope separation in order to enrich the uranium for small reactors and a bomb; they had to discover, mainly by trial and error, the right geometry and size for a critical reactor using unenriched uranium; and their industrial suppliers had to develop new techniques for producing sufficient quantities of uranium metal powder and rolled sheets of uranium. Later, they would have to cut the unusually hard metal sheets into cubes for the researchers' subsequent reactor designs.

Of the nine task-oriented research groups coordinated by Diebner and the Weapons Bureau, two concentrated on reactor construction: the Kaiser-Wilhelm Institute for Physics under Diebner's direction in Berlin and the experimental physics section of Heisenberg's Leipzig University physics institute. (In addition, Harteck performed an early experiment in Hamburg using dry ice as a moderator, and the inventive Manfred von Ardenne worked independently on reactor design and isotope separation in the Post Office laboratories in Berlin-Lichterfelde.) Although the Army had replaced Debye with Diebner as head of the Kaiser-Wilhelm Institute for Physics, Debye's staff, among them Wirtz and von Weizsäcker, remained in place. Regarding Diebner as unworthy, they called upon their mentor Heisenberg as an outside advisor. Until July 1942, when Heisenberg finally replaced Diebner as head of institute research, Heisenberg divided his weeks evenly between Berlin and Leipzig, providing (for better or worse) the main impetus to both of Germany's main reactor projects.

With Heisenberg in charge, the Leipzig team enjoyed unlimited access to nearly all of Germany's supply of heavy water. The Berlin team had to satisfy itself with using paraffin as a test moderator until production from German-occupied Norway became available. While the Leipzig team used concentric spherical shells of uranium and heavy water for ease of calculation, the Berlin experiments involved horizontal layers packed into metal cylinders and spheres. The results were disappointing. Most of the experimental arrangements failed to display any neutron multiplication—except for Leipzig's last attempt, involving two concentric aluminum spheres filled with uranium powder and heavy water. This test experiment achieved Germany's first actual neutron multiplication due to fission sometime late in 1941—a modest but real increase of 13% measured at the outer wall. This was the world's first neutron multiplication. As the Allies feared, the German head start was indeed paying off. "The simple expansion of the layer arrangement described here would thus lead to a uranium burner," Heisenberg and the Leipzig team reported to the Weapons Bureau.[14] Nuclear fission was no longer just a scientifically interesting exercise. The likelihood of controlled and uncontrolled fission had become very real.

The prospect of obtaining fissionable bomb material directly from the reactor, instead of using sophisticated isotope separation techniques, had also become very real at about the same time. Hahn's Berlin team had discovered that ^{239}U, created when ^{238}U, the most abundant isotope in natural uranium, captures a neutron, will decay on average in 23 minutes to element 93, which was later called neptunium (uranium being element 92). Apparently unaware of published American research along these lines, von Weizsäcker, in a secret report to the Army Weapons Bureau, suggested that neptunium would be as suitable as the rare and hard-to-produce ^{235}U for bomb construction. But neptunium is also unstable. As already reported by American researchers in 1940, neptunium decays in 2.3 days into the long-lived element 94, plutonium, which is equally fissionable. This opened up an alternative route to the atomic bomb. As Fritz Houtermans, working in von Ardenne's lab, reported to German authorities in August 1941, a working reactor using natural uranium as a fuel could be used to create plutonium, which can be extracted by chemical means and used as an explosive. In theory at least, a working German reactor would produce, not just energy to power the German military, but the material for an atomic bomb.

The Turning Point

With the basic theory of the nuclear chain reaction, the discovery of the plutonium alternative, the capture of the necessary raw materials, the backing of industrial concerns and the German Army, and a test reactor in Leipzig about to multiply neutrons, to those ignorant of the errors discussed earlier the German research effort seemed poised for early success in the Autumn of 1941. Events took a different course.

---

[14]R. and K. Döpel and W. Heisenberg, "Der experimentelle Nachweis der effektiven Neutronenvermehrung...." in *Heisenberg: Collected Works*, Vol. **A2**, p. 543.

As described more fully in the Prologue, the conditions for research in Germany grew more difficult as the situation at the front grew more desperate. As the German Army bogged down in Russia that winter, Hitler ordered total mobilization of the German economy, and the Army Weapons Bureau ordered a comprehensive review of all research projects. Schumann informed the Uranium Club in December 1941 that the Army could continue its support of fission research "only if a certainty exists of attaining an application in the foreseeable future."[15] When the scientists could give no guarantees, the Army slashed funding in early 1942, relinquished control of the Kaiser-Wilhelm Institute for Physics and concentrated modest support on a reactor project under the direction of its nuclear expert Diebner, who set up shop in the Gottow suburb of Berlin.

The uranium researchers quickly found new benefactors within the newly mobilized economy. In February 1942, shortly after the Army relinquished control of nuclear fission research, the Reich Research Council (*Reichsforschungsrat*) and Army Weapons Bureau jointly sponsored a program of nontechnical lectures at the Council's offices, with presentations by Hahn, Heisenberg, Harteck and several others. The Education Ministry subsequently assumed control of the project and assigned it to its Research Council, which placed it under Abraham Esau, head of the physics section and the newly named administrator, or "plenipotentiary" (*Bevollmächtigter*), for nuclear physics. But the Kaiser-Wilhelm Society, reclaiming its Berlin physics institute, enlisted the aid of Albert Speer, Hitler's new armaments minister, who induced Hitler to name Speer's boss, Hermann Göring, to head the Reich Research Council. At the same time the German Physical Society used the potential contributions of nuclear physics to the war effort to gain support and recognition for the ideologically maligned theoretical physics and to rehabilitate more fully its leading proponents, Heisenberg in particular. In July 1942 Heisenberg became scientific head of the main research effort, as Diebner's successor at the Kaiser-Wilhelm Institute for Physics. A year later Heisenberg persuaded Speer and Göring to replace Esau with Gerlach as nuclear plenipotentiary, that is, as chief administrator of both Heisenberg's and Diebner's reactor research projects.

As the scientific leader of the nuclear researchers, Heisenberg presented—in addition to his talk at the Research Council on February 26, 1942 (see Appendix 1)—two other important lectures to regime officials in the period after the Army relinquished control: a briefing to Speer and military commanders on 4 June 1942, and another to assembled dignitaries at Göring's aeronautical research academy on 6 May 1943. Each of these talks reflected both the political ends for which they were intended, as well as the state of German fission research. In each case he gained official backing for research by informing the authorities of the prospects for reactors and a bomb, but in each case he dampened expectations for rapid success by pointing to the problems still to be solved.

---

[15]Erich Schumann to research directors, 5 Dec. 1941, quoted in Bagge *et al.*, p. 28. See Walker, *German National Socialism*, pp. 46–60.

INTRODUCTION

Later at Farm Hall Heisenberg recalled the 26 February 1942 meeting as the time when he and the others first convinced Education Minister Bernhard Rust "that we had absolutely definite proof that it could be done."[16] In the manuscript of his talk that day, Heisenberg noted that the separation of isotope ^{235}U would yield an "explosive of totally unimaginable power," but he hastened to add that the techniques for separating isotopes were not yet available. He squarely informed the education minister and the other assembled leaders that an alternative route lay via the "engine" (reactor), which could lead to the acquisition of an equally powerful explosive—plutonium. He cautioned against expecting quick results, however, noting the technical difficulties that remained.

Although we do not have the manuscript of his talk to Speer three months later, Heisenberg apparently presented the same views in that meeting and in subsequent informal discussions. Speer responded with modest funding and priority ratings for the project until the end of the war—precisely to the satisfaction of Heisenberg and most of his colleagues. Believing themselves far ahead of the Allies right up to their hearing about Hiroshima, they were content to wait out the war developing a reactor. Their work at the time and their statements at Farm Hall all indicate that they believed that the technical hurdles to a bomb really were so high that they could not be surmounted by either side before the end of the war. As things stood, they had obtained permanent funding, regime recognition and support, ideological rehabilitation, draft deferments and the possibility of performing interesting research—all without running the risk of continuing research to develop a bomb, but very probably failing.

In his third nuclear fission lecture, a nontechnical presentation to Göring's institute in May 1943, Heisenberg acknowledged for the first time his understanding of explosive critical mass and fast-neutron fission in pure ^{235}U—notions essential to bomb design—but he did not enter into details.[17] He did not mention plutonium, nor did he need to mention it. The project was now haltingly on track toward a working reactor, a modest goal to which the scientists attached considerable urgency, believing that success would perhaps yield at least nuclear-powered electric generators. At any rate, the mere achievement of a sustained chain reaction would place German research far ahead of nuclear science in the Allied countries by war's end.

The Final Phase

As soon as Heisenberg settled into his new position in Berlin at the top of German nuclear research, he laid out plans for the construction of an actual working

---

[16] See p. 128.

[17] Heisenberg, "Die Energiegewinnung aus der Atomkernspaltung," in *Heisenberg: Collected Works*, Vol. **A2**, pp. 570–575. See Walker, *German National Socialism*, pp. 93–94.

reactor. Preliminary experiments had served their purpose: to provide precise measurements of nuclear parameters and to confirm the possibility of a chain reaction. The push for a working reactor would require large amounts of heavy water and large, industrially rolled metal uranium plates. The new materials did not arrive until nearly 1½ years later, and by then Allied bombing was becoming so intense that, despite relocation to a bunker laboratory in Berlin, construction of the reactor suffered numerous interruptions. Finally, in the middle of 1944, Speer ordered all research groups out of Berlin to safety. The Kaiser-Wilhelm Institute for Physics moved most of its staff to southwestern Germany, to the towns of Hechingen and Haigerloch. Hahn moved his Kaiser-Wilhelm Institute for Physical Chemistry to the nearby southern town of Tailfingen, while Diebner moved his independent reactor experiments to the town of Stadtilm in Thuringia.

While Heisenberg turned a larger fraction of his time to non-nuclear research starting in 1942, Bagge in Berlin and Clusius and Dickel in Munich developed several isotope separation methods but achieved little practical success. They never obtained enough ^{235}U to make proper measurements and certainly too little for a bomb. German researchers never obtained any plutonium, above all because they could not even achieve a reactor to produce it in quantity. Diebner, however, did make remarkable progress. While Heisenberg's group utilized plate designs, the more adept Diebner utilized cubes of natural uranium suspended on wires in a tank of heavy water. The observed neutron multiplication was far higher than Heisenberg's Leipzig group had ever achieved. Heisenberg insisted nevertheless that his Berlin researchers continue construction using the plate design, which cost the project another year.

By the time Heisenberg finally had his plates cut into cubes at the end of 1944 it was almost too late. Just as Heisenberg, Wirtz, and Bagge began to assemble their cube reactor in Berlin, Gerlach dispatched the remainder of the Heisenberg and Diebner teams to the south. Heisenberg planned to join von Weizsäcker, Korsching and the others in Haigerloch, where they had already set up facilities in a bombproof wine cellar cut into the side of a giant rock. But Gerlach and Diebner decided to stop, along with a sizable fraction of Germany's heavy water, halfway to Haigerloch at Diebner's new laboratory in Stadtilm. After a brief power struggle, all of Heisenberg's Berlin equipment finally arrived in Haigerloch just in time for one last attempt, but without Diebner's heavy water. Neutron multiplication turned out the highest yet achieved, but the reactor still fell short of going critical. In five years of research, Germany had failed to achieve even a self-sustaining chain reaction.

On April 23, 1945, an Alsos science intelligence unit swept into southern Germany on the heels of advancing French troops. The mission members found von Weizsäcker, von Laue, Korsching, Harteck, Bagge and Wirtz awaiting their arrival in Haigerloch and Hechingen, and they found Hahn in nearby Tailfingen. A week later a team of combat engineers under Colonel Boris T. Pash, military head of the Alsos Mission, traveled into German-held Bavaria in search of the mission's three remaining "targets." They found Diebner and Gerlach at the bombed-out University of Munich, and, on May 3, after a brief fire fight with retreating units, Pash captured Heisenberg at his country home in Urfeld, Bavaria. The German nuclear project was at an end. Five days later the German Army surrendered on all fronts.

BRIEF CHRONOLOGY*

1938

Dec. 22   Otto Hahn sends paper to Lise Meitner containing experimental results that are interpreted by Meitner and nephew Otto Frisch as nuclear fission.

1939

Jan. 6   Hahn and assistant Fritz Strassmann publish their results.

Jan. 26   Niels Bohr, informed by Frisch, announces the discovery in Washington, D.C.

Feb. 11   Meitner and Frisch publish a theoretical interpretation of the Hahn–Strassmann results as nuclear fission.

June–July   Heisenberg visits the United States.

Aug. 2   Einstein signs letter to President Roosevelt alerting him to the possibility of a bomb and urging government-sponsored research.

Sept. 1   Bohr and John Wheeler publish a comprehensive theory of nuclear fission.

Sept. 3   War breaks out in Europe.

Sept. 16   The German Army Weapons Bureau assembles scientists to begin fission research.

Oct. 5   The Weapons Bureau takes control of the Kaiser-Wilhelm Institute for Physics in Berlin-Dahlem.

Dec. 6   Heisenberg submits to the Weapons Bureau the first part of a two-part comprehensive report on the prospects and methods for exploiting nuclear fission.

1940

Feb. 29   Heisenberg submits the second part of his report to the Weapons Bureau.

---

*Allied wartime research developments are indicated in italics.

May 3   German troops occupy Norway, seizing the world's only heavy-water production plant at Vemork.

May 19   *Frisch and Rudolf Peierls submit a memorandum to the British government estimating the critical mass of ^{235}U needed for an atomic bomb and urging a bomb research project.*

June 15 *Using the Berkeley cyclotron, Philip Abelson and Edwin McMillan demonstrate that neutrons captured by ^{238}U lead to the creation of elements 93 and 94, neptunium and plutonium.*

July 17 C. F. von Weizsäcker suggests to the Weapons Bureau that neptunium bred in a reactor can be used as the explosive material in a fission bomb.

1941

Jan. 20 Walther Bothe and Peter Jensen report results on neutron absorption in graphite indicating, mistakenly, that graphite cannot be used as a moderator.

Mar. 28 *American physicists confirm that plutonium is fissionable, thus usable for a bomb.*

June 22 Germany invades the Soviet Union.

August   Fritz Houtermans reports to German authorities the possibility of using plutonium in a bomb.

Dec. 5   In the wake of total mobilization Erich Schumann, head of research in the Army Weapons Bureau, orders a review of all research projects.

Dec. 6   *The Manhattan Project to build the bomb is launched.*

Dec. 7   Japan attacks Pearl Harbor; America enters the war.

1942

February The Army Weapons Bureau decides to withdraw almost entirely from fission research and relinquishes the Kaiser-Wilhelm Institute for Physics.

Feb. 26 Heisenberg, Hahn, and other scientists deliver a lecture series on nuclear research to the Reich Education Ministry in Berlin, gaining ministry backing for the project under the Reich Research Council.

April   The first neutron multiplication is obtained in a Leipzig test reactor.

June 4   Heisenberg reports on fission research to Albert Speer, Germany's Minister for Armaments and War Production, and other senior officials.

June 9   Hitler issues a decree, placing the Reich Research Council under Göring and Speer.

July 1   Heisenberg becomes acting head of the Kaiser-Wilhelm Institute for Physics, Germany's main reactor research laboratory, and lays plans for the construction of a working reactor containing heavy water and uranium metal plates.

July   Kurt Diebner, supported by the Weapons Bureau, begins reactor construction using the alternative design of metal cubes suspended in heavy water, achieving positive neutron multiplication over the following year.

Nov. 5   *Construction of a uranium isotope separation plant begins at Oak Ridge, Tennessee.*

Dec. 2   *Enrico Fermi and collaborators in Chicago achieve the first self-sustained chain reaction in a pile consisting of uranium spheres embedded in graphite bricks.*

1943

January   *Planning begins for construction of reactors at Hanford, Washington, to breed plutonium for a bomb.*

May 6   Heisenberg, Hahn, and other scientists deliver lectures on fission research before Göring's German Academy of Aerodynamical Research.

Autumn   Berlin research institutes begin moving to southern Germany for safety against Allied bombing raids. The Kaiser-Wilhelm Institute for Physics is split between Berlin and the neighboring southern towns of Hechingen and Haigerloch.

1944

Jan. 1   Walther Gerlach is appointed "plenipotentiary" of all fission research sponsored by the Reich Research Council.

June 6   D-Day invasion of Europe.

August   The Alsos Mission, an American science intelligence unit, arrives in Europe.

November	The Alsos Mission determines that no German atom bomb exists.

1945

January	Gerlach orders the remainder of the Heisenberg and Diebner teams to move south.
March	The Heisenberg team in Haigerloch begins war time Germany's last attempt to achieve a critical reactor.
Apr. 23	The Alsos Mission captures scientists and equipment in Hechingen, Haigerloch, and nearby Tailfingen.
May 1–3	The Alsos Mission captures Diebner and Gerlach in Munich and Heisenberg in German-held Bavaria.
May 7–8	Germany surrenders.
July 3	Ten of the captive German scientists are flown from Belgium to England and interned at Farm Hall.
July 16	*The first atomic bomb, fueled by plutonium, is detonated in the New Mexico desert.*
July 17	Truman, Stalin, and Attlee meet at Potsdam near Berlin to discuss the future of Germany and the former Axis and Axis-occupied nations.
Aug. 6	*A uranium fission bomb destroys Hiroshima.*
Aug. 9	*A plutonium fission bomb destroys Nagasaki.*

1946

Jan. 3	The ten captive German scientists are returned to Germany and released under Allied supervision within the British zone of occupation.

wanted to annex. When the Munich treaty ceded Czechoslovakia to Germany, Heisenberg was demobilized. And so, when war broke out in 1939, Heisenberg was ready to be recalled. He was 37 and fit. His friend and fellow Nobelist Wolfgang Pauli referred to him as a "boy scout"—a somewhat sardonic reference to the fact that Heisenberg had been a long-time member of the *Pfadfinder*,[4] a branch of the German youth movement. On September 25, 1939 Heisenberg did receive his mobilization orders—but not to the front, to Berlin instead—where he was to join under the auspices of Army Ordnance what had become known as the *Uranverein* (the "uranium club").

The history of the uranium club illustrates some of the in-fighting that took place in the German nuclear project which was one of the several reasons for its eventual failure.[5] At about the same time Harteck sent his first letter to Army Ordnance, the Reich Research Council of the Ministry of Culture was contacted about the potentialities of fission by the Göttingen University professor of physics Georg Joos. The original "club" had been organized under the Research Council's auspices. Soon after war broke out in September, the army took over the project, simply muscling out the Culture Ministry, which generated some hard feelings. The army had, among other things, the power of the draft, which it used under Bagge's direction to induct any physicist who might be useful to the uranium project. When Heisenberg arrived in Berlin, he found several of his colleagues already assembled. Among them, besides Harteck, were Otto Hahn (the co-discoverer of fission), Hans Geiger (of Geiger Counter fame), Carl Friedrich von Weizsäcker (a protégé of Heisenberg and a first-rate theoretical physicist in his own right), and Walther Bothe (the leading nuclear experimental physicist left in Germany). A debate took place as to whether they should help to build a fission bomb. In 1945 Bagge recalled that Bothe and Geiger ended the discussion by Bothe's saying, "Gentlemen, it must be done," followed by Geiger's saying "If there is the slightest chance that it is possible it must be done."[6] Thus was launched the project to explore the potentialities of fission and to build a German atomic bomb if feasible. This was three and a half years before the opening of Los Alamos.

On January 2, 1939 Enrico Fermi, Italy's leading nuclear physicist, and his family landed in New York.[7] In December he had attended the ceremony in

---

[4] A valuable source of Heisenberg information is *Uncertainty; The Life and Science of Werner Heisenberg*, by David C. Cassidy (W. H. Freeman, New York, 1992). I will refer to this as UN. For more on "Pfadfinders" see UN, pp. 64–87.

[5] I have been much instructed in the details of the German program by Mark Walker's book *German National Socialism and the Quest for Nuclear Power* (Cambridge University Press, New York, 1989). I shall refer to this book as GNS. I am also grateful to Professor Walker for very useful correspondence.

[6] "Gentlemen..." the Farm Hall Transcripts Report 4.

[7] Much useful information about Fermi can be found in *Enrico Fermi—Physicist* by Emilio Segrè (University of Chicago Press, Chicago, 1970). I shall refer to this book as FER.

Stockholm where he was awarded the Nobel Prize in Physics for 1938 for his experimental work in nuclear physics. He had accepted a job at Columbia University and, in the wake of Mussolini's anti-Semitic laws, had decided to leave Facist Italy behind forever. His wife was Jewish. By the middle of March 1939 he had done experiments on fission with results that indicated that a chain reaction was possible, and these so alarmed the chairman of the Columbia physics department, George Pegram, that he alerted the United States Navy. Pegram happened to know Charles Edison, the Undersecretary of the Navy. Edison was unavailable, so Pegram wrote a letter to Admiral S. C. Hooper in the Office of the Chief of Naval Operations in which he informed the Admiral: "Experiments in the physics laboratories at Columbia University reveal that conditions may be found under which the chemical element uranium may be able to liberate its large excess of atomic energy, and that this might mean the possibility that uranium might be used as an explosive that would liberate a million times as much energy per pound as any known explosive. My own feeling is that the probabilities are against this, but my colleagues and I think the bare possibility should not be disregarded, and I therefore telephoned ... this morning chiefly to arrange a channel through which the results of our experiments might, if the occasion should arise, be transmitted to the proper authorities in the United States Navy."[8]

This letter led to an invitation for Pegram's colleague Enrico Fermi to go to Washington and lecture some of the Navy brass, which he did on March 18. There is some difference of opinion as to how this lecture was received. His biographer and colleague, Emilio Segrè, reports that Fermi's lecture was "understood and appreciated," and was a success at least inasmuch as the Navy allocated $1,500 to Columbia for fission research.[9] Other reports are less positive. According to one of them, when Fermi presented himself he overheard the desk officer, who went inside to announce him to the admiral, explain that "There's a wop outside." [10] It would be interesting to know how this individual would have announced Fermi after Hiroshima.

As it happens, Pegram's letter and Fermi's visit were *not* what launched the American nuclear weapons program. But why is it that physicists in both Germany and the United States alerted their respective militaries at almost the same time? This can be made clear with a small historical detour.

Unveiling the Nucleus

In 1907, the young physicist Ernest Rutherford left his native New Zealand for Manchester, England, carrying with him a list of possible research subjects.

---

[8] "Experiments..." FER p. 111.
[9] "...understood..." FER p. 111.
[10]"There's..." MAB p. 295.

One of them was to smash "alpha particles" (later identified as the nuclei of helium atoms) into various materials. He wanted, among other things, to explore the model of the atom that had been put forward earlier by Cambridge physicist J. J. Thomson. It was well known that the atom was electrically neutral and that somehow or other it was composed of a negative charge in the form of light, negatively charged particles called *electrons* (which Thomson had discovered) and a compensating positive charge. The positive charge was thought to be spread out uniformly in the atom, with the electrons scattered about like raisins in a positively charged "pudding." In this model, an alpha particle impinging on, say, a metal foil would pass through it like a bullet through so much tissue paper.

Rutherford had assigned the problem of studying these alpha-particle collisions to Geiger, who in time developed the particle-counting detector that bears his name. Assisting Geiger was a young undergraduate named Ernest Marsden. Marsden later recalled Ruthford's coming into the room where he was counting alpha particles and suggesting that he, Marsden, keep an eye out for alpha particles that might be scattered back at very large angles. None were expected in Thomson's model, since the atom was pictured as a loose structure through which the alpha particle would pass more or less undeflected. Why Rutherford made this suggestion is utterly mysterious. But, in fact, Marsden discovered that about one alpha particle in 8,000 was scattered at angles greater than 90 degrees from the forward direction. Rutherford, late in his life, described his reaction. "It was," he said, "quite the most incredible event that has ever happened to me in my life. It was almost as incredible as if you fired a 15-inch shell at a piece of tissue paper and it came back and hit you." This could only happen if the alpha particles had struck something massive buried in the atom. This lead him to the idea that all the mass of the atom was concentrated in a tiny ball in the center of the atom, in what was called after the analogy to a biological cell the atomic nucleus.[11]

This discovery radically changed the idea of the atom. The atom was now conceived to consist of a massive, postively charged, core nucleus surrounded by a cloud of light, negatively charged electrons. The great puzzle became: What kept this system stable? Why didn't the electrons radiate away their energy and simply come crashing into the nucleus? In 1913, the young Niels Bohr proposed an answer. He suggested that the electrons could only follow certain select orbits. We would now say that these orbits are "quantized." The orbit of least energy—the so-called "ground state"—was assumed to be absolutely stable. Electrons could undergo quantum jumps from higher to lower Bohr orbits emitting light and other electromagnetic radiation, in the beautiful spectral patterns we observe.

---

[11] A discussion of the discovery of the nucleus can be found in *The Tenth Dimension* by Jeremy Bernstein (McGraw Hill, New York, 1989). The Rutherford quote can be found on p. 78. MAB has an anecdotal history.

But what did the nucleus itself consist of? The simplest atom is that of hydrogen. It has one external electron and a single compensating nuclear positive charge. In the 1920s Rutherford coined the name *proton* for this particle and this term is the one we still employ. The next heaviest atom is helium. It has two circulating electrons and therefore two compensating positively charged protons in its nucleus. But can this be all? The answer is no because the helium atom is about *four* times as massive as the hydrogen atom, not twice as massive. Hence there must be one or more neutral objects together about as massive as the two protons to complement the two protons. Rutherford made the natural assumption, which was incorrect as it turned out, that these neutral objects consisted simply of two protons, each bound tightly to one electron. This was the commonly held nuclear model in the 1920s and early 1930s.

The realization that there had to be neutral objects in the nucleus gave rise to a new possibility, which was recognized a few years after Rutherford's discovery of the nucleus itself. One could now imagine two nuclei with the same number of protons, but different numbers of neutral components. Two such related nuclei are called "isotopes" of each other (from *isos*, the "same," and *topos*, "place," in Greek). Atoms with such isotopic nuclei have the same place in the periodic table of elements, and they have the same number of circulating electrons. Since it is the electrons that determine the chemistry of these atoms, isotopes have essentially the same chemistry so that they cannot be separated from each other by conventional chemical means. This fact will come to play an essential role in our story.

An important example of isotopic differences was discovered by the American physicist Harold Urey in 1932. Urey found that natural hydrogen—the kind you find in sea water—is 99.985% ordinary hydrogen, with one nuclear proton, and 0.015% heavy hydrogen, whose nucleus is known as deuterium, with a proton and an additional massive but neutral particle.

Besides being the year of Urey's discovery and Heisenberg's Nobel Prize, 1932 was also the year that the true nature of the neutral nuclear particle was revealed. The essential experiment was done by one of Rutherford's disciples at Cambridge, James Chadwick. It consisted of bombarding a beryllium target with alpha particles and observing that a penetrating beam of neutral radiation emerged. Chadwick identified this radiation with what Rutherford had speculated to be a bound-electron–proton combination. It took a bit of time before there was general agreement that this object, which was soon called the *neutron*, was an elementary particle in its own right: a noncharged particle somewhat more massive than the proton.

It was Rutherford, once again, who opened up the modern era of experimental nuclear physics by showing that when an alpha particle impinges on a nucleus it can do more than simply bounce off. It can be absorbed by the nucleus, providing the basis for a 20th-century alchemy using nuclear elements! Following up on this idea, by 1933 Pierre Joliot-Curie and his wife Iréne—the daughter of Marie—had produced "artificial" radioactive elements by bombarding stable elements with alpha particles.

The next step was taken by Fermi and his group in Rome. In 1934 Fermi had the inspired idea of using neutrons rather than alpha particles as the bombarding projectiles. The advantage of this was that as neutrons are electrically neutral they are not repelled by the electrostatic forces of the nucleus and can penetrate much more deeply. Fermi simply bombarded one element after another with neutrons to see what would happen. Finally he worked his way up to the then last-discovered element on the periodic table, uranium. The principal isotope of uranium, ^{238}U, has 92 protons and 146 neutrons. Fermi's expectation was that he would produce "transuranics"—that is, elements more massive than uranium none of which are found naturally on Earth. This, indeed, is what Fermi thought he had found. Ironically, a chemist named Ida Noddack had sent Fermi a paper in which she suggested that some of Fermi's results might mean that he had actually split, or "fissioned," the uranium nucleus with his neutrons, which, in fact, unknown to him, he had. Her paper was not very well argued and did not seem to fit the data on nuclear masses, so it was ignored.[12] One can only imagine what might have happened if nuclear fission had been recognized as such in Facist Italy in 1934.

Fast and Slow Neutrons

To appreciate the next step—and to anticipate an important element in the rest of our story—one must understand the distinction between what are known as *slow* (or *thermal*) neutrons and *fast* neutrons.[13] By definition, slow neutrons move with speeds of the order of a few kilometers a second, about the speeds that molecules at room temperature move in a gas. That is why these neutrons are also referred to as *thermal*. Fast neutrons, the kind that are emitted in many nuclear processes, move at speeds of tens of thousands of kilometers a second. Fermi's original experiments had been done with fast neutrons. In October of 1934—October 22 according to Segrè's recollection—Fermi, for no reason he could later reconstruct (shades of Rutherford) decided to put a piece of paraffin in front of his radon neutron source. Much to everyone's astonishment, neutrons filtered through this paraffin produced an extraordinarily enchanced activity in the nuclei they interacted with.

Fermi soon came up with an explanation. Paraffin acts like what we would now call a *moderator* for fast neutrons. Paraffin is a hydrocarbon: hydrogen and carbon. Neutrons scattering from the protons (hydrogen nuclei) in the paraffin are

---

[12]A discussion of Noddack can be found in FER p. 76.

[13]For a reader with some technical background a very useful nuclear physics text is *Introductory Nuclear Physics* by Kenneth Krane (Wiley, New York, 1987). See especially Chapter 13 on fission. I am grateful to Lowell Brown for many discussions on the technical aspects of fission.

rapidly slowed down. This is because the proton and neutron have about the same mass so the proton recoils after each collision, absorbing some of the neutron's momentum. A neutron hitting a brick wall would simply bounce off, changing its direction but not its speed. About 20 neutronic collisions in the paraffin are enough to slow it down to near thermal velocities. The nuclear reaction rates—this is what Fermi discovered—are sensitive functions of the speed, or energy, of the impinging neutron. At select energies the reaction rates can even increase by an order of magnitude (a power of 10) or more. This phenomenon is called a *resonance*. Even without the resonances, the reaction rates for these processes at low energies increase as the reciprocal of the speed of the incoming neutrons—the famous $1/v$ law. It was this increase that Fermi and his group had discovered more or less serindipitously.

By 1935, the Rome group began experimenting with slow neutrons impinging on uranium foils. In order to eliminate unwanted radiation, they covered these foils with aluminum, and this is why they failed to discover the evidence that fission was taking place. Slow neutrons readily fission natural uranium. When this happens energy is released: The fission products fly apart with a large kinetic energy. These energy pulses would have easily shown up in their detectors. But the aluminum foil absorbed these pulses and so, again, fission remained undiscovered.

The theorists, especially Bohr, now reenter our story. Bohr had become intrigued by results like those of Fermi and invented a picture, or model, of the nucleus that proved very helpful in interpreting it. A nucleus like uranium is composed of some 238 nuclear particles, which are generically called *nucleons*. No theory is capable of following the detailed evolution of 238 particles in an atomic nucleus. Bohr focused instead on the collective aspects of these heavy nuclei. For purposes of their gross structure, one can think of the nucleus as behaving something like a liquid drop. Such a drop has a surface tension—a force that makes its molecules tend to try to stick together—which gives the drop its shape. Still, an external force can deform the drops and, if they become distended enough, they can split—fission—into smaller droplets. In the nucleus similarly there are two forces that work against each other. The positively charged protons mutually repel each other so that the nucleus would fly apart if this tendency was not overbalanced by the strong attractive nuclear force.

The net effect of this interplay is to produce a surface tension something like that of a real liquid drop. When an external neutron is absorbed by such a structure, its energy is partitioned among the various nuclei and a new structure is formed, a so-called compound nucleus. This structure will, in general, not be stable. It will have various ways of decaying. These decay modes constitute the end result of the reaction. One prediction of the model, borne out by experiment, is that the compound nucleus loses all "memory" of how it was formed. Once it is formed, its properties, and not the properties of the initial particles, determine the characteristics of the reaction. Bohr published these results in 1937. The stage was now set for the discovery of fission.

The Discovery of Nuclear Fission

In 1938 Berlin radiochemist Otto Hahn was 59 years old—well past the age at which most scientists make their major discoveries. Always a handsome man, he had a special fondness for women, both as friends and colleagues. In an era when women were a rarity, and often an unwelcome rarity at that in scientific laboratories, Hahn had taken on Lise Meitner in his laboratory. Unmarried, she was a year older than Hahn. She had been born in Vienna and, like so many upper-class Viennese Jews, came from a converted, thoroughly assimilated family. Trained as a physicist, she joined Hahn's laboratory in 1907. Theirs became one of the foremost radiochemistry laboratories in the world.

In March of 1938, when Hitler annexed Austria, Meitner's world collapsed. She was now, baptized or not, a German Jew. She was warned by Max von Laue, a Nobel Prize-winning colleague of Einstein's in Berlin, that she was in grave danger. This act was typical of von Laue. Among the German physical scientists who remained in Germany, he was one whose character inspires much feeling of admiration. While Hahn was powerless to protect Meitner, he did help her to escape, and he gave her a diamond ring that he had inherited from his mother so she could sell it when needed. In July, with contacts made to Dutch physicists by Hahn, Meitner escaped to Sweden via Holland and Denmark and found a position in an institute near Stockholm. Hahn wrote her frequently about the work he was doing on uranium with their young associate named Fritz Strassmann.

Hahn and Strassmann continued the work they had been doing with Meitner; namely, irradiating uranium with slow neutrons and examining the resulting products. Their expectation was that they would produce some element, like radium, close to uranium in the periodic table. No one, Bohr included, had imagined that if you agitated a uranium nucleus with a slow neutron you could produce an element very distant from uranium in the periodic table. But, after painstaking chemical analysis Hahn found among the final products an element that seemed chemically indistinguishable from barium. The common isotope of barium has 56 protons and 81 neutrons, a little over half the number of nucleons found in uranium—hence very far from uranium on the periodic table. Hahn was dumbfounded. On December 19, 1938 he wrote to Meitner, "Perhaps you can suggest some fantastic explanation. We understand that it really can't break up into barium ... so try to think of some other possibility. Barium isotopes with much higher atomic weights than 137? If you can think of anything that might be publishable, then the three of us would be together in this work after all. We don't believe this is foolishness or that contaminations are playing tricks on us." [14] Hahn was a radiochemist and not a nuclear physicist, which Meitner was. That is why they made such a good combination, and that is why he turned to her now. One often says of a discovery

---

[14] "Perhaps..." MAB p. 253.

like this that it was a matter of "luck." What is not luck is the confidence of a careful scientist like Hahn that it was not "contaminations ... playing tricks on us." It was a real effect.

At first Meitner was equally dumbfounded. She wrote to Hahn, "Your results are very amazing. A process that works with slow neutrons and leads to barium! ... To me for the time being the hypothesis of such an extensive burst seems very difficult to accept, but we have experienced so many surprises in nuclear physics that one cannot say without hesitation about anything: 'It's impossible.'"[15]

It so happened that Meitner's nephew, Otto Frisch, was also a physicist. He too had been forced to leave Germany and was residing in Copenhagen, working at Bohr's institute. He decided, in late 1938, to visit his aunt in Sweden over his Christmas vacation.[16] Naturally, they began discussing Hahn's result. At first they were hindered by the notion that one could only produce barium by chipping away something like 100 nucleons from the uranium in a single interaction with the impinging neutron. This seemed crazy. But then they realized that Bohr's liquid drop model gave an alternate picture. The impinging neutron could possibly cause the droplet to deform. This could lead to a more energetically stable configuration than the original one, in which case the droplet would continue to distend. What would happen next was also a question of energetics. It might be energetically profitable for the droplet to distend even further until it split into smaller droplets.

In nuclear terms, the sum of the masses of the lighter nuclei into which the uranium nucleus splits might be less than the mass of the original uranium nucleus. Since, according to Einstein's formula $E = mc^2$, mass is energy, such a transition could be energetically favored. It was a question of putting in the numbers. As it happened, Meitner knew by heart the masses of the relevant nuclei. She and Frisch chose for illustrative purposes a splitting in which barium is produced as one product. For the electric charge to add up to the 92 of uranium, the other nucleus produced had to be an isotope of krypton. Meitner and Frisch proposed, following Bohr's liquid drop model, that the original drop had split into two droplets. Knowing the nuclear masses approximately they could estimate the energy released.

To get some sense of the magnitudes of energy involved, we note that the energy unit conventionally used in subatomic physics is the electron volt. It is not necessary to know the precise value of this unit in terms of more conventional energy units to appreciate the point. In a chemical reaction like burning, a few electron volts per atom are released. In contrast, in fission, a few *million* electron volts per atom are emitted. A useful number to keep in mind is that 1 kilogram or

---

[15]"Your results..."MAB p. 253.

[16]For a delightful account of this history see *What Little I Remember* by Otto Frisch (Cambridge University Press, New York, 1979). I shall refer to this book as WLI.

2.2 pounds of uranium completely fissioned would produce the energy equivalent of about *ten thousand tons* of TNT.

In a few days Frisch returned to Copenhagen to tell Bohr the news. As it happened, Bohr was about to leave for the United States and had only a few minutes for Frisch. In his autobiography Frisch records Bohr's reaction. He said, "Oh what idiots we have all been! Oh but this is wonderful! This is just as it must be! Have you and Lise Meitner written a paper about it?" [17] With that, he left for the United States; brimming with excitement. The resulting paper was published in the February 11, 1939 issue of the British journal *Nature* as a two-page letter.[18] It turned out to be one of the most important scientific communications of this era. Frisch had adopted the word *fission* for this process by analogy to the biological reference to cell division. The Frisch–Meitner Letter may be the only place in the physics literature where the word "fission" ever appeared in quotes. Unfortunately, as we shall see in the reports below, Hahn alone received the Nobel Prize for the discovery of fission, a circumstance that he accepted without any recorded complaint.

Bohr's excitement at Frisch's news did not have to do with what Bohr took to be the prospects of actually using the energy released by nuclear fission. The fact that laboratory fission experiments produced miniscule amounts of nuclear energy did not seem to have, at least to Bohr, any practical consequences. His excitement had to do with the nuclear physics. His theoretical ideas were apparently vindicated. However, it was not long before the possibility of practical consequences began to emerge.

Bohr landed in New York in January of 1939, two weeks after Fermi. Bohr had intended to keep the news of fission secret until Frisch and Meitner published their Letter, but due to a misunderstanding the word got out. His collaborator, Léon Rosenfeld, who had been on the boat with Bohr, thought that the Frisch–Meitner paper had already been published and informed a group of physicists. Among the first to hear it was the Hungarian-born polymath Leo Szilard. Szilard was a somewhat erratic visionary. In 1934, four years before fission was identified, Szilard conceived the notion of what he called a "chain reaction" involving neutrons. Szilard had no quantitative nuclear model in mind, but he imagined that some nucleus might be split apart and, in addition to the large nuclear fragments, neutrons might be emitted as well. These neutrons could then split other nuclei and the process would continue, increasing exponentially. If it happened fast enough, Szilard reasoned, it could cause a nuclear explosion. This was in 1934! Indeed, he took out a patent on the process and frequently emended it as new ideas came to him. When he heard about the fission of uranium his first thought was of the additional neutrons and hence the possibility of a chain reaction. If the neutrons were there, Szilard decided, then

---

[17]"Oh what..." WLI p. 116.

[18]The Frisch–Meitner paper was published in *Nature*, Feb. 11, 1939, p. 239.

this must be kept secret from the Germans, since the possibility of making an atomic bomb was now in view.

The Bohr–Wheeler Theory

After arriving in New York, Bohr moved to Princeton to take up residence as a visitor at the Institute for Advanced Study. He and the American physicist John Wheeler began a more systematic study of the theory of fission in terms of the liquid drop model. Not long into this work Bohr, reportedly turning red in the face, had a flash of insight that transformed nuclear energy research forever. Bohr realized that from the point of view of neutron-induced fission the two isotopes of uranium, ^{235}U and ^{238}U, would behave entirely differently. There is something Mozartian, at least to me, about this work: It is a perfect little jewel of physics.

Before discussing the implications of Bohr's insight, let us outline his reasoning, which went into the definitive theory of nuclear fission, the Bohr–Wheeler theory. By 1939, enough nuclear isotopes had been identified and studied so that certain regularities had become apparent. In making up nuclei, protons tend to couple with protons and neutrons with neutrons. Hence nuclei in which there are an odd number of protons and an even number of neutrons, or vice versa, are less tightly bound as a rule than nuclei with even numbers of protons and neutrons. (Nuclei with an odd number of protons and neutrons are also less tightly bound.) To take an example, ^{238}U has 92 protons and 146 neutrons, but ^{235}U has 92 protons and 143 neutrons and hence is less tightly bound.

Take, for illustration, the case of the fissioning of uranium into barium and krypton. We can imagine the uranium existing prior to fission as a kind of "virtual" state of barium and krypton, meaning that we can conceptualize the uranium nucleus as a sort of barium–krypton composite. The barium and krypton have positive charges that repel each other. If no other forces are at work, they would simply fly apart. But the strong nuclear force tends to hold them together. This creates a "barrier" of protons held together by the nuclear force. As the fission occurs, the fragments must somehow get over, or through, this charge barrier. There are two ways this can happen. Quantum mechanics allows tunneling through the barrier with varying degrees of probability. This leads to what is called *spontaneous fission*. It takes place even in the absence of an initiating neutron. The heavy nuclei, uranium and beyond, all undergo spontaneous fission with rates that increase as the nuclear charge increases. That is why very heavy stable nuclei do not exist in nature. On the other hand, the lifetime for the spontanous fission of uranium, for example, is so long—some 10^{16} years—that there is still uranium around.

But fission can also occur if an incoming neutron provides enough energy to lift the prospective fission fragments over the charge barrier. The minimum energy needed to do this is called the *activation energy*. To determine it, Bohr used his compound nucleus model of nuclear reactions. When a neutron impinges on ^{235}U, a ^{236}U nucleus is created. This is a nucleus with an even number of neutrons and protons; hence it is more tightly bound than the odd–even ^{239}U nucleus that is formed when a neutron impinges on ^{238}U. This results in a lower barrier, thus a lower activation energy for ^{235}U than for ^{238}U. Hence Bohr's crucial insight: *^{235}U is fissionable by slow or thermal neutrons, while ^{238}U is not.* But in natural uranium— the kind you find in a uranium mine—^{235}U is quite rare as compared to ^{238}U. Only about 1 in 139 natural uranium nuclei are ^{235}U.

What Bohr realized was that all the fission that Hahn had observed was from the rare ^{235}U nuclei in his sample. The much larger number of ^{238}U nuclei were essentially spectators to the fission process. Bohr decided, mistakenly as it turned out, that this fact made nuclear weapons, at best, an academic prospect. To make them, he realized, one would have to separate large amounts of ^{235}U from ^{238}U. Bohr thought that this would take the resources of an entire nation, and he could not imagine at that point any nation mustering the resources.

Bohr published his results, together with Wheeler, in the *Physical Review* in February of 1939. By the middle of March the additional neutrons that Szilard's theory of the chain reaction required had been observed. Two groups were responsible: Fermi, together with Szilard and a young postdoctoral assistant named Walter Zinn at Columbia, and a group headed by Frédéric Joliot-Curie in Paris.

In the process observed, in addition to the heavy isotopes created as fission products, on the average more than two neutrons—2.42 for ^{235}U— were emitted for each one absorbed to make fission. Therefore a chain reaction was possible, confirming Szilard's worst fears. He pressed to keep the result secret—to keep it away from the Germans. However, Joliot and his group published their result in the March 18 issue of *Nature*. This is the article that prompted German scientists like Harteck to contact the army. It was Fermi's result that made Pegram contact the United States Navy. The race to build an atomic bomb had begun.

Enter Einstein

As we have seen, by September of 1939 German Army Ordnance had become involved in the German project. That July, Szilard and his fellow Hungarian emigré Eugene Wigner had alerted Einstein to the possibility of a chain reaction. Einstein was suprised.*"Daran habe ich gar nicht gedacht! "*—"I never thought of that!" he remarked.[19] On August 2, Einstein wrote—largely at the dictation of Szilard—his celebrated letter to President Franklin D. Roosevelt alerting the President to the possibility of a German atomic bomb. It is worth quoting this letter in full if only to compare its impression of the German project with what we now know was actually taking place. The letter, dated August 2nd, 1939 reads:[20]

---

[19]"Daran..." MAB p. 305.

[20]"Sir..." The text of this letter and the circumstances surrounding it are given in *Einstein*, by Jeremy Bernstein (Penguin Modern Masters, New York, 1982), p. 225.

Sir:

Some recent work by E. Fermi and L. Szilard, which has been communicated to me in manuscript, leads me to expect that the element uranium may be turned into a new and important source of energy in the immediate future. Certain aspects of the situation seem to call for watchfulness and, if necessary, quick action on the part of the Administration. I believe, therefore, that it is my duty to bring to your attention the following facts and recommendations.

In the course of the last four months it has been made probable—through the work of Joliot in France as well as Fermi and Szilard in America—that it may become possible to set up nuclear chain reactions in a large mass of uranium, by which vast amounts of power and large quantities of new radium-like elements would be generated. Now it appears almost certain that this could be achieved in the immediate future.

This new phenomenon would also lead to the construction of bombs, and it is conceivable—though much less certain—that extremely powerful bombs of a new type may thus be constructed. A single bomb of this type, carried by boat or exploded in a port, might well destroy the whole port together with some of the surrounding territory. However, such bombs might very well prove to be too heavy for transportation by air.

The United States has only very poor ores of uranium in moderate quantities. There is some good ore in Canada and the former Czechoslovakia, while the most important source of uranium is the Belgian Congo.

In view of this situation you may think it desirable to have some permanent contact maintained between the Administration and the group of physicists working on chain reactions in America. One possible way of achieving this might be for you to entrust with the task a person who has your confidence and who would perhaps serve in an unofficial capacity. His task might comprise the following:

1. To approach Government Departments, keep them informed of further developments, and put forward recommendations for Government action, giving particular attention to the problem of securing a supply of uranium ore for the United States.

2. To speed up experimental work which is at present being carried on within the limits of the budgets of University laboratories, by providing funds, if such funds be required, through his contacts with private persons who are willing to make contributions for this cause, and perhaps also by obtaining the

cooperation of industrial laboratories which have the necessary equipment.

I understand that Germany has actually stopped the sale of uranium from the Czechoslovakia mines which she has taken over. That she should have taken such early action might perhaps be understood on the ground that the son of the German Under-Secretary of State, von Weizsäcker, is attached to the Kaiser-Wilhelm Institut in Berlin, where some of the American work on uranium is now being repeated.

Yours very truly,

A. Einstein

Viewed from the perspective of more than half a century later, there is something almost touchingly innocent about this letter. When we think of the sophisticated ways that have been devised to transport nuclear weapons halfway across the globe in minutes, to destroy entire countries, the idea of transporting one in a boat to blow up a port has a quaint naiveté.

The letter refers to experiments that might lead to a German atomic bomb program in the summer of 1939. In June of 1939 the German theoretical physicist Siegfried Flügge had written a detailed technical review of fission and an article in a widely read science journal. In the latter, he had pointed out that if all the uranium in a cubic meter of uranium oxide could be fissioned, the energy would be enough to equal the output of all the German coal-fueled power plants for 11 years. Perhaps it was these articles that had exercised Szilard. However, it was not until October 1939 that German Army Ordnance requisitioned the Kaiser-Wilhelm Institute for Physics for war work on nuclear energy. Its Dutch-born director, Peter Debye, was told either to take German citizenship or to emigrate. He came eventually to the United States, where he became a professor at Cornell University.

Finally, there is the reference to C. F. von Weizsäcker and his father. We have seen that the younger von Weizsäcker was an early recruit to the Army Ordnance program. We will have many occasions to meet him again, here and at Farm Hall.

But von Weizsäcker himself was only one of several recruits to the nuclear energy program and, in any event, the real work there did not begin until September, a month after this letter was written. The reference to his father, Ernst von Weizsäcker, is very interesting as it shows the tangled intertwining of politics and science—father and son—in Germany. Ernst von Weizsäcker was State Secretary in the German Foreign Office from 1938 to 1943. In a controversial decision he was convicted at Nuremberg in April of 1949 and sentenced to seven years in prison. After review, the sentence was reduced to five years and dealt only with his alleged responsibility for the deportation of Jews from France to Auschwitz in

March of 1942. There is little consensus on the justice of this conviction. At one end of the spectrum, it is claimed that he had the opportunity to object to these deportations, knowing full well what they meant, and did not. At the other end it is claimed that he did not know what the deportations really meant and realized that nothing he could do, save martyrdom, would be of any relevance. Of course there were many such dilemmas, many of which were faced by the Farm Hall detainees. It is certainly true that he was not a Nazi Party member and served them with some contempt. He later agreed that he should not have served them at all. As one writer put it, he should have known that "you cannot sup with the devil even with a long spoon."[21] This could equally well have been said of his son and most of the other recruits to the German nuclear program.

The British Impetus

The immediate result of Einstein's letter to Roosevelt, followed by a second one in 1940, was minimal. As is typical of bureaucracies, it led to the formation of a committee, the Advisory Committee on Uranium to the National Bureau of Standards. Nothing much was achieved in Allied research until well into 1940, and then progress took place mainly in Britain, where immigrants from Nazi Germany again played a crucial role.

Frisch, whom we had last seen in Copenhagen, had decided by 1939 that Denmark was not going to be safe for Jews much longer. The Germans occupied Denmark in April of 1940. Mark Oliphant—an Australian pupil of Rutherford who had worked with Paul Harteck and Rutherford on fusion—had by now become head of his own department at Birmingham. (One is struck again and again in this story by the criss-crossing of careers and countries. Physics was a small international club. In that spirit, it is not suprising, for example, that Rudolf Peierls, another immigrant to Britain whom we are about to meet, was able to convince himself during the war that the German atomic bomb program could not possibly be of a scale like our own by looking at German university catalogs. He discovered that the usual professors were in the usual places, teaching the usual courses.) Oliphant offered a job in Birmingham to Frisch, who had arrived there in the summer of 1939 on a visit and now, caught by the war, stayed. By the winter, he was looking for a research problem. Both he and Rudolf Peierls, who had arrived in England

---

[21] "...you cannot sup..." is taken from an essay entitled "The Conviction of Ernst von Weizsäcker on Count V at Nuremberg" by Leonidas E.Hill in: *Historians and Archivists. Essays in Modern German History and Archival Policy*, ed. George O. Kent (George Mason University Press, Fairfax, Virginia, 1991), pp. 83–114. Hill gives an objective account of Ernst von Weizsäcker's wartime activities. There is one odd statement in this essay: "At most there is in the entire corpus of his papers from 1900 to his death no more than evidence for the mildest antisemitism." One can only wonder in the case of von Weizsäcker what this is supposed to mean. I am grateful to Martin Heisenberg for sending me this article.

from Germany in 1933 and had also gotten a job in Birmingham, would have liked to work on radar, which is what Oliphant was doing. But radar was top secret and, since they were classified by the authorities as "enemy aliens," Frisch and Peierls were excluded from working directly on it. (Nonetheless Oliphant was able to make use of Peierls's encyclopedic abilities in theoretical physics by posing problems to him that seemed abstract but were in fact radar-related).

Frisch, in the meanwhile, had decided to continue his work on uranium. In particular, he wanted to test Bohr's prediction that ^{235}U was the isotope responsible for fission. To this end, he decided to try to separate a small quantity of the two isotopes. To do so, he proposed to use a method of isotope separation that had been invented by Klaus Clusius in Germany (it would later be discussed often at Farm Hall). In his autobiography, Frisch writes, "In its simplest form [the method] merely required a long tube standing upright with an electrically heated wire along its axis. This tube was to be filled with a gaseous compound of the element whose isotopes one wanted to separate, and the theory of Clusius (which had been confirmed by experiments) indicated that material enriched in the lighter isotope would accumulate near the top of the tube while the heavier isotopes would tend to go to the bottom. All simplicity itself."[22]

While he was waiting for the laboratory glass blower to produce his tube, Frisch received an invitation to write a report on fission for a chemical journal, to bring the chemists up to date. This gave him the opportunity to rethink the question of whether or not uranium could be used to make a bomb. Bohr himself had by now pronounced on its impossibility as a practical matter. Frisch's reasoning, whose elements we have anticipated, is very straightforward. Using the energy units we have already introduced, a typical neutron emitted in a fission of ^{235}U has a kinetic energy of about 2 million electron volts. The probability of a neutron of this energy fissioning a ^{238}U nucleus is tiny. (In fact, for neutron energies below 1 million electron volts, ^{238}U will not fission at all.) That is why natural uranium will not work for a bomb. This is what had stopped Bohr. It is worthwhile to be a little more quantitative. A crucial element in this reasoning is the notion of "cross section."

Physicists introduce the term *cross section* as a measure of the above-mentioned probabilities for fissioning a nucleus or indeed any other nuclear process involving collisions. A cross section has the dimensions of an area. Peierls has given a nice illustration. Suppose a window is constructed out of a type of glass that is sufficiently strong that it breaks only one in ten times when a boy throws a baseball at it. The effective area—or cross section—for breaking the window is then a tenth of its actual geometric area. The factor of a tenth gives us a measure of the strength of the glass. Nuclear cross sections are tiny by macroscopic standards, but large by subatomic standards. In centimeters, a typical nuclear cross section is something like 10^{-24} square centimeters. During the war, the physicists at Los Alamos from

---

[22]"...In its simplest..." WLI p. 124.

Purdue University, which is located in the farming state of Indiana, decided that this was such a big number, as compared, say, to the size of an electron, that they called it a "barn"—as big as a barn door. The cross section for a 2 million electron volt neutron to fission ^{235}U is about 1 barn. But if this neutron can be slowed down to thermal speeds, the cross section increases by a factor of about a thousand! At the time that Frisch was doing his contemplating, no one knew even the approximate values for these cross sections, since they had not yet been measured. The first actual separation of ^{235}U from ^{238}U was done by the American physicist Alfred Nier in late February of 1940. The large thermal cross section for fissioning ^{235}U was published by Nier and his collaborators in April of that year.

However, slowing the fast fission neutrons down in order to increase the cross section presents problems from the point of view of bomb design. Uranium has many neutron capture "resonances" in the energy region we are considering. A resonance in a cross section occurs when, for reasons involving whatever forces are in play, the cross section increases very rapidly at certain energies. For example, the cross section for swallowing a neutron, without fissioning the uranium nucleus, can jump up by a factor of 10,000 at such a resonance energy. The captured neutrons simply disappear into the nuclei and are lost to the chain reaction. To deal with this in a reactor, one embeds the uranium fuel elements in a matrix of a non-neutron absorbing material, such as graphite or heavy water. Such materials are known as *moderators*. Fast fission neutrons, as they emerge from the uranium fuel elements, flow into the moderator and are slowed down by collisions with the moderator nuclei, and when some of them eventually find their way back into the fuel elements, they are moving at thermal speeds, ready to fission the ^{235}U nuclei in the natural uranium.

But this slowing down takes time. So much time, in fact, that a nuclear explosion is impossible. It is as if it took days for the flame in a stick of dynamite to move from one end of the dynamite stick to the other. As Frisch writes in his autobiography, "At worst the material would heat up rapidly, melt, and some of it evaporate; the reaction would then stop because the neutrons would escape, having liberated no more than a microscopic fraction of the energy that was available in the mass of uranium. The result would be no worse than setting fire to a similar quantity of old-fashioned gunpowder." [23] Of course, having lived through the Three Mile Island and Chernobyl disasters, we are no longer as sanguine as Frisch appeared to be about nuclear reactor accidents. Still, no one who knows anything about the matter has suggested that reactors can blow up like an atomic bomb.

Critical Mass Is Critical

But suppose the Clusius process or some such process for separating isotopes really worked for uranium, Frisch thought. If one could actually do the separation,

---

[23] "At worst..." WLI p. 125.

one could then take advantage of the *fast* neutrons produced by each fission since one could use pure ^{235}U. The ^{235}U nuclei are fissionable by these neutrons. All the uranium nuclei would in such a sample be fissionable in a short enough time to produce a massive explosion. This was the key—fast neutrons and ^{235}U.

Frisch's next task was to attempt to estimate how much ^{235}U would be needed to support a chain reaction. This amount is now known as the *critical mass*. For reasons we will discuss shortly, an amount of uranium less than this mass will be inert, while an amount greater than this mass will self-destruct. Frisch thought initially that the critical mass would be tons, which would have made any practical use of fast ^{235}U fission in bombs essentially impossible. As it happened, Peierls, improving on a calculation of the French physicist Francis Perrin, had at just about this time produced an improved formula for the critical mass. He had published it because, as he had in mind natural uranium, it appeared to him to show that an atomic bomb was impossible, in agreement with Bohr.

To understand the relevant features of Perrin's formula and to get an insight into why there is a critical mass, let's ask how one would go about deriving it.[24] Suppose we take some arbitrary volume in the lump of uranium at hand. A fission occurs in this volume. Neutrons are released. It then takes a certain time before one of them can collide with the next uranium nucleus in the chain and produce a new fission. This time is what governs the rate at which neutrons can be produced in the volume since no new fission can take place before a neutron finds another uranium nucleus. The probability for fission will also affect this time since a neutron might simply collide elastically with a nucleus, producing neither nuclear energy nor additional neutrons. If the lump of uranium were infinitely big, the chain reaction would be unstoppable because every neutron would eventually find a new uranium nucleus to fission. But for a finite lump of uranium, neutrons can leak out of the surface and be lost to the process forever. The critical size of the lump is that size

---

[24]The technical details are described with wonderful clarity in *The Los Alamos Primer* by Robert Serber (University of California Press, Berkeley, 1992). These are the lectures given at Los Alamos by Serber in the spring of 1943, along with his delightful annotations. The reader is instantly struck by the fact that these people were serious about making a bomb. The first entry is entitled "Objective" and reads "The object of the project is to produce **a practical military weapon** in the form of a bomb in which the energy is released by a fast neutron chain reaction in one or more of the materials known to show nuclear fission."—the bold face is in the original. Nowhere in the German project do I find such a simple, down to earth, statement. There is much talk about the awsome power of nuclear weapons and how desirable it would be to have one. What is missing is a statement to the effect that we—the Germans—are going to have one, and these are the steps we are going to take to build one. I attribute this to the fact that, at least in the beginning, the Germans were sure they were going to win the war anyway, so there was no urgency about building a bomb. The Americans, on the other hand, were certain that the Germans were bulding a bomb and were ahead of them. This book also has reprints of the two original reports Frisch and Peierls sent to Tizard. I will refer to this book as LAP. I have taken critical masses and cross sections from this book.

at which these two effects just balance. To translate this into a mass we have to know how the lump is shaped. Let us suppose it is a sphere, the most favorable case. If we call the critical radius of this sphere r_c, then, remembering from elementary geometry, the associated critical volume V_c is related to r_c by the formula $V_c = \frac{4}{3}\pi r_c^3$. To find the mass of the corresponding volume we must multiply V_c by the density (mass/volume) of uranium, ρ_U. Under normal conditions the density ρ_U is 18.97 grams per cubic centimeter, as opposed to water, which has a density of 1 gram per cubic centimeter. To get a feeling for the size of things, let us suppose we have a kilogram of uranium in the form of a sphere. What would the radius of the sphere be? A short calculation shows that it is about 2.3 centimeters, about an inch. A ping-pong ball size lump of uranium weighs over 2 pounds!

The computation of r_c is central to the entire bomb enterprise—and to the discussions at Farm Hall. An underestimate of the critical size will persuade one that the task is easier than it is, while an overestimate might well discourage one from undertaking the project at all. We shall first discuss the Frisch–Peierls estimate and then, in due course, the various German estimates, insofar as one can pin them down. On the first of the year 1940, Frisch, a bachelor, moved into the Peierls home. (The late Genia Peierls—Mrs. Peierls—was, as I can testify from personal experience, a woman of nearly overpowering energy, which was largely devoted to hospitality.) Several generations of physicists lived in the Peierls home in Birmingham, and Frisch was one of them. Consequently, Frisch and Peierls found themselves in close proximity in the winter of 1940. Frisch continued his speculations.

To give a qualitative understanding of what Frisch did, we need to introduce the notion of the *mean free path* for fission. As the name might suggest, the mean free path for fission is the average distance a neutron travels between those collisions with ^{235}U nuclei that actually lead to fission. The more nuclei per cubic centimeter there are in the sample—the denser it is—the shorter the path, since there are more objects to collide with. If we call the mean free path d, then we must have d varying as $1/n$, where n is the number of ^{235}U nuclei per cubic centimeter. Remember, the denser the sample, the shorter the mean free path. But Frisch knew the density of uranium. He also knew the mass of the ^{235}U nucleus, which in grams is the absurdly small number 3.9×10^{-22} gram. One can divide these numbers to find that n is given by 4.86×10^{22} nuclei per cubic centimeter. But d also must depend on the probability for fission and that is related to the cross section. For example, if we were dealing with ^{238}U, and neutrons with less than a million electron volts of kinetic energy, the fission mean free path would be essentially infinite, since these neutrons cannot induce fission. The cross section is zero. The larger the fission cross section the smaller the mean free path. If we call the fission cross section σ_f, then putting these two effects together, we have $d = 1/n\sigma_f$.

At this point Frisch was stuck, because σ_f had not yet been measured. He made a guess. He took $\sigma_f = 10^{-23}$ cm^2. It turned out that this is an order of magnitude

(10 times) too big. It is so big that it appears to violate general principles of the quantum theory that limit the size of cross sections. The experimentally correct number for a 1 mega-electron-volt neutron is $\sigma_f = 1.22 \times 10^{-24}$ cm^2. In any case, with his number he found a mean free path of 2.1 centimeters—roughly 10 times shorter than the correct mean free path. In the Peierls theory of the critical size, r_c is proportional to the fission mean free path d. This mean free path is a sort of natural length that sets the scale of the size of things. If we take the d given by 2.1 centimeters, we are led to a critical mass of about 700 grams—less than a kilogram, not tons, a uranium sphere about the size of a ping-pong ball.

As Frisch later recounted, "Of course I discussed the matter with Peierls at once. I had worked out the possible efficiency of my separation system with the help of Clusius's formula, and we came to the conclusion that with something like 100 thousand similar separation tubes one might produce a pound of reasonably pure uranium-235 in a modest time, measured in weeks. At that point we stared at each other and realized that an atomic bomb might after all be possible." [25] As nearly as I can tell, they were the first people—German or Allied—to make this calculation and arrive at this conclusion. Although their calculation was wrong in detail, it made the crucial point that the amount of material needed to make a bomb was not out of reach.

It is interesting to speculate what they might have done if they had had available to them the experimentally correct value of the fission cross section. The same calculation would have given them a critical mass of about 400 kilograms—900 pounds of ^{235}U. (A better calculation, using different approximation techniques, done three years later at Los Alamos gave 60 kilograms for the critical mass, very close to the presently accepted value of 56 kilograms.) What conclusion would Frisch and Pierls have come to if their answer had been 400 kilograms? It is one thing to produce a pound of separated uranium and it is quite another thing to produce a half a ton of the stuff, and so, with the much bigger estimate, they might have given up.

But with their relatively tiny value for the critical mass, Peierls and Frisch pressed on. Would the stuff be explosive? The problem is the following. After the fission process begins, the uranium is rapidly heated up. The uranium turns into a hot gas. This gas expands and, as it expands, its density decreases. The uranium density we have been using of 19 grams per centimeter cubed is for solid uranium. With decreasing density the mean free path becomes longer and longer and the neutrons simply escape. The fission reaction turns itself off.

To take an example, the Hiroshima bomb, which was made of ^{235}U, fissioned only about 2% of the available uranium. In fact, a very small expansion is enough to turn the fission reaction off. One can estimate how fast the heated uranium

---

[25]"Of course I..." WLI p. 125.

nuclei are moving at this point. It turns out that this is about 10^8 centimeters a second. The neutrons released from the fission process had better be moving faster than this; otherwise they won't catch up and there will be no useful explosive chain reaction. But a fast neutron, with a million electron-volt kinetic energy, does move with a speed of about 1.4×10^9 centimeters a second—about 10 times faster than the uranium nuclei. This makes all the difference and shows why "fast" neutrons are absolutely essential in making an atomic bomb.

All of this was clearly understood by Frisch and Peierls by early spring of 1940. But what to do about it? They were still technically enemy aliens. They went to Oliphant, who advised them to write their work up so that it could be transmitted to Henry Tizard, then the most influential British scientist concerned with military applications. Frisch and Peierls wrote two reports. The second one—"On the Construction of a 'Super-bomb;' Based on a Nuclear Chain Reaction in Uranium"—is especially persuasive. It was sufficiently persuasive so that Tizard had a small committee formed composed of outstanding physicists and chaired by G. P. Thomson (the son of J. J. Thomson, the discoverer of the electron). The story of how this committee adopted the code name MAUD has often been told. A cable from Lise Meitner conveyed a request from the Bohr family to inform one Maud Ray Kent of their well-being. It was decided by the committee that Maud Ray Kent was a mysterious anagram for something atomic. A few years later, after Bohr had escaped to England, it was discovered that Maud Ray of Kent had been the governess who had taught English to Bohr's sons.

The release of the final MAUD report in the summer of 1941, and its transmittal to the United States, rescued the American project from stagnation and possibly extinction. It is not our purpose here to retell the story of the sucessful American and Allied effort to build the bomb. Our focus is on the German effort. It is striking, however, that while the Allies' motivation was a legitimate fear that the Germans would soon have the bomb, the German effort seemed to go ahead with the complacent certainty that the Allies would never have one—at least in time to influence the war. When asked after the war about this, Harteck responded, and this seems to be typical, "I was convinced that they [the Allies] would have a reactor in the early forties. But from a reactor, as you know, to a bomb there was a span of several years."[26] The Germans were so sure that the Allies were incapable of making a nuclear weapon that when the German nuclear scientists first heard of Hiroshima, they simply did not believe it. They thought it was a hoax.

Bothe and the German Project

When we left the German project in October of 1939, German Army Ordnance had just taken over the Kaiser-Wilhelm Institute for Physics in Berlin, and had excluded the Culture Ministry, which controlled the universities, from nuclear

---

[26]"I was convinced..." ABS p. 121.

research. The work on nuclear energy was parceled out. There were two major themes, isotope separation and the design of a reactor. In addition, Walther Bothe, who was the leading German nuclear experimental physicist, took charge of trying to measure various nuclear cross sections. The struggle of Bothe to construct a cyclotron in Germany during the war is a saga by itself. There would have been many uses in the program for a cyclotron. For example, one of the ways of separating small quantities of uranium isotopes was to accelerate them in the magnetic field of a cyclotron. The circular orbits of the two isotopes are slightly different. The one with the smaller mass moves in the orbit that has the larger radius; hence the separation. If the isotopes had been separated, even in very small quantities, Bothe could have measured the fast fission cross section in ^{235}U, a crucial parameter.

Among the reasons for Bothe's difficulties in constructing a cyclotron was the fact that he was not a Nazi. He had been deprived of his professorship at the University of Heidelberg by the Nazis in 1933 for not being sufficiently "politically correct." Then he had obtained a position at the Kaiser-Wilhelm Institute for Medicine, also in Heidelberg. Despite this, even before the war, he had begun a campaign to build a cyclotron in Heidelberg. In 1938 he made a world survey of cyclotrons. He discovered that there were 9 operating in the United States, with 27 under construction. There were none in Germany. Early in the war he ordered a cyclotron magnet to be built by the Siemens Company. It was finally delivered only in March of 1943. It took until 1944 before Bothe got the machine running— too late to have any relevance to the program.

The Moderator Problem

In January of 1941, inspired by some calculations by Heisenberg, who had taken charge of the theoretical aspects of reactor design, Bothe did an experiment with neutrons the result of which led to a major setback for the German nuclear program. It may well have prevented the construction of a successful reactor, which the Germans, like the Allies, regarded as the first step towards making an atomic bomb.

As we have seen, to make a reactor work, the fast fission neutrons must be slowed down by a moderator to thermal velocities. This moderator should be made of light elements to maximize the transfer of momentum with each collision. The more momentum transferred in each collision, the more rapidly the neutron is slowed down. But these elements must be chosen so that they absorb neutrons as little as possible, or otherwise the neutrons will be lost to the fission process. Pure hydrogen, the lightest element there is, might seem ideal. But hydrogen absorbs neutrons readily in inelastic collisions, producing a deuteron—a heavy hydrogen nucleus with a neutron and a proton in its nucleus as opposed to only a proton. Heavy hydrogen, which does not easily absorb neutrons, is potentially an excellent moderator, but it is rare and must be extracted at considerable cost from ordinary water.

Carbon would seem like a very good compromise as a moderator, since it is relatively light and very abundant. It also does not absorb neutrons. Graphite, a form of carbon mineral, is commonly used in pencils. The problem is that industrial graphite has impurities, boron, in particular, which soaks up neutrons like a sponge. One part of boron in 500,000, which is very pure graphite by commercial standards, is enough to render all but useless graphite as a moderator.

Unfortunately, Bothe used graphite that was not pure enough. He got an absorption cross section for neutrons that was about twice the value Fermi had gotten with purer carbon when he did a similar experiment at Columbia. Because of Szilard's insistence on secrecy, Fermi's number was not published in the open literature, so Bothe had nothing to check his result by. There is no reason to think that Bothe mismeasured the cross section for the graphite sample he had at hand. Bothe's experiment was repeated by a second group with different results. They seemed to have understood the impurity problem, which they communicated to German Army Ordnance. It is not clear that Bothe was ever informed. At this stage of the project the decisions appear to have been made by people like Diebner in German Army Ordnance and not by the working scientists. In any event, it was decided that graphite was not going to be pursued as a possible moderator. It was too expensive to purify it. This was a fateful mistake.

In an interview after the war Harteck was asked about the reaction to Bothe's result. He replied, "Since there was no publication it is difficult to say. I just did not know what Bothe did."[27] This observation illustrates how poor the communication appears to have been among the various groups. There was a German Army Ordnance publication by Bothe dated January 20, 1941 that described the experiment. Harteck, a key member of the nuclear energy program, apparently never saw it.

This is especially surprising as in the spring of 1940, Harteck had had one of his brilliant ideas, which involved using carbon as a moderator. He managed to extract a block of dry ice (frozen carbon dioxide) from the I. G. Farben company. He knew that in carbon dioxide he could reduce the impurities to 1 part in a million and that oxygen would not absorb neutrons. In the event, Farben sent him the dry ice before he could assemble enough uranium. Purified uranium supplied by the Auer Company, a company that still exists and most recently has been performing the same service for the Iraquis, was in short supply.

Harteck's "reactor" never did show any neutron multiplication. If he had been given enough uranium and enough dry ice at the same time, however, it is quite likely that he, and not Fermi, would have assembled the first chain-reacting pile. It was largely due to Szilard that our program obtained enough purified graphite—

---

[27]"Since there was..." ABS p. 102.

250 tons from the National Carbide Company—so that on December 2, 1942 Fermi and his team, having moved to the University of Chicago, made the first nuclear reactor. It had a purified graphite moderator.

Once the Germans abandoned carbon as a moderator, the only alternative for the German program was heavy hydrogen, in the form of heavy water. In March of 1941, Harteck reported to the war office that there were two urgent problems facing the project: the separation of uranium isotopes and the production of heavy water. He put the higher priority on the latter since a heavy-water reactor could, he felt, be made to work with natural uranium. The separation of ^{238}U and ^{235}U was so much more complicated and expensive than the production of heavy water that it should only, he wrote, be undertaken "for special applications in which cheapness is but a secondary consideration"—that is, for example, for making atomic bombs where price is no object.[28]

The principal source of heavy water in Europe was the Norwegian Hydro-Electric Company located at Vermork in southern Norway. The heavy water was a by-product of the plant's electrolytic separation of the hydrogen and oxygen in water. The hyrdrogen given off in such a process is relatively rich in heavy hydrogen (it is about 13% heavy hydrogen). It could then be further processed into nearly pure heavy water. By 1939, however the production of heavy water by Hydro-Electric was only some 10 kilograms per month. It was in no great demand until the German nuclear program began. After the German occupation of Norway in April of 1940, Harteck had a catalytic conversion process installed at the Vermork plant, which had been taken over by the I. G. Farben Company. With the new process, the Vermork installation was, in principle, capable of producing about 5 tons of heavy water a year. Harteck tried to hedge his bets by having similar installations set up in Germany, but Army Ordnance decided that this was too expensive and continued to tap into the Norwegian supply. This turned out to be another fatal mistake.

From 1941 on, British Intelligence was aware of the increase in the heavy-water activity at Hydro-Electric and that these supplies were being shipped to Germany. Since no one could think of any use for large quantities of heavy water other than in a nuclear reactor program, this seriously alarmed the British. By the

---

[28] "...for special applications..." See, for example, *The German Atomic Bomb*, by David Irving (Simon and Schuster, New York, 1967), p. 88. Much has been learned since Irving wrote his book. His book is still the most exciting account of the successful British and Norwegian attempts to block the production and shipment of heavy water to Germany. It reads like a spy novel. I shall refer to this book as GAB. For an authoritative account of our program to generate the essential materials for making a bomb see *Atomic Energy for Military Purposes* by Henry D. Smyth (Princeton University Press, Princeton, 1947). It is sometimes said that the "Smyth Report" revealed too much about how to make a bomb. In fact, it is suprising how little it reveals. It is a good source of the general history.

spring of 1942 the British, with the aid of some escaped Norwegians, had established a direct link to the plant. They acquired detailed plans of it. By October, a Norwegian team had been parachuted into Vermork and had reported back to England that the Germans had reinforced the security around the plant. In November the first commando raid on the plant took place with disasterous results. All the commandos were killed either in the landing or by the Germans after being captured.

The fact that these commandos were attacking a heavy-water facility tipped the Germans off not only to the fact that the Allies knew what they were trying to do, but that they had to be trying to do something similar, since the Germans also could only foresee using heavy water in reactor construction. Oddly, this did not seem to have lent a special urgency to the German program, although in February of 1942 in a report to General Emil Leeb, the head of Army Ordnance, the authors, who are anonymous wrote, "In the present situation preparations should be made for the technical development and ultilization of atomic energy. The enormous significance that it has for the energy economy in general and for the *Wehrmacht* [Armed Forces] in particular justifies such preliminary research, all the more in that this problem is also being worked on intensively in the enemy nations, especially in America." [29]

By the end of February, 1943, Allied commandos were back in Norway. This time, in one of the great exploits of the war, they completely destroyed the heavy-water facility. More remarkably, there was no loss of life on either side. The power station itself, which the Norwegians needed, was left intact. About a ton of heavy water was destroyed. It took several months before the Germans were able to get the plant back into operation. In November 1943 an air raid with 140 bombers was mounted against the plant and the neighboring fortifications. It was not very accurate, but it persuaded the Germans that making heavy water in Norway had no future. It was decided to evacuate all the remaining equipment to Germany.

In the meanwhile, Harteck had persuaded the I. G. Farben company to erect a small pilot plant in Leuna (Germany). The terms under which this plant was built illustrate another weakness in the German program, namely greed. The Farben Company, which had been making a fortune in the occupied countries, insisted on keeping a share of the patent rights to Harteck's heavy-water process and a share of any future profits to be derived from nuclear energy. These conditions were agreed to. By contrast, when the du Pont Company was selected by General Leslie Groves in the fall of 1942 to construct the plutonium-producing reactors in Hanford, Washington the terms were cost, plus 1 dollar, with all patent rights relinquished. This was typical.

---

[29]"In the present situation..." This quote can be found in UN p. 443. I am grateful to David Cassidy for calling my attention to it.

In January of 1944 the Germans decided to evacuate the last 14 tons of partially concentrated heavy water from Norwegian Hydro-Electric to Germany. A direct commando attack on the plant was now impossible because of the increased security. But the heavy water had to be shipped to Germany by train and then ferryboat across Lake Tinnsjö, one of the deepest lakes in the world. On February 20, 1944 the ferryboat Hydro was sunk by Norwegian commandos, with an unfortunate considerable loss of civilian lives. The drums carrying the heavy water disappeared into the lake.

The Plutonium Alternative

The motivation behind the German reactor project was essentially similar to that behind the Allies. No one had made a chain-reacting system and, until this was done, one could not be absolutely sure that a chain reaction would work. As for the military applications, the crudest was hinted at by Harteck after the war. He noted that, "If, for example, a carbon-dioxide reactor had been made a few years before the end of the war, it could have run. This could have placed nuclear research in an entirely new aspect." [30]

"You must be thankful that this didn't occur," he went on. "Not that an atomic bomb would have been made. But if you have a carbon-dioxide reactor and you let it run for a certain time, the cubes or rods of uranium would have become highly radioactive. Much highly radioactive material could have been made which could have been thrown around. That would have been very bad." Not an atomic bomb exactly, but still a very nasty weapon.

The most sophisticated military application of a reactor, however, was the possibility of using it to produce transuranic (heavier-than-uranium) elements, notably what came to be called plutonium. In June of 1940, the Princeton physicist Louis Turner published an article in *The Physical Review* entitled "The Missing Heavy Nuclei." [31] (It followed a brief communication on the same subject a few months earlier. Missing from *The Physical Review* was an article by Turner called "Atomic Energy from ^{238}U." He had submitted it on May 29, 1940, but Szilard, worried that it might be taken up by the Germans, persuaded Turner not to publish it until after the war. It was finally published in 1946.) Turner asked why there did not seem to be any elements heavier than uranium present in nature. He produced a very ingenious explanation, although not one that we accept today. Turner imagined that at some epoch there had been such elements, but that they had been irradiated by neutrons. Let us suppose that in this epoch there had been a substantial amount of ^{238}U.

---

[30] "If, for example..." ABS p. 128.

[31] See "The Missing Heavy Nuclei" by Louis A. Turner, *The Physical Review*, June 1, 1940, p. 950. Turner's suppressed paper was published in *The Physical Review* **69**, 366 (1946).

According to Turner's idea these ^{238}U nuclei are irradiated with neutrons. There is then a probability, which increases as the neutrons become slower, of a ^{238}U nucleus capturing a neutron, as discussed earlier, and releasing an energetic electromagnetic quantum—a gamma ray—and forming a ^{239}U nucleus. This nucleus, Turner reasoned, using general ideas of nuclear structure, was probably unstable. It was likely to shed one of its excess neutrons by emitting an electron, turning the neutron into a proton. The nucleus so formed would be an isotope of an element never previously observed with 93 protons and 146 neutrons. He called this element "Eka-rhenium." "Eka" was a prefix meaning "beyond" that had been employed by radiochemists. We now call this element neptunium, after the next planet beyond Uranus. He guessed that it too would be unstable against decay, producing an electron. He was right. It turns out that its half-life for electron decay is about 2.3 days, which became the signature for confirming its presence. Indeed, independently of Turner, the Berkeley experimenters Edwin McMillan and Philip Abelson had, at just about the same time, identified a 2.3-day electron-decaying element produced in the cyclotron bombardment of uranium by neutrons. They had discovered neptunium.

It was the decay product of "Eka-rhenium" that Turner was after. He did not know its stability, but he had a pretty good idea of its fissionability. Turner realized that this decay product, which he called "Eka-osmium"—which we now call plutonium, after the next planet beyond Neptune—consisted of 94 protons and 145 neutrons. If this plutonium isotope, ^{239}Pu, absorbed a neutron, it would become a "virtual" or even–even nucleus like ^{236}U, which is what is produced virtually when ^{235}U absorbs a slow neutron, and hence ^{239}Pu would be fissionable by slow neutrons in the same way that ^{235}U is. This was Bohr's argument now extended to plutonium.

This, Turner thought, would account for the absence of plutonium in nature. In his scenario, plutonium would have fissioned away by its accidental contact with slow neutrons. As an aside he pointed out, crediting John Wheeler, that an alternative possibility might be the heavy nucleus' instability against "spontanous fission." A heavy nucleus can, as we have mentioned, with a small probability fission spontaneously without any help from an external neutron. This, we now believe, is the correct explanation for the absence of plutonium in nature. There is no hint in Turner's paper that any of this might have anything to do with weapons. There is also nothing in the reports of Frisch and Peierls, written about the same time, to suggest that they had thought of transuranics made in reactors as fuel for nuclear weapons. That came soon.

Von Weizsäcker's "Open Road"

Szilard may have been the first person to think of using transuranics as a reactor fuel, but Turner was the first to suggest their use for bomb design. Close behind was C. F. von Weizsäcker on the German side.

Von Weizsäcker's recollections of his wartime activities have always been exceedingly murky. Decades after the war, in January of 1988 he gave a lecture at the international high-energy laboratory CERN, in Geneva, entitled "The Political and Moral Consequences of Science." In it he recounts his reaction when he first heard in 1939, in a seminar given by Otto Hahn, that Joliot-Curie had found the secondary neutrons emitted in fission. Von Weizsäcker said:[32]

> For every nuclear scientist, it was clear from the outset that if there was more than one secondary neutron per fission there would be a chain reaction. From that moment, it was clear that we were in a completely changed situation. We had an enormous, nearly unbearable responsibility for the world, which we had never sought, never wished for.
>
> I went immediately to my friend George Picht, who was a classical scholar and a philosopher, to discuss the question of how mankind was to survive given the fact that, if the chain reaction was possible, it would inevitably be carried out inasmuch as you could not stop elsewhere in the world doing it even if you did not do it yourself. If mankind was to survive, we concluded, it was necessary to abolish the institution of war. No other solution would work.

We, of course, have no way of knowing under what circumstances this pious conversation took place or what Picht and von Weizsäcker actually said. What we do know is that on 17th July of 1940, about a year after this alleged conversation took place, von Weizsäcker delivered a five-page document to German Army Ordnance—a copy was also sent to Heisenberg—explaining how to use transuranics to make bombs.[33] In his paper, copies of which are still extant, he speaks only of Eka-Rhenium (neptunium). (The notion of plutonium came to the Germans a year later when Fritz Houtermans raised it in another secret research report.) Using the Bohr–Wheeler theory, von Weizsäcker suggested that the next element beyond uranium would be fissionable and that it could be manufactured in a reactor from the radioactive decay of ^{238}U. Since it is chemically different from uranium, it could be removed from its uranium matrix by conventional chemical means. This would bypass the terribly difficult job of separating the uranium isotopes. The road to making a bomb appeared to open up. Indeed, one of the uses that von Weizsäcker gives for Eka-Rhenium at the end of his paper is *als Sprengstoff*—as an explosive.

It should be noted however, that in this document Weizsäcker only considered the fission of Eka-Rhenium by thermal neutrons. It is not clear whether he understood

---

[32] "For every nuclear scientist..." see "The Political and Moral Consequences of Science," *Transcriptions of Lectures held at CERN*, Geneva, January 1988, p. 30. We shall refer to this as PAM.

[33] I am grateful to David Cassidy for supplying a copy of von Weizsäcker's report.

the importance of fast neutrons in making a bomb. When pressed by a questioner at a later CERN lecture about how it was possible for physicists like himself and Heisenberg to work on a nuclear bomb for Germany, he gave a lengthy response, one which he had often given in previous interviews. In reading it, keep in mind that von Weizsäcker *voluntarily* offered the idea of using neptunium to German Army Ordnance. No one asked him to do it. He says in part:[34]

> I would not do the same now as I did at that time. I wanted to participate in the work. I did not expect that the bomb would be made during the war which Hitler had started. Still, this was not certain, and it might well have been possible, and if it had, Heisenberg and I and the others would have been in a horrible situation, because we did not actually want to give Hitler such a weapon.

> The motives for carrying on were different in different people. I had a long talk with Otto Hahn about this matter in October 1939, when I was quite active in the research. I said to him: "Please join the *Uranverein*, not to help us, but to help yourself, because you will protect your Institute by doing so. You will be doing something which is officially judged to be important for the war effort, and therefore your Institute will continue. Your people will not be dispersed to other projects or to the front." He said, "Well, I think you are right, I shall." Then he became quite emotional and said: "But if my work leads to a nuclear bomb for Hitler, I will commit suicide." "*Dann bring' ich mich um*." I can hear him saying it now.

> It was a very ambivalent situation. It was quite clear that Hahn was not the man to make a bomb. He continued to study radioactive substances, and that was not a great problem. Heisenberg was fully able to imagine a bomb, and to make plans for it, and what we did not publish at the time, but wrote in secrecy, will be published, I am told, in Heisenberg's collected works. Then it will be possible to read about that.

> In September or October 1939, Heisenberg told me the following: "Well, we must do it. Hitler will lose this war. It is like the end game in chess, with one castle less than the others. He will lose his war. Consequently, much of Germany will be destroyed, or its value will have disappeared. The value of science will still be there and it is necessary that science should live through the war, and we must do something for that. And therefore we must enter into that enterprise." Again, I can almost hear him say it word for word.

> My motive was far more ambitious and far less reasonable, far less sensible. I felt at that time that, by being somebody who

---

[34]"I would..." PAM p. 42.

was able to work on such an important assignment, I might obtain access to those responsible for the direction of policy, which I might thus be able to influence rather than simply being at the receiving end.

On the other hand, I have always been a very cautious person, even a little fearful. I always behaved in such a manner that no great damage was done, though great damage might have been done if we had been able to make a bomb.

Then, after a year or so, we realized that so much work was needed to make a bomb that we had no chance of making it. From that moment on, the moral problem more or less disappeared for us. The question was just how to survive. We did survive ...

The reader is invited to compare this curiously self-serving and ambiguous response to what von Weizsäcker actually said over a period of six months at Farm Hall.

The German Project, Continued

By 1942, the German Army Ordnance nuclear program involved some 40 physicists and chemists, spread out over nine different sites. Bothe was in Heidelberg, Hahn in Berlin, Harteck in Hamburg and Heisenberg in Leipzig and Berlin. In addition, there was a strange enterprise located in the Lichterfeld suburb of Berlin. It took place in the large private house of a man named Manfred von Ardenne.

Von Ardenne has been described as a "minor aristocrat but a major inventor of great ingenuity." [35] At the time he enters our story, he had found a sponsor for his work in an unlikely place—the Post Office. As a person who made his living by doing contract scientific work, he had done some research for the Post Office on improving communications. He had very little formal education in physics, but he had learned about fission, and when he turned his attention to it, he focused on isotope separation. Harteck later commented in an interview, "I met him once; he was a very bright boy. In his young years he started to make very good inventions. This impressed the Post Minister very much and he was given lots of money to develop his ideas. But I think nuclear energy was a bit out of his line. He was to a certain extent a type much like Werner von Braun ... They weren't what you would

---

[35] "...minor aristocrat..." This characterization can be found in an unpublished manuscript entitled *Heisenberg, German Morality, and the Atomic Bomb 1939–1945* by Paul Lawrence Rose. I am grateful to Professor Rose for sending me this manuscript. It is his thesis that Heisenberg did not understand the difference between a reactor and a bomb and this is why he was not able to make an atomic bomb. I believe the Farm Hall reports present a different picture. My sense of it is that Heisenberg understood the difference, but that he did not understand either one very well—certainly not the bomb.

call scientists but used very modern technology to overcome all their difficulties with imagination and hard work." [36]

Von Ardenne called his laboratory *Institut A*. In it he had several co-workers busily developing a variety of schemes for separating isotopes. Von Ardenne later claimed that in the late fall of 1941, he received successive visits from Heisenberg and Hahn who, independently, informed him that they had worked out the critical mass for a ^{235}U bomb and found it to be about 10 kilograms. What he was supposed to do with this information is unclear; but before he could do anything, von Ardenne claims that he was visited by von Weizsäcker, who told him that he and Heisenberg had decided, on theoretical grounds, that a ^{235}U bomb was impossible. They had, von Ardenne claims, gotten the notion that the fission cross sections dropped as the ^{235}U heated up, thus quenching any explosive reaction. Since Heisenberg is dead, and von Weizsäcker has essentially denied that any such conversation took place, one does not know what to make of all of this. It is one of several brick walls anyone who studies this subject runs into.

One also does not know what to make of the figure of 10 kilograms for the critical mass of ^{235}U that von Ardenne, who as of this writing is very much alive and living in Germany, insists he was told.[37] But in February of 1942, a 200-page report entitled *Energiegewinnung aus Uran* was produced for German Army Ordnance detailing all the work that had been done on uranium up to that point by the official project. In the report there is a figure—the author or authors are not named and the method of calculation is not supplied—of a critical mass between 10 and 100 kilograms. But during various stages of the war, this seems to have fluctuated upwards to the order of tons. In the summer of 1945, in a colloquy appearing below in the Farm Hall reports, Hahn asked Heisenberg whether the Hiroshima bomb—which used separated ^{235}U—required as much as 30 kilograms. Heisenberg replied, "I think so certainly, but quite honestly I have never worked it out as I never believed one could get pure '235.'" [38] How to reconcile this with von Ardenne's perhaps faulty memory is hard to fathom. Indeed, if Heisenberg "never worked it out," where did the estimate made for German Army Ordnance come from? Another unsolved mystery.

---

[36]"I met him once..." ABS p. 119. Von Ardenne has repeated his story in the May 8, 1993 issue of *Die Welt*. He was also featured in a recent Nova television program about his group, who went to the Soviet Union after the war to help build the first Russian atomic bomb. Rose claims that when von Ardenne returned to East Germany, after this adventure, he insisted that his daughter be addressed as "contessa" in her school. Rose describes von Ardenne as an "operator." This seems to understate the case.

[37]I am grateful to Mark Walker for correspondence about the German Army Ordnance figure for the critical mass. As far as one can discover, no wartime document exists with a detailed computation of this mass.

[38]"I think so..." Farm Hall transcripts Report 4.

The Plutonium Alternative, Continued

One thing is certain and that is that von Ardenne's laboratory came up with the idea of using plutonium—this time it definitely *was* plutonium, not neptunium. This had to do with the presence in his laboratory of the remarkable figure of Fritz Houtermans. Houtermans, who grew up in Vienna, had a half-Jewish mother and radical left-wing politics. He was a brilliant theoretical physicist and had no trouble in finding a job in the Soviet Union in the mid-1930s when it became clear that he could no longer remain in Germany. In 1937 Houtermans was arrested by the GPU, the Soviet secret police, as he was trying to emigrate from Russia. He spent 2½ years under terrible conditions in Soviet prisons. He kept his sanity by doing mathematics in his head. In April of 1940, as a "German," he was sent back to Germany where he was promptly jailed by the Gestapo for being a suspected Soviet spy. He managed to make contact with the Berlin physicists and was soon released. Von Laue found him a job in von Ardenne's laboratory, which was out of the way of the mainstream research enterprises.

By early 1941 Houtermans had rediscovered von Weizsäcker's transuranic idea. He wrote a report on it for von Ardenne in August of 1941, which was officially circulated only in 1944. But Houtermans was deeply shocked by his own discovery. He was persuaded that a German atomic bomb was now imminent. He, and von Weizsäcker, had no idea just how difficult it was to actually make a bomb out of plutonium. Assuming one had a reactor (the Germans never were able to build one) and one had learned how to separate the relatively tiny amounts of plutonium from the uranium fuel (a very difficult operation in its own right) one would then be in for an unpleasant surprise. Because of the intense neutron background in a reactor, the plutonium isotope ^{240}Pu is produced along with the isotope ^{239}Pu. The former absorbs an additional neutron to produce the latter. But ^{240}Pu spontaneously fissions. This is a disaster from the bomb point of view since the neutrons produced in these spontaneous fissions will cause the predominant ^{239}Pu nuclei to fission before a critical mass can be assembled. The result will be a fizzle, not an explosion.

Dealing with the above was probably the hardest problem solved at Los Alamos.[39] It took the enormous assembled talents of nearly the entire laboratory. Separating the two plutonium isotopes appeared hopeless, at least on any time scale that made any sense. If one tried to assemble the plutonium into a critical mass by mechanically shooting two subcritical masses against each other, as one does with a ^{235}U bomb, the assembly was much too slow to prevent predetonation.

---

[39] For example, Emilio Segrè's posthumous autobiography, *A Mind Always in Motion*, University of California Press, Berkeley, 1993, discusses the role of spontaneous fission in the plutonium story. Segrè was at Los Alamos and played a leading role in this aspect of the work. He and Fermi also realised that plutonium could be explosive. Segrè and collaborators made the first measurements of the plutonium cross section for fission, at Berkeley, in the spring of 1941, a result that was only published in the open literature after the war.

The problem was solved by implosion. A precisely shaped explosive charge was wrapped around the outside of the solid plutonium sphere, which became known as the "pit." This explosive is detonated at several points on the sphere nearly simultanously. The resulting shock wave implodes rapidly enough to overcome the predetonation problem.

The use of a *solid* pit was not obvious, but turned out to be much superior to a hollow sphere. It is structurally more stable and simpler to construct. It can be made to compress with the explosive shock wave. The critical mass of plutonium is substantially smaller than that of ^{235}U—11 kilograms as opposed to 56. This has to do with the fact that both the fission cross section and the average number of neutrons emitted per fission are larger. In the summer of 1957, I visited the Nevada test site where aboveground explosions took place. I was given a plutonium pit to hold. It had, as I recall, about the size and weight of a bowling ball. It was slightly warm to the touch, since plutonium is marginally radioactive.

In any event, the technology associated with implosion—the nearly simultaneous detonation of all points of the explosive shell, and the shaping of the detonation waves—was, when it was conceived during the war, so novel that one could not be sure that it would work. That is precisely what was successfully tested on July 16, 1945 in the desert in New Mexico. The Hiroshima bomb that was dropped on August 6, a pure ^{235}U weapon, had never been tested in prototype. The principles were considered so simple, relatively speaking, that no one had any serious doubts that it would work. It was a one-of-a-kind affair. We never built another atom bomb with pure ^{235}U. Plutonium was much more efficent and much simpler to produce, once the enormous problems of production and detonation had been solved.

The problems associated with plutonium never were recognized by the Germans during the war. There, the idea of using plutonium faded away. This is hardly surprising since, without a working reactor, it was impossible to make significant amounts. Even microscopic quantities produced in a cyclotron would have been sufficient to determine the relevant cross sections and other nuclear properties: the Germans did not succeed at this either. But, when Houtermans first thought of plutonium, he was so alarmed that he decided that he had to warn the Allies. He sent a message through a refugee who was leaving for America. The message said in effect that the Allied effort should be sped up, if there *were* such an effort. Houtermans did not know. The message also said that Heisenberg was trying to delay the work, fearing catastrophic results. This message brings us face to face with one of the most difficult issues to resolve in the history of the German nuclear program—the part or parts played by Heisenberg.

Werner Heisenberg

It is very unlikely that agreement will ever be reached on all the issues raised by Werner Heisenberg's war time role. One thing is certain; Heisenberg was a great physicist. He had the first truly quantum-mechanical mind—the ability to take the leap beyond the classical visualizing pictures into the abstract, all-but-impossible-to-visualize world of the subatomic. To a layperson it is very difficult to explain the difference between this kind of ability and the ability to do common-sense engineering physics. Heisenberg was simply not very good at that. Recently Peierls, who had worked with him in the 1920s wrote, "Though a brilliant theoretician he [Heisenberg] was always very casual about numbers. When I was his student in the late 1920s the first assignment he gave me was to check whether a recent observation in a spectroscopic experiment could be explained as an example of his uncertainty principle. A simple back-of-an-envelope estimate would have shown that the effect was 100 or even 1,000 times greater than could be explained by his hypothesis." [40] The one thing that an engineer cannot be is "casual about numbers." Fermi, in contrast, was a great engineering physicist—the better experimenters usually are—as well as a brilliant theorist. Fermi could estimate the order of magnitude of things within, as one witness put it to me, a "gnat's whisker." Heisenberg's inability to do this sort of thing made him, as far as the German program was concerned, often part of the problem rather than the solution.

In December of 1939 and in February of 1940, Heisenberg produced two reports for German Army Ordnance that set out the theory of a chain-reacting reactor, at least in principle. He concluded that a reactor moderated with heavy water could work with natural uranium. This is what inspired Harteck to begin investigating the possibilities of obtaining enough heavy water. By the summer, the Germans in Berlin began constructing a facility for their reactor experiments, which they called the "Virus House" to throw off suspicious visitors. The first experiments were done, partially under Heisenberg's direction, with an arrangement of layers of uranium oxide alternating with layers of a paraffin moderator. Heavy water was not available. There was also not enough uranium. The results were inconclusive, but were encouraging enough to suggest that the setup might go critical if heavy water were substituted for paraffin and sufficient uranium used. There was no sense of urgency about any of this work—no special pressure from German Army Ordnance. Indeed, people like Heisenberg and von Weizsäcker also spent time doing pure research and teaching. By contrast, Harteck did work full time on military applications. The reason for this relaxed attitude was that the German military was totally convinced that the war was as good as won. An atomic bomb might be icing on the cake, but for them the cake was plenty good enough without it.

By 1941, the atmosphere had changed. The Germans were now bogged down in Russia and winning the war now became a serious business. At this point,

---

[40] "Though a brilliant..." Rudolf Peierls, *New York Review of Books*, April 22, 1993, p. 6. I am grateful to Professor Peierls for discussions and correspondence over the last few years concerning the German nuclear program. I was very surprised when I read the Farm Hall reports carefully, to see Heisenberg's ineptness with this sort of numerical estimate. It was, therefore, especially interesting to me to learn that this was well-known among his colleagues.

Schumann, the general in charge of weapons research at German Army Ordnance, decided that unless the nuclear program could demonstrate its relevance to the war the Army would stop supporting it. A report was prepared, authored by a panel of anonymous experts from both inside and outside the project. This was the 200 page report mentioned earlier in which the critical mass of 10 to 100 kilograms of ^{235}U was given. The report was optimistic.

Optimism notwithstanding, German Army Ordnance decided to drop support of the project since it appeared to have no immediate relevance to the war effort. The natural entity to continue the project seemed to be the Kaiser-Wilhelm Society, the umbrella institution under which the Kaiser-Wilhelm institutes devoted to the various sciences operated. At about the time of the transfer, Schumann organized a conference in Berlin at which the nuclear scientists could parade their wares, both for other specialists—and in a separate venue—for a selected nontechnical public, especially from the government officials. This conference may have represented the high-water mark of the German nuclear program. The popular lecture series took place on the 26th of February 1942. Bormann, Göring, Himmler and Speer, as well as other very important Party figures, had been invited, but declined. Among the actual listeners was Bernhard Rust, the Minister of Education, and one of the most primitive of the Nazi racists. He took special pride in the fact that under his auspices the Jews had been forced out of the universities in 1933. Not long after he had succeeded in this, Rust found himself at a banquet in Göttingen seated next to David Hilbert, perhaps the greatest mathematician of the 20th century and a marvelous man. Rust asked, "And how is mathematics in Göttingen, now that it has been freed of Jewish influence?"[41]

"Mathematics in Göttingen?" Hilbert replied. "There is really none anymore."

This was the sort of man—Rust—who was about to take over the direction of the nuclear program.

Many of the figures we have already encountered addressed the group: Schumann, Hahn, Bothe, Harteck and, of course, Heisenberg. Heisenberg's lecture was a mixture of popular fission science with a tantalyzing glimpse of its military applications thrown in. He told his audience, "If one could assemble a lump of uranium-235 large enough for the escape of neutrons from its surface to be small compared with the internal neutron multiplication, then the number of neutrons would multiply enormously in a very short space of time, and the whole uranium fission energy, of 15 million-million calories per ton, would be liberated in a fraction of a second. Pure uranium-235 is thus seen to be an explosive of quite unimaginable

---

[41]"And how is..." This quote can be found in *Hilbert*, by Constance Reid (Springer, New York, 1987), p. 205. This book is a fine introduction to the life and work of this extraordinary man.

force." [42] He also managed a "commercial" for plutonium. When one has succeeded in constructing an operating reactor, he pointed out, "the question of producing the explosive receives a new twist: through the transmutation of uranium inside the pile, a new element is created [atomic number 94 (plutonium)], which is in all probability as explosive as pure uranium-235, with the same colossal force." [43]

In contemplating this lecture and its audience, one is struck by the question: What did Heisenberg think he was doing? What went through his mind at the sight of Rust and the other Nazis in this audience? Why was Heisenberg dangling before these people an "explosive of quite unimaginable force?" Certainly Heisenberg was not a Nazi. In fact he had been publicly denounced. In 1937, the Nazi Party member and Nobel Prize-winning physicist Johannes Stark inspired and partially wrote an article in the SS journal *Das Schwarze Korps*, attacking physicists like Heisenberg who believed in 20th century physics—relativity and the quantum theory—as "white Jews." Stark and his associates invented something they called *Deutsche Physik* consisting mainly of the classical physics they understood. The abstract thinking of the quantum theory and relativity was for them the work of Jews and their sympathizers. Heisenberg had family connections with Heinrich Himmler, the head of the SS and future principal organizer of the "final solution," who was persuaded to take a personal interest in what was a potentially very serious and dangerous matter. People had ended up in concentration camps for much less. This resulted in a letter Himmler wrote on July 21, 1938 to his subordinate, SS *Gruppenführer* Reinhard Heydrich, which reads in part:[44]

> Dear Heydrich,
>
> I have received the good and very objective report on Professor Werner Heisenberg, Leipzig. I enclose herewith a very proper letter of Professor Prandtl, Göttingen [Ludwig Prandtl was a very distinguished aeronautical engineer who strongy supported the case for modern physics.], with which I agree. ... I also enclose a copy of my letter to Heisenberg for your information. I believe that Heisenberg is a decent person and that we cannot afford to lose or to silence this man, who is still young and can still produce a rising generation in science...

On the same day he wrote to Heisenberg: [45]

---

[42]"If one could..." GAB p. 108.

[43]"...the question of..." GAB p. 110.

[44]"Dear Heydrich..." This quote is taken from Samuel Goudsmit's book *Alsos* (American Institute for Physics, New York, 1995), pp. 117–118. This is a reissue of Goudsmit's classic. This letter, and several others, are given in translation alongside the originals. It gives one something of a shock to see the original letters. I shall refer to Goudsmit's book as ALS.

[45]"Very esteemed..." ALS p. 117.

Very esteemed Herr Professor Heisenberg:

Only today can I answer your letter of July 21, 1937, in which you direct yourself to me because of the article of Professor Stark in *Das Schwarze Korps*.

Because you were recommended by my family I have had your case investigated with special care and precision.

I am glad that I can now inform you that I do not approve of the attack in *Das Schwarze Korps* and that I have taken measures against any further attack against you.

I hope I shall see you in Berlin in the fall, in November or December, so that we may talk things over thoroughly man to man [*von Mann zu Mann*].

With friendly greetings,
Heil Hitler!
Yours,
H. Himmler

P.S. I consider it, however, best if in the future you make a distinction for your audience between the results of scientific research and the personal and political attitude of the scientists involved.

Himmler's remarkable postscript became the compromise formula that the physicists working in the German nuclear energy program adopted in order to enable them to use results of the relativity theory and the quantum theory while avoiding a confrontation with the advocates of *Deutsche Physik*. They attempted to divorce the scientific results from any context, or they invented a false context. This activity culminated in a meeting (called "religion discussions") attended by some 30 scientists in November of 1942, in Seefeld, in the Tyrolean Alps. Heisenberg was there and the final report was co-authored by von Weizsäcker. By citing only "Aryan scientists" it managed to deprive Einstein of any real credit for the relativity theory. "Einstein," it said," merely followed up the already existing ideas consistently and added the cornerstone." [46] The final paragraph, which was von Weizsäcker's work, reads, "At the Seefeld meeting the opinion was expressed, however, that one must reject the imposition of the physical relativity theory into a world philosophy of relativism, as has been attempted by the Jewish propaganda press of the previous era." [47] Throughout the war the German nuclear physicists carried with them the excess baggage of these political compromises. This is another of the many reasons why their project failed.

---

[46]"Einstein..." ALS p. 153.
[47]"At the Seefeld..." ALS p. 153.

The Project's New Sponsors

The earlier 1942 meeting in February in Berlin, the one that Rust attended, was even more successful than its sponsors may have intended. Rust, apparently impressed by Heisenberg's lecture, decided that nuclear energy was too important to be left to the Kaiser-Wilhelm Society and he took it over himself, placing it under the aegis of the *Reich* Research Council. The head of its physics department was a loyal Nazi, Abraham Esau. News of Heisenberg's lecture even filtered up to Joseph Goebbels, the Reich's Minster of Propaganda.

Goebbels got it into his head that a nuclear weapon could be built rapidly enough to actually win the war. This was a dangerous situation for the scientists to find themselves in. They did not see the slightest chance for an atomic bomb to be built by them in the immediately forseeable future. After all, they had not yet even succeeded in building a reactor. The general brouhaha caught the attention of Albert Speer, who had just been appointed Minister of Armaments and Munitions. On June 4, 1942 a meeting was arranged among Speer, several military figures he brought with him, and the nuclear scientists. All the participants in our story were there. Heisenberg gave a lecture that was presumably a repeat performance of his lecture of February. After the lecture, Speer asked Heisenberg directly about the possibility of atomic bombs. Heisenberg was now under the gun and, as Speer later recalled, said, "The technical prerequisites for production would take years to develop, two years at the earliest, even provided that the program was given maximum support." [48] But, when Speer asked him specifically how much support would be needed, Heisenberg mentioned a few million marks, a figure that Speer thought was absurdly low. It became clear to Speer (as he later claimed) that, at this point, for whatever reasons, the German nuclear scientists were no longer serious about building a bomb. Nonetheless, he felt that nuclear energy was a technology of great promise for the future of Germany and his office lent its support, which was essential, for the rest of the war.

All of this had a dramatic effect on Heisenberg's position. In June of 1942, the same month as the conference with Speer, he was named director of the Kaiser-Wilhelm Institute for Physics and a professor at the University of Berlin. This made Heisenberg the de facto director of the nuclear program, the goal of which was, at the very least, to build a working reactor. Heisenberg's appointment did not please everybody. When Harteck was asked about it after the war he replied angrily, "But how can you be a leader in such technological matters when you have never run an experiment in your whole life? That's ridiculous! That's no excuse whatsoever!

"While Heisenberg is one of the best theoreticians of our age and Weizsäcker, in addition to being a very good theoretical physicist and philosopher, could also

---

[48] "The technical..." MAB p. 404.

expound his views very well, nevertheless both had never been involved in a large experimental venture before. How could they think they could lead the development of a new technology? That was poor judgement; it is almost unbelievable." [49]

Harteck had some reason to complain. In February of 1943, he and a colleague Johannes Jensen proposed using a double centrifuge for separating isotopes. In a centrifuge, particles of different mass are acted on by different forces, which results in the isotope separation. In the double centrifuge, two centrifuges are connected and the gas is periodically pulled from one chamber to the other, multiplying the separation effect. Harteck estimated that about 100 of these centrifuges would be enough to enhance the percentage of ^{235}U so that a reactor would operate with substantially less uranium. The so-called "ultracentrifuge" was one of the few enduring technological innovations to come out of the German project. For his own part, Heisenberg certainly set back the reactor project by his insistence on inferior designs of his own devising. His original construct (in Berlin) consisted of alternating layers of metal uranium and a paraffin moderator. The layer design was simpler to compute, which is what appealed to Heisenberg but apalled his more experimentally oriented colleagues. In addition to experimenting with a layer design in Berlin, Heisenberg had also worked with spherical designs in Leipzig. They consisted of concentric spheres of uranium alternating with heavy water. These too lent themselves to theoretical computation. They yielded Germany's first neutron multiplication, in the spring of 1941, and convinced Heisenberg and co-workers that controlled and uncontrolled nuclear fission were not just theoretical possibilities but technically feasible.

In 1942 the young theorist Karl-Heinz Höcker was able to return from the Russian front where he had been sent. The liberation of some of the young scientists who had been sent to fight at various fronts was one of the dividends of Speer's interest in the project. They were given military exemptions. This preserved at least some part of a generation of young physicists. Höcker, upon his return, had gone with von Weizsäcker to the German-occupied University of Strassburg where the latter had accepted a professorship. Höcker made a careful analysis of the optimal design of the fuel elements and the moderator in a reactor and concluded that Heisenberg's Berlin layer design was about the worst. The best would be to make uranium spheres with radii about the size of the neutron's mean free path—a few centimeters—and embed these in the moderator. Fermi's reactor used uranium, shaped into ovoid lumps. Cubes, Höcker concluded, would be better than layers, but like spheres, would be difficult to mould. He thought cylinders, which seemed easier to build, would make a good compromise.

At this point a tug of war ensued between Heisenberg, who wanted the available heavy water for his Leipzig reactor experiments, and Esau, who wanted it to test

---

[49]"But how can you..." ABS p. 115.

Höcker's theory. In fact, since 1941 Diebner, who was working for Army Ordnance, had been using a reactor design involving cubes and had already shown experimentally that it was better than either of Heisenberg's constructions. By 1943, Esau and his people were able to do tests with uranium metal cubes suspended in heavy water that showed that Höcker had been right. It took a year and a half—until after his uranium plates arrived from the manufacturer—before Heisenberg would back down. By that time, air raids had forced the evacuation of Heisenberg's Berlin group. He had left Leipzig in 1942 for the village of Hechingen in southern Germany, where his group occupied the wing of a textile factory. Diebner struggled on a Stadtilm with the blessing of Esau's replacement, Walther Gerlach. Heisenberg's reactor experiments—what was left of them—were carried out in a cave in the town of Haigerloch near Hechingen. For all practical purposes the large-scale German nuclear energy program was at an end, although some research was carried out until the war was over.

Heisenberg's Travels

The centerpiece of this book is what happened just after the war and the light it throws on what the German physicists did during the war. Before turning to it, I would like to discuss another aspect of Heisenberg's wartime activities, his visits abroad, which were mainly to occupied countries.[50] These visits have left a residue of doubt about Heisenberg's intentions. After Germany began the war in 1939, visits to occupied countries by distinguished German academics became part of the German cultural propaganda program. On these countries was forced an entity called a "German Cultural Institute," which, not to put too fine a point on it, was a Nazi propaganda instrument. The visitor was to touch bases with this institution and, upon returning to Germany, had to report to the Ministry of Education as to the attitudes towards Germany of the colleagues visited—a kind of cultural espionage.

In September of 1941, about a year and a half after the German occupation of Denmark, Heisenberg visited Copenhagen.[51] The ostensible reason was to attend a scientific conference that had been arranged by the German Cultural Institute in Copenhagen. In fact this conference followed on an earlier visit by von Weizsäcker, and it took a bit of arm twisting of the authorities to include Heisenberg as well as von Weizsäcker, on the second visit; the senior von Weizsäcker's influence was brought to bear. All of the physicists at Bohr's institute, including Bohr, refused to have anything to do with this conference. According to one report this did not stop

---

[50] An excellent source for this aspect of Heisenberg's wartime activities is "Physics and propaganda: Werner Heisenberg's foreign lectures under National Socialism," by Mark Walker, *Historical Studies in the Physical Sciences*, 22:2 (1992). I thank Professor Walker for sending me this article. I shall refer to it as PNP.

[51] PNP p. 365.

von Weizsäcker from bringing the director of the German Cultural Institute, uninvited, to Bohr's institute, pushing past his secretary and forcing a confrontation.

On the evening of 16 September Bohr and Heisenberg had a private meeting. The intent and content of this meeting remain one of the most controversial events in this history. One thing is certain. Bohr came away from this meeting very shaken. It appears that Heisenberg had raised the prospect of nuclear weapons with Bohr. To what end is totally unclear. Whatever Heisenberg intended, Bohr was left with the impression that the Germans were working on an atomic bomb.

In the fall of 1943 Heisenberg visited occupied Holland. During the visit he took a walk with an old friend and colleague, Hendrik Casimir, with whom he had spent time in Copenhagen. Casimir has recounted their conversation on occasion with varying degrees of anger. One of the kinder descriptions is the following:[52]

> It was during this walk that Heisenberg began to lecture on history and world politics. He explained that it had always been the historic mission of Germany to defend the West and its culture against the onslaught of eastern hordes and that the present conflict was one more example. Neither France nor England would have been sufficiently determined and sufficiently strong to play a leading role in such a defense, and his conclusion was—and now I repeat in German the exact words he used—"*da wäre vielleicht doch ein Europa unter deutscher Führung das kleinere Übel*" (and so, perhaps, a Europe under German leadership might be the lesser evil). Of course, I objected that the many inequities of the Nazi regime, and especially their mad and cruel anti-Semitism, made this unacceptable. Heisenberg did not attempt to deny, still less defend, these things; but he said one should expect a change for the better once the war was over.

This was a common theme among the so-called "good Germans." They wanted Germany to win the war, but Hitler to lose it. I do not think any other formulation describes the mixed motivation of these people.

In December of 1944 Heisenberg made his last visit abroad during the war, this one to Switzerland. He went to a dinner at a Swiss colleague's house. Sometime during the evening he had an exchange with the well-known Swiss phyicist Gregor Wenzel. Wenzel said to him, "Now you have to admit the war is lost." As Wenzel

---

[52]"It was during..." This is quoted in *Heisenberg's War* by Thomas Powers (Knopf, New York, 1993), p. 328. I have strong disagreements with the conclusions of this book that Heisenberg, on moral grounds, held up the German nuclear project; that he knew how to make a bomb but didn't and that he kept this knowledge secret from his colleagues. On this matter I think the Farm Hall transcripts speak for themselves. The reader will have to decide.

later told many people, Heisenberg replied, *"Es wäre so schön gewesen, wenn wir gewonnen hätten"* (it would have been so sweet if we had won).[53]

There seems to be little doubt on the basis of these quotations and others that Heisenberg, at various stages of the war, wanted the Germans to win it.

Intelligence

During the war neither side knew in detail the progress of the other. The Germans heard rumors about some sort of atomic bomb program in the United States, but they did not take them seriously. Hiroshima caught them totally off guard. The British had a certain amount of hard intelligence. We have seen that there was was enough intelligence for the destruction of the German heavy-water program in Norway to be ordered and executed.

The heroic figure of Paul Rosbaud was an especially significant source for the Allies. Rosbaud was an Austrian with a background in chemistry who had gotten into scientific publishing. He knew all the leading figures in the German program. They knew of his anti-Nazi feelings. Furthermore, they trusted him. He managed to get some information about the program to England via Switzerland and some through the Norwegian underground. After the war the principal British intelligence officer R. V. Jones reported, "We also [through Rosbaud] had been able to follow the movements of ... Werner Heisenberg, and to establish that he had not been associated with any large-scale construction project such as the production of an atomic bomb ... As a result of these contacts, we were fairly confident that the German work was very substantially behind that in America; and we never seriously considered, for example, that the V1 or V2 warheads would be nuclear, even though the V2, in particular, would have been an ideal means of nuclear delivery, and even though we had traced one nuclear physicist, Pasqual Jordan, to *Peenemünde* [the site of V2 development]."[54] (The V1 and V2 were rockets, many of which landed on London.)

In contrast to this apparent British calm, the Americans became more and more concerned—frenzied might not be too strong a word—about the Germans, the closer the Allies got to the successful completion of their own program. This might seem paradoxical unless one has observed scientists at work in a competitive situation. The more one has solved one's own problem, the simpler it seems. Indeed, it sometimes seems so simple that one cannot understand why everyone else had not solved it long ago. In particular, one is certain that one's competitors must have seen through everything and have now gone on to the next step. Of course, much

---

[53] "Es wäre..." Several of my colleagues have confirmed that this is what Wentzel told them Heisenberg said.

[54] "We also..." ALS, p. xi.

more was at stake here than simply an academic scientific problem. If the Germans had been able to build an atomic bomb, it would have changed the whole course of the war. To some people on the Manhattan project, the fact that we had been able to solve these very difficult technological problems suggested, erroneously as it turned out, that the Germans must have solved them as well, and that it was only a matter of time before the first atomic bomb fell on London. On the other side, the Germans, believing themselves ahead, were convinced that since they had not solved the technical problems, neither had the Allies. One wonders what would have happened if the leaders of our project, such as General Groves, had been able to see the following letter written by Rudolph Mentzel, who was in charge of the Reich Research Council and all the war related research in the German universities, to one Dr. Görnnert in Hermann Göring's office. The *Reichsmarschall* Göring had caught the atomic bomb fever, and Mentzel felt obliged to set him straight. He wrote on July 8, 1943:[55]

> Dear Party Brother Görnnert:
>
> Enclosed I send you a report by State Counsel Prof. Dr. Esau, Plenipotentiary for Nuclear Physics, on the present state of the work with the request to inform the *Reichsmarschall* about this. As you can see from the report the work has progressed rather considerably in a few months. Though the work will not lead in a short time towards the production of practically useful engines or explosives, it gives on the other hand the certainty that in this field the enemy powers cannot have any surprise in store for us.
>
> With best regards
> Heil Hitler!
> Your
> Mentzel

At the time this letter was written Los Alamos had been in operation for several months.

Alsos

Mentzel's letter was, of course, not known here, but in September of 1943 a scientific intelligence mission was proposed to follow the Allied armies into Europe, to learn as much as possible, and as rapidly as possible, about the German nuclear program and other war-related research. The mission had the strong backing of General Groves and, indeed, was named, without his prior knowledge, *Alsos*—the Greek word for "grove." How this whimsey came about, I have not been able to ascertain.

---

[55]"Dear Party Brother..." ALS, p. 5.

The mission's first assignment was to follow General Mark Clark's troops into Rome to interview any of the Italian physicists who might know something about the German program. This was done without learning a great deal. But soon Groves had another idea. Since Heisenberg was the most celebrated physicist left in Germany and an acknowledged German patriot besides, and since by this time Heisenberg's visit to Bohr was well known and Bohr saw in Heisenberg a serious threat, Groves, and a number of otherwise quite sensible people in the American program, got the notion that it would be a good idea to capture or kill Heisenberg.

What dissuaded them, it would appear, was that such an attempt would be like a siren going off alerting the Germans to what the Allies were doing. As I have tried to make clear, and as will become, I think, even clearer in the sequel, disposing of or interrogating Heisenberg would have been of little relevance in hindering the German program. In fact, as Harteck made amply clear, it might have improved it. In retrospect, one wonders what Heisenberg contributed to the program after his initial studies on the potentialities of fission and his not very successful work with the Leipzig reactor.

Plutonium was due to Houtermans and von Weizsäcker; the ultracentrifuge and the carbon-dioxide reactor to Harteck; the use of carbon as a reflecting mantle to reflect neutrons back into the reactor and improve the efficiency to Bothe; the use of cubes or spheres as fuel elements to Höcker and Diebner, and its experimental verification to Karl Wirtz at the Kaiser-Wilhelm Institute; and the construction of the only working cyclotron in Germany again to Bothe. Harteck put the matter bluntly, "Theoretical physics was not highly thought of in the Third Reich. But certainly theoretical physics is one of the basic sciences in modern history. Now Heisenberg represented theoretical physics. We, including myself, backed him purposely, to improve his standing at that time in Germany. But after a year he disappointed us. He thought he was the man to direct the whole show, even though to my knowledge he had not initially contributed any basic ideas to the uranium fission problem."[56] The only person who thought that he was indispensable to the German program seemed to be Heisenberg himself and some of the politicians who did not understand its technical aspects.

Enter Goudsmit

Very soon after it was initiated, it became clear to the people who had invented the Alsos Mission that they needed a scientific associate. In short order they found the perfect man, Samuel Goudsmit. Goudsmit had been born in Holland and, like many Dutch people, was fluent in nearly all the European languages. Curiously, when he had been a student in Amsterdam he had taken a course in the scientific methods then used in crime detection.

---

[56]"Theoretical physics..." PAM, p. 123.

In the 1920s, Goudsmit and George Uhlenbeck had introduced the notion of the electron spin into physics. This was a very important discovery and ensured Goudsmit entré among the German physicists who were later involved in the nuclear program—especially Heisenberg, whom he had known for over a decade.

In 1927, Goudsmit took a job at the University of Michigan in Ann Arbor and he was instrumemental in organizing a celebrated summer school there. Indeed, in late July of 1939, Heisenberg lectured at the school for a week and stayed in Goudsmit's home.

Goudsmit was not a nuclear physicist. When he was tapped for the job with the Alsos Mission, he did not know of the existence of the Allied program. He had never heard of Los Alamos. He was briefed, but not extensively. In his fascinating book *Alsos*, Goudsmit writes, "[I]n other words I was expendable and if I fell into the hands of the Germans they could not hope to get any major bomb secrets out of me." [57] As the mission progressed, and the Alsos team learned more and more about the paucity of the German program, the concern focused on not letting the Russians get at the Germans and so glean "any major bomb secrets." One wonders what would have happened to the mission if Groves's obsession had not shifted from the Germans to the Russians. Would there still have been an Alsos mission at the end of the war?

Goudsmit Returns Home

Goudsmit also had a personal reason for wanting to get back to Europe. His parents had remained in Holland and, although he suspected the worst, he did not know for certain what had happened to them. There is no passage so moving in the book *Alsos* as Goudsmit's description of visiting The Hague just after the liberation of Holland. He writes:[58]

> My trip gave me the chance to visit the house of my parents in The Hague, where I had been brought up and where I lived all during my high-school and college days. Driving my jeep through the maze of familiar streets that seemed somehow to have become smaller and narrower than I remembered, I dreamed that I would find my aged parents at home waiting for me just as I had last seen them. Only I knew it was a dream. In March, 1943, I had received a farewell letter from my mother and father bearing the address of a Nazi concentration camp. It had reached me through Portugal. It was the last letter I had ever received from them or ever would.

---

[57]"...in other words..." ALS, p. 15.
[58]"...my parents..." ALS, p. 46.

...Climbing into the little room where I had spent so many hours of my life, I found a few scattered papers, among them my high-school report cards that my parents had saved so carefully through all these years ... . As I stood there in that wreck that had once been my home I was gripped by that shattering emotion all of us have felt who have lost family and friends at the hands of the murderous Nazis—a terrible feeling of guilt. Maybe I could have saved them. After all, my parents already had their American visas. Everything had been prepared; all was in readiness. It was just four days before the invasion of the Netherlands that they had received their final papers to come to the United States.

It was too late. If I had hurried a little more, if I had not put off one visit to the Immigration Office for one week, if I had written those necessary letters a little faster, surely I could have rescued them from the Nazis in time. Now I have wept for the heavy feeling of guilt in me ... . Alas! My parents were only two among four million victims taken in filthy jampacked cattle trains to the concentration camps from which it was never intended they were to return.

The world has always admired the Germans so much for their orderliness. They are so systematic; they have such a sense of correctness. That is why they kept such precise records of their evil deeds, which we later found in their proper files in Germany. And that is why I know the precise date my father and my blind mother were put to death in the gas chamber. It was my father's seventieth birthday.

Goudsmit Arrives in Europe

The first venture that Goudsmit participated in on the European continent was in Paris. The Alsos Mission entered the city with the Allied troops and made contact with Joliot-Curie at the Collège de France. Joliot-Curie, it turned out, had been involved with the French resistance. His laboratory had been used for the manufacture of "Molotov cocktails." He informed Goudsmit that shortly after the Germans had occupied Paris, he was visited by Schumann and Diebner. They were thinking of removing Joliot-Curie's cyclotron to Germany. However, they were persuaded to leave the machine in Paris, but to send a German group to work on it in Paris. As it happened, the leader of the group was an assistant of Bothe named Wolfgang Gentner. Genter was a courageous anti-Nazi and he helped shield Joliot-Curie and to keep anything of military usefulness from being sent back to Germany.

In December of 1944, the Alsos group entered the French city of Strasbourg (Strassburg in German). It had been occupied by the Germans. The university had been taken over and von Weizsäcker installed as a professor. He was nowhere to be found, but he had left behind a treasure trove of papers. After studying them Goudsmit was certain that the Germans were very far from having built a nuclear weapon. He could see that they had not even been able to construct a successful chain-reacting pile. Remarkably, the group found the remains of a recent letter from Heisenberg to von Weizsäcker with his latest street address and telephone number in Hechingen. Someone suggested that they fly to neutral Switzerland to place a phone call to Heisenberg to see how he was doing.

In a certain sense, this visit to Strassburg was for Goudsmit the end of his mission. He had come to Europe to learn if the Germans had an atomic bomb and now, as far as he was concerned, he had learned that they did not. In fact, Goudsmit returned to Washington for Christmas. That was the December that Heisenberg visited Zurich and explained how sweet a German victory would have been. On January 31, 1945, the three nuclear physicists Walther Gerlach, Kurt Diebner and Karl Wirtz left Berlin with a caravan of trucks that carried what was left of Germany's uranium and heavy water, except for what was already moved to Haigerloch. Their destination was Stadtilm in southern Germany, about 200 miles from Hechingen. Here, Diebner had planned to continue his own reactor project. Upon arriving in Stadtilm, Gerlach, who had taken over from Esau as director of the project in 1943, found nothing in the way of a real laboratory. He then agreed to have the material moved to Hechingen where Heisenberg was planning a last desperate attempt to build his reactor. Heisenberg was still convinced—and indeed remained convinced even after Hiroshima—that his reactor experiments were significantly ahead of the Allies—something that could eventually be used as a bargaining chip with the Allies.

In the meantime in Washington, General Groves made explicit his real obsession—the Russians. He decided to try to prevent anything nuclear, whether it was nuclear material or human talent, from falling into the hands of the Russians and French. As a start, having learned that metallic uranium was being manufactured by the Auer company, in what was going to be the Russian zone of occupation, he arranged for the plant to be completely destroyed from the air.

Alsos Redux

By early 1945, Goudsmit had returned to Europe to begin the second phase of his mission—to capture and interrogate the German nuclear scientists, thereby keeping them out of other hands. In March, Goudsmit followed the troops into Heidelberg. The aim was to occupy Bothe's laboratory. Bothe was in residence and he and Goudsmit had a somewhat surreal conversation. Bothe was willing, even eager, to discuss his nonmilitary research and to show Goudsmit the cyclotron, but he was unwilling to discuss, before the German surrender—which he thought was imminent—any military work he had done. As soon as VE day came, he submitted a full report. Goudsmit found Gentner by chance in Heidelberg. Gentner was totally forthcoming. He was able to tell Goudsmit about the Stadtilm and Hechingen projects. The group headed for Stadtilm only to learn that the Gestapo had preceded them and had escorted most of the scientists to somewhere in the Bavarian Alps.

In late April, the Alsos group got to Hechingen and the neighboring town of Haigerloch. Von Weizsäcker and Heisenberg had departed for different destinations. Before doing so, von Weizsäcker helped lower the group's essential research papers—sealed in a metal drum—into a cesspool behind his Hechingen residence. They were fished out by two American soldiers. In *Alsos* Goudsmit commented, "Sometimes we wondered if our government had not spent more money on our intelligence mission than the Germans spent on their whole project." [59]

In Hechingen and its environs the Alsos group rounded up von Laue, Wirtz, Bagge, Hahn and a relatively young physicist named Horst Korsching. It had been decided to leave Bothe alone. Goudsmit felt he had nothing more to reveal. A little later von Weizsäcker was also picked up. The decisions of whom to pick up and whom to leave appear to have been largely Goudsmit's. He anguished over the cases of von Laue and Hahn. Von Laue had had nothing to do with the program, and Goudsmit felt that both he and Hahn might have a constructive influence in a postwar Germany. As he wrote in an official communication, "I strongly recommend that they be given an early opportunity to confer with a few prominent Allied colleagues on the general state of science in Germany before and during the war. They may have constructive suggestions about postwar matters. If any small-scale revival of German scientific education occurs, whether planned by the Allies or without our interference, it would be desirable to have these men in key positions." [60] Despite Goudsmit's opposition they were rounded up with the rest.

Heisenberg had made a harrowing three-day bicycle journey through a beaten and bombed out Germany from Hechingen to his home in Urfeld. On the third of May, he was picked up by the Alsos Mission. Two days earlier Gerlach had been located in Munich and, the day after, Diebner in a nearby town. Heisenberg, Gerlach and Diebner were taken to Heidelberg. The rest had already been sent to the Allied European headquarters in Reims. Goudsmit and Heisenberg had a brief conversation in Heidelberg during which Heisenberg said, "If American colleagues wish to learn about the uranium problem I shall be glad to show them the results of our researches if they come to my laboratory." [61] Goudsmit could only feel pity. Harteck was picked up in Hamburg and sent directly to what was known as "Dustbin," an internment center in Versailles for important civilian prisoners.

In *Alsos* Goudsmit describes his first encounter with Harteck. He writes:[62]

> Harteck was brought to my office, I had not met him before.
> At first he was rather reluctant to talk. He was not aware of how
> much we already knew about him and his work.

---

[59]"Sometimes we..." ALS, p. 108.

[60]"I strongly recommend..." ALS, p. 106.

[61]"If American..." ALS, p. 113.

[62]"Harteck was brought..." ALS, p. 122.

"Tell me something about your efforts to make volatile uranium compounds," I said, knowing that he had undertaken this research in the hope of finding some substance suitable for isotope separation by gas diffusion methods.

Harteck admitted having directed such work, "It was not successful," he said. "The nearest we came was with some complicated organic compounds containing a uranium atom surrounded by atoms of hydrogen and carbon. Very complex molecules indeed, hard to describe," he said. "I'll try to show you," he continued. Pointing at the paperweight cube on my desk, he said: "Now let us assume that represents uranium." He moved to pick it up. "But this is uranium!" he cried.

That incident ended his hesitancy. He recognized the uranium cube as coming from the German pile experiments, and he proceeded to give a complete account of what he knew.

From Dustbin to Farm Hall

To an interviewer Harteck later described how he had arrived at "Dustbin." As he was driven through Paris he "had on a beret and a blue coat; I must have looked like a dignified Allied officer in civil dress when I saluted the people lining the streets who were evidently waiting for a parade. That was very amusing to me." [63] He went on:

When I was taken into custody by the Allied Military I was very happy. I had no family cares and I was in best humor. I was in high spirits. All the dangers were over. Looking back I am sometimes astounded that I survived all the dangers of the Third Reich and the war.

I was taken to a small flophouse run by American or Canadian military people. Then Gerlach was brought in. He looked as if his whole world had collapsed. When Gerlach had asked for a glass of water, his guard said, "Look for an empty can in the trash barrel!" Gerlach was shocked at things like this; he expected people, including his guard, to speak respectfully to him, the Plenipotentiary for Nuclear Physics in Germany. But I took it more from the amusing side.

When I came to the detention camp, Hahn, Heisenberg, Weizsäcker, and others were already there. They had been transported in a truck guarded by soldiers with machine guns while I had been driven in very nicely. En route my captor and I stopped overnight at a comfortable home in Heidelberg. A black soldier took my luggage to my room, which overlooked the Neckar River.

[63] "...had on..." ABS, p. 125.

> I don't know why the others weren't treated as well as I
> was. They acted a bit depressed. When I saw Heisenberg I said,
> "It was always my wish that after the war I would be brought to
> a nice place for relaxation...," he laughed.

Once they had been assembled, the question was what to do with them. By this
time, British intelligence had become part of the operation. The man at the scene
was Lieutenant Commander Eric Welsh. He reported to his superior, Dr. R. V.
Jones, that an American general had suggested shooting them. Not sure whether or
not this was a joke, Welsh proposed that Jones get them moved to England. As it
happened, there was what has been described as a "lovely Georgian country house"—
a manor called Farm Hall—in the town of Godmanchester near Cambridge that
had been used as a staging area for various resistance groups who were air-dropped
in Europe, and was now free. It seemed like an ideal place to put the ten Germans.
While it was being prepared, the Germans were transported to Belgium in June.
Here they settled into the routine that they would follow for the next six months.
Heisenberg played the piano. The younger men participated in whatever sports
were available.

Then there was the weekly "colloquium"—a lecture series that was taken very
seriously especially by von Laue, who organized them. Harteck recalls an incident,
an amusing one made more so by the fact that Harteck thought he was in Holland,
when in fact he was in Belgium. He remembers that von Laue[64]

> ...always planned on colloquiums in physics in his institute
> in Berlin on a certain day of the week and at a certain time. Even
> in our detention we had a colloquium on the same day and at the
> same time; good papers given; it was very interesting.
>
> One day when we were in camp in Holland [sic] an English
> officer came to von Laue and said, "Please be ready tomorrow to
> leave for England by airplane."
>
> Laue replied, "That's impossible!"
>
> "Why is it impossible?" asked the officer. Laue said,
> "Because I have my colloquium then." "I understand, Professor,"
> said the officer, "but couldn't you have your colloquium some
> other time?" And Laue answered, "But could you not have the
> airplane come some other time?"

On July third, the ten Germans were taken by a Dakota aircraft to England and
then by road to Farm Hall. Harteck recognized the cathedral of Ely and realized
that they were not far from Cambridge where he had studied with Rutherford. At
Farm Hall each of them was assigned a prisoner-of-war batman to look after his
needs. There was a tennis court and a piano for Heisenberg. The bedrooms were

---

[64]"...always planned..." ABS, p. 126.

paneled and the food was good. What none of them seem to have realized, at least initially, was that the estate had been wired to record conversations.

For the next six months everything the Germans said was audited. Thousands of words per day were then taken down and later translated, or summarized and then made into reports—the Farm Hall transcripts. The reports were classified "Top Secret" and had a very limited distribution. The officer in charge of Farm Hall, Major T. H. Rittner, sent a copy to a Colonel M. W. Perrin of the British nuclear program and to Lieutenant Commander Welsh. A few other people saw it. A copy was sent to the American Embassy in London to the military attaché. It was transmitted to Washington, where it was given to General Groves. He initialed each copy. Goudsmit was shown them. Books appeared; Goudsmit's own, General Groves's memoirs, a book by Jones, which contained what were either purported to be direct quotes or accurate summaries. But the original transcripts were tightly held.

When, in 1981, the historian of science Gerald Holton asked to see them for scholarly reasons he received a reply from the Foreign and Commonwealth office which said in part, "It is, as you probably know, the general policy of the British government to release documents to the Public Record Office 30 years after their date of origin. But there are exceptions. We do not, for instance, even after 30 years, release documents which contain information about individuals, the disclosure of which could cause distress or embarrassment to themselves or their immediate descendants. I am afraid there can be no doubt that the Farm Hall transcripts fall into this category and the British Government, after very careful consideration, has decided that the transcripts cannot at present be opened for public inspection." [65]

Whose "distress or embarrassment" might have been at issue, one can only conjecture. By this time several of the Farm Hall detainees—Hahn, Diebner, von Laue, Gerlach and Heisenberg—were already dead. But von Weizsäcker's brother Richard had become the President of Germany. Was that the reason? On the 20th of December 1991, a very distinguished delegation of the Royal Society wrote an impassioned letter to Lord Mackay asking for the release of the transcripts. Whether this letter made the difference—there was no explanation and no apology—on February, 24, 1992 the Public Record Office at Kew finally released the reports. Soon afterward, the National Archives in Washington, D.C., released their files of the Farm Hall reports.

Not long afterwards, thanks to the efforts of Robert Silvers, the editor of *The New York Review of Books*, I obtained a copy of the reports from England. I had had a long interest in the history of the German nuclear program and had tried to talk to as many people as I could about it—especially Sam Goudsmit, who was my

---

[65]"It is..." I thank Gerald Holton for a copy of this letter.

first boss when I went to work at the Brookhaven National Laboratory in 1960. When I finally saw the reports—written as they are mostly in dialogue form—I thought that they would make, if properly interpreted, a great play—just as the Oppenheimer hearings make a great play. I wanted to call the excerpts I put together for the *New York Review of Books* "Nuclear Shakesphere." I now realize that that would have been wrong. "Nuclear Kafka" would have been much better.[66]

Here were ten brilliant, very complicated, often egocentric, men, including two Nobel Prize winners and one future Nobel Prize winner—Hahn—held for six months without explanation and without being charged with anything. They did not understand why and I believe that, even after a few months, their wardens hardly understood why. The real reason, to keep them from falling into Soviet hands, they could only guess at. They were treated not exactly as prisoners, but as "guests." Indeed, this is the term that is used in the reports.

All their complaints and anxieties were known to their monitors who, from time to time, descended *deus ex machina* to magically respond to them. During these months their illusions fell away. They realized that they had failed and that their country had failed. They blame each other. They blame Hitler. They blame the Americans. The young blame the old. The old blame each other. Each week there is von Laue's colloquium. Heisenberg plays the piano. There are one or two visitors. It all passes like a surreal dream. Then, after six months, they are released to return to a Germany in ruins. All of this is recorded in the transcripts, along with a choruslike commentary of the monitors.

Jeremy Bernstein

---

[66]My excerpt appeared in the *New York Review of Books* August 13, 1992.

CAST OF CHARACTERS*

Erich Bagge:	A junior physicist and former Heisenberg student who had helped Diebner establish German fission research and later worked on isotope separation.
Captain P.L.C. Brodie:	Rittner's assistant and editor of the later Farm Hall reports.
Kurt Diebner:	Physicist and organizer of the German Army's fission project; later performed reactor experiments independently of the Heisenberg group.
Walther Gerlach:	Senior physicist and administrator of German fission research beginning in 1944.
Samuel A. Goudsmit:	Distinguished Dutch-American physicist and scientific head of the Alsos Mission.
Major General Leslie R. Groves:	Military commander of the Manhattan Project and Washington administrator of the Alsos Mission.
Otto Hahn:	Eminent radiochemist and co-discoverer of nuclear fission, for which he received the Nobel Prize in chemistry while at Farm Hall.
Paul Harteck:	Physical chemist and Hamburg professor; worked on isotope separation and reactor designs.
Werner Heisenberg:	Eminent quantum physicist and Nobel Prize winner; leading scientific figure of the German effort; headed main reactor experiments in Leipzig and Berlin.
Horst Korsching:	Junior physicist in the Kaiser-Wilhelm Institute for Physics in Berlin; worked on isotope separation.
Max von Laue:	Eminent physicist and Nobel Prize winner for his work on x rays; outspoken anti-Nazi; did not engage in fission research.

---

* The names of the Farm Hall detainees are italicized.

Michael Perrin:	Physicist and official of the British atomic bomb program.
Major T. H. Rittner:	British officer in charge at Farm Hall and editor of most of the reports.
Carl Friedrich von Weizsäcker:	Theoretical physicist; influential younger colleague and friend of Heisenberg.
Lieutenant Commander Eric Welsh:	Rittner's superior, a British naval intelligence officer stationed in London.
Karl Wirtz:	Physicist and head of reactor construction in the Berlin Kaiser-Wilhelm Institute for Physics.

PART I

SETTLING IN
1 May – 6 August 1945

[The British code name for the recording of the ten German scientists at Farm Hall was "Operation Epsilon." Until the group arrived in England on July 3, 1945, they were not being recorded. Hence the cover memorandum or "Preamble" to headquarters covering this period has a narrative character. It deals with the two months from the first of May to the thirtieth of June and describes the complications of getting "the professors," as they are called, although not all were professors, from the Continent to Farm Hall. We have already given some of this history in the Introduction, but it is interesting to see how it appeared to the Allied administrators involved at the time. The "I" in the narrative is Major T. H. Rittner, the officer in charge. The tone is very much his. It is not clear if it had been explained to him who these Germans really were and why they were significant. There is no indication that he knew of the atomic bomb project—either that of the Allies or the Germans. His comments show a mixture of frustration and bemusement.[1]

My own comments are set off by square brackets. Errors of grammar are retained from the original; the spelling of the names Weizsäcker, Korsching, and Goudsmit has been corrected. J. B.]

---

[1] Three other first-hand accounts of events and impressions from this period are also available: (1) Excerpts from a diary maintained by Erich Bagge, one of the German detainees, published in Erich Bagge, Kurt Diebner, and Kenneth Jay, *Von Uranspaltung bis Calder Hall* (Rowohlt, Hamburg, 1957), pp. 42–72; (2) Max von Laue's lengthy unpublished letters to his son Theodor, then at Princeton University, in Deutsches Museum, Munich, Handschriftenabteilung, 1976–20; and (3) unpublished field reports of the Alsos Mission on the location, capture and detention of the German scientists, through 21 May 1945, in National Archives, Washington, D.C., Microfilms M1109, Roll 2.

TOP SECRET

To: Lt. Col. M. W. Perrin
and Lt. Comdr. E. Welsh
From: Major T. H. Rittner

OPERATION "EPSILON"

I. PREAMBLE

[Perrin and Welsh are at Headquarters; Perrin is Michael Perrin, an official of the British bomb program. Welsh is Eric Welsh of British naval intelligence and a colleague of R. V. Jones, a leading figure in British science intelligence.[2]]

1st May 1945

I received at H.Q. from Lt. Comdr. Welsh instructions to proceed to Rheims (France) to report to G2 SHAEF and collect a party of German scientists. *[G2 stood for Army Intelligence; SHAEF for Supreme Headquarters Allied Expeditionary Force, which was commanded by General Dwight D. Eisenhower.]* A chateau at Spa (Belgium) had been prepared for their detention. A number of distinguished British and American scientists would be visiting them in the near future and my instructions were that these Germans were to be treated as guests. No one, repeat no one, was to contact them except on instructions from H.Q.

II. RHEIMS (2ND–7TH MAY)

(2nd May 1945)

I proceeded by air to Rheims and reported to SHAEF where I was informed by Major Keith, P.A. to A.C. of S. G2 *[Personal Aide to Army Chief of Staff]* that the chateau at Spa was no longer available and that the party was to be held at Rheims at 75 Rue Gambetta until other arrangements could be made.

Arrangements had been made to draw American "A" Rations ready-cooked and a staff of two British Orderlies and an American cook had been provided by SHAEF in addition to the necessary guards.

The same evening, the following arrived at 75 Rue Gambetta, escorted by Major Furman, U.S. Army *[Robert Furman was General Groves's intelligence aide;*

---

[2] See R. V. Jones, Introduction Goudsmit, *op. cit.*, p. xiv.

*according to an Alsos roster of 15 April 1945, he was attached to the scientific
section of the Alsos Mission. For background, see Introduction.[3]]:*

Professor Hahn.

    "   von Laue.

Doctor   von Weizsäcker.

    "   Wirtz.

    "   Bagge.

    "   Korsching.

Professor Mattauch, whom I had been told to expect was not among the party.
*[This is a reference to the Austrian physicist Josef Mattauch. He had come to work
with Hahn after Meitner had left. Goudsmit seems not to have included him in his
list of scientists to be detained.]*

The professors were friendly and settled down well. They expressed appreciation
of the good treatment they were receiving and a very pleasant atmosphere prevailed.
At my request they gave me their personal parole not to leave the house or that
portion of the garden which I allotted to them.

3rd May 1945

The following day I telephoned H.Q. (Lt. Comdr. Welsh) and informed him of the
situation regarding Spa. In the meantime I was informed by SHAEF that
arrangements were being made to accommodate the party at a chateau at Versailles
where the original policy regarding these detainees could be carried out. I met
Major Calvert *[a member of the Alsos Mission's scientist team]* and explained the
situation to him.

5th May 1945

I was asked by SHAEF H.Q. Commandant to release Allied Personnel who were
required in connection with the impending VE *[Victory in Europe]* Day negotiations
and who, in any case, had shown some reluctance to wait on Germans. I pointed
out that it was essential for me to have staff for this purpose and it was suggested
that I take on German P. W. *[prisoner of war]*. It seemed to me that this would
solve the staff problem and I accordingly agreed and acquired from the Rheims
P. W. stockade a German P. W. waiter and a cook, but I stipulated that these men
would have to remain with me as long as the professors were detained.

The professors were by this time beginning to get restive and they were particularly
worried about their families. They asked permission to write letters, and after

---

[3] Alsos Mission Files, National Archives, Microfilms M1109, Roll 2.

referring the matter to H.Q. (Lt. Comdr. Welsh) and obtaining sanction, the letters were written and, after being censored by me, handed to General Strong's secretary (Jun. Comdr. Frazer) at SHAEF for transmission.

7th May 1945

SHAEF informed me that arrangements had been made to accommodate the party at Versailles and that H.Q. had agreed to the move. A Dakota was put at our disposal and the party took off at 1700 hours *[5 P.M.]* in the expectation that at last the long awaited contact with their British and American colleagues was about to take place.

III. VERSAILLES

(7th–11th May)

On arrival at Versailles, I reported to G2 SHAEF and found that the party was to be accommodated in a detention centre known as "Dustbin" at the Chateau du Chesnay. This centre had been set up for the purpose of interrogating German Nazi scientists and industrialists.[4] The conditions were most unsatisfactory from my point of view as complete segregation was impossible and there was great danger of undesirable contacts being made with the professors. In addition, only camp beds were provided and there was scarcely any other furniture. The food was the ordinary P.W. rations. It was obviously impossible to carry out my mission in these surroundings but I was able to pacify the professors, who accepted the situation with as good a grace as possible. The Camp Commandant did his best to make them comfortable.

8th May 1945

In spite of the general holiday atmosphere at SHAEF and in London consequent upon the declaration of VE Day, I managed to contact H.Q. (Lt. Comdr. Welsh) by telephone and explain the new situation. He told me to contact Major Furman, U.S. Army, in Paris and try and make other arrangements through him. This I did and we decided to try and get the party back to the Rue Gambetta at Rheims.

9th May 1945

Major Furman informed me that he was arranging for us to return to Rheims and that in the meantime the following Germans were to join the party:

Professor Heisenberg
Doctor Diebner

---

[4] For more on "Dustbin," see John Gimbel, *Science, Technology, and Reparations: Exploitation and Plunder in Postwar Germany* (Stanford University Press, Stanford, 1990), pp. 17–20.

The situation at the Chateau du Chesnay was becoming more and more difficult as the professors were highly indignant at being treated as "war criminals," as they put it; Professor von Laue was almost in tears. In spite of the fact that other German scientists including Professor Osenberg were in the house, and were being interrogated by British and American Officers, I was able to prevent the identity of my party being revealed. *[Werner Osenberg was an SS officer who had been appointed by Göring in 1943 to coordinate scientific research through the Reich Research Council (Reichsforschungsrat).]* I had refused to submit a nominal roll or to allow any contact with them. Dr. Robertson, Scientific Advisor to SHAEF, did, however, see Professor von Laue out for exercise and spoke to him, but I was able to persuade him to break off the conversation and he accepted the situation well. *[H. P. Robertson was a distinguished Princeton cosmologist who had come to Britain to be the scientific liaison with British intelligence.]*

10th May 1945

The professors were becoming more and more restive and they begged me to contact Professor Joliot in Paris *[Pierre Joliot-Curie, son-in-law of Marie Curie, who, together with his wife Irène Curie, were leading French researchers in nuclear fission]* whom they assured me would help them. This request was of course refused and I told them they must have patience and that everything possible was being done for them.

In order in some way to alleviate conditions I took them in parties by car to Versailles to see the gardens and palace. On one occasion a guide asked for their identity cards in order to visit the Hall of Mirrors and we left the premises hurriedly having pleaded a previous engagement.

11th May 1945

It was now clear that the difficulties which had arisen were due mainly to an order issued by the Supreme Commander *[Eisenhower]* stating that no preferential treatment was to be given to any German nationals. This order was given after reports had appeared in the press describing the good treatment being meted out to Reichsmarschal Göring.

General Strong refused to agree to my party returning to Rheims but arrangements were made by MIS *[Military Intelligence Services]*, on the instructions of Brig. General Conrad, to accommodate the party for a short time at a villa at Le Vesinet, near St. Germain. The professors were overjoyed at the prospect of leaving what they called the concentration camp and after I had inspected the villa, I left Versailles with the party in command cars on the evening of 11th May after informing H.Q. by cable of the arrangements which I had made.

IV. LE VESINET

(11th May–4th June)

The Villa Argentina, 89 Allee du Lac Inferieure at Le Vesinet, was a large house standing in its own grounds. MIS provided a guard and arranged for us to draw American "B" rations in a semicooked condition from their mess. They also supplied us with canteen goods. During our whole stay at Le Vesinet, MIS gave me every possible assistance.

The professors were delighted with their new surroundings and the old atmosphere of cordiality quickly returned. There was some trouble with the plumbing and electric light in the villa, which had been empty for some time, and the professors all helped to remedy the defects. When outside help was necessary, such as on an occasion when the basement was flooded owing to a burst pipe, they were confined to their rooms whilst a very voluble and inquisitive French plumber dealt with the matter.

On the evening we arrived, Major Furman brought Professor Harteck to join the party. As the party had now grown from six to nine, I asked the professors to renew their parole, which they did.

12th May 1945

As we could only have the use of the villa for a very limited period, I cabled H.Q. through Colonel Robin Brook urging that efforts be made to bring the party to England as it was obvious that it would not be possible to arrange accommodation on the Continent suitable for carrying out my mission.

There was considerable speculation amongst the U.S. troops and the French civilian population regarding the identity of the party. I was accused of harboring Marshal Petain. A number of inquisitive people, including the owner of the villa who came post haste from Paris when he heard from the concierge that his house was being occupied, were dealt with. I was able to spread the story that my party consisted of active anti-Nazis who were being kept by us for their own protection.

The information, inadvertently let out by Major Furman, that French colonial troops were still in occupation at Hechingen and Tailfingen caused consternation amongst the professors, who had been told that American troops would be taking over. Professor Heisenberg asked permission to write a letter to his friend Dr. Goudsmit of the U.S. Army, who he believed was in Paris, asking him to get news of the families. *[Goudsmit was still a member of the Alsos mission and was questioning some of the Germans.]* On receipt of a cable from Mr. Perrin *[there are several Perrin's in this story; which one this is, is not clear]* sanctioning this, I handed the letter to Dr. Goudsmit, who offered to do what he could. He subsequently gave me a letter from Professor Heisenberg's wife, which I handed to him, for which he was duly grateful. *[There is a point worth commenting on here concerning Goudsmit's generosity in contacting Heisenberg's wife under these circumstances. In 1943, a Dutch friend and colleague of Goudsmit's named Dirk Coster wrote to Heisenberg with a plea to try to save Goudsmit's parents from deportation. Heisenberg, after some delay, wrote a letter for Coster to use as he saw fit in which he described Goudsmit's hospitality to visiting Germans and containing the phrase that he, Heisenberg, "would be very sorry, if for reasons unknown to me, his [Goudsmit's] parents would experience any difficulties in Holland." When he wrote this letter, Goudsmit's parents had already been deported to Auschwitz. Goudsmit never held Heisenberg responsible for his parents' death. He blamed himself, and it is typical of him that he would have tried to contact Heisenberg's wife and to offer what help he could.]*

Major Gattiker was sent by Mr. Perrin to get some information from Professor Harteck and Dr. Wirtz regarding the whereabouts of certain apparatus. I was present at the interview. All questions were answered.

17th May 1945

Brig. Gen. Conrad came to the villa and I showed him over. He did not speak to any of the professors. He expressed his satisfaction with the arrangements that had been made and agreed that the "B" scale of rations should continue although MIS wanted to reduce them to the "C" scale, which was that authorized for P.W. On the following day, however, the rations were cut without warning and I protested to Colonel Ford of the C.O. of MIS who eventually agreed to restore the original scale.

Major Furman sent Lt. Dietesheim, U.S. Army, to ask Professor Harteck about certain apparatus at Celle. I was present at the interview. *[A Lt. Ditesheim is listed as serving with Col. Pash among the "special officers" of the Alsos Mission.]*

The professors spent their time in Le Vesinet working in their rooms or sunbathing in the garden. They developed a passion for physical exercise and even the more aged Professors von Laue and Hahn could be seen running solemnly round and round the garden at six o'clock in the morning clad only in thin underpants. On Tuesdays and Fridays they assembled in the common room to hear a lecture by one of themselves. I was able to supply them with books, technical journals, and games.

During this time, Major Furman was endeavoring to find suitable permanent accommodation. He had obtained a letter from Brig. Gen. Betts, D.A.C. of S. G2 SHAEF *[Deputy Army Chief of Staff, attached to G2 (intelligence)]* asking all concerned to assist in finding accommodation for the party. He informed me that he had found a chateau near Liège (Belgium) and I arranged to inspect it.

20th May 1945

I received a cable from V.C.S.S. *[presumably headquarters]* informing me that Washington had been asked to agree to the professors being brought to England, and I replied stating that I proposed to inspect the chateau in Belgium, and asking for instructions pending a decision from Washington. V.C.S.S. replied telling me to proceed as though I knew nothing about these negotiations.

25th May 1945

I flew to Liège with Major Furman to inspect the Chateau de Facqueval near Huy. Lt. Col. Watkins, U.S. Army, the Area Intelligence Officer, took us to the chateau. He pointed out that the administration would come under the local American Military Authorities and that it would have to be strictly in accordance with General Eisenhower's order regarding treatment of enemy nationals. Apart from this, the security appeared unsatisfactory as there were Belgian civilians working on the estate, and I was also informed that the political situation was very tense and that serious disturbances were expected. In addition, the owner of the chateau, a very wealthy Belgian lawyer, Mr. Goldschmit, had just returned from five years as a P. W. in Germany *[and is not to be confused with Goudsmit of the Alsos Mission]*. I spoke to him, and he was naturally very distressed at having his home requisitioned. Of course he did not know the purpose for which it was going to be used but he told me that he proposed to contest the validity of the requisition as the house had not been occupied by the Germans, and, according to an agreement between the Allies and the Belgian Government, only such houses could be requisitioned. I checked this later and found it to be the case. He told me that he was a friend of General Erskine, head of the SHAEF mission to Belgium, and that he intended to appeal to him. As a matter of fact, a request for derequisition was received from General Erskine later, shortly before we left.

Lt. Col. Watkins wanted the American guard troops accommodated in the best rooms in the house and suggested that the professors should be put in the attics. I refused to agree to this.

I reported to H.Q. (V.C.S.S.) by cable.

In the meantime MIS were pressing me to vacate the Villa Argentina, which was urgently required to accommodate their own staff who were passing through Le Vesinet for redeployment. I saw Colonel Ford and informed him that it was impossible for us to move until other suitable accommodation had been found and assured him we were doing our best in this respect.

28th May 1945

I received a cable from Lt. Comdr. Welsh informing me that he proposed to visit me and telephoned him arranging to meet him in Paris on 30th May.

30th May 1945

Lt. Comdr. Welsh arrived and I took him to the villa. I explained the whole situation to him and arranged to take him to see the Chateau de Facqueval. He was very cordially received by the professors, but they were disappointed that he was unable to give them any news of their families or any information regarding their future.

31st May 1945

Lt. Comdr. Welsh and I flew to Liège and were taken to the Chateau de Facqueval by Captain Mueller, U.S. Army, Colonel Watkins' deputy. After inspecting the house and grounds and talking to Mr. Goldschmit we agreed that the place was unsuitable and we returned to Le Vesinet.

1st June 1945

A conference took place at Major Furman's office in Paris at which Major Calvert was present. Lt. Comdr. Welsh said that we considered the Chateau de Facqueval unsuitable and that we were trying to get sanction to take the party to England where suitable accommodation was available. It was agreed that efforts should be made to remain at Le Vesinet pending a decision on this point and Major Furman proposed sending a cable to General Groves, which was drafted. I understand that after I left the conference it was decided not to send this cable. Lt. Comdr. Welsh then returned to London.

I saw Colonel Ford at MIS who informed me that the Villa Argentina was required immediately for a party of WACs [members of the Women's Army Corps] and after some discussion he agreed to put other accommodation at our disposal for a few days.

3rd June 1945

Major Furman told me that the party were to move at once to Belgium on the orders of Brig. Gen. Conrad. I refused to move before Monday 4th June and telephoned H.Q. (Lt. Comdr. Welsh), who confirmed that the move should take place.

It was not possible to arrange air transport and MIS provided two command cars with trailers and a saloon car for the journey.

4th June 1945

A movement order was obtained from Col. Ford and we left Le Vesinet at 1300 hours [1 P.M.] on 4th June and arrived at the Chateau de Facqueval at 2345 hours [11:45 P.M.].

During the whole of my stay in France I received valuable assistance from Colonel Brook and his staff.

V. HUY

(4th June–3rd July)

Although Major Furman has assured me that the arrangements he had made at the Chateau de Facqueval were in accordance with the agreed policy, I found on arrival that this was not the case. Only P.W. rations were available and no provisions had been made for a meal for the professors, who had been travelling since midday. Fortunately I had brought American "K" rations, which we had eaten by the roadside.

Captain Davis, U.S. Army, had been temporarily placed in command pending the arrival of Lt. Toepel of the A.L.S.O.S Mission, who had been appointed to command the unit. *[Regarding Rittner's punctuation of "Alsos," he obviously did not know of the Greek pun the name was based on; Toepel is listed in the April 15 Alsos roster as a "special officer" of the Mission.]* Mr. Oates, an American C.I.C. *[Combined Intelligence Committee]* man, was also attached to the unit. These officials did everything in their power to help me.

It was pointed out to me that the American troops would object to any signs of fraternization and that I would not be allowed to provide any extra food or comforts for the professors. As a matter of fact I did later provide additional food and drink with the connivance of the American officer in charge, but without the knowledge of the American G.I.s.

5th June 1945

I received a cable from H.Q. (Lt. Comdr. Welsh) stating that the whole future policy regarding the professors was being examined and that I was to use all my endeavors to keep them in a good frame of mind pending a decision.

In view of the attitude of the American troops it was impossible for me to live with the professors as I had done up to now. Ordinary "A" rations were drawn for the officers and troops, whereas only P.W. rations *[C rations]* were drawn for the professors, and two separate messes had to be set up. I reported the unsatisfactory position to Lt. Comdr. Welsh at H.Q.

The professors had no alternative but to accept the position but they were getting to the end of their tether. They had been promised contact with British and American scientists and had been assured that full provision was being made for their families. They could not understand why they were being treated in this way. I explained to them some of the difficulties that had arisen and was able to reassure them and keep them reasonably happy.

The routine at the chateau was much the same as it had been at Le Vesinet and, the weather being mainly fine, the professors spent most of their time in the garden. The guard troops had been provided with a piano and as they rarely used it, I persuaded them to give it to the professors. This instrument was in a very bad condition, a number of notes were missing, but it did not take them long to take the whole thing to pieces and repair it with improvised tools. I borrowed a local piano tuner's kit and they soon had it tuned. I also bought a wireless set, which proved a very welcome addition to the amenities of the house.

Speculation as to the identity of the professors was as great in Belgium as it had been in France. The most popular guess was that the party consisted of von Ribbentrop and his staff. There was considerable danger to security owing to the fact that the American troops, who were not trained in intelligence work, mixed freely with the village girls. They also made nightly trips to Liège. There were three Belgian civilians engaged as cooks, etc., for the mess and these people could not be confined to the premises.

Lt. Col. Watkins insisted upon the establishment being run as an American Military Station, *[and]* he even wanted the Stars and Stripes flown from a flag staff in the grounds; this suggestion I vetoed. The Chateau was officially designated "Special Detention Centre, Area No. 5, Channel Base Section, ETOUSA" *[European Theatre of Operations, U.S. Army]* and this had to appear on all correspondence and requisitions. This drew attention to the nature of the establishment and there was the obvious danger of Swiss or Red Cross representatives claiming the right of entry.

9th June 1945

The professors were very worried when they read in the newspapers that the Russians were extending their zone of occupation in Germany. Dr. Diebner was frantic as it appeared that the town of Stadtilm (Thuringia), where his wife and son were, was to come under Russian occupation. He begged me with tears in his eyes to get his wife and son moved into the British or American zone. I pointed out that his previous activities hardly warranted our doing him a favor but said I would see what could be done. In the meantime Professor Heisenberg had told me that Mrs. Diebner had worked with her husband and knew about all his work and that of the others and thought it would be unfortunate if she fell into Russian hands. I consequently cabled this information to H.Q. with the request for the family to be moved. During the next few days Dr. Diebner showed signs of mental aberration and threatened first to attempt to escape and, when he realized that this was impossible, he threatened to commit suicide. It was a great relief when I was able to inform him that his family had been moved to Neustadt Nr. Coburg. The receipt of this news moved him to such an extent that he asked to be taken to church although he admitted that he had no religion and had not been inside a church for many years. I took him to the village church to mass the following Sunday, where he caused a sensation by appearing dressed up as though for a church parade.

10th June 1945

Lt. Toepel arrived to take over command of the unit. This officer was an Alsos man and had been present at Hechingen and Tailfingen when the professors were taken into custody. He knew those who came from there and they recognized him.

Lt. Toepel handled a difficult situation very well indeed, cooperating in every way and turning a blind eye to my fraternization whilst maintaining his position as O.C. *[Officer in Command]* of the troops.

14th June 1945

Professor Gerlach was brought from Paris to join the party. The professors were delighted to see their old colleague. *[This completes the group of ten German scientists held prisoner.]*

15th June 1945

By this time the professors were again becoming very, very restive and they hinted to me that the time might soon come when they would take desperate measures to let the world know of their situation. They did not say what action they contemplated but said they would give me due warning. They showed a certain loyalty to me personally as they appreciated what I had been able to do for them. They assured me that they would not break their parole without withdrawing it. I had a long talk with Professor Heisenberg, who is the most sensible of them, and he told me that their main worry was the lack of information about their families. He also said that they suspected that their potential value was being judged by the documents found at their institutions. He said that these did not give a true picture of the extent of their experiments which had advanced much further than would appear from these documents and maintained that they had advanced still further as a result of pooling of information since their detention. He begged for an opportunity of discussing the whole matter with British and American scientists in order to acquaint them with their latest theories and work out a scheme for future cooperation. Professor Heisenberg and Dr. Harteck suggested that Professor Bonhoeffer of Leipzig, who they believed was at Friederichsbrunn in the Ostharz, should be brought to join this party. They said he was an active anti-Nazi who had worked with them and that it would be unwise to let him fall into Russian hands. The above information was passed to H.Q. via cable. *[Karl-Friedrich Bonhoeffer, a Leipzig colleague of Heisenberg's, was a physical chemist who had worked with Harteck on the production of heavy water. He was the brother of Dietrich Bonhoeffer, the courageous anti-Nazi Protestant minister whom the Nazis murdered shortly before the German capitulation. The Germans knew, as we have seen, that the Allies had destroyed their capacity for making heavy water. Heisenberg and Harteck seem to have inferred from this that the main interest in keeping them had specifically to do with heavy water. The theme of Heisenberg believing himself to be in a position to teach the Americans and British about nuclear energy will recur to the end.]*

The professors again asked to be allowed to write to their families and I said I would try and arrange for the letters to be delivered. Letters were written and after censorship, which necessitated a lot of rewriting, these were handed by me to Lt. Comdr. Welsh in London.

Lt. Cdr. Welsh told me on the telephone that permission had been given for the professors to be brought to England and he asked me to come over as soon as possible to inspect Farm Hall.

16th June

As we required additional staff, I got two more P.W. from the stockade at Namur, a second cook and a man who was a barber by profession. This enabled us to be more or less independent of outside domestic help. The laundry was done in the house. A group photograph was taken by Mr. Oates. (The negative and all copies of this photograph are in my possession.) *[A Mr. Oates is listed as a Combined Intelligence Committee agent attached to the Alsos Mission.]*

17th June

In order to get an air passage to the U.K., I had to get myself temporarily attached to a British unit stationed at Brussels and I accordingly got myself attached to 21 Army Group and got an Authority from them and proceeded to London.

Lt. Comdr. Welsh and I went to Farm Hall where arrangements had already been made to install microphones. I had asked for such an installation from the day I took charge of the professors. We arranged with Colonel Kendrick to transfer the necessary staff of technicians from CSDIC (U.K.) to man the installation. We were fortunate also in obtaining the services of Captain Brodie from CSDIC to act as Administrative Officer. *[Capt. P.L.C. Brodie will appear later as one of the on-site administrators of the detainees. CSDIC was most likely a military organization.]*

26th June

I returned to Belgium, leaving Captain Brodie to complete the arrangements at Farm Hall.

On arrival at Brussels airport I was informed that Lt. Colonel Watkins was making an inspection of the Chateau de Facqueval that afternoon. He was allowed to inspect only the American troops and their quarters and the professors were confined to the house during his visit.

The professors received the news of the impending move to England with mixed feelings. On the one hand they looked on it as a step forward in that they expected to meet their British colleagues, but on the other hand England seemed much further from home than Belgium.

Certain difficulties arose regarding the journey of the professors to England as Lt. Col. Watkins insisted upon orders directing him to release them from American custody. Eventually orders were obtained in Paris directing him to release all personnel detained at the Special Detention Centre to me personally or to my representative, at Liège airport.

30th June 1945

I left for England leaving Lt. Toepel in charge. All the professors gave me their word to carry out any instructions given by Lt. Toepel and they were handed over to Mr. Oates, whom I had designated for the task, at Liège airport on the 3rd of July and flown by special aircraft to Tempsford.

Lt. Col. Page and his staff were extremely helpful during the whole of my stay in Belgium.

VI. SUMMARY

The operation has been successful to date in that,

(1) The professors have been detained for over ten weeks without any unauthorized person becoming aware of their identity or place of detention, and,

(2) They have, with considerable difficulty, been kept in a good frame of mind.

[The following character sketches appear as an appendix to this preamble, though on a separate page at the end of the report before the signature. The sketches were apparently made by Major Rittner after being with the "professors" over two months. They are dated, along with this "Preamble," 14 July 1945. By that time, the party had spent nearly two weeks in Farm Hall, during which time they were being secretly recorded. The first Farm Hall report will cover the first weeks of confinement.]

The following are brief character sketches of the professors:

VON LAUE:

A shy mild mannered man. He cannot understand the reason for his detention. He has been extremely friendly and is very well disposed to England and America.

HAHN:

A man of the world. He has been the most helpful of the professors and his sense of humor and common sense has saved the day on many occasions. He is definitely friendly disposed to England and America.

HEISENBERG:

He has been very friendly and helpful and is, I believe, genuinely anxious to cooperate with British and American scientists although he has spoken of going over to the Russians.

GERLACH:

Has a very cheerful disposition and is easy to handle. He appears to be genuinely cooperative.

HARTECK:

A charming personality and has never caused any trouble. His one wish is to get on with his work. As he is a bachelor, he is less worried about conditions in Germany.

DIEBNER:

Outwardly very friendly but has an unpleasant personality and is not to be trusted. He is disliked by all the others except Bagge.

VON WEIZSÄCKER:

A diplomat. *[Remember: von Weizsäcker's father was the number two man and top civil servant in Hitler's Foreign Ministry.]* He has always been very friendly and cooperative and I believe he is genuinely prepared to work with England and America but he is a good German.

WIRTZ:

An egoist. Very friendly on the surface but cannot be trusted. I doubt whether he will cooperate unless it is made worth his while.

BAGGE:	A serious and very hardworking young man. He is completely German and is unlikely to cooperate. His friendship with Diebner lays him open to suspicion.
KORSCHING:	A complete enigma. He appears to be morose and surly. He very rarely opens his mouth. He has, however, become more human since his arrival in England.

14th July 1945

T. H. Rittner *[signature]*
Major

[With the first installment of the reports from Farm Hall, covering the period between July 3rd and July 18th, the form of the reports emerges. The transcribed, translated and edited dialogues begin. When the transcripts were first released, the question was raised as to whether the Germans suspected they were being monitored. The colloquy between Diebner and Heisenberg below appears convincing to me. There is some evidence—see later in the transcripts—that by the following November the Germans may have had a hint that they were being listened to. The report opens with Rittner's commentary. Mr. M. Perrin, to whom the report is addressed, is Michael Perrin, an official of the British atomic bomb project. Lt. Comdr. Welsh is at Rittner's headquarters.]

TOP SECRET

Mr. M. Perrin for Gen. Groves

through Lt. Comdr. Welsh

Copy No. 1

Ref. F. H. 1

To: Mr. M. Perrin and Lt. Comdr. Welsh
From: Major T. H. Rittner

OPERATION "EPSILON"
(3rd–18th July 45)

I. GENERAL

1. A report covering the operation on the continent from May 2nd until 3rd July 1945 has already been submitted.

2. The arrangements for bringing the party to England went according to plan and the following landed at Tempsford on the afternoon of 3rd July and were taken to Farm Hall by car:[5]

Professor von Laue.

Professor Hahn.

Professor Heisenberg.

Professor Gerlach.

Doctor Harteck.

Doctor von Weizsäcker.

Doctor Wirtz.

Doctor Diebner.

Doctor Bagge.

Doctor Korsching.

together with four P.W. orderlies. A further P.W. orderly has since been added to the party. *[In the American transcripts a hand—no doubt Groves's—has carefully checked off each man, making sure that everyone*

---

[5] Farm Hall is a spacious English country estate in the village of Godmanchester near Cambridge and the air field from which Allied bombers flew missions over Germany. The estate had been used during the war as a "safe house" for MI6 agents and resistance fighters preparing to drop behind enemy lines. R.V. Jones, *The Wizard War: British Scientific Intelligence 1939–1945* (New York, 1978), p. 481; Introduction, in Goudsmit, *op. cit.*, p. xiv.

was there. "Professor" clearly was (and is) much the more prestigious title in Germany, as few PhDs obtained (or obtain) professorships. But it is not clear how the distinction between "professor" and mere "doctor" in this list was made. Harteck, for example, was certainly a professor, as we would use the term. There were social and professional distinctions here, also. Throughout the war, Heisenberg, von Weizsäcker, and Wirtz worked on nuclear fission at odds with, and in the end independently of, Diebner and Bagge. Tensions existed between the two groups throughout the war. These were partly reflected in distinctions of status. Heisenberg and the other academic scientists tended to look down on Diebner, the German Army's long-time expert on nuclear physics and explosives. Although Bagge had been Heisenberg's student and assistant, he had allied himself with Diebner just before the war, since he was in need of a job. As a result of this factionalism, von Weizsäcker, Goudsmit reports, objected to being grouped by Goudsmit with the younger, non-elite scientists. "What kind of selection is this!" he commented.[6] Goudsmit picked people, especially the younger ones, because he thought they might have some interesting ideas. One of the many failures of the German program was not taking the ideas of the younger people seriously enough.]

3. All the professors have renewed their parole to me in writing in respect of Farm Hall and grounds and I have warned them that any attempt by any one of them or by the orderlies to escape or to communicate with anyone will result in them all having their liberty considerably restricted. *[For Major Rittner they are all "professors."]*

4. Ordinary army rations *[probably A rations]* are drawn for the professors and the officers and troops and these are prepared for all by the P.W. cooks.

5. Microphones have been installed in all the bedrooms and living rooms used by the professors. *[There have been suggestions that microphones were also placed among the trees outside.]* This installation has proved invaluable as it has enabled us to follow the trend of their thoughts. *[They also had access to newspapers, on which Rittner hoped they would comment.]*

In the following conversation, Diebner and Heisenberg discussed the possibility of there being microphones in the house. The conversation took place on 6th July in the presence of a number of their colleagues:

DIEBNER: I wonder whether there are microphones installed here?

HEISENBERG: Microphones installed? (laughing) Oh no, they're not as cute as all that. I don't think they know the real Gestapo *[Secret Police]* methods; they're a bit old fashioned in that respect.

---

[6] Goudsmit, *Alsos*, p. 104.

II. MORALE

1. The party has settled down well at Farm Hall but they are becoming more and more restive. The question of their families is causing them the greatest anxiety and I believe that if it were possible to make arrangements for an exchange of messages with their families, the effect on general morale would be immediate.

2. Most of the recorded conversations are of a general nature and show that they are pleased with the treatment they are receiving but completely mystified about their future.

3. Lt. Comdr. Welsh visited Farm Hall on 7th July. The atmosphere was somewhat tense as can be seen from the following conversations:

(a) Conversation between Heisenberg, Harteck, Wirtz, Diebner, and Korsching after the announcement of Lt. Comdr. Welsh's visit:

HEISENBERG: I can see the time is coming when we must have a very serious talk with the Commander. Things can't go on like this.

HARTECK: It won't do. We have no legal position since they have to keep us hidden.

HEISENBERG: Apparently they feel guilty about their own scientists, *[as]* otherwise one can't understand it. I tell you what we'll do; one evening we'll make the Commander drunk and then he'll talk. We'll play bridge and then talk seriously from one o'clock onwards.

WIRTZ: I think you should speak to the Commander and tell him we are very dissatisfied and then we can make him drunk one evening.

HEISENBERG: Yes, that is the right sequence of events. First there will be an afternoon when we will go for him and break him down and then an evening when we will make it up.

HARTECK: Yes, and tell him in no uncertain terms that we are being wronged.

HEISENBERG: Yes, of course.

DIEBNER: You appear to have a certain influence on him and I think that you could achieve something with him.

HEISENBERG: Well, I think I am more or less in his good books. I will point out to him that he has let Stark and Lenard go on living happily in Germany whilst we poor wretches have to let our wives and children starve. *[Philipp Lenard and Johannes Stark were both Nobel Prize winners in physics who had joined the Nazi Party even before Hitler came to power. They had led the campaign to replace modern physics in Germany by "German" physics, attacking Heisenberg in particular. By the 1940s, their physics was so out of date and mediocre that Goudsmit decided that there was no point bothering with them. As a rabid Nazi, however,*

Stark was tried and convicted by a criminal tribunal. Lenard was deemed too old and ill for prosecution. When the Alsos Mission found Lenard, he identified himself as Germany's greatest physicist. This dialogue is the beginning of the Germans' attempt to distinguish themselves from one another by comparing their relative degrees of Nazism or lack of Nazism.]

HARTECK: In the meantime the British and American soldiers are looting everything at home.

WIRTZ: He doesn't mind that.

HEISENBERG: Oh, yes, he does.

DIEBNER: With a bit of cunning, we may get something out of this. First of all they are keeping this whole business here secret and secondly the idea seems to be to be friendly to us.

HEISENBERG: I should say that the point is that they don't yet know what they want. That's the whole trouble. They don't want us to take part in any discussion regarding our future as they don't want us to have any say in the matter. They want to consider what to do and they have not yet agreed among themselves.

HARTECK: But they can't say to you: "You <u>must</u> stay here." They can merely ask: "Do you want to stay here under these conditions?" Or can they say: "You must stay here."

HEISENBERG: Of course they can if they want to. Of course it is possible they will agree to ask us whether we want to stay in England or go to America but *[say]* that we cannot stay in Germany.

DIEBNER: When the Commander comes he is sure to bring some letters or some good news with him. As soon as he comes he will try and pacify us with all sorts of excuses.

KORSCHING: Then he will talk for hours and afterwards think to himself: "Well that's all right, now I've calmed them down for a bit."

(b) Conversation between von Weizsäcker, Hahn, Heisenberg, and Wirtz after Lt. Comdr. Welsh had had a talk with them.

WEIZSÄCKER: I was very annoyed with the way the conversation began. That was when you started about the letters *[presumably to their families and colleagues]*. When he said: "Yes, they have gone but there has been no reply yet." It's all very mysterious.

HAHN: No, he said they had not yet been sent. That's what he said.

WEIZSÄCKER: That came out bit by bit after we had really questioned him. And then the remarks about "misfortunes," etc. Of course it's easy to bring things up like that and I can understand an Englishman being annoyed at our bringing that sort of thing up but that was not the proper way to reply to your questions. I felt I didn't want to listen to it all and I didn't want to give the impression that I disagreed when the man said things like that. That's why I left the room; also of course to make it easier for you.

HAHN: I would be pleased, Mr. Heisenberg, if you would have a talk with him. You needn't know the details of my conversation with him. *[Even in these circumstances Hahn refers to Heisenberg as "Mr." No one seems to be on a first name basis with anyone else. This was, and still is, commonplace in German academic life. Among men with the same title or status, titles are dropped and Mr. (Herr) is used. I have been told that Hahn was on a first-name basis with only three people. Presumably one of them was his wife.]*

HEISENBERG: He started of his own accord at lunch. I got the impression that he is rather depressed about the whole situation here and the fact that he got a somewhat hostile reception.

WIRTZ: Hahn told him that we are living here like princes but what use is that to us when we have no news of our families, have no idea what is to happen to us, and are out of touch with our work. Although we are well treated, we are nevertheless prisoners.

HEISENBERG: It certainly made an impression on him and he wanted to talk to me about it at lunch but I refused and said: "We will have a private discussion afterwards."

WEIZSÄCKER: I don't think we ought to spoil our chances with this man as he may be the one who can help us against others who are more hostile to us. He probably came here expecting us to be more cheerful and to receive him as well as we did last time at Le Vesinet. He felt at once that that was not the case and was naturally annoyed.

---

4. The general lines upon which the professor's minds are working can be seen from the following conversations.

(a) Conversation between Diebner, Heisenberg, Harteck, Wirtz, and Korsching on 6th July.

DIEBNER: Suppose you *[apparently speaking to Heisenberg]* were to escape and get to Cambridge. You have a lot of friends there. That would cause a terrific sensation. The whole thing would become known. Surely you would do that if they detain you here for a year.

HEISENBERG: If nothing happens now, I will certainly go to the Major (Rittner) in a comparatively short time and say to him: "I ask permission to break my parole." Then he will be in the awkward position of having to post an armed sentry outside my door. That will cause trouble higher up.

DIEBNER: That would at any rate result in some action being taken. What could they do to you? If you escaped and really tried to get to Cambridge, they could do nothing. They could get the police to bring you back but the damage would be done.

HARTECK: They seem to be afraid that one might do something hostile to England but they are hiding us from their own people and that is the amazing thing. If it had been the other way round—we never hid a foreign scientist in Germany, the other scientists all knew about it. *[If, at this stage, one had asked Rittner or Welsh why these particular people were being held in this particular way, one wonders what they would have said. Presumably, they knew nothing about the involvement of the Germans in a nuclear weapons project.]*

DIEBNER: The awful thing with the English is that it takes ages before they make up their minds to do something.

WIRTZ: The Empire has been built up through centuries; they have plenty of time. They can't understand it when someone is in a hurry.

HEISENBERG: One can say that they do things better than others because they take their time.

DIEBNER: They have money and in consequence have time.

HARTECK: The longer one is here, the more anxious one is to get home. In addition, it annoys one to be left in doubt. One gets terribly bitter.

DIEBNER: That's it—terribly bitter.

HEISENBERG: It may be that the British Government are frightened of the communist professors, Dirac and so on. They say "If we tell Dirac or Blackett where they are, they will report it immediately to their Russian friends *[such as]*, Kapitza, and Comrade Stalin will come and say: "What about the Berlin University Professors? They belong in Berlin." *[Dirac and Blackett may have had leftist sympathies, but neither was a communist. Patrick M.S. Blackett was a British Navy man, turned physicist, who had also been a protegé of Rutherford. Blackett was an early recruit to the British nuclear weapons program. He won the Nobel Prize in physics in 1948. He died Lord Blackett. Paul A. M. Dirac was a theoretical physicist whose accomplishments matched those of Heisenberg. He shared the 1933 Nobel Prize in Physics with Erwin Schrödinger. Heisenberg had won it the same year, but for 1932. The reference to Kapitza is particularly grotesque. Peter Kapitza had been another Rutherford associate who had come to work for him in 1921 and who had gone back to his native Russia in the 1930s. Kapitza was an early recruit to the Soviet atomic bomb project but he resigned from it in the mid-1940s. He claimed he could not get along with its director Lavrenti Beria. He was then placed under house arrest until Stalin's death in 1953.]*

DIEBNER: It's quite possible they just don't want to say anything.

KORSCHING: Then of course they will have to wait until everything has been settled by the "Big Three". *[Heads of state of the Big Three victor countries—the U.S., U.K. and Soviet Union—met at the end of July in Potsdam, outside Berlin.]*

DIEBNER: I think the right thing in that case would be for the English to give us a hint in some way. They may not be able to say it openly because of Comrade Stalin.

HEISENBERG: It is possible that the "Big Three" will decide it at Potsdam and that Churchill will come back and say: "Off you go, the whole group is to return to Berlin" and then we'll be in the soup. *[Presumably Heisenberg is worried here about being taken to task in Germany for failing to build a bomb.]*

[The last World War II meeting of Allied leaders took place in the Potsdam suburb of Berlin from July 17 to August 2, 1945. Its purposes were to plan how to conclude the war against Japan and to lay down the guidelines for the post-war treatment of Germany and former German-occupied lands, as prescribed in the three-power Berlin Declaration of 5 June 1945. The leaders of the Big Three attending were Stalin, Truman (who had become president after Roosevelt's death) and Clement Attlee (who replaced Churchill after the Labor Party victory in the parliamentary elections, 5 July 1945, though the results were not announced until 26 July 1945). France, one of the four occupation powers in Germany, was not present. The Potsdam Accords, signed on 2 August 1945, provided general guidelines on territorial and occupation issues, including the treatment of German science.

Ironically, this was the conference at which Truman informed Stalin of the atomic bomb. Stalin reportedly showed little surprise. The Soviets were already at work on their own bomb and knew about the Allied bomb through espionage agents such as Klaus Fuchs.]

(b) Conversation between Wirtz and von Weizsäcker on 7th July:

WEIZSÄCKER: These people have "detained" us firstly because they think we are dangerous; that we have really done a lot with uranium. Secondly, there were important people who spoke in our favor and they wanted to treat us well. These two facts were mixed up. Now they have got into this awful political muddle.

The decent thing for them to do now would be to say to us: "It is not possible to come to a decision about you so quickly. What shall we do? Would you like to remain with your families for the time being or ...?" They don't do that but prefer to keep us on ice. That's not nice of them. As a matter of fact I believe them when they say it has to do with the election *[in England between the Labor and Conservative parties during the Potsdam conference]* and all sorts of political muddles. I don't believe it is due to malice that they do nothing with us but it is just that they cannot come to a decision about us.

WIRTZ: Yes, I could quite understand that, but they could say, "We will come to some arrangement now about your families." What's the idea of the whole thing?

WEIZSÄCKER: Yes, but of course that is difficult—the French zone of occupation.

But the damnable thing is that they won't let one have any say in what is to happen to one or one's family or give one any hopeful indication of what is going to happen.

(c) Conversation between Wirtz, Hahn, and Diebner on 16th July after reading in the newspaper that Lord Cherwell was attending the Potsdam conference. *[Cherwell—Frederic A. Lindemann—was Churchill's science advisor during the war. He had been a German national who had emigrated earlier to Britain. He had received his doctorate with Walther Nernst in Berlin, while working on the quantum behavior of solids at low temperature. It is not clear whether he knew that the Germans were being detained.]*

WIRTZ: That's the man who has had us detained.

HAHN: If Cherwell knew we were detained here, something would happen. He doesn't know; he would certainly speak to one and discuss what he should or could do.

DIEBNER: Things like that will certainly be discussed. I imagine that they will decide at the "Big Three" conference which scientists are to go to Russia.

HAHN: How should Cherwell know anything? He doesn't know anything about us; that's the stupid part about it. But perhaps he does know.

III. ATTITUDE TOWARDS BRITISH AND AMERICANS

---

1. Some interesting sidelights on the attitude of some of the professors towards Britain and America appear from the following conversations between Bagge and Korsching.

(a) 8th July

KORSCHING: It makes me furious when people are so childishly Anglophile. It was just the same in Hechingen.

BAGGE: How do you mean?

KORSCHING: They handed them the *[heavy]* water on a platter, they did the same thing with the uranium and all the instruments and all the secret files in duplicate and—I don't know—20 grams of radium. That's awful. *[When the Alsos mission entered Hechingen, it will be recalled, they confiscated the uranium and the heavy water. Apparently some radium was overlooked.]*

BAGGE: Wirtz and Bopp buried 2 (10?) grams of radium, which they will sell privately later. *[The uncertainty about the amount is in the original. Different amounts are mentioned. Fritz Bopp who was a physicist was left in charge of the facility at Hechingen. It was eventually occupied by the French and Bopp had a hard time of it.]*

KORSCHING: Weizsäcker, although he is clever, imagines he can negotiate with them regarding the handing over of the *[heavy]* water and on what conditions. They discussed it with the Commander. At first they wanted to say: "We will only tell you on condition that you let us go working on it." They imagined they could get away with that. He need only threaten them with bread and water and they will give way.

(b) 11th July

BAGGE: If we want to continue working on our subject *[nuclear fission]*, we will certainly have to work together with the Anglo-Americans. No one has any money in Germany.

KORSCHING: If one is convinced that Germany will be occupied by the Russians for a long time and you work on the production of weapons for the English, the end result will be that you will make Germany into the (future) battlefield. The English are, of course, really much too careful to think of fighting Russia. Of course I would have no pangs of conscience in making neutron sources for the Americans. Of course we could not separate uranium for them with the existing separation apparatus. I would be perfectly willing to carry on working with that, as it is completely harmless (laughs).

From what I know of the Anglo-Americans, I don't relish the idea of their assimilating us as easily as all that. The result will be that all the good work we may do in our lives will, one could almost say, go to the credit of Anglo-American brains. You can't imagine Weizsäcker and Wirtz doing nothing *[sic: anything]* but remaining in Germany for the rest of their lives.

BAGGE: What do you mean? The first thing Wirtz did was to ask, "Will we be given British nationality?"

KORSCHING: He had all sorts of discussions beforehand. Don't imagine it was his idea. I was once talking to Wirtz and Heisenberg and I said: "It would certainly be a clever move for anyone who is thinking of working in England to acquire British nationality as otherwise he would be shot if he fell into Russian hands." They both agreed that one would have to do that. If one is taken to England, one may have to stay there. I would rather take Swedish nationality than stay in Germany and wait for the next war. On the other hand I would not make any effort to become British. If there is nothing more to be made out of Germany one should at any rate get away from Russia. Von Weizsäcker is more or less resigned to the idea of becoming Russian one day.

Suppose the English were to come and say: "You can carry on with your work, in fact you are to go on working on uranium. We will take everything back to Hechingen but you must sign a paper." Then presumably one would have to sign in order to get away from here. But would you really do it?

BAGGE: I would say that even during the war I was able to carry on my scientific work freely and I would ask whether I could continue to do so. *[In fact, Bagge had worked for German Army Ordnance on weapons research.]*

KORSCHING: I would say the same, of course. If they said "No," I would sign all the same and do it in spite of that.

On the other hand, of course, they will not give us the heavy water any more. They may say: "Go back and work but not on the uranium machine." They know we cannot get hold of two tons of uranium secretly. *[I am not sure how Korsching has arrived at this figure.]* And then of course they may say: "The uranium machine people are to go back but the isotope separators must carry on working at separating isotopes under American control."

BAGGE: Men like Wirtz will want to do something too. Wirtz may construct his curious machine again then.

KORSCHING: He will not be able to separate even 1 milligram of anything. Wirtz has the same problem as I have with my apparatus. *[Korsching was applying the Clusius method discussed in the Introduction, a glass tube and heating coil, to separate isotopes. It never worked well for uranium.]* It is a question of solubility. As long as he uses fluids which are not mercury, you get the solubility effect just the same with him as with me. The difference between his apparatus and mine is that his stages are single and mine more compact. But of course he will try and play about with it even if it is no good. But I believe the English may be satisfied with the fact that they have the apparatus. But I imagine we will have to sign one thing: that we must keep silence about all the apparatus they have taken away from us. I can't believe they will let us go; we could then publish the theory of both apparatus. We will certainly have to sign a declaration that we will not publish it. One must be very careful not to let ourselves in for anything.

---

2. Diebner and Bagge somewhat surprisingly expressed a desire to acquire British nationality in the following conversation on the 17th of July:

DIEBNER: I would be glad Bagge if we could stay here.

BAGGE: It would be a wonderful thing if we could become English.

DIEBNER: And then have nothing more to do with the *[Nazi]* Party again. I would willingly take an oath never to have anything to do with the Party again.

IV. TECHNICAL

---

1. The biweekly lectures are being continued. In fine weather these take place out of doors.

2. The following remarks were made by Bagge in conversation with Korsching on 9th July.

BAGGE: I have now solved the wave equation. *[Bagge is referring here to the*

Schrödinger wave equation. A former student of Heisenberg's, Bagge is working on the problem of finding the correct wave function to describe the heavy hydrogen nucleus—the deuteron. A deuteron is a proton and a neutron bound together into a nucleus by the nuclear force. When an electron orbits the nucleus, it forms an isotope of hydrogen known as deuterium. When deuterium combines with oxygen, it forms heavy water. Finding the wave function of the deuteron was a very fashionable nuclear theory problem at this time. Bagge does not seem to have contributed much to its solution.] Now I have to calculate the correct distribution of the charge from the wave function and the quadrupole moment from the distribution of the charge. That is what I am doing just now. First of all it is known that the deuteron is near enough spherical, *[and]* hence you can get the forces acting between proton and neutron from the intrinsic energy of the deuteron; i.e., you can find a force which gives the correct mass of the deuteron. This force, of course, corresponds to a certain relative direction of the spin of the particles. But in the deuteron a definite spin position is realized, the spins of the proton and neutron are parallel, and for this relative position of the spins you can calculate the force. A priori we know nothing about the spin position, but something can be calculated from the scattering experiments. Namely, if the spins are antiparallel, the force is only half as great. You can find a function giving the force as function of the spins which has just this property. Heisenberg has pointed this out. If you assume with Heisenberg that the force depends on the spins in this way, the forces are twice as big in that position as compared with this position, and the spherical symmetry of the deuterons is preserved. Now we have the function of Heisenberg's and the quantity of the forces, and we can take the scattering experiments correctly into account. In other words, with the help of Heisenberg's functions, we can explain the experimental scattering results <u>and</u> the intrinsic energy without contradiction.

[Hans] Bethe has shown that within the theory of Yukawa you can make assumptions which will give Heisenberg's function of the spins. *[Hidekei Yukawa was a Japanese physicist who first had the idea of nuclear forces being generated by the exchange of elementary particles called mesons.]* To make the calculation invariant from the point of view of relativity, you have to introduce additional terms which also depend on the spin directions and which can explain the quadrupole moment of the deuteron. Bethe has assumed forces in such a way that (1) They agree with the results of the scattering experiments. (2) They give the correct mass of the deuteron. (3) They give the quadrupole moment of the deuteron correctly.[7] That is all correct, but it is correct only because he introduces a new term for every effect he wants to explain. The starting point was the mass of the deuteron which is obtained with a ... *[ellipsis from original]* Then come the scattering experiments which require Heisenberg's term. To obtain the quadrupole moment correctly you need the Yukawa term which Bethe has used. Each term is introduced for a specific purpose. Of course it is a

[7] Hans Bethe, "The Meson Theory of Nuclear Forces," *Physical Review*, **55**, 1261–1263 (1939); **57**, 260–272, 390–413 (1940).

possible theory. You put as much ... into it, as you need to explain new (experimental) results.

[At this point in the transcript the conversation appears to involve Hahn and Laue, not Korsching. It concerns the question of breeding plutonium. There is no indication of how the transition occurred; probably editing by the British.]

HAHN: We don't know the properties of uranium-94 *[he means plutonium]*, but we know those of "93" *[neptunium]*.

BAGGE: You wait until the "93" has completely disintegrated, and then you should really have pure "94."

HAHN: That is far too little, you can't do anything with that. You will get nothing of an element with a period of decay of 10,000 years through the disintegration of a 2.3-day element.

BAGGE: Why? You have the 93 element with a period of decay of 2.3 days and now you wait for 20 days. Then there will be nothing left of the 93 element which will have completely transformed itself into the 94 element. *[Bagge seems to me to have the correct side of this argument. I do not understand what point Hahn is trying to make. The procedure Bagge is outlining is how plutonium is actually produced.]*

LAUE: That is too little.

HAHN: There are as many atoms as correspond to the "93." But you can prove the (existence of) "93" for the simple reason that in 2.3 days—that means actually (in) seconds—it disintegrates by one five-thousandth.

BAGGE: Now Korsching does the following: he takes your trace of the 93 element which you have concentrated.

HAHN: Every ten years one alpha ray will be emitted. How can you demonstrate that?

BAGGE: If so far you have been able to demonstrate 10,000 years by alpha counting methods, i.e., to confirm 10,000 as a lower limit, then you should be able to improve on this by approximately another 1,000 by the use of a "Plattenmethode" as Korsching has stated; but the zero effect (Null Effekt) will upset the measurements.

V. FINANCE

The professors told me some time ago that they all had German money with them which they would like to send back to their families. In consequence I asked them on 7 July to let me know how much each individual had. The following conversation took place between Diebner and Gerlach:

DIEBNER: I wanted to put down that I am carrying a certain sum.

GERLACH: I would just write, "I have so many thousand marks; it was money to pay... ."

DIEBNER: Funds of the Reich Research Board (<u>Reichsforschungsrat</u>). *[This board oversaw the nuclear project during the last half of the war.]*

GERLACH: No, not Reich Research Board but Research Society.

DIEBNER: Yes.

GERLACH: For the payment of the salaries of assistants and technical personnel. The money was at my home and I took it with me; I had no chance of banking it.

DIEBNER: I have just counted it. I should have had RM 95,000 with me but it is only RM 79,000 and something. I gave some of it to Kremer (?). I should have RM 35,000 of my own money and RM 60,000 belonging to the Research Board. But I have only got a total of RM 79,000. Perhaps I gave some to my wife.

Subsequently I *[Major Rittner]* was given the following list of money carried by each individual:

Von Laue	RM	201
Hahn		785
Heisenberg		1,809
Harteck		10,400
Gerlach		400
von Weizsäcker		550
Wirtz		726
Diebner		79,246
Bagge		1,238
Korsching		1,034
	RM	96,389

[One wonders if any of this currency had any purchasing power in 1945. The German currency system was not reformed until 1948, when two currencies were introduced: one each for East and West Germany. To set some scale for these numbers, a well paid research physicist during the war was earning about 8,000 marks a year. When I was in Germany in the summer of 1947 the currency, at least in the American zone of occupation, was the cigarette.]

VI. PERSONALITIES

1. The Professors

   (a) VON LAUE: Appears from monitored conversations to be disliked by his colleagues. *[One regrets that one does not have the full German transcript at this point. There is certainly nothing in the English version that reflects this, nor is it reflected in von Laue's long letters to his son in this period. In 1959 von Laue wrote two angry letters to Paul Rosbaud explaining his disagreements with some of his fellow Farm Hall detainees. Although this was many years after Farm Hall, I will discuss these letters in the concluding section of this book.]*

(b) HAHN: Unpopular with the younger members of the party *[Diebner and Bagge]* who consider him dictatorial. *[Here again one misses the full transcript.]*

(c) HEISENBERG: Has been accused by the younger members of the party of trying to keep information on his experiments to himself. *[The transcripts, unfortunately, do not tell us what these experiments were. Perhaps they refer to the reactor experiments that the Döpels carried out under Heisenberg's oversight in Leipzig, or to the Berlin reactor experiments from which Diebner and Bagge were excluded.]*

(d) VON WEIZSÄCKER: Told Wirtz that he has no objection to fraternizing with pleasant Englishman *[sic]* but felt a certain reluctance in doing so "this year when so many of our women and children have been killed."

(e) DIEBNER: Is very worried about his future and has told Bagge that he intends to send in a formal request to be reinstated as a civil servant. He hopes we will forget that he was a member of the Nazi party. *[All former party members faced denazification proceedings.]* He says he only stayed in the Party as, if Germany had won the war, only Party members would have been given good jobs.

2. Others

(a) BOTHE: There has been a lot of speculation as to why Professor Bothe has not joined the party *[the party at Farm Hall]* as expected. They imagine he has been clever enough to be able to stay in Germany and carry on with his work!

(b) EWALD (?): *[This is Heinz Ewald, a radio chemist who worked at Hahn's institute on isotope separation.]*: Stated by Gerlach to have possessed an exceedingly good mass spectrograph able to produce an unusually large number of lines.

(c) MAUER (?): *[This is probably a reference to Werner Maurer, one of the people on the nuclear project interrogated by Goudsmit and released.]* One of the professors in conversation with Gerlach said he was afraid of a physicist named Mauer who was an ardent Nazi but a poor research worker. Mauer worked with Strassman (?) *[Fritz Strassmann, Hahn's collaborator in the discovery of fission]* on the disintegration of molybdenum and uranium.

(d) MEYER: A physicist head of the Development Section of the torpedo experimental station. He is in his middle thirties and is a graduate of Karlsruhe University. He is an ardent Nazi. *[This cannot be Erwin Meyer, apparently mentioned earlier, since Erwin Meyer was born in 1899.]*

(e) STRASSMANN (?): Worked with Maurer on the disintegration of molybdenum and uranium. (See above.)

	(signature)
Farm Hall	T. H. Rittner
19th July 1945	Major

TOP SECRET

To: Mr. M. Perrin and Lt. Comdr. Welsh
From: Major T. H. Rittner

OPERATION "EPSILON"
(18–31 July 45)

I. GENERAL

There has been very little change in the position at Farm Hall since the last report. Outwardly the guests are serene and calm, but it is clear that their restiveness is increasing. Suggestions have been made that one of the guests should attempt to get a letter to Cambridge. Steps have been taken to prevent this.

II. MORALE

The following conversations show the general trend of morale:

---

1. Conversation between Heisenberg, von Weizsäcker, Wirtz, Harteck and Diebner on 18 July:

WEIZSÄCKER: I would say we must wait for the "Big Three." The whole thing is connected with that. *[A reference to Potsdam, where the post-war occupation was discussed. Von Weizsäcker has convinced himself that the fates of the ten German scientists will be decided by the three heads of state!]*

WIRTZ: This is the position. Why don't they want to send letters? Not because there is no post; that's all rot; of course they could send a letter. For some reason or other no one must know that Professor Heisenberg, etc., are here. That's the point. The moment anyone, even your wife is told, "Professor Heisenberg is well and happy," they will realize that he is still in captivity.

HEISENBERG: Everyone in Hechingen knows that I have been arrested, but the moment news gets through, they will know: "Ha! They are still alive."

WEIZSÄCKER: They know that in any case. *[The following passage represents the first place in the transcripts where there are significant marginal marks of various kinds—presumably by General Groves. As he received the reports from London every couple of weeks, Groves signed for them with the date.]*

89

HEISENBERG: I could also imagine that they are afraid of the following: Assume that it became known that we are here; some clever journalist would turn up and, of course he would not be allowed in. He would have a look at the place from the outside, see us playing all sorts of games in the garden, sun bathing, etc. The next day there would be a terrific article in the newspaper just like it was with Goering: "German Nazi scientists enjoying life in England. For lunch they have... ." He could write a wonderful article like that and that would of course be awkward for everyone concerned. I could well understand that that is the reason they want to keep it secret here. Of course if our colleagues who know something about the business—Goudsmit for instance—were clever, they would put another article in the newspaper, about anti-Nazis. It could start with Pastor Niemoeller and Bishop Gahlen. *[These are references to Martin Niemöller and Clemens August Graf von Galen, Bishop in Münster, both of whom were noted for opposing Nazism within Germany.]*

WIRTZ: A man like Goudsmit doesn't really want to help us; he has lost his parents. *[How Wirtz knows this is not clear. Perhaps he learned of it from Goudsmit during Goudsmit's interrogation of the scientists. It appears that Goudsmit did learn the exact fate of his parents from Hahn, but how Hahn learned about Goudsmit's parents is not clear.]*

HARTECK: Of course Goudsmit can't forget that we murdered his parents. That's true too and it doesn't make it easy for him.

[The British archival file of the reports contains a letter from Major Calvert, containing the original German of the above exchange. It reads as follows:

American Embassy
Office of the Military Attache
1, Grosvenor Square, W.1.
London England

1 September 1945

Subject: Farm Hall, "Epsilon" Report No. 2.—Re Goudsmit

To: Major Francis J. Smith, Room 5004, New War Dept. Bldg., Washington, D.C.

Attention: Mr. Ryan.

1. Major Smith asked that this office get the original transcript of that part of the Farm Hall Report No. 2 wherein Harteck mentioned Goudsmit's parents and made the statement, "Of course we murdered them." The German text of that statement is as follows:

WIRTZ: "Ein Mann wie Goudsmit will uns garnicht richtig helfen, der hat ja seine Eltern verloren.

HARTECK: Ja, also natürlich, ganz kann der Goudsmit nicht davon absehen, dass wir seine Eltern <u>umgebracht</u> haben. Das ist ja auch wahr, ich meine, dass ist nicht so ganz leicht für ihn."

2. The word "umgebracht" is probably best translated to mean "killed" rather than "murdered."

For the Military Attache:

H. K. Calvert,

Major, F.A. (Field Artillery)

Assistant to the Military Attache.]

DIEBNER: I would imagine that we will be given more freedom the moment the Russians say: "We agree, you will take over the scientists." They are negotiating with the Russians as to who shall be handed over to Russia and who shall not. Presumably that is being discussed in Berlin now.

WIRTZ: Surely the Major must have noticed that our morale has sunk.

HARTECK: He's noticed that all right.

WIRTZ: It's another question whether our attitude is directed against him personally.

HEISENBERG: No, he knows it is not against him personally.

WIRTZ: You can see it in the William Joyce case, which has been postponed until 11 September. The English are like that. *[William Joyce, nicknamed "Lord Haw-Haw" for his derisive speech, broadcast English-language Nazi propaganda to Allied troops from Berlin during the war. He was captured in May 1945 and brought to London. Since he was traveling on a British passport, although he was American, he was charged with high treason against Britain. According to The Times (London), of July 18, p. 2, the trial was postponed for summer vacation and the delay of documents. He was convicted that fall and hanged in 1946.]*

HARTECK: Yes. They've got plenty of time.

WIRTZ: If I were ever to land with airborne troops in England I would have all the men arrested straight away and they would be separated from their wives for two years just to show them what it's like.

HEISENBERG: I think there is a 90% chance of our getting back to Germany.

HARTECK: Yes. I think that is most likely. At first I thought they would really be more interested in getting information out of us. But they don't do that.

HEISENBERG: Perhaps they won't do so.

HARTECK: Apparently not. They will wait until they can do it better themselves. Then we will have to swear an oath not to talk about the thing, etc., and then perhaps they will pay each of us £500.

WIRTZ: Not on your life! We will have to pay for having been here.

---

2. Conversation between Wirtz, Harteck, Heisenberg on 21 July:

WIRTZ: I think there is a very good chance we will get back to Germany. There is a 25% chance we will get back before 1 December. The chance of getting back between 1 December and the end of next year, I would put at 70%. I think there is a 40% chance that we will never get back at all. Of course the percentages don't add up to 100. I think there us a 15% chance that we will never see our wives again.

HEISENBERG: That's all much too pessimistic. I think there is a 35% chance that we will get back before 1 December. The chance of our getting back within a reasonable time after that date, I would put at 50%. The chance of our never getting back except perhaps in totally different circumstances after many, many years, I would put at 14%. There is a 1% chance that we will never see our wives again. I can see no reason to assume that they want to treat us badly, but I can see a reason to assume that they don't want to have us in Germany as they don't want us to pass on our knowledge to other people. *[It is significant that Groves has flagged this paragraph. While the Germans had very little knowledge that would have been of any use to the Allies, they had a great deal of knowledge that would have been very valuable to a government such as that of the Soviet Union, trying, as they were, to catch up to the Allied program—or to France, for that matter. Groves's desire to keep them out of French hands will also be evident, and is suggested by the Alsos Mission's efforts to snatch the Germans from Hechingen before the French knew what happened. For example, Harteck's ultracentrifuge would have been an extraordinarily useful thing for any country to possess. This desire to keep knowledge out of the "wrong" hands clearly is a root motive for the base of the Farm Hall detentions.]*

HARTECK: That is one point but on the other hand we may be shot; not by the English but by the people there. If one of us went to Hamburg University some mad student might come and shoot one.

HEISENBERG: I still feel very strongly that they are making an exception in our case in that they are treating us better than most others and therefore I should say we will see our wives again even if we don't return to Germany. That would only be prevented if something unforeseen occurred. Of course one never knows, something astounding may suddenly happen.

WIRTZ: That's what I think. I consider there is a 15% chance of that.

---

3. The thing which is worrying the guests more than anything else is the fact that they are unable to send news to or get news from their families. The following conversation between Wirtz, Korsching, and Heisenberg took place shortly after I had discussed this question with Heisenberg on 26 July.

WIRTZ: I can't understand that. My wife will tell every Frenchman that the English have taken me away.

KORSCHING: I don't believe that is the real reason.

HEISENBERG: Then what do you think is the real reason?

KORSCHING: They want to keep us as long as possible from contact with anyone.

WIRTZ: I don't quite understand that because, if that were really the case, they ought to have taken our wives too. But in any case everyone in Hechingen knows we were taken away. I can't understand that.

HEISENBERG: The whole position with regard to Russia depends upon the outcome of this election. It is obvious that if Atlee becomes prime minister— *[Heisenberg and Korsching seem to think that if the Labor Party wins, Britain will become pro-Soviet.]*

KORSCHING: We will be handed over to Russia. That's just it.

HEISENBERG: That would change the whole political situation.

WIRTZ: They have done wrong in detaining us and now they can't get out of it. It is unpleasant for them. I can see that one of us will have to get to Cambridge one day.

HEISENBERG: Yes in certain circumstances.

WIRTZ: We'll have to fix that, or send a letter to Cambridge. That should be possible.

KORSCHING: Of course, I will put it in the letter box.

HEISENBERG: That's all right but so far you have not been able to do it because you have given your parole.

KORSCHING: That's why I always said we should give it for a limited time.

WIRTZ: We will just say: "We take it back," and then one day—

HEISENBERG: The first thing they will do will be to post a sentry with a tommy gun.

KORSCHING: They can't do that so quickly; if we do it cleverly, it can be done at 10 o'clock in the evening. (laughter)

HEISENBERG: We could just throw it out of the window over the wall. You might do that in any case but let's wait a bit.

---

4. Speculation as to the reason for their detention is still a favorite topic of conversation as can be seen from the following talk between Heisenberg, Harteck, and Gerlach on 26 July:

HEISENBERG: It looks as though the Americans fear nothing so much as the possibility of the French getting even an inkling of the uranium business—very odd. The Americans know that Joliot is interested in the business and they are afraid that Joliot, who is a communist, will do something with the Russians. At any rate, if Joliot gets to know all about it, the Americans can't prevent the Russians from finding out all about it. If they were forbidding us to write letters merely in order to annoy us, there would be no reason for treating us so well here; and they have always treated our families well. *[Some physicists were moved from the French and Russian zones of occupation into the American and British zones. Groves flagged this entire statement.]*

HARTECK: They are probably not really frightened of the French but only of the Russians.

GERLACH: Certainly.

HEISENBERG: The Russians are certainly two years behind us in the separation of uranium but if they put people like Lenko (?) and Landau, etc., on to it they will most certainly succeed. *[The Soviet atomic bomb program began in 1939. The first Russian nuclear explosion took place on September 23, 1949. One thing the Russians in fact did was to remove von Ardenne and his entire group, along with others, such as Gustav Hertz, who had earlier worked on isotope separation, to the Soviet Union, where they did work on uranium separation. "Lenko" here may refer to Yakov Frenkel, a well-known Russian theorist, or to Dimitri Ivanenko, who was a nuclear physicist. Landau refers to Lev Landau, the best of the Russian theorists. Landau was always in some trouble with the regime during the Stalin era. After the war he was involved in the nuclear weapons program. Groves flagged this exchange.]*

HARTECK: Is that the Landau from Goettingen?

HEISENBERG: No, that is the man who was often in Copenhagen. He worked on—

GERLACH: Geomagnetism. *[Landau did outstanding work in nearly every branch of physics.]*

HEISENBERG: He worked with me at Leipzig. He's a very clever Russian Jew.

HARTECK: Doesn't Joffe have anything to do with it? *[Abram Joffe was a senior academician who was an important member of the first Soviet advisory committee on nuclear weapons. The fact that these men all knew who all the others were is another testimony to the small, close knit community that these scientists were part of. When the Allies stopped publishing about fission, the Russians knew at once that they must have a nuclear weapons program. The Germans did, too, but apparently did not take it seriously, as we shall see.]*

HEISENBERG: He deals with the political side. Lenko (?) is a good man too.

GERLACH (?): *[The question mark is in the original transcripts. Perhaps the transcribers had difficulty identifying the voice.]* The whole thing as far as we are concerned is really a political question. They're not interested in us as physicists.

GERLACH: Laue has only heard about the uranium machine since we have been in detention. *[Laue was never trusted by the Nazi government. Although he remained deputy director of the Kaiser-Wilhelm Institute for Physics until 1945, he would not have been invited to work on the nuclear program even if he had wanted to. It* *does, however, seem odd that he did not know of the nuclear research effort in that institute, especially after he moved with the institute to Hechingen. In any event, he was not a nuclear physicist.]*

HARTECK: He knew absolutely nothing.

5. The following conversation between Bagge and Diebner on 26 July shows their respective attitudes:

DIEBNER: Do you think Gerlach wants to stay here for five years?

BAGGE: We want to get the position clear.

DIEBNER: Do you think von Weizsäcker wants to stay here for five years?

BAGGE: Oh yes, he wants to stay here. He likes it here. He says every day that he has never had such a good opportunity to think and work as he has here.

You must see that the situation is getting worse. Up to now I always hoped that the thing would come to end in some sensible way but I have lost hope, that is the tragedy. When I see how slowly everything goes, how it is being kept more and more secret, the fact that even here in England they have to hide us from their own people, from their Lord Cherwell, from Churchill, and everybody, that's what I can't understand.

DIEBNER: They can't do that for ever. They must realize that something will happen if we don't acquiesce.

BAGGE: I'm frightened. I'm reaching the end of my tether. (half sobbing)

DIEBNER: About your family?

BAGGE: Yes, of course, that's one reason.

DIEBNER: If I have to stay here for a year and then go back to Germany, then I shall have the support of these people in some way.

BAGGE: And in the meantime my family will be dead. After all I feel responsible for my family. I saw it for myself. The first day the French arrived in Hechingen and raped the women one after the other and a few days later they took me away. *[There is no confirmation of the rape claim.]* The day I had to leave, three Moroccans were billeted in the house—that's been going on for three months and I'm supposed to look happy here. I shall go mad. I can't stand it much longer.

DIEBNER: You must stick it.

BAGGE: I shall refuse to go downstairs. I shall eat nothing. I shall go on a hunger strike.

(Note: *[from Rittner]* Bagge is much too fat and a course of bread and water would be good for his health.)

DIEBNER: Bagge, you mustn't think we're all complete fools. Heisenberg is no fool. Do you think men who have wangled things to their own advantage all the time are going to let themselves be fooled?

BAGGE: You must also realize that if, during the war, we (put) people in concentration camps—I didn't do it, I knew nothing about it, and I always condemned it when I heard about it—if Hitler ordered a few atrocities in concentration camps during the last few years, one can always say that these occurred under the stress of war, but now we have peace and Germany has surrendered unconditionally and they can't do the same things to us now.

---

5. Hahn and Diebner had a long talk on 30 July part of which is reproduced elsewhere in this report. *[See below, Sec. III of this report. The "5" heading in this section is an error in the original and should read "6."]* The following extract shows their attitude to the letter question and Hahn's philosophical acceptance of the situation:

HAHN: I read an article in the <u>Picture Post</u> about the uranium bomb; it said that the newspapers had mentioned that such a bomb was being made in Germany. *[This was before the bomb was used on Japan, when its existence was kept in strict secrecy!]* Now you can understand that we are being "detained" because we are such men *[who would build such a terrible weapon]*. They will not let us go until they are absolutely certain that no harm can be done or that we will not fall into Russian hands or anything like that. To my mind it is a mistake to do anything. All my hopes and efforts are now directed towards getting in touch with my family. Of course I also think of my Institute as I am actually the only original member of the Kaiser-Wilhelm Gesellschaft left who was there when it was formed. *[Apparently he did not know that Max Planck was still alive.]* Of course one is sad when one sees it all disappear but I can't do anything about it. One must be a fatalist here. The longer one is "detained" here and knows nothing, the more one gets into a state where one racks one's brains to discover what is going to happen. I fight against it and make jokes. Also I don't take life too seriously in that I always look on the bright side of things.

DIEBNER: I would have been just the same in Germany. The day before I went away I said to my wife, "I suggest we commit suicide." I had reached that stage then.

HAHN: My wife was like that sometimes and that is why I am worried whether she will hold out without news. See what Laue did against National Socialism and I think I worked against it too. We are both innocent but I am not allowed to write to my wife. *[Von Laue was almost the only German physicist who publicly continued to lecture on relativity, attributing the theory to Einstein, and he courageously opposed Nazi physicists at every step in their efforts to gain control of German physics.]* I have told the Major: "If my American and English friends knew how I am being repaid for all my work since 1933, that I am not even allowed to write my wife, they would be very surprised." We are being well treated here, our slightest wish is granted if it is possible, everything except writing letters.

DIEBNER: It is the future that worries me.

HAHN: The outlook for the future is dark for all of us. I have not got a long future to look forward to. *[Hahn actually lived for another 23 years.]* Suppose you want to work later with Gerlach; do you think he will work on the uranium machine? Men are not idealists and everyone will not agree not to work on such a dangerous thing. Every country will work on it in secret. Especially as they will assume that it can be used as a weapon of war. *[It is remarkable that Hahn is expressing these views less than a week before Hiroshima, when the bomb was still secret. Groves was apparently also amazed, as indicated by his heavy, emphatic marginal lines here.]*

We have no contacts abroad now. No foreigner can find out where we are and they will wonder. My Swedish friends with whom I used to correspond will wonder what has happened and will assume I am dead. *[We will see in the sequel that Hahn's "Swedish friends" have not forgotten him. Hahn may also be referring to his former colleague Lise Meitner, who had fled to Sweden after the German annexation of Austria in 1938.]*

DIEBNER: I am becoming more and more pro-English. They do everything very decently. The Major takes great trouble.

HAHN: He takes great trouble and he would probably consider us ungrateful if we suddenly sabotaged everything. We can't do that.

DIEBNER: No, no, that's out of the question.

III. THE NAZI PARTY

Some of the guests appear to be worried about their previous adherence to the Nazi Party and its effect upon their future. The following conversations show their fears. *[Only two of the captives, Diebner and Bagge, were Party members. But since all German professors were civil servants of the state, they were required to adhere to certain practices and to make certain accommodations with the regime.[8]]*

---

1. Conversation between Bagge and Gerlach on 30 July: *[In the following, Gerlach, professor of physics at the University of Munich, drops the names of a number of Munich physicists. Munich, the seat of several Party students' and professors' organizations, had been a hotbed of the Nazi physics movement.[9]]*

---

[8] For more on Heisenberg's experiences, see UN.

[9] The identities of some of the German names in the passages that follow are taken from the German translation of selected Farm Hall reports: Dieter Hoffmann, *Operation Epsilon*, translated by Wilfried Sczepan. (Rowohlt, Berlin, 1993). The identities given by Hoffmann have not been independently verified.

BAGGE: All the young assistants I knew had to join the Party; those from Munich too, Renner (?) and Welker (?). *[The question marks are in the transcript; Welker is probably Heinrich Welker, a German physicist.]*

GERLACH: They didn't all do it.

BAGGE: Those who wanted to go to the university had to.

GERLACH: Kappler (?) and Buhl (?) who were with me didn't. *[These are probably Eugen Kappler, one of Gerlach's assistants in Munich, and Otto Buhl, a physicist at the University of Munich.]*

BAGGE: Do you know Euler, who was one of Heisenberg's assistants? *[Hans Euler was a brilliant but somewhat unstable young physicist. He was a Soviet sympathizer whom Heisenberg tried to protect. After the Hitler–Stalin pact, Euler joined the German air force and was killed in action over the Soviet Union in June of 1941.]* He did not get a job in Leipzig because he wasn't a member of the Party. The fight lasted 18 months and Heisenberg and Hund and heaven knows who else couldn't manage it. *[Friedrich Hund was a Leipzig colleague of Heisenberg's.]*

GERLACH: I managed it. Blumenthal (?) was not in the Party. He had to go in 1937 because they said his wife was partly of Jewish extraction. He went into business. Grimmen (?) was not in the Party either.

BAGGE: Meyer (?) ? *[probably Erwin Meyer, a German physicist]*

GERLACH: Meyer (?) was in the party. He was at one time a big man in the SS but got fed up afterwards. We cured him. I don't know whether Duhn (?) was in or not.

BAGGE: I was not in the Party. In 1933 I was taken by the high school SA people and pushed into the SA just like all the other young assistants I know. For instance, Wirtz—I don't know about von Weizsäcker—and Bopp, they were all in the SA. It was compulsory and one could do nothing about it. *[The SA or Brown Shirts were Hitler's storm troopers. Hitler liquidated the division during the Röhm Putsch in 1934. "High school" is short for Technische Hochschule or polytechnic school.]*

GERLACH: I didn't join the Teacher's Union (Lehrerbund) *[a Nazi organization]*.

BAGGE: In our Institute all the assistants had to join the Lecturer's Union (Dozentenbund) *[a Nazi organization]*.

GERLACH: Ruecherz (?) didn't join *[probably Eduard Rüchardt, a physics professor at the University of Munich]*. They tried to force us and we got letters and they made difficulties. We just threw everything into the wastepaper basket and didn't answer.

BAGGE: That is one way of doing it.

GERLACH: I maintain that it is not right to say one <u>had</u> to do it. I never put anything in writing. Dr. Barth was not a member of the Party. He had been an assistant in Russia for three years and was a proper assistant *[that is, state-sponsored,* *as opposed to privately funded]* in the Institute. Schuetz (?) was a Party member without realizing it *[probably Wilhelm Schütz, one of Gerlach's doctoral students]*.

BAGGE: That's what happened to me. In the autumn of 1936 my mother wrote to me in Leipzig asking whether I wanted to join the Party. Someone had asked. My mother thought it was a good thing and had sent my name in. A few months later I received my Party book which stated that I had been in the Party since 1 May 1935. It had been back-dated 12 months. It also said that I had sworn an oath to the Fuhrer in May 1935. Not one word of it was true.

GERLACH: I don't believe Hilschi (?) *[probably Rudolf Hilsch, a German physicist]* was a Party member or Meissner (?) either, but I'm not sure *[Walther Meissner, a physics professor at the University of Munich]*. Only a few of the Munich men were members. They kept on complaining and making their silly speeches. I let them make them and occasionally I was really rude as, for instance when I said in the faculty, "I don't care a damn what the Reichs Chancellery *[Hitler's office]* says."

DIEBNER: Taking the line of least resistance as so many did was of course not the right course.

GERLACH: I had a half Jew as assistant until the autumn of 1944; I kept on saying: "It's impossible to remove the man as so much depends on him." There was a girl who got into trouble later. We lost the assistant Neumann (?), who went into business later. None of the female personnel I had were Party members. I had no picture of Hitler in my Institute. They kept on coming and saying we should buy a picture of Hitler. I always said: "No, I already have one." I had a very small picture I had bought for 5 pfennig *[5 cents]*. The Nazis treated me badly. They reduced my salary and withdrew my allowances.

BAGGE: Didn't that happen to other people too?

GERLACH: No. Then they brought an action against me and I didn't go to the Institute any more. I said: "I won't go back until you withdraw the case." That was my trump card.

BAGGE: On what grounds did they reduce your salary? You had an agreement.

GERLACH: I just got a letter saying: "The agreement between the Bavarian State and yourself is cancelled; from now on your salary will be as follows." And that was that.

(Gerlach leaves the room.)

BAGGE: They could do nothing against him. He knew Goering personally. His brother was in the SS and that's how he managed to stay on. *Gerlach gets a certain personal amusement out of annoying people. It wasn't just his convictions.

[Rittner has appended a remark:] *Note: In a conversation with Hahn, Gerlach said that his brother was involved in certain big money deals with the SS. He found

this out when a sum of money was once transferred to his account in Berlin instead of his brother's. He expressed his disapproval of his brother's association with the SS to Hahn.

DIEBNER: He has rows with everyone.

BAGGE: There's something behind it. Why do they keep talking to us about the Party. Heisenberg started it and now Gerlach has brought it up.

2. Part of a conversation between Diebner and Hahn on 30 July:

[In this conversation, Diebner seems to be rationalizing his past to himself, or perhaps rehearsing how he will explain it. It is unlikely that he knew he was being recorded.]

DIEBNER: I wanted to tell you how I came to join the Party and how I have suffered under the Nazis. In 1933 I became a Freemason in opposition to National Socialism. I never voted for Hitler. That became known in Halle and the result was that I got into difficulties at the Institute. Then I went to the "Waffenamt" *[German Army Ordnance]* and was to have become a civil servant, but I did not. Schumann didn't forward my application. He said he couldn't do it because I was a Freemason. Schumann *[Erich Schumann, head of German Army Ordnance Office, which initially oversaw nuclear research]* did his best for me and sent me to a man in Munich and after a year the thing went through and I became a civil servant, a "Regierungsrat".

HAHN: The fact of being a Party member does not necessarily tell against a man. The newspapers say that.

DIEBNER: Everyone knows my views. Gerlach knows them; I was never a National Socialist and never took any part in politics. Wirtz knows my views. I told him: "I am a Party member. We'll see what happens. If the Nazis win, I shall still be a Party member and that will help us and if things go the other way, you will have to help me." That's what we arranged at that time. Now I feel rather isolated here.

HAHN: Do you feel that you are treated here differently to the others?

DIEBNER: That's just it. Wirtz knows that Heisenberg will help him no matter what happens. I am sure that Gerlach would help me; he has always been very decent to me.

HAHN: The fact that you were in the Party hasn't really done you any harm.

DIEBNER: When I get back to Germany now everyone will say: "Party man. Party man!"

HAHN: None of us know what will happen to us. In my opinion it's no good worrying too much about the future as we have no idea what will happen to us. You got on quite well with Joliot, didn't you?

DIEBNER: I have helped so many people. I persuaded Schumann to see that

Professor Pieterkowski (?) in Poland *[probably Stefan Pienkowski]* should be given facilities to go to Germany before the SS came. I often helped Joliot vis-à-vis the Gestapo.

HAHN: What happened to the Pole?

DIEBNER: I don't know. He didn't come. At Copenhagen Schumann wanted to remove the cyclotron. I prevented Copenhagen from being touched. *[This is a reference to a controversial trip that Heisenberg and Diebner took to Copenhagen in late January 1944. Diebner's statement is self-serving. Heisenberg did manage to have Bohr's institute returned to the control of the Danes, but at the price of further compromises with the regime. Note that Diebner does not seem at all curious about what happened to the Pole.]* I have done <u>so much</u> against these people. For instance, we prevented people being arrested in Norway. *[Since Diebner himself was a member of the Nazi party, it is not clear why he feels entitled here to distinguish himself from other Nazi scientists.]*

HAHN: Then I don't understand why you are worried. We can only hope that we will be able to send letters home but I don't think we can expect anything else just yet.

---

3. In the following conversation on 18 July, Heisenberg relates how he tried to help some of his colleagues and Wirtz admits German atrocities: *[This discussion is evidence that well-placed people in Germany, during the war, knew of the camps and what was happening in them as well as other atrocities the Germans were committing.]*

HEISENBERG: During the war I had five calls for help in cases where people were murdered by our people. One was Soloman (?), Hoffman's (?) son-in law. *[Hoffmann is Gerhard Hoffmann, who was Debye's successor in Leipzig after Debye moved to Berlin in 1936. He had been one of Diebner's mentors.]* I could do nothing in his case as he had already been killed when I got the letter. The second one was Cousyns the Belgian cosmic ray man; he disappeared in a Gestapo camp and I couldn't even find out through Himmler's staff whether he was alive or dead. I presume he is dead too. Then there was the mathematician Cammaille; I tried to do something about him through Sethel (?) *[probably Sethke, a foreign office official]* but it was no good and he was shot. Then from among the Polish professors there was a logistician with a Jewish name—and then with the other Poles the following happened: his name was Schouder, a mathematician. He had written to me and I had put out feelers in order to see what could be done. I wrote to Scholz (?) *[probably Heinrich Scholz, philosophy professor at the University of Münster]* who had something to do with Poland. Then Scherrer *[Paul Scherrer, a Swiss physicist, a close friend of Heisenberg's, and an invaluable source for Allied intelligence]* wrote me the following ridiculous letter saying he also had something to do with the case. He wrote: "Dear Heisenberg, I have just heard that the mathematician Schouder is in great danger. He is now living in the little Polish town of so-and-so under the false name of so-and-so." That came in a letter which was of course opened at the frontier. It is unbelievable how anyone can write that from Switzerland. I heard nothing more about Schouder and I have now been told that he was murdered.[10]

WIRTZ: We have done things which are unique in the world. We went to Poland and not only murdered the Jews in Poland, but for instance, the SS drove up to a girls' school, fetched out the top class and shot them simply because the girls were high school girls and the intelligentsia *[standard British usage]* were to be wiped out. Just imagine if they arrived in Hechingen, drove up to the girls' school and shot all the girls! That's what we did.

IV. THE FUTURE

Speculation by the guests as to the future in general has been dealt with under the heading "Morale," but the following conversation between Diebner, Korsching, and Bagge on 21 July goes rather further:

BAGGE: For the sake of the money, I should like to work on the uranium engine; on the other hand, I should like to work on cosmic rays. I feel like Diebner about this. *[The word "engine" throughout these reports is probably a translation of the German word "Maschine," which was commonly used during the war for what the British, Americans, and French called a "reactor" or "pile." The contemporary German usage is "Meiler" (pile).]*

KORSCHING: Would you both like to construct a uranium engine?

DIEBNER: This is the chance to earn a living.

KORSCHING: Every layman can see that these ideas are exceedingly important. Hence there won't be any money in it. You only make money on ideas which have escaped the general public. If you invent something like artificial rubies for the watch making industry, you will make more money than with the uranium engine. Well, Diebner, we'll both go to the Argentine.

DIEBNER: I shall come with you.

KORSCHING: I know Merkada (?) *[A. Mercader, an Argentine physicist]* there. I could write to him. Of course the letter must not be opened on the way.

BAGGE: Who is he, a physicist?

KORSCHING: Yes, he has worked with Schüler. *[Hermann Schüler was a spectroscopist at Hechingen, at the Kaiser-Wilhelm Institute for Physics.]* He came over to look around a bit. He came from the University of La Plata; not stupid, but of course he could not compete with Schüler. You can only build a uranium engine of your own in the Argentine.

---

[10]Other cases in which Heisenberg was involved are discussed in Cassidy, *loc. cit.*, pp. 483–484.

DIEBNER: That is right, there are advantages to that.

BAGGE: I think we should approach the Argentinian ambassador.

KORSCHING: The man ought to understand something about physics and that is always difficult as such people know nothing about it.

BAGGE: He knows nothing about it, but the Argentinian ambassador will know that there is something in it.

KORSCHING: But you have to consider that the Argentinian ambassador has to be careful that the British and Americans don't put one over on him somehow. They set one of their agents to work for instance, if you can talk to the Argentinian ambassador in Madrid or so, you might perhaps succeed, but I don't think you would here in England.

BAGGE: But if you disclose your identity and explain to him the whole situation?

KORSCHING: Yes, but then you will not be in a very strong position.

BAGGE: Then I get to La Plata and if I get the job as an assistant, let us say, that would not be bad at all.

(Pause)

KORSCHING: Actually I find it somehow very typical, perhaps, but quite possible that Heisenberg really continues to work on the uranium engine, in the end several really productive ideas will have been contributed by all sorts of people but people will say in the end: "It has been Heisenberg's work."

Is there any uranium ore in the Argentine at all?

DIEBNER: I don't think so.

KORSCHING: It again makes it awkward if they have to import it—to have to import ten tons of uranium!

BAGGE: You can't get that at all; only from the Russians perhaps and they will not part with it either.

KORSCHING: Still I should like to get to Hechingen once more to collect the rest of my things. After all I still have all my books there and the telescope—though mind you I have hidden it from the French. Of course I did not hand that over. I have got all my glass prisms, lenses, etc. I lifted a floorboard, hid the stuff, and nailed the board down again.

BAGGE: In the Institute?

KORSCHING: In my private lodgings.

(Diebner leaves the room)

If you work together with Heisenberg on a uranium engine, then you can write off your share. If you want to work on a uranium engine, then you would have to do it somewhere else. Of course it would be an idea to go to the Argentine with two people and say: "Here we are, we know how to do this and that; we have a good method for the separation of isotopes, we do not need to produce heavy water." Somehow in this fashion we have to do it. It would not come to anything if you collaborated with Heisenberg on a uranium engine. They did not even bring along the small fry to this place; that is how outsiders judge the work. They get there and read all the secret reports before they take people away from there.

BAGGE: How long before did they have the secret reports?

KORSCHING: Two or three days before. The principal question which Goudsmit put to me was: "Is that your idea? Has that been published already, is that anything new?"—that is all he wanted to know. And Bopp and Fischer they just ignore one and say, "Oh well, they just made some calculations for Heisenberg. Apart from that for instance, the ordering of the apparatus from the firms and all the other various things which we have done, Wirtz just told him (Goudsmit): "I have done that." Do you think Wirtz is going to be modest in front of Mr. Goudsmit? No, he says: "I have built this here, I conducted the negotiations with the firms, I had that built here and I have done the experimental work, and as far as the countings are concerned—everybody knows only too well how easy it is to count particles— Messrs. Fischer and Bopp did that." *[Fischer and Bopp were researchers at the Kaiser-Wilhelm Institute for Physics.]* And that is how Wirtz has excluded them. Goudsmit takes his word for it. Bopp was quite disgusted and astonished that suddenly he was dropped like that. And that is how it is all over the world. A scientist is asked, "What have you thought out, where is your idea?" If you then make the strategic mistake of moving in the shadow of a man who is already world famous, then you are out of the limelight for the rest of your life and if you raise your voice against that, then on top of it you will be called a trouble maker. *[A hand, probably that of Groves, has made the marginal note, "Ain't it the truth."]*

BAGGE: Did you notice how Heisenberg wiped the floor with Weizsäcker?

KORSCHING: And how! I rubbed my hands with joy. It is of course very degrading that he (Weizsäcker) cannot even do a few simple calculations.

BAGGE: Heisenberg can now of course make it up with him, if later he publishes the thing together with Weizsäcker.

KORSCHING: As far as I know Heisenberg, he will not do that.

BAGGE: I don't think he will either.

KORSCHING: He will publish it and mention Weizsäcker, etc., and in the end the whole effort of Weizsäcker will have been in vain because it will be said, "Heisenberg is behind this." *[I am not aware of such a publication.]*

BAGGE: For what remains in the end is the mathematical structure. The little bit of roundabout thinking which Weizsäcker did will be forgotten. *[It is quite unclear what work is being discussed here. There is no hint in the transcript.]*

KORSCHING: If Weizsäcker does not now try hard to write down a few more formula*[s]*, then he is squashed altogether. I think it serves him right, for Weizsäcker has unlimited ambition. (Pause) Now the really positive point about the Chief (Heisenberg) is the following: If you do some work of your own, which he acknowledges to be sound and worthwhile, then you have complete liberty to do it. In Weizsäcker's institute you become a slave—"Now you do this, what you are doing is ridiculous, etc." Weizsäcker would never let people work in his institute as the Chief would.

BAGGE: That you can see from Höcker. *[It will be recalled that Karl-Heinz Höcker made the correct analysis of the geometry of the reactor fuel elements, which Heisenberg chose to ignore.]*

KORSCHING: Höcker is clever enough to wiggle out of it as a rule. But as we have said, if you want to work on the uranium engine, it is obviously completely useless to do it <u>with</u> the Chief.

BAGGE: If you want to build an aircraft today then first you have to ignore your own interests, because the state is too much interested in it, to grant you liberty to work on it as you please. I would say, the aircraft is today comparable to the uranium engine. That is why, if one has purely scientific interests, one should slowly withdraw from it.

KORSCHING: On the other hand Heisenberg will say, if we cannot build a cyclotron anyway—and it is obvious that we cannot build one in Germany with the American ...—then we will have to hold back as a source of neutrons, at least a neutron generator, for the production of artificial radioactive elements, etc.

BAGGE: Why can't we build a cyclotron?

KORSCHING: Because we have no money. It takes too long—over there they have them ready made and if we do not now make some progress in nuclear physics, then Germany will slowly lose her place, where nuclear physics is concerned. A 2.50 meter cyclotron—even if you <u>could</u> ... start on it, would ... only be ready when the Americans would have completed all their work on the "2.50 meter."[11] One can of course still build a small cyclotron, 1 meter or 80 centimeter. It is obvious that you can do a lot of things with the engine, enormous quantities, enormous concentration of neutrons, in fact there are any amount of possibilities ... . I think the Chief has the right ideas slowly to wangle permission to run his own uranium engine for scientific purposes. He will probably obtain it, if the others do not in the meantime study the heavy water.

---

[11]It is unclear which accelerator Korsching has in mind. The main accelerator under construction at that time in the United States was Lawrence's 184-inch diameter synchrocyclotron, completed in 1946. M. Stanley Livingston, *Particle Accelerators: A Brief History* (Harvard University Press, Cambridge, 1969).

BAGGE: I am convinced they (Anglo-Americans) have used these last three months mainly to imitate our experiments. *[This is another illustration of German illusions about the Allied nuclear program. They were quite convinced right up to Hiroshima that, as so often in the past, their work set the standard to be "imitated."]*

KORSCHING: Not even that. They used them to discuss with their experts their possibilities and to study the secret documents. They probably examined a few specimens of our uranium blocks. From these specimens they can see for instance whether the engine has been running already. It could have been run; the blocks must have undergone some internal chemical change.

BAGGE: But they know already, that it did not run; that they were told.

KORSCHING: That's just it. They were told practically everything up to approximately the last series of measurements. It is the same to them whether it ever came to an increase in neutrons of 5 or 50. The issue must be quite clear to them. *[In the last experiments the Germans did with their reactors they were getting a small amount of neutron multiplication—more neutrons being produced than were being used to initiate the reactions. This is the first step towards a self-sustaining chain reaction, which they were never able to achieve.]*

BAGGE: But they will certainly have the ambition to imitate our experiments as soon as possible and for that purpose they need the D_2O *[heavy water]*. Once they have worked with that—(int.) *["int." probably stands for "interrupted." Bagge is still convinced that deuterium is the only workable moderator. The Germans will remain convinced of this throughout these reports. Fermi used graphite in the reactor he built successfully at the University of Chicago in 1942.]*

KORSCHING: They'll obviously never let go of it. If that is so, then a uranium engine can only run in Germany without the production of heavy water—which as Harteck thinks is so frightfully easy, but connected with great expense, but can be run only with an efficient method for the separation of isotopes, which is technically workable with ordinary water. *[Korsching is saying that normal water can be used as a moderator if the ^{235}U content in natural uranium is enriched by separating out some of the more plentiful isotope ^{238}U but that the method is much more costly.]*

BAGGE: Quite so. But with ordinary water you need 15 tons of uranium even with an increase in concentration of 5%. *[Bagge apparently means uranium enriched in ^{235}U to 5%, but since the Germans never built a successful reactor, it's not clear how he arrived at these figures.]*

KORSCHING: No. Just consider, you can increase the concentration of uranium from 0.7% to 1% or 2%. *[This is the increase in the ^{235}U concentration that Korsching postulates would make a light water reactor possible.]* If they will not let us work on uranium and we must sign the following statement: "I pledge myself, not to run a uranium engine for anybody anywhere in this world," then you must sign it.

BAGGE: I would sign under one condition: That they grant me enough money for other purposes, so that I have the possibility to carry on with my experiments.

KORSCHING: Of course we can say that. But then they will say: "Then we will contribute to your funds."

BAGGE: That would have to be a contribution of RM 100,000 per year.

KORSCHING: That we will never get, but perhaps we may get RM 30,000 a year. They do not want to destroy Germany but what England wants is to weaken her, otherwise they will never be able to achieve hegemony in Europe, if they immediately boost us up again.

BAGGE: They seem now to plan a "United States of Europe."

KORSCHING: Yes, if Russia would not constantly interfere. They know perfectly well that once they have let us go back to Germany they'll only have 50% control over us. They can put somebody in my room, and I guarantee you, that without that fellow noticing it, I'll be able to make an experiment. I just know he goes to see his girlfriend on Saturday, so I'll just work on Saturday night. It is possible that they themselves have already great quantities of heavy water and uranium.

BAGGE: That I do not believe.

KORSCHING: But there are many military men in England who say, "Once we let those swine go back then they'll construct the uranium engine and in the end they'll blow it up." *[This is a possible reference to using the reactor as an explosive.]* They might also say: "These people are so clever that our guard troops will be blown up with it, but not they themselves." There are also many people in England who say: "On no account must these people be treated generously; they must be made to work constantly under the threat of machine guns." I do not believe the Commander will achieve so much, that he will be able to say: "Here is your heavy water, here is your uranium, now carry on with your work."

BAGGE: There is also the question, whether the Commander wants that.

KORSCHING: Quite, if the man says: "I assure you on my word of honor." What does it mean? He did not give it to us in writing. Also he has never said: "I shall take care that your position as scientists is safeguarded." He has not even done that, but all he has said was: "I assure you on my word of honer that I—" (int.) *[presumably an interruption]*

BAGGE: You have heard that yourself?

KORSCHING: No, not the "word of honor," but the word "assure." Of course he will not have us beheaded, that is quite clear. After all he is more or less favorably disposed towards us. I am sure there are also people who say, "Behead them!" There you have to be glad that there is such a man as the Commander. If they put a piece of paper before you: "Here, please sign," there is nothing left for you to do but sign. You cannot write: "I pledge myself not *[to]* work on the uranium engine in any state, except the Argentine." In that case you would find yourself in jail for the next hundred years (laughs). I do not believe they will send us away without our signatures or without any assurance. The Argentine would perhaps be quite nice as a sort of bold adventure; as I said before, if one were so far advanced with the separation of isotopes that one knew for sure one can increase the concentration of uranium by 1% with a certain small expenditure of energy, then it would have sense, but otherwise to do the same all over again would of course not make much sense.

I shall be glad when I have liberty of movement again and be able to walk in the street and buy a scientific book, when I can do anything at all, and can write letters to friends who have survived the war.

BAGGE: I got into contact with the uranium engine only through the war, and I have always felt an outsider and for me it would mean to take a step which I do not want to take at all, because if it had been my endeavor to make a lot of money, I could have stayed home with my parents. I would have probably kept clear of the war equally easily. If I had joined my father's business, I do not like to think how much money we could have earned. *[According to his own account and Leipzig university records, Bagge, a former student of Heisenberg's, was a researcher on nuclear physics in Heisenberg's institute in the 1930s, when he received military orders to report to the Army Weapons Bureau on 8 September 1939 to plan to research on nuclear fission.[12]]*

KORSCHING: That you can also do with the uranium engine; if you really put a uranium engine before the Argentines, then you can say: "I am a scientist, I only want to build up a laboratory for myself; pay me 500,000 pesetas, but otherwise leave me in peace." Then you can of course work on cosmic rays at the University of La Plata as much as you like and on top of that you have the 500,000 pesetas. You would get them, if you got into the good books of the right professors and politicians.

BAGGE: But it could easily be, over there, that there is an awful lot of intriguing as well. Perhaps there are a lot of people like Wirtz.

KORSCHING: Of course you will not get the amount of pesetas which you should get according to the value of the proposition, but even so, if you only get 3% it would be a fortune.

BAGGE: Actually you derive no benefits from your patent either. *[These were presumably patents for various isotope separation methods. These turned out to have no standing. The Allies had independently invented and used them all during the war. All patents were placed under Allied control, and the records on many were confiscated and transferred to the United States and United Kingdom through the operations of the technical intelligence unit FIAT (Field Intelligence Agency, Technical).]*

KORSCHING: I did not tell them at all that it is a patent. I could have done so but then I would have lost everything. As it is now, if I find some third person in

---

[12]See Bagge, Diebner and Jay, *op. cit.*, p. 22, and Cassidy, *loc. cit.* p. 400.

Sweden—if I say, "This is the position, I have the patent, they do not know anything about it, take it out in Sweden; all I want for myself is 5% of what you can get from any firm." Then, when the Americans suddenly see that the patent has been taken out, they cannot do anything about it. Perhaps it will already be superfluous in a year or so. That is why I have not given it to them. I admit it is still with the Patent agent in Zehlendorf *[a fashionable section of Berlin]*. Fortunately there is nothing in the Institute; there I have, of course, hidden everything. In Zehlendorf it is in his private flat, thank God. So if the Russians have not pilfered everything there—it may be that it has been burnt, then it is lost anyway—and if the British do not search every private house in Zehlendorf now, then they will not find it at all. *[Zehlendorf was in the U.S. sector of Berlin.]* About these 20 grams of radium, of which Diebner talked and which seem to belong to the German Radium Institute— I ask myself, why do these people do that? If I had been there, I would have said: "Do you know that I have radium at all?" Then: "Do you know the exact amount?" Then I would have hidden 1 or 2 grams somewhere.

BAGGE: Wirtz has hidden 2 grams. Only Wirtz knows where these 2 grams are and then Diebner has some as well.

KORSCHING: But even so, it is too much that 20 grams still fell into their hands. One could have done it like that everywhere. I saw it myself, there they pinched some measuring apparatus. Those two apparatus which I took along, they could not pinch. On the other hand of course they must not notice it, because they say, "All right, you starve in Germany, you will not get any money from us." But our two engines they need not have got of course. *[The two "engines" are probably the two reactor experiments directed by Diebner in Gottow and Heisenberg in Berlin.]* The childish thing is, we need only have put them on the lawn at the back and it would have been perfect. They did not even look into the ... loft. I put umpteen things up there. They did not even notice the apparatus which was in that box in the chemistry room—the box was 2 meters long. *[All of this equipment was presumably connected to Korsching's experiments to separate isotopes. The Soviets soon stripped the Berlin institute of everything, including the door knobs. A reactor sitting on the back lawn would have been a sight!]*

V. TECHNICAL

The usual biweekly lectures have been given. These have been confined to general subjects.

(Signed)
T. H. Rittner
Major

FARM HALL
1 August 1945

[The preceding report was transmitted to Washington on the eleventh of August 1945 by Major H. K. Calvert, who was the assistant to the Military Attache at the American Embassy in London. He appended a note which contains the following paragraph:]

"Attached is report No. 2 of Operation "Epsilon." Report No. 1 has been furnished your office through British channels. Report No. 3 indicating the reaction of the guests to Valhalla Day will follow in the near future." *["Valhalla Day" was the day of the dropping of the atomic bomb on Hiroshima, the sixth of August 1945. It is uncertain how it came to be known by this name. The Germans' reaction to this is one of the most revealing moments in these reports. We will come to it shortly, but first there is a relatively brief report covering the period between the first and the sixth of August.]*

Report 3
TOP SECRET

Capt. Davis for Gen. Groves
Copy No. 1
Ref. F. H. 3

To: Mr. M. Perrin and Lt. Comdr. Welsh
From: Major T. H. Rittner

OPERATION "EPSILON"
(1–6 August 1945)

I. GENERAL

This report covers the period since my last report up to the evening of 6 August when the announcement of the use of the atomic bomb was made.

The effect of the announcement and the subsequent reaction of the guests forms the subject of a separate report Ref. FH4. *[Report 4, in Part II.]*

II. MORALE

In conversation with a British officer regarding the position of communication with the families, Hahn completely broke down. Bagge also came very near to tears when he described the fate worse than death which he pictured was that of his wife and children at the hands of the Moroccan troops.

General morale has, however, improved since I was able to tell the guests that permission had been granted for them to write letters to their families and that it was hoped to obtain answers. This permission was contained in a cable from Lt. Comdr. Welsh to Mr. Perrin dated 1 August.

Letters were written and it was almost pathetic to see the efforts made by the guests to convey information that they were in England. The look of discomfort on their faces when asked to delete certain sentences was obvious and subsequent monitored conversations showed that the sentences I had blue-pencilled were the ones which were intended to convey this information. The letters have all been rewritten, and I am trying to make arrangements through Captain Davis to have them delivered.

III. THE GUESTS AND THE NAZIS

The guests have been at great pains to clear themselves of any suggestion that they had any connection with the Nazis. Gerlach in particular has done his best to make this clear to his colleagues and one wonders whether this may not be due to a guilty conscience on his part. In this connection Gerlach had a long conversation with me in the course of which I suggested that there must have been Gestapo agents working in their institutes. We also discussed the question of how much they had known of the scientific work being carried out in other countries. This conversation had the desired effect and Gerlach proceeded to discuss these points with the other guests. The following conversations ensued:

---

1. Conversations between Gerlach, Hahn, and Heisenberg on 4 August.

GERLACH: The Major asked me what we had known about scientific work in enemy countries, especially on uranium. I said, "Absolutely nothing. All the information we got was absurd."

HEISENBERG: In that respect one should never mention any names even if one knew of a German who had anything to do with it.

GERLACH: For instance, I never mentioned the name of that man Albers (?). The "Secret Service" people kept asking me: "From whom did you get information?" and I always replied: "There was an official in Speer's ministry and in the Air Ministry who gave it *[presumably information]* out officially." I did not say it was Albers (?) who did it.

HEISENBERG: I had a special man who sent me amazing information from Switzerland. That was some special office. Of course I have burnt all the correspondence and I have forgotten his name. *[This man remains a mystery.]*

HAHN: Did you actually get any new information from him?

HEISENBERG: At that time I always knew exactly what was being discussed in the Scherrer Institute regarding uranium. Apparently he was often there when Scherrer lectured and knew what they were talking about. It was nothing very exciting but, for instance, he once reported that the Americans had just built a new heavy water plant and that sort of thing.

---

2. The following conversation took place between Gerlach and Heisenberg on 5 August:

GERLACH: I have just been talking to Diebner about whether there may have been an SS man amongst our colleagues. There was that business with Dr. Gruenzig (?); he was some sort of patent man who had once been a Hitler Youth leader.

HEISENBERG: I remember. He was at Hechingen.

GERLACH: Yes he was at Hechingen and we were always trying to get rid of him. Rosenberg (?) sent him to us *[possibly a reference to Alfred Rosenberg, the infamous Nazi ideologue]*.

HEISENBERG: Oh yes. That's right. But that was right at the end, during the last six months perhaps.

GERLACH: Well the Gruenzig (?) business was in the summer of 1944. At first he wanted me to send him to Munich. I mistrusted him and didn't let him see anything and we got rid of him with a lot of difficulty. I always said, "The man is too valuable to be used in an office job." Didn't Gruenzig (?) once want to put someone in your Institute? We discussed it with you at the time and warned you. (Pause) Then Diebner told me he was always suspicious that someone from the British Secret Service had been with Bothe, a certain Dr. Gehlen (?) *[Heinrich Gehlen, a German physicist]*. Did you ever know him?

HEISENBERG: Yes I knew Gehlen (?). I must say I can understand your suspicion of Gehlen (?). I knew Gehlen (?) at Leipzig, he worked with Döpel *[Robert Döpel, who worked together with his wife Klara, was an experimental colleague of Heisenberg's at Leipzig who had shown that heavy water was a good moderator]*, and I couldn't quite make him out. He was recommended to me by his cousin, Philosophy Professor Gehlen who had been at Leipzig and was then moved to Königsberg. *[This is Arnold Gehlen, philosophy professor in Leipzig 1934–1938.]* His wife was Swedish and I knew he had contacts abroad.

GERLACH: He had been with the English Bank before.

HEISENBERG: What I didn't like about the man was the fact that he had had such a varied career. He was a man of about 36 or 37; he had worked in a bank in Italy and then in an English bank; then he had some technical job in Sweden and had had all sorts of other jobs. He had never really completed his studies. Döpel took him on as he made quite a good impression. I often discussed the matter with Döpel and we agreed that Gehlen should at any rate be told nothing about the uranium business. *[This raises a point we shall return to later. If, as the Germans were shortly to claim, the "uranium business" was unrelated to the war, why did it matter if Gehlen, or anyone else, was told about it? And why were all of the reports labeled "secret" throughout the war?]* Later he went to Bothe. We could not make him out and I believe I spoke to Bothe about it and told him I was not sure of him. On the other hand there was some business about his having been denounced to the Gestapo in Leipzig. He was supposed to have had contacts abroad and the matter was investigated and he was acquitted. I can't remember exactly what happened. I wouldn't mention the Gruenzig (?) business to the Major as it might cost him (Gruenzig (?)) his life.

GERLACH: No I wouldn't do that. As I said I didn't mention Albers. I didn't say anything about him in Paris either. *[Gerlach visited Joliot's laboratory in Paris where there were Germans working.]*

HEISENBERG: I suspected two persons of belonging to the foreign "Secret Service." The first one is Dellenbach and I am pretty certain about him, and the second one is *[Heinrich]* Gehlen (?) but I am not sure about him. *[Dellenbach is* *probably Walter Dällenbach, a Swiss engineer who came to Germany during the war to work on the nuclear project.]*

GERLACH: I am quite certain about Dellenbach. You know how he got his job?

HEISENBERG: I presume through his connections with Bormann's cousin. *[Martin Bormann was Hitler's personal aide.]* I once discussed it with Vögler (?).

GERLACH: I also spoke to Vögler (?) about Dellenbach and also spoke to Speer's man Goerler (?) about it. *[This is a reference to the German industrialist Albert Vögler who became the president of the Kaiser-Wilhelm Gesellschaft in 1940.]* Then there was that unpleasant business about Dellenbach and the Swiss telegram about the uranium engine which our "Secret Service" intercepted. It all seemed to point to Dellenbach. There were two other people mixed up in it, an engineer and a professor. He (Dellenbach) wouldn't tell me his name but I heard afterwards that he had a very curious position and that he was continually at (Hitler's) Headquarters. His name was said to be Schmitt. He was one of those mysterious people and Hitler made him a professor during the war. Later that SD *[the Security Service of the SS, an intelligence unit]* man Pohl (?) came to me and told me the whole thing had been cleared up and that it had been an act of revenge on the part of one man who had pretended it was Dellenbach in order to harm him. They didn't get the other man as he had got to Switzerland in the meantime.

HEISENBERG: I'd like to talk to Vögler (?) about that, as I raised so many objections to taking Dellenbach into my Institute and Vögler (?) and I nearly had a row about it. Otherwise Vögler (?) is such a sensible man and he must have had his reasons.

IV. THE POTSDAM CONFERENCE

[Truman, Stalin and Attlee met in the Potsdam suburb of Berlin 17 July to 2 August 1945 to establish the general guidelines for peace treaties, the postwar treatment of Germany and former German-held nations, and the war against Japan. The Accords, announced on 2 August, provided only generalities about Germany and left responsibility for specifics, such as the treatment of captured Germans, to the newly established Council of Foreign Ministers (which relied in turn on the four-power Allied Control Authority in Berlin). The Potsdam Accords called for the complete disarmament and demilitarization of Germany and the breakup of "the present excessive concentration of economic power." They called for Allied controls on the German economy to the extent necessary, among other things, "to control all German public and private scientific bodies, research and experimental institutions, laboratories, et cetera, connected with economic activities."[13]]

---

[13]Paragraph 15.e. of the Accords, published in *Documents on Germany under Occupation, 1945–1954*, edited by Beate Ruhm von Oppen (London, 1955), pp. 47–57. For more on German science and the Allied occupation, see D. Cassidy, *HSPS*, **24** (2), 197–235 (1994).

The announcement of the communiqué at the end of the Potsdam conference caused a certain amount of alarm and despondency among the guests. They were particularly upset about the clauses referring to the probable cession of eastern German provinces to Poland *[Section VIII of the Accords]*. They noted the reference to German science but made very little comment. Heisenberg's remark to the others was: "At any rate it would have been infinitely worse if we had won the war." *[It is unclear whether Heisenberg refers here to postwar German science, postwar Germany or the postwar world order as a whole. This is a point where one misses having the full original transcripts or recordings.]*

V. PROFESSOR BOTHE

1. Heisenberg and Gerlach discussed Bothe in the course of their conversation on Gestapo and other agents. The following is the text of their talk:

GERLACH: The Bothe business is very odd. *[The Germans do not understand why Bothe, who did important work on selection of a moderator, was not included among them. Goudsmit decided who would be held and who released. In Alsos, Goudsmit recounts his interrogation of Bothe and his suspicion at the time that Bothe had hidden his research papers; Bothe maintained that he had burned them, which turned out to be the truth.[14] Apparently Goudsmit decided that there was nothing further to learn from Bothe. Heisenberg, below, indicates that Goudsmit did not detain Bothe because Bothe fell ill.]*

HEISENBERG: I think the following may be the solution. Bothe was a lot with Joliot. When Bothe got ill and thereby escaped detainment, Fleischmann *[Rudolf Fleischmann, a physicist at Göttingen]* managed to get in touch with Joliot and suggested that he should put in a word for him. Joliot would certainly have been delighted to do so partly because of the uranium and partly for Bothe's own sake. The others may then have been unable to get hold of Bothe again. In the meantime, Joliot may have made them think that Bothe was the only man who could really do anything in that line. It is obvious that Bothe had contact with Joliot, he certainly treated him well during the war and that may be what has happened. But I wonder whether it will do Bothe any good in the long run as I can't believe the Americans will allow Joliot much freedom. *[In his book (p. 86) Goudsmit reports that the Americans jailed Bothe briefly in June until Goudsmit intervened. Bothe won the Nobel Prize in Physics in 1954 for his work on nuclear physics.]*

2. Bagge and Diebner also discussed Bothe on the same day as follows:

DIEBNER: It doesn't look as though Bothe will join us.

---

[14]Goudsmit, *op. cit.*, 78–80.

BAGGE: I think Gehlen (?) is behind it. It looks as though Gehlen (?) had the decency to keep Bothe informed of what was going on so that Bothe could make his plans as far as these people are concerned and act accordingly.

3. Another reference to Bothe and Gehlen (?) appears*[s]* in Section III of this report.

VI. TECHNICAL

1. The usual biweekly lectures on general scientific subjects have taken place.

2. The following conversation between Diebner and Bagge took place on 5 August.

DIEBNER: In the end we really had no more radium. There was an awful row as someone wanted some. I fetched another 3 grams at the last moment.

BAGGE: Didn't firms like Braunschweigische Chemiefabrik have any more?

DIEBNER: I don't know. They may have had 1 gram; all the rest had been requisitioned by the State. I got mine from the Harz, I sent a car specially for it.

BAGGE: That was the Reichsstelle for radium?

DIEBNER: Yes. The Reichstelle for Chemistry had the radium—25 (?) lb. (sic) *[in original]*.

BAGGE: It's a pity they didn't hide 10 grams out of the 24 grams.

DIEBNER: I wasn't there. If I had been there we wouldn't have handed it over. The cars drove up and it disappeared. A pity, I had made up my mind not to hand it over.

[This conversation about the missing radium, and how it should have been hidden, took place the day before Hiroshima.]

FARM HALL,   (Signed)
GODMANCHESTER   T. H. Rittner
8 August 1945   Major

PART II

THE BOMB DROPS
6–7 August 1945

[After Robert Oppenheimer saw the first atomic bomb explosion at Trinity at 5:30 on the morning of July 16, 1945, he recalled a line from the Bhagavad–Gita spoken by Vishnu, "Now I am become Death, the destroyer of worlds." Among the worlds that were destroyed by the announcement of Hiroshima was the world of the ten German scientists interned at Farm Hall. As we have seen, prior to this announcement, such was their sense of importance that they had persuaded themselves that their personal fates were being decided in a conference involving Truman, Stalin and Attlee. They were sure that their superior knowledge was a ticket to riches in places as far flung as Argentina. Then came Hiroshima—"the destroyer of worlds."]

Report 4
TOP SECRET

Capt. Davis for Gen. Groves
Copy No. 1.
Ref. F. H. 4

To: Mr. M. Perrin and Lt. Comdr. Welsh
From: Major T. H. Rittner

OPERATION "EPSILON"
(6–7th August 1945)

I. PREAMBLE

1. This report covers the first reactions of the guests to the news that an atomic bomb had been perfected and used by the Allies. *[This was the uranium bomb made of 89%-enriched ^{235}U.]*

2. The guests were completely staggered by the news. At first they refused to believe it and felt that it was a bluff on our part, to induce the Japanese to surrender. After hearing the official announcement they realized that it was a fact. Their first reaction, which I believe was genuine, was an expression of horror that we should have used this invention for destruction.

3. The appendices to this report are:

1. Declaration signed by all the guests setting out details of the work in which they were engaged in Germany.

2. Photographs of the guests with brief character sketches of each. *[Actually, the photographs and character sketches are the first appendix and the declaration is the second. The declaration appears after this report, but the photographs appear as a separate insert.]*

II. 6TH AUGUST 1945

1. Shortly before dinner on the 6th of August I informed Professor Hahn that an announcement had been made by the BBC *[British Broadcasting Company]* that an atomic bomb had been dropped. Hahn was completely shattered by the news and said he felt personally responsible for the deaths of hundreds of thousands of people, as it was his original discovery which had made the bomb possible. He told me that he had originally contemplated suicide when he realized the terrible potentialities of his discovery and he felt that now these had been realized and he was to

119

blame. With the help of considerable alcoholic stimulant he was calmed down and we went down to dinner where he announced the news to the assembled guests.

2. As was to be expected, the announcement was greeted with incredulity. The following is a transcription of the conversation during dinner.

HAHN: They can only have done that if they have uranium isotope separation.

WIRTZ: They have it too.

HAHN: I remember Segrè's, Dunning's and my assistant Grosse's work; they had separated a fraction of a milligram before the war, in 1939. *[Segrè is Emilio Segrè, whom we have already met. John Dunning was an experimental physicist who worked with Fermi on the early fission experiments. Aristide von Grosse, who was at Columbia University at the outbreak of the war, collaborated with Dunning and Alfred Nier on the early experiments to show that ^{235}U was the fissionable isotope of uranium. He had been Hahn's assistant in the early 1930s.]*

LAUE: "235"?

HAHN: Yes, "235."

HARTECK: That's not absolutely necessary. If they let a uranium engine run, they separate "93."

[The Germans understood that what Harteck refers to as "93," and which is now called neptunium, was unstable. It decays into "94"—plutonium—with a half-life of 2.36 days. Hahn published a paper on this decay in <u>Die Naturwissenschaften</u> in 1942. To make sense, if sense can be made of the colloquy that follows, let us review briefly here the remarks made in the Prologue about the German knowledge of the use of transuranic elements, such as plutonium, for weapons. Independently of developments in the United States regarding transuranic elements, on the 17th of July 1940 von Weizsäcker produced a report for the German project in which he suggested using element 93 as a fissionable weapons fuel. It was not until 1942 that Hahn published the paper referred to above that showed that this element was unstable and completely unsuitable for this purpose. In the meantime in August of 1941 Houtermans came up with the idea of using element 94—plutonium—which is long lived and as fissionable as ^{235}U. This idea must have made its way into the project since at his lecture before the Nazi dignitaries on 26 February of 1942, Heisenberg refers to using "94." In the experiments that the Germans did to make a reactor they must have produced trace amounts of plutonium. It did not seem to have occurred to them to do any radiochemistry on these. Of course without a functioning reactor they never could have made enough plutonium to use in a bomb. In what follows Harteck and Hahn seem to have forgotten that element 93 is unstable.]

HAHN: For that they must have an engine which can make sufficient quantities of

"93" to be weighed. *[It is not clear what Hahn has in mind here. He is still talking about "93."]*

GERLACH: If they want to get that, they must use a whole ton. *[This reference to a "ton" is equally obscure. A "ton" of what?]*

HAHN: An extremely complicated business, for "93" they must have an engine which will run for a long time. If the Americans have a uranium bomb then you're all second raters. Poor old Heisenberg.

LAUE: The innocent!

HEISENBERG: Did they use the word uranium in connection with this atomic bomb? *[The British newspaper accounts of the next day did discuss uranium and even described how some of it had been mined in Canada.[1]]*

ALL: No.

HEISENBERG: Then it's got nothing to do with atoms, but the equivalent of 20,000 tons of high explosive is terrific.

WEIZSÄCKER: It corresponds exactly to the factor 10^4. *[Probably what Weizsäcker has in mind here is that 1 kilogram of uranium completely fissioned would correspond in energy to about 10^4 tons of exploding TNT (trinitrotoluene). This is the sort of "back of the envelope" calculation that the Germans had presented to Army Ordnance.]*

GERLACH: Would it be possible that they have got an engine running fairly well, that they have had it long enough to separate "93"? *[As noted earlier, the word "engine" is apparently a translation of the German word <u>Maschine</u>, which the German scientists used throughout the war when referring to the reactor or pile.]*

HAHN: I don't believe it. *[The first plutonium-producing reactor went into operation at Clinton, Tennessee, on November 4, 1943. By the summer of 1944, several grams of metallic plutonium had been delivered to Los Alamos. The mass production of plutonium took place at Hanford, Washington, a huge operation involving some 60,000 people. It began in the fall of 1944. Groves predicted that there would be enough plutonium to make several bombs by the summer of 1945, and he was right.]*

HEISENBERG: All I can suggest is that some dilettante in America who knows very little about it has bluffed them in saying: "If you drop this it has the equivalent of 20,000 tons of high explosive" and in reality doesn't work at all.

HAHN: At any rate, Heisenberg, you're just second-raters and you might as well pack up.

HEISENBERG: I quite agree.

---

[1] See *The Times* (London), 7 August 1945, p. 4.

HAHN: They are 50 years further advanced than we.

HEISENBERG: I don't believe a word of the whole thing. They must have spent the whole of their £500,000,000 *[$2 billion at the then-official exchange rate]* in separating isotopes; and then it is possible. *[In President Truman's account, released on August 6, Truman claimed: "We spent $2,000,000,000 on the greatest scientific gamble in history—and won" [The Times (London), 7 Aug. 1945, p. 4], making this the most expensive scientific-technological project ever carried out until that time. Isotope separation accounted for a large share but by no means the whole of that; Groves was wont to say that ^{235}U was more valuable per gram than diamonds.]*

WEIZSÄCKER: If it's easy and the Allies know it's easy, then they know that we will soon find out how to do it if we go on working.

HAHN: I didn't think it would be possible for another 20 years.

WEIZSÄCKER: I don't think it has anything to do with uranium.

HAHN: It must have been a comparatively small atomic bomb—a hand one.

HEISENBERG: I am willing to believe that it is a high pressure bomb and I don't believe it has anything to do with uranium but that it is a chemical thing where they have enormously increased the speed of the reaction and enormously increased the whole explosion.

GERLACH: They have got "93" and have been separating it for two years, somehow stabilized it *[a reactor]* at low temperature and separated "93" continuously.

HAHN: But you need an engine for that.

DIEBNER: We always thought we would need two years for one bomb. *[I am not sure whom Diebner includes in his "we" here or on what this estimate is based. But his use of the word "bomb" is unchallenged by the others.]*

HAHN: If they have really got it, they have been very clever in keeping it secret.

WIRTZ: I'm glad we didn't have it.

WEIZSÄCKER: That's another matter. How surprised Benzer (?) (Menzel ? SAG) would have been. *[This may possibly be a reference to Rudolf Mentzel, who, toward the end of the war, was head of the Reich Research Board.]* They always looked upon it as a conjuring trick.

WIRTZ: Döpel, Benzer (?) and Company.

HAHN: Döpel was the first to discover the increase in neutrons. *[In 1942, the Döpels, working under Heisenberg in Leipzig, did a pile experiment with uranium and heavy water as moderator in which they obtained the first clear multiplication of neutrons—indicating the possibility of a chain reaction.]*

HARTECK: Who is to blame?

(?)VOICE: Hahn is to blame.

WEIZSÄCKER: I think it is dreadful of the Americans to have done it. I think it is madness on their part.

HEISENBERG: One can't say that. One could equally well say "That's the quickest way of ending the war."

HAHN: That's what consoles me.

HEISENBERG: I still don't believe a word about the bomb but I may be wrong. I consider it perfectly possible that they have about ten tons of enriched uranium, but not that they can have ten tons of pure ^{235}U. *[This estimate clearly illustrates Heisenberg's confusion about the physics of atomic bombs. It is difficult to comprehend how he could have told the people at German Army Ordnance or von Ardenne that 60 pounds or so was enough to make a bomb and now could talk about ten tons! Clearly something is wrong, as will become evident shortly.]*

HAHN: I thought that one needed only very little "235."

HEISENBERG: If they enrich it slightly, they can build an engine which will go but with that they can't make an explosive which will... *[This statement is correct. A slightly enriched uranium mixture is very good for a reactor, but it cannot be made to explode like a bomb.]*

HAHN: But if they have, let us say, 30 kilograms of pure "235," couldn't they make a bomb with it? *[The correct answer is "yes," but Heisenberg has other ideas.]*

HEISENBERG: But it still wouldn't go off, as the mean free path is still too big. *[This statement shows that at this point Heisenberg has no idea how a bomb works. The meaning of the mean free path will be discussed below.]*

HAHN: But tell me why you used to tell me that one needed 50 kilograms of "235" in order to do anything. Now you say one needs two tons. *[We do not know what argument Heisenberg gave Hahn for the 50 kilograms, and when he gave it, but evidently he did. The Germans later continually denied that they ever had any interest in building a bomb, but this discussion proves otherwise.]*

HEISENBERG: I wouldn't like to commit myself for the moment, but it is certainly a fact that the mean free paths are pretty big.

HARTECK: Do you want 4 or 5 centimeters—then it would break up on the first or second collision.

HEISENBERG: But it needn't have the diameter of only 4 or 5 centimeters.

HAHN: I think it's absolutely impossible to produce one ton of uranium-235 by separating isotopes.

WEIZSÄCKER: What do you do with these centrifuges? *[Presumably meaning: what do you think we would or could do with these centrifuges?]*

HARTECK: You can never get pure "235" with the centrifuge. But I don't believe that it can be done with the centrifuge. *[The Allies made several different kinds of separation plants, including centrifuges. The method that was used at Oak Ridge to separate the uranium for the Hiroshima bomb was electromagnetic and involved use of mass spectrographs. That technology increasingly was superseded by gaseous diffusion enrichment; centrifuge technology was perfected only in the 1950s and 1960s.]*

WIRTZ: No, certainly not.

HAHN: Yes, but they could do it with the mass spectrographs. Ewald has some patent. *[Heinz Ewald, who was a young physicist working in Hahn's institute, invented an electromagnetic separation method that seemed very promising. It was taken up by von Ardenne and probably delivered later to the Russians. What is curious here, and characteristic, is that these Germans, all of whom were nominally working towards the same goal, had, apparently, so little knowledge of each other's work. That was the great virtue of the Allied project. There were people in charge who made it their business to know about everything.]*

DIEBNER: There is also a photochemical process. *[There is no such known process. What Diebner has in mind is unclear.]*

HEISENBERG: There are so many possibilities, but there are none that we know, that is certain.

WIRTZ: None which we tried out.

HAHN: I was consoled when, I believe it was Weizsäcker *[who]* said that there was now this uranium—23 minutes—I found that in my institute too, this absorbing body which made the thing impossible consoled me because when they said at one time one could make bombs, I was shattered. *[Hahn may be referring here to ^{239}U, an unstable isotope of uranium with a half-life of 23.5 minutes. One wonders who the "they" are who told Hahn bombs could be made. It could well have been Heisenberg, who wrote of the possibility as early as his first report to Army Ordnance in 1939.]*

WEIZSÄCKER: I would say that, at the rate we were going, we would not have succeeded during this war.

HAHN: Yes.

WEIZSÄCKER: It is very cold comfort to think that one is personally in a position to do what other people would be able to do one day. *[A very strange statement whose meaning is obscure.]*

HAHN: Once I wanted to suggest that all uranium should be sunk to the bottom of the ocean. I always thought that one could only make a bomb of such a size that a whole province would be blown up.

HEISENBERG: If it has been done with uranium-235, then we should be able to work it out properly. It just depends upon whether it is done with 50, 500 or 5,000 kilograms and we don't know the order of magnitude. *[At this point the published accounts available to the Germans have not given the quantity of ^{235}U used in the Hiroshima bomb.]* We can assume that they have some method of separating isotopes of which we have no idea.

WIRTZ: I would bet that it is a separation by diffusion with recycling. *[The diffusion method of isotope separation rests on manufacturing a uranium gas and forcing it through porous barriers with billions of holes each of submicroscopic dimensions. Atoms of the gas with different masses diffuse through the holes at slightly different rates. The original estimate was that 5,000 of these barriers would be needed for nearly complete separation, as opposed to 22,000 centrifuges. A gaseous diffusion plant was constructed in Clinton, Tennessee and put into operation in 1945. It cost half a billion dollars. Since it went into operation after August 1945, it did not affect the outcome of the war.]*

HEISENBERG: Yes, but it's certain that no apparatus of that kind has ever separated isotopes before. Korsching might have been able to separate a few more isotopes with his apparatus.

WIRTZ: We only had one man working on it and they may have had 10,000.

WEIZSÄCKER: Do you think it is impossible that they were able to get element 93 or 94 out of one or more running engines *[reactors]*?

WIRTZ: I don't think that is very likely.

WEIZSÄCKER: I think the separation of isotopes is more likely because of the interest which they showed in it to us and the little interest they showed for the other things. *[This must refer to Goudsmit's line of questioning after von Weizsäcker was captured.]*

HAHN: Well, I think we'll bet on Heisenberg's suggestion that it is a bluff.

HEISENBERG: There is a great difference between discoveries and inventions. With discoveries one can always be skeptical and many surprises can take place. In the case of inventions, surprises can really only occur for people who have not had anything to do with it. It's a bit odd after we've been working on it for five years. *[The sense here is: If we decided not to do it, it cannot be done.]*

WEIZSÄCKER: Take the Clusius method of separation. *[This is the method that Otto Frisch tried to use.]* Many people have worked on the separation of isotopes and one fine day Clusius found out how to do it. It was just the separation of isotopes which we neglected completely partly knowingly and partly unknowingly, apart from the centrifuges.

HEISENBERG: Yes, but only because there was no sensible method. The problem of separating "234" from "238" or "235" from "238" is such an extremely difficult business.

HARTECK: One would have had to have a complete staff and we had insufficient means. One would have had to produce hundreds of organic components of uranium, had them systematically examined by laboratory assistants and then had them chemically investigated. There was no one there to do it. But we were quite clear in our minds as to how it should be done. That would have meant employing a hundred people and that was impossible.

HAHN: From the many scientific things which my two American collaborators sent me up to 1940, I could see that the Americans were interested in the business.

WEIZSÄCKER: In 1940 van der Grinten wrote me, saying that he was separating isotopes with General Electric. *[This is probably a reference to W. van der Grinten, one of Debye's assistants at the Kaiser-Wilhelm Institute for Physics in Berlin, who emigrated to the United States after German Army Ordnance took control of the institute.[2]]*

HARTECK: Was van der Grinten a good man?

WEIZSÄCKER: He wasn't really very good but the fact that he was being used showed that they were working on it.

HAHN: That wicked Bomke was in my institute. *[This is a reference to Hans Bomke, who had worked in Stark's German Bureau of Standards, then in Hahn's Kaiser-Wilhelm Institute for Chemistry, from 1939 to 1941. He finished out the war in the research laboratories of the German Post Office.]*

HARTECK: I never came across such a fantastic liar.

HAHN: That man came to me in 1938 when the non-Aryan Fraülein Meitner was still there—it wasn't easy to keep her in my institute. I will never forget how Bomke came to us and told me that he was being persecuted by the State because he was not a Nazi. We took him on and afterwards we found out that he was an old fighting member of the Party. *["Old fighting member" is a literal translation of the German word Altkämpfer, which referred to a party member who had joined before Hitler came to power in 1933.]*

WEIZSÄCKER: Then we might speak of our "Bomke-damaged" institutes. (Laughter)

---

3. All the guests assembled to hear the official announcement at 9 o'clock. They were completely stunned when they realized that the news was genuine. They were left alone on the assumption that they would discuss the position and the following remarks were made:

---

[2] The identities of many of the German names below are derived from Dieter Hoffmann, *Operation Epsilon* (Rowohlt, Berlin, 1993), but they have not been independently confirmed.

[Transcripts of the 9 P.M. BBC news report, including a statement by the British government on the British role in making the bomb, follow in Appendix 3. The statement, which Prime Minister Attlee said Churchill had prepared before the change of government, also appeared in full in The Times (London), 7 August 1945, p. 4, and elsewhere. Truman at that time was still at sea, returning home from Potsdam. A report on Truman's prepared statement, issued by the White House on Aug. 6, appeared on the same page of The Times. Both statements emphasized competition with the German scientists, beginning in 1942, and the relative failure of the Germans.]

HARTECK: They have managed it either with mass spectrographs on a large scale or else they have been successful with a photochemical process.

WIRTZ: Well I would say photochemistry or diffusion. Ordinary diffusion. They irradiate it with a particular wavelength (all talking together). *[It is not clear what this process is.]*

HARTECK: Or using mass spectrographs in enormous quantities. It is perhaps possible for a mass spectrograph to make 1 milligram in one day—say of "235." They could make quite a cheap mass spectrograph, which, in very large quantities, might cost a hundred dollars. You could do it with a 100,000 mass spectrographs. *[This is essentially what the Allies did.]*

HEISENBERG: Yes, of course, if you do it like that, and they seem to have worked on that scale. 180,000 people were working on it. *[The Times report of Truman's statement said: "The number of people employed at one time on these projects was 125,000, and more than 65,000 were still engaged in operating plants." The Manchester Guardian, 7 August 1945, p. 5, reported that 78,000 people had been employed at Clinton, Tenn. plant, "the first atomic-bomb factory."]*

HARTECK: Which is 100 times more than we had.

BAGGE: Goudsmit led us up the garden path.

HEISENBERG: Yes, he did that very cleverly. *[Goudsmit, of course, never gave any hint to the Germans about the Allied program during their interrogation.]*

HAHN: Chadwick and Cockcroft. *[James Chadwick and John Cockcroft were very distinguished British physicists who were involved with the nuclear weapons program. Churchill noted in his press statement that a technical advisory committee had been formed early in the war, consisting of Sir James Chadwick, Rudolf Peierls and Drs. Halban, Simon and Slade.]*

HARTECK: And Simon too. He is the low-temperature man. *[Franz Eugen Simon was a Jewish-German refugee at Oxford who worked on isotope separation by gaseous diffusion.]*

KORSCHING: That shows at any rate that the Americans are capable of real cooperation on a tremendous scale. That would have been impossible in Germany. Each one said that the other was unimportant.

GERLACH: You can't really say that as far as the uranium group is concerned. You can't imagine any greater cooperation and trust than there was in that group. You can't say that any one of them said that the other was unimportant. *[Gerlach was the administrative head of fission research during the last years of the war.]*

KORSCHING: Not officially, of course.

GERLACH: (Shouting). Not unofficially either. Don't contradict me. There are far too many other people here who know.

HAHN: Of course, we were unable to work on that scale.

HEISENBERG: One can say that the first time large funds were made available in Germany was in the spring of 1942 after that meeting with Rust when we convinced him that we had absolutely definite proof that it could be done. *[It will be recalled that Truman and Churchill had placed the beginning of competition with the Germans in 1942, when the Manhattan Project got under way. Bernhard Rust was Hitler's cabinet minister in charge of the Reich Ministry for Research and Education who presided over the February 26, 1942 meeting where the nuclear scientists exhibited their wares. The "it" here is an atomic bomb. Funds were continued to support a research program, but at a level that was absurdly small compared to what would have been needed to achieve a bomb.]*

BAGGE: It wasn't much earlier either.

HARTECK: We really knew earlier that it could be done if we could get enough material. Take the heavy water. *["It" here may refer to obtaining a chain reaction in a reactor. At this point the Germans still have not realized the possibility of using graphite rather than heavy water as a moderator.]* There were three methods, the most expensive of which cost 2 marks per gram and the cheapest perhaps 50 pfennigs. And then they kept on arguing as to what to do because no one was prepared to spend 10 million if it could be done for three million.

HEISENBERG: On the other hand, the whole heavy-water business which I did everything I could to further cannot produce an explosive.

HARTECK: Not until the engine is running. *[This dialog shows clearly that the Germans were aware of the plutonium route. I bring this up again because of a mistake in Goudsmit's book Alos. The paragraph in question, on p. 243, contains the following sentences which have been much commented on. "Heisenberg never hit on the idea of using plutonium, although in principle it was suggested by his colleague Houtermans, who did not belong to the inner circle. Yet if that idea had been taken up, the German uranium project might have gone farther. As it was, their immediate goal was only a slow uranium pile and beyond that, their eventual goal was the erroneous idea of an explosive pile." The reason plutonium did not get taken up, as has been said, was that the Germans never were able to make a reactor—the first step to manufacturing plutonium. I do think that Heisenberg understood the difference between the requirements of making a reactor as opposed to a bomb in that he realized that fast neutrons were essential to making a bomb. I* *do not think—and the rest of the dialogue will make this clear—that he had any real understanding of the physics of a bomb, other than a few qualitative generalities, many of which were totally wrong.]*

HAHN: They seem to have made an explosive before making the engine and now they say: "In future we will build engines." *[Hahn, of course, had this completely wrong, probably because peaceful applications—i.e., reactors—were mentioned in the press reports as something for the future.]*

HARTECK: If it is a fact that an explosive can be produced either by means of the mass spectrograph—we would never have done it as we could never have employed 56,000 workmen. *[See the numbers quoted above. In the British newspapers of the next day it was stated that 78,000 people were employed at Oak Ridge.]* For instance, when we considered the Clusius–Linde business combined with our exchange cycle we would have needed to employ 50 workmen continuously in order to produce two tons a year. *[Harteck is referring to heavy water. Linde was a German company that held the patent right to this process.]* If we wanted to make ten tons we would have had to employ 250 men. We couldn't do that.

WEIZSÄCKER: How many people were working on V1 and V2? *[The rockets, some of which landed on London.]*

DIEBNER: Thousands worked on that. *[Mostly slave labor. The nuclear project made some indirect use of slave labor. The Auer Company, which was producing uranium oxide for the nuclear project, employed 2,000 female slave laborers taken from the Sachsenhausen concentration camp. This was the uranium that Heisenberg and the rest were using in their reactor experiments.[3]]*

HEISENBERG: We wouldn't have had the moral courage to recommend to the government in the spring of 1942 that they should employ 120,000 men just for building the thing up. *[What Heisenberg seemed most to have feared was that he would promise a weapon he couldn't deliver. That was his situation beginning in 1942.]*

WEIZSÄCKER: I believe the reason we didn't do it was because all the physicists didn't want to do it, on principle. If we had all wanted Germany to win the war we would have succeeded. *[As has been emphasized in the Introduction, this became the basis for one of the myths surrounding the German nuclear weapons effort: We could have done it, we knew how to do it but we didn't do it on principle. If von Weizsäcker really believed this, then why did he willingly and voluntarily turn over his idea for using plutonium to German Army Ordnance? How better to help Germany win the war? In 1959 Max von Laue had a correspondence with Paul Rosbaud that we shall present in detail at the end of the book. In it von Laue reminisces about his days at Farm Hall. One of his principal memories is that of*

---

[3] Walker, *op. cit.*, p. 133.

von Weizsäcker leading the attempt to create the myth that the Germans did not succeed because they did not want to succeed. He wrote: "Heisenberg gave a lecture on the subject in one of the colloquia which we prisoners had arranged for ourselves. (This is the lecture Heisenberg gave on August 14 on his understanding of nuclear weaponry. It appears in full in the next section of the reports.) Later during our table conversation, the version (Lesart, or a "way of reading") was developed that the German atomic physicists really had not wanted the atomic bomb, either because it was impossible to achieve it during the expected duration of the war or because they simply did not want to have it at all. The leader in these discussions was Weizsäcker. I did not hear the mention of any ethical point of view. Heisenberg was mostly silent." The ineluctable fact, born out by the documentation in German Army Ordnance and elsewhere, was that, at least in the beginning, von Weizsäcker and the others wanted the project to succeed.]

HAHN: I don't believe that but I am thankful we didn't succeed. *[It is important to notice that when Hahn says that he does not believe von Weizsäcker, no one contradicts him.]*

HARTECK: Considering the figures involved I think it must have been mass spectrographs. If they had had some other good method they wouldn't have needed to spend so much. One wouldn't have needed so many men.

WIRTZ: Assuming it was the Clusius method they would never have been able to do anything with gas at high temperatures. *[The Clusius method of isotope separation does not work very well for uranium.]*

HARTECK: When one thinks how long it took for us to get the nickel-separating tube—I believe it took nine months.

KORSCHING: It was never done with spectrographs.

HEISENBERG: I must say I think your theory is right and that it is spectrographs.

WIRTZ: I am prepared to bet that it isn't.

HEISENBERG: What would one want 60,000 men for?

KORSCHING: You try and vaporize one ton of uranium. *[Korsching has in mind that the isotope-separation processes work with gaseous uranium.]*

HARTECK: You only need ten men for that. I was amazed at what I saw at I. G. [Farben].

HEISENBERG: It is possible that the war will be over tomorrow.

HARTECK: The following day we will go home.

KORSCHING: We will never go home again.

HARTECK: If we had worked on an even larger scale we would have been killed by the "Secret Service." *[Harteck probably has in mind the fact that every time a large-scale German nuclear effort was detected, such as the obtaining of heavy*

[This was originally printed as the first appendix to Report 4.]

PHOTOGRAPHS OF FARM HALL AND THE GUESTS DETAINED THERE

[Photographs of Farm Hall and the Farm Hall detainees are courtesy of the U. S. National Archives and were provided by Professor Mark Walker.]

FARM HALL

The most friendly of the detained professors. Has a very keen sense of humor and is full of common sense. He is definitely friendly disposed to England and America. He has been very shattered by the announcement of the use of the atomic bomb as he feels responsible for the lives of so many people in view of his original discovery. He has taken the fact that Professor Meitner has been credited by the press with the original discovery very well, although he points out that she was in fact one of his assistants and had already left Berlin at the time of his discovery.

PROFESSOR OTTO HAHN

A shy, mild-mannered man. He cannot understand the reason for his detention as he professes to have had nothing whatever to do with uranium or the experiments carried out at the Kaiser-Wilhelm Institute. He is rather enjoying the discomfort of the others as he feels he is in no way involved. He is extremely friendly and is very well disposed to England and America.

PROFESSOR MAX VON LAUE

Has always been very cheerful and friendly, but from his monitored conversations is open to suspicion because of his connections with the Gestapo. As the man appointed by the German government to organize the research work on uranium, he considers himself in the position of a defeated general and appeared to be contemplating suicide when the announcement was made *[about the use of the atomic bomb]*.

PROFESSOR WALTHER GERLACH

Has been very friendly and helpful ever since his detention. He has taken the announcement of the atomic bomb very well indeed and seems to be genuinely anxious to cooperate with British and American scientists.

PROFESSOR
WERNER HEISENBERG

A very charming personality. Appears to be interested only in his research work. He has taken the announcement of the atomic bomb very philosophically and has put forward a number of theories as to how it has been done.

PROFESSOR PAUL HARTECK

Outwardly very friendly and appears to be genuinely cooperative. He has stated, both directly and in monitored conversations, that he was sincerely opposed to the Nazi regime and anxious not to work on an atomic bomb. Being the son of a diplomat he is something of one himself. It is difficult to say whether he is genuinely prepared to work with England and America.

PROFESSOR CARL FRIEDRICH
VON WEIZSÄCKER

DOCTOR KARL WIRTZ

A clever egoist. Very friendly on the surface, but cannot be trusted. He will cooperate only if it is made worth his while.

DOCTOR ERICH BAGGE

A serious and very hard-working young man. He is completely German and is unlikely to cooperate.

A complete enigma. On the announcement of the use of the atomic bomb he passed remarks upon the lack of courage among his colleagues which nearly drove Gerlach to suicide.

DOCTOR HORST KORSCHING

Outwardly friendly but has an unpleasant personality and cannot be trusted.

DOCTOR KURT DIEBNER

water in Norway, it was destroyed by the Allies.] Let's be glad that we are still alive. Let us celebrate this evening in that spirit.

DIEBNER: Professor Gerlach would be an Obergruppenführer *[Lieutenant General, roughly]* and would be sitting in Luxembourg as a war criminal.

KORSCHING: If one hasn't the courage, it is better to give up straightaway. *[Korsching probably means the courage to mount a major effort.]*

GERLACH: Don't always make such aggressive remarks.

KORSCHING: The Americans could do it better than we could, that's clear.

(Gerlach leaves the room.) *[Probably upset at the criticism.]*

HEISENBERG: The point is that the whole structure of the relationship between the scientist and the state in Germany was such that although we were not 100% anxious to do it, on the other hand we were so little trusted by the state that even if we had wanted to do it it would not have been easy to get it through. *[Matters would have been totally different if early in the war a reactor had been successfully built. Heisenberg's statement is questionable. While it is true that early in the war the scientists were not very trusted, by 1942 they, especially Heisenberg, were. How else could he and others have gotten permission to travel to occupied territories and even to neutral Switzerland, if they were not trusted? Also, his direct connections with Speer, Goering and Himmler could have enabled him to push this project through if he had seen the need and the possibility to do so.]*

DIEBNER: Because the official people were only interested in immediate results. They didn't want to work on a long-term policy as America did.

WEIZSÄCKER: Even if we had gotten everything that we wanted, it is by no means certain whether we would have gotten as far as the Americans and English have now. *[He is now speaking about the bomb as a reality.]* It is not a question that we were very nearly as far as they were but it is a fact that we were all convinced that the thing could not be completed during the war.

HEISENBERG: Well that's not quite right. I would say that I was absolutely convinced of the possibility of our making a uranium engine but I never thought that we would make a bomb and at the bottom of my heart I was really glad that it was to be an engine and not a bomb. I must admit that.

WEIZSÄCKER: If you had wanted to make a bomb we would probably have concentrated more on the separation of isotopes and less on heavy water. *[Note again that graphite is not a consideration.]*

(Hahn leaves the room.)

WEIZSÄCKER: If we had started this business soon enough we could have got somewhere. If they were able to complete it in the summer of 1945, we might have had the luck to complete it in the winter 1944–45. *[Von Weizsäcker forgets that the Germans began their program in the fall of 1939, while the Manhattan Project was launched in December 1941. It is ironic that the German Army stopped major support of the bomb project at the same time that the Manhattan Project got under way. The Germans began well ahead in the race. Their problem—one of many problems—was that they did not see it as a race. They simply did not believe that the Allies could build a reactor, let alone a nuclear weapon.]*

WIRTZ: The result would have been that we would have obliterated London but still would not have conquered the world, and then they would have dropped them on us.

WEIZSÄCKER: I don't think we ought to make excuses now because we did not succeed, but we must admit that we didn't want to succeed. If we had put the same energy into it as the Americans and had wanted it as they did, it is quite certain that we would not have succeeded as they would have smashed up the factories. *[This may be true. Witness what happened to the Auer factory. But this is a far cry from saying that we did not succeed because "we did not want to succeed."]*

DIEBNER: Of course they were watching us all the time.

WEIZSÄCKER: One can say it might have been a much greater tragedy for the world if Germany had had the uranium bomb. Just imagine, if we had destroyed London with uranium bombs it would not have ended the war, and when the war did end, it is still doubtful whether it would have been a good thing. *[One wonders in Weizsäcker's scenario who is supposed to have won the war.]*

WIRTZ: We hadn't got enough uranium.

WEIZSÄCKER: We would have had to equip long-distance aircraft with uranium engines to carry out airborne landings in the Congo or Northwest Canada. We would have had to have held these areas by military force and produce the stuff from mines. That would have been impossible.

HARTECK: The uranium content in the stone in the radium mines near Gastein was said to be so great that the question of price does not come into it.

BAGGE: There must be enormous quantities of uranium in Upper Silesia. Mining experts have told me that.

DIEBNER: Those are quite small quantities.

HARTECK: If they have done it with mass spectrographs we cannot be blamed *[for not succeeding?]*. We couldn't do that. But if they have done it through a trick, that would annoy me.

HEISENBERG: I think we ought to avoid squabbling amongst ourselves concerning a lost cause. In addition, we must not make things too difficult for Hahn.

HARTECK: We have probably considered a lot of things which the others cannot do and could use.

WEIZSÄCKER: It is a frightful position for Hahn. He really did do it. *[This appears to be a reference to Hahn's discovery of fission.]*

HEISENBERG: Yes. (Pause) About a year ago, I heard from Segner (?) *[probably Sethke, who worked in the German Foreign Office]* from the Foreign Office that the Americans had threatened to drop a uranium bomb on Dresden if we didn't surrender soon. At that time I was asked whether I thought it possible, and, with complete conviction, I replied: "No." *[On what information about uranium such a question would have been based on is difficult to imagine. If Heisenberg had wanted the war to end without a German victory, he might well have said "yes," but then he might have been ordered to build a bomb too.]*

WIRTZ: I think it is characteristic that the Germans made the discovery and didn't use it, whereas the Americans have used it. I must say I didn't think the Americans would dare to use it. *[Here we can see the German Lesart already taking shape. Von Weizsäcker will soon give it its fullest elaboration. In 1956 a Swiss journalist named Robert Jungk wrote a best-selling book whose English title was Brighter Than a Thousand Suns. He interviewed several of the Farm Hall veterans. Heisenberg declined to see him, but later praised his book. Von Weizsäcker appears to have been one of his principal sources. In his book, Jungk makes the following statement: "It seems paradoxical that the German nuclear physicists, living under a saber-rattling dictatorship, obeyed the voice of conscience and attempted to prevent the construction of atomic bombs, while their professional colleagues in the democracies, who had no fear, with very few exceptions concentrated their whole energies on production of the new weapon." The resemblance between this statement and that of Wirtz is uncanny and certainly not accidental. Very recently, Jungk has stated that he was "misled" by these scientists. It is a pity he and all of us did not have access to the Farm Hall transcripts in 1956.]*

---

4. Hahn and Laue discussed the situation together. Hahn described the news as a tremendous achievement without parallel in history and Laue expressed the hope of speedy release from detention in the light of these new events.

5. When Gerlach left the room he went straight to his bedroom where he was heard sobbing. Von Laue and Harteck went to see him and tried to comfort him. He appeared to consider himself in the position of a defeated general, the only alternative open to whom is to shoot himself. Fortunately he had no weapon and he was eventually sufficiently calmed by his colleagues. In the course of conversation with von Laue and Harteck, he made the following remarks:

GERLACH: When I took this thing over *[in 1943, with the backing of Speer, Gerlach took over as "plenipotentiary" (German: Bevollmächtigter) of the nuclear program]*, I talked it over with Heisenberg and Hahn, and I said to my wife: "The war is lost and the result will be that as soon as the enemy enters the country I shall be arrested and taken away." I only did it because, I said to myself, this is a German affair and we must see that German physics are preserved. I never for a moment thought of a bomb but I said to myself: "If Hahn has made this discovery let us at least be the first to make use of it." *[In Gerlach's case this is probably a truthful statement. He had been working for the German Navy and had until his appointment no real connection with the nuclear project.]* When we get back to Germany we will have a dreadful time. We will be looked upon as the ones who have sabotaged everything. We won't remain alive long there. *[Gerlach died in 1979.]* You can be certain that there are many people in Germany who say that it *[losing the war because they did not build the bomb]* is our fault. Please leave me alone.

---

6. A little later, Hahn went up to comfort Gerlach when the following conversation ensued:

HAHN: Are you upset because we did not make the uranium bomb? I thank God on my bended knees that we did not make the uranium bomb. Or are you depressed because the Americans could do it better than we could?

GERLACH: Yes.

HAHN: Surely you are not in favor of such an inhuman weapon as the uranium bomb?

GERLACH: No. We never worked on a bomb. *[Gerlach cannot be referring to the group as a whole, since they certainly did work on a bomb in the beginning.]* I didn't believe that it would go so quickly. But I did think that we should do everything to make the sources of energy and exploit the possibilities for the future. When the first result, that the concentration was very increased with the cube method appeared *[Gerlach is no doubt referring to using Diebner's cubical fuel elements in the reactor as opposed to Heisenberg's layer design]*, I spoke to Speer's right-hand man, as Speer was not available at the time, an Oberst Geist *[Col. Friedrich Geist, Chief of Technical Research in Speer's Ministry for Weapons Production]*, first, and later Sauckel at Weimar *[Fritz Sauckel, District Leader of Thuringia and head of worker mobilization]* asked me: "What do you want to do with these things?" I replied, "In my opinion the politician who is in possession of such an engine can achieve anything he wants." About ten days or a fortnight before the final capitulation Geist (?) replied: "Unfortunately we have not got such a politician."

HAHN: I am thankful that we were not the first to drop the uranium bomb.

GERLACH: You cannot prevent its development. I was afraid to think of the bomb, but I did think of it as a thing of the future, and that the man who could threaten the use of the bomb would be able to achieve anything. That is exactly what I told Geist, Sauckel and Murr *[Wilhelm Murr, Party District Leader and Reich Governor of Württemberg, the province in which Hechingen and Haigerloch lay]*. Heisenberg was there at Stuttgart at the time. *[This, of course, contradicts what he said in the preceding section about never "for a moment" having thought of a bomb.]*

(Enter Harteck)

Tell me, Harteck, isn't it a pity that the others have done it?

HAHN: I am delighted.

GERLACH: Yes, but what were we working for?

HAHN: To build an engine, to produce elements, to calculate the weight of atoms, to have a mass spectrograph and radioactive elements to take the place of radium.

HARTECK: We could not have produced the bomb but we would have produced an engine and I am sorry about that. If you had come a year earlier, Gerlach, we might have done it, if not with heavy water, then with low temperatures *[his dry ice idea]*. But when you came it was already too late. The enemy's air superiority was too great and we could do nothing.

Hahn, Gerlach, and Harteck go on to discuss their position if they return to Germany and Gerlach considers that they will have to remain here another two years because they will be in danger. Hahn, however, feels that he could return to Germany without any danger to himself. Gerlach goes on to explain that the Nazi party seemed to think that they were working on a bomb and relates how the Party people in Munich were going round from house to house on the 27th or 28th of April last telling everyone that the atomic bomb would be used the following day. *[It is not clear who was supposed to be using this weapon and against whom. Note, however, that people like Heisenberg had been giving lectures to important Party members about nuclear explosives of "quite unimaginable force."]* Gerlach continues:

GERLACH: I fought for six months against Esau and Beuthe (?) taking over all the heavy water and the uranium and having the engine made by the Reichsanstalt. *[Abraham Esau was Gerlach's predecessor in nuclear administration and president of the German Bureau of Standards or Physikalisch-Technische Reichsanstalt. Hermann Beuthe was a researcher at the Reichsanstalt and an SS functionary who had worked on the investigation of Heisenberg before the war.]* Esau told me more than once: "The cube experiment is my experiment and I am going to take everything." And as I was stubborn and refused to give in, Beuthe (?) sent a letter to Himmler through the S.D. *[Security Service]* regarding my political attitude.[4] I

---

[4] The relationships among the SD, the SS, SA, Gestapo and other organizations were complex and changing. The SA (Brown Shirts) had been Hitler's private army until the unit was purged in the Röhm Putsch of 1934, while the SS continued as Hitler's personal body guard. Within the SS, the SD (Sicherheitsdienst) served as an intelligence gathering unit. In 1936 Hitler placed Himmler in command of the SS and all security, subordinating the Security Police (Sicherheitspolizei, or Sipo) and the Secret State Police (Gestapo), along with the SD, to the SS. See Karl Dietrich Bracher, *The German Dictatorship* (Holt, Rinehart, and Winston, New York, 1970) and Franz Neumann, *Behemoth* (Octagon Books, New York, 1983).

know all about it and you have no idea the trouble I had with Esau and what my position was in February and March of last year because of Beuthe's (?) accusations. I wouldn't have given much for my chances of life at that time. That went on till September or October until Esau eventually officially gave up his claim to the uranium and the heavy water. *[This internecine bickering over scarce materials was another reason why the German project failed. There was no General Groves to make rapid final decisions for the entire project.]*

HARTECK: Of course we really didn't do it properly. Theory was considered the most important thing and experiments were secondary, and then almost unintelligible formulas were written down. *[This was a favorite complaint of Harteck and he had a point. An example is the Heisenberg layer design for a reactor. Heisenberg liked it primarily because it was simple to calculate. But it was not very good, as subsequent experiments showed. When Robert Oppenheimer was appointed the director of Los Alamos there was a great deal of surprise, and some distress, because he was a theorist. There were several reasons why it worked. He had a polymathic grasp of physics and radiated authority and competence. He also surrounded himself with equally brilliant experimenters and provided an atmosphere in which they could all talk freely to one another. That was one of the reasons why they were not given military ranks and uniforms. Furthermore, Fermi, who was a brilliant experimenter as well as theorist, had already built the reactor.]* We did not carry out experiments with sufficient vigor. Suppose a man like Hertz had made the experiments, he would have done it quite differently. *[Gustav Hertz was an outstanding German experimenter whose uncle Heinrich Hertz, one of the great 19th century physicists, was Jewish. Because of his Jewish ancestry, Hertz was driven from his professorship in Berlin. He was able to remain in Berlin in private industry and then, as a Marxist, he went to the Soviet Union after the war, where he worked on the Russian bomb. He died in East Germany. Although he was an expert on isotope separation, he was not allowed to work on that problem during the war.]*

GERLACH: They did make experiments. They measured the heat of uranium.

HARTECK: For instance, if you measure the emission of heat and at the same time make the 23-minute body *[^{239}U]*.

GERLACH: What Schütze (?) was to have done later? *[Werner Schütze was a doctoral student and co-worker of Hertz's.]*

HARTECK: Why was that not done?

GERLACH: Perhaps it was.

HARTECK: You might perhaps have boiled the metal, so obtaining a large surface area which would behave towards neutrons as in *[Otto]* Stern's experiments. Then you would see that in one case it was better by a few percent and in another case worse. But such experiments were not made, or rather they wanted to persuade you against it.

HAHN: Hertz did that.

GERLACH: Yes. He had all the material he could find.

HAHN: When was that—in 1944?

GERLACH: Yes, the end of 1944. But he had measured the emission of heat already two years before. I just went to Hertz and said "Look here, Hertz, let's discuss the uranium business." He said: "I know nothing about it," so I told him all about it. Then he told me that Schutze had made such heat experiments and then we discussed it and decided that that really was the best thing.

HAHN: So he (used) a small radium preparation and beryllium preparation ...

GERLACH: 25 milligrams and about a hundred grams of uranium powder (?). He only used powder. When I heard about it, I said straightaway that that was the right method of examining small bodies.

HARTECK: We had 27 grams of radium. If we used—say—5 grams of radium as neutron sources we could easily have measured with the best-shaped bodies.

GERLACH: We must not say in front of these two Englishmen Welsh and Rittner *[the two senior British military officers in charge of Farm Hall]* that we ought to have done more about the thing. Wirtz said that we ought to have worked more on the separation of isotopes. It's another matter to say in front of an Englishman that we did not try hard enough. They were our enemies, although we sabotaged the war. *[Gerlach may mean they sabotaged the war by failing to build a bomb.]* There are some things that one knows and one can discuss together but that one cannot discuss in the presence of Englishmen.

HAHN: I must honestly say that I would have sabotaged the war if I had been in a position to do so.

---

7. Hahn and Heisenberg discussed the matter alone together. Hahn explained to Heisenberg that he was himself very upset about the whole thing. He could not really understand why Gerlach had taken it so badly. Heisenberg said he could understand it because Gerlach was the only one of them who had really wanted a German victory, because although he realized the crimes of the Nazis and disapproved of them, he could not get away from the fact that he was working for Germany. *[Despite the claim Heisenberg makes here, considerable evidence suggests he himself held the views he attributes to Gerlach.]* Hahn replied that he too loved his country and for that, strange as it might appear, it was for this reason that he had hoped for her defeat. Heisenberg went on to say that he thought the possession of the uranium bomb would strengthen the position of the Americans vis à vis the Russians. They continued to discuss the same theme as before that they had never wanted to work on a bomb and had been pleased when it was decided to concentrate everything on the engine. *[Here again one misses the full transcript, but clearly the scientists were already groping toward the Lesart that will emerge in full the next day.*

Note that they need to explain their failure to themselves, to the German public and to the public abroad.] Heisenberg stated that the people in Germany might say they should have forced the authorities to put the necessary means at their disposal and to release 100,000 men in order to make the bomb, and he feels himself that had they been in the same moral position as the Americans and had said to themselves that nothing mattered except that Hitler should win the war, they might have succeeded, whereas in fact they did not want him to win. Hahn admitted, however, that he had never thought a German defeat would produce such terrible tragedy for his country. They then went on to discuss the feelings of the British and American scientists who had perfected the bomb, and Heisenberg said he felt it was a different matter in their case as they considered Hitler a criminal. They both hoped that the new discovery would in the long run be a benefit to mankind. Heisenberg went on to speculate on the uses to which America would put the new discovery and wondered whether they would use it to obtain control of Russia or wait until Stalin copied it. They went on to wonder how many bombs existed. *[At that moment, there was one—"Fat Man"—the plutonium bomb that was to be dropped on Nagasaki on August 9th. A second plutonium bomb could have been delivered a few days later.]* The following is the text of this part of the conversation.

HAHN: They can't make a bomb like that once a week.

HEISENBERG: No. I rather think Harteck was right and that they have just put up 100,000 mass spectrographs or something like that. If each mass spectrograph can make 1 milligram a day, they have got 100 grams a day *[of separated ^{235}U].* *[The scientists do not consider plutonium, which would require a working reactor, because the newspapers and BBC had spoken only of uranium and did not mention reactors and probably because they had failed to build a reactor.]*

HAHN: In 1939 they had made only a fraction of a milligram. They had identified the "235" through its radioactivity.

HEISENBERG: That would give them 30 kilograms a year.

HAHN: Do you think they would need as much as that?

HEISENBERG: I think so certainly, but quite honestly I have never worked it out as I never believed one could get pure "235." I always knew it could be done with "235" with fast neutrons. That's why "235" only can be used as an explosive. One can never make an explosive with slow neutrons, not even with the heavy-water machine, as then the neutrons only go with thermal speed, with the result that the reaction is so slow that the thing explodes sooner, before the reaction is complete. It vaporizes at 5,000° and then the reaction is already ...

[He ends here. One is struck by two things in this statement. The first is Heisenberg's admission to Hahn that he had never "worked out" the amount of ^{235}U—the critical mass—of uranium needed to make a bomb—some 56 kilograms. It is difficult not to

take this statement at its face value. Why at this stage of things would Heisenberg have told Hahn, whom he seemed to trust, a deliberate falsehood? But then how are we to reconcile this statement with the figures apparently obtained during the war: the 50 or so kilograms that, von Ardenne later claimed, Heisenberg quoted to him during the war, and a figure of the same order of magnitude found in the anonymous German Army Ordnance report of January 1942 that Heisenberg had presumably read and had probably had helped to write? I can only conclude that by this time, over three years later, Heisenberg had somehow forgotten these earlier estimates—if, indeed, he ever made them. This seems supported by the next part of the colloquy in which Heisenberg, attempting to perform the calculation for Hahn, gets it wrong at every level. Knowing how scientists work, I find it implausible that he ever did the calculation correctly before. One can imagine even a Heisenberg forgetting a number—he was, in any case, not very good with numbers—but it is very difficult to imagine his forgetting a general method of calculation, a method that once led him to a more reasonable answer.

The second thing I find striking is that Heisenberg understood the difference between a reactor and a bomb. His presentation of this to Hahn speaks for itself.]

HAHN: How does the bomb explode?

HEISENBERG: In the case of the bomb it can only be done with the very fast neutrons. The fast neutrons in "235" immediately produce other neutrons so that the very fast neutrons which have a speed of—say—1/30th that of light make the whole reaction. Then of course the reaction takes place much quicker so that in practice one can release these great energies. In ordinary uranium a fast neutron nearly always hits "238" and then gives no fission. *[This is because the cross section in ^{238}U for a fast neutron causing a fission is much smaller than the cross section for the other possible reactions.]*

HAHN: I see, whereas the fast ones in the "235" do the same as the "238," but 130 times more. *[What Hahn had in mind here is that the cross section for fission produced by fast neutrons in ^{238}U is about a 100 times smaller than that for ^{235}U.]*

HEISENBERG: Yes. If I get below 600,000 volts I can't do any more fission on the "238," but I can always split the "235" no matter what happens. If I have pure "235" each neutron will immediately beget two children and then there must be a chain reaction which goes very quickly. Then you can reckon as follows. One neutron always makes two others in pure "235." That is to say, in order to make 10^{24} neutrons I need 80 reactions, one after the other. Therefore I need 80 collisions and the mean free path is about 6 centimeters. In order to make 80 collisions, I must have a lump of a radius of about 54 centimeters and that would be about a ton.

[We must now attempt to sort out this essential paragraph line by line. It, and particularly the completely erroneous figure of 1 ton, represents what Heisenberg understood, and did not understand, about bomb physics as of the time of Hiroshima.

I find absurd the idea that, as some have recently tried to argue, Heisenberg really had a deeper understanding but even at that time in history chose not to reveal it to Hahn.

Heisenberg's first sentence is correct and is in accord with the observation that it takes a neutron with a kinetic energy of at least about one million electron volts to initiate fission in ^{238}U. Neutrons with a smaller energy either get absorbed or elastically scattered. There is some significant probability for neutrons with energies greater than one million electron volts (hence faster neutrons) to fission ^{238}U. This process can be used to increase the yield of a weapon—the released energy—but ^{238}U by itself cannot sustain a chain reaction. On the other hand, neutrons of any energy can fission ^{235}U. That was Bohr's insight. In a ^{235}U fast fission, on the average, about two and half neutrons are emitted. This is somewhat larger that Heisenberg's example of two, but for the sake of simplicity, and without changing anything essential, we can stick with his two.

His next sentence is also correct and is based on the energetics of the situation. It is something any physicist who had read even the Frisch–Meitner paper could calculate. The argument goes as follows: We shall use the physicist's energy unit— the erg—in this argument. The Hiroshima bomb produced an energy release equivalent to that of 20,000 tons of TNT. This Heisenberg knew from the news reports. Also, for reasons I will now explain, 20,000 tons of TNT is a convenient reference figure and one that Heisenberg used in his demonstration talks during the war. Essentially all this energy comes from the fissioning of individual ^{235}U nuclei. (The Hiroshima bomb contained an admixture of about 11% ^{238}U, which contributed something to the energy release.) As was known since the Frisch–Meitner paper, each of these fissions produced about 2.7×10^{-4} ergs. This is a minuscule number of ergs compared to the amount needed to fry an egg. However, there are a lot of nuclei per kilogram of ^{235}U—about 2.58×10^{24} of them. Putting these numbers together, there are about 10^{18} ergs of fission energy available in each gram of ^{235}U. This is to be compared to the approximately 4×10^{10} ergs of chemical energy available in each gram of TNT. If we convert from grams to English tons we arrive at the famous result that the fission energy available in 1,000 grams of ^{235}U—one kilogram—is equivalent to 20,000 tons of TNT. This calculation Heisenberg had certainly done before. In fact, it was already given in rough estimate earlier in these reports by von Weizsäcker. In addition, Siegfried Flügge in his August 1939 article in Die Naturwissenschaften (comparable to Science or Nature) on fission presented a similar calculation. Thus any physicist familiar with fission knew that the Hiroshima bomb, with its announced energy release of the equivalent of about 20,000 tons of TNT, corresponded to the successful fissioning of one kilogram of ^{235}U out of the total material of the bomb.

How many nuclei does this involve? As we have remarked, there are about 2.58×10^{24} nuclei in each kilogram of uranium. But it is at this point that

Heisenberg's calculation becomes unstuck. The picture he gives of how the bomb works is that there is a neutron that fissions a ^{235}U nucleus, producing two neutrons, that in turn fission two more ^{235}U nuclei, producing four neutrons and so forth. In n generations this will fission 2^n of ^{235}U nuclei, always assuming that two neutrons are produced with each fission. To fission a kilogram we need to fission the approximately 10^{24} nuclei that compose it. It is a simple exercise in logarithms to show that this figure corresponds to about 80 generations. That is, $2^{80} \approx 10^{24}$; fissioning 10^{24} nuclei will, under Heisenberg's assumptions, produce about 2^{80} neutrons. Then Heisenberg argues that this involves 80 successive collisions each producing a fission. He then notes that a neutron moves on the average about 6 centimeters between fission-producing collisions. The actual number is closer to 17, which Heisenberg could not know precisely since he did not know the relevant fission cross section. But that is not the real issue here. One might then naively say, following this line of reasoning, that the size of the lump of uranium needed is his 6 centimeters times the 80 collisions. But Heisenberg was, of course, not that naive. As any physicist would know, the problem is analogous to the drunkard who is allowed to step three feet in any direction away from a lamppost against which he has been leaning. How far from the lamppost will he get after many such successive steps in random directions? This is a famous "random walk" problem solved in every statistical physics class. For a large number of steps the answer turns out to be the square root of the number of steps, multiplied by the step length. In Heisenberg's picture, the neutrons are doing a random walk away from where the first collision was initiated. They are bouncing off nuclei, without inducing fission, in random directions. Hence the size of the lump is, according to Heisenberg, $\sqrt{80} \times 6 \approx 54$ centimeters.

Before describing why this calculation nevertheless turns out to be irrelevant to the actual case of a bomb, let me describe how Heisenberg uses it. He would like to use this length of 54 centimeters to calculate the mass of the lump. For simplicity, let us assume that it is spherical and call the radius of the sphere r. Then the volume of the sphere V is related to the radius by the expression $V = (4/3) \pi r^3$. But the mass density of uranium—the amount of mass in a unit volume—has long been known to be 19.04 grams per cubic centimeter. If we multiply this density by the volume we will have the total mass of the lump. If we use Heisenberg's 54 centimeters and do the multiplication correctly, which he did not—he made an arithmetical error—we come out with a mass of his "bomb" of 13 tons! He erroneously gives 1 ton for the same calculation. What is surprising is that Heisenberg did not realize that there had to be something wrong with the totality of his various numbers. Only a few minutes earlier he told Hahn that the Americans were able to accumulate about 30 kilograms—60 pounds—of ^{235}U a year. This is a very sensible answer and about right. But now he concludes that they needed a ton—a ton being a metric ton (not an English ton), that is, 1,000 kilograms or about 2,200 pounds. Dividing 60 into 2,000 gives about 33 years instead of 1! He does not seem to realize that the two figures are incompatible. It is this sort of thing that inspired a very distinguished *colleague of mine to comment that while Heisenberg was a very great physicist he was not a very good one—a man you could trust to think things like this through sensibly. If he had done his own incorrect calculation correctly, he would have discovered that it would take four centuries to accumulate the stuff and that the resultant bomb would have been 3 tons heavier than the total payload of any World War II bomber.*

But his whole calculation, even if he had done the arithmetic correctly, is irrelevant to how a bomb really works, or even to how a critical mass is defined. Indeed, once the fission reaction is initiated, then in any volume, the reaction proceeds at a rate determined by the time it takes between fission-producing collisions. In ^{235}U this rate is about one fission every hundredth of a microsecond. These fissions produce neutrons. Some of them will eventually produce more fissions in the ^{235}U while others will escape out of the volume and be lost. We can now get a feeling of how big this volume must be so as to allow enough neutrons to be produced to compensate for the number being lost through the surface. If we take the size to be much larger than the mean free path, then very few neutrons will get out before fissioning something. If we take it to be much smaller than the mean free path, then most of the neutrons will get out before doing any fissioning. It is then reasonable to say that the radius is very roughly the mean free path size. In the next part of these reports we will go into this in more detail. I am being somewhat imprecise here since there are actually two mean free paths involved (see Part III for the details). If we use Heisenberg's 6 centimeters for the mean free path we would get a bomb size of about 6 centimeters as opposed to his 54—a factor of 9 smaller—and because the mass varies as the cube of this size the critical mass would be about 700 times smaller than Heisenberg's number. This very crude calculation gives a much too small answer—about a kilogram—for the critical mass, but it gives the essence. To do better, one must do a real calculation. As we shall see, over the next week or so, Heisenberg took time to think the problem over and he presented the outlines of such a calculation to his colleagues on the 14th of August. But there is no convincing evidence, as far as I can see, that he had ever done it earlier during the war.

There is an equally important point that he does not consider at all here. What happens in a real bomb is that as the fissions begin, the bomb material heats up. This is discussed later in these reports. Indeed, it becomes a gas. This happens very rapidly. But as the gas expands the distance between the nuclei becomes larger and larger and the fission reaction will shut itself off, long before all the material has been fissioned. Indeed, the critical mass for ^{235}U is, as we have noted in the Introduction, 56 kilograms. The energy released in the Hiroshima explosion was caused by the fissioning of only a small part of that—1 kilogram of ^{235}U—about 2% of the material in the bomb. In Heisenberg's discussion this effect is ignored. Hence the obvious question is why, according to Heisenberg, is not the whole ton fissioned, which would have produced an explosion 1,000 times bigger than what was reported.

This seems to be at the back of Hahn's mind all throughout this discourse. Recall he says at one point, "It must have been a comparatively small atomic bomb—a hand one." And later, "I always thought that one could only make a bomb of such a size that a whole province would be blown up." He has not understood how, even taking the 50 kilograms he remembered Heisenberg telling him during the war, one could get a bomb equivalent to only 20,000 tons of TNT. Why not 50 times more or, if Heisenberg is right with his ton, 1,000 times more; indeed, enough to blow up a small province. This problem does not seem to bother Heisenberg, which once again shows that at the time he had not really understood bomb physics.]

HAHN: Wouldn't that ton be stronger than 20,000 tons of explosive? *[Hahn is once again picking at the same issue.]*

HEISENBERG: It would be about the same. *[Why? Why wouldn't it be 1,000 times "stronger"? It is the same problem, which Heisenberg apparently still does not understand.]* It is conceivable that they could do it with less in the following manner. They would take only a quarter of the quantity but cover it with a reflector which would turn back the fast neutrons. For instance, lead or carbon, and in that way they could get the neutrons which go out to come back again. It could be done in that way. It is possible for them to do it like that. *[Here Heisenberg has once again half understood something. As early as 1941 the Germans, including Heisenberg, had understood the utility of surrounding a reactor with a mantle of material that would reflect escaping neutrons back into the volume with the fuel elements. They realized that if they used such a mantle they could decrease the size of the reactor. One of the mantles used was ordinary water. At Los Alamos it was realized from the beginning that such a mantle would be useful also in the construction of a bomb. It was known there as a "tamper." The tamper was to serve two purposes—three if uranium was used. It would reflect neutrons. If the tamper were massive enough, it would retard the expansion of the exploding bomb and increase the amount of time for fission to take place. If it were uranium it could also produce additional energy with subsidiary fissions. The tampers considered included gold, tungsten and rhenium as well as natural uranium. A thick tamper of natural uranium reduces the critical mass of a bomb from 56 to 14 kilograms. But it was also realized that there was a limitation to the use of a tamper material. If the tamper were a good moderator, like carbon, the neutrons would bounce around in it for a considerable time before returning to the primary uranium fuel. For a reactor this is no problem since one does not want a fast buildup of the fission energy. But for a bomb, it is disastrous since it can slow the whole process up, causing a fizzle. For Heisenberg to have proposed using carbon as a tamper shows that he had not understood this aspect of bomb physics either. Indeed, it shows he was thinking like a reactor physicist, which, for the last two years, he was.]*

HAHN: How can they take it in an aircraft and make sure that it explodes at the right moment?

HEISENBERG: One way would be to make the bomb in two halves, each one of which would be too small to produce an explosion because of the mean free path. The two halves would be joined together at the moment of dropping when the reaction would start. They have probably done something like that. *[They did.]*

[Rittner remarks:] Heisenberg went on to complain bitterly that Goudsmit had lied to him very cleverly and thinks that he might at least have told him that their experiments in America were further advanced. *[Mrs. Heisenberg wrote in her later recollections of Heisenberg that Goudsmit had lied to Heisenberg when, after his capture, Heisenberg asked if atomic bomb research had been done in America. "With a smile, Goudsmit answered that there had been more important things to do during the war, and that there had been no efforts in that direction."[5] Why Heisenberg in his right mind would think that in a time of war Goudsmit would transmit any military secrets to him is beyond reason. On matters of this sort, Heisenberg often seems totally removed from reality.]* They agreed that the secret was kept very well. Hahn remarked on the fact that there had been no publication of work on uranium fission in British or American scientific journals since January 1940, but he thought there had been one published in Russia on the spontaneous fission of uranium with deuterons. Heisenberg repeated all his arguments saying that they had concentrated on the uranium engine, had never tried to make a bomb and had done nothing on the separation of isotopes because they had not been able to get the necessary means for this. He repeated his story of the alleged threat by America to drop a uranium bomb on Dresden and said that he had been questioned by Geheimrat Segner (?) of the Foreign Office about this possibility. The conversation concluded as follows:

HEISENBERG: Perhaps they have done nothing more than produce "235" and make a bomb with it. Then there must be any number of scientific matters which it would be interesting to work on.

HAHN: Yes, but they must prevent the Russians from doing it.

HEISENBERG: I would like to know what Stalin is thinking this evening. Of course they have got good men like Landau, and these people can do it too. There is not much to it if you know the fission. The whole thing is the method of separating isotopes.

HAHN: No, in that respect the Americans and in fact all the Anglo-Saxons are vastly superior to them. I have a feeling that the Japanese war will end in the next few days *[right]* and then we will probably be sent home fairly soon *[wrong]* and everything will be easier than it was before. Who knows that it may be a blessing after all?

---

[5] Elisabeth Heisenberg, *Inner Exile: Recollections of a Life with Werner Heisenberg*, translated by S. Cappellari and C. Morris (Birkhäuser, Boston, 1984), p. 108.

8. The guests decided among themselves that they must not outwardly show their concern. In consequence they insisted on playing cards as usual till after midnight. Von Weizsäcker, Wirtz, Harteck and Bagge remained after the others had gone to bed. The following conversation took place:

BAGGE: We must take off our hats to these people for having the courage to risk so many millions.

HARTECK: We might have succeeded if the highest authorities had said, "We are prepared to sacrifice everything."

WEIZSÄCKER: In our case even the scientists said it couldn't be done. *[Only beginning in the middle of 1942.]*

BAGGE: That's not true. You were there yourself at that conference in Berlin. I think it was on 8 September *[Bagge is, no doubt, referring to the conference of September 16, 1939]* that everyone was asked—Geiger, Bothe and you Harteck were there too—and everyone said it must be done at once. Someone said, "Of course it is an open question whether one ought to do a thing like that." Thereupon Bothe got up and said, "Gentlemen, it must be done." Then Geiger got up and said, "If there is the slightest chance that it is possible—it must be done." That was on 8 September '39.

WEIZSÄCKER: I don't know how you can say that. 50% of the people were against it.

HARTECK: All the scientists who understood nothing about it all spoke against it, and of those who did understand it, one third spoke against it. As 90% of them didn't understand it, 90% spoke against it. We knew that it could be done in principle, but on the other hand we realized that it was a frightfully dangerous thing. *[In fact, it was not until the middle of 1942 that the German scientists said a bomb could not be built in time to affect the outcome of the war.]*

BAGGE: If the Germans had spent 10 billion marks on it and it had not succeeded, all physicists would have had their heads cut off.

WIRTZ: The point is that in Germany very few people believed in it. And even those who were convinced it could be done did not all work on it.

HARTECK: For instance, when we started that heavy-water business the Clusius method was apparently too expensive, but I told Esau that we should use various methods all at once; there was the one in Norway; and that we should have a Clusius plant to produce 2–300 liters a year, that is, a small one and then a hot-cold one. As far as I can see we could never have made a bomb, but we could certainly have got the engine to go.

WIRTZ: Korsching is really right when he said there wasn't very good cooperation in the uranium group as Gerlach said *[i.e., contrary to what Gerlach said]*. Gerlach actually worked against us. He and Diebner worked against us the whole time.

[Gerlach supported both the Diebner and the Heisenberg projects almost to the very end.] In the end they even tried to take the engine away from us. If a German court were to investigate the whole question of why it did not succeed in Germany it would be a very very dangerous business. If we had started properly in 1939 and gone all out everything would have been all right. *[He seems to regret that the Germans did not succeed more than he is grateful that Germany did not attain a bomb.]*

HARTECK: Then we would have been killed by the British "Secret Service."

WIRTZ: I am glad it wasn't like that, otherwise we would all be dead.

(Pause)

BAGGE: It must be possible to work out at what temperature the thing explodes.

HARTECK: The *[neutron]* multiplication factor with "235" is 2.8, and when one collides with the other *[another 235 nucleus]* how long is the *[mean free]* path until it happens? 4 centimeters. Rx is the *[critical]* radius. Then you have to multiply that by the mean free path and divide it by the square root of the multiplication factor. That should be 3.2. R is about 14 centimeters, the weight is 200 kilograms; then it explodes. *[This apparently off-hand calculation of the critical mass by Harteck, which does lead to a sensible answer, unlike Heisenberg's, shows some evidence that he had done this problem before. It is difficult to believe that he would have known, for example, that the critical radius involves the inverse square root of the multiplication factor if he had not thought about it. How Harteck got the number of 2.8 for the multiplication factor is unclear. During the war the Los Alamos people who certainly knew more about it than he did used 2.2. Only after the war was the number increased to 2.52 as the measurements became better. Perhaps it was Harteck who supplied the German Army Ordnance report of January 1942 with its numbers in the scientists' attempt to interest the Army in continuing support of bomb research.]*

---

9. Gerlach and Heisenberg had a long discussion in Gerlach's room, which went on half the night. In the course of this conversation they repeated most of the statements that had been made in the course of the general conversation downstairs and have already been reported. The following are extracts from the conversation:

GERLACH: I never thought of the bomb, all I wanted was that we should do everything possible to develop Hahn's discovery for our country. *[What did he think the consequences would have been? Gerlach keeps contradicting himself about whether or not he ever thought in terms of a bomb. It is difficult to believe that he had never thought that the project could lead to a bomb, since that was one of its goals from the very beginning.]*

Heisenberg went on to stress the fact that they had concentrated on the development of the engine and stated that although the Allies appeared to have concentrated on the bomb they could presumably also make the engine now. He attributed that they failed to perfect the engine to the attacks on the factories in Norway. He blamed Hitler for the fact that, as he puts it, "Hahn's invention has now been taken away from Germany." He went on:

HEISENBERG: I am still convinced that our objective was really the right one and that the fact that we concentrated on uranium may give us the chance of collaboration. I believe this uranium business will give the Anglo-Saxons such tremendous power that Europe will become a bloc under Anglo-Saxon domination. If that is the case it will be a very good thing. I wonder whether Stalin will be able to stand up to the others as he has done in the past.

GERLACH: It is not true that we neglected the separation of isotopes—on the contrary, we discussed the whole thing at Tübingen in February, and there was a meeting at Munich. Clusius, Harteck and I said that this photochemical thing must be done. It took till the end of the year before the people who could do it were got together and the spectrograph obtained and special accommodation acquired, as the Litz (?) *[probably a reference to Linz, an Austrian town between Munich and Vienna]* Institute had been smashed up.

HEISENBERG: You shouldn't take remarks like the one Korsching made too seriously. He now thinks because the Americans have done it that he could have succeeded in separating isotopes if he had more means at his disposal. That is, of course, sheer and utter nonsense. His experiment was interesting, that's why we carried it out, but I am convinced that the Americans have done it by completely other methods.

GERLACH: If Germany had had a weapon which would have won the war, then Germany would have been right and the others in the wrong, and whether conditions in Germany are better now that they would have been after a Hitler victory...

HEISENBERG: I don't think so. On the other hand, the days of small countries are over. Suppose Hitler had succeeded in producing his Europe and there had been no uranium in Europe.

GERLACH: If we had really planned a uranium engine—in the summer of 1944 we would not have had a bomb—and that had been properly handled from a propaganda point of view...

HARTECK *[This is probably a typographical error for Heisenberg; there is no indication that Harteck is present.]*: That might have been a basis for negotiation. It would have been a basis for negotiation for any other German government, but not for Hitler.

GERLACH: I went to my downfall with open eyes, but I thought I would try and save German physics and German physicists, and in that I succeeded.

HEISENBERG: Perhaps German physics will be able to collaborate as part of a great Western group.

Gerlach then went on to repeat how Esau had tried to get all the heavy water and uranium in order to have the experiment made at the <u>Reichsanstalt</u>. Heisenberg then continued.

HEISENBERG: Now that the whole thing has been made public, I assume that in a comparatively short time they will tell us what is to happen to us as I can't see the sense in keeping us detained as it is obvious that they are <u>much</u> further advanced than we were. There may be some details in which we could help them as they appear to have done very little in the heavy-water line. *[By the end of the war, there were very large plants producing heavy water in both the United States and Canada.]*

GERLACH: The only thing to do now would be to say: "We will get all the uranium people together—Chadwick, Fermi, etc.—and let them discuss it."

HEISENBERG: I wouldn't be surprised if in a comparatively short time we meet some of those people and perhaps something will come of it. It seems to me that the sensible thing for us to do is to try and work in collaboration with the Anglo-Saxons. We can do that now with a better conscience because one sees that they will probably dominate Europe. It is clear that people like Chadwick and Cherwell have considerable influence.

(Pause)

GERLACH: I would really like to know how they have done it.

HEISENBERG: It seems quite clear to me that it is the separation of isotopes. Although it is possible as Harteck says that it is done with 100,000 mass spectrographs.

GERLACH: I am not sure whether perhaps the Bagge method... *[This was an isotope separation method invented by Bagge in which a beam of uranium molecules was sent through rotating blades. Faster and slower molecules were sorted out since if a molecule had the "wrong" speed it would hit one of the blades.]*

HEISENBERG: That would never produce pure "235." The Bagge method is not bad for enriching but the centrifuge is good for that too.

GERLACH: The Bagge method enriches more.

HEISENBERG: Yes. It is a terrific lot to expect pure "235."

GERLACH: How pure must it be?

HEISENBERG: I should say 80% "235" and 20% "238" is all right, 50-50 would be all right, but there must not be much more "238" than "235."

---

10. Wirtz and Weizsäcker discussed the situation together in their room. Von Weizsäcker expressed the opinion that none of them really worked seriously on uranium with the exception of Wirtz and Harteck. He also accused Gerlach and Diebner of sabotage. *[It is at places like this where*

one misses the full transcript, if it exists. What is it that Gerlach and Diebner were supposed to have "sabotaged"? As administrator, Gerlach had supported Diebner's reactor project almost to the end, in addition to Heisenberg's project. Probably von Weizsäcker thinks that this division of labor ultimately sabotaged the Heisenberg project, which would have succeeded.] Wirtz expressed horror that the Allies had used the new weapon. They went on to discuss the possibility of the Russians discovering the secret and came to the conclusion that they would not succeed under ten years. *[As mentioned before, the first Soviet A-bomb test, referred to by the Allies as Joe I, took place on September 23, 1949. The time for this development was, it is now known, substantially shortened by the espionage activity of Klaus Fuchs. He was part of the British team at Los Alamos. When the British left Los Alamos they were not allowed to take any classified documents with them—a humiliating situation since, as we have seen, it was the work of Peierls and Frisch that really started the program. But Fuchs had a photographic memory and left Los Alamos with the final engineering drawings in his head. These he reproduced for the Russians. The hydrogen bomb they found for themselves.]* They went on as follows:

WIRTZ: It seems to me that the political situation for Stalin has changed completely now.

WEIZSÄCKER: I hope so. Stalin certainly has not got it yet. If the Americans and the British were good imperialists they would attack Stalin with the thing tomorrow, but they won't do that, they will use it as a political weapon. Of course that is good, but the result will be a peace that will last until the Russians have it, and then there is bound to be war.

At this point Heisenberg joined Wirtz and von Weizsäcker. The following remarks were passed:

WIRTZ: These fellows have succeeded in separating isotopes. What is there left for us to do?

HEISENBERG: I feel convinced that something will happen to us in the next few days or weeks. I should imagine that we no longer appear to them as dangerous enemies.

WEIZSÄCKER: No, but the moment we are no longer dangerous we are also no longer interesting. It appears that they can get along perfectly well by themselves.

HEISENBERG: Perhaps they can learn something about heavy water from us. But it can't be much—they know everything.

WEIZSÄCKER: Our strength is now the fact that we are "un-Nazi." *[This may be a reverse play on the German adjective* underdeutsch *("un-German"), a word used pejoratively by the Nazis to characterize anyone or anything non-German or non-Aryan. It is interesting that von Weizsäcker does not use the term "anti-Nazi."]*

HEISENBERG: Yes, and in addition, uranium *[fission]* was discovered by Hahn and not by the Americans.

WEIZSÄCKER: I admit that after this business I am more ready to go back to Germany, in spite of the Russian advance.

WIRTZ: My worst fears have been realized with regard to the complications which will now arise about us.

HEISENBERG: I believe that we are now far more bound up with the Anglo-Saxons than we were before as we have no possibility of switching over to the Russians even if we wanted to. *[As will become clearer later, Heisenberg uses the word "Anglo-Saxon" to refer to the British and Americans, including the European émigrés.]*

WIRTZ: They won't let us. *[In the end, this was one of the real reasons for their internment. Groves wanted to keep the German scientists out of the hands of the Russians and the French.]*

HEISENBERG: On the other hand, we can do it with a good conscience because we can see that in the immediate future Germany will be under Anglo-Saxon influence.

WIRTZ: That is an opportunistic attitude.

HEISENBERG: But at the moment it is very difficult to think otherwise because one does not know what is better.

WEIZSÄCKER: If I ask myself for which side I would prefer to work of course I would say for neither of them.

---

11. Diebner and Bagge also discussed the situation alone together as follows:

BAGGE: What do you think will happen to us now?

DIEBNER: They won't let us go back to Germany. Otherwise the Russians will take us. It is quite obvious what they have done, they have just got some system other than ours. If a man like Gerlach had been there earlier, things would have been different.

BAGGE: Gerlach is not responsible, he took the thing over too late. On the other hand it is quite obvious that Heisenberg was not the right man for it. The tragedy is that Korsching is right in the remarks he made to Gerlach. I think it is absurd for von Weizsäcker to say he did not want the thing to succeed. That may be so in his case, but not for all of us. Von Weizsäcker was not the right man to have done it. Heisenberg could not convince anyone that the whole thing depended on the separation of isotopes. The whole separation of isotopes was looked on as a secondary thing. When I think of my own apparatus—it was done against Heisenberg's wishes.

DIEBNER: Now the others are going to try and make up to the Major and sell themselves. Of course they can do what they like with us now, they don't need us at all.

BAGGE: I won't do it. I will work on cosmic rays. Do you remember how von Weizsäcker said in Belgium, "When they come to us we will just say that the only man in the world who can do it is Heisenberg." von Weizsäcker is very upset about the whole thing.

(Pause)

BAGGE: You can't blame Speer, as none of the scientists here forced the thing through. It was impossible as we had no one in Germany who actually separated uranium. There were no mass spectrographs in Germany.

DIEBNER: They all failed. Walcher (?) *[Wilhelm Walcher, a German physicist who worked on isotope separation]* and Hertzog (?) *[probably Richard Herzog, an Austrian physicist]* wanted to build one, but they didn't succeed.

12. Although the guests retired to bed about 1:30, most of them appear to have spent a somewhat disturbed night judging by the deep sighs and occasional shouts which were heard during the night. There was also a considerable amount of coming and going along the corridors. *[Von Laue wrote to his son the next day that "probably none of us got to sleep last night." Bagge recorded in his diary that von Laue knocked on his door about 2 A.M. to say that he was very worried about Hahn. They all stayed awake until they were sure that Hahn was asleep.[6]]*

III. 7 AUGUST

1. On the morning of 7 August the guests read the newspapers with great avidity. Most of the morning was taken up reading these. *[The Times (London), 7 August 1945, took the unusual step of publishing a headline, "The First Atomic Bomb," in large letters next to the title on page one. Page 4 contained several stories devoted to the bomb, including Churchill's statement in full and a report entitled, "How the Bomb Was Made, Mr. Truman's Account." The upper left side of the page contained the large heads: "First Atomic Bomb hits Japan. Explosion equal to 20,000 tons of T.N.T. Anglo–U.S. Secret of Four Years' Research. 'Rain of Ruin' from the Air."]*

2. In a conversation with Diebner, Bagge said he was convinced it had been done with mass spectrographs.

3. Hahn, Heisenberg and Harteck discussed the matter in the following conversation:

---

[6] Max von Laue to his son, 7 Aug. 1945. Bagge, in Bagge, Diebner, and Jay, *op. cit.*, p. 58.

HAHN: What can one imagine happens when an atomic bomb explodes? Is the fission of uranium 1%, 10%, or 100%? *[Hahn is still worried about the question that bothered him the previous day and Heisenberg, as the following response shows, has still not understood the issue.]*

HEISENBERG: If it is "235," then for all practical purposes it is the whole lot, as then the reaction goes much quicker than vaporization as for all practical purposes it goes with the speed of light. In order to produce fission in 10^{25} atoms you need 80 steps in the chain reaction so that the whole reaction is complete in 10^{-8} seconds. Then each neutron that flies out of one atom makes two more neutrons when it hits another uranium-235. Now I need 10^{25} neutrons and that is 2^{80} neutrons. I need 80 steps in the chain and then I have made 2^{80} neutrons. One step in the chain takes the same time as one neutron to go 5 centimeters, that is 10^{-9} seconds, so that I need 10^{-8} seconds, so the whole reaction is complete in 10^{-8} seconds. The whole thing probably explodes in that time. *[This calculation—the elements of which we have commented on before—would be fine if the bomb material did not expand. Then the bomb would use up its uranium with 100% efficiency. But when a real bomb has expanded by some 10% of its original radial size the fission reaction shuts itself off. The actual efficiency is a few percent. What is typical is that Heisenberg does not appreciate the contradiction between his analysis giving 100% efficiency and the yield of the bomb—20,000 tons of TNT corresponding to 1 kilogram of completely fissioned uranium—which had been publicly announced. What does he think has happened to the rest of uranium? His figure of 10^{-8} seconds is about right for fissioning of 1 kilogram of ^{235}U. But before it can fission the rest, the reaction shuts itself off. By claiming that the "whole lot" is fissioned in 10^{-8} seconds Heisenberg has put himself in an impossible position since, on the one hand, he claims that the bomb consists of hundreds of kilograms of ^{235}U and, on the other, the yield only corresponds to the fissioning of a single kilogram. Hahn is not a theoretical physicist, but he has enough common sense to understand that something is wrong. The fact that Heisenberg does not have this common sense, combined with his exaggerated self-importance and the fact that people around him like von Weizsäcker were convinced that he could do no wrong in physics, made him a terrible director for a program like this. This is what Harteck said in the interview he gave after the war from which we have quoted extensively, and it is what Bagge had just said the day earlier: "It is quite obvious that Heisenberg was not the right man for it."]*

(Pause)

HEISENBERG: They seem to have made the first test on 16 July. *[At Trinity. The Times reported this in a separate article, titled "A Trial Bomb."]*

HAHN: They must have had more material then. They could not make 100 kilograms of new uranium-235 every fortnight. *[Hahn now seems to have decided that the mass of a uranium bomb is about 100 kilograms and not Heisenberg's metric ton. It occurs to none of the Germans at this point, or later in the transcript* *even after Nagasaki, that the Allies made any other sort of weapon besides the uranium bomb. Most seemed to believe that the Allies had not yet achieved a critical reactor, as indicated by von Weizsäcker's statements to von Laue under paragraph 5 of this report. Despite the fact that they themselves had thought of using plutonium, they simply can't imagine that the Allies had thought of the same thing and have actually made a bomb with it. As we have mentioned before, the uranium-based Hiroshima bomb was one of a kind.]*

HEISENBERG: They seem to have had two bombs, one for the test *[actually it was plutonium]* and the other *[uranium]* for...

HARTECK: But in any case the next one will be ready in a few months. *[Harteck too is thinking only of uranium. Nagasaki had not yet taken place.]* Stalin's hopes of victory will have been somewhat dashed.

HAHN: That's what pleases one about the whole thing. If Niels Bohr helped, then I must say he has gone down in my estimation. *[This is a theme that will be repeated. It never seems to occur to these Germans what Niels Bohr's estimation of them might be, having collaborated with a government which perpetrated almost unimaginable crimes.]*

---

4. Gerlach and von Laue discussed the position of Niels Bohr and the part he had played. Gerlach said he was very upset about this as he had personally vouched for Bohr to the German government. *[After reading a statement like this, one is convinced that Gerlach must then have been living on a plane of profound unreality. What does he think is now going to happen? Is the dead Hitler somehow going to reprimand him for having vouched for Bohr?]* von Laue said that one could not believe everything that appeared in the newspapers. *[In addition, The Manchester Guardian, 7 August 1945, p. 6, reported how Bohr had escaped the German occupation of Denmark in a fishing boat in 1943.]*

5. In a conversation with von Laue, von Weizsäcker said it will not be long before the names of the German scientists appear in the newspapers and that it would be a long time before they would be able to clear themselves in the eyes of their own countrymen. *[Clear themselves of what? Collaborating with the Nazis? Failing to build the bomb? Working on the bomb? For the last 50 years von Weizsäcker and most of the others have been trying to clear themselves in general.]* He went on to quote from the newspaper that we *[the Allies]* were unable to control the energy from which he assumed that we were not yet in possession of a uranium engine, so that their work would still be of considerable value. *[The American Secretary of War, Henry L. Stimson, did issue a statement on the 6th of August that appeared in the British press the next day (The Manchester Guardian, 7 August 1945, p. 6) to the effect that the Allied scientists had found nonexplosive means of releasing nuclear energy, but*

that wartime necessity had prevented a full exploration of these matters. He did not describe, however, the reactor development specifically.] He ended by saying:

WEIZSÄCKER: History will record that the Americans and the English made a bomb, and that at the same time the Germans, under the Hitler regime, produced a workable engine. In other words, the peaceful development of the uranium engine was made in Germany under the Hitler regime, whereas the Americans and the English developed this ghastly weapon of war.

[The Lesart is born! This statement, which was repeated, without quotes, almost verbatim in Jungk's book, is in a nutshell the Lesart that von Laue warned Rosbaud had been invented at Farm Hall. It was, of course, clear to his listeners there what he was doing, for they knew all too well that the Germans were never able to build a reactor—a "workable engine." As for "ghastly weapons of war," for what purpose did he turn his realization that plutonium would be an ideal fuel for a bomb over to German Army Ordnance? For the "peaceful development of the uranium engine"? Over the years von Weizsäcker has developed a considerable following in Germany as a peace advocate. His lectures at CERN, one of which is quoted in the Prologue, are typical of the genre. One of the important benefits of the release of the Farm Hall reports is to reveal the character of the person quoted.]

6. Gerlach continued to complain to Diebner about the attitude of Korsching the evening before. They went on to discuss the methods by which information concerning their work may have leaked out. They reminded themselves that Heisenberg and von Weizsäcker once spent four weeks in Switzerland *[in 1944]* and had discussions with Scherrer. Gerlach and Diebner went on to discuss the political aspects of the atomic bomb, and expressed satisfaction that the Russians appear not to have the secret.

7. In a conversation between Wirtz, von Weizsäcker and Heisenberg, Heisenberg repeated that in July 1944 a senior SS official had come to him and asked him whether he seriously believed that the Americans could produce an atomic bomb. He said he had told him that in his opinion it was absolutely possible as the Americans could work much better and quicker than they could. *[The previous day, when Heisenberg still believed the bomb was a bluff, he told exactly the same story, except when asked the same question he said he had told the same official "with complete conviction ... No."]* von Weizsäcker again expressed horror at the use of the weapon and Heisenberg replied that had they produced and dropped such a bomb they would certainly have been executed as war criminals, having made the "the most devilish thing imaginable."

8. At 6 o'clock the guests all heard Sir John Anderson speak on the wireless. *[John Anderson, trained as a scientist, was Churchill's Chancellor of the Exchequer. He was the cabinet official in charge of the British nuclear*

program.] The subsequent conversation was merely a repetition of the previous ones, and was chiefly concerned with somewhat caustic comments on the usage to which the new discovery had been put. Heisenberg's final comment was:

HEISENBERG: If the Americans had not gotten so far with the engine as we did—that's what it looks like—then we are in luck. There is a possibility of making money.

9. Later, Gerlach and Heisenberg had a long discussion in which they discussed the future. Gerlach said he hoped they would be able to discuss the whole question with people like Chadwick. Heisenberg said he felt sure something of the sort would be done, but he felt they should wait and see what happened. They went on to discuss references in the newspapers to the alleged work which had been done in Germany on the bomb, and said they hoped it would be possible to prevent the newspapers from continuing to make such statements. *[This is probably a reference to two statements that appeared in the British newspapers on August 7, one from Truman and one from Churchill. Truman said, "By 1942, we knew the Germans were working feverishly to find a way to add atomic energy to other engines of war, but they failed. We may be grateful to Providence that the Germans got V1's and V2's late and in limited quantities, and even more grateful that they did not get the atomic bomb at all." Churchill's statement, released through Prime Minister Attlee, had a similar tone. He wrote, "By God's mercy British and American science outpaced all German efforts. These were on a considerable scale, but far behind. The possession of these powers by the Germans at any time might have altered the result of the war and profound anxiety was felt by those who were informed. Every effort was made by our intelligence service and by the Air Force to locate in Germany anything resembling the plants which were being created in the United States. In the winter of 1942–43 most gallant attacks were made in Norway on two occasions by small parties of volunteers from the British Commandos and Norwegian forces, at very heavy loss of life, upon stores of what is called 'heavy water,' an element in one of the possible processes. The second of these two attacks was completely successful." One may imagine the effect on the Farm Hall detainees of these two statements.]* They ended their conversation by expressing surprise that they had known nothing about the preparations that had been made in America. Heisenberg said that someone from the German Foreign Office had told him that 70% of their Gestapo agents in Spain had just stayed there to work for the other side.

10. Heisenberg, von Weizsäcker, Wirtz and Harteck also discussed the future and came to the conclusion that they would probably be sent back to Hechingen and allowed to continue their work. They realized, however,

that we might be afraid of telling the Russians too much. In this connection they mentioned that Bopp, Jensen, and Flügge could also tell them a lot if they wanted to. They came to the conclusion that Groth was probably in England. *[Probably Johannes Jensen, a physicist who worked with Harteck. Wilhelm Groth had been an associate of Harteck and there is no reason to think he was in England at this time.]*

IV. THE MEMORANDUM SIGNED BY THE GUESTS

All the guests have been extremely worried about the press reports of the alleged work carried out in Germany on the atomic bomb. As they were so insistent that no such work had been carried out, I suggested to them that they should prepare a memorandum setting out details of the work on which they were engaged, and that they should sign it. There was considerable discussion on the wording of this memorandum, in the course of which Diebner remarked that he had destroyed all his papers, but that there was great danger in the fact that Schumann had made notes on everything. Gerlach wondered if Vögler had also made notes. *[Diebner and Gerlach are obviously worried that any surviving papers and notes would contradict the Lesart.]* From the conversation it did, however, appear that they had really not worked on a bomb themselves, but they did state that the German Post Office had also worked on uranium, and had built a cyclotron at Miersdorf. *[As far as I know, no such cyclotron was ever built.]* Gerlach stated that the Scwab group *[probably a reference to Georg-Maria Schwab, a German physical chemist]* also had some uranium, and he remembered that the SS had come to him once and tried to obtain large quantities of heavy water. Harteck also mentioned an SS Colonel whose name he could not remember, who had previously been with Merck (?) who had shown considerable interest in the subject. Wirtz remarked that they should remember that there was a patent for the production of such a bomb at the Kaiser-Wilhelm Institute for Physics. This patent was taken out in 1941. *[I have never seen such a document, but if it exists, it would be fascinating. Patents aside, the paper trail of reports, technical papers and lectures tracing the Germans initial foray into bomb physics is a long one. See the references in the Bibliography.]* Eventually a memorandum was drawn up and a photostat copy of it is attached to this report. Wirtz, von Weizsäcker, Diebner, Bagge and Korsching at first did not want to sign it, but were eventually persuaded to do so by Heisenberg.

[Other documents fill in some of the background. Bagge's diary entry for 7 August 1945 suggests that the factional split noted above played itself out in discussions over the memo and the Lesart it presented. Those not wanting to sign were among the younger members of the group and were perhaps worried what effect a signed admission to having worked on nuclear fission in wartime Germany might have on their careers. Heisenberg drafted the memo together with Gerlach on the blank pages of a British military school notebook. The notebook, with a working draft of the memo in Heisenberg's handwriting, survives in his papers (Heisenberg Archive,

Max Planck Institute for Physics, Munich). Von Laue informed his son of the position taken in the memo on 7 August. Later he tried to send a copy of the memo to his son in Princeton, N.J. for distribution in the United States.[7] Apparently at that time he was not yet so consciously opposed to the Lesart. Bagge wrote in his diary on 10 August 1945 that "our older men" hit on the idea of writing a memo "from which the view arose that we in Germany did not work on an atomic bomb but rather on a stabilized engine. The story found widespread but not general agreement." Heisenberg and Gerlach presented the memo to the group, "which was then signed after some difficulties."[8] The careful wording of the memo betrays the difficult public situation of the scientists and their internal disagreements.]

FARM HALL   (signed)
GODMANCHESTER   T. H. Rittner
11 August 1945   Major

[There are a few places in the transcripts where the German original is given in full: for example, Heisenberg's August 14th colloquium on the physics of the atomic bomb; the songs and pastiches written for the November 16th celebration of Hahn's winning the Nobel Prize for Chemistry; and the memorandum appearing below. In the first and last instances the English translation is also given in the reports, while for the Hahn Fest only the German is given. The English translation of the memorandum is given first, followed by the original German. Readers with a knowledge of German can judge for themselves the quality of the translations in the transcripts.[9]]

TRANSLATION

8 August 1945

As the press reports during the last few days contain partly incorrect statements regarding the alleged work carried out in Germany on the atomic bomb, we would like to set out briefly the development of the work on the uranium problem.

1. The fission of the atomic nucleus in uranium was discovered by Hahn and Strassmann in the Kaiser-Wilhelm Institute for Chemistry in Berlin in December 1938. It was the result of pure scientific research, which had

---

[7] Max von Laue to his son, 22 Sept. 1945.

[8] Bagge, in Bagge, Dieber, and Jay, *op. cit.*, p. 58.

[9] The German text is also published in Heisenberg, *Collected Works*, Vol. C5, pp. 26–27, where it is dated 7 August 1945. A typewritten copy of the memo, dated 8 August 1945 and slightly revised by hand, is among Max von Laue's letters to his son. The English translation of points 1 to 5 was first published in Groves, *Now it Can Be Told*, pp. 336–337.

nothing to do with practical uses. It was only after publication that it was discovered almost simultaneously in various countries that it made possible a chain reaction of the atomic nuclei and therefore for the first time a technical exploitation of nuclear energies.

2. At the beginning of the war a group of research workers was formed with instructions to investigate the practical application of these energies. Towards the end of 1941 the preliminary scientific work had shown that it would be possible to use the nuclear energies for the production of heat and thereby to drive machinery. On the other hand, it did not appear feasible at the time to produce a bomb with the technical possibilities available in Germany. Therefore the subsequent work was concentrated on the problem of the engine for which, apart from uranium, heavy water is necessary.

3. For this purpose the plant of the Norsk Hydro at Rjukan was enlarged for the production of larger quantities of heavy water. The attacks on this plant, first by the commando raid, and later by aircraft, stopped this production towards the end of 1943.

4. At the same time at Freiburg and later at Celle, experiments were made to try and obviate the use of heavy water by the concentration of the rare isotope ^{235}U.

5. With the existing supplies of heavy water the experiments for the production of energy were continued first in Berlin and later at Haigerloch (Wurtemburg). Towards the end of the war this work had progressed so far that the building of a power-producing apparatus would presumably only have taken a short time.

Remarks (referring to previous paragraphs)

Para. 1. The Hahn discovery was checked in many laboratories, particularly in the United States, shortly after publication. Various research workers—Meitner and Frisch were probably the first—pointed out the enormous energies which were released by the fission of uranium. On the other hand, Meitner had left Berlin six months before the discovery and was not concerned herself in the discovery.

Para. 2. The pure chemical researches by the Kaiser-Wilhelm Institute for Chemistry on the elements produced by uranium fission continued without hindrance throughout the war and were published. The preliminary scientific work on the production of energy mentioned in paragraph 2 was on the following lines:

Theoretical calculations concerning the reactions in mixtures of uranium and heavy water. Measuring the capacity of heavy water to absorb neutrons. Investigation of the neutrons set free by the fission. Investigation of the increase of neutrons in small quantities of uranium and heavy water. With regard to the atomic bomb the undersigned did not know of any other serious research work on uranium being carried out in Germany.

Para. 3. The heavy water production at Rjukan was brought up to 220 liters per month, first by enlarging the existing plant and then by the addition of catalytic-exchange furnaces which had been developed in Germany. The nitrogen production of the works was only slightly reduced by this. No work on uranium or radium was done at Rjukan.

Para. 4. Various methods were used for separating isotopes. The Clusius separating tubes proved unsuitable. The ultracentrifuge gave a slight concentration of the isotope 235. The other methods had produced no certain positive result up to the end of the war. No separation of isotopes on a large scale was attempted.

Para. 5. Further power-producing apparatus was prepared which was to produce radioactive substances in large quantities artificially without the use of heavy water but at very low temperatures.

Paras. 3 and 5. On the whole the funds made available by the German authorities (at first the Ordnance Department and later the Reich Research Board) for uranium were extremely small compared to those employed by the Allies. The number of people engaged in the development (scientists and others, at the institutes and in industry) hardly ever exceeded a few hundred.

Signed: Otto Hahn   M. v. Laue
         Walther Gerlach   W. Heisenberg
         P. Harteck   C. F. v. Weizsäcker
         K. Wirtz   E. Bagge
         H. Korsching   K. Diebner

(My signature signifies that I share responsibility for the accuracy of the above statement, but not that I took any part whatever in the above mentioned work. Signed—M.v. Laue)

[This document is remarkable for what it does not say. Meitner is given lukewarm credit—"probably the first"—and her departure from Berlin is made to seem like some sort of natural event. No mention is made as to why she was forced to leave. There is also no mention of the fact that Hahn wrote her frequently asking for and obtaining her advice and even proposing collaboration, and that she and Frisch interpreted Hahn's data to mean that fission had occurred, thus contributing in an essential way to the discovery. All of this is buried in the sentence, "On the other hand, Meitner had left Berlin six months before the discovery and was not concerned herself in the discovery."

We also see in this document the beginning of the systematic campaign that has lasted to the present time in which these scientists—and, after their deaths, their descendants—claim some lofty high ground for their wartime nuclear research. One of the ironies of their incarceration was that it gave them the opportunity to synchronize and make plausible their version of history—hence their worry about any surviving papers and notes that might contradict their story. The bomb, according to them, was a passing fancy, briefly considered, found too difficult to make, and then passed by for the benign reactor. Forgotten is the dangling before the likes of Bernhard Rust and assorted field generals and officials of the regime uranium weapons of unimaginable explosive force, or von Weizsäcker's 1940 five-page report to the War Office on the use of a reactor for creating and obtaining a new transuranic explosive, or even Harteck's frequent explanation to representatives of the German Navy how a functioning reactor could be used to power submarines.

Von Ardenne and his group are dismissed implicitly as being nonserious: "...the undersigned did not know of any other serious research work on uranium being carried out in Germany." This despite Houtermans's realization of the utility of the more stable plutonium as a nuclear explosive and the group's progress towards isotope separation, subsequently exported bodily to the Soviet Union. There is also the misconception that "heavy water is necessary" for the functioning of a reactor, leading to the excuse for the German failure in the destruction of the heavy water plant at Rjukan. After the war, when Heisenberg learned that graphite had been used as a moderator in the first reactor, he began a campaign in 1946 to discredit Bothe for his "mistake" in his measurements of the neutron absorption properties of graphite.

Although intended for public consumption, this Farm Hall memorandum was not released to the public at that time. The Germans were still being held incommunicado and would continue so for the next five months. But the memo did serve as the model for everything most of them said about their wartime activities for half a century. Apparently only von Laue later repudiated this memo. The original German is as follows.]

TOP SECRET

Copy No. 1
FH4
Appendix 2
*[Appendix 1 contains the photos of the detainees.
It appears here as an insert, separate from this report.]*
8 August 1945

Da die Presseberichte der letzten Tage über die angeblichen Arbeiten an der Atombombe in Deutschland zum Teil unrichtige Angaben enthalten, möchten wir die Entwicklung der Arbeiten zum Uranproblem im Folgenden kurz beschreiben.

1) Die Atomskernspaltung beim Uran ist im Dezember 1938 von Hahn und Strassmann am Kaiser-Wilhelm-Institut für Chemie in Berlin entdeckt worden. Sie war die Frucht rein wissenschaftlicher Untersuchungen, die mit praktischen Zielen nichts zu tun hatten. Erst nach ihrer Veröffentlichung wurde ungefähr gleichzeitig in verschiedenen Ländern entdeckt, daß sie eine Kettenreaktion der Atomkerne und damit zum ersten Mal eine technische Ausnutzung der Kern–Energieen ermöglichen könnte.

2) Beim Beginn des Krieges wurde in Deutschland eine Gruppe von Forschern zusammengerufen, deren Aufgabe es war, die praktische Ausnutzbarkeit dieser Energieen zu untersuchen. Die wissenschaftlichen Vorarbeiten hatten gegen Ende 1941 zu dem Ergebnis geführt, daß es möglich sein werde, die Kern–Energieen zur Wärme–Erzeugung und damit zum Betrieb von Maschinen zu benutzen. Dagegen schienen die Voraussetzungen für die Herstellung einer Bombe im Rahmen der technischen Möglichkeiten, die Deutschland zur Verfügung standen, damals nicht gegeben zu sein. Die weiteren Arbeiten konzentrierten sich daher auf das Problem der Maschine, für die außer Uran "schweres" Wasser notwendig ist.

3) Für diesen Zweck wurden die Anlagen der Norsk Hydro in Rjukan zur Produktion von größeren Mengen von schwerem Wasser ausgebaut. Die Angriffe auf diese Anlagen zuerst durch ein Sprengkommando, dann durch die R.A.F., haben diese Produktion gegen Ende 1943 zum Erliegen gebracht.

4) Gleichzeitig wurden in Freiburg, später in Celle, Versuche angestellt, durch Anreicherung des seltenen Isotops 235 die Benutzung des schweren Wassers zu umgehen.

5) Mit den vorhandenen Mengen des schweren Wassers wurden zuerst in Berlin, später in Haigerloch (Württemberg), die Versuche über die Energie–Gewinnung fortgeführt. Gegen Ende des Krieges waren diese Arbeiten so weit gediehen, daß die Aufstellung einer Energie liefernden Apparatur wohl nur noch kurze Zeit in Anspruch genommen hätte.

Anmerkungen

Zu 1) Die Hahn'sche Entdeckung ist kurz nach ihrer Veröffentlichung in vielen Laboratorien, insbesondere in den Vereinigten Staaten, nachgeprüft worden. Auf die großen Energieen, die bei der Uranspaltung frei werden, wurde von verschiedenen Forschern, zuerst wohl von Meitner und Frisch, hingewiesen. Dagegen hatte Professor Meitner bereits ein halbes Jahr vor der Entdeckung Berlin verlassen und war an der Entdeckung selbst nicht beteiligt.

Zu 2) Die rein chemischen Arbeiten des Kaiser-Wilhelm Institutes für Chemie über die Folgeprodukte der Uranspaltung sind im Kriege ungestört fortgeführt und veröffentlicht worden. Die unter 2) genannten wissenschaftlichen Vorarbeiten über die Energie–Gewinnung umfaßten Untersuchungen von folgender Art: Theoretische Abschätzung über den Ablauf der Reactionen in Gemischen aus Uran und schwerem Wasser. Messungen des Absorptionsvermögens von schwerem Wasser für Neutronen. Untersuchungen über die bei der Spaltung frei werdenden Neutronen. Untersuchungen über die Neutronenvermehrung in kleinen Anordnungen aus Uran und schwerem Wasser. Zur Frage der Atombombe sei noch festgestellt, daß den Unterzeichneten keine ernst zu nehmenden Untersuchungen etwa anderer Gruppen in Deutschland über das Uranproblem bekannt geworden sind.

Zu 3) Die Schwer–Wasser-Produktion in Rjukan wurde zunächst durch den konsequenten Ausbau der schon vorhandenen Anlage und dann durch den Einbau von in Deutschland entwickelten katalytischen Austausch–Öfen auf etwa 220 Liter pro Monat gesteigert. Die Stickstoffproduktion des Werkes wurde hierdurch nur unwesentlich vermindert. Mit Uran und Radium ist in Rjukan nie gearbeitet worden.

Zu 4) Zur Isotopentrennung wurden verschiedene Verfahren angewandt. Das Clusius'sche Trennrohr erwies sich als ungeeignet. Die Ultra-Zentrifuge ergab eine geringe Anreicherung des Isotops 235. Die anderen Verfahren hatten bis zum Ende des Krieges noch keine sicheren positiven Ergebnisse geliefert. Eine Isotopentrennung in großen Maßstab ist nicht in Angriff genommen worden.

Zu 5) Ferner wurde eine Energie liefernde Apparatur vorbereitet, die zwar ohne schweres Wasser, jedoch bei sehr tiefer Temperatur künstlich-radioaktive Substanzen in großer Menge erzeugen sollte.

Zu 3)–5) Im Ganzen sind von den deutschen Behörden (zuerst Heereswaffenamt, später Reichs–Forschungsrat) für das Uranvorhaben Mittel bereit gestellt worden, die gegenüber den von den Alliierten eingesetzten Mitteln verschwindend gering sind. Die Anzahl der Menschen, die an der Entwicklung beteiligt waren, (Wissenschaftler und Hilfskräfte in Instituten und Industrie), hat wohl in keiner Phase einige Hundert überschritten.

[The document is signed by all ten detainees with von Laue's disclaimer.]

*Meine Unterschrift bedeutet, daß ich mich für die Richtigkeit der obigen Darstellung mit-verbürge, nicht aber, daß ich an den darin erwähnten Arbeiten irgend welchen Anteil gehabt habe. M. v. Laue.

PART III

PUTTING THE PIECES TOGETHER
8–22 August 1945

[As the reports proceed, the ten German scientists settle into a restless waiting period. They are sure that they are about to be released. They, of course, do not know that British law permits them to be held for six months—and only six months— without a charge being brought. One wonders whether anyone at this point was giving much thought as to their eventual disposition. At times the tension becomes almost unbearable. Their discussion continues to focus on how the atomic bomb was made. Their speculations culminate in Heisenberg's lecture to his colleagues on August 14, in which he reveals once again his superficial understanding of bomb physics.]

TOP SECRET

To: Mr. M. Perrin and Lt. Comdr. Welsh
From: Major T. H. Rittner

OPERATION EPSILON
(8th–22nd August 1945)

I. GENERAL

1. The guests have recovered from the initial shock they received when the news of the atomic bomb was announced. They are still speculating on the method used to make the bomb and their conversations on this subject, including a lecture by Heisenberg, appear later in this report. The translation of the technical matter has been very kindly undertaken by a member of the staff of D.S.I.R. The original German text of Heisenberg's lecture has been reproduced as an appendix to this report.

2. There is a general air of expectancy as the guests now feel there is no further need for their detention and they assume that they will shortly be told what plans have been made for their future and that they will soon be reunited with their families. They are eagerly awaiting replies to their letters which have now been dispatched.

3. The declaration of the surrender of Japan was greeted with relief rather than enthusiasm. The guests listened with great interest to the King's broadcast on "VJ" *[Victory in Japan]* Day and all stood rigidly to attention during the playing of the National Anthem.

4. Sir Charles Darwin paid a visit to Farm Hall on 18th August. This was the first time the guests had had contact with a scientist since their detention and they were delighted to have the opportunity of meeting him. Conversations during the visit and subsequent reactions are dealt with elsewhere in this report. *[This Charles Darwin was the grandson of the great naturalist. He was a distinguished physicist who had been one of the original members of the British uranium group. It is uncertain whether or not he knew he was being bugged.]*

II. THE FUTURE

1. A number of the guests have discussed their attitude towards cooperation with the Allies. The following conversation took place between Heisenberg, von Weizsäcker and Gerlach on 10th August.

GERLACH: If you were faced with the opportunity of cooperation in order to make the bomb useful for mankind, would you do it?

HEISENBERG: It is unlikely to arise in that form, as it can't be done. "Useful for mankind" means only that the Russians shouldn't get it, but that can't be prevented as the Russians are certain to have the bomb in five year's time *[he was right]*, possibly in a year. From what Chadwick said in that interview *[not found]* I would say that the Allies will try and form a Control Commission <u>with</u> the Russians, and they will control the manufacture of uranium-235, and the uses to which it is put. They will try and come to a peaceful understanding with the Russians in some way. I would have no objection if one could be included in such an organization so that we could share, in some way, control of it for Germany. I imagine that there will be some sort of organization embracing all the nuclear physicists in the world.

WEIZSÄCKER: What are your feelings about that?

GERLACH: I would join.

---

2. Hahn and von Weizsäcker discussed their future in the following conversation on 11th August.

HAHN: I have been thinking, and it is quite possible that they will not send us back to Germany unless we undertake to do quite different work, and they will say: "Stay here; if you like we will let your wives come over, but you must be a long way from Russia."

WEIZSÄCKER: If I was faced with the alternative of working on uranium in England or America, or not working on uranium in Germany, I would very quickly choose not working on uranium in Germany.

HAHN: So I should think.

WEIZSÄCKER: In fact I think I should say "Even if you keep me here I would prefer not to work on uranium for the time being. I would like to wait a bit and see whether I can overcome the antipathy I have to the bomb."

HAHN: I have really come to the conclusion, sad as it is, that as far as I am concerned, I shall probably do nothing more. I might have been able to do something if they had let me carry on with my harmless chemistry; assuming I had been sent 10 grams of this stuff which had in some way given off something without exploding, then one could have that stuff and use it as an indicator for chemistry or even biology; I would enjoy that and then perhaps I could help a bit, but I don't see anything for me. *[What Hahn seems to be asking for is a small amount of uranium to do chemical and biological experiments.]*

WEIZSÄCKER: I would like it best if they just said to me, "You needn't sign any paper, you can just go back to Germany."

HAHN: They won't do that. If they let you go back to Germany, you will have to give an undertaking on oath not to work on uranium.

WEIZSÄCKER: One could do that. If I was in Germany, I don't feel that I would want to carry on any opposition to the Anglo-Saxons there. There will be plenty of that in any case. On the contrary I would feel more inclined to persuade people to come to a sensible understanding with them. If I can help in this respect as far as the Germans are concerned, I feel I should be in a much stronger position if I could say that I was under no obligation to them. If I have to say I am working for their Armed Forces I would have no moral authority, and I consider that more important in Germany than for me to continue to work on uranium.

HAHN: If I could choose, although things look bad in Germany, I should prefer to go to Germany than stay here, provided I had some means of livelihood.

WEIZSÄCKER: Of course.

---

3. Heisenberg and von Weizsäcker also discussed international scientific cooperation in the future. The first part of the conversation could not be recorded, but it appeared that they would consent to cooperation only if they were treated as equal partners personally. They seem to consider international physics as being almost synonymous with work under the leadership of Niels Bohr. The conversation continued:

HEISENBERG: I think each of us must be very careful to see that he *[each one of us]* gets into a proper position.

WEIZSÄCKER: That was not possible under the Nazis. The right position would really have been in a concentration camp, and there are people who chose that. Of course it is a question how one can get into the right position with the present regime, but one can try.

HEISENBERG: It will certainly be easier than it was before, there is no doubt about that.

WEIZSÄCKER: I have a lot in common with the Anglo-Saxons, but not with their governments.

HEISENBERG: I believe Bohr and his friends, particularly the politicians, might have certain doubts about you—partly because of your father, and possibly even more because of the Strassburg business. *[C. F. von Weizsäcker had accepted a professorship at the University of Strassburg after Strasbourg was occupied and renamed Strassburg by the Germans and the university turned into a "Reich university."]*

(Pause)

There is also the difference between you and me that a man of my age <u>must</u> be in an organization of that kind whether he wants to or not. *[Heisenberg was 43 and von Weizsäcker 33. It is not clear what he is talking about. As far as is known, Heisenberg did not belong to any of the party organizations.]*

WEIZSÄCKER: If you are in Germany, a great deal of the responsibility for the continuation of physics in Germany will be yours.

(Pause)

WEIZSÄCKER: Wirtz is no longer keen on working on uranium.

HEISENBERG: I think it more likely that he is no longer interested because he sees that the others were able to do it better than we were.

WEIZSÄCKER: I think it is more than that. I think that he and I think much the same way about it.

---

4. Von Weizsäcker also discussed the future with Wirtz and repeated his previously expressed views. The conversation then continued:

WIRTZ: So you don't want to work on uranium in Germany under Allied control.

WEIZSÄCKER: I wouldn't like to do that at the moment. I would not like to be less free than other Germans, but I would not like to work for the Allied governments on something which is so closely connected with the means by which they finished the war with Japan. What I would like to do would be to lecture on physics at some German university and to study cosmology and philosophy. What I would not like to do would be for us all, including Heisenberg, to go back to Germany, and for none of us to remain in touch with this business. *[The Allies did forbid fission research for nearly a decade.]* I have a feeling that Heisenberg has quite different ideas to me *[sic]*, and that he would very much like to continue working on the uranium engine. Personally, I would like very much if Heisenberg were to work on the machine in Germany and keep personal contact with the English and Americans, and that I should have contact with Heisenberg, but not work on the engine myself. I believe that there will probably be a long period of peace, during which time the Anglo-Saxons will be the strongest people in the world. The Russians will not be overrun by them, but they will probably have to curtail their expansionist policy in Europe because of the bomb. The only alternative will be war very soon between the Russians and the Anglo-Saxons, in which I will be just as unwilling to help the Russians as the Anglo-Saxons.

---

5. Diebner and Bagge had the following character-revealing conversation on 12th August:

DIEBNER: If I knew anything I would not be here.

BAGGE: If you run away or if you escape you will be shot. You must realize these people are not interested in Mr. Diebner's life when you consider the danger that might arise if Mr. Diebner got to Russia.

DIEBNER: There is no danger because I don't know anything. For instance, I don't know why it is easier to produce fission in element 94 *[plutonium]*. I didn't know all that. It is not in any book.

BAGGE: People like Döpel are sure to be already in Russia and working there. If people like Döpel and Bohse (?) realize that by this means they cannot only save their lives but improve their position, I am sure they will work there. *[This is almost certainly a reference to Heinz Pose, who was a physicist on Esau's staff, which probably meant that he had close affiliations with the Nazi Party. He and Robert Döpel, Heisenberg's colleague at Leipzig, did in fact volunteer to go to the Soviet Union where they joined von Ardenne and others in work on the Russian atomic bomb. Indeed the German nuclear scientists in the Soviet Union were treated very well, kept in a kind of gilded isolation. When the Russians had used them to build the bomb, they unloaded them back into East Germany.]* I will tell you something, Diebner, during the war you (helped) Bohse and now if they are making the atomic bomb for the Russians and have got themselves a good...

DIEBNER: They won't forget me.

BAGGE: That's it.

DIEBNER: I have got good connections there.

BAGGE: After all you did the best you could for them.

6. The views of the guests on cooperation can be summarized as follows:

(a) BAGGE: In previous reports Bagge has shown himself to be thoroughly German and he has expressed a hearty dislike of the Allies. He has shown slightly pro-Russian sentiments. He has suggested to Diebner that some of his (Diebner's) friends, who may be working for the Russians, might help him.

(b) DIEBNER: Has suggested in previous reports that he would like to stay in England but has not expressed himself on the subject of cooperation with the Allies. He welcomed Korsching's suggestion of working in the Argentine on uranium. In a conversation with Bagge, Diebner agreed that some of his friends, who may be working for the Russians, might help him.

(c) GERLACH: Told Heisenberg that he would be prepared to join an international body of physicists.

(d) HAHN: Has not expressed himself in the past on the subject of cooperation with the Allies. In a conversation with von Weizsäcker he said that he could see no future for himself and he wanted to go back to Germany at all costs.

(e) HARTECK: Has not expressed himself on the subject of cooperation.

(f) HEISENBERG: In previous reports Heisenberg has expressed the hope of being able to continue his work as part of an international group of physicists. He repeated this hope in conversation with Gerlach and said he would like to be responsible, as part of an international body, for the work in Germany.

(g) KORSCHING: Has often expressed annoyance at Anglophile behavior of some of his colleagues. He does not appear to be willing to work for the Allies and has suggested going to the Argentine.

(h) VON LAUE: Has not expressed himself on the subject of cooperation.

(i) WIRTZ: In a previous report Wirtz said he considered it useless to continue work on nuclear physics in Germany.

(j) VON WEIZSÄCKER: In previous reports von Weizsäcker has shown that he is somewhat shocked at the idea of cooperation with the Allies so soon after the war. He has advocated State Control of Science. In conversation with Wirtz he said that he wants to return to Germany and is prepared to sign an understanding not to work on uranium or to tell anyone about such work. He does not want to work for the Allies either in Germany or elsewhere but he says he has no intention of working for the Russians. He would like to lecture on physics at a German university and work on cosmology and philosophy.

III. TECHNICAL

1. There has been a lot of discussion of the technical aspects of the atomic bomb. Eventually Heisenberg was asked to give a lecture on the subject which took place on 14th August.

2. The following conversation took place between Diebner, Harteck and Bagge:

DIEBNER: We had to fetch the heavy water from Norway.

HARTECK: Just think of the hot and cold tube method, that would have cost R.M. *[Reichsmark]* 15 million for which I.G. *[Farben, the giant chemical conglomerate]* guaranteed five tons a year, though perhaps we would have got six tons. Then they said they couldn't build it and in their case it was only a few thousandths of their annual turnover. *[It is impossible to imagine any of the American corporations with which General Groves dealt telling him that the work he asked them to do was too small a fraction of their annual revenue to be bothered with.]* That was in fact the first method ready for industrial development though perhaps not the cheapest. I.G. did build the small apparatus for about 50 liters a year and that cost R.M. 300,000. Of that R.M. 100,000 was for measuring instruments and 200,000 for the apparatus. For an apparatus 100 times as big which was *[is what would have been]* needed industrially, these R.M. 200,000 would have increased as the two-thirds power *[of the number of liters of heavy water produced, i.e., less than one-to-one]*, that is, they *[the total cost]* would have been R.M. 2½ million and then we should have got the five tons. Suddenly they said that was a mistake and that for a 100 times the size, the cost would be a 100 times. They always said, "We'll build it after the war." When I first talked with Herr Basche I wanted to bring Dramm into it, and it appeared that Dramm could not take part because he was a quarter Jewish. *[H. Basche was a civil servant who was Diebner's immediate superior in German Army Ordinance; Dramm is not further identified.]* He left RuhrChemie because he had a row—the whole senior staff was changed—and he was one who had followed the whole construction through. Just think if we had had him! He would have built the thing for us, with him we could have built it.

DIEBNER: I.G. had Esau on their conscience.

HARTECK: In practical matters I was the stupid one. I worked for almost six years on this thing alone and the people who've done other things turn out to be the lucky ones.

It seems clear to me that if we had had a machine for 10 or 12 tons *[of uranium]*, mixing with paraffin and cooling by liquid air would have been good in every case. If one has one part of uranium and one part of hydrogen and mixes them homogeneously and cools it to liquid air temperature, then it is reduced by half and the absorption *[of neutrons]* becomes very strong and might fall to 20%. Since there is so much uranium, the $2n$ *[a reference to neutrons]* process is very probable, and on the other hand the absorption by water, if it is homogeneous, is almost zero, only 2% or 3%. Heavy water absorbs nothing at all, perhaps 1%, but paraffin absorbs 2%. In our machine absorption at the resonance position was about 10% to 12%, at lower energies it was 15% or 16% with heavy water. The $2n$ multiplication was perhaps 12% to 14%, I can no longer remember. In the machine it was stronger. Taken altogether there were certainly regions where the *[neutron]* multiplication factor was bigger than in the uranium machine. It seems beyond dispute that it works. *[The reference here appears to be a reactor design of Harteck's.]*

BAGGE: That would mean that at these temperatures the apparatus would run.

HARTECK: Then we could get it running—quite simply, for we need only the metal and this big cask, you just put liquid air in on top and pump it out—then it starts.

BAGGE: Yes, then it only makes neutrons, heats up and stops again.

HARTECK: Yes, quite right. You let it run for a period, for you can cool with a certain number of kilowatts, and when it has run a certain time, the others have been enriched and then you get them out. That is one special way in which you could do the thing. They wouldn't all run all the time, but you need them all to start up, with a colossal expenditure of cold. The other way is the photochemical *[enrichment of ^{235}U. The reference to "photochemical" seems to be a misprint or mistranslation, since no such separation process seems to exist. It occurs several times in the manuscript.]*—that you just go on trying at it with a big staff *[making the procedure industrial]*. As soon as one has the photochemical process it is much cheaper than the mass spectrograph and in any case naturally for other purposes you would try out the isotope lock *["lock" (<u>Schleuse</u>) as in a canal]* and the centrifuge and such methods, for one should not rely on one method. If you consider this whole program of work with the heavy water and low temperatures and the photochemistry and all that involves, I'm not certain whether these fellows can do it at all.

---

3. The following conversation took place between Gerlach and Harteck on August 8th, 1945.

HARTECK: We want chiefly to have a machine just as a means of studying it.

GERLACH: The technical difficulty in the present *[heavy]* water machine is the preparation of the uranium and then the whole subsequent process like casting it *[the uranium metal]* to shape. Therefore, it would be better if it were something with a *[uranium oxide]* powder.

HARTECK: I first proposed the scheme 2½ years ago because I thought one would have to make other experiments on account of stabilization and it has been proved step by step and that was the only sensible thing to do. *[Heisenberg had earlier informed his colleagues that a working reactor would stabilize by itself, without the need for external controls.]*

---

4. The following conversation took place between Hahn, Gerlach and Bagge on August 11th, 1945.

HAHN: In Germany they could prepare a few grams of ionium per annum. *[Ionium is an isotope of thorium.]*

GERLACH: No, we prepared 60 kilograms of pure ionium.

HAHN: I reckon that is impossible. Is that supposed to have been done in Germany?

GERLACH: No, in Belgium. I don't know where it was done but I do know that it played a big part in some espionage business. Stetter *[Georg Stetter, a Viennese physicist, and one of the early recruits to the German program]* interested himself in it and there was some S.S. business *[Hitler's notorious elite troops]*, some agent— one doesn't know who he was—was sent to me. I was to work with him, an Indian. They said he was a Japanese spy. He was determined to find out where we got the ionium from. That was 1944–5.

[In the following conversation, the attributions to Hahn and Gerlach in the manuscript seem to be reversed. The proper attributions are given in brackets.]

GERLACH *[HAHN]*: Did Stetter work with the S.S. on ionium?

HAHN *[GERLACH]*: No. The fission of ionium was experimentally proved in the Radium Institute at Vienna, but for that one does not need to build a machine— they get 50 times as much ionium from pitchblende *[a uranium ore]* weight for weight as radium. If therefore, you prepare 1 gram of radium you also prepare 50 grams of ionium. The ionium must, therefore, correspond to a production of 1 kilogram of radium if they have carried it out quantitatively.

GERLACH *[HAHN]*: Can one make a bomb out of it?

HAHN *[GERLACH]*: The neutron energy in ionium has only been approximately calculated. *[The Allied project also considered using thorium isotopes but decided that it had no advantages over uranium.]* One had no pure ionium but one took this mixture of ionium and thorium *[presumably the common isotope ^{232}Th]* in Vienna which contains about 50% ionium, and in that they believed that they had demonstrated fission at a lower voltage than with thorium alone. In any case there is a report from the year 1941 from the Vienna Radium Institute; who wrote it I do not know, probably Stetter.

GERLACH *[HAHN]*: Can you make a bomb out of 2 kilograms of ionium?

HAHN *[GERLACH]*: I don't know.

BAGGE: Can one prepare ionium in large quantities?

HAHN: Yes, but not at all with thorium—80% thorium would not be too bad.

BAGGE: You get so much more ionium than radium?

HAHN: Ionium has a half-life of 80,000 years and radium only 1,500, and since they are produced in the same series, they are proportional to their half-lives, but in all uranium pitchblende there is always some thorium and they prepare this thorium with it. Thorium has an exceedingly long half-life of 10^{10} years. Thorium undergoes fission—we did that by January 1939. Ionium is also fissile but it's still a question with what sort of neutrons. *[The thorium that Hahn used was presumably natural thorium with all its isotopes, so the fission he observed may well have been from ionium.]*

GERLACH: That depends chiefly on the cross section *[a measure of the probability of the process]*.

HAHN: It has the atomic number 90 and *[atomic weight]* 232.

BAGGE: Then you see that it'll undergo fission with difficulty *[like uranium-238]*. All the heavy elements with even numbers undergo fission with difficulty. *[This is a point we discussed in the Prologue in connection with the Bohr model of fission.]*

GERLACH: If, however, it had a very short mean free path and a very big cross section?

BAGGE: It wouldn't have those. If it's of even number, then it would not be split by thermal neutrons but with neutrons of higher energy and then it cannot have anything like so large a cross section; for the cross section *[for fission]* must be of the order of the geometrical cross section of the nucleus. That is about 2.5×10^{-24} *[cm²]*. And 2.5×10^{-24} *[cm²]* gives I think a mean free path of 6 centimeters.

HAHN: I don't know how they did it because unlike us they had no pure radio-thorium.

5. After reading the newspapers on 8 August *[this was one day prior to the dropping of the plutonium bomb on Nagasaki]*, the following comments were made:

BAGGE: It says in the newspapers that "236" will be used, which results from the bombardment of "235". This they call "Pluto." This might be "93" but this would mean they had a running stabilized machine *[reactor]*. On the other hand, they say they have not got one. Therefore it is still difficult to believe. *[There appears to have been one authorized reporter within the project, William Laurence of the New York Times. Mr. Laurence was then considered the doyen of newspaper science writers. His science background appears to have been limited. Feynman used to recount that at the first atomic bomb test known as Trinity he stood next to Laurence. There came the flash and a few seconds later the noise. When he heard the noise Laurence asked Feynman, "What was that?" What Bagge is grasping at is that when ^{238}U is bombarded by a neutron it becomes ^{239}U, which then decays into neptunium, which in turn decays into plutonium. When ^{235}U is struck by a neutron it becomes ^{236}U, which can then fission. Bagge, perhaps misled by some probably garbled newspaper account, has made a salad out of all of this.]*

(Pause)

HEISENBERG: But if they are working with heavy water the material will be lost to them ... . Here they have, however, quite slow reaction times, since heavy water implies thermal neutrons and thermal neutrons indicate reaction times of the order of 10^{-3} seconds or so. *[Heisenberg still seems to be treading in heavy water. As far as I can see, what he is saying makes no sense at all.]*

WIRTZ: They only need that to produce additional neutrons. *[Ditto.]*

HEISENBERG: I see, simply for the increase in energy production. That I agree. But I do not see how the reaction can take place in 8 pounds of something, since the mean free paths are fairly long. They have always got free paths of 4 centimeters. In 8 pounds they will surely get no chain reaction whatsoever. But still it may not necessarily be true what is written in the newspaper. *[Insofar as I can make any sense of this, I suspect that it is connected with Heisenberg's previous confusion between the critical mass—many kilograms—and the mass that is actually fissioned in the explosion—about a kilogram.]*

I still do not understand what they have done. If they have this element 94, then it could be that this "94" has quite a short mean free path. *[This was Houtermans's and von Weizsäcker's idea, which they apparently obtained independently of Turner—that plutonium would be highly fissionable so that the fission mean free path would be smaller than in ^{235}U.]* We have done little research in the field of completed fast neutron reactions because we could not see how we could do it because we did not have this element, and we saw no prospect of being able to obtain it. *[By doing "it" Heisenberg is referring to building a nuclear weapon. There would have been no other reason to produce plutonium.]* How they have obtained this element is still a mystery.

WIRTZ: Yes, but I believe that they have got it and I feel sure the bomb is not big.

HEISENBERG: That is to say it might be of the order of 400 kilograms.

---

6. The following day *[August 9]* the newspapers mentioned that the atomic bomb *[used on Hiroshima]* weighed 200 kilograms and the following conversation took place between Harteck and Heisenberg:

[The bomb actually weighed over 4000 kilograms, or about 9,700 pounds. The 200 kilograms mentioned here probably represents the approximate weight of the ^{235}U and the ^{238}U tamper. The Hiroshima bomb—known as <u>Little Boy</u>—looked, as one of the pilots who delivered it remarked, like an "elongated trash can with fins." Fully assembled with its casing, it was 10½ feet long and 29 inches in diameter.]

HARTECK: Do you believe that it is true that this is the weight of the bomb or that they wish to bluff the Russians?

HEISENBERG: This has worried me considerably, and therefore this evening I have done a few calculations and have seen that it is more probable than we had thought on account of the substantial multiplication factors which one can have with fast neutrons. *[This is the number of neutrons produced with each fission.]* We have always calculated with a multiplication factor of 1.1 because we had found this in practise with uranium. *[This is presumably a reference to the number of fission neutrons produced for each thermal neutron absorbed in a reactor. This is a much smaller number than the total number of fast neutrons produced in each fission since some of the produced neutrons will not cause further fissions. They will get absorbed. The total number of fast neutrons produced per fission is, on average, about 2.5. But the effective number in a typical reactor operating with natural uranium, which is mostly unfissionable ^{238}U, is only 1.33. The situation in separated ^{235}U is entirely different since all the ^{235}U nuclei can undergo fission.]* If they have a multiplication factor of 3 or 5, then naturally it is a different matter. We said we need about 80 links in the chain reaction; now the mean free path is 4 centimeters. *[The mean free path for fission for fast neutrons is actually about 17 centimeters.]* Therefore we must have 80 long divisions (so was the rough estimate) and this would come to about a ton *[1,000 kilograms]*. *[This is a repeat of Heisenberg's erroneous argument that he had given to Hahn a few days earlier. In that argument he took the mean free path to be 6 centimeters, which he has now reduced to four. But his arithmetic is still wrong. His original arithmetic should have given him 13 tons. The new arithmetic should give him $(4 \text{ cm}/6 \text{ cm})^3 \times 13$ tons $\simeq$ 4 tons, not 1 ton. I will come back to the multiplication factor in a moment.]* This calculation is right if the multiplication factor is 1.1 because even then we use really every neutron which "escapes" *[from a uranium nucleus]* for multiplication. If, on the other hand, the multiplication factor is 3, things are quite different. Then I can say, if the whole thing is only as big as the mean free path, then one neutron which walks around therein once meets another and makes three neutrons. From these three neutrons one will already come back, the other two can go off *[be "sterile" as far as further fissions are concerned]*; the one that comes back will for certain make another three. In practice therefore I need only the mean free path for the thing to work. *[It seems that Heisenberg is about as confused here as he was earlier, although he appears to be trying to close in on the right answer, which he has apparently read in the newspapers. The critical size does depend on the number of fission neutrons produced in a single fission. Let us call this number n. Then the quantity that enters the correct calculation is n–1 because it has taken one neutron to initiate the fission. In uranium 235, n is 2.52, so that n–1= 1.52. Heisenberg wants to raise n to 3 so that n–1 would be 2. But, as Harteck noted, what enters the calculation of the critical radius of say, a sphere of uranium, is one over the square root of n–1; i.e., 1/ $\sqrt{n-1}$. To get the critical mass, this must be cubed since the volume varies with the cube of the size. Thus Heisenberg would argue that the critical mass would be reduced by a factor of $(1.52/2)^{3/2}$ = 0.66. His new arithmetic, correctly done, will still not give him a small enough critical mass, since two-thirds of 4 tons is more than 1 ton.]*

HARTECK: What are these 100–200 kilograms which are around it?

HEISENBERG: This will be the reflector *[tamper]*. For instance, they might have lead as a reflector and of course part of the weight could be apparatus; you must remember that it is a dangerous business. They must arrange it so that it is at first taken apart into two pieces between which a reflector—of shall we say lead or some other material—is placed, and then at the right moment this lead will be pulled out and the thing clapped together.

(Pause)

Well how have they actually done it? I find it is a disgrace if we, the professors who have worked on it, cannot at least work out how they did it.

HARTECK: I believe it would be technically possible to produce 2 kilograms of proto-actinium *[sic]* though of course an enormous amount of materials would have to be used. *[Protactinium—element 91—is fissionable by fast neutrons. But it is rare, and uranium-235 has the great advantage of being fissionable by neutrons of all energies.]* For ten such bombs this would mean 50 kilograms of radium in three years, which is unbelievable. *[Protactinium is isolated from pitchblende, a uranium ore, in which it occurs with about the same frequency as radium. Hence, to get enough protactinium for a bomb, one would produce also fifty kilograms of radium, which Harteck finds, with reason, incredible.]*

HEISENBERG: Nevertheless they have quite obviously worked on a scale of quite fantastic proportions.

HARTECK: I believe rather in a machine *[a plutonium-producing reactor]* than in the production of so many kilograms ... because it has never yet been found in the world. One finds always a ... . Yes, but on these grounds ... they could not produce this. They would have to have a billion tons to get out sufficient material for man to weigh. Rutherford in his time made it *[presumably a reference to protactinium]* artificially and on that basis they have made their calculations. There are perhaps 10^{-15} grams in the world. Or they must have had unbelievable luck and somewhere they found this element, in the same way that suddenly cesium in large quantities was found in Sweden.

HEISENBERG: In the newspapers is the statement that the essential element was discovered in 1941.

HARTECK: This could be the decay product of 23 minutes half-life uranium from which they have made "93." *[Uranium-239, which is created when a neutron is captured by uranium-238, does decay spontaneously in about 23 minutes into neptunium-239, which is itself unstable, and decays in about 2.3 days into plutonium-239.]*

HEISENBERG: There is something else. If they have made it with a machine, then there is the fantastically difficult problem that they have had to carry out chemical processes with this terrifically radioactive material. *[He is right. This is what had to be done.]*

HARTECK: Then they must have to start by letting it cool off for 6 months.

HEISENBERG: Right. They built a machine *[reactor]* from which they must start by removing a large amount of energy so that the chemical change takes place; therefore they must have let the machine run at a constant temperature so that they could take out the total energy, which is in order of magnitude the equivalent of a power station working for ten years. *[The reader who wants to learn some of the details on what had to be done by the Allies is well advised to read the relevant sections of the "Smyth Report." Here we note that early in the project it was realized that to produce a kilogram of plutonium a day would require a reactor that would release energy, mostly in the form of heat, at a rate of somewhere between 500,000 and 1,500,000 kilowatts of power. Roughly the argument was that each fission produced about 200 million electron volts of energy—this is 3×10^{-9} watt-seconds of energy—and about two and half neutrons. To keep the reactor running, one of these neutrons must make a new fission. The others can in principle be absorbed by the ^{238}U to begin the plutonium-producing cycle. Adding up the energies to make 1 kilogram a day, one arrives at the above result. Smyth observes that the Grand Coulee Dam, which was then under construction, would produce hydroelectric power at a rate of 2,000,000 kilowatts. This sets the scale of what had to be done.]*

HARTECK: The machine need only work slowly.

HEISENBERG: It does work slowly.

HARTECK: That again is the difficulty. I believe that if 1% conversion has taken place, then the machine stops. *[Harteck probably has in mind that making this much plutonium requires enough fissions of ^{235}U so as to use it up in the fuel elements of the reactor. Fuel elements are the bundles of fissionable material used in a reactor.]*

HEISENBERG: Then if 1% conversion has taken place, then they must dismantle the machine.

HARTECK: To refurbish? *[To put in new fuel elements.]*

HEISENBERG: Yes, and thereby they will of course be able to take out "94"; nevertheless one could say that if they have done it with a machine of 1 ton they will be able to take out not an inconsiderable amount of material. For instance, if 1% conversion has taken place, then they can take out 1%—that is to say 10 kilograms of "94" out of the machine.

HARTECK: It is, of course, not only "94" which is formed.

HEISENBERG: I do not believe that the Americans could have done it. They would have had to have had, shall we say, a machine running at least not later than 1942 and they would have had to have had this machine running for at least a year and then they would have had to have done all this chemistry. *[The Germans were simply unable to accept the fact that the Allies had both the competence and the capacity to do this.]*

HARTECK: Highly improbable.

HEISENBERG: I believe it almost more likely that they have done something quite original such as getting out proto-actinium in quantity from colossal quantities of material. It says in the newspaper that enormous quantities of material went in and practically nothing came out. This appears to me to fit in with such a chemical process or isotope separation, but one does not get an impression from the newspapers that "235" has been used for it. Do you know when the work was carried out by the Americans which showed that proto-actinium could be disintegrated at 150,000 volts?

HARTECK: That was about 1940–1941. It was certainly before 1942.

HEISENBERG: Perhaps the facts are that thereby they discovered the element "Pluto." "Pluto" is a code name. Proto-actinium also starts with "P." Perhaps they simply say to themselves, "If we now extract the proto-actinium, then we can do the thing."

HARTECK: Then as a by-product they will have about 50 kilograms of radium. They will be able to warm their feet with it!

HEISENBERG: Is proto-actinium really so active?

HARTECK: No, not so active as the equivalent radium. Proto-actinium has a much weaker activity. It is in the ratio of 30,000:1,500, i.e., 20 times weaker. One has the same quantity of proto-actinium pitchblende, on the basis of equivalent weight, although it is 20 times weaker because only 4% or 5% comes out of the neighboring chain of uranium-235. Assuming that proto-actinium had a parent substance, such as *[that?]* the parent substance of radium is present mixed in the ratio of 1:1, then on the basis of equivalent weight there would be 20 times as much proto-actinium in pitchblende as there is radium, because it has a half-life 20 times longer than radium. From uranium both are produced simultaneously. One is "235" which makes proto-actinium, which builds up to 4.6% in the course of uranium decay, so that in fact 50 kilograms by weight of radium have the same activity as 50 kilograms of uranium whilst 50 kilograms of proto-actinium only have the same activity as 2.5 kilograms of radium. *[Harteck is describing the radioactive chain that leads from uranium to protactinium. Since this element was never used for anything, I do not think it is worthwhile to try to sort out his remarks here.]*

HEISENBERG: Well I see now that it is possible with fast neutrons. Just now we have discussed proto-actinium; this is almost easier to imagine than all other methods.

HARTECK: If Grosse *[Aristide von Grosse, Hahn's former assistant, who had moved to the United States]* helped them who has produced pure proto-actinium and is a very good chemist who is very interested in proto-actinium and has something, he has placed it at their disposal; then they have tried to split it to establish whether proto-actinium undergoes fission.

HEISENBERG: We knew that proto-actinium undergoes fission below about 50,000 or 100,000 *[electron]* volts—much lower than in the case of thorium—and this means that if one has pure proto-actinium in considerable quantity, then the whole thing would blow up. At one time we spoke about this I know. I once came to you and asked how much proto-actinium there was.

HARTECK: Then I said there was perhaps half a gram.

HEISENBERG: Then I said, "Well with that amount it certainly won't work." *[This is surely a reference to a bomb.]* Perhaps they are making this stuff on a kilogram scale; and if they then make a good reflector, then they can work well with 1 or 2 kilograms.

HARTECK: I would estimate that during the last one to two years 1–1½ kilograms of radium have been produced in the world. Naturally this could be increased by a factor of about 10, and one would obtain then in one year about 1 kilogram, but they must have more. *[Again a reference to the fact that the production of protactinium and radium are linked.]*

7. Later the same day *[August 9]* the guests discussed the new bomb in the following conversation *[Apparently they were not yet aware of the plutonium bomb used on Nagasaki.]*:

WEIZSÄCKER: I find, having regard to the Russians, they are telling a little too much about the bomb.

GERLACH: But each time they make exactly different statements. I am of the opinion that there is as little truth in one as in another.

HEISENBERG: It is still not clear which method has been adopted. Either they have taken pure proto-actinium or they have really separated the isotopes; or they have made element 94 with machines.

HARTECK: If it had been that we had been in Russia and had the necessary material and had to start from nothing, then we would undertake to make a machine work in nine months.

HAHN: No, no, no.

HEISENBERG: If one had the necessary material. The machine is now no more of a problem.

WIRTZ: If you had no heavy water, or if you had too little, how would you do it?

HARTECK: Production of heavy water would begin within six months in a properly designed chemical plant.

HEISENBERG: This is the question, is the fission cross section for fast neutrons in "238" and "235" substantially different? *[The first measurement of the fast neutron cross section in ^{235}U was done in the spring of 1941 by a group at the Carnegie Institute in Washington under the direction of Merle Tuve. It is amazing that the Germans never separated enough ^{235}U to do this absolutely crucial measurement. It could have been done, and was done in the United States, with micrograms of ^{235}U. If the Germans had concentrated on getting one mass spectrograph, or Bothe's cyclotron, to work, they could easily have separated this amount. This part of the transcript, and its sequel, is filled with vapid speculations about this cross section, where one decent measurement would have settled the matter.]*

HARTECK: What indeed is the biggest fission cross section that one can take?

HAHN: Doesn't this depend on the exploitation of "238," also for instance on the Japanese elements for which it is much smaller?

HEISENBERG: For "235" it is smaller. *[For the neutrons relevant to the bomb, which have a kinetic energy of about a million electron volts, the ^{235}U cross section is about 100 times larger.]*

HAHN: Yes, "235" is 0.7% of "238." *[Hahn is referring to the relative isotopic amounts in natural uranium.]* "238" is obviously split by fast neutrons into exact halves—<u>also</u> in exact halves not <u>only</u>. But this exploitation into exact halves is considerably smaller than for normal fission products with fast neutrons. In this instance the Japanese for once published something original; it appeared as if only these Japanese elements, as we have called them, came out. This is, however, not the case. They are very much less than the others. *[To me this resembles some of the passages in plays by Samuel Beckett. Sense is struggling to reach the surface, but not quite getting there. For anyone who reads this discussion, and who has the appropriate technical background, the notion that the Germans had extensive* *knowledge of these matters, but which they kept to themselves for moral reasons, will appear absurd.]*

HARTECK: I had only thought what is believed to be the highest.

HEISENBERG: What could one have as the highest?

HAHN: About 2½ centimeters.

HEISENBERG: No, what do you take as the cross section?

HARTECK: Tell me, what is the geometrical diameter, how big is it?

HEISENBERG: The radius is 0.8×10^{-12} centimeter.

(Diebner produces a book)

[From the later discussion this seems to be a set of tables.]

I want to have the fission cross section for fast neutrons.

DIEBNER: 0.5×10^{-24} *[cm²]. [Diebner's number is wrong. The correct number is 1.22×10^{-24} cm². Even as late as 1943 the Allied project did not have a very good number for this fission cross section. At Los Alamos the number 1.5×10^{-24} cm² was used, which is 20% off. As Serber has pointed out, there were accidental compensating errors in the calculations where this was used so that the final result was nearly correct.[1]]*

HAHN: And what is the cross section for slow ones?

DIEBNER: For medium fast ones it is 0.1 *[$\times 10^{-24}$ cm²]* and for slow ones 1,000 *[$\times 10^{-24}$ cm²] or thereabouts. [The actual value for slow ones is about 640×10^{-24} cm². This is so much bigger than the cross section for fast neutrons that it raises the issue of slowing down the neutrons in the bomb by using a moderator to take advantage of the huge increase in the cross section. The reason that it will not work is that then the sequential fission processes will be too slow to make an explosion. Shortly, we will find the Germans coming up with the idea of slowing down the neutrons. They will, once again, be totally confused about the effects of this on producing a bomb.]*

HEISENBERG: Then the mean free path is 8 centimeters. If it is 0.5, then it is of course bigger by a factor of 4½.

HAHN: I do not understand that. How can then 0.5×10^{-4}—how big must it then be for slow ones? Obviously much bigger.

HEISENBERG: With pure "235," a couple of hundred.

HAHN: I see, times 10^{-24}? *[This is the slow neutron cross section, which is actually 640×10^{-24} cm².]*

---

[1] Serber, *op. cit.*, p. 15.

HEISENBERG: Yes. In a mixture of "238" plus "235" *[natural uranium]* the fission cross-section ratio is approximately 3.3. If I recalculate for "235," then I must multiply by 100 or 140 and then I get the value of 400. But for fast neutrons it is quite small. *[Heisenberg is again groping for the 640 referred to above. One decent measurement would replace all this floundering. The "quite small" is the relatively small cross section for the fast neutrons in ^{235}U.]*

(Pause)

If, for example, you put round it ordinary uranium as a reflector, then things are quite different. You can, of course, have luck if you make element 94. With uranium the mean free path is almost 40 centimeters. *[Heisenberg is not telling us, or Hahn, what mean free path he is talking about. As we have said several times, the fission mean free path for fast neutrons in ^{235}U is 17 centimeters.]*

KORSCHING: What would happen if there were a mixture of "94" and—is it simply proportional to the mixture, or would it be more favorable?

HEISENBERG: I would say proportional.

HARTECK: It is usually worse because the mean free path becomes longer and the weight goes in the Kubus. *[As usual, Harteck is trying to salvage something sensible out of the chaos. His point is that the mean free path in the mixture is longer than in pure plutonium, and that the critical mass depends on the cube of the path, since it depends on the volume.]*

HEISENBERG: The best arrangement is to place the pure element, which is quite pure, in the middle and to place round it the best possible reflector.

(Pause)

I would say in the most favorable circumstances one would obtain a geometrical cross section of about 8 centimeters, *[Heisenberg's discussion (or the translation of it) is now incoherent. A "cross section" is not measured in centimeters but in units of area—square centimeters. What I think he is trying to say is that if one took the fission cross section as large as quantum mechanics allows, one would get a mean free path of 8 centimeters.]* and if one, by some process, obtained out of it 5 neutrons *[but how is he going to produce five neutrons per fission?]*, one need not make the radius *[of the bomb]* any bigger than one mean free path. *[If the man would only do the calculation, and stop talking about it, he would find the relationship between the critical radius and the mean free paths. He would then see that the multiplication factor is not the key point here. This discussion takes place on August 9th. He must have done the calculation for the first time in the next few days since he presents a much better, albeit not entirely correct, version of it in his August 14th lecture.]*

HARTECK: Is there actually also a metal which will reflect back principally fast neutrons? Actually there is none, there is always a forward persistence.

HEISENBERG: Yes, but on the contrary, the heavy ones have the tendency to scatter under little corners. *[An obvious mistranslation for: "scatter through small angles." The German word <u>Winkel</u> can mean either "corner" or "angle."]* In the case of the light ones it is fairly spherically symmetric, but in the case of the heavy ones there is an elastic scattering which goes in a strong forward direction, but they do not then move.

(Pause)

I would rather think if we are dealing with such small quantities that it must be that they will obtain so many neutrons.

HARTECK: This would again suggest the already working machine and "Pluto"— for the heavy...

HEISENBERG: For the "94," yes. I do not know, perhaps just as many come out in the case of proto-actinium.

GERLACH: What is the case with ionium?

HEISENBERG: This is the parent substance of radium. This has no chances as a result of fission. Fission would most likely occur with fast neutrons. With fast neutrons I might believe it possible.

(Pause)

Let us assume that they have done it with proto-actinium, which to me at the moment appears to be the most likely. *[The Germans still don't believe that the atomic bomb was made with separated uranium or plutonium.]* Proto-actinium can be separated chemically if one is willing to take the necessary effort. These stories of radiation screens fit it, although proto-actinium is about 20 times weaker in activity than radium. If they are making kilograms of it, it will be terrible. I have the impression that for this expenditure (of £ 500,000,000) *[about 2 billion dollars, a figure that was quoted in the papers]* they could have produced the quantity of proto-actinium.

BAGGE: If they had made 20 kilograms of proto-actinium how many tons of uranium would they have had to work with?

HEISENBERG: Approximately the same as with radium.

BAGGE: That is to say from 7 tons, 1 gram.

HEISENBERG: They would have had to work with 140,000 tons of material.

BAGGE: Have they got this?

HEISENBERG: But of course.

DIEBNER: There are still 10,000 tons lying in Belgium.

HEISENBERG: Was there ever so much proto-actinium in Germany?

HARTECK: No, no, out of the question.

HEISENBERG: At one time I spoke to Hahn. We dismissed the proto-actinium problem as being impracticable.

HARTECK: What is the decay constant of proto-actinium?

HEISENBERG: The α decay constant is 3.2×10^4 years.

HARTECK: And how many neutrons ... proto-actinium.

HEISENBERG: It is the same thing as in the case of "235." Approximately the same will come out as in the case of "235." But the relationship of neutrons to protons is somewhat higher in the case of proto-actinium. In the case of uranium-235 two neutrons come out per fission. In the case of proto-actinium it is perhaps 2–5.

BAGGE: On the other hand, it does not fit in that it was only in 1941 that the element "Pluto" was discovered.

HEISENBERG: Yes, but in the first place "Pluto" may be a code name. At the end of 1940 or the beginning of 1941, the American work appeared to establish that proactinium was fissionable below about 50,000 *[electron-]* volts. During the discovery they might also have thought they had discovered that it was spontaneously fissionable.

BAGGE: Already in the work of Bohr and Wheeler *[John Wheeler, his collaborator in the 1939 paper on fission]* ... it was stated that it was fissionable.

HEISENBERG: No, the actual facts were that in the case of proto-actinium, I believe Bohr and *[John Wheeler]* had made a miscalculation. And then when the American work appeared, a memorandum came from Bohr in which he announced that there was a mathematical mistake in his formulae and if the formula was correctly set up, something came out of proto-actinium.

WIRTZ: Well, I am prepared to take on a bet that they have separated isotopes.

HEISENBERG: Yes, I will of course not deny it, but there are now three quite clear ways in which they can have done it and only three: isotope separation, proto-actinium and a machine with D_2O *[heavy water]* and element 94.

WIRTZ: My method is a machine with light water and the separation of element 94. I do not believe that they have so much heavy water at their disposal that they could really have many working uranium machines.

BAGGE: For what purpose have they hitherto used the heavy water?

HEISENBERG: Yes; this would fit in with Wirtz's hypotheses. If one has heavy water for only one machine, then from one machine, one can take out quite a lot of "94" in the course of time.

WIRTZ: Yes, and then I believe they also put a little heavy water in the bomb in order to raise the factor 2.

HEISENBERG: That may be so.

(Pause)

One has the impression that the English must have done something else other than the mass spectrograph.

8. On 13 August, Hahn and Wirtz made the following remarks:

HAHN: Element 93 decays in 2–3 days into "94." They have of course "94." This is obviously plutonium. They have "93" as a nice stable conversion product resulting from the bombardment with fast neutrons of uranium-237. *[He is unwilling to accept the idea that the Allies had a reactor working with uranium-238.]*

WIRTZ: Today it states in the newspaper that they could not work with the rare element plutonium because they reckoned it would take 70,000 years to obtain sufficient *[amounts]* before they could make a bomb. This means that until now they have not got a running machine.

HAHN: "93" can be quantitatively separated from "92." Strassmann and I have worked out the quantitative separation.

Heisenberg's Lecture on Atomic Bomb Physics

August 14, 1945

[See my Prologue for the setting. Major Rittner included a copy of the German text as transcribed by the British eavesdroppers in an appendix to this report. The version of the English translation below, reproduced from the reports in the U.S. National Archives, differs slightly from the British version of this report, published in Operation Epsilon. However, the German text in the Appendix to this report is identical to the British version. For clarity, I have simplified some of Heisenberg's notation and corrected some obvious algebraic mistakes. The interested reader will find the original notation in the appended German text, with no grammatical or algebraic corrections.]

9. Heisenberg gave the following lecture on 14 August in which he described his ideas of how the atomic bomb was made. As this is highly technical the full German text is reproduced in the Appendix.

HEISENBERG: I should like to consider the ^{235}U bomb following the methods we have always used for our uranium machine. It then turns out in fact that we can understand all the details of this bomb very well. *[The reactor analogy has very serious limitations. Reactors make use of slow neutrons, unlike the bomb. They also run on natural or slightly enriched uranium. The whole point of a reactor is to run it under controlled conditions so that the energy is released in a steady state. Reactors, if they are operating properly, do not expand and turn themselves off. One of the oddities of the reactors designed by Heisenberg was that he assumed that somehow the reactor would turn itself off once a certain temperature had been reached. This was an untested hypothesis and, considering Heisenberg's modest level of competence in these matters, it is probably lucky for him that his reactors* *never went critical. He might have generated a miniature Chernobyl or Three Mile Island.]* I will begin then by recapitulating once more the chief data on ^{235}U. I may repeat briefly what happens in this bomb. If a neutron is present in ^{235}U, it travels on and soon meets a ^{235}U nucleus. Then two things can happen. Either it is scattered elastically or it causes a fission. If it is scattered, the scattering may be either elastic or inelastic, and so the neutron goes on with the same or lower velocity. *[One of the maddening things about Heisenberg's expositions is the sort of thing he has just said. He starts by saying a neutron can be scattered elastically or can cause fission. Then he says a scattering can be either elastic or inelastic. What is a reader to make of this? The correct dichotomy is between fission versus elastic and inelastic scattering where inelastic scattering includes the capture of neutrons.]* This does not prejudice the power of the neutron to cause fission later *[because neutrons of any energy can fission ^{235}U].* There is therefore no probability of neutrons being lost anywhere. The process naturally goes on; the neutron at some time meets a ^{235}U and splits it. In the fission, several neutrons are produced. These neutrons behave like the first, and so the chain reaction goes on. If one had an indefinitely large amount of ^{235}U, the chain reaction could go on indefinitely, for two or three neutrons would always result from each one by fission. These two or three would repeat the process, and so it would go on. Thus the total number of neutrons would increase exponentially. The multiplication of neutrons is, however, in competition with the process by which the neutrons escape from the mass. *[This is the first inkling in these reports that Heisenberg has begun to grasp the notion of a critical mass properly.]* If in fact one has a finite mass of uranium, those neutrons at the surface which are moving outwards escape, and have no chance of taking part in fissions. So the question arises whether this loss of neutrons by escape from the mass is greater or less than the gain of neutrons arising from the production inside. To calculate this, or convince oneself, it is necessary to have the cross sections and mean free paths. I have a handy formula for this, and here it is: the mean free path for any process in uranium-235 is 22 centimeters per cross section, the cross section being measured in 10^{-24} cm^2. *[The derivation goes as follows. The mean free path d is given by $d = 1/\sigma n$, where σ is the cross section and n is the number of ^{235}U nuclei per cubic centimeter. The number of ^{235}U nuclei per kilogram is 2.58×10^{24} while the density is 19.1 grams per cubic centimeter. If we measure the cross section in units of 10^{-24} cm^2, the result follows, although I get 20.4 rather than Heisenberg's 22. One wonders what he had available to him to do arithmetic at Farm Hall—a slide rule?—or was it all done by hand?]* This means that if, for example, the cross section for fission is 1×10^{-24} *[cm^2]*, then the mean free path (MFP) for fission is 22 centimeters. The scattering cross section is empirically about 6×10^{-24}, and so the MFP is 3.7 centimeters. *[It is not clear which cross section Heisenberg is talking about here. For natural uranium, the scattering cross section for thermal neutrons is about 3.4×10^{-24} cm^2. This is probably what Heisenberg means.]* The most difficult part is the cross section for fission. This naturally depends markedly on the velocity. For thermal neutrons, as far as we know, it is in the neighborhood of 300 to 400 $\times 10^{-24}$ cm^2, i.e., very big. *[This cross section the Germans could measure, since for* *thermal neutrons all the fission is by means of ^{235}U.]* For fast neutrons I cannot now recall the figure exactly. *[This remark is very puzzling. How would Heisenberg be able to "recall" a figure? The Germans never measured this quantity and, as far as I know, Tuve's result was not published in the open literature.]*

There is a figure of 0.5×10^{-24} cm^2 in Diebner's tables *[presumably a compilation of data Diebner made]* but perhaps it refers to "238" and not "235." *[What it probably refers to is natural uranium. The fission cross section in natural uranium, σ_f, we can write as*

$$\sigma_f = \frac{0.72}{100} \times \sigma_f(235) + \frac{99.28}{100} \times \sigma_f(238),$$

where we have taken into account the isotopic content of natural uranium. What the Germans could measure was σ_f. What they could not do was to decompose it into its two parts. Indeed, σ_f is about 10^{-24} cm^2.] I think though that we can only know this figure accurately for "238" because with fast neutrons the "238" and "235" are both subject to fission, and so when you measure the fission it is that of "238" in most cases, and I don't quite see how the two fissions can be properly differentiated *[in the formula above, the factor in front of σ_f is 0.0072, and so it contributes rather little to the sum].*

HAHN: Because there was only 0.7% of it? *[The point I made above.]*

WEIZSÄCKER: It will never be possible to measure that. I do not see how it could be done. *[It does not occur to von Weizsäcker that the Allies might have separated "235," apparently because the Germans couldn't do it.]*

HEISENBERG: Perhaps you could do it like this: you would take neutrons of velocity slightly below the critical limit for "238," but not thermal; let us say 10^5 volt neutrons. With these you would measure the cross section and then calculate the ratio.

WEIZSÄCKER: Yes, but then you don't know exactly how the cross section is going to depend on energy. *[Indeed, at the threshold for fission of ^{238}U the fission cross section for ^{238}U increases very rapidly as a function of neutron energy.]*

HEISENBERG: One could perhaps say that at these very high energies the cross section would be comparable with the geometrical cross section of the nucleus. It would not depend so greatly on energy. Bohr's theory even suggests that it would be constant over the whole energy range. *[Heisenberg is again not clear about which cross section he is talking. The cross section for ^{235}U fission is roughly constant in this energy range while the cross section for ^{238}U is rapidly varying. The Bohr theory referred to here is the calculation of the fission cross sections using the liquid-drop model that Bohr and Wheeler published in the open literature in 1939.]*

HARTECK: If they have a good enough spectrograph in the U.S.A. to effect a complete separation, then you need do no more than to have a thin layer and to multiply correspondingly. For if a nucleus breaks up, it gives off more than one α particle, which you find with counters, and thus the ratio of thermal to fast neutrons. In this way you would solve it experimentally. They have certainly determined it exactly.

HEISENBERG: Yes. I have indeed made an estimate of 0.5 to 2.5 *[always in units of 10^{-24} cm²]* for the cross section, since I argued that it was 0.5 for "238," which must be a lower limit as "235" is more fissile and 2.5 is the nuclear cross section, the true collision cross section, and it cannot be much greater. Admittedly, it might be a little more than πr^2, but it must lie within these limits. *[This is called the "geometric cross section," since πr^2 is the area of a disk of radius r. For high-energy neutrons the total cross section is about the geometric cross section—about 2.5—in Heisenberg's units. Half of this is due to scattering and half to fission. For thermal neutrons the geometric approximation is totally wrong. For these low energies, the fact that these neutrons have a wave nature as well as a particle nature plays an essential role.]* Therefore, if you take the limits between 0.5 and 2.5, the resulting MPF *[mean free path]* for fission is from 9 to 44 centimeters. For scattering *[not fission]* again, we know that for all the heavy elements the cross section is about 6 at high energies. In uranium we know it pretty exactly, for it is, I think equal to 6.2×10^{-24} in "238." In lead it is slightly less, but they are all in this region. So we can say that for scattering the cross section is pretty certainly in the neighborhood of 6×10^{-24} and so the MFP *[for scattering]* is about 3.7 centimeters. Then there is an important quantity we need, the multiplication factor; i.e., the number of neutrons produced from a collision which results in the fission of "235." Since we know the multiplication factor for thermal neutrons very closely from our Berlin experiments, we calculate not per fission, but per thermal neutron absorbed. Now for thermals, the cross section for fission is about 3 and that for absorption about 6.2; i.e., we actually get only half the true multiplication factor if we take our figures.

Our figure is 1.18, so we can say the multiplication factor is really 1.18×2 or, roughly speaking, between 2 and 2.5. *[The actual number is 2.52, but now Heisenberg is giving sensible numbers and not his chimerical 5 of some days earlier.]*

LAUE: I don't follow that.

HEISENBERG: We have always experimented with ordinary uranium, in which "235" is rather less than 1% and the rest "238." In this ordinary uranium we have the following relations for thermal neutrons: we have a cross section of 6×10^{-24} for the capture of a thermal neutron, which may be simply captured to form "239," which decays with a period of 23 minutes, or may cause fission, which must be fission of "235."

HAHN: Are you still thinking of thermal neutrons?

HEISENBERG: For the moment I am speaking only of thermals. For thermals, the fission cross section of "235" is naturally frightfully high—it is actually in the neighborhood of several hundred *[always in units of 10^{-24} cm²]*—but because it only occurs with a frequency of 1% *[i.e., roughly the percentage of the fissionable*

^{235}U *in natural uranium]*, it only plays a small role in the whole. Thus the effective cross section *[for fission]* calculated in "238" is only about 3. *[Heisenberg actually means natural uranium here, not pure ^{238}U.]* This figure 3 was I think determined by *[Gottfried von]* Droste in your lab.

HAHN: Yes.

HEISENBERG: I think Droste got a result of 3.1 or thereabouts. If two neutrons are absorbed you have a fission in only one case, because the total cross section is 6 and the fission cross section is 3. *[In other words it is equally likely that one thermal neutron will fission a ^{235}U nucleus as it is that it will be absorbed by a ^{238}U nucleus. Thus if, say, two neutrons are produced in a fission, one of them will get "swallowed" by a ^{238}U nucleus and be lost to the fission process.]* Hence if the multiplication factor for a fission is x, then the effective multiplication factor is simply ½x, because every second neutron is killed by being captured. *[The "effective multiplication factor" is what the experimenter actually measures. To infer the actual multiplication factor one must multiply, in this example, by 2.]*

HARTECK: If you have ... *[The German text reads: "Wenn man die Resonanz ... hat," which translates to: "If you have ... resonance."]* Would you think that in this case the Breit–Wigner formula, which gives 1/v exactly for low temperatures, held, or could there be a small difference at low temperature between the extrapolation from the Breit–Wigner formula and direct (fission?)? *[Harteck appears to be worrying about the energy dependence of the fission cross section at low energies, which is not relevant to the discussion of the bomb. His line of questioning threatens to derail things entirely. But he goes on.]* You see, is there a relative deviation of 10% between them, or is the 1/v law exact at low temperatures?

HEISENBERG: I should think it would go exactly as 1/v.

WEIZSÄCKER: This formula simply means that the probability of the process per unit time is constant.

HARTECK: That is quite clear, but there is still the exact influence of the resonance level.

HEISENBERG: Yes, but it is so distant.

WEIZSÄCKER: All the same I should say the smaller the v to which you go, the better ... (interrupted) *[The concern here is still the behavior of the cross sections at small energies. None of this has any real relevance to what matters here.]*

HEISENBERG: But the whole resonance band plays no part at all in the bomb. *[Heisenberg now gets the discussion back on track.]* I wanted to make this brief digression into the thermal region only to say that the multiplication factor in fission of "235" is about 2 to 2.5, or more exactly we should say 2 × 1.18. That means that when "235" is split there are 2 to 2.5 neutrons produced. It seems to me that the Americans or the English are of the opinion that the figure is a bit higher, because in the paper there was a picture of the uranium process, and for each fission they showed three neutrons produced. *[It is possible that the paper in question showed* *plutonium where nearly three neutrons are produced.]* So I think it is quite conceivable that in actual fact the number is about 3, and that the cross section which Droste found is slightly high, the true one being a little less. The Americans had actually determined the fission cross section as 2 sometime earlier, and then the number comes out as exactly 3.

DIEBNER: The last values—the calculated values—were a little higher. In our last experiment, they came out somewhat higher.

HEISENBERG: Yes, that was a question of 1%, which doesn't count for much. I have therefore recently taken a multiplication factor of, I think, 2.5. So now we have collected the most important data. Now we must ask what happens in uranium when a fast neutron sets off on its journey? We can say this: if we had an indefinitely large amount of uranium-235, and neutrons in it, it is clear that the number of neutrons would grow exponentially. *[Each fission would produce 2.5 more, and on and on.]* Next we must consider how the exponential growth takes place. So I wrote down the equation n *[the number of neutrons in a cubic centimeter of ^{235}U, which is changing exponentially in time]* proportional to e^{vt}, where v is a characteristic reciprocal time for this exponential growth. This characteristic time, which we shall need later as the reaction time, can easily be estimated, if we note that the time before a neutron makes one fission is plainly the ratio of the MFP for fission to the velocity. *[In the formulas, $v = v / \lambda_f$ where v is the neutron's average speed and $\lambda_{fission}$ is the fission mean free path.]* Thus a neutron travels about 9 centimeters *[actually 17 centimeters]* to the next fission, and I have to calculate how long it travels before covering 9 centimeters. This time is $\lambda_{fission}$/(velocity). *[This is the reciprocal of the quantity above.]* In this time the multiplication of neutrons is exactly by a factor x; i.e., instead of 1 neutron I now have x neutrons. So for the determination of the quantity $v(x)$ I get the equation

$$e^{\lambda_f / v \times v(x)} = x$$

In other words, the characteristic reciprocal time $v(x)$ is $v / \lambda_f \times lnx$. We can take the velocity as approximately 1/20 that of light, for they are neutrons of about 1,000,000 volts. *[In the theory of relativity there is a simple expression that relates the square of the ratio of the speed of a particle like a neutron to the speed of light, to its mass m, and its kinetic energy T. It is*

$$\left(\frac{v}{c}\right)^2 = \cfrac{1}{\left(1 + \cfrac{m^2 c^4}{T^2 + 2mc^2 T}\right)},$$

where c is the speed of light. Heisenberg is using neutrons with a kinetic energy T of 1 million electron volts—fast fission neutrons. In the same units the mass-energy of the neutron, mc^2, is given by 939.573 million electron volts. Putting these numbers in, the result follows. If the advocates of <u>Deutsche Physik</u>—*Germanic physics— had prevailed in Germany, this calculation would have been illegal to carry out* *during the war, since it involves Einstein's relativity theory.]* We know then how a large number of fast neutrons would increase in an indefinitely large mass of uranium. *[In such a huge mass none of the neutrons would escape and the production would go on indefinitely.]* But when the distribution of neutrons is not uniform *[when it depends on where inside the volume one is]*, and if we ask, not how the total number changes, but how the number in a definite small volume changes, then naturally neutrons can leave the small volume by diffusion. So I must write down a diffusion equation for the neutrons, and I must know their diffusion coefficient. *[Diffusion is related to the random or drunkard's walk we discussed earlier. The basic idea of the diffusion equation is to keep track of how the neutrons can be created and lost in the finite volume and its surface. A very clear derivation of the equation Heisenberg is about to write down is given in papers from Los Alamos.[2] Serber points out that the conditions needed to derive this equation are not very well satisfied in the case at hand, so a more exact procedure is necessary to get a reliable critical mass. This was carried out by Serber and his collaborators at the time he gave his lectures in the spring of 1943.]* According to the kinetic theory of gases, the diffusion coefficient *[which measures the ease of the diffusion]* is equal to the MFP for scattering, multiplied by the velocity and by the factor 1/3. *[At this point Heisenberg makes what appears to me to be a technical mistake. His diffusion coefficient involves only what he refers to as "scattering." These are all the processes by which neutrons can interact that do not include fission. But, as Serber makes clear,[3] the diffusion coeffcient should also include fission. Even if there were none of the other processes, neutrons would proceed to diffuse out of the volume. The correct mean free path to use is what is called the "transport mean free path," which includes both scattering and fission.]* Now the MFP for scattering is known, it is 3.7 centimeters. *[Including both effects gives, according to Serber,[4] a mean free path of 5 centimeters as opposed to Heisenberg's 3.7 centimeters for natural uranium, so his calculation will still, somewhat fortuitously, give a qualitatively correct idea of the critical radius.]* Finally then I have for the time rate of the neutron density at any *[spatial]* point $\dot{n}$ (time rate of change of the density) = (diffusion coefficient) $\times \nabla^2 n$, (where ∇^2 is the Laplace operator)+ νn. *[Here D is the diffusion constant and I have used the more customary notation for the Laplace operator, ∇^2 opposed to Heisenberg's notation. It represents the rate of change of the rate of change in the spatial dependence of n. If we call the diffusion coefficient D, then we can write the full equation as $\dot{n} = D\nabla^2 n + \nu n$, where, as Heisenberg will point out, this ν is the same reciprocal characteristic time for fission reactions as discussed above.]* We see that if there were no term νn and so no multiplication, this would be simply the known equation for heat conduction *[the equation that tells us how heat dissipates in a heated object].* This term expresses the continued multiplication of the neutrons. *[Indeed, if we set D = 0 in the equation*

---

[2] *Ibid.*, pp. 25–28.

[3] *Ibid.*, p. 26.

[4] *Ibid.*, p. 27.

above, we have the equation ṅ = vn whose solution is just n = n₀eᵛᵗ; the exponential shown above.] One also notices the dimensions, and this is rather important, that the ratio D/v is evidently the square of a length, for if I divide through *[the entire equation]* by v I have D/v as a factor of the Laplace operator applied to n, and this must have the same dimensions as n. *[The Laplace operator has dimensions of inverse length squared and, to compensate, D/v must have the dimensions of length squared.]* Since the date of Fermi's work this quantity D/v has been called the square of the diffusion length l^2. *[In the early 1930s Fermi had treated slow neutrons as if they acted like molecules in a diffusing gas.]* This l comes out as 6.2 centimeters divided by the square root of the fission cross section, expressed in units of 10^{-24} *[cm²]. [Here, Heisenberg's technical mistake has caught up with him. The correct expression for the quantity D/v is*

$$D/v = \frac{1}{3} \frac{1}{N^2 \sigma_f \sigma_t},$$

where N = 4.92 × 10²² per cubic centimeter is the density of ²³⁵*U nuclei. In units of 10^{-24} cm², σ_f = 1.22, while σ_t = 4. (Where σ_t is the transport cross section.) Putting these numbers in, I find a diffusion length l of 5.31 centimeters. Heisenberg certainly cannot mean dividing by the square root of the fission cross section. That makes no sense at all. In the end, he comes out with a diffusion length that is close to the correct number—somehow.]* If the fission cross section is just 1×10^{-24}, the diffusion length is 6.2 centimeters. Perhaps for a moment we can at this point consider the comparison with our machines *[reactors]*. In our machines the diffusion length was always much greater. I have not the figures exactly in my head, but I think I remember that the diffusion length in the best machine that we had in the end was 35 centimeters. On that account the machines had to be of tremendous size. This arises in two ways. In the first place, the multiplication factor was much smaller. Here it is 2.5, there is only 1.18 because the "238" removes so little. *[This is a very puzzling statement. In both cases it is the fission of* ²³⁵*U that causes the creation of the neutrons. In both cases each fission produces, on the average, 2.5 neutrons. Heisenberg may be talking about an erroneous value with which he had been working previously. In any event, in a reactor some of the neutrons are absorbed by the* ²³⁸*U, so it is customary to define a quantity*

$$\eta = v \frac{\sigma_f}{\sigma_f \sigma_a},$$

where, in this expression η is the effective number of neutrons available for fission, v is the actual number produced in a fission—the 2.5—and σ_f and σ_a are the fission and absorption cross sections. For thermal neutrons, the kind that Heisenberg is talking about, this η is 2.08, which is still not the 1.18 he mentions.] In the second place—and this is much more important—a neutron travels a long way from the place where it is produced, before it becomes thermal and is absorbed. Thus, in the machines we had, it was slowed down in D₂O *[heavy water]* and then captured as a thermal. It traveled something like 20 centimeters before it was finally captured. This length is naturally added to l [*the diffusion length in uranium*], and is compounded with it; and so the diffusion length here is only about 6.2 centimeters, whereas there it was in the neighborhood of 35 centimeters. We have then the diffusion equation according to which the neutrons spread. I now solve the equation for a sphere of uranium of given radius R and I assume that the uranium sphere is surrounded by some other substance [*the tamper*]. We can consider later, what sort of substance. Naturally we can take it as a vacuum [*no tamper*] but in any case we assume a sphere so as to solve the equation easily. There will certainly be solutions in which the neutron density on the whole decreases exponentially and others in which it increases exponentially. Indeed the following clearly holds: If the uranium sphere is small, more neutrons travel outwards than are produced in the interior, and the neutron density diminishes exponentially. On the other hand, if the sphere is made enormously large, the flux of neutrons outwards is negligible compared with the multiplication inside, and then the density increases exponentially. I substitute arbitrarily therefore the neutron density

$$n = n_0 e^{\mu t}$$

[*where n_0 is the number density of neutrons as a function of space*] and try to determine the characteristic exponential factor [*μ*] in the exponent. If μ is positive, the machine works and the bomb explodes. If μ is negative, this means that any neutrons which are in the mass immediately travel away and are of no further interest. So when you put $n = n_0 e^{\mu t}$ you obtain the equation $D\nabla^2 n + (\nu-\mu)n = 0$.
We have to solve this equation. For this, we introduce another appropriate characteristic length

$$\frac{D}{(\nu - \mu)} = l_1^2 .$$

[*In the transcript there is what is clearly a misprint. The quantity I have given as $\nu-\mu$ is given as $\nu \times \mu$. This misprint does not occur in the German original.*] The solution of this equation is known [*and found in any book on mathematical physics*]; it is simply the equation of the known type, $\nabla^2 \phi + k^2 \phi = 0$. The spherically symmetric solution [*the one that depends only on the distance from the center of the sphere and not on the direction*] is $(\sin x)/x$ (x is therefore in this case the variable) or r/l_1. [*I have written r/l_1 rather than the $1/l_1$ that appears in the original.*] The solution in the interior of the sphere is therefore $(1/r) \sin(r/l_1)$ [*here r is the distance from the center of the sphere*] and the internal neutron density is diluted according to this formula. [*This function has a maximum at the center of the sphere and then falls off until the surface is reached.*] Indeed this must be the case if I do not assume that there is a source of neutrons anywhere [*as was the case with their reactor experiments*]. If I had an internal source of neutrons, it could naturally follow that I should need a solution which was singular, for example, at $r = 0$, because there was a source there. But I will assume that there is no source at all, so that neutrons are distributed continuously over the sphere, and this can only be according to the formula $(1/r) \sin(r/l_1)$.

LAUE: Is that a source independent of the uranium?

HEISENBERG: Yes. So inside the sphere we certainly have this distribution $(1/r) \sin(r/l_1)$. What happens outside? Here we can say we are dealing with fast neutrons, which are scattered and slowed down in the external surrounding substance. The slowing, however, does not harm, for a slow neutron can also cause fission, and so I can say that on the whole the external neutron density does not alter. *[I do not see what Heisenberg is getting at here. Is he thinking of a surrounding sphere of natural uranium? In this case there would be a certain amount of fission. He does not seem to understand that the slowing-down process takes time during which the material has expanded and the primary fission reaction shut down. He still does not seem to have grasped the significance of Hahn's original line of questioning.]* So outside, there is no absorption, either positive or negative, and there is the pure diffusion of fast neutrons. Again, I can say that on the outside I have a medium in which neutrons only diffuse but are neither absorbed or multiplied. In this external medium a diffusion equation like the one above holds but with the simplification that $v = 0$ and so there is no multiplication. The solution to this simplest form of diffusion equation is naturally that n decreases as $1/r$. Thus in the exterior space the density decreases as $1/r$, because we are dealing with ordinary diffusion without accompanying absorption. I have somewhat simplified the matter, by neglecting μ, which is in any case small compared with v. *[He is neglecting the possibility of neutron production in the exterior space.]*

HAHN: They come back then from the outside, I think.

HEISENBERG: Yes. A notable fraction of the neutrons flow outwards, and a part are always scattered back. So I must set down the boundary conditions. These are that at the separating surface between the uranium sphere and the surrounding reflector the density and the flux must both be continuous. I have already given the internal density as $(1/r) \sin(r/l_1)$ and the external density as α/r. *[Here α is a constant to be fixed by the boundary conditions.]* I must choose α *[such]* that for $r = R$ at the boundary of the sphere both expressions are equal *[where R is the radius of the uranium sphere]*.

LAUE: Why must the density be continuous?

HEISENBERG: The neutron density cannot have a sudden discontinuity. The neutrons move very rapidly backwards and forwards across the boundary. So there cannot be a sharp change in density. Thus I have in these two terms described the flux density. The flux of neutrons is easily obtained by differentiating the density with respect to r, and then the flux is the product of the density gradient and the diffusion coefficient. *[A well-known calculation—outlined for example in Serber's papers—shows that if the number of neutrons per centimeter cubed is n, and if the neutrons are moving in random directions with an average speed v, then the number of neutrons moving across a square centimeter of the surface of a sphere per second, j, is given by j = lv/3 × dn /dr. Here l is the transport mean free path, v the average velocity, and the 1/3 comes from the averaging over directions. The combination* *lv/3 is just what is meant by the diffusion coefficient. If the uranium sphere is surrounded by a tamper, then the tamper will, in general, have a different diffusion coefficient and the boundary condition will have to reflect this. Modifying Heisenberg's notation slightly, let us call the interior diffusion coefficient D_i and the exterior coefficient D_e. Heisenberg now presents a verbal description of what happens when one applies the conditions that both the density n and the current j are continuous at the surface of the sphere of radius R. This leads to two equations that can be used to eliminate the coefficient of 1/r, α, in the external solution. I will precede Heisenberg's verbal description of this by writing down the condition that emerges; namely, $\cot (R/l_1) \times R/l_1 = 1 - D_e/D_i$, where $\cot x = \cos x / \sin x$. In deriving this expression, Heisenberg has made an implicit simplification that he does not bother to mention. A real tamper does not extend forever. At its boundary there is also a boundary condition—usually that outside the tamper there are no neutrons. His derivation is equivalent to assuming that the radius of the tamper is very, very large. All of these simplifications and confusions make it very clear to me that Heisenberg had never done this problem before. An interested reader is invited to compare his inadequate treatment with the one found in Serber's talks.[5]* On the left-hand side we have the differential coefficient with respect to r multiplied by the diffusion coefficient D_i, where the subscript i refers to the interior, and outside we have the differential coefficient of α/r with respect to r; that is, $-\alpha/r^2$ multiplied by the external diffusion coefficient. And now I simply write down the condition that the two should be equal, and ask you to believe me that α cancels out and one is left with the ratio of the two coefficients of diffusion coefficients D_e/D_i, which must equal

$$D_e/D_i = 1 - (R/l_1) \cot(R/l_1).$$

BAGGE: If there is a vacuum or simply air outside, what happens then?

HEISENBERG: You can still use this formula, but D_e must be taken as infinite. You say that each neutron which goes out of the sphere is immediately carried right away. *[It cannot be reflected back.]* That leads to the neutron density at the surface of the sphere being zero, because they are carried away with arbitrarily great speed. Now we see that to get an unequivocal result we must know not only the internal coefficient of diffusion which we know already, but also the external.

That means, we must assume something about the material which surrounds the uranium sphere. We also see that it is expedient to surround it with something which scatters as many neutrons as possible back, that is, which has as high a scattering cross section as possible. But here we are concerned with scattering of fast neutrons, for which there are no great variations in scattering cross section. One can say that if lead or ^{238}U or anything of that sort surrounds it, the scattering cross section is always of the order of 6×10^{-24}. If graphite is used, to take a very

[5] *Ibid.*, pp. 30–33.

light example, we have about 4×10^{-24}, as the carbon atoms are somewhat more closely packed than in uranium. Do what you will, you always get MPF *[mean free paths]* in the region of 4 centimeters. Thus I think there would be little gained by seeking out some rare element, but it probably always lies in the neighborhood of 4 centimeters. *[In this paragraph Heisenberg reveals that, after over a week of reading public accounts, thinking about the problem, and the explosion of one more bomb, Nagasaki, he still has not clearly understood the key difference between a reactor and a bomb. As has been emphasized here again and again, a bomb must work with fast neutrons because otherwise the expansion of the material will shut the reaction off before an explosion takes place. The time scale for this is about 10^{-8} seconds. When a neutron gets into the tamper it scatters around. This takes time. It takes so much time that this time scale, which is about 10^{-7} seconds, becomes the time scale for these neutrons. Hence they get back into the ^{235}U sphere too late to participate in the explosion. In a reactor, this does not matter because the chain reaction is going on continuously. Thus graphite, if pure, is a very good material for a reactor moderator but a terrible material for a tamper. It slows the neutrons down and is not massive enough to hold the expansion back. The use of a tamper reduces the critical mass substantially, but it does not improve the efficiency of the bomb much. Heisenberg appears to have understood none of this.]*

WEIZSÄCKER: The wording of the announcement was that the uranium was mixed with graphite, in order to slow down the neutrons. *[Unfortunately one does not know to what announcement von Weizsäcker is referring. There seems to be a confusion in the discussion that follows as to whether what is being discussed is a reactor or a bomb. In the reference below Heisenberg is clearly talking about using graphite as a tamper.]*

HEISENBERG: I suppose they mixed it with graphite, increasing the scattering coefficient, and so diminishing D_i and thus made a slightly smaller machine possible. But you don't gain much in that way because, for fast neutrons, graphite scatters about as well as "235."

HARTECK: The volume goes up as the cube of the radius, which is always disadvantageous. *[I will not try to analyze this colloquy until it begins to make sense again.]*

HEISENBERG: You must always take one "235" *[nucleus]* to "plug up" one carbon atom.

WEIZSÄCKER: On the whole I get more material from a substance with the same MFP for scattering.

HARTECK: But there is not only the scattering MFP to consider, but also the MFP for capture. If, let us say, I put in one half, then I must have only half as much uranium per unit volume, and so I need four times the volume of uranium. Admittedly I gain very little by it, but I lose more by scattering. It gets worse all the time.

WEIZSÄCKER: But in that case the neutrons are notably slower and so have a considerably greater scattering cross section.

HEISENBERG: That has practically no effect. The $1/v$ law first goes astray much lower. Here, on the contrary, the effective cross section is independent of the velocity, simply the cross section of the nucleus. *[It is by now quite obscure what nucleus Heisenberg is talking about. He seems to be discussing bomb design again.]* But round the outside, as we said, one must put something, and if possible something with as small a scattering MFP as possible, and I have as a trial assumed that this external MFP was the same as the internal; and indeed carbon on the outside approximately does this. On account of the uncertainty which enters here, I have yet to consider this μ term on the outside, for it is open to us to choose D_e as 4 or 6 centimeters. at will. *[Heisenberg has decided, as a first approximation, not to include the fact that neutrons can be created or absorbed in the tamper. For example, if the tamper is made of natural uranium, fast neutrons can fission the ^{235}U in it and neutrons will be created.]*

GERLACH: Do you think they put graphite in, to prevent melting? If uranium carbide powder was reduced, you have already a very high density. *[Gerlach now threatens to derail the exposition.]*

HEISENBERG: It could be something like that. Some such technical trick seems to me most likely. Perhaps we can consider that later. So if the internal and external diffusion coefficients are equal, $D_e/D_i = 1$ and the cotangent is zero *[recall the formula* $\cot (R/l_1) \times R/l_1 = 1 - D_e/D_i$, *which means the angle is $\pi/2$ [the angle at which the cosine vanishes and hence the cotangent], so that the radius must be $(\pi/2)l_1$. [That is, $\pi/2 = R/l_1$.]* We see that it would be less favorable to have no scattering material outside, for if there were empty space around the uranium sphere, D_e would be infinite; i.e., the cotangent on the right-hand side would be $-\infty$, which happens when the angle is π [$\cos(\pi)/\sin(\pi) = -\infty$] and the radius is doubled *[Here, $\pi = R/l_1$.]* Thus we can say quite roughly that if there is nothing around the uranium sphere, the critical radius, at which it goes off *[explodes]*, is twice as big as if the sphere is surrounded by graphite or lead or "238." I have therefore assumed that the ratio of the scattering cross-sections inside and out is unity. Then the sphere radius $[R]/l_1$ is $\pi/2$ *[$\pi/2 = R/l_1$]* and now I insert the value for l_1 and obtain an equation for μ. It is *[again I have simplified Heisenberg's notation]* $\mu = v - D\pi^2/4R^2$ or $\mu = v(1 - R_k^2/R^2)$ where R_k is a critical length equal to $1/2\pi l_1$ and μ_k is approximately 9.7 cm/(fission cross section)$^{1/2}$.

[Here Heisenberg's various previous confusions have caught up with him. Let us derive the correct expression. Comparing the two expressions for μ we see that $R_k^2 = D\pi^2/4v$. But

$$D/v = \frac{1}{3} \frac{1}{N^2 \sigma_f \sigma_t} .$$

Thus

$$R_k^2 = \frac{\pi^2}{12} \frac{1}{N^2 \sigma_f \sigma_t} .$$

If we call the transport mean free path l, with $l = 1/N\sigma_t$, we may write $R_k^2 = (\pi^2/12)l^2(\sigma_t/\sigma_f)$. If we take $l = 5$ centimeters, $\sigma_t = 4$ and $\sigma_f = 22$ in units of 10^{-24} cm^2, we find $R_k = 8.2$ cm. Shortly we will give the range of Heisenberg's answers. Readers of Serber's Los Alamos talks will notice that the 8.2 centimeters given above is about half of the value for R_k Serber gives first. That is because his first calculation is done with no tamper. If one uses a tamper having a diffusion coefficient whose value is the same as the interior diffusion coefficient, then his number and ours are in agreement. We now return to Heisenberg's discussion.]

From this we see that µ is actually negative if R is very small *[compared to R_k—see above]*. If I take then a very small sphere, the term R_k^2/R^2 is dominant compared with unity and the neutron density diminishes exponentially. If on the other hand R is greater than R_k, then µ is positive and the neutrons increase exponentially, that is, the whole thing explodes. We see therefore that R_k is the critical magnitude which the uranium sphere must have as a minimum if the affair is to explode.

The explosion then follows exponentially with the time factor µ. Now we see that the critical radius is pretty sensitive to the value of the fission cross section. If I assume the smallest value, 0.5, I get a critical radius of 13.7 centimeters, and if I assume the greatest, 2.5, I get 6.2 centimeters.

HARTECK: Is that with a reflector?

HEISENBERG: With a reflector for which the MFP outside equals that inside. Now these 6 centimeters are notably greater than the value which those people claim. They claim that the whole explosive weighed 4 kilograms and this sphere of 6.2 centimeters weighs about 16 kilograms. *[The calculation needed here is that the mass $M = 4/3 \times \pi R^3 \times \rho$ where ρ is the uranium density of 19.1 kilograms per cubic centimeter. With Heisenberg's numbers I find a mass of about 19 kilograms.]* There are two possibilities. One is that the fission cross section is really much bigger, and it is not wholly inconceivable that it is practically as big as the scattering cross section; i.e., about 6×10^{-24} *[cm^2]*, and then it doesn't quite reach what we want. So I do not know what else can be changed in the data. They may have a better reflector, but it couldn't help them much. *[It is, and it is not, remarkable that the reason for this discrepancy completely eludes the Germans. It is remarkable because von Weizsäcker, who is in this audience, actually thought of using plutonium as a nuclear explosive. Of course the reported critical mass of about 4 kilograms with which Heisenberg begins this paragraph referred to plutonium—the Nagasaki bomb. For plutonium the untampered critical mass is 11 kilograms, and with a uranium tamper it is 5 kilograms. This is the mass that Heisenberg is trying to understand. On the other hand, it is not remarkable that the Germans have not thought of plutonium here, because to admit that this explosive is plutonium would be to admit that the Allies had a successful reactor program. This the Germans still cannot believe. As the transcript shows, they do not accept the fact that the Allies can have done the chemistry, let alone build a reactor for making plutonium. To admit this is to admit that they have nothing to offer to the British and American programs.]*

WEIZSÄCKER: You said earlier that the $1/v$ term begins much lower. It begins then when the wavelength of the neutrons is greater than the geometric cross section of the nucleus. *[Wolfgang Pauli used to describe exchanges like this as "desperation physics." We are about to see several vivid examples.]*

HEISENBERG: Yes.

WEIZSÄCKER: Perhaps they have added graphite so as to have slow neutrons and a larger fission cross section. *[Just what one does not need. This discussion clearly refers to reducing the critical mass in the bomb by reducing the critical length which one could do if one could increase the cross sections.]*

HEISENBERG: But graphite slows down very slowly at first.

WIRTZ: But if you had heavy hydrogen—say as many deuterium atoms in the form of heavy paraffin as there are uranium atoms—pressed together. *[I will not try to disentangle these exchanges either, until they begin to be relevant to actual bomb physics.]*

HEISENBERG: In any case it would be better lighter than heavier.

WEIZSÄCKER: At what neutron energy is the wavelength equal to the nuclear cross section?

HEISENBERG: At 100,000 volts it is 10^{-11} centimeters.

WEIZSÄCKER: For the nucleus you might take about 10^{-12}; thus, at a million volts the nuclear cross section and the wavelength are comparable. If only they succeeded in getting neutrons of a half million volts, the effective cross section would be a great deal greater.

HEISENBERG: I don't believe that at all, because here we are not in the resonance region. Naturally at the resonance level the cross section can be the simple square of the wavelength.

WEIZSÄCKER: For thermal neutrons this cross section then is about 50,000.

HEISENBERG: We know that for thermals, the fission cross section is 400×10^{-24}. If then you go to 100,000 volts, the cross section according to the $1/v$ law, if it is valid, is already 0.4. So you can say at 100,000 volts you would get something, according to the $1/v$ law, which was rather smaller than what is certainly there.

WEIZSÄCKER: Then there is the further question how strongly are the neutrons slowed down, for is it indeed true that practically every collision is inelastic?

HEISENBERG: I should say, after three or four collisions it would be about 10% or perhaps even less.

WEIZSÄCKER: If you simply apply *[Victor]* Weisskopf's formula, you can say that a neutron which enters the nucleus with an energy *[E]* emerges perhaps with energy of the order of $E/4$.

HEISENBERG: On the other hand if you have a scattering cross section of 6, at least 50% of the scattering cross section is elastic scattering and the neutrons are thrown out with a change of direction.

HAHN: If you have a uranium reflector you get disintegration by fast neutrons; admittedly that does not give much but it does give some multiplication.

HEISENBERG: So I would like to propose the following explanation: I believe that what they've got in the centre is a mixture of "238" and "235," probably 5C% of each, for they are not likely to have succeeded in separating "235" completely. *[The separation achieved in the end was 89%.]* From this mixture, which is certainly not much worse than pure "235," they will have made a sphere say, of 8 centimeters but in this 8 centimeter sphere there is correspondingly little ^{235}U and they have given that as the weight. *[The opposite of the uranium bomb.]*

HAHN: Lise Meitner says here something about heavy water.

HEISENBERG: She certainly doesn't know anything about it. *[She certainly did.]* Heavy water doesn't make sense because here it's only a question of fast neutrons and for these, light water is just as good as heavy.

HAHN: If a fast neutron is shot into uranium metal it multiplies itself by 1.4 or 1.35 before it slows down.

HEISENBERG: That naturally depends on the size and it is again a sort of diffusion process but as the most favorable, for an infinitely large sphere of good quality "238," it is increased by 40%. Probably one could use a mixture in which "235" was only, say, 10% and "238" 90%. The "238" has anyway the advantage that, if it once causes a fission, it gives a large number of neutrons, about five. So it may be, as we have just found out, as much a question of the fission cross section as of the particular mixture. I have up to now assumed a sphere whose radius was only 5% greater than the critical radius. *[The following sentence, missing from the American version, appears in the British version and it corresponds with the original German: Now one must inquire, if one has such a sphere, how does the explosion proceed?]* On that I must say that I do not think they have much exceeded 5% for they must be certain that the halves of the sphere are definitely less than the critical limit. So apparently they put the sphere together from two hemispheres.

KORSCHING: Can they not simply be cylinders?

HEISENBERG: They could be cylinders but I would say that spheres are always the simplest case, because in the end one wants the neutrons in the smallest possible volume.

KORSCHING: Hemispheres are very difficult to put together.

HEISENBERG: Yes there may well be an iron cylinder behind. A possible construction would be that one had hemispheres attached to an iron cylinder, and this iron cylinder moving in a gun barrel would be shot from the gun on to the other hemisphere, which would be held in some way. *[The actual construction was* *something like this: A uranium-235 "bullet"—a heavy projectile of uranium—was fired into rings of ^{235}U and tamper. Imagine "catching" the uranium projectile in surrounding rings of uranium. Each of these components—projectile and rings— was subcritical but, when fitted together exceeded the ^{235}U critical mass. The problem is to do this assembly fast enough so as to avoid predetonation—fizzles. At the time, the United States Army gun with the maximum projectile velocity could shoot a 50 pound projectile with a muzzle velocity of 3,150 feet per second. Unfortunately this gun was 21 feet long; too long for a practical bomb. It turned out that a 1,000 feet per second muzzle velocity was enough, which reduced the length of the gun to only 6 feet—small enough to fit into a bomber as was the case for the Hiroshima bomb. As we have mentioned, plutonium bombs do not use "guns" but rather use explosive lenses to implode the plutonium sphere.]* If one assumes that the sphere after being put together has a radius about 5% more than the critical radius, then the hemispheres if we consider them as spheres—in reality they have another form— have a radius about 85% of the critical radius. In other words, you have to go with the hemispheres pretty close to the critical conditions and they must have measured these very exactly so that nothing happens to them. *[They did. Since the shapes actually used did not lend themselves easily to calculation, the design relied on actually measuring the critical mass for various shapes—a tricky business.[6]]* In any case they naturally have the following factor of safety: These hemispheres are surrounded on one side by air when they stand empty and so the backscattering is much poorer.

WEIZSÄCKER: These geometrical forms seem unsatisfactory to me. From these hemispheres you could surely cut a little figure with rounded edges which would be more practicable, for the gadget with sharp angles does not help at all. *[The word Zeug can be translated as "gadget," but "thing" or "object" would be better. The use of the word "gadget" for a nuclear weapon was Los Alamos jargon. This use by the British translators is probably coincidental.]*

HEISENBERG: Agreed. So a possible construction would be still to have the hemispheres in an iron cylinder and say an iron cylinder underneath, the hemisphere above it and then a gun barrel below it so that the plane sides of the hemispheres are facing each other. Then you have a little charge above so that at a determined moment this upper cylinder is shot down to the lower one and the whole thing into a sphere. Why this must be done so fast I will now explain. The process goes according to the equation $n = n_0 e^{\mu t}$, where μ is the reciprocal time which was worked out earlier in the formula. If one now assumes that the radius is only 5% more than the critical radius, then what you find is $\mu = 0.5 \times (10^7 \text{ second})^{-1}$. Therefore in 10^{-7} second the intensity increases *e*-fold *[by a factor of 2.72]*. This means, in other words, the whole reaction is complete in 10^{-5} second. *[What Heisenberg appears to have done is to equate $e^{\mu t}$ with 2^{80}, the number of generations needed to*

---

[6] *Ibid.*, pp. 56–63.

completely fission one kilogram of ^{235}U. Taking the logarithm of both sides produces his answer.] Now the question is in the first place why must one bring the two hemispheres together so rapidly. Could one not put the whole thing together slowly and say, "All right, if I bring them together slowly the thing will go off at sometime when I've brought them near enough together and that's all right." That seems wrong to me for the following reason. If I bring them slowly together, the thing begins at a certain time when I have exceeded the critical radius by much less than 5%, let us say when I am only 1/10 per 1,000 over the critical radius. At this time the time factor with which the affair goes is much slower and is not 10^7 (seconds)$^{-1}$ but only about 10^{-4}. Then the whole explosion would mean not 10^{-7} but 10^{-4} second. In this time the thing would heat up so fast that one would reach 5,000 or 10,000 or 20,000 degrees. As soon as you get to these high temperatures the whole affair disintegrates. This disintegration follows then in a time comparable with 10^{-4} second, which means that the reaction doesn't run to completion but runs practically until 10,000 degrees is reached and then it stops. *[While Heisenberg has finally come to grips with the problem of the expansion of the bomb material, it appears to me that he still has not fully understood the situation. He acts as if the reaction, as he puts it, must run to "completion." By this, I understand him to mean that all the fissionable material is fissioned. But this is not what happens in a bomb. Typically the efficiencies are only a couple of percent. That is what it was in the Hiroshima bomb. That means to fission 1 kilogram of material requires having 50 kilograms of ^{235}U available. The real reason for wanting the assembly to be rapid is to avoid predetonation. If, for example, natural uranium is used as a tamper, then, since it is radioactive and can decay with the emission of neutrons—as well as other particles—one must have the assembly rapid enough so that these decay neutrons will not start the chain reaction before enough material is assembled for it to go critical. This problem, which is less severe for uranium than plutonium, can be solved with the gun assembly. For plutonium, because of the presence of the ^{240}U isotope, the assembly must be much faster, and that is what motivated the development of the implosion method.]* So I must choose an exceedingly short time so that it doesn't fly apart too soon. I have worked this out roughly and I find that the time must not be longer than 10^{-6} second, perhaps half, but that is about the limit. One could reach this by shooting the two hemispheres together, but cannot reach it if they're brought together slowly. I might say there is a critical distance, say a centimeter, and if they are more than 1 centimeter apart nothing happens; it doesn't go off. If I bring them nearer than 1 centimeter then the thing goes off explosively. This last centimeter must be covered in 10^{-6} second.

HARTECK: That won't do: they would need 10,000 meters a second. *[300 meters a second works fine.]*

HEISENBERG: Well 10^5 *[means 10^{-5} second]* is perhaps just possible. *[Ten times faster than Harteck wants.]* Perhaps they could not quite use that.

HARTECK: "As fast as possible" is not good enough. *[The American version now contains the sentence: There must be a "very" to it. The British has: It is important.*

The German reads: "... sondern es kommt sehr darauf an," which means, "for this is very crucial."]

HEISENBERG: There is still the possibility of arguing otherwise. You could in fact say that if one brings no neutron source in the neighborhood and leaves it only to cosmic radiation, then you could say, "If I bring it slowly together there will at first be no cosmic ray neutron there." But this is playing with chance. It might just happen that at that very moment when the critical radius was passed, a neutron might be present and then the efficiency of the bomb would be very low. *[The Los Alamos scientists considered cosmic ray neutrons and concluded that there were too few to play any role in the predetonation problem.]*

WEIZSÄCKER: How often do cosmic ray neutrons occur in such a small region?

HEISENBERG: That's the question of priming. *[Heisenberg is worried about what starts the chain reaction in a bomb or the "initiator" as it was called at Los Alamos. The idea developed at Los Alamos was to use a mixture of materials—in the end polonium and beryllium—that is assembled in the center of the bomb when the two halves come together. Polonium is radioactive, and the α particles it produces scatter from the beryllium, in turn producing secondary neutrons. These neutrons are what initiate the explosive chain reaction.]* I've estimated it as follows: Priming might be done by means of spontaneous fission. That is indeed a possibility. But one sees that it is not satisfactory. The mean life for spontaneous fission is about 10^{14} years, if I remember right. *[Experiments to detect spontaneous fission were begun in 1939 and the results published in the open literature. Spontaneous fission is the source of the unwanted neutrons I discussed above. The last thing one wants to do is to use such a chance process as the initiator of a bomb.]*

HARTECK: 10^{14} to 10^{16} years.

HAHN: How do we know that "235" undergoes spontaneous fission?

HEISENBERG: Well there is probably "238" as well. They're approximately equivalent. That comes to about 10^{22} seconds and if I want a neutron in 10^{-6} second I must have 10^{38} atoms; naturally I haven't.

WEIZSÄCKER: Conversely one could naturally say that if there is definitely no other priming mechanism, then it must be put together slowly and it will go off.

HEISENBERG: Yes, but I think not. Possibly they've adopted some such trick. If so they may naturally have bad luck, which they must risk, and the bomb will have a very low efficiency.

WEIZSÄCKER: If you put it together relatively fast, then the probability that it will go wrong is very small.

HEISENBERG: Only if you put it together rapidly you must take care that it doesn't bounce apart again.

HAHN: What would happen if you introduced 1/1000 milligrams of radium? *[Hahn* *is on the right track. Radium by itself won't work since the α particles it emits, being electrically charged and therefore repelled by the uranium nuclei, cannot initiate fission. But if you also introduce beryllium, as suggested above, then neutrons will be produced, but several grams of radium are needed. Polonium is better because it emits less unwanted radioactivity.]*

HEISENBERG: That would certainly work.

GERLACH: If a hemisphere is 85% of the critical size what is the life of a thermal neutron? *[Gerlach seems not to have followed this discussion.]*

HEISENBERG: Do you mean, if you're considering thermal neutrons from cosmic radiation?

GERLACH: Yes, for they make more neutrons in the hemisphere.

HEISENBERG: That doesn't last long.

HARTECK: A thermal neutron has a velocity of 10^5 centimeters *[per second]* and if you have pure "235" the MFP is only a few hundredths of a centimeter. So the order of magnitude would be 10^{-7} second.

HEISENBERG: Yes, I agree that is much too small.

GERLACH: But again there is another neutron there.

HEISENBERG: That runs away, it's too fast.

GERLACH: There was a formula for such decay times.

WEIZSÄCKER: It's already been worked out. Yes, in our big machine *[the last Berlin–Haigerloch reactor experiments]* the decay times were much longer.

HEISENBERG: It could be that you'd work it like this; you bring the two parts together as fast as possible and say, "We'll hope that we don't have bad luck, that just as we exceed the critical size the first neutron will be there."

KORSCHING: If the decay time is so sharply dependent, then you must, if you screw things together quite slowly with a micrometer screw, be able to burn the stuff as slowly as you like.

HEISENBERG: Fluctuations come in then. Naturally in principle it would be possible. I've also considered it from the energy point of view. *[Things now get back on track.]* Let us suppose there are 4 kilograms *[of]* "235" which are actually burnt. *[He has presumably chosen 4 kilograms because he confused it with the reported critical mass of the Nagasaki bomb.]* In this there would be 3×10^{21} ergs set free, which is quite trivial. *[The simple arithmetic here is that fission in uranium produces 7×10^{17} ergs of energy per gram fissioned. Multiplying this by 4 kilograms gives Heisenberg's answer.]* For each fission 3×10^{-4} ergs are set free, which I must multiply by some factor. Now I ask how high does the temperature go in this block of uranium? That can easily be calculated by assuming that this whole energy is practically converted into radiation, for the specific heat of the metal is independent of *T* *[temperature]* and so the energy increases proportionally to *T*. *[This brings us to another aspect of bomb physics—what happens to the fission energy once it is produced? The fission fragments come away with substantial kinetic energy, which in turn is transferred to the uranium nuclei. These nuclei are therefore heated up very rapidly—in less than a microsecond—to tens of millions of degrees. The electrons in the uranium metal are liberated at these high temperatures so that one is dealing with a uranium gas. In such a gas, the energy is proportional to the temperature; E ≈ T. But radiation is also being produced. This is the so-called "black body" radiation generated by the oscillations of charged particles in any material at any temperature above absolute zero. The energy density—the amount of energy per cubic centimeter—of this radiation increases as the fourth power of the temperature, E/(cm³) ≈ T⁴. Because of this high power, this radiation energy will, when the temperature becomes high enough, equal the kinetic energy of the uranium gas. For temperatures above this critical temperature the energy will be essentially all in radiation energy. One can show that this happens at a temperature of about 60 million degrees. This is the temperature Heisenberg is about to calculate.]*

LAUE: You are dealing with a uranium gas.

HEISENBERG: Yes. The radiation which results instantaneously in this space has an energy content which according to Boltzmann's law increases with T^4. Therefore at exceedingly high temperatures radiation preponderates over everything else. Therefore in practice the whole energy is converted into radiation, and I can calculate the temperature by saying that it increases like the neutron density according to a law e^{ut}. *[Energy increases as the number of fissions build up. These produce a buildup of neutrons, according to Heisenberg's exponential.]* It will rise to a maximum, in fact, until the whole energy is used up. The total energy up to this time must have flowed through the surface, because radiation travels with the speed of light, so it spends practically no time inside the uranium. Now according to the Stefan–Boltzmann law energy σT^4 *[the fourth-power law discussed above]* goes through the surface, where σ is the constant 5.8×10^{-5} erg per second per square centimeter and degree to the fourth power. *[The actual number is 5.67 and not 5.8.]* The total energy must therefore be equal to the time integral of the surface F of the uranium lump times σT^4. *[Heisenberg has in mind that the sphere containing this radiation is expanding so that the surface area is increasing in time, which means that the energy per unit area passing through this surface will decrease.]* This time integral is simply equal to

$$\frac{F \times \sigma \times (\text{maximum temperature})^4}{4 \times (\text{increase factor due to expansion})}$$

and if I insert the data which we have assumed above, I find a maximum temperature of 3×10^7 degrees. That is somewhat higher than the papers give. In the papers I saw a figure 3.6×10^6 degrees. *[It is not clear if the reports Heisenberg saw had to do with the Nagasaki bomb. His computed figure is close to Serber's number for the uranium bomb.[7]* It seems as if the whole energy is not converted. Maybe we do not get the right power of ten because we do not know the exact conditions of the bomb and it is also a question of whether the figure in the newspaper is right. If one has the sphere put together before the thing goes off, then it practically doesn't expand in 10^{-7} second. I've calculated by how much the sphere expands and at 10^{-7} second it is the order of a few millimeters.

LAUE: For the reflector, radiation pressure is the most important.

HEISENBERG: Radiation pressure at the maximum is about 10^9 atmospheres; in itself that is wildly enormous but it does not affect much in this extraordinarily short time towards expanding the affair noticeably.

HARTECK: Well, how was the temperature calculated?

HEISENBERG: I've simply calculated as follows. At the end of the reaction practically all the energy which is liberated has gone as radiation. Naturally this is not quite right because a certain fraction of the energy is employed in accelerating the particles and in moving the molecules. But practically radiation at the high temperature plays the main part. Therefore most of the energy goes in radiation and only very little in the momentum of the fragments. This radiation energy emerges with the velocity of light. Therefore I said that at the end of the reaction practically the whole energy which has been liberated has flowed through the surface. Radiation of 3×10^7 degrees, because it is Planckian radiation is roentgen *[x-ray]* radiation of which the maximum lies at a wavelength of about 1 ångstrom *[10^{-8} centimeters]* or more exactly 0.86 ångstrom. *[Still more exactly, 0.96 ångstrom.] [Max Planck produced the first correct formula for the characteristics of black-body radiation. Among the properties of black-body radiation is a relation that connects the most likely wavelength of the radiation, λ_{max}, and its temperature. It states that $\lambda_{max} = 0.29°cm / T$. This is the formula Heisenberg is about to use. Incidentally, since these reports were made, a convention has been adopted according to which temperatures measured, as they are here, on the absolute, or Kelvin scale, do not require the degree symbol. We have kept the degree symbol because it is in the transcript.]* The main part of the radiation comes out as x-rays and is absorbed in the surrounding air.

The first thing that happens is that the first 10 meters of air are brought to a white heat. What one will see right at first is a glowing ball of about 20 meters diameter which glows white in consequence of the absorbed x rays. This radiation naturally sends out further radiation and so the affair generally spreads.

WEIZSÄCKER: Since radiation at the beginning is only a small part of the energy, as soon as the thing has reached a reasonable temperature is not the greater part of the pressure gas pressure and the rest a pressure wave? *[This is the first sensible*

---

[7] *Ibid.*, p. 41.

contribution von Weizsäcker has made to this discussion. The initial damage effect of the bomb is a shock wave caused by this gas pressure, followed by a high-velocity wind. In the two aboveground nuclear tests I witnessed in Nevada in 1957, I recall that the effect of this shock wave was something like a disagreeable click in my ears rather than a rolling explosion. Of course, that was preceded by the visible display, which is what Heisenberg is speculating about.]

HEISENBERG: In the beginning the affair is remarkably spherical.

WEIZSÄCKER: I should distinguish three phases: a radiation phase; then a phase where a pressure wave is the main effect and finally convection sets in and lifts the whole thing *[produces the mushroom-shaped cloud].*

LAUE: How much energy is sent out as visible radiation?

HEISENBERG: I should compare this inner uranium sphere with a glowing body at say 1,000 degrees. Then it would radiate in the visible 10^4 times as much as this glowing body. The surface of this uranium sphere radiates about 2,000 times more than the surface of the sun.

WEIZSÄCKER: That means that if you see it from a distance so that it looks as big as the sun, then it radiates 1,000 times more than the sun.

HEISENBERG: It would be interesting to know whether objects can be knocked down by the pressure of the visible radiation. *[No.]*

Discussing the Lecture

[The title "Discussing the Lecture" is in the transcripts and presumably reflects the fact that at this point Heisenberg and Hahn were conversing alone.]

HEISENBERG: In our machine every neutron has one chance in 20 of being captured by resonance and so 1/20 of element 94 is made for each fission.

HAHN: I don't understand that.

HEISENBERG: In our machine it was so arranged that every neutron had one chance in 20 of being captured by resonance before it became thermal.

HAHN: Oh I see.

[I will reserve much of my further commentary on this lecture for the coda to this book. Here let me make two observations. The first should be obvious. The Germans had no comprehensive understanding of bomb physics. This goes way beyond Heisenberg's confusion about the value of the critical mass. Nearly everything Heisenberg says in this lecture misses essential points and the comments are worse. I make this observation because there have been many assertions to the contrary— some post facto by the Germans themselves and most recently by Thomas Powers in his book Heisenberg's War. Powers writes, "The general discussion prompted by Heisenberg's lecture on August 14 made it clear that only some of the scientists

*really understood bomb physics—Heisenberg, Harteck, von Weizsäcker, and Wirtz—
while the others were evidently hearing much that was new to them."[8] The notion
that this lecture showed that the four scientists mentioned "really understood bomb
physics" is so ludicrous that one wonders if Powers has any understanding at all
of the physics contained in this lecture and the comments made during it. Moreover,
the fantasy that Heisenberg understood how to make a bomb all along but kept
"the secret" to himself is equally absurd. This lecture was given to show that the
"professors" could figure out how a bomb was made. It represented the high-water
mark of their understanding.*

*The second comment I want to make is related to the first. In reading this lecture,
I am once again struck by the intellectual thinness of this group. Here are ten
German nuclear scientists—nine if one does not count von Laue—who are supposed
to be the cream of the crop, the intellectual elite, of German nuclear physics, men
who had been working on these questions for several years. And look at the
discussion it produced. To see what I have in mind, let us entertain the following
fantasy. Suppose the tables had been turned and ten of the best Allied scientists
had been interned in Göttingen when a hypothetical German atomic bomb went
off. Whom shall we include? Fermi, Bethe, Feynman, Serber, Wigner, von Neumann,
Oppenheimer, Peierls, Ulam, Teller, Bohr, Frisch, Weisskopf ... . What would the
technical conversation have been like? No doubt there would have been
disagreements and some fumbling. But like this? The question answers itself.*

*The report now turns to the first contact the Germans had with an Allied scientist—
the visit of Sir Charles Darwin. It is not known if Sir Charles was aware that he
was being recorded. It is also uncertain whether or not he had seen the scientists'
August 8 memorandum on their work. Both are probably the case; if so, Sir Charles
was deliberately asking leading questions of the scientists. Bagge wrote in his
diary (entry for 20 August) that they had all placed great hopes on Darwin's visit,
but that they were all greatly disappointed that he could not make any promises
regarding their release.]*

IV. VISIT OF SIR CHARLES DARWIN

1. Sir Charles Darwin, who was accompanied by Lt. Comdr. Welsh, arrived
at Farm Hall in time for tea on 18 August. After meeting the guests at tea
he had a conversation alone with Hahn and they were later joined by
Heisenberg. Both expressed appreciation of the treatment they were
receiving here and stated their chief worry was the absence of news of
their families. Heisenberg gave Sir Charles some details of the work carried

---

[8]Powers, *op. cit.*, p. 451.

out at his institute. The following are extracts from the conversation, which took place in English.

HEISENBERG: We have tried to make a machine which can be made out of ordinary uranium.

DARWIN: With a little bit of enrichment?

HEISENBERG: No, not at all.

DARWIN: With heavy water?

HEISENBERG: Yes. That worked out very nicely and so we were interested in it.

(Pause)

After our last experiments, if we had 500 liters more heavy water, I don't doubt that we had got the machine going.

DARWIN: What heat could you have got?

HEISENBERG: Such an apparatus stabilizes itself at a certain temperature. *[This again is Heisenberg's curious notion of reactor design—the idea that the reactor would stabilize itself at a certain temperature. The whole reason for having neutron-absorbing control rods is to shut the reactor off so it won't run away. His belief that it would stablize without control rods was a big mistake that could have had disastrous consequences.]* If one wants to fix the temperature of the reactor, this can be done by varying the amount of heavy water in it. If you have got enough uranium, more heavy water will raise the temperature.

As soon as we had the machine going, we could have made almost any intensity of radioactive isotopes. Because, just by taking enough energy out, you can raise the intensity as high as you want.

DARWIN: Had you got enough heavy water to do this?

HEISENBERG: We actually had in Germany two tons *[2,000 kilograms or about 2,000 liters]* of heavy water. That would be just sufficient to do it. Actually we had only 1½ tons, and the remaining 500 liters of heavy water had some impurities of light water in it. And so we could not use them and intended to make them pure again. By then the war was over.

DARWIN: Did you contemplate anything about developing an engine, a real engine?

HEISENBERG: There had been plans to use this heat and to make an engine.

DARWIN: Had you any ideas about that?

HEISENBERG: One plan was to enrich the isotope "235" a little bit, so that that thing would run with ordinary water; then you can simply pump the ordinary water through.

DARWIN: You were thinking of getting up (to?) 400 degrees, that sort of thing?

HEISENBERG: Yes. But the main trouble is in the corrosion of the uranium, the chemical change. We tried different schemes to perfect it.

DARWIN: You <u>tried</u> some, or were you only talking about it?

HEISENBERG: We have done some work on it, but it was not very successful.

HAHN: The prevention of corrosion was not finished yet. Harteck knows about that and about heavy water.

HEISENBERG: The other scheme would be to work with heavy water and ordinary uranium and then, of course, you can only go to low temperatures. Then the water should be pumped through and should give off the heat to ordinary water, but we have not got very far. We in our institute were only interested to make such a machine which would give us high neutron intensities with which we intended to play.

DARWIN: Have you thought much about "94" ?

HAHN: You can produce it only by having a machine like this. There must be a fairly stable "93" too.

There is produced a "93" from the *[uranium]* "237" by fast neutrons which decays in seven days into this inactive "93." You are probably more interested in the thing of the <u>slow</u> neutron. With ordinary uranium with slow neutrons you get an active "93" and an inactive "94." But there is produced by fast neutrons a "93" by means of the decomposition of uranium of the atomic weight 237, not 239. If a neutron hits a (239?), two neutrons are sent off. *[This is incomprehensible.]*

DARWIN: There is a "239" which gives off two neutrons and forces (?) the two ...

HAHN: You have "238." When this "238" gets hit by neutrons, two neutrons are sent away. Therefore you get uranium-237. And this uranium-237 decomposes in seven days to ...(int.)

DARWIN: Is that on a very narrow absorption band? Or something of that kind, so that you cannot get much of it?

HAHN: We don't know anything about it, because it is not active (enough).

HEISENBERG: I should not expect any narrow band. I should say, that any high-speed neutron would do it, but it must be a very high-speed neutron, because it must also have the energy to knock another neutron out.

DARWIN: I see your point. It is not a resonance level?

HAHN: No. In my laboratory, where I had no strong substances at all, I could make this "237," decaying in seven days into an inactive element.

DARWIN: That was "β-active"?

HAHN: "237" gives (off) "β rays" *[electrons]*.

DARWIN: Having done that, it is stable?

HAHN: Fairly stable. It may even be 10,000 years. Nobody knows—<u>we</u> don't know it anyhow.

DARWIN: You were doing it with radium and/or beryllium?

HAHN: Yes. In the Heisenberg laboratory in Berlin, they had a high-tension plant *[a Van de Graaf accelerator]*, and there we got some stronger preparations.

DARWIN: What sort of high tension was that?

HEISENBERG: We had about 10^6 volts.

HAHN: In Berlin, we could have these preparations. In Tailfingen, we had not got them anymore; we tried to get them from the <u>Reichspost</u> *[von Ardenne's group]*; they had something too. And we hoped to get something from the cyclotron of Bothe.

---

2. After dinner there was a general discussion. Sir Charles raised the question what they, the scientists, were going to do about things in light of the atomic bomb. Gerlach replied that he did not think there would be "free science" in the world from now on. Gerlach, Hahn, Heisenberg and Harteck strongly expressed the opinion that Russia would never play the game. While scientists in other countries would publish their work, they did not think the Russian government would allow Russian scientific work to be made public. Von Weizsäcker put forward the opinion that either every physicist in every country refuses to hand over the secret of atomic force to any government—which all agreed was impossible—or scientists must lead the governments themselves. Harteck wondered whether Russia would agree to international control of the atomic bomb, whereupon Hahn and Gerlach suggested that it would be a good thing, perhaps, if every one of the big countries had 500 such bombs. Then everybody would be afraid of everyone else. Heisenberg thought that if there are two powers of equal strength, there is bound to be war, because there are always problems when each power will think that the right is on their side and there would be no way of settling it except by war. Hahn again emphasized that they were all very much afraid of Russia and that they felt a profound distrust of Stalin. If conditions in Germany should get very bad, even British- and American-controlled Germany would be driven into the arms of Stalin. They themselves would rather see Germany lean towards the West and they hoped that the Western Allies would help Germany to such an extent with food, etc., that such bad conditions would not arise. Heisenberg in the end stated that at present all scientists were too dependent on their governments and he thought scientists must try and get some political influence.

3. Later in the evening the following conversation took place in the presence of Lt. Comdr. Welsh, who had shown them a copy of the White Paper dealing with the atomic bomb. *[On August 12, 1945 a lengthy statement*

was issued by the British government on the development of the atomic bomb with special emphasis on the British contributions. It is reproduced in Smyth's report as Appendix 7. Some of the commentary that follows reflects the fact that the British report does not go into the American contributions. The British report does mention the possible use of carbon as moderator for a reactor, but is very unspecific on the details of bomb design. The Smyth report was also issued on the 12th of August, but it was not then available to the Germans.]

WEIZSÄCKER: They have decided to do it by gaseous diffusion. *[This is a reference to isotope separation. The British report describes the British decision to focus on the gaseous diffusion method. Most of the uranium in the Hiroshima bomb was separated electromagnetically.]*

HARTECK: Hertz tried that and even he didn't succeed. *[The reader will recall Harteck's lament that Gustav Hertz was not allowed to participate in the program because he was not "100%" Aryan.]*

I persuaded *[Henry]* Albers *[a physical chemist]* who was at Celle to make a compound which would have a vapor tension the same as mercury *[presumably a gaseous uranium compound to use in diffusion]*, at room temperature—such a substance is suitable for (testing) differences in speed of vaporization *[the orthography is inconsistent in this report]*. If you make 10,000 kilograms of such a substance the whole thing becomes automatic; it is vaporized and condenses. You can make 10,000 one after another and then it must work.

GERLACH: We had discussed a sort of continuous belt, it would have to be done in a high vacuum. That is the difficulty. These differences in the speeds of vaporization...

HARTECK: You can work out how it would go and you will see that you get quite fantastic results (?). *[The question mark is in the transcript with no explanation.]* It must work with the speed of vaporization. We know from Hevesy's experiments that is simply the kinetic gas theory. *[George de Hevesy was another one of the brilliant Hungarians. He worked at Bohr's institute in Copenhagen in the 1930s on biological uses of isotopes.]*

GERLACH: But Hevesy only got fractions of thousandths.

HARTECK: Those were fraction of thousandths in thickness. If the thing was to be *[of]* any use, one would have to build thousands of them one behind the other.

GERLACH: I have never worked it out, but I know that the difficulty is that you can get only such very small quantities. I would do it, as I told you recently, by this variation in the Maxwellian law. I think one ought to try the radiometer method. You have a radiometer which is bombarded from one side which produces a current round the radiometer from the warm to the cold side, and you can put a whole lot of warm–cold surfaces warm-cold, warm-cold.

HARTECK: If I were allowed to cooperate on this problem with large means at my disposal I would go out for photochemistry. I have no doubt that it could be done.

4. Heisenberg and Korsching discussed their position in the light of Sir Charles Darwin's visit in the following conversation:

HEISENBERG: I don't see how war between Russia and America can be prevented as Russia appears determined to cut herself off from the rest of the world because they have a different ideology. The Anglo-Americans want the balance of power in Eurasia. The only balance of power they can achieve now is the whole of Europe against Russia. The only choice for us is either to join this Western European bloc or join up with Russia. My own feelings are that the Western European bloc is better, but I can understand someone saying that we ought to join up with Russia. That is a standpoint which could be discussed.

KORSCHING: What depresses me is the thought that all the work we may do in Germany will, so to speak, fall into the hands of other people.

HEISENBERG: That attitude would not be correct if there were to be a united Europe, as we would then be part of it. I think that if a United States of Europe were to be formed it would be in our interests to fight for it as all our old traditions would remain in such a united Europe whereas if we were to start now as part of the Russian Empire everything that had ever been in Germany would disappear. I admit that something would then start which augers well for centuries to come, but after all we have been brought up in the other tradition.

KORSCHING: It annoys me that Germany is not clever enough to work for England without losing her soul, so to speak. It is not so much a question of, "Shall we let the Russians onto the Rhine," as no one can honestly want the Russians on the Rhine, but "Will this pan-Europa eventually be predominantly German or English?" that is the question. *[Two lines in the margin next to the quotes, presumably by Groves.]*

HEISENBERG: There is no doubt about it, it will be predominantly English. We can't do anything about that. When pan-Europa has existed for 300 years, then I should say Germany will play an important part, but the spirit of the whole thing will be English.

5. The following morning *[August 19]* Heisenberg and Bagge had the following conversation:

HEISENBERG: My general impression is that apparently a large proportion of the people who are handling this business are of the opinion that we should go back to Germany and even continue to work on this uranium business as that really has nothing directly to do with the bomb. I am not really very happy about the result of this visit. They don't want to tell us anything definite as long as they have not come to a definite decision, and they can't come to any definite decision, because it is all so completely new, and they don't know what to do. Apparently, the tendency among these people like Darwin is to consider very carefully a long-term plan, to consider the state of Europe in four years time and how gradually to return to peace conditions. They are not so much concerned with the next three or four years, the main thing being gradually to arrive at a stabilized Europe in a few years time. Of course that is right, that is the important thing. For that reason it doesn't matter to them if we are detained for three months or six months. They say to themselves, "A few weeks one way or the other won't matter as it is a question of the whole problem." They intend to let us play some part in it in the long run. They seem to be thinking along the lines of a United States of Europe and they say to themselves, "The German scientists are among the most important people as they have a certain amount of influence in Germany and because, in addition, they are sensible people with whom one can discuss things." But they are not in a hurry.

BAGGE: There can't be any hurry about it until they have made up their minds whether they want to bring the Russians in on the atomic bomb or not.

HEISENBERG: True.

BAGGE: Of course at the moment I am only interested in my own fate. *[Two lines in the margin, probably made by Groves.]*

HEISENBERG: Yes, of course. That was the great difficulty in the discussion yesterday, the fact that our first interest is our future, whereas Darwin and the others are interested firstly in the fate of the world. *[Two lines in the margin next to the previous sentence, probably by Groves.]* That is understandable as for them there is no difficulty about the next three or four years, but their big problem is what will happen after that, as they are naturally frightened that one fine day they will be attacked just as we were attacked (sic). *[Major Rittner has inserted "sic" here just to make sure that we have not missed Heisenberg's reading of the history of the Second World War.]* Our most important problem is the question of our families.

FARM HALL,   (signed)
GODMANCHESTER   Major T. H. Rittner
                                                                  23 August, 1945

TOP SECRET

Copy No. 1
Appendix to F. H. 5

GERMAN TEXT OF LECTURE GIVEN BY PROFESSOR HEISENBERG ON AUGUST 14TH, 1945

[This appendix to Report 5 contains the German text of Heisenberg's August 14 lecture. I present it without commentary or any attempt to change or correct any of the typographical errors.]

HEISENBERG: Ich moechte die ^{235}U Bombe nach den Methoden behandeln und besprechen, die wir bisher immer bei unserer Uran–Maschine angewendet haben. Da stellt sich dann in der Tat heraus, dass man alle Einzelheiten dieser Bombe wirklich sehr gut verstehen kann. Ich will damit anfangen, noch einmal die wichtigsten Daten vom ^{235}U zu rekapitulieren. Ich will vielleicht ganz kurz noch mal wiederholen, was passiert in dieser Bombe. Wenn im Uran 235 ein Neutron vorhanden ist, dann läuft dieses Neutron ein Stück weit und trifft dann auf einen 235–Kern. Dann kann es zwei Sachen machen. Entweder es wird elastisch gestreut, oder es spaltet. Wenn es gestreut wird, dann kann die Streuung elastisch oder unelastisch sein; dann fliegt das Neutron also mit derselben oder einer niedrigeren Geschwindigkeit weg. Das tut aber der Fähigkeit dieses Neutrons weiterzuspalten keinen Eintrag. Es ist also keine Wahrscheinlichkeit, dass Neutronen irgendwie verloren gehen. Der Vorgang geht natürlich so: es trifft also nach einiger Zeit auf ein 235 und spaltet es. Bei der Spaltung kommen wieder einige Neutronen 'raus. Diese Neutronen machen dasselbe, und so läuft die Kettenreaktion. Wenn man beliebig viel Uran 235 haette, dann würde die Kettenreaktion auf jeden Fall beliebig lange weiterlaufen, denn es würden immer aus einem Neutron 2 bis 3 bei der Spaltung entstehen. Diese 2 bis 3 würden wieder den Prozess machen, und so würde es weitergehen. Also würde die Gesamtmenge von den Neutronen exponentiel anwachsen. Mit diesem Prozess der Vermehrung der Neutronen steht aber in Konkurrenz der Prozess, wo die Neutronen nach aussen aus dem Stück weglaufen. Wenn man nämlich ein endliches Uran–Stück hat, dann werden die Neutronen, die an der Oberfläche sind und nach aussen gerichtet sind, eben auslaufen ohne, dass sie weiter an der Spaltung teilnehmen koennen. Also es fragt sich, ob der Neutronenverlust dadurch, dass die Neutronen aussen aus dem Stueck 'rauslaufen, grösser oder kleiner ist als der Neutronengewinn, der durch die Vermehrung im Inneren kommt. Wenn man das nun rechnen oder sich überlegen will, dann muss man zunaechst mal die Wirkungsquerschnitte haben und die freien Weglaengen haben. Da habe ich zunaechst einmal eine Faustformel hingeschrieben. Die heisst so: die freie Weglänge für irgendeinen Prozess im Uran 235 ist gleich 22 cm/ Wirkungsquerschnitt, und den Wirkungsquerschnitt diesmal gemessen in 10^{-24}. Das heisst also, wenn den Wirkungsquerschnitt, z.B. für Spaltung 1×10^{-24} ist, dann ist die freie Weglänge für Spaltung 22 cm. Der Wirkungsquerschnitt für Streuung ist empirisch etwa 6×10^{-24}, daher ist die freie Weglänge 3,7 cm. Nun is das Schwierigste dabei der Wirkungsquerschnitt für Spaltung. Der Wirkungsquerschnitt für Spaltung hängt erstens natürlich sehr stark ab von der Geschwindigkeit. Bei thermischen Neutronen ist er, soviel wir wissen, in der Gegend, von etwa 300 bis 400×10^{-24}, also sehr gross. Bei schnellen Neutronen is mir die Zahl nicht mehr genau in Erinnerung. Eine Zahl, die in den Doerrig'schen (?)[sic: Diebner?] Tabellen steht, die aber vielleicht für 238 und nicht für 235 gilt, die ist $0,5 \times 10^{-24}$. Ich glaube auch, dass man nur diese Zahl für 238 wirklich gut wissen kann, weil ja bei schnellen Neutronen das 238 und das 235 gleichzeitig spaltet, und man also, wenn man Spaltungen misst, eben in den meisten Fällen die vom 238 misst, und ich nicht so recht sehe, wie man die beiden Spaltungen überhaupt unterscheiden kann.

HAHN: Weil das nur 0.7% davon wären?

WEIZSÄCKER: Das wird man also nie messen koennen. Ich wüsste gar nicht, wie.

HEISENBERG: Man könnte vielleicht folgendes machen; man müsste Neutronen nehmen, die eine etwas kleinere Geschwindigkeit haben als die kritische Grenze beim 238, aber nicht thermisch; also sagen wir, Neutronen von 10^5 Volt. Mit denen müsste man dann den Wirkungsquerschnitt messen und dann mit dem Verhältnis umrechnen.

WEIZSÄCKER: Ja, aber da weiss man auch nicht genau, wie dann der Wirkungsquerschnitt weiter von der Energie abhängt.

HEISENBERG: Man könnte vielleicht sagen, so ungefähr wird der Wirkungsquerschnitt in diesen grossen Energien doch vergleichbar sein mit der Kernoberfläche. Von der Energie wird es wohl nicht so toll abhängen. Die Bohr'sche Theorie gibt sogar an, dass er eigentlich im ganzen Energiegebiet konstant sein soll.

HARTECK: Wenn die so einen guten Spektrographen haben in U.S.A., dass sie restlos trennen können, dann braucht man nichts anderes zu machen als so eine dünne Schicht zu haben und dann entsprechend zu multiplizieren. Denn wenn ein Kern aufbricht, gibt es ja viel mehr als ein Alpha–Teilchen, die findet man immer mit dem Zählen, und dann gibt man das Verhältnis von thermischen zu schnellen. Da würde man es experimentel lösen. Die haben es sicherlich daher genau bestimmt.

HEISENBERG: Ja. Ich habe jetzt mal abgeschätzt 0,5 bis 2,5 für den Wirkungsquerschnitt, indem ich mir gesagt habe, 0,5 ist der beim 238, das wird ja die untere Grenze sein, denn 235 wird leichter spalten. Und 2,5 das ist der Querschnitt des Kerns, der richtige Stossquerschnitt, und viel höher kann es auch nicht sein. Nun könnte es natürlich ein bisschen grösser sein als πr^2 aber so in den Grenzen wird es liegen. Wenn man also die Grenzen zwischen 0,5 and 2,5 annimmt, dann ist die zugehörige freie Weglänge für Spaltung 9 cm bis 44 cm. Bei der Streuung dagegen weiss man, dass der Streuquerschnitt bei all diesen schweren Elementen ungefähr 6 ist bei hoher Energie. Beim Uran kennen wir ihn ziemlich genau, da ist er, glaube ich, $6,2 \times 10^{-24}$ beim 238. Beim Blei ist er ein bisschen niedriger, aber die sind alle ungefähr in der Gegend. Also kann man sagen, für Streuung ist der Wirkungsquerschnitt ziemlich sicher in der Gegend von 6×10^{-24} und daher die freie Weglänge etwa 3,7 cm. Dann ist eine wichtige Grösse, die man noch braucht, der Vermehrungsfaktor, also die Anzahl der Neutronen, die bei einem Stoss, bei einer Spaltung von 235 herauskommen. Da kennen wir aus unseren Berliner Arbeiten sehr genau den Vermehrungsfaktor bei thermischen Neutronen, der aber nicht pro Spaltung sondern pro thermische Absorption gerechnet wird. Nun ist im thermischen der Spaltungsquerschnitt etwa drei und der Absoptionsquerschnitt etwa 6,2, d.h. wir kriegen eigentlich nur die Hälfte von wahren Vermehreungsfaktor, wenn wir unsere Zahl nehmen. Unsere Zahl ist, also kann man sagen, der Vermehrungsfaktor ist in Wirklichkeit $1,18 \times 2$, wird also, grob gesprochen, zwischen 2 und 2,5 liegen.

LAUE: Ich habe das nicht verstanden.

HEISENBERG: Wir haben immer experimentiert mit gewöhnlichem Uran, wo also nur etwas weniger als 1% 235 drin ist und sonst 238. In diesem gewöhnlichen Uran haben wir bei thermischen Neutronen folgende Verhältnisse: man hat einen Wirkungsquerschnitt von 6×10^{-24} dafür, dass ein thermisches Neutron verschwindet, und zwar entweder einfach wegabsorbiert wird und damit den 239 Körper macht, der in 23 Minuten zerfällt, oder dass es spaltet, und zwar spaltet dann zwar das 235 ... (int.)

HAHN: Ist das für thermische jetzt gedacht?

HEISENBERG: Ich spreche im Moment nur über thermische. In thermischen ist natürlich der Wirkungsquerschnitt für Spaltung für das 235 furchtbar hoch, der ist in der Wirklichkeit in der Gegend von ein paar Hundert, aber weil es nur mit 1% Häufigkeit vorkommt, spielt das dann im Ganzen doch nur eine geringe Rolle: das heisst, der Wirkungsquerschnitt umgerechnet auf 238 ist dann auch nur etwa 3. Diese Zahl 3 ist, glaube ich, von Droste (phon.) mal bei Ihnen bestimmt worden.

HAHN: Ja.

HEISENBERG: Droste (phon.) hat, glaube ich, eine Messung von 3,1 oder so etwas 'rausgebracht. Wenn zwei Neutronen absorbiert werden, hat man nur in einem Falle eine Spaltung, denn der gesamte Absorptionsquerschnitt ist 6, Spaltungsquerschnitt ist 3. D.h., wenn der Vermehrungsfaktor bei der Spaltung x ist, dann ist die effektive Vermehrung bloss $\frac{1}{2}x$, weil eben jedes zweite Neutron einfach vorher stirbt und eingefangen wird.

HARTECK: Wenn man die Resonanz ... hat, da hat man doch am Schluss $1/v$ für die geringen, und wenn das ... ist, gilt auch $1/v$. Würden Sie glauben, das bei dieser Breit–Wiegner Formel das ganz genau $1/v$ gibt für die niederen Geschwindigkeiten, oder könnte es, wenn man zu tieferen Temperaturen geht, ein kleiner Unterschied sein, wenn man die Breit–Wiegner Formel extrapoliert und die direkte Fission (?)? Verstehen Sie, dass es sich da um 10% verschiebt relativ züinander, oder ist da unten schon ganz haarscharf $1/v$?

HEISENBERG: Ich würde denken, dass es doch sehr genau $1/v$ ist.

WEIZSÄCKER: Diese Formel bedeutet doch gar nichts anderes als dass die Wahrscheinlichkeit des Prozesses pro Zeiteinheit konstant ist.

HARTECK: Das ist ganz klar, aber es ist ja noch die gewisse Einwirkung von der Resonanzstelle.

HEISENBERG: Ja, aber die ist so weit weg.

WEIZSÄCKER: Jedenfalls würde ich sagen, zu je kleinerem v man geht, desto besser ... (int.)

HEISENBERG: Also das spielt ja bei der Bombe gar keine Rolle, die ganzen Resonanzgeschichten. Ich wollte ja diese ganze kleine Abschweifung ins Gebiet der thermischen Neutronen nur machen, um zu sagen, dass wir auf Grund unserer Experimente schliessen würden, dass der Vermehrungsfaktor bei der Spaltung des 235 etwa 2 bis 2,5 ist. Also genaür würden wir $2 \times 1,18$ sagen. D.h., wenn ein 235 spaltet, dass dann 2 bis 2,5 Neutronen dabei 'rauskommen. Es scheint mir, dass die Amerikaner oder die Engländer der Ansicht sind, dass die Zahl ein bisschen höher ist, denn in der Zeitung war so ein Bild von dem Uran–Prozess, und da waren bei einer Spaltung immer drei Neutronen gezeichnet, die 'rauskamen. Also ich halte auch für durchaus denkbar, dass in Wirklichkeit die Zahl doch etwa 3 ist, und dass eben der Spaltungsquerschnitt, den Droste (phon.) seinerzeit bestimmt hat, doch noch ein bisschen hoch ist, dass der in Wirklichkeit ein bisschen niedriger ist. Die Amerikaner haben tatsächlich früher mal für den Spaltungsquerschnitt 2 bestimmt, und dann käme genau die Zahl 3 'raus.

DIEBNER: Die Werte wurden ja auch immer höher, die berechneten Werte. Bei unseren letzten Versuchen waren sie doch etwas höher geworden.

HEISENBERG: Ja, da handelt es sich aber um 1%, dass schafft nicht viel. Ich habe also nachher gerechnet mit einem Vermehrungsfaktor, ich glaube 2,5. Dammit haben wir also die wichtigsten Daten beieinander. Jetzt müssen wir fragen; Was passiert um Uran, wenn ein schnelles Neutron da auf die Reise geschickt wird. Dazu kann man nun folgendes sagen: Wenn wir ein beliebig grosses Stück Uran 235 hätten und darin Neutronen, dann ist es ja klar, dass die Anzahl der Neutronen exponentiel anwächst, weil ja die Kettenreaktion einfach beliebig weitergeht. Jetzt muss man sich noch überlegen wie es exponentiell zuwächst. Ich habe also da die Formel hingeschrieben, n ist proportional e^{vt}, wo eben v eine charakteristische reziproke Zeit ist für dieses exponentielle Anwachsen. Diese charakteristische Zeit, die man nachher als Reaktionszeit braucht, kann man einfach so abschätzen, dass man sagt, die Zeit, bis ein Neutron eine Spaltung macht, ist offenbar gegeben durch das Verhältnis der freien Weglänge für Spaltung geteilt durch die Geschwindigkeit. Also ein Neutron läuft etwa 9 cm bis zu der nächsten Spaltung. Nun muss ich einfach mir ausrechnen, wie lange läuft es, bis es eben die Strecke 9 cm zurückgelegt hat. Diese Zeit ist $\lambda_{Spaltung}$/Geschwindigkeit. In dieser Zeit ist die Vermehrung des Neutrons gerade dieser Faktor x; d.h., statt eines Neutrons habe ich nacher x

Neutronen. Also bekomme ich für die Bestimmung dieser Grösse υ die Gleichung $e^{(\lambda.\text{Spaltung}/\upsilon)} = x$. Oder in anderen Worten die charakteristische reziproke Zeit $\upsilon = (\upsilon/\lambda_{\text{Spaltung}}) \log x$. Die Geschwindigkeit kann man ungefähr gleich 1/20 Lichtgeschwindigkeit annehmen, denn es sind Neutrone von etwa 1000000 Volt, so ganz voll gesprochen. Also jetzt wissen wir, wie eine Menge schneller Neutronen in einem beliebig grossen Uran–Block sich vermehrt. Aber wenn die Verteilung der Neutronen ungleichförmig ist, und ich frage nicht, wie sich die gesamte Anzahl von Neutronen in einem bestimmten kleinen Volumen ändert, dann können natürlich aus diesem kleinen Volumen die Neutronen auch durch Diffusion wegkommen. Also muss ich so eine Diffusionsgleichung aufschreiben für die Neutronen und muss dazu die Diffusionskonstante der Neutronen wissen. Die Diffusionskonstante ist nach der kinetischen Gastheorie immer gleich der freien Weglänge für Streuung υp mal der Geschwindigkeit mal dem faktor 1/3. Also die freie Weglänge für Streuung ist bekannt, die ist 3,7 cm. Die Geschwindigkeit ist auch bekannt, das ist 1/20 Lichtgeschwindigkeit. Daraus kriege ich die Diffusionskonstante. Schliesslich habe ich also für die zeitliche Veränderung der Neutronendichte an irgendeinem Punkt die Gleichung ρ (das ist die zeitliche Änderung der Dichte) = Diffusionskonstante mal $\Delta\rho$ (Δ ist der Laplace Operator) $+\upsilon\rho$. Also man sieht ja, wenn das $\upsilon\rho$ nicht dastünde, also die Neutronenvermehrung, dann wäre das einfach die Wärmeleitungsgleichung die man ja kennt. Dieses Glied $\upsilon\rho$ bedeutet eben, dass die Neutronen sich ausserdem noch vermehren. Man sieht auch dimensionsmässig—das ist noch wichtig—das Verhältnis d/υ ist offenbar das Quadrat einer Länge, denn wenn ich mit υ durchdividiere, dann habe ich eben als Faktor, vom Laplace Operator angewandt auf ρ, d/υ, und da muss ja dieselbe Dimension haben wie ρ. Dieses d/υ nennt man seit den Fermi'schen Arbeiten das Quadrat der Diffusionlänge l^2. Dieses l kommt also jetzt hier numerisch 'raus zu 6,2 cm geteilt durch Wurzel aus dem Spaltungsquerschnitt, wobei der letztere wieder in 10^{-24} gerechnet ist. Wenn der Spaltungsquerschnitt also gerade 1×10^{-24} ist, dann ist diese Diffusionslänge 6,2 cm. Vielleicht kann man an dieser Stelle jetzt einen Moment den Vergleich machen mit unseren Maschinen. Bie unserer Maschine war die Diffusionlänge immer viel grösser. Ich habe die Zahlen jetzt nicht mehr genau im Kopf, ich glaube aber, mich erinnern zu können, dass die Diffusionslänge bei unserer besten Maschine, die wir zuletzt gehabt haben, etwa 35 cm war. Deswegen werden ja auch die Maschinen immer so furchtbar gross. Das liegt an folgenden zwei Punkten: erstens ist der Vermehrungsfaktor viel kleiner. Also hier ist etwa 2,5, dort ist er nur 1,18, weil das 238 eben so viel wegnimmt. Zweitens—und dieser Einfluss ist noch wichtiger—läuft eben ein Neutron sehr weit von der Stelle, wo es ausgesendet wird, bis es thermisch wird und wieder absorbiert wird. Also in den Maschinen, mit denen wir zu tun haben, wird es durch D_2O abgebremst und dann als thermisches Neutron eingefangen. Es läuft eben immer schon ungefähr 20 cm weit, bis es schliesslich eigenfangen wird. Diese Länge addiert sich natürlich zu dem, sie wird in das l verarbeitet. Also hier ist die Diffusionslänge eben nur etwa 6,2 cm, während sie dort in der Gegend von 35 cm war. Jetzt haben wir also die Diffusionsgleichung, nach der die Neutronen sich ausbreiten. Jetzt will ich diese Gleichung lösen für eine Uran–Kugel von einem vorgegebenen Radius R, und ich will annehmen, dass diese Uran–Kugel R wieder umgeben ist von irgendeiner anderen Substanz. Was für eine Substanz, können wir uns nacher überlegen. Wir können natürlich auch Vakuum annehmen, aber jedenfalls nehmen wir eine Kugel an, dann kann man die Gleichung bequem lösen. Dann wird es sicher Lösungen geben, bei denen die Neutronendichte auch im Ganzen exponentiel zunimmt oder auch exponentiel abnimmt. Und zwar wird sich doch offenbar folgendes herausstellen: Wenn die Uran–Kugel klein ist, laufen immer mehr Neutronen nach aussen ab als innen produziert werden. Dann nimmt die Neutronendichte exponentiel ab. Wenn ich dagegen die Kugel hinreichend gross mache, dann kommt der Neutronenabfluss nach aussen nicht auf gegen die Neutronenvermehrung im Inneren, und dann nimmt die Neutronendichte exponentiel zu. Ich setze also willkürlich an, dass die Neutronendichte gleich $\rho = \rho 0 e^{\mu t}$ sein soll, und suche zu bestimmen diesen charakteristischen Faktor μ im Exponenten. Wenn das μ positiv ist, dann geht die Maschine, und die Bombe explodiert. Wenn μ negativ ist, dann heisst es, dass irgendwelche Neutronen, die in dem Stück sind, sofort herauslaufen und weiter nicht mehr interessant sind. Also wenn man das einsetzt, $\rho = \rho_0 e^{\mu t}$, dann kommt die Gleichung 'raus: Diffusionskonstante mal $\Delta\rho + \rho(\nu-\mu) = 0$. Diese Gleichung muss man lösen. Dazu führt man wieder zweckmässig eine charakteristische Länge, nämlich $d/(\nu-\mu) = l_1^2$. Die Lösung dieser Gleichung kennt man. Das ist einfach die Gleichung von dem bekannten Typus $\Delta\phi + K^2\phi = 0$. Die Kugelsymmetrische Lösung lautet $\sin x/x$ (x ist also in dem Fall die Variable) oder $1/l_1$. Die Lösung im Liesung im Inneren dieser Kugel heisst also $(l/r)\sin(r/l_1)$. Also die Neutronendichte muss sich im Inneren verteilen nach dieser Formel $(l/r)\sin(r/l_1)$. Und zwar muss das dann der Fall sein, wenn ich nicht annehme, dass innen irgendeine Neutronenquelle ist. Wenn ich innen eine Neutronenquelle hätte, dann könnte es natürlich sein, dass ich eine Liesung *[Lösung?]* brauchen kann, die an der Stelle $r = 0$ z.B. singulär ist, weil dort eine Quelle liegt. Aber ich will annehmen, dass gar keine Quelle da ist, so dass die Neutronen sich alle irgendwie gleichmässig über die Kugel verteilen, und das geht nur nach der Formel $(l/r)\sin(r/l_1)$.

LAUE: Ist das eine vom Uran unabhängige Quelle?

HEISENBERG: Ja. Also im Inneren der Kugel haben wir sicher diese Abhängigkeit $(l/r)\sin(r/l_1)$. Wie ist es aussen? Da kann man folgendes sagen: Wir haben es mit schnellen Neutronen zu tun, die werden in der äusseren umgebenden Substanz irgendwie gestreut und dabei verlangsamt. Das Verlangsamen aber schadet gar nichts, denn auch ein langsames Neutron kann spalten. Also kann ich so sagen: die Neutronenanzahl ändert sich aussen überhaupt nicht. Also aussen habe ich keinerlei Absorption, weder positive noch negative, und ich habe aussen reine Diffusion von schnellen Neutronen. Ich kann also sagen, aussen habe ich ein Medium, in dem die Neutronen nur diffundieren, aber nicht absorbiert oder vermehrt werden. In diesem Medium aussen gilt also auch so eine Diffusionsgleichung, wie sie da oben steht, bloss mit der Vereinfachung, dass $\nu = 0$ ist also keinerlei Vermehrung stattfindet. Die Lösung dieser einfachsten Diffusionsgleichung heisst natürlich, ρ nimmt ab wie $1/r$. Also im Aussenraum muss ρ, die Dichte, abnehmen wie $1/r$, weil es sich um gewöhnliche Diffusion handelt ohne zugehörige Absorption. Ich habe es mir da etwas erleichtert, indem ich das μ weggelassen habe, das μ ist doch gering gegen das ν.

HAHN: Die kommen doch von aussen wieder zurück, denke ich.

HEISENBERG: Ja. Ein erheblicher Teil der Neutronen fliesst nach aussen ab, und ein Teil wird immer nur nach innen zurückgestreut. Also ich muss dann die Grenzbedingungen ansetzen. Die heissen so: An der Trennungsfläche zwischen Uran–Kugel und umgebendem Mantel muss die Dichte stetig übergehen, und muss der Strom stetig übergehen. Die Dichte innen habe ich schon hingeschrieben, die ist $(l/r)\sin(r/l_1)$. Die dichte aussen α/r. Ich muss das α so wählen, dass für $r = R$ am Kugelrand die beiden Ausdrücke gleich sind.

LAUE: Warum soll die Dichte stetig übergehen?

HEISENBERG: Die Neutronendichte kann ja nicht springen. Die Neutronen bewegen sich ja doch sehr schnell 'rüber und hinüber über die Grenzfläche. Also ich kann nicht einen Dichtesprung aufrecht erhalten. Also dann habe ich unter diese beiden Glieder mit der Dichte die Ströme geschrieben. Den Strom bekommt man ja einfach, indem man die Dichte nach r differenziert. Der Strom ist ja gegeben durch ein Gradienten der Dichte, multipliziert mit dem Diffusions–Köffizienten. Also steht auf der Linken Seite der Differential–Quotient nach r, multipliziert mit der Diffusions–Konstante d_i, und zwar habe ich jetzt im Index "i" dazugeschrieben, weil es die Diffusionskonstante im Inneren bedeutet, und aussen steht der Differentials–Quotient nach r von α/r, das ist $-\alpha/r^2$ multipliziert mit die *[den?]* Diffusions–Konstante aussen. Und schreibe ich einfach die Bedingung auf, dass die beiden gleich sein sollen, und das werden Sie mir glauben wenn man das also hinschreibt, dann fällt das heraus, das kann man eliminieren. Es bleibt stehen, das Verhältnis der beiden Diffusions–Konstanten d_a/d_i muss sein 1—Kugelradius/l_1 mal ctg r/l_1.

BAGGE: Wenn aussen freies Vakuum oder einfach Luft ist, wie es da?

HEISENBERG: Dann können Sie diese Formel auch anwenden, bloss müssen Sie dann da gleich unendlich setzen. Sie müssen sagen, dass jedes Neutron was nach aussen kommt, sofort abtransportiert wird. Das läuft darauf hinaus, dass am Kugelrand die Neutronendichte Null wird (sic!) *[from original transcript]*, weil sie aussen mit beliebiger Geschwindigkeit abtransportiert wird. Jetzt sieht man also, damit man zu einem klaren Resultat kommt, muss man kennen nicht nur die Diffusions–Konstante im Inneren, die kennen wir ja, sondern auch die Diffusions–Konstante aussen. Das heisst, man muss nun irgend etwas annehmen über das Material, was man um die Uran–Kugel drumtut. Man sieht auch, es ist offenbar zweckmässig, um die Uran–Kugel etwas drumzutun, was möglichst viel Neutronen zurückstreut, also in anderen Worten, etwas drumzutun, was einen möglichst grossen Streuquerschnitt hat. Andererseits handelt es sich hier um Streuung von schnellen Neutronen. Bei schnellen Neutronen hat man keine grossen Variationen der

Wirkungsquerschnitte. Man kann sagen, wenn ich etwas Blei drumtü oder Uran 238 oder so etwas, dann habe ich immer Streuquerschnitte von der Grössenordnung 6×10^{-24}. Wenn ich Kohle drumtü, um ein ganz leichtes zu nehmen, dann habe ich etwa 4×10^{-24}, dafür sind die Kohle–Atome etwas dichter gepackt als im Uran. Man kann es eigentlich machen wie man will, man kriegt immer freie Weglängen in der Gegend von 4 cm. Also ich glaube eigentlich nicht, dass man irgend etwas damit profitiert, wenn man sich da besonders raffinierte Elemente 'raussucht, sondern wahrscheinlich liegt es halt immer in der Gegend von 4 cm.

WEIZSÄCKER: Der Wortlaut der Meldung war, man mische das Uran mit Graphit, um die Neutronen zu verlangsamen.

HEISENBERG: Ich könnte mir denken, dass man dadurch, dass man es mit Graphit vermischt, den Streuquerschnitt noch heraufsetzt, das heisst, also dass die verringert und dadurch die ganze Maschine noch ein bisschen enger kriegen kann. Aber viel profitiert man damit nicht, denn für schnelle Neutronen streut die Kohle eigentlich genau so gut wie 235 ... (int.)

HARTECK: Das Volumen nimmt kubisch zu, das ist immer schlecht.

HEISENBERG: Sie müssen doch immer ein 235 'rausnehmen, ein Kohle–Atom 'reinzustopfen.

WEIZSÄCKER: Ich kriege doch im Ganzen von einer Substanz mit derselben Streuweglänge mehr Material.

HARTECK: Aber es kommt uns doch nicht nur auf die Streuweglänge sondern auch auf die Einfangweglänge an. Wenn ich, sagen wir, die Hälfte dazugebe, dann habe ich in der Volumeneinheit die halbe Menge an Uran; ich muss also einen doppelt so langen Weg zurücklegen bis zur Spaltung, und dadurch bekomme ich die vierfache Menge an Uran. Ich gewinne zwar ein bissel etwas dadurch, dass ich mehr dann drin herumstreü. Es wird immer schlechter.

WEIZSÄCKER: Aber dafür werden die Neutronen erheblich langsamer und haben dann einen wesentlich grösseren Streuquerschnitt.

HEISENBERG: Das macht fast nichts aus. Das $1/v$ Glied geht ja erst viel tiefer los. Hier im Gegenteil ist doch der Wirkungsquerschnitt immer unabhängig von der Geschwindigkeit, einfach immer der Kernquerschnitt. Aber aussen 'rum wie gesagt, muss man 'was tun und zwar möglichst etwas, was keine kleine Streuweglänge hat, und ich habe jetzt mal versuchsweise angenommen, dass diese Streuweglänge aussen genau so gross ist wie die innen. Also z.B. Kohle aussen tut das schon ungefähr. Ich habe wegen der Ungenauigkeit, die hier hereinkommt, dann auch unterlassen, dieses µ–Glied aussen noch zu berücksichtigen, denn ist ja ganz willkürlich, ob ich aussen d_a gleich 4 cm oder gleich 6 cm annehme.

GERLACH: Ob die den Kohlenstoff zugesetzt haben, um das Schmelzen zu sparen? Wenn man nämlich Uran–Karbid–Pulver nimmt und das reduziert, dann sind das zusammen schon eine sehr hohe Dichte.

HEISENBERG: So 'was könnte es sein, ja. Das könnte ich mir eher vorstellen, so eine technische Geschichte (?). Vielleicht können wir das nachher noch weiter besprechen. Also wenn die Diffusions–Köffizienten aussen und innen gleich sind, dann ist $d_a/d_i = 1$, dann muss also einfach der ctg $s = 0$ sein, und der ctg s ist null, wenn das Argument $\mu/2$ ist, also muss dann der Radius gleich $\pi l_1/2$ sein. Man sieht auch, dass es ungünstiger wäre, etwa kein Streumaterial drumzutun, denn wenn ich etwa leeren Raum drum hätte, um die Uran–Kugel, dann wäre d_a gleich unendlich, d.h. der ctgs auf der rechten Seite müsste gleich minus unendlich sein, und das ist er dann, wenn das argument π ist, und dann müsste also der Radius doppelt so gross sein. Also ganz grob kann man sagen, wenn ich gar nichts drumtü, um die Uran–Kugel, dann ist der kritische Radius, bei dem es los geht, doppelt so gross als wenn ich die Uran–Kugel mit Kohle oder Blei oder Uran 238 umgebe. Ich habe also jetzt angenommen, dass der Verhältnis der Streuquerschnitte innen und aussen eins ist; dann ist Kugelradius/$l_1 = \pi/2$, und jetzt sehe ich den Wert von l_1 aus der Gleichhung ein und bekomme damit jetzt eine Gleichung für μ. Es kommt heraus $\mu = \nu - d\pi^2/4R^2\,\pi$, oder $\mu = \nu(1 - R_K^2 R^{-2})$ wo R_K eine kritische Länge ist, $R_K = \pi/2l$ und ungefähr $\pi_K = 9{,}7$ cm /Spaltungsquerschnitt hoch$^{-1/2}$. Daraus sieht man, das π ist tatsächlich negativ, wenn R sehr klein ist. Wenn ich also eine sehr kleine Kugel nehme, dann überwiegt das Gleid $\pi_K^2 R^{-2}$ gegenüber der 1, und die Neutronendiche nimmt exponentiell ab. Wenn dagegen R grösser ist als R_K, dann wird π positiv, und dann nehmen die Neutronen exponentiel zu, d.h., die ganze Geschichte explodiert. Man sieht also, dieses R_K ist die kritische Grösse, die Uran–Kugel mindestens haben muss, damit die Sache explodiert. Die Explosion erfolgt dann exponentiel mit diesem Zeitfaktor π. Nun sieht man, dieser kritische Radius hängt noch ziemlich empfindlich vom Spaltungsquerschnitte ab. Wenn ich den kleinsten Wert annehme, nämlich 0,5, dann bekomme ich einen kritischen Radius von 13,7 cm, und wenn ich den grössten annehme, nämlich 2,5, dann komme ich 6,2 cm.

HARTECK: Ist das mit Rückstreumantel?

HEISENBERG: Mit einem Rückstreumantel, für den eben aussen die freie Weglänge so gross ist wie innen. Nun sind diese 6 cm. eigentlich noch erheblich grösser als das, was die anderen behaupten. Die anderen behaupten ja, dass die ganze Explosivmasse nur 4 kg gewogen habe, und diese Kugel von 6,2 cm. wiegt ungefähr 16 kg. Nun gibt es zwei Möglichkeiten: das eine ist dass der Spaltungsquerschnitt in Wirklichkeit doch noch höher ist, und es ist ja nicht ganz undenkbar, dass er praktisch so gross ist wie der Streuquerschnitt, also etwa 6 × 10^{-24}, und auch dann reicht es nicht ganz. Also ich weiss nicht, was noch viel geändert werden könnte in den Daten. Sie können also noch einen besseren Rückstreumantel haben, aber da können sie auch nicht viel dabei verdienen.

WEIZSÄCKER: Du hast vorhin gesagt, das $1/v$ Glied fängt erst viel weiter unten an. Das fängt doch sofort dann an, wenn die Wellenlänge der Neutronen grösser wird als der geometrische Kernquerschnitt.

HEISENBERG: Ja.

WEIZSÄCKER: Vielleicht haben sie eben doch deshalb Graphit dazugegeben, damit sie langsamere Neutronen haben und einen grösseren Spaltungs querschnitt.

HEISENBERG: Aber erstens bremst doch Kohle furchtbar schlecht ... (int.)

WIRTZ: Aber wenn sie etwas schweren Wasserstoff—nehmen wir an so viele schwere Wasserstoff–Atome, sagen wir mal, in Form von schwerem Paraffin ... das zusammenzupressen, wie sie Uran–Atome haben.

HEISENBERG: Jedenfalls leichter wäre es noch besser als schwerer.

WEIZSÄCKER: Bei welcher Energie der Neutronen ist die Wellenlänge gleich dem Kernquerschnitt?

HEISENBERG: Bei 100000 Volt ist sie 10^{-11} cm.

WEIZSÄCKER: Beim Kern darf man doch ansetzen etwa 10^{-12}; das heisst, bei einigen Millionen Volt sind die Kernquerschnitte und die Wellenlängen der Neutronen vergleichbar. Wenn es also nur gelingt, die Neutronen herunterzubringen auf, sagen wir, eine halbe Million Volt, dann wird sofort der Wirkungsquerschnitt um ein ganzes Stück grösser sein.

HEISENBERG: Das glaube ich gar nicht, weil es ja nicht so ist, dass wir hier an der Resonanzstelle sind. Natürlich bei der Resonanzstelle kann der Wirkungquerschnitt einfach Quadrat der Wellenlänge sein.

WEIZSÄCKER: Bei thermischen Neutronen ist dieser Querschnitt doch eben 50000 oder so 'was.

HEISENBERG: Wir wissen, dass in thermischen der Spaltungsquerschnitt 400 × 10^{-24} ist; wenn du nun auf 100000 Volt gehst, ist nach dem $1/v$ Gesetz, wenn es gilt, der Wirkungsquerschnitt bereits 0,4 geworden. Also kann man sagen, bei 100000 Volt würde nach dem Gesetz schon etwas Kleineres 'rauskommen als sicher da ist.

WEIZSÄCKER: Nun kommt die weitere Frage, wie stark werden die Neutronen gebremst, denn es ist ja so, dass praktisch jede Streuung unelastisch ist?

HEISENBERG: Ich würde sagen, nach drei bis vier Stössen wird es vielleicht schon so auf den 10ten Teil, vielleicht sogar auf weniger 'runtergegangen sein.

WEIZSÄCKER: Wenn man einfach so die Weisskopf'sche (phon.) Formel anwendet, dann wird man doch immer sagen, ein Neutron, das mit einer bestimmten Energie E in den Kern hineingeht, kommt mit einer Energie der Grössenordnung $E/4$ vielleicht wieder 'raus.

HEISENBERG: Andererseits, wenn du einen Streuquerschnitt von 6 hast, dann sind mindestens 50% dieses Streuquerschnitts rein elastische Streuung, die so da aussen dran vorbeigeht und abgelenkt wird.

HAHN: Wenn man einen Uran–Mantel hat, dann gibt es ja doch noch das Auseinanderkrachen durch schnelle Neutronen; das gibt zwar nicht viel, aber doch eine kleine Vermehrung.

HEISENBERG: Also ich wollte überhaupt eigentlich folgende Deutung vorschlagen: ich würde glauben, dass das, was die im Zentrum haben, eben eine Mischung aus 238 und 235 ist; etwa so, das 50% 235 und 50% 238 ist, denn wahrscheinlich werden sie das 235 auch nicht gerade beliebig 'reingemacht haben. Von dieser Mischung, die sicher nicht viel schlechter ist als das reine 235, werden sie schon eine Kugel haben, die einen Radius von, sagen wir, 8 cm hat, aber in dieser Kugel von Radius 8 cm ist dann entsprechend wenig Uran 235 drin, und das haben sie angegeben als Gewicht.

HAHN: Die Liese Meitner sagt doch aber hier vom Schweren Wasser etwas.

HEISENBERG: Die weiss ja sicher nichts. Schweres Wasser has sicher überhaupt keinen Sinn, denn es handelt sich ja nur um Prozesse mit schnellen Neutronen, und für schnelle Neutronen ist Leichtes Wasser genau so gut wie Schweres.

HAHN: Wenn man ein schnelles Neutron hineinschiesst in Uran–Metall, dann vermehrt sich das auf 1,4 oder 1,35 bis es abgebremst ist.

HEISENBERG: Das hängt natürlich ganz von der Grösse ab, also das ist auch wieder so ein Diffusionsprozess, aber als Günstigstes für eine unendlich grosse Kugel aus gutem 238 vermehrt es sich um 40%. Wahrschleinlich könnte man schon eine Mischung verwenden, in der bloss, sagen wir, 10% 235 und 90% 238 sind. Das 238 hat immerhin doch den Vorteil, dass, wenn es mal spaltet, es dann gleich kolossal viele Neutronen abgibt, ungefähr 5 Stück. Es kann also, wie wir gerade festgestellt haben, sowohl am Spaltungsquerschnitt liegen als auch daran, dass die solche Mischungen verwenden. Jetzt muss man also fragen, wenn man nun wirklich eine solche Kugel hat, wie geht die Explosion vor sich? Da habe ich jetzt mal angenommen eine Kugel, deren Radius nur um 5% grösser ist als der kritische Radius. Ich muss dazu sagen, ich glaube nicht, dass sie viel mehr gemacht haben als etwa 5% mehr, denn sie müssen ja sicher sein, dass die Hälfte der Kugel sicher unter der kritischen Grenze ist. Also sie setzen die Kugel zusammen aus zwei Halbkugeln offenbar.

KORSCHING: Können das nicht einfache Zylinder sein?

HEISENBERG: Das können auch Zylinder sein, aber ich würde sagen, Kugeln ist eigentlich immer der einfachste Fall, denn man will ja doch am Schluss die Neutronen mit einer kleinen Menge möglichst in einmen Raum drinhalten.

KORSCHING: Halbkugeln kann man schlecht so aufeinander schieben.

HEISENBERG: Da ist ja sowieso ein Eisenzylinder dahinter und so. Eine mögliche Konstruktion wäre, man hat die Halbkugeln an einen Eisenzylinder drangemacht, und dieser Eisenzylinder läuft in einem Kanonenrohr und wird in dieser Kanone auf die andere Halbkugel geschossen, die dann auch so gehalten wird. Wenn man annimmt, dass die Kugel, nachdem sie zusammengesetzt ist, einen um 5% grösseren Radius hat als den kritischen Radius, dann hätte die halbe Kugel, wenn ich das als Kugel betrachte—in Wirklichkeit hat sie eine andere Form—einen Radius von etwa 85% des kritischen Radius. In anderen Worten, muss man schon auch mit den halben Kugeln ziemlich dicht 'rangehen, an die kritische Daten, und das müssten die also sehr genau gemessen haben, dass ihnen da nichts passiert. Immerhin haben sie natürlich auch noch folgenden Sicherheitsfaktor: sie haben diese Halbkugel ja auf der einen Seite mit Luft umgeben, wenn sie leer noch da steht, und dadurch ist die Rückstreuung dort viel schlechter.

WEIZSÄCKER: Ich finde diese geometrische Form doch ungünstig. Eigentlich müssete man aus dieser Halbkugel eine kleinere Figur mit runden Ecken ausschneiden, die wirklich wirksam ist, denn das Zeug mit den spitzen Kanten hilft ja nichts.

HEISENBERG: Eben. Also eine mögliche Konstruktion wäre. sie haben immer diese Halbkugel in einem Eisenzylinder drin. Nun sagen wir, unten steht ein Eisenzylinder, die Halbkugel nach oben, nun kommt ein Kanonenrohr, und oben drüber ist wieder ein Eisenzylinder mit der Halbkugel nach unten, so dass sie flachen Seiten der Halbkugel sich zugewandt sind. Nun habe ich oben eine kleine Sprengladung, so dass zu einer bestimmten Zeit dieser obere Zylinder 'runterstosst auf das untere und das Ganze nun zu einer ganzen Kugel zusammengesetzt wird. Warum das so schnell gehen muss, will ich gleich sagen. Der Prozess läuft nun ab nach der Gleichung $\rho = e^{\upsilon t}$, wo μ diese reziproke Zeit ist, die jetzt da oben in der Formel ausgerechnet ist. Wenn man mal annimmt, dass eben der Radius nur 5% grösser ist als der kritische Radius, dann kommt also 'raus $\mu = 0,5 \times (10^7$ Sekunden$)^{-1}$. Also in 10^{-7} Sekunden nimmt die Intensität jeweils auf das e–fache zu. Das heisst in anderen Worten, die ganze Reaktion läuft ab in etwa 10^{-5} Sekunden. Nun ist die Frage: erstens, warum muss man die beiden Halbkugeln so schnell aufeinandersetzen? Könnte man nicht die ganz langsam aufeinandersetzen und sagen: "Na gut, wenn ich sie eben langsam aufeinandersetze, irgendwann mal geht eben dann die Geschichte los, wenn ich sie nahe genug beieinander habe, und dann ist ja alles gut?" Das scheint mir aus folgendem Grund schlecht zu sein. Wenn ich es langsam zusammensetze, fängt die Sache an zu einem Zeitpunkt, wo ich nur viel weniger über dem kritischen Radius bin als diese 5%, also sagen wir, bloss 1/10 pro mille über dem kritischen Radius. Zu dieser Zeit ist der Zeitfaktor, mit dem die Geschichte geht, sehr viel langsamer, also nicht $(10^7$ Sekunden$)^{-1}$, sondern eben nur 10^{-4} oder so was. Dann würde die Ganze Explosion eben nicht 10^{-7} sondern 10^{-4} Sekunden brauchen. In dieser Zeit würde also die Sache sich so schnell so weit erwärmen, dass man auf 5000° oder 10000° oder 20000° kommt. Sobald ich aber diese hohen Temperaturen habe, dann platzt die ganze Geschichte ja auseinander. Dieses Auseneinanderplatzen erfolgt dann auch die Zeiten vergleichbar mit 10^{-4} Sekunden. Das heisst, die Reaktion läuft gar nicht bis zu Ende ab, sonderen sie läuft eben praktisch nur ab, bis sie etwa 10000° erreicht hat, und dann ist sie schon zu Ende. Also ich muss die Zeit schon hinreichend kurz wählen, damit das nicht vorher auseinanderfliegt. Das habe ich nun mal so überschlagen, und da kommt eben 'raus, die Zeit darf eigentlich nicht länger als 10^{-6} Sekunden sein, vielleicht noch $1/2 \times 10^{-6}$, aber das ist dann so etwa die Grenze. Das kann man erreichen, wenn man die beiden Halbkugeln aufeinanderscheisst. Man kann es aber nicht erreichen, wenn man sie etwa bloss langsam aufeinander legt. Ich kann sagen, es gibt einen kritischen Abstand, sagen wir mal, 1 cm. Wenn ich sie mehr als 1 cm auseinander habe, passiert gar nichts, geht es überhaupt nicht los. Wenn ich sie näher als einen Zentimeter zusammen habe, dann geht die Sache explosiv los. Dieser letzte Zentimeter muss in 10^{-6} Sekunden zurückgelegt werden.

HARTECK: Das geht ja nicht, das wären ja 10000 m pro Sekunde.

HEISENBERG: Na ja, 10^5 (means 10^{-5} Sekunden?) *[sic]* ist vielleicht gerade noch möglich. Darum werden sie es auch nicht ausnutzen können.

HARTECK: Es genügt nicht nur "möglichst schnell," sondern es kommt sehr darauf an.

HEISENBERG: Es kommt sehr darauf an. Es gibt noch eine Möglichkeit, da anders zu agumentieren. Man könnte nämlich folgendes sagen: wenn man gar keine Neutronenquelle in die Nähe bringt und es sozusagen der Höhenstrahlung überlässt, dann könnte ich ja so sagen: "Ich bringe es verhältnismässig langsam zusammen, dann wird zunächst gar kein Höhenstrahlungsneutron da sein." Aber das ist ein Spiel des Zufalls. Da kann es eben passieren, dass doch gerade in dem Moment, wo der kritische Radius überschritten ist, schon das Neutron da ist, und dann ist der Wirkungsgrad der Bombe viel schlechter.

WEIZSÄCKER: Wie oft entstehen in so einem kleinen Gebiet Höhenstrahlen–Neutronen?

HEISENBERG: Das ist jetzt die Frage der Zündung. Da habe ich folgendes abgeschätzt: Erstens kann die Zündung etwas durch die spontane Spaltung erfolgen. Das ist ja eine Möglichkeit. Da sieht man aber, das reicht nicht. Die Lebensdaür für spontane Spaltung ist etwa 10^{14} Jahre, wenn ich mich recht erinnere.

HARTECK: 10^{14} bis 10^{16}.

HAHN: Woher weiss man, dass 235 spontan spaltet?

HEISENBERG: Ach so, da ist 238 wahrscheinlich auch dabei. Die beiden sind auch ungefähr vergleichbar. Das wären also in Sekunden etwa 10^{22} Sekunden, und wenn ich nun in 10^{-6} Sekunden ein Neutron haben will, dann müsste ich 10^{38} Atome haben; die habe ich natürlich nicht.

WEIZSÄCKER: Man könnte natürlich umgekehrt sagen, wenn bestimmt kein andere Zündungsmechanismus da ist, dann führt man es ganz langsam, und dann geht es los.

HEISENBERG: Ja, ich weiss auch nicht. Vielleicht haben sie so einen Trick gemacht. Dann können sie natürlich Pech haben, sie müssen dann riskieren, dass ihnen die Bombe einen sehr schlechten Wirkungsgrad gibt.

WEIZSÄCKER: Wenn sie es dann noch relativ schnell zusammenführen, ist die Wahrscheinlichkeit, dass es schief geht, doch sehr gering.

HEISENBERG: Bloss wenn sie es da schnell aufeinanderschiessen, müssen sie dafür sorgen, dass es nicht wieder durch Reflektion auseinandergeht.

HAHN: Was würde passieren, wenn die 1/1000 mg Radium da 'reinnähmen?

HEISENBERG: Das würde sicher reichen.

GERLACH: Wenn die eine Hälfte so 85% von der kritischen Grösse ist, wie lange lebt dann ein thermisches Neutron drin?

HEISENBERG: Sie meinen, wenn mal also die thermischen Neutronen von der Höhenstrahlung betrachtet?

GERLACH: Ja, denn die machen doch wieder neü Neutronen in der Hälfte drin.

HEISENBERG: Das lebt nicht lange.

HARTECK: Das hat doch die Geschwindigkeit von 105 cm, ein thermisches. Und wenn wir reines 235 haben, dann ist die freie Weglänge nur einige Hunderdstel Zentimeter. Also wird die Grösserordnung sein etwa 10^{-7} Sekunden.

HEISENBERG: Ja, stimmt, das ist viel zu klein.

GERLACH: Dafür ist aber wieder ein Neutron da.

HEISENBERG: Das läuft weg, das ist zu schnell.

GERLACH: (Für) solche Abfallzeiten war doch mal eine Formel angegeben.

WEIZSÄCKER: Hier ist es ja ausgrerechnet. Ja, in unseren grossen Maschinen sind die Abfallzeiten viel grösser.

(Pause).

HEISENBERG: Kann ja sein, dass sie es doch so machen: sie führen die beiden Teile möglichst schnell zusammen und sagen: "Wir hoffen eben, dass wir nicht das Pech haben, dass gerade, wenn die kritische Grösse überschritten ist, schon das erste Neutron da ist."

KORSCHING: Wenn die Zerfallszeit so ungeheür abhängig ist, dann müsste man, wenn man ganz langsam mit einer Mikrometerschraube die Dinger zusammenschraubt, dann erreichen können, dass man die beliebig langsam abrennen lassen kann.

HEISENBERG: Da kommen Schwankungserscheinungen. Natürlich, im Prinzip wäre das möglich. Dann habe ich also noch eine energetische Betrachtung drangefügt. Nehmen wir an, es sind 4 kg 235 was wirklich 'verbrennt.' Dann werden dabei frei 3×10^{21} erg. Das ist ganz trivial. Pro Spaltung werden ungefähr 3×10^{-4} erg. frei, das muss ich dann mit irgendwelchen Faktoren multiplizieren. Nun kann ich fragen, wie hoch wird die Temperatur in diesem Uran–Block? Da kann man nun einfach so rechnen, dass diese ganze Energie praktisch in Strahlung umgesetzt wird, denn die spezifische Wärme von dem Metal ist von T unabhängig, also die Energie geht etwa mit T.

LAUE: Es handelt sich um Uran–Gas.

HEISENBERG: Ja. Dagegen die Strahlung, die auch in diesem Raum gleichzeitig entsteht, die hat einen Energie–Inhalt, der nach dem Boltzmann'schen Gesetz mit T^4 geht. Also bei hinreichend hoher Temperatur überwiegt immer die Strahlung über alles andere. Also praktisch wird die ganze Energie in Strahlung umgesetzt, und ich kann die Temperatur so ausrechnen, dass ich sage: die Temperatur wird ebenso wie die Neutronendichte exponentiel zunehmen, wieder nach einem Gesetz e^t. Sie wird bis zu einem Maximum zunehmen, bis nämlich die gesamte Energie verbraucht ist. Die gesamte Energie muss bis zu diesem Zeitpunkt dann durch die Oberfläche auch abgeflossen sein, denn die Strahlung geht ja mit Lichtgeschwindigkeit, also praktisch braucht sie keine Zeit im Inneren des Urans. Nun geht durch eine Oberfläche nach dem Stephan–Boltzmann'schen Gesetz pro cm und Sekunde die Energie σ, wobei die Konstante ist—$5{,}8 \times 10^{-5}$ Erg pro Sekunde, cm^2 und Grad⁴. Es muss also das Zeitintegral von Oberfläche F des Uranstücks mal σT^4 gleich der gesamten Energie sein, und dieses Zeitintegral ist bei expansieller Zunahme einfach gleich

$$\frac{F \times \sigma \times (\text{Maximal Temperature})^4}{4 \times (\text{Expansionellen Zunahmefaktor})}$$

und wenn ich nun die Daten einsetze, die wir da oben angenommen haben, dann kommt man auf eine Maximaltemperatur von 3×10^7 Grad. Das ist etwas hoher als die Zeitungen angeben; in den Zeitungen habe ich mal die Zahl $3{,}6 \times 10^6$ Grad gelesen. Es scheint, dass nicht die ganze Energie umgesetzt wird. Es kommt ja vielleicht auch nicht <u>so</u> auf die letzte zehner Potenz an, denn die Bedingungen kennen wir ja nicht genau von der Bombe, und es ist ja auch wieder die Frage, ob diese Zeitungszahl richtig ist. Wenn man wirklich die Kugel zusammen hat, bevor die Sache losgeht, dann dehnt sie sich in den Sekunden auch faktisch nicht aus. Ich habe ausgerechnet, um wieviel die Kugel sich ausdehnt, und da kommt man eben bei 10^{-7} Sekunden erst auf Ausdehnung von Grössenordnung von wenigen Millimetern.

LAUE: Vor allen Dingen kommt ja doch der Strahlungsdruck in Frage für den Streumantel.

HEISENBERG: Der Strahlungsdruck ist bei der Maximaltemperatur etwa 10^9 Atmosphären; das ist an sich irrsinnig viel, aber es reicht eben nicht, um in dieser ungeheür kurzen Zeit schon merklich die Geschichte auszudehen.

HARTECK: Also wie ist die Temperatur ausgerechnet worden?

HEISENBERG: Also ich habe einfach so ausgerechnet: es soll praktisch bei Ende der Reaktion die gesamte Energie, die frei geworden ist, durch Strahlung weggegangen sein. Das ist natürlich deswegen nicht ganz richtig, weil ja auch ein gewisser Bruchteil der Energie dazu verwendet wird, um wirklich die Teilchen zu beschleunigen, also die Moleküle zu bewegen. Aber praktisch spielt eben bei diesen ganz hohen Temperaturen eigentlich die Strahlung die Hauptrolle. Also das meiste von Energie geht in Strahlung, und nur relativ wenig Energie geht in Bewegung von Teilchen. Diese Strahlungsenergie kommt mit Lichtgeschwindigkeit 'raus. Also habe ich gesagt, es muss bis zum Ende der Reaktion praktisch die gesamte Energie, die überhaupt frei wird, durch die Oberfläche nach aussen abgeströmt sein. Die Strahlung von 3×10^7 Grad ist, weil sie Planck'sche Strahlung ist, eine Röntgenstrahlung, deren Maximum bei etwa 1 Ångstrom Wellenlänge liegt, also die genäure Zahl ist 0,86 Ångström. Der Hauptanteil der Strahlung kommt 'raus als Röntgenstrahlung, und wird nun in der umgebenden Luft absorbiert. Das erste, was dann passiert, wird sein, dass die ersten 10 m Luft zur Weissglut gebracht werden. Was man zu allerest sehen wird, wird ein glühender Ball von etwa 20 m Durchmesser sein, der weiss glüht infolge der absortierten Röntgenstrahlung. Diese Strahlung wird natürlich wieder weitere Strahlungen nach aussen schicken, und so wird sich die Geschichte allmählich ausbreiten.

WEIZSÄCKER: Wobei dann allerdings wohl nur noch ein kleiner Teil Strahlung ist von Energie, denn, sowie das Ding auf vernünftigere Temperaturen gekommen ist, dann ist der grössere Teil des Drucks Gasdruck, und dann geht der Rest als Druckwelle weiter.

HEISENBERG: Dann wird die Geschichte am Anfang wunderbar kugel–symmetrisch sein, und dann allmählich erst kommen die Konvektionserscheinungen dazu, und dann wird es kompliziert.

WEIZSÄCKER: Ich würde drei Phasen sagen: eine Strahlungsphase, dann eine Phase, wo zunächst einmal eine Druckwelle erzeugt wird, und nun dehnt es sich mit dieser Druckwelle gleichzeitig aus, und dann wird eine Konvektion einsetzen und das Ganze nach oben getragen.

LAUE: Wieviel Energie geht von vornherein als sichtbare Strahlung weg?

HEISENBERG: Ich vergleiche etwa diese innere Uran–Kugel mit einem glühenden Körper, sagen wir einmal, auf 1000°. Dann würde es um 10^4 mal mehr strahlen im sichtbaren als dieser glühende Körper. Die Oberfläche dieser Uran–Kugel strahlt also um etwa 2000 mal mehr als die Sonnenoberfläche.

WEIZSÄCKER: D.h., wenn man es aus einer Entfernung sieht, in der es so gross ist wie die Sonne, dann strahlt es eben 1000 mal mehr als die Sonne.

HEISENBERG: Es wäre interessant, ob z. B. Gegenstände von dem sichtbaren Strahlungsdruck schon umgeworfen werden können. Das ist durchhaus denkbar. (Pause). Jedes Neutron hat in unserer Maschine die Chance 1/20 eingefangen zu werden im Resonanzkörper, also auf jede Spaltung ist praktisch 1/20 "94" gemacht.

HAHN: Das habe ich jetzt nicht verstanden.

HEISENBERG: In unsere Maschine ist es immer so eingerichtet gewesen, dass jedes Neutron mit der Chance 1/20 weggefangen wurde durch die Resonanzstellen, bevor es themisch geworden ist.

HAHN: Ach so.

PART IV

LOOKING TO THE FUTURE
23 August–15 September 1945

[It is now late August and the "guests" have been interned for some four months. As the transcripts make clear, tempers are beginning to fray on both sides.]

Report 6
TOP SECRET

Capt. Davis for Gen. Groves
Copy No. 1
Ref. F. H. 6

To: Mr. M. Perrin and Lt. Comdr. Welsh
From: Major T. H. Rittner

OPERATION "EPSILON"
(23 August–6 September 1945)

I. GENERAL

1. The principal incident during the period under review has been the receipt of replies to the letters written by the guests to their families. This is dealt with in detail later in this report. Although the letters show that the families are apparently well, the guests are picking on quite trivial remarks in the letters as giving cause for anxiety. They have already asked that further letters should be sent in the near future. In this, as in many other ways, they show complete lack of appreciation of the fact that they are nationals of a defeated nation and seem to think that the Allied military authorities have nothing better to do than to send couriers round Germany for their benefit.

2. As the weather deteriorates the guests are unable to spend so much time out of doors. This is having the effect of making them bored and querulous and will tend to get worse as time goes on. Heisenberg has threatened to withdraw his parole unless some decision is come to regarding his future and that of the rest of the guests. *[It will be recalled that each of the Germans had given his word—parole—that he would not try to escape.]*

3. Professor Hahn was lent a copy of the American magazine Life of 20 August containing articles on the atomic bomb and a number of photographs of personalities, including himself, connected with atomic research going back some hundreds of years *["The Atomic Bomb: Its First Explosion Opens A New Era," Life, 19 (20 August 1945), 87B–95]*. Von Weizsäcker was looking at this journal when he was heard to remark, "Of course they are mostly Germans." The fact that this statement was untrue merely emphasizes the inborn conceit of these people, who still believe in the Herrenvolk. This applies to every one of the guests with the possible exception of von Laue. *[Major Rittner has not commented on an obvious irony in von Weizsäcker's thoughtless remark. Most of the "Germans" in question were Jewish refugees who had been forced out of Germany*

235

precisely because the regime that he had collaborated with had declared them to be not German enough.]

4. The usual biweekly lectures have been given, but they have been confined to general physics. There have been no other technical discussions worth reporting.

5. Major Calvert, Major Smith, Captain David and Lieutenant Volpe, all of the U.S. Army, visited Farm Hall on Sunday August 26th, and dined with the guests.

II. NEWS FROM HOME

1. The American Military Authorities sent Lieutenant Warner, U.S. Army, to Germany with the letters the guests had written to their families, with instructions to bring back replies if possible. This officer returned with a number of replies and visited the guests at Farm Hall on 28 August.

2. Replies were received from the wives of von Laue, Hahn, Gerlach, Heisenberg, Wirtz, and Bagge, showing that these families were well and living under reasonable conditions.

3. Von Weizsäcker's wife had gone to her parents in Switzerland. Harteck and Korsching are bachelors and had not written.

4. The only unfortunate case was that of Diebner. It will be remembered that arrangements were made in June, at Diebner's request, to move his wife and child from Stadtilm in Thuringia, which was about to be occupied by the Russians. They were taken to Bagge's parents at Neustadt bei Coburg. When the American officer arrived at the home of the old Bagges to deliver Diebner's letter he found that Diebner's wife and child had left for an unknown destination accompanied by a certain Herr Rackwitz. Old Mrs. Bagge made it quite clear to the American officer, and also in a letter to her son, that she disapproved of the "goings on" between Frau Diebner and Rackwitz. Diebner has merely been told that it was impossible to deliver his letter and he appears to be satisfied that his friend Rackwitz is protecting his interests in looking after his wife and child.

5. The following points of interest emerged from the letters:

> (a) Frau Wirtz wrote on 30 June that there was a rumor that Heisenberg had been brought to England by plane and there was also a rumor that the rest of them were in the U.S.A. She also stated that Professor Joliot had been in Hechingen. He told her that they would soon be home.

> (b) On 2 July, Frau Wirtz mentioned that there had been a lot of Russians in Hechingen. She also mentioned that Bopp had been dismissed from his post as Deputy Director *[of the Laboratory at*

Hechingen] of the Institute and had been imprisoned for five days. Schüler had persuaded the French to appoint him Deputy Director in place of Bopp. *[Fritz Bopp did not get on with the French. In fact the French Navy imprisoned him for five days. While in prison he was replaced by the spectroscopist Hermann Schüler with whom the French got on better.[1]]*

(c) In a letter, Frau Wirtz stated that the institute was still working and that she and the other wives were being paid 60% of their husbands' salaries. *[The Kaiser-Wilhelm Institute for Physics, which had recently moved from Berlin to Hechingen. It was the location of Germany's main reactor experiments and the place where most of these scientists were captured at the end of the war.]*

(d) Frau von Weizsäcker has gone to Switzerland. She wrote in a letter to Frau Wirtz that she had heard a rumor that their husbands were in England.

(e) Frau von Laue also mentioned the presence of the Russians in Hechingen, and stated that she had heard that the entire staff of the Kaiser-Wilhelm Institute in Berlin, together with all the apparatus and documents, had been taken to Russia.

(f) Frau von Laue also stated that she had heard that Professor Hahn had been elected President of the Kaiser-Wilhelm Gesellschaft. *[This was the umbrella organization under which the different Kaiser-Wilhelm Institutes functioned. The fact that the promotion of Hahn was considered a matter of importance a few months after Germany's defeat says a great deal about the priorities governing German academic life.]*

III. WIRTZ'S RADIUM

1. Reference has been made in previous reports to a quantity of radium which Wirtz was alleged to have hidden.

2. The following conversation took place between Wirtz, von Weizsäcker and Heisenberg on 27 August. A copy of the original text was immediately sent to Lt. Comdr. Welsh.

WIRTZ: I hope the radium is still in Hechingen. I only discovered afterwards that it had been buried under the case containing the uranium cubes (?) *[The question mark is in the original. This is presumably a reference to the cubes of uranium that were to be used as fuel elements in the reactor.]*

HEISENBERG: Oh there!

---

[1] See Walker, *op. cit.*, pp. 186–187, for further details.

WIRTZ: Yes there. The Americans had taken these cubes (?) out and then someone shouted to Geismann (?) *[One of the institute technicians]*: "Must I take the case out?" Geissmann (?) said he didn't care, so they didn't take the case out and threw the rubble back into the hole on to the case—it was quite a job as it was a big case and they had only taken away about a third of the rubble, just enough to get the lid open, and it would have been quite a job to have got it right out. The radium was underneath it; it is still there. Geissmann (?) succeeded in putting one of the cubes (?) on one side whilst those 14 or 15 men were searching. We made a mistake, we ought not to have handed it over. *[Hechingen was occupied by French and Moroccan troops on April 22 of 1945, followed closely by a contingent from Alsos. The episode being described must have occurred at that time.]*

[The Farm Hall files in the U.S. National Archives contain several items of correspondence regarding this section of the report. Major H. K. Calvert wrote a memo to Major Francis J. Smith, War Department in Washington, dated 13 September 1945, in which he summarized a discussion about Wirtz's radium. It states in part:

> This matter has been discussed by Major Smith, Lt. Comdr. Welsh and myself and it was decided that as far as this material is of no direct use for TA *[probably Technical Agency]*, and, as the operation of securing of this material would likely be detected by the French, it was thought best to take no action at the present in regard to securing it. If your office is not in accord with this, please advise.

This was followed in the file by an undated handwritten memo from Maj. Amos E. Britt, Corps of Engineers, to Gen. Groves: "WAC (?) I do not see any need for our trying to get the radium—." At the bottom of this memo, Groves wrote: "Write to tell Calvert OK. G."

On 26 September 1945 Maj. Britt wrote to Calvert to inform him: "This office concurs in your decision not to make any attempt to secure the radium reported hidden at Hechingen."

It is unknown what finally happened to the radium.]

IV. THE FUTURE

1. A number of the guests have discussed their future with me. In the main their ideas expressed to me correspond to those expressed in private conversation with their colleagues, which have already been reported.

2. Heisenberg made it quite clear to me that he wishes to continue work on uranium, although he realizes that this could only be done under Allied control. His main interest at the moment is to get back to Germany to look

after his family, who appear to be in some difficulty as they live in the mountains near Munich, and his wife has no one to help her with her seven children. He is very distressed to hear from his wife that his mother died two months ago, and that a woman friend of his wife, who had been helping her, had also died. He is perfectly prepared to give an undertaking on oath not to work on uranium, except under Allied control, if he is allowed to return to his family. Heisenberg has threatened to withdraw his parole, which he gave me in writing some time ago, unless some arrangement is made regarding the future of himself and his family.

3. Bagge had a long conversation with me regarding his future. He professes to be no longer interested in uranium, and would prefer to concentrate on work on cosmic rays. He says he only took up research on uranium because of the war. Bagge appears to be more concerned about his family than any of the other guests. It will be remembered that he had pictured his wife being raped day and night by Moroccan troops, and when it was clear from his wife's letter that this was not the case, he did not show the relief and joy that I expected. He now complains that his wife is expected to cook for the French troops that are billeted in his house. Like many others he just fails to realize that Germany has lost the war. He is working himself up into a possibly dangerous state of nerves.

4. The following conversation took place on 25 August between Heisenberg, Harteck and Wirtz:

HEISENBERG: I would think that one could come to an arrangement with the Anglo-Americans so that they would on the one hand superintend the work—which they will do in any case—and that at the same time they would see that we got sufficient material.

HARTECK: I can tell you that as soon as that happens we will be looked upon as traitors in the eyes of the masses.

HEISENBERG: No. One must do that cleverly. As far as the masses are concerned, it will look as though we unfortunately have to continue our scientific work under the wicked Anglo-Saxon control, and that we can do nothing about it. We will have to appear to accept this control with fury and gnashing of teeth.

HARTECK: One couldn't get away with that at Hamburg.

HEISENBERG: One could get away with it in Hechingen.

WIRTZ: I don't understand why you are so optimistic about the Anglo-Saxons; Hahn and the others are the same. Surely the last five months have shown you that there is not much ground for optimism.

HEISENBERG: It is true that they have now held us prisoners for five (sic) months, but when you consider the position the Allies are in, then it is understandable. Now that they have got the atomic bomb, and realize what a terrifically important thing they have in their hands, it is not very easy for the politicians to allow German uranium specialists to be at large. You can't expect that.

---

5. The following conversation took place between Heisenberg and Korsching on 6 September:

HEISENBERG: I have the feeling that the only thing they really fear is that we might go over to the Russians. The English say to themselves quite rightly: "They don't know our technical details, but they know so much about the whole business that they could be a very considerable help in speeding the thing up in Russia."

KORSCHING: But these people know us so well by now and know we are not pro-Russian.

HEISENBERG: But if in a year or six month's time we find that we are only able to eke out a meagre existence under the Anglo-Saxons, whereas the Russians offer us a job for say 50 thousand rubles, what then? Can they expect us to say: "No, we will refuse these 50 thousand rubles as we are so pleased and grateful to be allowed to remain on the English side."

KORSCHING: No. We must simply say that if the English expect us not to work for the Russians, then we expect them not to let us starve, but to let us live decently.

FARM HALL   T. H. Rittner
GODMANCHESTER   Major
                                              8 September 1945

[The next report, Report 7, covers the week from the 7th to the 13th of September. In his letter of 26 September 1945 transmitting Reports 7 and 8 to Major Smith (for Gen. Groves) in Washington, Calvert, now a Lieutenant Colonel, stated, "Inasmuch as these reports contain information of an extremely valuable nature which should aid in making the ultimate decision [about the] disposition of our prisoners, it is being forwarded without taking time to add comments however, our comments will follow shortly."]

Report 7
TOP SECRET

Capt. Davis for Gen. Groves
Copy No. 1
Ref. F. H. 7

To: Mr. M. Perrin and Lt. Comdr. Welsh
From: Major T. H. Rittner

OPERATION "EPSILON"
(7th–13th September 1945)

I. GENERAL

1. The guests are now in a cheerful and friendly mood expecting, since the visit of Professor Blackett, an early return to Germany. *[Bagge wrote in his diary (12 September 1945): "Blackett promises that something will happen in 14 days at the latest."]*

[It will be recalled that early in the transcript Heisenberg refers to Patrick M. S. Blackett as one of the "communist professors" the British government was "frightened of." I pointed out then that Blackett was a British naval officer turned physicist who was one of the original British workers on the atomic bomb program, although he did not stay with the program for long. While he was known for his leftist sympathies, to my knowledge, Blackett was never a communist and certainly gave his government no reason to be frightened of him. He was at that time professor of physics at Manchester. He received the Nobel Prize for Physics in 1948 for cosmic ray discoveries using an automatic Wilson cloud chamber that he had developed.]

2. Indeed, on Tuesday, 11th September, Professor Hahn came to ask about the possibility of using two Swiss 20-franc notes, which he has with him, to buy certain little luxuries for his wife.

3. An easing of the letter difficulty is also expected, Professor Hahn having asked for a supply of plain envelopes for possible letters to Professor Blackett, Sir Charles Darwin, Herr Schumacher, and so on. *[This is a reference to Heisenberg's brother-in-law Fritz Schumacher who was living in England—see below for more.]*

II. VISIT OF PROFESSOR BLACKETT

1. Professor Blackett and Lt. Comdr. Welsh arrived at Farm Hall on Saturday, 8th September, in the early evening, staying until after lunch on Sunday.

[As indicated below, with the change of government, Blackett had been appointed to a science advisory committee and had just learned three days earlier of the German detainees. His visit also had an official purpose. The heads of state meeting at the Potsdam Conference in July–August had transferred all decisions about Germany to a Council of Foreign Ministers, made up of the Allied foreign ministers. The council's first meeting was scheduled for September 20, 1945 in London. According to Bagge (diary entry for 12 September), Blackett informed the detainees that after their general deliberations, the foreign ministers would meet in a special session to decide the fate of the German scientists at Farm Hall, though no such meeting ever took place as far as we know. The decision would be relayed immediately to them. "Now we are waiting again," wrote Bagge on the 12th, "and hope that this day will bring something good for us."]

---

2. Before and after dinner on Saturday *[September 8]* Professor Blackett had long conversations in English with Heisenberg, who was an old friend, about the future of German science, about the guests at Farm Hall and their immediate prospects and about Heisenberg's family troubles. *[Blackett and Heisenberg knew each other quite well. Both had worked in the field of cosmic rays (high-energy physics) before the war, and during his several prewar trips to England, Heisenberg had stayed in Blackett's home.]*

(a) Before dinner:

HEISENBERG: We had some discussions with Darwin and he told us that Bohr held very strongly the opinion that everything (concerning the bomb) should be made quite public and not be kept secret; on the other hand, of course, it is such an important thing for politics that it is almost impossible to do away with all secrecy.

BLACKETT: A great many serious people are in favor of it. I think, the arguments are very strong. Of course, if you do, it is a little difficult logically, because why don't you do it with all other armaments? After all, the bomb is only one. Dale, in his letter to the Times, said he believes one should have no secrets about armaments at all. *[Sir Henry Dale, President of the Royal Society and wartime head of the Scientific Advisory Committee to the Cabinet, had written a letter to the editor of the Times (London), which was published on 8 August 1945 (p. 5) under the headline: "Science in War and Peace. The Atomic Bomb. Secrecy or Freedom of Research."]*

HEISENBERG: That is probably not possible to achieve. You will not be able to force the different governments to give their armaments away unless you can actually get a total disarmament of the world, which would obviously be the best thing to do.

BLACKETT: How does one start?

HEISENBERG: Yes, I am afraid that the Russians for instance simply won't.

BLACKETT: The Americans are the only people who have got it and what they do is according to what the Russians do and, clearly, the Russians are behind the Americans. How many years, I do not know.

HEISENBERG: At least three.

BLACKETT: Yes, at least three. I have not had anything to do with it. I was a little connected with it in '41 and I have only recently come in through this committee— you saw it in the paper—which is partly a result of the change of government and things. You have seen the British White Paper?

HEISENBERG: Yes.

BLACKETT: There is a very much more detailed one coming out in America *[the Smyth report]*. It has not yet been published in England.

HEISENBERG: From the things I have seen in the papers and in the White Paper which Darwin gave us, I think that I can imagine all the details of what they have done. The physics of it is, as a matter of fact, very simple; it is an industrial problem. *[There is no reason to believe that he understood the physics much better at this point than he had at his lecture three weeks earlier. The White Paper contains very few details and would, indeed, have been misleading since it describes only the British effort. That was its purpose. Reading it one could get the impression that heavy water was the only suitable moderator for a reactor. For example, the report speaks of the need for "tons" of heavy water.]* It would never have been possible for Germany at all to do anything on that scale. In some way, I am glad that it has not been possible because it would have been terrible for us all. We have started on a very small scale. We were interested in a kind of machine, but not a bomb, the idea being first of all that we knew that there was no chance to do anything on that scale and we knew that in order to separate the isotopes, we would have to do it on that scale. *[Typically, Heisenberg is remembering what he wants to remember and forgetting the rest, such as his wartime lectures about the wondrous prospects for nuclear weapons.]* Then we thought we could, with much smaller industrial effort, actually build a small machine which gives us energy.

BLACKETT: Which is a sensible thing; that is what we want to do.

HEISENBERG: Yes, and we knew also, if we did that, then our government will be satisfied with it and we have had a good time in working on it. Actually, I think we have almost succeeded in doing it. However, all the plants producing heavy water were destroyed by the R.A.F. *[Royal Air Force]* and that was really why it was not completed. But still, from the scientific side, one knows all the things. The Russians certainly also know it, Kapitza and Landau.

BLACKETT: Frankly, there aren't any secrets, there are some tricks of the trade. You know the recipe for making an omelette, but you can't necessarily cook a nice one. There aren't any scientific secrets. In fact, Bohr told me, in '39 there was a discussion on the whole thing in Copenhagen; it was extraordinarily complete. *[This is such a bizarre statement on the part of Blackett that one wonders if he was setting Heisenberg up. In 1939 Bohr was convinced that nuclear weapons were impossible because of the isotope separation problem. The use of plutonium had not yet been thought of, and no successful reactor had been built.]* Tell me about yourself.

HEISENBERG: There are many subjects, I don't know which we can discuss, because, of course, there are some limits. What do you think will happen in Germany at all, for science, etc? Of course, we are interested whether one can make a living in Germany or not. Then the special question: If there is a possibility to have science reestablished in Germany, which would be a practical scheme for, say, our group? I thought that you probably would know the conditions which your government has in mind in this respect and I thought that perhaps within the frame of these conditions we could have a discussion, that we would both agree—within this frame—what we both think would be the most reasonable scheme.

BLACKETT: That we certainly can do.

HEISENBERG: Of course, it is another question whether your advice would be taken by the government.

BLACKETT: I have only been on the fringe of the Control Commission and things. *[After the war an Allied Control Authority was established in Germany by the four occupying powers to govern the country. When the military occupation ended in 1949, a civilian Allied High Commission maintained control until 1955.]* Frankly speaking, it is in a pretty bad mess. We were not very well prepared for the war, but we were probably better prepared for war than we were for the peace.

HEISENBERG: Exactly what Darwin has told me!

BLACKETT: You must remember that we just were not prepared for winning the war and the people did not see far enough. There obviously are, from what I have heard, a lot of different opinions; you get the military against the other people. In fact, generally in America and England there is a formative period going on in which we are really trying to think out what is practical politics. And this question of science; well, all kinds of different ideas have been put about by different people. I have got a perfectly clear idea of my own and I think I can say that a great majority of English scientists agree. Whether our views will be accepted, I don't know. Only a few points are certain. In my view, all universities should be re-started and encouraged with their teaching and their research. It seems to me that the universities are, to a great extent, the key to what is commonly called "reeducation." I believe that ordinary research should go on quite freely. I think it will come—this is only my own personal view—in not too long a time that ordinary academical *[sic]* research and private research in the smaller industries, in the light industries, would be fairly uncontrolled, fairly free. There may be some inspectorate.

HEISENBERG: The first question would be: "What do you think will happen to Europe as a whole?" Then I would probably say: In some ways, I don't fear the controls, because I think, the world is anyway going into a state in which everything is more controlled than it has been before. All industry will be controlled; it is partly socialism, I should say. Socialism always means that you can get things more effectively done by the government taking over the organization. As a matter of fact, we see in Russia and, partly, we have also seen in Germany perhaps how effectively such a thing can work. *[If it were not Heisenberg, one might take this* *evaluation to be a joke. Apparently he means it.]* Insofar I wouldn't mind if there were control in many respects, even to some degree at the universities.

BLACKETT: In a way, we have oversold science. A lot of people are thinking that scientists are magicians who, by themselves, are dangerous; what is dangerous is the great machine which makes use of these things and produces them. We have to prevent people from thinking that scientists as such are dangerous people, that is rather current. Whether nuclear physics will ever become clean open subjects *[sic]* again, we are as much in the dark as you are there.

HEISENBERG: That is what I have felt. And also, necessarily, after the atomic bomb had been dropped, I knew it must be an extremely difficult subject.

BLACKETT: Many of us who knew about it being done just really prayed that it would not come off because it is a great complicating factor. It is going to need a very very great deal of political and technical courage to get the world ... under control.

HEISENBERG: If your people would agree that science in general can be encouraged in Germany and also that, say, nuclear physics is allowed again—of course not preparing a bomb, but just ordinary physics, high tension and all this old game—what scheme, do you think, could be applied in our case, because our case is difficult? Our institute is really in Berlin. Now, Berlin is almost Russian and, therefore, I would understand that your politicians would not like us just to work in Berlin, because they would be afraid that we could in some way combine with the Russians and so on. We have transferred our institute from Berlin to Hechingen, as there was so much bombing in Berlin. Now Hechingen is in the hands of the French. (Laughs) We moved as far west as possible because we preferred to be occupied by you or the Americans instead of the Russians, but then we had the bad luck that the French came. And now they probably would not like us to work in the French zone. On the other hand, in this respect you have managed it very badly because they have just imprisoned part of us *[the Farm Hall contingent]* and the other half stays in Hechingen and can tell the French everything they want. Von Laue, for instance, he had never heard anything about uranium during the whole war, he never knew anything about the machine we were building and Mr. Bopp, for instance—he is a theoretical physicist working in my laboratory—he was acquainted with every small detail in the whole business and he stayed in Hechingen. *[If, as Heisenberg and the others claim, their program had only to do with peaceful reactors, what was there to hide from von Laue, the French, or anyone else?]* And Joliot visited him and (Joliot) told me, he had told Joliot everything about it. *[It appears from the parenthesis inserted by Major Rittner that Joliot told Heisenberg about Bopp, but it is not clear how this could have happened. This would make somewhat more sense if Rittner had inserted "Bopp" instead of "Joliot."]* Well, I could not help it, it was not my business to prevent him.

BLACKETT: My own personal views are that the majority of you should go back reasonably soon. *[Why the "majority"? Who should not go back? It's a pity that*

Blackett does not explain.] Whether you should leave nuclear physics for the time being and work in other things—I don't know whether it will be necessary or not. I don't think there is any danger in working in nuclear physics, provided that no great uranium or ...plants are built. Obviously, the subject is perfectly right. I am quite sure, personally, that the rest of physics and science generally will be clear for you within a fairly reasonable time in Germany. That is my own view and nothing will shake it. Whether the people agree with me, I am not quite sure. I know most scientists do. It is obviously ludicrous to take any other view in the long run.

HEISENBERG: There is still one other question in this connection, this control we spoke about. This is almost a necessary thing in Germany now in order that everything should work in science. We have not got any German government. In ordinary times, I would have gone to my government and said: "Well, this is the situation, I would like you to give me some money," and so on. And this is the difficult situation in Germany as a whole. Since you don't allow a German government, you must rule Germany yourselves. You can't have the cake and eat it and, therefore, if it is done as it seems to be done now, then really it <u>ought</u> to be done and then there should be a control to every institute of physics, either American or English. In any case, there should be some provision made that the English adviser or the local government can see that we get money or anything like that.

BLACKETT: The trouble has been that we were not really prepared for the end of the war and the whole conception of what is going to happen in Germany was very vague, but is now a little clearer since the Berlin conference. *[This is a reference to the Potsdam Conference of July–August 1945, officially known as the Berlin Conference.]* The rough outlines are settled and what is clear and, I think, fundamentally sensible is that the government starts locally, building up, rather than to start right at the top.

HEISENBERG: Yes, obviously.

BLACKETT: I don't know what the group is going to be, whether there will be, roughly speaking, the English, the French and the Russian groups, but, as regards getting resources, there will have to be an economic and financial administration. Presumably there will be largely German personnel with a few Allied people at the top. I should have thought, supposing you and some of your colleagues went back to the English zone, Göttingen or somewhere ... (int.)

HEISENBERG: There are only two universities which are still intact in the English zone, Göttingen and Heidelberg. Of course, Heidelberg is in the American zone. But these institutes are filled with people already, they would not need any more.

BLACKETT: It is a question of mere accommodation?

HEISENBERG: It is a question of accommodation and also the following: I am a professor at the University of Berlin and hitherto I got the money from there, but since the end of the war I have not got any money at all and I don't know whether my wife can live or not. Of course, the same problem arises for everybody, and this is a matter which must be settled in some way.

BLACKETT: Those domestic things, there I would be in a very good position to get something done. I think we can get a reasonable policy adopted. I don't think I should be frightfully worried about the bread and butter side of it. Things are difficult, well, they are difficult for the whole of Europe. I don't think you need to be frightfully worried.

HEISENBERG: There is really very much trouble in my family. You have probably heard that two members of my family have died during the last months when I was away. My mother has died and then a friend of my wife. She did not actually belong to the family, but she used to live with us. These things happen, but I was a little angry with the Americans because, when they took me, they told me they would take care of my family. My wife was not even allowed to write me that my mother was ill. So I could not see my mother before she died. Also, after she had died, I did not get any letter from my wife. I only got it two months later. I think something must be done to see whether the people have anything to eat or not.

BLACKETT: Those are the things that will right themselves in the end.

HEISENBERG: The situation was this: I had lived in Leipzig. Our house was destroyed in 1943 and I moved the family to a cottage I owned before the war in the Bavarian Alps. This cottage was meant for a very few people and at the end of the war there were about 13 people in this very small house. My family is still there. The last day, when this Colonel Pash *[of Alsos]* came to take me to Heidelberg, I told him about the extreme difficulty of the food situation and he was very kind and allowed me to go with an American jeep to some place where I could buy bread for about a week.

BLACKETT: When have you last heard from your family?

HEISENBERG: That was about three weeks ago. That was the first letter I had since we were taken prisoner. Since that time I have felt that something must be done about the family and I told our Major about that. Let us speak about the general questions. If we go back, say to Göttingen, then the terrible question arises where should people live in Göttingen, because all the houses in Göttingen are certainly overcrowded to the last. That would be so in practically every German city. Have you been to Germany?

BLACKETT: Only in Frankfurt. That is pretty bad. What universities are in the American sector?

HEISENBERG: Heidelberg. I should say that Heidelberg would be the best, in so far as the city of Heidelberg is still intact.

BLACKETT: Munich University is gone, is it?

HEISENBERG: That is completely burned out. Well, it may be that in the outskirts of Munich you would perhaps be able to find some room. Heidelberg would be a good place in so far as there are several institutes which are empty now. Then Bothe is in Heidelberg, so there would be cooperation with Bothe. From the accommodation point of view, it would be best if we could simply stay in Hechingen until something is found. I was the only one who had no accommodation for my family in Hechingen, but probably I would be able to find a flat.

BLACKETT: All the people except von Laue and Hahn worked in Hechingen?

HEISENBERG: Even von Laue and Hahn were in Hechingen. We were practically all in Hechingen except for Diebner.

BLACKETT: The institute is running?

HEISENBERG: Yes, the institute is running, as far as I know. If it is simply the problem that it should be avoided that we discuss matters of nuclear physics with the French, of course, we would be able to give our word of honor not to do it or something like that.

BLACKETT: I don't personally believe—that is, when people wake up to the facts—that there is anything in it. There is more published in the American document than we know, at least more than I know. *[As detailed as the Smyth report appears to be, it tells surprisingly little about the physics and engineering of the bomb. For example, it certainly does not give the critical masses of anything. What it does give is a good idea of the extent and scope of the project.]* It is published, it is not secret. There are only about a dozen copies in England yet. It is extremely detailed *[but not compared to Serber's Primer, which was classified until 1965].* It is all about plutonium, separation processes, etc. I don't think there are any secrets.

HEISENBERG: No, from a reasonable point of view there is, of course, not the slightest reason to keep us here whilst Mr. Bopp is in Hechingen.

(b) At this point the conversation was interrupted and was resumed again after dinner, as follows:

HEISENBERG: Apparently there will only be a kind of provisional arrangement now and the final decision about what shall happen to German science will be made later.

BLACKETT: Yes, I think it has been formulated now, but it will take some time to get finally settled. As to your own future, action is going on very energetically at the moment.

HEISENBERG: When do you think that will be decided so that we could perhaps leave here?

BLACKETT: I am a little bit new here to the position, only having heard of your position here three days ago, but I think, I am now in a position to put my weight about. It is the change of government and this new committee. We are very much junior partners in the collaboration with America, and your position here is really

American. It is not a British responsibility. They have said what they want done and we have done it. We have taken part in this bomb project only in a very small way, and we are not, in fact, free agents. One can see, till the bomb was dropped, that there was an argument for our extreme secrecy, but after that there clearly is not. But now the bomb has been dropped and this committee has been formed, it is quite possible to outline a reasonable policy for it and push for it. I think the circumstances are quite favorable for pushing for a decision. The decision may be made in Washington, not here, but, obviously, we will have a say in the decision. The decision should be—one extreme would be that you should all be sent back to Germany, just carry on your ordinary work with some restrictions on nuclear physics. And then I can say to you, there is a possibility of some of you being invited to work in England or America. I don't know, and I don't know whether it will be made and I don't know what the reactions would be. I am quite sure there wouldn't be any compulsion about it. You will be given the option. At least, in my own view. Remember, I am talking very much as a private individual. You know, no one can talk, in a sense, anything but as a private individual, because the decisions are made by an enormous number of people, and you never know what is going to happen. But I suggest this as a possibility. I don't think, it will be many of you, frankly. You and Hahn or somebody like that. What your reactions would be, and what my advice to you would be, I don't even quite know.

HEISENBERG: I can tell you what my feelings would be. I think that von Laue, if he were asked, would always say "yes" because he has his son living in America. That is what I could imagine. But for the rest of us, in some way, we feel that it is our duty to stay in Germany. Now, of course, if the situation in Germany becomes so bad that one should say, "We'll never have the opportunity of doing any reasonable research work," that is a different matter again because finally my life is bound to physics. Therefore, I really don't know, but I feel more inclined to say: "If possible, I should like to be in Germany and rebuild the thing."

BLACKETT: I think you are right. I think, the future of Germany is extremely important for Europe. You are one of the people who can help to get things going again.

HEISENBERG: There is one thing which we haven't mentioned: what shall Hahn do with his institute? First of all, he is the discoverer of the fission. All the experiments which he carried on in his laboratory are pure chemistry of radioactive substances and certainly are not of the slightest danger to anybody.

BLACKETT: No, I agree entirely.

HEISENBERG: The third is that it is difficult to convince a politician that Hahn is not a dangerous person. But just in the discussions which you have with Mr. Anderson *[Sir John Anderson, had been the member of Churchill's cabinet responsible for the British nuclear program.]*, I think it would perhaps be convenient to say it is good that there should be a control in every German scientific institute because, if they make such a control, then perhaps they are less afraid of, say, Mr. Hahn continuing his experiments.

BLACKETT: If I had my way, I would say, subject to a very rigorous, overriding control on heavy industry and production and prototypes, I would leave you free to get on with some work. I would allow you to have uranium in kilograms or so. Whether this will happen, I don't know.

HEISENBERG: Personally, I would go entirely away from experimental physics. But I have had this institute for about five years and I think that these people in some way depend on me and it is nice to go on. The idea always was, I would like to have some small uranium machine going, just so much that one can get very strong radioactive preparations so that Hahn could get ... (int.)

BLACKETT: I agree. And all the biological aspects.

HEISENBERG: Well, we were interested in having a strong activity of neutrons. I thought, I can make some nice experiments with high intensity neutron beams and things like that. This will be allowed?

BLACKETT: It may happen, but I don't even know whether I can get back. We don't know ourselves what the status of nuclear physics in England is going to be. Are we going to have a Shangri-la? We don't know. To you generally as a group I would say: "In general, go back and study the harmless part of physics and be as good as you can and do your very best to build up a new Germany."

HEISENBERG: If I am going to rebuild the institute then, of course, I would be glad if I could rebuild it in this place where it really is going to be. The difficulty is, that, as present, people are in Hechingen. Now I don't know whether Hechingen will, in the long run, be the best place. In some way, of course, it would be best to say: "Let us go back to Berlin where I think we have an institute which is still entirely intact." I think, Berlin would be the best solution in the long run or, maybe, one of the big cities.

BLACKETT: I entirely sympathize with your concern with these practical difficulties. But the real difficulty is on a broader level. There are differences of opinion about this question. There is the view that all scientists are dangerous, and, if we can get over that and substitute for "the scientists are dangerous," "the application is dangerous and wants control," then one can find individual ways of sorting the practical difficulties. The biggest difficulty is the question of the different *[occupation]* zones and the relations with Russia. That is a very serious one. I simply don't know. I don't believe there is a policy about it yet. But it seems quite clear that there is a very, very strong feeling that one must not risk any of you brilliant key people working for Russia. There is an interim period when America alone has it. And in that case it may be sensible to prevent you working for the Russians.

HEISENBERG: Obviously. Of course, I would not mind at all if we should give a kind of word of honor never to join the Russians. But, if in the long run it turns out that living conditions in Germany are just impossible and if then, say, the Russians would make very good offers to some of the physicists, it would be difficult for those to say: "I'd rather starve in Germany than go to Russia." Then the situation is this, that you will get some decision on the principal questions first, and then all private problems will be discussed.

BLACKETT: I think, that, if they can get the right decisions on the main issues, it will be quite easy to take steps to get private things right. But I can't be certain about how the primary decision will go. I don't think it will go adversely in the long run, it may easily be delayed. I just don't know.

HEISENBERG: If it is delayed, that would mean that we would be detained still longer.

BLACKETT: Well, I don't think so. I suspect that you wouldn't be detained (longer). I mean, this is an absolutely pure guess.

HEISENBERG: With regard to my family, I think that something must be done. When I got this letter from home, I felt that, if I only told the Major that I am worried about the family, then exactly nothing will happen. He, perhaps, tells it to the next one, but the next one certainly does no..., so I decided to tell him that I am taking back my word of honor that I would not go out of this house. This, apparently, has had the consequence that they told you about the whole thing, and, insofar, already something very good has come out of it, but I rather think that something must be done about my family, and I suggested, which the Major approved, that one should perhaps try to get in connection with my wife's brother. *[Heisenberg had married into the Schumacher family of Bonn and Berlin. Elisabeth Heisenberg's father was a well-known economist. Her brother Fritz, also an economist, had emigrated to England in 1939. We will hear more about him in a moment.]*

BLACKETT: I know him well, he stayed with us a few days ago.

HEISENBERG: Did he tell you about my family?

BLACKETT: Oh yes, he tried to get in touch with you, but he was not allowed to.

HEISENBERG: Do you think there is a chance that I could get in touch with him? Or do you think that would not be allowed?

BLACKETT: There is absolutely no conceivable reason, in my view, for this complete blackout on information about your being here, and the fact that you have been kept incommunicado from everybody is just silly now. Up to the bomb being dropped there was a blackout on everything, now I don't see the slightest reason from any point of view why Schumacher should not come to see you, but this is not, in fact our responsibility ... (int.)

HEISENBERG: Who is going to decide, Washington?

BLACKETT: Well, it will have to be settled in Washington and I think we are in a strong position to be pretty firm about it and take steps. *[One wonders if Blackett* *knew he was being recorded and that the transcripts were being sent directly to General Groves. There is a double check mark next to this paragraph in the copy of the document that went to America.]* I can see no conceivable objections on any grounds and I cannot understand why there is this extreme blackout about the whole thing at all.

HEISENBERG: Did my brother-in-law tell you what he thinks should be done about the family, because he has been there?

BLACKETT: He stayed with us one night before he went to Germany the last time.

HEISENBERG: Did he know at that time that I was taken away in Germany?

BLACKETT: Yes, he knew you were not in Germany. He did not know where you were. I see no objective reasons at all why Schumacher should not come and see you and should not, if necessary, go over there and get your family going. The difficulty is that it is not, in fact, at the moment our responsibility, but I think, we are in a position now to do something about it.

HEISENBERG: How long ago is it that my brother-in-law has been with you?

BLACKETT: I should guess, about the end of July.

HEISENBERG: That was before he went to Germany?

BLACKETT: He had been before. He is in American uniform on the Bombing Research Mission. You know, he has become rather an extremely successful economist here. He is very friendly with Morrison *[Herbert Stanley Morrison]*, the Lord President of the Council, and is very much in with the Labor Party. He is rather the sort of private advisor to the Labor Party on economics. He is very well thought of indeed. I met him two years ago with *[Sir Stafford]* Cripps. He was one of this new, what I call, neo-Keynesian school of economists.

HEISENBERG: Of course, I would be very glad to see him also. But if you perhaps could just telephone to him and ask him what he thinks one could do perhaps ... (int.)

BLACKETT: I think the chief thing to do is for me to try and get some contact to be allowed in general between you people and other people. And later that will come too. I don't see any reason why other scientists should not come and see you here too. There was laid down a law that no one should see you. We didn't lay it down.

HEISENBERG: That is clear. Only the problem is, it may take again weeks until you get this permission. If you could just telephone ... (int.)

BLACKETT: I don't think Schumacher is in England at the moment, actually.

HEISENBERG: The important thing would be that somebody takes care of my family in some way, the best thing would be if Schumacher could go there.

BLACKETT: I think that can be arranged quite easily. Tell me, on the whole, everybody here would be glad to get back to Germany as soon as possible, roughly speaking?

HEISENBERG: Yes.

(Pause)

I have a few more questions. One is that Bohr has his 60th birthday on October 5th. I would have liked to write to him and to send him a paper which I had intended as a kind of "Festschrift" for him. I don't know whether you think that this would be possible.

BLACKETT: Send it to me and I see [sic] what can be done. If the decision is made that you should be allowed to go back, it will want a visit to Germany from myself or someone to the Control Commission to go round and explore the possibilities of ... . But we got quite a good, very sympathetic scientist on the Control Commission now who will be in charge of that sort of arrangement. I don't think there will be much doubt about the majority of your junior colleagues here. They will be allowed to go back to Germany very soon. But I think there is a possibility of you key people being asked whether you would like to work in this country. I don't know. [We will discuss what happened to these Germans after Farm Hall in the coda to this book; but here, let me point out that restrictions on German nuclear research remained in force until 1955.]

HEISENBERG: There is one thing I would also ask in this connection. Could you just keep us in touch with things. Of course, you are not allowed to tell us about all the discussions. That is obvious. Only it is very difficult just to have to sit here and know nothing about what is happening.

BLACKETT: I cannot make any promises, because I am a bit new to the job. I am fairly optimistic that things will clarify fairly quickly now.

HEISENBERG: This question of my family, do you think that in a short time I could get some statement on the business?

BLACKETT: Yes, you will get a statement quickly.

HEISENBERG: What do you mean by quickly?

BLACKETT: A fortnight.

In connection with the above, it is worth noting the following remarks made by Heisenberg to Hahn on 5th September, 1945:

HEISENBERG: I have the feeling that we shall be nearer getting out of this detention once we get permission to contact my brother-in-law. If I could talk to him, we could achieve a good deal more because, after all, he has got various connections here. And he, on his part, could contact Blackett for instance or somebody like that. Besides, he could perhaps send some food to my family.

3. On the morning of 9th September, Hahn told Professor Blackett of his anti-National-Socialist feelings and willingness to cooperate with the Allies in the following conversation in English:

HAHN: As I know from the letters from Hechingen and Tailfingen, the institutes seem to be allowed to work now as before, but you think, Heisenberg told me, it will not be allowed ... (int.)

BLACKETT: No, I did not say that, I said there is no policy settled yet. There are certain differences of opinion in the Allied Control Commission about German science, but I have no doubt at all that the view of the majority of English scientists and the sensible people is that ordinary academic and pure and fundamental physics will be completely uncontrolled. There may conceivably be some bar on nuclear physics. Already there is a bar on nuclear physics in England. The trouble is that nuclear physics in a big way can only be done with big government support. You have got to have cyclotrons and things like that and so it ceased to be, even in England, a free subject. If I had my way, I would say that nuclear physics in a small way will be as open to you as it will be to us.

HAHN: It was really a more secret subject in your country than in ours, because I published my papers. *[He did publish his measurement in 1942 of the half-life of ^{239}U, which decays into element 93, neptunium (which decays in turn into plutonium). It appeared in Otto Hahn and Fritz Strassmann, Die Naturwissenschaften, 30, 256–260 (1942).]* I told the people that if I do not publish our harmless things, we make the American and English people think we are making bombs, etc. Therefore, we show them that we do quite harmless things, but I told them you never can tell what will happen tomorrow. Therefore I saved the people in my laboratory. They did not go to war because I told them, it was awfully important; of course we knew that it was of no importance at all. We really were cheating our government. The same as my friend Mattauch *[Josef Mattauch, the Austrian physicist who succeeded Lise Meitner in Hahn's laboratory]*, he was just as much a fanatical anti-National-Socialist as I was. *[Hahn's description of all of this is, of course, self-serving and only partially true. When the original uranium group of which Hahn was a member was assembled for the particular purpose of investigating nuclear weapons, the subject of uranium was made a state secret. There is no reason to think that at that time Hahn and the others thought they were "cheating" their government. It should also be recalled that at the popular lecture series given on the 26th of February 1942 before such authorities as Bernhard Rust, the title of the first speaker's lecture—Eric Schumann's—was "Nuclear Physics as a Weapon." Hahn was the second speaker—he spoke about uranium fission—and the third speaker was Heisenberg. That was the lecture at which Heisenberg spoke about the use of reactors to power submarines and about plutonium as an explosive fuel. Does Hahn really believe that they were all there "cheating" their government?]*

BLACKETT: I don't think there will be restrictions. *[One wonders what Blackett* *really thinks about all of this. He is obviously being very careful about what he says.]*

HAHN: I have some people—for instance, my friend Strassmann, and there are other young people—who have really good experience in separating isotopes or, say, indication method *[using isotopes as biological and chemical tracers?]* and I think it would be interesting even for Americans, because I don't know whether they have so very many chemical people with that experience and therefore it is a waste of manpower *[for the German chemists to be unoccupied]*, even in the interest of the Americans. Of course, we would welcome any amount of English and American friends or people who look at our work, perhaps they could even learn something chemically.

BLACKETT: I think that you need not worry very much, that is coming out quite all right: what is annoying to you is the delay. People have been working here very hard to help you and to get things right and my own view is that their effort will succeed quite soon.

HAHN: I am not speaking for myself but for the young people. What shall they live on if they are not allowed to work?

BLACKETT: Are they working?

HAHN: I suppose so.

BLACKETT: That I can find out.

(Pause)

HAHN: My great trouble is really my institute. What is the future of people who really behaved well during the war? I hardly had a man who was in the Party. If I had not discovered this uranium fission, so that the people said, "Oh that is very important," I think I should have lost my place *[position]*.

BLACKETT: I may say that your reputation is very well known over here because of your very fine record as anti-Nazi. It is very much appreciated, so don't you worry.

HAHN: I always think that one might persuade the people that we can be of use and help to the Americans and, of course, English scientists, if they really allow us to continue.

BLACKETT: We are very sympathetic. You have been stopped, through circumstances of war, for some months. Heaps of us have been stopped in our own subjects for six years.

---

4. In the following conversation in English Professor Blackett advised von Laue to return to the rebuilding of Germany and offered to try to arrange meetings with Professor Born *[Professor Max Born, a very*

distinguished German theoretical physicist of Jewish origin who had found refuge in Britain] and Sir William Bragg *[a Nobel Prize-winning British physicist].*

BLACKETT: You are very keen to get back to Germany?

LAUE: Yes.

BLACKETT: It ought to happen soon. It is all very unfortunate. Great efforts have been made over here by the people concerned to get everything cleared up, but, of course, we have had a very difficult position. We have not, in fact, been able to do what we want, and I think they tried to make it as comfortable as you can be under conditions which we did not invent.

LAUE: Some of our younger colleagues have the wish to go for one or two years to America or England. Is that perhaps possible?

BLACKETT: Who?

LAUE: Bagge.

BLACKETT: You mean for ordinary pure science?

LAUE: Yes.

BLACKETT: I don't think that it is any use trying to do that immediately. I think the sensible thing is for you to be sent back as soon as possible and to get going under the best conditions and then perhaps, in a year's time, visits may be possible. But I cannot tell at all about that. I don't think it is worth looking ahead to ask when you will be able to move about. We don't know ourselves when we will be able to move about Europe freely.

LAUE: Do you think it is possible for me and my wife to go to our son at Princeton? *[von Laue's son, Theodor von Laue, studied history at Princeton University and later became a professor of history in Massachusetts.]*

BLACKETT: When I don't know, but there is no doubt the time will come. The strain on transport is extremely great and it will be quite impossible to make a case for you to have priority of transport. That I think is not reasonable to expect, but what I think is reasonable is that we shall try and do our best to make sure, when you are back in Germany, that you have reasonable conditions for working. It is easier for you as a theorist. I can assure you that we scientists in England are very sympathetic. I am very keen that publications will start properly again and also the exchange of periodicals. If you went back to Germany, what would you do?

LAUE: I would go to the seat of the Kaiser-Wilhelm Institute. *[He was still vice-director of the institute for physics.]*

BLACKETT: That is now moved to Hechingen.

LAUE: Only a part of it has moved to Hechingen and I don't think it is possible to go to Berlin yet.

BLACKETT: I feel that you are one of the people who should, in my own personal view, be back there helping to rebuild academic and scientific life. Your reputation is very high as a very wise man who has taken a very good line and you are respected enormously. I remember talking about your attitude to the Nazi movement—do you remember—right back in '38. I feel, you ought to be one of the people back there, trying to get the right views across and rebuilding things. That you would like to do?

LAUE: Yes.

BLACKETT: I would like it to be possible to have wider discussion between you and other people about the future of German science. I do not know why you should not see Bragg. As I say, we have not been in control of this, but I will certainly remember it and see what I can do. Born and Bragg are the two people whom you would like to see again?

LAUE: Yes, and G. P. Thomson *[another Nobel Prize-winning British physicist]*.

---

5. Later on Sunday morning, Professor Blackett had another talk with Heisenberg in which they discussed the guests at Farm Hall, as follows:

HEISENBERG: Weizsäcker is not interested much in going back to the uranium business, he is more interested in astrophysics at present. He was professor at the University of Strasbourg but that of course is finished. *[The Allies took the city from the Germans, restoring it to France.]* But every German government will always be glad to give ... (int.)

BLACKETT: He is extremely good?

HEISENBERG: He is a very good man.

BLACKETT: He wants to go back to Germany?

HEISENBERG: Yes, I think so. He feels the same way as I do *[that]* we are needed in Germany and that we are not needed in the United States.

BLACKETT: I agree with you about that. What about Korsching?

HEISENBERG: He is not a brilliant physicist, but he is a very good experimenter and he had a nice idea on the separation of isotopes. *[Here one of the problems with the German nuclear program is put in a nutshell: the relative lack of respect for experimental physics and physicists on the part of theorists like Heisenberg. We have seen the role that played in Heisenberg's inability to make a functioning reactor.]* He had an apparatus going which was in some way a combination of the idea of Clusius and Nichol and the ... diffusion *["Nichol" is certainly a reference to Gerhard Dickel, who had collaborated with Clusius on a method of separating isotopes—one which we have already discussed.]*.

BLACKETT: He looks a little unhappy.

HEISENBERG: He is the type of man who has never been abroad. He is German and has never come out of his German cities. He thinks it is terrible to stay here, he has no work to do.

BLACKETT: Bagge?

HEISENBERG: His primary quality is great energy. He is a very active man and insofar he has done good work *[sic]*. He has done partly theoretical, partly ... work. I don't know whether you have seen his papers on cosmic radiations. In some ways he is a proletarian type *[Blackett must have appreciated this for he had left Cambridge in the 1930s to teach at Birkbeck, a "workingman's college" in London]*, he comes from a proletarian family and that is one of the reasons why he went into the Party, but he never was what one would call a fanatical Nazi. In some way I like him quite well. He has his great ability to work ... . If I tell him, "You try to build up this apparatus," then I can be sure that in a short time he actually has done it.

BLACKETT: He is mainly an experimenter but does a little theory?

HEISENBERG: Yes.

BLACKETT: Wirtz?

HEISENBERG: He is a much better physicist, he really knows the whole game of physics. He is an experimenter and he has been very helpful to the organization. He is the type of man who knows how to organize an institute. If Wirtz had not been in our institute, we certainly would not have come so far in the uranium business and all the other things; especially when we had to try to get some apparatus, he was the man to organize it. *[One way the project got apparatus was to take it from the so called <u>Beutelager</u>. These were depots all over Germany where scientific and other equipment, looted from the occupied countries, was stored. German scientists could, and did, simply help themselves.]* In some way he is perhaps the most important of the younger people in my institute. He really managed the whole thing, I could not manage an experimental institute at all. Wirtz is very good. He has never made a real mistake in his experiments.

BLACKETT: What was he working on before?

HEISENBERG: He has been working on thermodiffusion.

BLACKETT: What would he go back to?

HEISENBERG: For instance, if we restarted the institute for cosmic rays, that would be nice. Then he certainly would be able to do any kind of work connected with cosmic rays.

BLACKETT: There is nothing special about him, politically or anything else?

HEISENBERG: No, he was politically always on the good side, on our side.

BLACKETT: Korsching is the same, has he always been neutral politically?

HEISENBERG: Yes, entirely neutral. The only ones of our party who have been in the National Socialist Party are Diebner and Bagge. Diebner is of course politically perhaps the most difficult case of all. *[I will discuss more fully in the coda the* *interaction between Heisenberg and Diebner, and what its consequences were after Farm Hall. Here, let me mention that one of Heisenberg's postwar activities was writing testimonials for German scientists and others whom he was willing to proclaim free of Nazi taint. These testimonials were given the nickname <u>Persilscheine</u> or Persil certificates, after Persil, the well known laundry soap. In this colloquy Heisenberg is already beginning to distance himself from the German Army Ordnance physicists who would be difficult to "launder."]*

BLACKETT: He is a physicist?

HEISENBERG: He has got his degree in physics, but he is not really a physicist, he is more a kind of <u>Verwaltungsmann</u> *[administrator]*. He was connected with the <u>Heeres–Waffenamt</u> *[German Army Ordnance]*. He was the organizer of this whole uranium business on a very small scale from the beginning. *[It is a pity that Blackett does not take this opportunity to ask Heisenberg why this "whole uranium business" was in domain of the German Army in the first place. The sense one has of this dialogue, and what happened after Farm Hall, is that Allied officials like Blackett had determined to have scientists like Heisenberg reanimate German science at all costs, and that it was better not to ask too many questions.]*

BLACKETT: Under Gerlach?

HEISENBERG: He was not under Gerlach. In the beginning, it was wholly a matter of this department of ordnance; his man was a General Schumann (?) *[The fact that Rittner has put a question mark next to the name of Erich Schumann indicates that he had not yet understood the organization of the German nuclear project.]* Then Schumann (?) was replaced by Esau.

BLACKETT: What would he do, if he went back, what would Diebner do?

HEISENBERG: That is one of the difficulties. He suggested several plans. The one plan said in some way he could be connected with the administration of scientific work; the other possibility would be that he could be connected with industry.

BLACKETT: There are innumerable thousands of people in Germany who have got to find a new occupation. We have a sort of scientific responsibility for the good people, the not-so-good people will have to find their own way. That is the lot? We have been through all?

HEISENBERG: Harteck is professor at Hamburg.

BLACKETT: He just goes back, I suppose?

HEISENBERG: He just goes back.

III. REACTION TO PROFESSOR BLACKETT'S VISIT

The only detailed reaction to Professor Blackett's visit was a conversation between Heisenberg and von Weizsäcker, showing concern for the future of the Kaiser-Wilhelm Institute in particular and of science in general. Von Weizsäcker, whilst admitting the necessity—in their own interest—to work at present for science on an international basis, admits doubt whether this would be a paying proposition to any nation while national sovereignty still exists.

HEISENBERG: On the whole, I find the situation satisfying.

WEIZSÄCKER: I should say, Blackett is a sensible man with whom one can get down to brass tacks.

HEISENBERG: Yes.

WEIZSÄCKER: Is it your impression that the rest of us might get back to Hechingen long before you and Hahn?

HEISENBERG: That is conceivable, although I think that once the first change in the manner of our detention is made, the whole thing must soon come to an end.

WEIZSÄCKER: There is just one snag; if you don't go to Hechingen while Laue does, the institute will have the most incompetent leadership imaginable.

HEISENBERG: In fact, Wirtz, would have the actual control. We would have to think over carefully how to work that. It will be difficult officially to take away Laue's authority. I might well do it in a friendly manner, saying: "You are the official head, but I recommend that, for the time being, you let Wirtz do everything."

WEIZSÄCKER: I would even undertake a little intrigue to see that Laue doesn't get back either until you get back, but I should say that is rather difficult to bring about, as one should not do too much in that direction.

HEISENBERG: As Laue is the only one who would gladly go to America, it might be possible to do it in that way.

WEIZSÄCKER: I don't mean to be unkind to Laue, but one must think of the institute.

HEISENBERG: My impression is, even if they are still doubtful about us, that it is most likely they will say: "We don't want you to go to the French sector for any length of time, but by all means go there with Blackett and have a look round, but actually we should like to set up the final show in Göttingen."

WEIZSÄCKER: On the other hand, I don't want to give too much power to Wirtz, which he, himself, doesn't want anyway. If for instance Wirtz gets back, then the question arises what the attitude will be towards Schüler. *[This is Hermann Schüler, the spectroscopist whom the French placed in charge of Hechingen. The Germans did not trust him.]* You are the only one who can deal with him. It is obvious that you will take Schüler's place when you get back and, if Wirtz gets there before you, then he would have to be the nominal head. But the whole problem of subsequent relations with Schüler is so unpleasant that it will be pointless for anyone else but you to deal with it.

HEISENBERG: I am actually not pessimistic in this respect as, even if the

Americans did offer me an opportunity to go to America, I could still say that I should have to return to Germany first in order to see how I stand or something like that. Blackett repeated again and again that he was firmly convinced that it would be senseless to control science in the future as science as such is not all that dangerous. Only the industrial use of science presents a danger. He said that one must make a clear difference between science as such and its application.

WEIZSÄCKER: It is not in our interest to say so but—and even Blackett must realize this—if we, in Germany, had withheld the publication of Hahn's discovery for only about a year, then the Americans would not have been able to complete the atomic bomb in this war. *[There are so many more ironies in the atomic bomb story that one hardly knows where to begin. If Fermi had discovered fission in 1934 ... . If Lise Meitner had not still been in communication with Hahn ... . If Frisch and Peierls had not been able to collaborate, and on and on ...]* From the point of view of pure science, it is clear that every limitation is primarily a hindrance to progress. From the point of view of the politician, however, I should say that the discovery of a principle such as a dynamo is of the utmost interest just at the stage before it has been developed technically. Because, if you get it at such an early stage, you have a chance to get ahead of your competitors. On the other hand, once the principle has become common knowledge, then every country has enough competent people to develop it. However, ... not say that now, as it might spoil our own chances but it is true nonetheless.

HEISENBERG: The consequence of what you say would be that <u>all</u> science would be kept a close secret everywhere, but I do not think that things will turn out that way, because for instance, it appears that the Americans have in fact published pretty well all the details of their atomic bomb. *[Not so.]*

WEIZSÄCKER: I am by no means in favor of that happening either. It depends on what one wants. One can say: "We want politics to be international and so we also want science to be international." But if for instance the Americans are afraid of the Russians or the Russians of the Americans, then you cannot say with a clear conscience: "We want science to be international." If the theory I am now propounding were to be accepted, then it could only mean that we should be forbidden to do scientific work in Germany. Thus, obviously, we must work for international science.

HEISENBERG: Yes, I am convinced that the only possible thing for us in Germany is to adopt the international theory.

WEIZSÄCKER: Obviously.

HEISENBERG: The international theory will win in the end, even though there may be five more wars fought with atomic bombs in the meantime.

WEIZSÄCKER: Actually, this would necessitate the abolition of national power. As long as there is anybody who is interested in power, he must try, under present circumstances, to monopolize the results of scientific research. Only when all national power has been abolished, will it be possible to have an international science.

HEISENBERG: Yes, and that is exactly the theory the Americans have adopted and therefore they are gaining practically all the power.

WEIZSÄCKER: But I must say that, what they have really achieved, they have achieved through secrecy.

(Laughter)

HEISENBERG: Blackett thought nevertheless that nuclear physics and uranium physics would be impossible for us for some time so that one would perhaps have to see for the time being what Hahn does is not so defined. It seems to me that one must wangle one's way around these things by clever definitions. We shall have to see what can be done in my institute, but I would just as soon work on cosmic rays.

WEIZSÄCKER: Have you the impression that Blackett has influence?

HEISENBERG: His influence is certainly increasing at present, because he has been a Labor man for a long time and is now slipping into politics. Whether or not he is clever enough to retain his influence later on is unforeseeable.

WEIZSÄCKER: Do you think he is now working for political influence? Is he at heart a scientist who is glad to get back to science or is he prepared to sacrifice science for politics?

HEISENBERG: Certainly partly the latter. Although, of course, he wants to do scientific work, he realizes that he has an influential position and wants to do something in that sphere as well.

WEIZSÄCKER: Yesterday I overheard him saying something which prejudiced me enormously in his favor. I do not know exactly what question he was asked, but he replied that, in his experience, when physicists start meddling in politics, then they become just like other politicians. That seems to me so realistic compared to all other physicists' opinion that I feel that he may be the only physicist who could really be of any use as a politician.

IV. LECTURES

The usual biweekly lectures have been given but have been confined to general physics and there has been no other technical discussion worth reporting.

FARM HALL   P.L.c.Brodie
GODMANCHESTER   Capt. 1.C.
15th September 1945   For Major T. H. Rittner

Report 8
TOP SECRET

Capt. Davis for Gen. Groves
Copy No. 1
Ref. F. H. 8

To: Mr. M. Perrin and Lt. Comdr. Welsh
From: Major T. H. Rittner

OPERATION "EPSILON"
(14th Sept.–15th Sept. 45)

[Blackett's visit inspired Heisenberg to write him a letter restating his position. This letter is a remarkable document for what it reveals and does not reveal. This report is concerned with it.]

---

1. This report deals only with a letter written by Heisenberg to Professor Blackett and the discussions attending the writing of the letter.

2. Before mentioning the letter, Heisenberg discussed the future with Gerlach in the following conversation on the afternoon of Sept. 14th.

Heisenberg proposes the <u>Deutsche Physikalische Gesellschaft</u> *[identified below]* as a central authority, suitable to control physics in Germany and, he hopes, able to overcome the difficulties of the several separate zones of occupation. *[By this time, the Americans, British, French and Russians had partitioned Germany into four zones, each with its own military government.]*

There is also mention of certain funds held by the "Kaiser-Wilhelm Institute" and by Gerlach.

HEISENBERG: <u>Die Deutsche Physikalische Gesellschaft</u> (German Physical Society) is a useful organization, as it would see to it from the beginning that the various zones will not be isolated from each other.

GERLACH: Yes, it has already occurred to me that the <u>Deutsche Physikalische Gesellschaft</u> is an organization which is politically harmless.

HEISENBERG: Quite, it has been in existence since before the Nazis and it has not been nazified.

GERLACH: It hasn't been a member of these various Nazi organizations, but last year or the year before these two Nazi leaders were put in.

HEISENBERG: But that wasn't the Society's fault. Of whom were you thinking?

263

GERLACH: Of Finklenburg in the first place. *[Wolfgang Finklenburg was an experimental physicist who had opposed the Deutsche Physik movement although he was a Party member. He was vice president of the German Physical Society.]*

HEISENBERG: Yes, Finklenburg of course is slightly Nazi (int.)

GERLACH: ...whom *[Carl]* Ramsauer wanted to have for purely political reasons *[to bolster the effort against Deutsche Physik and to obtain increased government funding of physics]. [Ramsauer was a leading German industrial physicist who, during the period being discussed, was the president of the German Physical Society. Although a student of the radical Nazi Philipp Lenard, he had opposed the Deutsche Physik movement.]*

HEISENBERG: Although, I believe, Finklenburg is not of Esau's type.

GERLACH: No, he has conducted himself in this discussion on religion ... (int.)

HEISENBERG: ...very decently. *[This is a reference to the so-called Religionsgespräche (religion discussions) during the war, the subject of which was not religion, but the political ideology of physics. Finklenburg, von Weizsäcker, and other physicists met several times with representatives of Deutsche Physik to defuse the attacks by reaching common agreement on key issues.[2]]*

GERLACH: Also when this discussion *[on "religion"]* was being prepared, he always was on the right side.

HEISENBERG: As far as I know him, I never had the impression at all that he was wildly Nazi. I don't think he would have joined any Jew baiting. I think he was at one time a member of the S.S. I suppose that is true. I would say, the Deutsche Physikalische Institut has now got to choose clever people who can cope with the others. Indeed, I think, one should have people on the executive who can cope with the Russians and also people who can cope with the Americans. They will have to negotiate with the Inter-Allied Control Commission from whom they will have to get fundamental decisions, so that they can carry on and do any necessary wrangling. I would very much like to go to Berlin now, for instance, and have a talk with Sauerbruch. *[Ferdinand von Sauerbruch was a noted anti-Nazi surgeon, and an acquaintance of Heisenberg. His code name for Hitler was "Schimpanski."]* I am sure he could do something for me. By now, he must have one or two things running and then one could probably get quite a decent position in Berlin. My feeling is that the solution which has to come and probably will come is that the Anglo-Saxons will see to it that we shall have again a unified administration for all zones.

GERLACH: With the Deutsche Physikalische Gesellschaft there were also the Gauvereine *[district branches]*. I should think it is quite likely that these Gauvereine as such will carry on independently for the time being until there is a central controlling administration.

---

[2] Beyerchan, *Scientists Under Hitler*, *op cit.* and Cassidy, *op cit.*

HEISENBERG: Besides, there must be a chief whom we can choose ourselves, as in the past, and this chief can then direct affairs all round.

GERLACH: And he would have to try also in the Russian zone ... (int.)

HEISENBERG: Yes, especially there. I would say that the Berlin Gauverein in particular must work with all three at the same time. We still had money from the Reichsforschungsrat *[the Research Board]* left in Haigerloch—100,000 marks. I put it in my institute's account for safety. That, of course, is at our disposal again when it is wanted.

GERLACH: Officially I have half a million marks in a special account in Munich. Whether it is still there, I don't know, of course. That was money which had got lost on its way from Berlin: so I went to Ettal, where the Kultusministerium *[the Ministry of Culture]* was and asked them to sign a letter for me to the Reichsbankstelle *[the Reich's Bank branch]* in Munich asking them to advance half a million marks to the Bayrische Staatsbank *[the Bavarian State Bank]* and to debit the amount to the Kultusministerium. The president of the Reichsbank did it and the president of the Bayrische Staatsbank acknowledged it. From there, it was transferred to my bank, the Hypotheken-und-Wechselbank.

HEISENBERG: If we can save that money somehow, we should do so at all costs and use it for research in some form.

---

3. Early in the morning of 15 September, Heisenberg proposed to Harteck, von Weizsäcker and Wirtz that he should write a letter to Professor Blackett setting out their own wishes for the future which he could bring up at a supposed conference on Thursday, 20th of September. *[This is a reference the special meeting of the Council of Foreign Ministers on the Farm Hall scientists. Capt. Brodie is apparently skeptical that it will take place. In the end, it did not.]*

All believe that their best hope for the future is to work under Allied, including Russian, control, as they will then be given more ample facilities.

There is an undercurrent of German nationalism *[underlining in the original]* in the minds of von Weizsäcker and Wirtz.

This was the discussion:

HEISENBERG: What do you think of my once more putting the different points of view in writing for Blackett? The things we have discussed may well have gone in at one ear and out the other, but if they have been put down in writing, they can look them up again during their discussion and say: "It is like this."

WEIZSÄCKER: What would you want to write?

HEISENBERG: With regard to our institute I would say: I would prefer a wider field of control to a very restricted one without control. If there is no control, we would certainly not be able to do any work on uranium and certainly nuclear physics only on a very restricted scale. That leaves only work on cosmic rays. If there were no control, we would certainly do no work on cosmic rays that needed aeroplanes or balloons either. Perhaps, if we were lucky, we might just do something in connection with the Jungfraujoch. *[This referred to a cosmic ray observatory set part way up the Jungfrau mountain in Switzerland.]* That means all that will really be left to us would be a kind of tuppenny-ha'penny physics with cosmic rays. The Americans have worked in that field so thoroughly that it would take many years' work to catch up technically. That is not really worthwhile. In fact, it would be better for the institute if they allowed a wider field of research and controlled it. If they don't want to do that under any circumstances, then it would be better for the institute if, say, Debye came and worked on quite a different branch of physics. *[It will be recalled that the Dutch-born director of the Kaiser-Wilhelm Institute for Physics in Berlin, Peter Debye, left for the United States in 1940, rather than take German citizenship and do war work for the Germans. Heisenberg was later appointed to Debye's position. There were many Dutch physicists who felt Debye had stayed in Germany too long and who regarded him with suspicion.]* We ought to consider whether we should not simply put that as another suggestion. Then the institute would have to be changed completely to something where there are no problems of secrecy and so on. I would then go back to theoretical physics and we'll have to see how things develop. In favor of control we might also mention that a reasonable control is the beginning of collaboration which, after all, should be desirable for them as well. If we write that to Blackett in a private letter, I don't believe that there is any danger of being hanged by the Werewolves later on. *[Heisenberg seems to be afraid that his fellow Germans will accuse him of collaborating with the "Anglo-Saxons." This is a theme that runs throughout the transcripts.]* We might also consider whether we should not actually suggest that we shall work only on cosmic rays and not on nuclear physics but that we should at least work in Berlin under a control which will make it possible for us to get aeroplanes for our work. There will always be English pilots who can fly them, and, if there is an English or American supervisor in our institute, then he would have the right connections in that quarter.

WEIZSÄCKER: (gloomily) This, of course, could even more easily be interpreted as "collaboration." In any case, I think it is an excellent thing for Blackett to know exactly what we would like. Didn't you tell him?

HEISENBERG: Well, I told him more or less what we have discussed tonight. (Pause) If we had to work in a field that has been exhausted, then we would have to interest ourselves in experimental precision methods. I am a completely unsuitable person to organize that. But Debye could find solutions and entirely different ways to be able to work in some field not considered dangerous.

HARTECK: Then comes the question: Do they want us to start highly qualified work in Germany again?

HEISENBERG: Blackett certainly does.

HARTECK: One could imagine some physical institute in Hamburg on the lines of the <u>Reichsanstalt</u> *[the Bureau of Standards]*. I don't believe that the English would allow that.

HEISENBERG: I am not so sure. The <u>Deutsche Physikalische Gesellschaft</u> ought now to do this: Firstly, they ought to tell the <u>Gauvereine</u>, each <u>Gauverein</u> should get on good terms with its local government. But, secondly, the <u>Physikalische Gesellschaft</u>, as a whole continues to exist. The others are not likely to forbid that, because it is a very good position politically. And now, if they are clever, they'll get people onto their board who know how to deal with the various people. There will be enough to deal with the Americans, but there ought to be somebody who can somehow deal with the Russians. In that way, we'll have to see to it that there is a central scientific organization in Germany. I don't believe others will prevent that.

WEIZSÄCKER: We have been told that the future of German research is still under discussion. We don't know what the results of these discussions will be. If they decide that research in Germany is not to be encouraged, there is no future for our institute. Apart from that, it is, of course, as well if Blackett knows in time what we would like to do in case we get permission to work.

HARTECK: Will they, for instance, allow us to continue work on the benzine syntheses (<u>Benzinsynthesen</u>) in the chemistry of carbohydrates? *[This is probably a reference to synthetic fuels. "<u>Benzin</u>" in German is equivalent to the American word "gasoline."]* If there is anything that interferes in the slightest with their own business, are they likely to prohibit it?

HEISENBERG: They will prevent all types of organization which will again make Germany an independent industrial power.

WEIZSÄCKER: These things will change. If they now, for instance, forbid research, it is important that we do university work, that is train young people who actually can't do anything now. But in five years' time, when they have learned something, research may perhaps be allowed again after all, and then we shall need these people. I am quite convinced that after a few decades research will be done again in Germany on a large scale. So now the main thing is to bridge the gap during which, perhaps, it won't be possible.

WIRTZ: Well, I think, we might just as well ask for as much as we can hope to get done for us. (Pause) To return to the letter to Blackett, I am all for telling him, we would like to work on as many different subjects as possible and we would have no objections against some sort of control. Perhaps you could add that he should keep this letter as private as possible.

HEISENBERG: Naturally, the Commander and all these people will see it.

WEIZSÄCKER: It does not matter if they see it, only the Werewolves shouldn't. I would like to know if any of you has any doubts about this letter because that is a matter on which we can decide now.

HEISENBERG: I wanted him to have this letter before Thursday's meeting *[the "supposed conference" of September 20, referred to above by Rittner and Brodie]* because it is important that he should by then thoroughly understand the position. I am a little afraid that the easiest solution for the English would be to say: "They must not do nuclear physics. They may work on cosmic rays." After all, that is the easiest way out for them and one should not make it so easy for them.

WIRTZ: I think, if we can keep things going now, then later on perhaps we might achieve more instead of being tied to the best we can get for ourselves at present.

HEISENBERG: I don't know about that.

WEIZSÄCKER: I think that, with people like Blackett, one should ask for things on a grand scale and, above all, make proposals that will keep us in permanent contact with Blackett or some of their people. After all, that is quite a good thing.

HEISENBERG: Yes.

WEIZSÄCKER: I would say, it is fundamentally very good for us if an Englishman is obliged to be personally present in our institute all the year round.

HEISENBERG: Yes.

WEIZSÄCKER: I would, therefore, say, the control is not at all unpleasant, but rather it is desirable, just as I think it desirable that the Allied Government of Germany lasts as long as possible so that the Anglo-Americans have full responsibility for whether the people starve or not. Of course, we must get a man who is not too awful. But perhaps Blackett can see to that. Naturally, if we get a man like Diebner, that would be intolerable. I would not like to have the Commander of course; he again is too high up for that, nor would I even like to have his son. *[Perhaps Lt. Comdr. Welsh had a son engaged in these activities.]* The only problem is whether that will later be held against us as "collaboration."

HEISENBERG: Actually, I think so.

WIRTZ: If the whole thing is properly worded I see no danger.

WEIZSÄCKER: Of course, one could consider starting a big low-temperature laboratory, if everything else fails.

HEISENBERG: That would have to be in Berlin as well and I don't know at all whether one shouldn't perhaps say, the best solution is to go back to Berlin in a year's time or so. Wouldn't it really be the best solution if we were to work in Berlin on cosmic rays and low-temperature physics and be controlled by an American as well as by a Russian?

WEIZSÄCKER: Now, that's ideal. Probably that won't be possible, that would be too much to expect. Because once they let us go to the Russians, then they'll let us work on uranium. That is the same thing.

HEISENBERG: Through my letter to Blackett, I want to prevent him from adopting the solution which is easiest for the English. Such a solution annoys me as it would merely mean that we may go home and they would take no further interest in us. That is just what I want to prevent. I would say in that case collaboration with Hahn's institute is also a point in favor of that as it would facilitate a more favorable solution insofar as the English will say, from the point of view of prestige, it is hardly possible to stop Hahn from working on uranium. That would be so niggardly that they could hardly bring themselves to do it. If we could now continue to work together with Hahn on such things under control, then they'll say to themselves, "We'll have to give permission to Hahn, we shall have to control him anyway; we might as well allow the whole group Hahn–Kaiser-Wilhelm Institut to continue to work under control. That does not apply to the rest of German science which shall be free, but this is a special case. That is perhaps after all the most reasonable solution."

WIRTZ: I am pessimistic on that point, because they are so terribly afraid of German research.

HEISENBERG: In any case, if they discuss whether Hahn should go on working on uranium, all physicists on the American commission, on which Oppenheimer is, or the people here will say: "Yes we'll have to give him permission, we can't do anything else." *[Oppenheimer was at that time on the Scientific Panel of the so-called Interim Committee formed to deal with all the aspects of atomic energy. It is highly unlikely that he knew any of the details about the detainees at Farm Hall.]*

HARTECK: Are you sure?

HEISENBERG: I am certain about that.

WEIZSÄCKER: There is a certain trend in the world which is now beginning to appear; let us call it "internationalism." There are quite a number of people, especially in England and America, who think that way and I don't know at all whether they're doing their countries any good. But they are the people to whom it is best for us to attach ourselves and we'll have to support that. Those people who don't want to keep any secrets about the atomic bomb are the people who are useful to us.

---

4. Later on the morning of the 15th *[of September]* Heisenberg, having read his letter *[to Blackett]* to Hahn, discusses it with him.

He says that the letter *[which we shall see in full shortly]*, in fact, implies that, unless he is generously treated by the Western Allies, he will seriously consider working for the Russians.

HEISENBERG: How do you feel about the whole thing?

HAHN: I am afraid they want to stop us doing nuclear physics.

HEISENBERG: In your case, there is a good chance that they won't do that. It would be very hard for them, also from the point of view of prestige, to stop you from working, as without any doubt you discovered the whole thing *[with considerable help from Strassmann, Meitner and Frisch]*.

HAHN: I think that what you have written there *[in the letter to Blackett]* is excellent. Do you think it would be wiser if Debye joined us?

HEISENBERG: I would say that, if they are determined to curtail nuclear physics, then Debye is certainly a good solution. Debye would then reorganize the institute completely to suit his own work ... (int.)

HAHN: No, I mean that you should be there, only that a man like Debye, being definitely "non-Nazi," should be there as well. *[Here again is the term "non-Nazi." We don't have the German original, but the word is probably* <u>unnazi</u>*, which, as indicated earlier, may be a play on words and is not equivalent to "anti-Nazi."]*

HEISENBERG: Yes.

HAHN: I don't believe Debye would ever go to Hechingen.

HEISENBERG: Certainly not to Hechingen, but perhaps, say, to Heidelberg. Actually, he would perhaps prefer above all to go back to Berlin. In some ways, Debye's return would of course be the simplest way to get over the difficulties. If Debye takes over, then he has got to do everything and then it is a question whether I should simply not go to Munich or do something else. After all, why shouldn't I simply do theoretical work? I would say, if nuclear physics can be done in a big enough way, or cosmic rays with sufficient means, then I should, of course, like that. *[It should be noted that cosmic ray research involved the study of elementary and nuclear particles at energies often far above 10^8 electron volts, which was higher than the energies then attainable in accelerators.]* If however, one has to work with a few shabby measuring tubes (<u>Zaehlrohr</u>) *[these are counting tubes, for counting numbers of detected particles]* on subjects which have already been exhausted by the Americans, that just is not worthwhile.

HAHN: Can you do work on cosmic rays in Germany at all? Have we got mountains 3,500 and 4,000 meters high?

HEISENBERG: What I should like would be firstly: I should like to put apparatus into an aeroplane. There is an immense number of aeroplanes in Germany which, of course, cannot be used by Germans. But I don't at all see why any American pilots, who have to practice flying anyway, should not take up with them some apparatus or, for instance, one could send people with apparatus up to the <u>Jungfraujoch</u>. I think that this slightly more international cooperation is definitely the right thing. I had imagined doing nuclear physics and cosmic ray work in greater style in peace time. To do modern physics in a small way is of no use at all. There is a great temptation now for the Anglo-Saxons to say: "These people shall, of course, continue to work. We don't want to take away all their chances, but these big technical things are quite out of the question for them." That means, we are permanently put on ice and can do physics on the Roumanian or Bulgarian scale. But that is exactly what we must endeavor to prevent these people from doing.

Then it is greatly preferable that they, themselves, should take the responsibility for what is done in Germany, and then it will be in their own interest to see that it is done properly.

HAHN: Actually, it ought to be quite agreeable to the English at least, if not everything is done in America.

HEISENBERG: I would also say the English ought really be interested in rebuilding Europe, and they are bound to say to themselves—I am not going to tell them that, because then they would detain us still longer—if the English tell me, "At the very best, you will be allowed to work with tupenny-ha'penny apparatus" and the Russians say "You will get an institute with a yearly budget of half a million," then I would consider if I shouldn't go to the Russians <u>after all</u>. Because that is simply idiotic. After all, we are there to work sensibly. Up to now, it is certainly so that in these scientific matters the Russians are much more generous than the English. I am firmly convinced of that, because the Russians have already learned the modern way of thinking which the English, of course, have not up to now. I don't know at all that the future of Europe does not lie with the Russians after all. What impressed me again so very much in that direction recently was the reaction of the very nice American Major who said: "Yes, we Americans want to go home again. We don't want to see those destroyed towns. We are going to send our boys home and we are going to leave here just as many as absolutely necessary, but we don't want to have anything to do with the whole business." Well, my God, if that is what they want, then we are <u>bound</u> to work with the Russians.

HAHN: Unless the English take the initiative.

HEISENBERG: They can't, they are much too weak. They can't do anything against the Russians.

HAHN: If we could achieve being allowed to carry on under English supervision, that would, of course, be by far the best.

HEISENBERG: Yes. I find, there are only these two possibilities: either the Anglo-Saxons take so much interest in Europe that they really want to hold it, and holding in that case means that they take part in nearly everything which is being done and see to it that it is being done properly. But if they don't want to and say, "No, for all we care Europe can go bankrupt," then there is nothing left for Europe but to turn to Russia. Because the Russians wouldn't let it go that way, they would do something. I think we ought to make it a little more difficult for them to take the line of least resistance, and naturally the line of least resistance is: "Well, yes, we will allow you Germans to do a little physics again on a small scale." But that is exactly what we don't want.

HAHN: But, of course, it is dangerous to threaten them with Russia.

HEISENBERG: We can't do that. After all, that is implied when I say, I don't want to do petty physics. Either I want to do proper physics or none at all. If the final decision is that I can't do proper physics and I go back to Germany again, naturally they, too, will realize that I am then going to consider doing physics with the Russians after all.

5. The letter *[to Blackett from Heisenberg]*, the original of which was passed on on September 17th to Lt. Comdr. Welsh:

Dear Blackett,

After our recent talk, I thought matters over and came to the conclusion that it might be well to tell you about the special situation of my institute before we discuss the future of our institutes in general. The Kaiser-Wilhelm Institut for physics in Berlin was built by Debye *[in 1936]* and was under his direction until January 1940. After Debye's departure, Diebner was in charge of the administration for some time. He was responsible for the conversion of the institute to nuclear physics. From spring 1941 onwards, I was practically in charge and later also officially. Since that time, the bulk of our work was done on uranium and on nuclear physics in general (high-tension apparatus); besides that, work was done on cosmic rays, as you will know from our book *[Kosmische Strahlung, edited by Heisenberg (Springer, Berlin, 1943)]* and also work in the various departments (x-ray laboratory, low-temperature laboratory and optics) was continued on a reduced scale. As the first aim of our scientific work we had intended to build a <u>Brenner</u> (burner) *[reactor]* with D_2O *[heavy water]*, graphite and uranium metal. This burner was to be a strong source of neutrons. In wartime, naturally, these results would have been followed by technical developments which would have been aimed at a practical use of the energy. We had, however, hoped that the burner could in peacetime be used for the preparation of powerful radioactive substances for chemical research at Hahn's institute and also perhaps at my institute with neutron beams of great intensity. The quantities of D_2O, graphite and uranium at Haigerloch and Stadtilm would probably have been just sufficient for the construction of the burner.

The first question regarding the future of the institute is whether Debye will return and take charge once more. We managed for Debye to be still in charge officially, therefore it depends only on him whether he is willing to take charge again and, if so, there would probably be no political difficulties since he is of Dutch nationality. If, on the other hand, Debye does not return, the question of the future subject of our research will arise. If we are to choose between the following two possibilities, either a very much reduced field of work without control or a wider one but controlled by Allied physicists, then I should certainly prefer the latter possibility for the following reasons: If there were no control, policy would probably prohibit work on nuclear physics in general. In that case, provided the line of research is not completely changed, the institute could only work on cosmic rays. And in that case any collaboration with Hahn's institute would stop. Besides, in the field of cosmic rays all possibilities would be closed to us if they involve considerable technical means; i.e., experiments with aircraft and such like. Then the institute would have to rely on working with the most modest technical means in a field in which others have already done such thorough work that the result would not justify such an effort. In that case, it might be better to switch over the institute to quite different subjects with which I have nothing to do. If, however, work on nuclear physics could be continued, at least with high-tension apparatus, so that the collaboration with Hahn's institute would continue, I would certainly be prepared to put up with control. Then perhaps one might be able to get the support of the authorities for experiments on cosmic rays so that a considerably greater technical effort becomes possible. After all, in the long run, it will be possible for physicists who are themselves interested in science to exercise a control.

The question of the location of the institute can probably be decided only when the future of the "Kaiser-Wilhelm Gesellschaft" as a whole is being discussed. Perhaps Hechingen is a suitable interim solution which, however, should be replaced as soon as possible by a permanent solution. Probably there would be empty institutes in Heidelberg and Göttingen which could be used, but no living accommodation. The institute in Berlin is undamaged and is occupied by American troops. It is possible that the Russians had previously removed apparatus and equipment. Perhaps it would be easier in Berlin to get our old flats back, but the specific difficulties of Berlin are not in favor of that town.

I hope, we shall be able to discuss all these problems once more when the fundamental questions have been settled.

With kindest regards,

Yours (sgd) W. Heisenberg

[According to Bagge (diary entry of 19 September), Major Rittner had fallen sick and returned over a week earlier to his family in London. That left only his second in command, Capt. Brodie, as their overseer, and it is he that now signs these reports.]

Farm Hall	(signed) P.L.c. Brodie
18 Sep 45	Captain
	For Major T. H. Rittner

[It is a pity that we do not have Blackett's reaction to Heisenberg's remarkable letter. Did he have available to him the intelligence data from the Alsos mission so

that he would understand what it meant when Heisenberg notes that Diebner "was responsible for the conversion of the institute to nuclear physics"? What, if anything, did Blackett make of this? Did he realize that Diebner represented German Army Ordnance, which had taken over nuclear research? More significantly, what did Blackett make of the sentence, "In wartime, naturally, these results [the reactor experiments] would have been followed by technical developments which would have aimed at a practical use of the energy"? Did Blackett ask himself how would the energy from a reactor be used practically in wartime? It is very unlikely Blackett knew that on February 26, 1942, in the course of his address to the Nazi Party officials, including Bernhard Rust, Heisenberg said, "As soon as such a pile [reactor] begins to operate, the question of producing the explosive receives a new twist: through the transmutation of uranium inside the pile a new element is created (atomic number 94 [plutonium]), which is in all probability as explosive as pure uranium-235, with the same colossal force."]

PART V

LOOKING TOWARD HOME
16 September–11 November 1945

[After Blackett's visit, the Germans were sure they were about to go home. They did not, at least for four months. The Council of Foreign Ministers, established by the Potsdam Accords to oversee occupation policies and to formulate peace treaties with the former Axis powers, met for the first time in London beginning on September 20. Apparently a special session of the Council (or part of a session) was scheduled for September 20 to decide the scientists' fate and other matters. The special session did not take place, for the two meetings held that day to formulate peace treaties for Finland and Romania broke up without agreement. Capt. Brodie traveled to London the next day to see what had happened. When he returned, he informed the detainees nearly in passing that no decision had been made.[1] When the delay began to register, the situation, as the following report shows, grew very tense.]

---

[1]Bagge, *Diary*, in Bagge, Diebner, and Jay, *op. cit.*, p. 61.

Report 9
TOP SECRET

To: Mr. M. Perrin and Lt. Comdr. Welsh
From: Major T. H. Rittner

OPERATION "EPSILON"
(16th–23rd Sept. 45)

I. GENERAL

1. This has been a difficult week, chiefly spent in placating Heisenberg, who had expected rather more from Professor Blackett than was perhaps justifiable.

2. Heisenberg's letter to Professor Blackett—mentioned in F.H. 8 *[Report 8]*—was delivered to Lt. Comdr. Welsh on September 17th.

3. On 20th September, I *[Capt. Brodie]* had an involuntary conversation with Bagge *[not given here]* in which I tried to prepare the ground should there be, as I expected, no immediate result of the Conference *[of Foreign Ministers]* supposed to take place on that day.

II. THE MEETING ON 20TH SEPTEMBER

4. On 21st September, I went to London at the request of the professors to find out the result of the meeting.

5. On my return, without immediate permission to return everyone to Germany, a tense situation arose.

6. Professors Hahn, Heisenberg and Gerlach impressed upon me that the vital question was really the future of Frau Heisenberg and his *[sic]* children. Unless they were looked after, Heisenberg would feel morally bound to withdraw his parole and the rest would loyally do likewise.

7. I gained a breathing space by repeating that the meeting was still in progress and that a definite decision was expected shortly. It is always disastrous to give a definite date, as, when nothing happens on that date, the effect on our guests is unfortunate.

8. I also agreed to get in touch with Professor Blackett through Lt. Comdr. Welsh to see whether he had made any arrangements with Heisenberg's

brother-in-law, Herr *[Fritz]* Schumacher at Oxford, to look after Heisenberg's family.

9. Heisenberg discussed this conversation withi von Weizsäcker, Wirtz, Korsching and Diebner that evening without, however, referring to Herr Schumacher:

HEISENBERG: We were talking about my family and, generally speaking, the result of today's meeting was such that one still doesn't know what they want. This is certainly a plausible result, but not one one might have wished for. There will be another meeting next week and it is hoped that a decision will be taken then.

DIEBNER: Nobody knows what, I suppose.

HEISENBERG: Everything up to now seems to point towards the one thing that, if anything, will be decided at all, it will be decided that we should go home. But the point is that they cannot make up their minds to do that.

KORSCHING: Is this an all-British committee?

HEISENBERG: On the contrary, Blackett told me, I should realise that in these matters the British are very much playing second fiddle.

WIRTZ: I think that one should turn completely to America.

HEISENBERG: That is why it is a pity that we have so little connection with leading Americans. To talk to a mere American major is of no use. *[Unbeknownst to him, General Groves, as his underlining and initials on the reports show, was reading every word.]*

WIRTZ: The tragedy is that we are in England. We should either be flown to America or be sitting at American Headquarters in Germany. But here in England we are right off the map.

HEISENBERG: Yes, there is something in that.

DIEBNER: What did the British hope for in bringing us here? If they don't have any influence, what does it all mean?

HEISENBERG: They obviously have some influence.

WEIZSÄCKER: One should nurse friendly relations with both of them. The Americans may be stronger, but Britain may have more to say during the coming years in determining our fate. I have the feeling that the Americans are less interested.

HEISENBERG: At any rate, the British have a really vital interest in Europe, because if they do not succeed now in making a lasting arrangement in Europe, they will be in for it next time. This is quite obvious.

10. On Saturday morning *[Sept. 22]*, Heisenberg asked me whether I could not bypass Lt. Comdr. Welsh and telephone to Professor Blackett direct. I refused, but explained that it was much better not to bother Professor

Blackett unduly who was doubtless doing all he could and that veiled threats such as a withdrawal of parole would undoubtedly have the effect they least desired. In a conversation later on, Heisenberg expressed his annoyance to Hahn as follows: "I can wait a bit, but it is nevertheless annoying that the Captain *[presumably a reference to Captain Brodie, who is preparing these reports for Major Rittner]* may not telephone Blackett."

III.TECHNICAL

11. On Tuesday, 18th September, Harteck gave a lecture on "Atmosphere," based on the work of Fowler and Milne.

12. There has been nothing else of technical interest during the week.

FARM HALL   (signed) P. L. C. Brodie
GODMANCHESTER   Captain,
                                             For Major T. H. Rittner
                                                          27 Sep 45

[This report contains a technical appendix, which is presented here. It concerns a method of producing heavy water invented by Harteck.]

Copy No. 1
Appendix to F.H. 9

To: Mr. M. Perrin and Lt. Comdr. Welsh
From: Major T. H. Rittner

OPERATION "EPSILON"
(Production of Heavy Water)

1. On 23rd September Harteck described to Hahn a method of producing D_2O *[heavy water]* which he and *[Hans]* Suess had discovered and which is considered more economical than any other method known to them.

2. As adequate facilities for translation were not available at Farm Hall, this has been done in London.

3. The translated conversation was as follows:

HARTECK: It is a question of an ammonia distillation. The most expensive part is the vessel for distillation. Then you have to take some substance which has as high a vapour pressure difference as possible at the highest possible pressure. Apparently that is ammonia. Moreover, that has three hydrogen atoms and will exchange with water when you want.

HAHN: Does the ammonia gas flow straight through the water?

HARTECK: No, you continually fractionate the ammonia and exchange the ammonia which has been regenerated with water. You have a column in which there are 5 or 10 tons of ammonia.

HAHN: There is more light ammonia above ...

HARTECK: And the heavy is at the bottom. Then you take the ammonia, the light upper fraction, allow it to exchange by flow against water until it has its old content. So all I need is really just a few tons of ammonia which is certainly not dear *[expensive]*.

HAHN: Do you then impoverish the water?

HARTECK: No, it is any old water.

HAHN: And the ammonia that you get again from the water ...

HARTECK: That is again normal.

HAHN: And the light ammonia just disappears?

HARTECK: No, the light ammonia is not lost.

HAHN: Well, then the hydrogen exchanges ...

HARTECK: With the water and is driven out again later. It is as if for example you take 20 percent out and 80 percent is normal, then you carry out the exchange. It is just a question of economy.

HAHN: How much does it affect it if you have 5 tons of ammonia? How long must you distil this fractionally so as to get a reasonable enrichment at the bottom?

HARTECK: One step is 2.4 percent. You would have to have a column about 80 meters high if you want to get twelve-fold enrichment.

HAHN: For one step ...

HARTECK: No, the important thing is how many kilowatt-hours must you expend in order to get 1 gram of heavy water.

HAHN: I believe yours is cheaper. I would like to know just how you work it. Would you put 12 columns side by side?

HARTECK: No, one giant column. Diameter about 2 meters, height 80 meters. It works like this: If I have cold water and hot water, say at 5 and 20 degrees, then I have got an evaporator at 20 degrees and condensor at 5 degrees.

HAHN: And in what form is the ammonia?

HARTECK: Liquid ammonia.

HAHN: Under a certain pressure then?

HARTECK: Yes, at 9 or 10 degrees it has a pressure of 4,000 millimeters *[of mercury]* or so. That's the best.

HAHN: Then you get a few atmospheres on it?

HARTECK: Several atmospheres. In a column with so many bends you have a pressure drop of about 1½ atmospheres. You can estimate that straight away. And this fall of pressure of 1½ atmospheres corresponds to several degrees difference of temperature. And then it boils down to this: I can heat with hot water and cool with cold water. But I could, however, have a heat pump, that is, a refrigerator, and if I have this, then I need continuously 2,000 kilowatts. To make 5 tons per annum. For 1 gram one needs 3 to 4 kilowatt-hours. That is, if you use a heat pump. If you use hot and cold water, it is very much less and of course costs very much less. I only got that worked out after we had designed the column.

The procedure is cheaper. It seemed so to everybody that I spoke to about it according to any means of estimating. Yet apparently these people work with graphite blocks and not with heavy water. *[This is the first evidence in these reports of the Germans' learning that the American reactors were designed to use graphite as a moderator.]* But perhaps heavy water has difficulties, if it picks up neutrons and becomes radioactive. And if one has in fact played about far too long with the thing, like I have, and has a definite solution, it is not at all good, to be stopped in such a way. Don't you think so?

HAHN: Yes, I agree.

HARTECK: Now the question is, in Germany apparently we cannot do any more.

HAHN: Certainly not with heavy water.

HARTECK: What I would really like, would be, if I could have a talk with one of the physical chemists, that is Rideal *[?]* or H. S. Taylor. If they have not already got this process, then I certainly would not show up badly. *[H. S. Taylor was a physical chemist at Princeton. He had developed a method for producing heavy water that bears a resemblance to Harteck's.]*

HAHN: Agreed. You talk to them and they say to you, "Yes, we knew that long ago," and they go out and take out the patent afterwards, or they would use the process.

HARTECK: Oh, a patent application is all the same to me. But all the same one would at least like to be able to collaborate a bit or to come a bit more in contact with the scientific people. We became so discreet in Germany. It is a pity that we put so much time into the thing and this is the result. We have built several columns and the I. G. *[Farben]* constructed ...

HAHN: You would really like Taylor or Rideal to come here? They do not let anybody come in here, that is the shame of it.

HARTECK: But this you could say to the people, that of all that has been done so far you got the impression that the process that we have for heavy water is better than what they have by an appreciable factor. So it is rather an act of friendship on our part in the special case of heavy water. I do not want to press myself on these people, but it is about half a year since we are *[have been]* here and you could not say we were running after them. *[At this point the Germans actually have been at Farm Hall less than three months, but it has been nearly six months since they were taken into captivity.]* The Major can say to the Commander that I would very much like to see Rideal on such and such a matter.

HAHN: That you had a method whereby you were convinced that you could prepare heavy water 2 to 3 times as cheaply as by previous processes.

HARTECK: I won't exaggerate but you can certainly say 3 times. The director *[at I. G. Farben]* said if it was set up and you could sell heavy water at 20 pfennigs *[cents]* per gram you could do quite good business. There is nothing in writing that you could show. In my notes I have only, "According to the new process from the Institute for Physical Chemistry—Method for Heavy Water—an apparatus will be built at a cost of 1.2 million marks to be capable of producing 5 tons of D_2O." Otherwise there is no word about it. Right from the highest levels it was admitted that that was naturally quite unreasonable last February. The vapour pressure of ammonia had not even been measured and then you need an exchange apparatus; that is, in fact the point, that one fractionates not only the ammonia but that one continuously exchanges it with water. These are in fact the two dodges.

HAHN: Now then at the bottom you have your ordinary ammonia which you gradually enrich.

HARTECK: Yes, indeed.

HAHN: What happens to it?

HARTECK: This ammonia flows into the second column and the second column is set vertically in the interior of the first column. Then in the second you set a third inside. The first is round about 2 meters in diameter, the internal one is perhaps 40 centimeters and the innermost 15 centimeters. Can I draw it for you? This is the first column, the big one. That is, we will say, normal, that is, perhaps 30% impoverished and here threefold. It exchanges here with water and comes here again against the counter current. Then here comes the threefold—here we have the column inside, then the lower material comes up here, that is threefold. In reality it may be much more here, it is already tenfold. So here it is tenfold and here it is round 80-fold.

HAHN: For what reason then?

HARTECK: Because it then goes on being fractionated. It runs down and the gas rises. Then they both go through again. Here the 80-fold and here 800-fold.

HAHN: What happens to the light fractions? Are they always carried off by the water?

HARTECK: Yes, they act on each other, and here is the light one, that is simply the counter current, the ammonia flows in here, water in the opposite direction and it is only a few seconds before they have come into equilibrium and then the water which flows away with of course all the ammmonia in it, has to be boiled. And the remainder which I have, that is already let us say 10%, that is simply burnt, it plays no more part. Now we have 20% water with which I can do what I like.

(signed) P.L.c. Brodie
Capt.
24 XI 45

TOP SECRET

Lt. Col. Calvert for Gen. Groves
Copy No. 1
Ref. F. H. 10

To: Mr. M. Perrin and Lt. Comdr. Welsh
From: Major T. H. Rittner

OPERATION "EPSILON"
(24th–30 Sept. 1945)

I. GENERAL

1. This has been a quiet week, the guests being largely engaged in writing a memorandum concerning their own future. They all seem quite happy at present.

II. THE MEMORANDUM

2. On 24th September, Professor Hahn discussed the situation with Major Rittner *[in London; Rittner, who was still ill, had asked Hahn to visit him[2]].* Professor Heisenberg, in a conversation with Professors von Weizsäcker and Wirtz, having nevertheless already made it clear that he no longer really wished to withdraw his parole:

HEISENBERG: I have had another talk with Hahn. He will tell the Major that we are, on the whole, really very depressed and that it has become increasingly clear to us that nothing will be decided about us as soon as we had hoped, as it won't be allowed on account of higher politics, and that perhaps it would be a good thing if some kind of limit could be fixed by which at least something could be decided about our families. Besides, he shall make it quite clear to the Major that he (Hahn) had only succeeded after tremendous trouble in persuading me to wait at least for a few days before proceeding with this parole business. I think, it is quite a good thing to continue exerting pressure this way, although my personal feeling is that I should not withdraw my parole in the immediate future.

WEIZSÄCKER: Actually I think that today being the date on which they had expressly told you that you would be given some news, you are perfectly justified, in fact, it is actually your duty, to apply pressure in this direction if you want to have a basis for further negotiations.

---

[2]*Ibid.*, p. 61.

HEISENBERG: Yes.

WIRTZ: However, we must not push matters so far that we have suddenly no alternative left.

WEIZSÄCKER: We must not push matters so far that we have to carry out our threat.

3. Hahn reported his discussion with Major Rittner to Heisenberg, Major Rittner having suggested, as they were getting restive, that they should write a memorandum on their political convictions and hopes for the future, but Heisenberg did not wish to be associated politically with Diebner:

HAHN: The Major thought that we should put something about our political convictions into this memorandum; that is, something about the anti-Nazi convictions of our whole group. *[Apparently it was Major Rittner who suggested that they highlight their "anti-Nazi" activities, if any, rather than giving a full account of their complex relationship with the German government.]*

HEISENBERG: Yes, but if we put down something in this memorandum about a general anti-Nazi attitude and Diebner signs it, then I could not conscientiously sign it as well. You know as well as I do that Diebner has joined the Nazi game.

4. Gerlach, in a conversation with Hahn, expressed similar doubts:

GERLACH: Diebner could never sign with a clear conscience that he had never taken part in war work of any kind. *[Has Gerlach forgotten that, before he took over the nuclear program, he was in charge of the research for the German Navy that developed magnetic proximity fuses for torpedos?]*

5. Korsching, who is unmarried, in a conversation with Bagge and Diebner, thought that this was not the time for making demands, but felt that, once back in Germany, it would be easier to get permission to work on an uranium engine:

BAGGE: I do think this memorandum must be compiled with great care.

KORSCHING: The main thing is to make them send us home. Later on, things will arrange themselves. I mean, in a year's time we can certainly build a uranium engine again, nobody will give a damn. *[He was very wrong. As mentioned before, work on applied fission in Germany was controlled until 1955.]* But if we say now that we won't go unless we can build a uranium engine, they will just keep us here. We must just renounce our wishes in that respect, to start with at any rate. Later on we must just ask these people for permission again, then they are bound to say "yes" after a while. That is also in the interest of the English. The English obviously want the Americans to keep their hands out of it. The Americans, of course, will only do that, if, for the time being, we promise that we will not work on uranium at all. If after a year we go to the English and say: "Give us permission," then they will certainly grant it, then they will have able assistance. In a year's time all this will be out of date: then it will simply be an English enterprise. Then you may have to work in England but there is no reason why one should not go there.

6. In a general discussion, the guests found some difficulty in composing the memorandum, as their principal desire is for something to be done for their families and not to protest their political convictions which they feel are well enough known. Nothing of interest transpired from this discussion which has not already come to light in previously monitored conversations.

7. A photostat copy of the memorandum is attached as Appendix I. *[We have provided an English translation following the German text.]*

III. LETTERS

8. Letters arrived from Tailfingen on 25th September and, after translations had been made here—which translations were handed to Lt. Comdr. Welsh on 28th September—the letters themselves were handed to the guests on 26th September, together with letters from Prof. Blackett and Frank. *[Sir Charles Frank is a British physicist who was deeply involved in the British nuclear intelligence effort during the war. He had worked at the Kaiser-Wilhelm Institute for Physics in Berlin before the war.]*

9. The letters gave general pleasure except to Bagge, who is something of a masochist and immediately thought the worst of everyone when there was no letter for him. In a conversation with Diebner, he said: "That man *[the courier]* was in Hechingen and I have had no letters. Have we really deserved that? We have told them everything and now they simply detain us. What have we done?"

10. On 28th September, letters arrived from various scientific friends which have further improved the temper of the household and given some anxiously awaited news of the "Kaiser-Wilhelm Gesellschaft." These were not previously opened here. *[They learned that the aged Max Planck had assumed the presidency of the society, although the Russians had appointed Robert Havermann to that post in Berlin.[3]]*

IV. THE FUTURE

11. Von Weizsäcker, à propos of nothing in particular, suggested in a conversation with Hahn and Gerlach that it would be unwise to return the party to Germany.

---

[3]Max von Laue to his son, 29 September 1945.

WEIZSÄCKER: If I were in charge of the whole question, I would certainly think it over most carefully before letting us go home.

GERLACH: I have also come to the conclusion that they probably will not let us go to Germany now.

V. TECHNICAL

12. On Friday, 28th September, Hahn gave a lecture on his first discoveries on uranium fission, as previously published.

13. There was nothing else of technical interest during the week.

FARM HALL,   (signed) P.L.c.Brodie
GODMANCHESTER   Captain,
                                          For Major T. H. Rittner
                                                      3 Oct 45

[This appendix contains the German memorandum translation, which follows. Significantly, it was signed by all ten detainees, although again apparently with some difficulty. In his diary, Bagge pointed out that in the end it was signed "in order of age."[4]]

---

[4]*Ibid.*, Bagge diary entry of 27 Septemhber 1945, in Bagge, Diebner, and Jay, *op. cit.*, p. 61.

Die unterzeichneten deutschen Wissenschaftler befinden sich etwa fünf Monaten in Haft, offenbar weil ein Teil von ihnen zu der Arbeitsgruppe gehört hat [*ruled pen underlining*]; die in Deutschland während des Krieges das Uranproblem bearbeitet hat {note (1)}. Da die alliierten Behörden bisher noch keinen endgültigen Beschluss über das weitere Schicksal der Unterzeichneten haben fassen können, möchten wir darum bitten, die folgenden Gesichtspunkte in Erwägung zu ziehen.

Die unterzeichneten Wissenschaftler haben vor dem Krieg, insbesondere soweit sie auf dem Gebiet der Kernphysik gearbeitet haben, stets reine Grundlagenforschung betrieben, und zwar in der gleichen Weise, wie dies international in der Wissenschaft überall üblich war. Sie haben die brauchbaren Ergebnisse ihrer Arbeiten veröffentlich, haben sie auf internationalen Tagungen vorgetragen, und ihre Institute waren regelmässig von ausländischen Physikern oder Chemikern besucht. {note (2)} Erst im Verlauf des Krieges sind in den Instituten auch Kriegsaufträge bearbeitet worden; trotzdem ist die rein wissenschaftliche Arbeit weitergegangen {note (3)} und es ist uns gelungen, einen wertvollen Teil der wissenschaftlichen Tradition und des wissenschaftlichen Nachwuchses durch den Krieg zu retten. Die Unterzeichneten glauben, dass der Wiederaufbau der Wissenschaft und der Universitäten in Deutschland auch im internationalen Interesse liegt, und dass man dafür sorgen soll, dass das durch den Krieg Gerettete nicht nachträglich noch verloren gehe. Die Unterzeichneten werden für diesen Wiederaufbau dringend gebraucht; sie haben den Wunsch, die Arbeit in der gleichen internationalen Weise wie vor dem Krieg fortzusetzen. Wenn die Politik zur Zeit hierin gewisse Einschränkungen verlangt, sind sie bereit, diese in Kauf zu nehmen.

Schliesslich möchten die Unterzeichneten darauf hinweisen, dass die völlige Trennung von ihren Familien bei den äusserst schweren Lebensbedingungen in Deutschland für diese Familien und damit für sie selbst eine sehr grosse Härte bedeutet {note (4)}.

Aus diesen Gründen möchten die Unterzeichneten bitten zu erwägen, ob nicht die folgende Regelung möglich wäre:

1. Es wird den Unterzeichneten gestattet, nach Deutschland zurückzukehren und dort für ihre Familien zu sorgen.

2. Sie nehmen ihre Lehr—und Forschungstätigkeit wieder auf wobei der Umfang ihres Arbeitsgebiets und der Ort ihrer Arbeit noch im Einzelnen (etwa im Einvernehmen mit den alliierten Behörden in Frankfurt a.M.) festzulegen ist.

3. Umfang des Arbeitsgebiets. Wenn die Wahl besteht zwischen einer sehr starken Einschränkung des Arbeitsgebiets ohne Kontrolle einerseits und weiteren

Arbeitsmöglichkeiten mit Kontrolle andererseits, so ist die zweite Möglichkeit vorzuziehen. Denn erstens würde eine starke Einschränkung, zusammen mit den schon durch die Wirtschaftslage gegebenen Schwierigkeiten den Wiederaufbau wertvoller Forschungsarbeit fast unmöglich machen, zweitens würde eine Kontrolle jedes Misstrauen beseitigen und vielleicht von Wissenschaftlern ausgeübt werden können, die an der Arbeit selbst Interesse haben.

4. Arbeitsort. Die Kaiser-Wilhelm Institute für Chemie und Physik haben ihren eigentlichen Sitz in Berlin (amerikanische Besatzungszone), sie sind jetzt in Verlagerungsstätten in Tailfingen und Hechingen (französische Besatzungszone) untergebracht. Wenn aus äusseren Gründen für die Weiterarbeit weder Tailfingen—Hechingen noch Berlin in Betracht kommt, so schlagen die Unterzeichneten vor, Heidelberg, München oder Göttingen in Erwägung zu ziehen, wo es wahrscheinlich leere Institute bzw. geeignete Anlagen gibt. Die Beschaffung von Wohnraum würde hier allerdings die grössten Schwierigkeiten machen.

Anmerkungen

1) Inzwischen sind Dr. Bopp von der gleichen Arbeitsgruppe und Prof. Schüler von den Franzosen verhaftet und nach Frankreich gebracht worden. Es wäre wohl zweckmässig, wenn auf diese Institutsmitglieder die gleichen Gesichtspunkte angewendet würden, die auf uns angewendet werden.

2) Einige der Unterzeichneten haben Institute geführt, in denen eine Reihe von englischen und amerikanischen Wissenschaftlern gearbeitet oder einen Teil ihrer Ausbildung erhalten hat. Z.B. haben wissenschaftlich gearbeitet an dem von Prof. Hahn geleiteten Kaiser-Wilhelm Institut für Chemie: Dr. M. Francis, Prof. King.

An dem von Prof. Gerlach geleiteten Physikalischen Institut der Universität München: Dr. Bragg, Dr. Colby, Dr. Lane, Dr. Goudsmit, Dr. Little, Dr. R. W. Wood, Dr. Wulff.

An dem von Prof. Heisenberg geleiteten Institut für theoretische Physik an der Universität Leipzig: Dr. Eckart, Dr. Houston, Dr. Jahn, Dr. Feenberg, Dr. Podolski, Dr. Slater, Dr. Uehling, Dr. Nordsieck, ferner die später nach Amerika oder England ausgewanderten: Dr. Bloch, Dr. Weisskopf, Dr. Halpern, Dr. Placzek, Dr. Teller und Dr. Peierls.

3) Die Arbeiten des Kaiser-Wilhelm Instituts für Chemie über die Spaltungsprodukte des Urans sind während des Krieges fortgesetzt und in vollem Umfange veröffentlicht worden. Das Kaiser-Wilhelm Institut für Physik hat noch 1943 ein Buch über die Kosmische Strahlung herausgegeben. Ausserdem wurden verschiedene Arbeiten aus dem Gebiet der theoretischen Physik, über magnetische, elektrische und optische Probleme veröffentlicht.

4) In diesem Zusammenhang ist zu berücksichtigen, dass die Familien der Unterzeichneten zum Teil ihre eigentliche Wohnung durch Luftangriffe verloren haben und in Notquartieren wohnen. Die derzeitigen Lebensbedingungen in Deutschland, besonders in der französischen Zone, machen es einer Frau, die Kinder zu betreuen hat, fast physisch unmöglich, auch für Lebensmittel und Brennholzvorräte für den Winter zu sorgen. Wahrscheinlich sind die Familien wegen unserer Abwesenheit auf den Winter überhaupt nicht vorbereitet. Ausserdam erhalten sie zum Teil sicher keinerlei Zahlungen mehr. Die Unterzeichneten glauben auf Grund ihres persönlichen Verhalten in den vergangenen Jahren die Erwartung aussprechen zu dürfen, dass man ihre Familien nicht im Winter in Deutschland verkommen lässt.

(signed) Otto Hahn, M. v. Laue, Walther Gerlach, W. Heisenberg, P. Harteck, K. Diebner, K. Wirtz, Erich Bagge, C. F. v. Weizsäcker, H. Korsching

26/9/45

TRANSLATION

The undersigned German scientists have been in custody for five months, evidently because a part of them belonged to a group that was working on the uranium problem during the war {note (1)}. As the Allied authorities have not been able so far to reach a final decision on the further fate of the undersigned, we wish to ask that the following viewpoints be taken into account.

Before the war, the undersigned scientists, especially insofar as they were working in the field of nuclear physics, always did pure basic research, namely in the same manner as was practiced in science internationally. They published the useful results of their work, they presented them at international congresses and their institutes were regularly visited by foreign physicists or chemists {note (2)}. It was first during the course of the war that military assignments also were worked on in these institutes; nevertheless, purely scientific work continued {note (3)}, and we were able to save a valuable part of the scientific tradition and posterity during the war. The undersigned believe that the reconstruction of science and the universities in Germany is in the international interest also, and that one must take care that what was saved during the war does not become lost thereafter. The undersigned are urgently needed for this reconstruction; they have the wish to resume work in the same international manner as before the war. If policy at this time demands certain restrictions therein, they are prepared to take this into account. Finally the undersigned would like to note that the complete separation from their families, who are living under extremely difficult conditions in Germany, means a great hardship for these families and so also for themselves {note (4)}.

For these reasons the undersigned would like it to be considered whether the following arrangements might be possible:

1. The undersigned will be allowed to return to Germany and to provide for their families there.

2. They will take up their teaching and research activites again, the scope of their area of work and their place of work to be determined in detail (say, in agreement with the Allied authorities in Frankfurt a.M).

3. Scope of the area of work. If there exists a choice between a very strict restriction on the area of work without inspection on the one hand or broader possibilities for work with inspection on the other, the second possibility is to be preferred. For, firstly, a strict restriction, together with the difficulties already presented by the economic situation, would make the reconstruction of worthwhile research work almost impossible; secondly, supervision would remove any distrust and perhaps could be performed by scientists who themselves have an interest in the work.

4. Place of work. The Kaiser Wilhelm Institutes for Chemistry and Physics have their actual seat in Berlin (American occupation zone); they are now housed in evacuation sites in Tailfingen and Hechingen (French occupation zone). If, for external reasons, neither Tailfingen–Hechingen nor Berlin come into consideration for further work, the undersigned suggest taking into consideration Heidelberg, Munich or Göttingen, where there are probably vacant instititutes or suitable facilities, though in this case procurement of living quarters would surely pose the greatest difficulties here.

Notes

1) Meanwhile Dr. Bopp, from the same working group, and Prof. Schüler have been arrested by the French and taken to France. It would probably be useful if the same viewpoint would be taken toward these institute members as toward us.

2) Some of the undersigned have led institutes in which a series of English and American scientists have worked or received part of their education. E.g., the following have done scientific work at the Kaiser Wilhelm Institute for Chemistry, led by Prof. Hahn: Dr. M. Francis, Prof. King.

At the Physical Institute of the University of Munich, led by Prof. Gerlach: Dr. Bragg, Dr. Colby, Dr. Lane, Dr. Goudsmit, Dr. Little, Dr. R. W. Wood, Dr. Wulff.

At the Institute for Theoretical Physics led by Prof. Heisenberg at the University of Leipzig: Dr. Eckart, Dr. Houston, Dr. Jahn, Dr. Feenberg, Dr. Podolski, Dr. Slater, Dr. Uehling, Dr. Nordsieck; further the later emigrants to America or England: Dr. Bloch, Dr. Weisskopf, Dr. Halpern, Dr. Placzek, Dr. Teller and Dr. Peierls.

3) The work of the Kaiser Wilhelm Institute for Chemistry on the products of uranium fission were also continued during the war and were published in their full scope. *[This claim that Hahn's group published all of their results on uranium in the open literature during the war seems only partially correct.]* The Kaiser Wilhelm Institute for Physics produced in 1943 a book on cosmic radiation *[but it had nothing to do with the main research of the institute, nuclear fission]*. In addition, various works from the field of theoretical physics, on magnetic, electrical and optical problems were published.

4) It is to be taken into consideration in this connection that the families of the undersigned, in part, have lost their actual homes in air attacks and live in emergency quarters. The current living conditions in Germany, especially in the French zone, make it almost physically impossible for a woman who must look after children to take care of supplies of food and firewood for the winter. Probably, because of our absence, our families are not at all prepared for the winter. In addition, some of them certainly are not receiving any kind of income any more. The undersigned believe that on the grounds of their personal conduct in the past years they may be allowed to express the expectation that their families not be left abandoned in Germany this winter.

Signed: Otto Hahn, M. v. Laue, Walther Gerlach, W. Heisenberg, P. Harteck, K. Diebner, K. Wirtz, Erich Bagge, C. F. v. Weizsäcker, H. Korsching

9/26/45

[This document, as we see, was signed by the ten detainees in order of age and dated September 26, 1945. It was not translated into English as part of the report, and there is no indication that it was ever sent anywhere. If it had been, what would a reader have made of it in September of 1945? Would such a reader have understood the, at best, half truth about the open publication "in full scope" of the group's work on uranium during the war? While Hahn published some of his work, the vast majority of the group's work was in classified Army Ordnance reports. Would such a reader have appreciated the irony of Heisenberg's citing, as references to the utility of his institute in Leipzig for American and English scientists, a group of Jewish refugees—Peierls, Weisskopf and so on—that the government he had been collaborating with had later forced out of Germany? To say nothing of Gerlach's citing Goudsmit. What would an English reader have made of the complaints of the Germans about living conditions in Germany, when such a reader was still suffering the deprivations of a war started by the compatriots of these scientists?

The next day a letter was sent by Michael Perrin to James Chadwick. Michael Perrin was one of the first recruits to what the British called "Tube Alloys." This was their code name for the equivalent of their "Manhattan Project." Perrin's job was nuclear intelligence—namely monitoring the German nuclear program. The person to whom the letter is addressed is Sir James Chadwick, the discoverer of the neutron. He was one of the original Tube Alloy physicists. He had also witnessed the first nuclear explosion at Trinity. The letter appears as a photocopy in the British version of the transcripts. It is a short letter and I give it in full, including the wonderful letterhead. (Imagine a Manhattan Project letterhead indicating the street address and telephone number, including the extension! The people at Los Alamos were not even allowed to give a mailing address—only a postal box number— and had no telephone numbers.)]

DEPARTMENT OF SCIENTIFIC & INDUSTRIAL RESEARCH

Directorate of Tube Alloys

Telephone: Whitehall 1632   16 Old Queen Street
(Extension 202)   Westminster, S. W. 1

27th September 1945

Sir James Chadwick, F.R.S.
Technical Section, B.S.C.
P.O. Box 680,
Benjamin Franklin Station,
Washington 4, D.C.

TOP SECRET

Dear Chadwick,

I enclose two further reports in connection with Operation Epsilon *[Reports 9 and 10 just presented].*

We gave copies of these to Blackett who has, of course, had the original of Heisenberg's letter *[the one quoted in Part IV]*, before having the discussions here which led to the sending of ENCAM 424 from *[Sir John]* Anderson to F. M. Wilson.

Yours sincerely,

M. W. Perrin

[This letter shows that Blackett had received all the Farm Hall reports that pertained to his visit. From those, it had to have been obvious to him that what he had actually seen of the Germans was only the tip of a very murky iceberg. We now rejoin the reports at the beginning of October.]

Capt. Davis for Gen. Groves
Copy No. 1
Ref. F. H. 11

To: Mr. M. Perrin and Lt. Comdr. Welsh
From: Major T. H. Rittner

OPERATION "EPSILON"
(1st–7th October 1945)

I. GENERAL

1. All interest this week centres on a meeting between Professors Hahn, von Laue, and Heisenberg with various British scientists *[Blackett, Hill and Bragg]* at the Royal Institution *[in London]* on Tuesday, 2nd October, and a letter *[yet another]* which Heisenberg has written to Professor Blackett as a result.

II. THE MEETING

2. In addition to the various British scientists, Heisenberg also met his brother-in-law, Herr Schumacher, who apparently gave him an encouraging report about conditions in the British zone, and whom Heisenberg is most anxious to meet again in the near future. He has asked for this second interview as he thinks Schumacher will be able materially to assist him in selecting a site for the future Kaiser-Wilhelm Gesellschaft.

3. On returning from the London meeting, Heisenberg gave the following account of what had been taking place:

> Blackett has told me the following: The Americans have decided that we should return to Germany. They have made a condition, however, that we are not to return to the French zone. Blackett has expressly told me that he does not believe that we are to join our families at home in order to fetch them from Hechingen, but he thinks it is more probable that the families will be brought to us from Hechingen. The Americans do not appear to raise objections against our going to the British sector. In accordance with a very detailed report, which my brother-in-law gave me, conditions seem to be best in the English sector at present. Göttingen, Hamburg and Bonn came under discussion. The idea is that some central organisation is going to be set up which will somehow arrange the reconstruction of German science. Göttingen was mentioned in this connection, as, first of all, the Kaiser-

Wilhelm Gesellschaft has been evacuated to Göttingen and, secondly, the Academy *[of Sciences]* is there and, thirdly, on account of the university. The only snag about Göttingen is the proximity of the Russian sector and Blackett thought that the Americans would not consider Göttingen for that reason. The plan now seems to be that the Allies want to agree on a place where to send us. It will naturaly be a tremendous task for any Allied organization to endeavor to obtain an institute and accommodation for us, to get us there and to have our families and furniture brought along as well, but, fundamentally, that would be the only solution to make this plan attractive for us. The second alternative would be that the furniture will be left there and only our families brought along. In that case, only a few flats would be vacated for us. I have the impression that the Americans consider this latter alternative as the easier one and actually intend to carry it out. But I think that we can still exert some influence in this matter and I almost feel that we shall be able to choose between our families staying in Hechingen until a move on a larger scale will be possible and us remaining detained in the meantime on the one hand, and being united with our families as soon as possible but not being able to take our furniture along on the other hand. According to what Blackett told me, it will probably be fairly easy to arrange for those whose homes are already in the American sector simply to join their families now. When talking of my own family, I sort of asked whether there was a chance for me to return to my own family. Blackett considered this very probable. As we stand at present, we can influence matters considerably as they themselves don't know yet what they shall do. All this, naturally, within the scope of what they have said.

III. LETTER TO PROFESSOR BLACKETT

4. Later that evening Heisenberg suggested writing a letter to Professor Blackett outlining their wishes for the future on the strength of matters discussed during the meeting. The following is a report of the conversation which took place:

HAHN: Well, what do you think we should decide upon now?

HEISENBERG: I feel we should do the following: I should simply write another letter to Blackett tomorrow or the day after in which I shall put on record firstly what has been discussed in the meeting this afternoon and secondly what we shall now have discussed amongst ourselves. We should decide upon a strategy in accordance with which we can make suggestions to these people, as I feel that at present we have a fair amount of influence on what will be done. For instance, I think we could get a decision through, that within the next few days an Englishman, an American and one of us is to go to Germany in order to inspect the various places to which the institutes could be moved, and they, together, will then make a report on the possibilities. Perhaps even a programme could be worked out as to what this commission should do in Germany.

HARTECK: To judge from my experience, it is always better if several people go, say two or three.

HAHN: I doubt whether they will let three of us roam about, but perhaps we could get them to agree to two.

HEISENBERG: I should say that something could be achieved in this direction as this would not contravene the condition imposed by the Americans to the effect that we are not to leave here until something definite has been decided upon. It is, after all, an obvious and reasonable demand that somebody should travel about to find things out.

HAHN: But the French zone would be out of bounds during such [a] trip.

HEISENBERG: I should say, the places to visit would be Munich, Heidelberg, Göttingen, Bonn and Hamburg.

BAGGE: Heidelberg has not been mentioned anymore earlier on. Why not?

HEISENBERG: Actually only because we would rather steer clear of the American zone of occupation at present which, after all, is very much in the interests of the British just now.

WEIZSÄCKER: The only ones who have really got a vital interest in the well-being of Germany are the British apparently. By the way, I think that the results of the conference this afternoon have been unexpectedly positive.

WIRTZ: Yes, but I think that if the institutes or even some of their members could not join us from the French zone, these positive results are very doubtful.

WEIZSÄCKER: Of course, but these are difficulties of which we have known already.

LAUE: I should think that the English place more importance on general questions than on our institutes.

HEISENBERG: Yes, that is the difference between Britain and America. The Americans place more importance on people and the uranium bomb and the English are more interested in science in general.

WEIZSÄCKER: That is well and good, but, as we are pawns in this game, we must stress that to be able to work is the main thing for us.

GERLACH: It would be unthinkable to waste us on scientific education.

WEIZSÄCKER: The only thing we can do is to work ourselves in a place where we are in a position to talk with these people. But we cannot be made into just an official administrative body.

HEISENBERG: That is surely not the intention of the English.

5. Having slept on the matter, the drafting of the letter was discussed again on the morning of the 3rd October. In this discussion it appears that the meeting at the Royal Institution has greatly encouraged the guests, even to the point of dictating their own terms. Von Weizsäcker's diplomatic cunning is especially worthy of note.

HEISENBERG: The key to the whole problem seems to be that we cannot work in any place in Germany without our institutes. It is, therefore, vital that if we are to be moved, all the institutes and at the same time all our furniture and everything belonging to the families must be moved as well. We must make it clear to Blackett, therefore, that the Allied authorities cannot avoid negotiations with the French under any circumstances. The most important point of the letter to Blackett must, therefore, be: "Negotiations with the French will have to be taken up to get their agreement on the institutes moving from Hechingen and Tailfingen to another place yet to be decided upon." Then it is to be hoped that, once these negotiations have been successfully concluded, we will be allowed to join our families in Hechingen and Tailfingen. The official reason for this could be that we are to prepare the move. But I don't know whether one should stress this point already now as this probably belongs to a later stage.

WEIZSÄCKER: I suggest, we keep on telling the English that we wish to leave here but, at the same time, keep making suggestions which are difficult to comply with. And whilst these suggestions are pending, we are kept here and that will serve as a further moral pressure until our suggestions have been carried out. But if we now make suggestions which can be easily complied with but are not worth very much to us, then they will be accepted immediately and then these unsatisfactory conditions will last for years. Blackett will encounter tremendous difficulties now. Mr. Bevin *[Ernest Bevin, British Foreign Secretary]* will say: "How can you expect me to do such a thing with the French at this stage, it is quite out of the question." Then Blackett will say: "The only famous German scientists who have never been Nazis are sitting about here and not even their families are cared for," and thus again, Bevin will be obliged to do something. But if they tell him: "They are in Godesberg or Urfeld and everything is taken care of," then Bevin will say: "Good, then let us wait for five years."

LAUE: The fact that we are in England, however, is favourable as the English simply will have to take an interest.

WEIZSÄCKER: The English are responsible for us now and we must make use of that.

HAHN: From month to month we have stiffened our attitude towards them and just through that our situation has improved.

WIRTZ: The firmer we are, the more results we will get.

WEIZSÄCKER: Strategically, it is a wonderful situation for us, if they have to refuse us something, as we can then say: "Allright, but then give us this or that."

But, if from the start we suggest something which they don't have to turn down, as it is easy to carry out and yet is not of much use to us, then we shall have to do everything for ourselves.

6. The final letter to Professor Blackett was handed to me *[Capt. Brodie]* on the 4th October and was given to Lt. Comdr. Welsh the following day. The following is a translation of the letter:

Dear Blackett,

We were very grateful for the manner in which our discussions in London were carried on and the subjects discussed and, on the strength of these, we have once again amongst ourselves discussed the pending questions in detail. Perhaps it will be useful if I report to you on this.

After what we have been told by you and your colleagues, we appear to be bound to the following conditions: The Allied authorities agree on the whole to our return to Germany. However, for the time being, a return to the French zone of occupation is not intended, but rather the scene of our activities is to be shifted to a place within the Anglo-American zone of occupation, such a place to make it possible to resume work in accordance with the former scientific tradition and thus be suitable as a starting point for the rebuilding of science as a whole.

Bearing these conditions in mind, the following difficulties have to be pointed out: The resumption of our work is completely dependent on our institutes. Our removal to a larger town with a university will only prove useful if our institutes with all their equipment and their members—who are at present still working in Hechingen and Tailfingen—are also moved to that town. Such removal, under the conditions prevailing at present in the zone of occupation, will necessitate the authority of the French government which, as you know, has taken a lively interest in the work and equipment of the institutes. *[This is an interesting euphemism for the fact that, at least in the beginning, the French cleaned these institutes out and installed their own directors. There was, for obvious reasons, not much love lost on the part of the French toward the Germans.]* I, therefore, believe that negotiations about the future of the institutes cannot be avoided between the Anglo-American and French authorities. It can be rightly added in favour of such a removal into the Anglo-American zone that these institutes are actually stationed in Berlin–Dahlem, i.e., the American sector, and that Württemberg only represents a temporary place of evacuation of the Dahlem institutes. Furthermore, it can be stressed that these institutes represent the private property of the Kaiser-Wilhelm Gesellschaft, which is at present administered from Göttingen, and that these institutes are not the property of the German state.

Quite independent of the results of these negotiations with the French authorities, one should start immediately to look for a suitable place to which to move the institutes. In the discussions which we had amongst ourselves on this question, various arguments were put forward which, if such a place has to be in the English sector, were more in favour of Hamburg than of Bonn. The decision as to the sector itself will hardly depend on us. In any case, we were all agreed that it would be most desirable if two people of our lot here and perhaps also members of the institutes in Hechingen and Tailfingen were given an opportunity to inspect for themselves the respective places of work, the possibilities for accommodation, etc., before the removal of the institutes is finally decided upon. In order to commence work in this direction immediately, we should like to ask you whether the following decisions cannot be brought about:

1) A commission comprising suitable persons of the Allied authorities and two members of our party here (perhaps Wirtz and I) will be asked to find a suitable place for the institutes and to make a report on their findings. The following should be part of the task set *[for]* this commission: Visit to the various likely towns (Munich, Heidelberg, Göttingen, Bonn, Hamburg) and connect with the respective authorities. The head office of the Kaiser-Wilhelm Gesellschaft and several of the Hechingen and Tailfingen institutes would also have to solve the problems of finance and supplies.

2) At the same time, the Anglo-American authorities will start negotiations with the French authorities on the subject of the intended move of the institutes.

3) As, for instance, Gerlach (Munich) and Harteck (Hamburg) could give valuable assistance to the commission in their work in Munich and Hamburg, there should be no objections if such members of our circle who have their families or institutes in the Anglo-American sector were to return to Germany immediately—perhaps under the condition that they don't leave their respective sectors.

If this scheme would prove useful in its main points, I should imagine my own activities to be as follows: I would return to Germany at the earliest possible date with the group mentioned under (3), that is to start with, I would return to Urfeld in order to try and attend there to the most dire needs. Then, perhaps a few days later, I would be at the disposal of the commission who could perhaps start their work in Munich and fetch me there. After completion of our trip, I could return to England for a further conference or I could await the final decision in Urfeld and then commence with the removal myself. On the whole, it would be— probably also for deciding the starting point— advisable for me to have frequent opportunities to discuss these questions with you, but I don't know, of course, to what extent transport could be made available for such purpose.

As regards the question of starting point, we are all agreed here that, as far as natural science is concerned, the Kaiser-Wilhelm Gesellschaft would be a suitably central organisation and that, for historical and philosophical subjects, it should be the Kartell der Deutschen Akademien [Organization of German Academies]. Connection with the universities could be maintained from both these places.

Once again, many thanks and kindest regards.

Your (sgd) W. Heisenberg"

[I will return at the end of this part to indicate how this optimistic prospectus was greeted by the British occupation authorities.]

IV. OTHER LETTERS

7. Letters, from Hahn to Geheimrat *[Privy Councilor] [Max]* Planck, Professor *[A.]* Westgren *[a Swedish scientist to whom some German scientists had written during the war to register their moral objections to Hitler and Nazism]*, Professor Lise Meitner, from von Laue to Geheimrat Planck and Professor Lise Meitner and from von Weizsäcker to his wife, were handed to Lt. Comdr. Welsh on the 6th October, translations having been made.

V. THE FLY IN THE OINTMENT

8. Bagge, true to his character, made the following comment to Hahn: "If we go to Bonn now, what should I do there alone? Then I shall be sitting all alone in a furnished room and have all the trouble of getting my own food."

VI. TECHNICAL

9. There were no lectures and no matters of technical interest during the week.

FARM HALL,   (signed) P.L.c. Brodie
GODMANCHESTER   Captain,
                                           For Major T. H. Rittner
                                                 8th October 1945

TOP SECRET

To: Mr. M. Perrin and Lt. Comdr. Welsh
From: Major T. H. Rittner

OPERATION "EPSILON"
(8th–14th October 45)

I. GENERAL

1. This has been a quiet week, but the guests are showing increasing signs of restiveness.

2. Captain Speer, U.S. Army, arrived on Monday, 8th October, a relief as welcome as it was necessary.

3. On Tuesday, 9th October, first Heisenberg and then Hahn approached us, complaining that nothing was being done about their families and that their own detention was altogether immoral. The usual threat of a withdrawal of parole was brought up and, as usual, we were able to prevent this for the time being.

II. TECHNICAL

4. On Tuesday, 9th October Hahn gave a lecture on previously published experiments and fission carried out by himself, *[Fritz]* Strassmann and Götte *[possibly a reference to Hahn's prewar assistant Aristide von Grosse]*.

5. There was nothing else of technical interest.

FARM HALL
GODMANCHESTER

(signed) P. L. c. Brodie
Captain,
for Major T. H. Rittner
18th October 1945

Copy No. 1
Ref. F. H. 14

To: Mr. M. Perrin and Lt. Comdr. Welsh
From: Major T.H. Rittner

OPERATION "EPSILON"
(14th–21st October 1945)

[At this point the reference system in the reports becomes unstuck. This should be "Ref. F. H. 13" (Report 13). I will leave the numbers as they are on the original.]

I. GENERAL

1. Another quiet and uninteresting week, in which the main emphasis has been on our guests' worries about their families.

2. Wirtz suggested to me on Sunday, 21st October, that, as he and some of the others did not expect that they would be allowed to return to Germany for some considerable time, it would be a good idea to bring their families over here.

II. FOREIGN RELATIONS

3. There is at meal times an increasing tendency among the guests to cavil at the behaviour of the occupying powers in Germany, the Russians and the French being considered particularly wicked.

4. The general attitude seems to be that the German war was a misfortune forced on the Germans by the malignancy of the Western Powers, who should by now have forgotten that it had taken place (the guests seem to have done so) and that the United Nations should all be largely concerned to set Germany on her feet again.

5. Both Wirtz and von Weizsäcker have argued that the Japanese war was engineered by President Roosevelt who deliberately allowed the attack on Pearl Harbour without giving the due warning he was in a position to give. In any case, Commodore Perry's first expedition to Japan was the prime cause of the war which was, therefore, the responsibility of the Americans.

III. LITTLE HITLERS

6. Diebner is considered something of a Nazi by his hosts *[i.e., by Rittner and his staff]*. The compliment is apparently returned as can be seen in the following conversation between Bagge and Korsching:

BAGGE: Tell me, what is Diebner so excited about?

KORSCHING: He is quite rightly annoyed about our Nazi-nationalist English guards.

IV. TECHNICAL

7. There was nothing of technical interest during the week.

[Bagge noted: "Our colloquia have died a quiet death."[5]]

FARM HALL   (signed) P. L. c. Brodie
                                                           Captain,
                                               for Major T. H. Rittner
                                                    25th October 1945

---

[5]*Ibid.*, Bagge diary entry of 21 October 1945, p. 63.

Report 16
TOP SECRET

Copy No. 1
Ref. F. H. 16

To: Mr. M. Perrin and Lt. Comdr. Welsh
From: Major T. H. Rittner

OPERATION "EPSILON"
(22nd–28th October 45)

[This should be report number 15.]

I. GENERAL

1. Yet another quiet week. The guests are becoming apathetic, no longer bothering to hold colloquia and, according to Wirtz, none of them now troubles to do any scientific work. *[Bagge reported that the "guests" had become quite dejected and had ceased planning for their release after Welsh told Heisenberg bluntly that he no longer wanted to discuss the matter.[6]]*

II. CONSERVATISM

2. The guests do not easily accept new ideas. On Thursday, 25th October, I mentioned that Professor Oliphant *[a British physicist]* had said that uranium was not the only source of atomic energy. This suggestion was greeted with derision, but on showing them the relevant article in <u>Picture Post</u> for Saturday 27th October, it was generally agreed that there was something in the suggestion. *[This is a very strange reaction on the part of the Germans, since they had thought of using plutonium themselves.]*

III. LETTERS

3. All the guests and orderlies have written letters for eventual delivery to their next-of-kin. These, together with duplicate translations, were delivered to Lt. Comdr. Welsh on Tuesday, 23rd October. A letter from von Laue to his son in America was handed to Lt. Comdr. Welsh on Friday, 26th October.

---

[6]*Ibid.*, Bagge diary entry of 24 October 1945, p. 63.

IV. MONITORING

4. The monitoring service, which is continuous during the guests' normal waking hours, had produced nothing at all this week.

FARM HALL
GODMANCHESTER

(signed) P. L. c. Brodie
Captain,
for Major T. H. Rittner
31st October 1945

Report 16-A
TOP SECRET

Copy No. 1
Ref. F. H. 16

To: Mr. M. Perrin and Lt. Comdr. Welsh
From: Major T. H. Rittner

OPERATION "EPSILON"
(29th Oct.–4th Nov.)

I. GENERAL

1. Capt. Speer, U.S. Army, left on October 29th.

2. A visit from Dr. *[Charles]* Frank, on Friday 2nd of November was the highlight of the week.

II. WEREWOLVES

3. A paragraph in the <u>Daily Express</u> for Tuesday 30th October suggesting that Hahn might work at Didcot *[the site of the British nuclear enterprise]* provoked him to say that it was monstrous to write so, and so to provoke the "Werewolves." *[German fanatics still in Germany.]*

III. THE FUTURE

4. In the late evening of 31st October, Heisenberg, Harteck and Korsching discussed their future in the following conversation; they thought the British more likely to find a use for them than the Americans.

5. **HARTECK:** Do you think that the offer of the Russians for the German scientists has any influence on our remaining here?

HEISENBERG: I would say: There is a party quite high up near Mr. Truman and this party says: "One must lock up those Germans for years, because wherever they are they are a danger. If they are just anywhere, they can go over to the Russians, and even if they don't want to go, the Russians can kidnap them." And then there is another party who says: "That is a quite impossible approach. Firstly they are anti-Nazis. Secondly they are upright scientists. Thirdly this whole secrecy is nonsense in any case. We must make use of these people, in order to build up science again in Germany." This second party has now obviously achieved a principal concession from the opposition party: the fact that we are going back to Germany. But now the opposition party says: "If you are so insistent on that point, then you must arrange everything before hand *[so]* that they can on no account get somehow kidnapped by the Russians." I should think that if we get back to Germany at all, this factor will perhaps even get us into a favourable position in Germany. For they will say to themselves: "Firstly we have got to put up guards, of course, so that they don't get kidnapped. Secondly, however, we also have to offer them such good terms that they will willingly stay with us." *[General Groves has initialed this sentence on his copy.]*

HARTECK: But it would be too much trouble for them to have the main party messing around in Munich and me in Hamburg.

HEISENBERG: Yes, that's just it. That's the great difficulty. I can't see yet how they want to do it. Of course, it is possible that at some point this opposition party up there will also say that they are no longer interested and will then say: "After all they don't know very much about the secrets, and fundamentally, the Russians already know everything." Nevertheless I would still think that in any case it would be unpleasant for them if we went to the Russians. *[The last sentence is underlined in the original, probably by Groves.]*

HARTECK: Anyway, have they got enough people?

HEISENBERG: The English or the Americans?

HARTECK: The English. I have an idea that the Americans have an abundant supply of people, and the English simply have too few.

HEISENBERG: Yes, I can imagine that the English would say: "Well, that's quite good. Let's take these people to England." I should think that there is perhaps one party here who want*[s]* that. But I believe that the Americans wouldn't allow that either because they say and they are justified to some extent: "The English won't give them a huge salary, and especially they won't employ all of them." Then let's say, there are Nazis among *[this sentence is underlined up to here]* them and they certainly will incline more towards Russia than towards England. And if they are at large, who can stop them from simply going to the Russian Embassy in London and saying: "We put ourselves at the disposal of Russia." I don't know whether the Americans would allow that. Now the fact is that the Americans are not so greatly interested in the English starting a gigantic atom factory over here in the near future.

HARTECK: But can they prevent that at all?

HEISENBERG: No, they can't stop them from doing any amount of atomic research over here. But they can stop them from employing us over here by saying: "This is an inter-Allied affair. You are looking after these Germans but we want to have a say in what is to be done with them."

HARTECK: The Americans can draw from a huge number of institutes. This is not the case in England.

HEISENBERG: They have not such an abundance of people.

HARTECK: And if they are joined by a dozen or so people, that would be quite nice.

KORSCHING: But I too believe the Americans will be against it. People of whom one doesn't know how far one can trust them—I mean there are certainly enough people who are going to say: "One might trust Professor Hahn and perhaps Professor Heisenberg, but one doesn't know exactly what the others are like."

HEISENBERG: Yes, a couple of us are Party members. *[Sentence underlined. Bagge and Diebner have acknowledged Party membership.]* That will certainly cause a certain amount of difficulties. One must realize that there are certainly some high-ups in America who will say, and from their point of view quite rightly so: "The easiest way out would be if these ten Germans were dead." The Americans don't need us at all. There is no doubt that they can do it better than we can. They are not at all interested in seeing that the English are assisted by us. It is quite nice if the English are some years behind. And under no circumstances must they go to the Russians. But naturally these people aren't the only ones who have a say in these matters. Particularly as these people are being strongly attacked by the American scientists for other reasons.

HARTECK: After all, I must say if one knows the Russians and the Nazis, these people here are really very decent to take so much trouble with us. *[Statement underlined, probably by Groves, who is worried about their working for the Russians.]*

HEISENBERG: The English say: From their point of view, the American policy to smash Europe to pieces *[!]* is just as logical as the corresponding Russian policy, but from the English point of view it is the worst thing that could happen, because the English must still control Europe. And therefore for the English it is of the utmost importance to reconstruct Europe, and for that purpose we are useful to the English. It is quite clear that they could use us, because up to now they haven't got a large number of trained young people. They could even use us in Germany. Again they might say: "Let these people work in Germany on this problem, and let them promise to let us have any new results first, and only produce what we tell them to." This control plan might well be quite acceptable to them.

KORSCHING: That would mean that the people concerned would not publish anything.

HEISENBERG: No, it is like that. It would mean that one could, of course, not publish these technical details any more, but one could publish the purely scientific matters on which one could work just as well. I would prefer to run the institute on a purely scientific basis. One could easily tackle problems, which even from the point of view of nuclear physics, still tend to the side of pure science, for instance cosmic rays. In this respect I am for waiting until these people have decided what to do with us. The trouble is that up to now they are completely at loggerheads. There are some who are extremely friendly towards us, and on the other hand there are these obstinate people, these American Heydrichs and Kaltenbrunners who say: "What? The best thing these German scientists can expect from us is to stay locked up." *[Reinhard Heydrich and Ernst Kaltenbrunner were two notorious SS officers. It is interesting that Heisenberg does not mention his family acquaintance Heinrich Himmler in his list.]* I think the English have got every reason to wish for the help of German science *[a note written in the margin adds: that is to assist German science]*, because in a manner of speaking this is going to be their sphere of influence and they'll get something out of it. On the other hand, it doesn't matter to the Americans.

IV. DR. FRANK'S VISIT

6. The contemplation of Dr. Frank's visit aroused the usual pleasure that is given by contacts with the outside world.

7. It was not thought to be anything but a social call, and Heisenberg, answering a question of Korsching, did not propose any special plan of campaign for the day:

8. **KORSCHING:** How shall we behave when Frank comes?

HEISENBERG: The best thing is just as usual.

9. Dr. Frank had long talks with Wirtz, who was the hero of the day, but nothing new was said, at least in the House. *[It is not clear whether or not the bugging system at Farm Hall also extended to the grounds. This statement seems to imply that, at least at this time, it only functioned in the building itself. In his introductory essay to* Operation Epsilon, *Frank notes that at the time of his conversation with Wirtz—whom he knew well from his work at the Kaiser-Wilhelm Institute for Physics in Berlin prior to the war—the Germans had begun to suspect that they were being bugged. They had found some unexplained wires in the back of a cupboard. One should consider this when evaluating statements made by them from November on.]*

10. There was little reaction to the visit, but in conversation with Hahn, Wirtz thought Dr. Frank had worked hard to be able to visit them at all. Heisenberg detected the bogey of Party Politics:

11. **WIRTZ:** Frank said the whole business of our detention is purely political.

HAHN: If it had nothing to do with physics we would not be here.

WIRTZ: He himself *[Frank]* says what is being done is, of course, all quite nonsensical. The wrong people are detained, nearly everything that can be known has already been published, etc., and he laughs about Truman and these people, but he says there is nothing one can do at the moment. I mean actually he has achieved quite a lot by the fact that he comes here, after Blackett has apparently been excluded for the time being. Frank says he himself is conservative, while Blackett is not.

HEISENBERG: There you are, it is, after all, that party business.

[Bagge noted that if they were to take Frank's opinion seriously, they would still be at Farm Hall five years from now.[7]]

---

12. Von Laue's reaction to Hahn is to show the first signs of impatience, but Hahn recommends waiting until Mr. Attlee returns from the U.S.A. *[Attlee was in Washington for three-power talks on nuclear energy problems with Truman and Canadian Prime Minister Mackenzie King, 10–16 November, followed by a visit to Ottawa until 19 November 1945.]*

---

13. **LAUE:** But now at last something must happen, after all we can't sit here for ever.

HAHN: We must wait until Mr. Attlee comes back from the conference with Truman before doing anything further.

---

14. Korsching suggested to Bagge a secret separatist movement in which the younger scientists should dissociate themselves from the older, as the former have nothing to do with the atom bomb. Korsching would write about this to Lt. Comdr. Welsh offering to give their word to abandon nuclear physics, provided they may continue to work in some other spheres. They also decided to await Mr. Attlee's return from the U.S.A.

V. FRENCH SCIENCE

---

15. The article in The Times (London) of Saturday 3rd aroused no comment other than angry resentment at the French having removed scientific equipment from Germany, and some scorn for the reported French achievements during the occupation.[8]

Farm Hall,   (signed) P.L.c. Brodie
Godmanchester   Capt.,
                                           for Major T. H. Rittner
                                                   5th Nov. 45

---

[7]*Ibid.*, Bagge diary entry of 6 November 1945, pp. 64–65.

[8]"Science in France. Bold and Rapid Planning for National Welfare. Research under German Rule." *The Times* (London), 3 November 1945, p. 5. The article reported on a meeting of the Association Française pour l'Avancement des Sciences in Paris the previous week, attended by delegates from Britain and ten other nations, to discuss the past and future of French science, especially regarding nuclear research.

TOP SECRET

To: Mr. M. Perrin and Lt. Comdr. Welsh
From: Major T. H. Rittner

OPERATION "EPSILON"
(5th–11th Nov. 1945)

I. GENERAL

1. The week began with Heisenberg proposing drastic action and ended with a very successful and pacifying visit from Lt. Comdr. Welsh.

II. HEISENBERG'S PLANS

2. In conversation with Hahn on 5th November, Heisenberg discussed the possibility of taking some action to clarify their own position and future. Hahn agreed that things were becoming impossible. *[Recall that Welsh had reportedly informed Heisenberg that he no longer wished to discuss the scientists' release, provoking a severe sense of hopelessness among the "guests."]*

3. **HEISENBERG:** I don't know whether it would not be a good idea after all for one of us to return his parole and scram.

HAHN: I consider that to be a dangerous undertaking, because then people would have a good reason for saying: "We have treated them well and now they are obstinate. Therefore, we shall treat them badly." Perhaps one should speak with the Captain again *[a reference to Captain Brodie, who has taken over from Major Rittner]*, at any rate, about the sinking spirits of several of us, and then I should say to him: "Listen, some of our people have just about reached the end of their tether ...". He can see that for himself. Laue staying in bed for a day and that sort of thing, and that Gerlach gets fits of hysteria; he can hear that when Gerlach suddenly gets a fit in the kitchen and starts shouting at the staff. I can tell him that, in the long run, it will not be possible anymore to calm people down again and again.

HEISENBERG: I think, what they are doing is so very unnecessary. I simply cannot understand why they don't tell us what is going on.

HAHN: Shall we go there together, perhaps the day after tomorrow?

HEISENBERG: I just think that talks with the Captain are somehow futile, they don't help. He listens to us and then passes it on to the Commander, already with certain reserves. Then they have a talk about it, air their feelings a bit as to how unpleasant the whole thing is and with that things have really come to an end as already the Commander does not pass this on to a higher authority anymore. Perhaps, if we are very lucky, the Commander tells the competent Colonel or General who is sitting here in London. It is impossible that it will ever reach America where a decision could be made. *[This last sentence was underlined and initialed by General Groves!]*

HAHN: Then let us tackle the problem in such a way that we really ask for a visit of the American Colonel *[probably Lt. Col. Calvert]*. We shall never see the superior of the Commander, he keeps him away from us.

---

4. Speaking to Wirtz on November 6th, Heisenberg elaborated three possible means of forcing a decision. Wirtz, as usual, tried to exert a restraining influence.

---

5. **HEISENBERG:** I should like to have your opinion about three possibilities I have thought of. The first one is that we should make an application for an interview with Sir John Anderson. The second plan would be that I would withdraw my parole. I have thought of the following rather daring plan: Let us assume I had no further obligation on account of my parole. Then I could run away one day and could go to the Danish Embassy. I would ask them for shelter and could establish contact with Bohr, or the Danish Embassy could do that, and from there I could then somehow negotiate independently through Bohr. I would tell them that I am quite prepared to return to English or American captivity, but only under certain conditions. These conditions we would have to think out. To start with, we would want to know how the negotiations about our future are progressing, we don't want to be treated as stupid schoolboys. Secondly, we would want to have contact with our families or something of that nature. The third would be that we have a general discussion here in which we would decide that we shall all withdraw our parole on, say, 1st December. In that case, Hahn could go to the Captain and tell him that the utmost he was able to achieve with us was that we would wait until the 1st of December, but it had already been decided to withdraw the parole on that date and he should ask at the same time that a note to that effect should be made on our written parole now: "terminates on 1st December" or something like that. Those are the three possibilities. How would you feel about them?

WIRTZ: Well, to start with at any rate, I would not be against making an application to be received by Sir John Anderson.

HEISENBERG: In my opinion, I don't think, this has any chance for success.

WIRTZ: Well, I don't think much of anything connected with escape. I can't tell you exactly why, but...(int.)

HEISENBERG: Too forceful, you think. My impression would be that at best we could force an issue now, but we should have to pay for it later on. In any case, those circles who now detain us here would be so badly disposed towards us for all time that, in the end, the result would be detrimental after all. I should say that the only chance for lasting success would be, after we have achieved something temporarily, that those people who are badly disposed towards us will definitely disappear from American politics and will be replaced by people like Oppenheimer who mean well. But it is a very risky game and there is a very good chance that if we make such a daring coup, the opposition will bring forth all its hatred of Germans and they will say: "Well, on the whole, they have, after all, all tried to help the Nazis; they would have naturally given it to Hitler" and so on forth.

6. Discussing the matter with Wirtz, von Weizsäcker showed the same caution:

7. **WEIZSÄCKER:** If we really must have an outlet for our bad humour and our worries, then I would much rather insult the Captain (Brodie) three times during the course of a meal than compose just one document which might do us harm for years to come.

WIRTZ: Yes, one must not shoulder responsibilities—as Heisenberg apparently is willing to do—only to vent one's own feelings and thereby causing [cause] great harm.

WEIZSÄCKER: Hahn is also in the mood for action now, but when he does something, it will be sensible.

III. LT. COMDR. WELSH'S VISIT

8. Lt. Comdr. Welsh came down [from London] on 10th November and had long and satisfying talks with various members of the company, particularly Wirtz.

9. Wirtz repeated his conversation with Lt. Comdr. Welsh to Heisenberg and then said:

10. **WIRTZ:** My object this evening was to let him know that we understand his difficulties, but it is very valuable to us to have regular contacts with him.

HEISENBERG: I quite agree.

11. On 11th November, Hahn also expressed his satisfaction with the visit:

12. **HAHN:** I am very glad that the Commander was here again and that we could put our views before him.

WIRTZ: I think, if the Commander were to discuss things with us often and as thoroughly as yesterday he did with me, it would be much easier for us to put up with all of this.

HAHN: I quite agree.

IV. TECHNICAL

13. Colloquia are again in fashion which indicates an improvement in morale.

14. On 6th November, Bagge gave a lecture about the chemical properties of the transuranic elements, based on work by Fermi.

15. On 9th November, Wirtz lectured on the subject of chemical reactions of elements.

16. There was nothing else of technical interest during the week.

V. ADMINISTRATION

17. During my absence from Farm Hall on 8th and 9th November, Mr. Oates *[a CIC agent formerly attached to Alsos]* was very kindly brought over from Paris to take my place. *[Brodie was in London, conferring with Welsh and Rittner, probably about the deteriorating morale of the "guests." He returned with Welsh on the 10th.]* He stayed until the 11th of November.

FARM HALL   (signed) P.L.c.Brodie.
                                                                   Captain,
                                                         for Major T. H. Rittner
                                                          15th November 1945

[Some measure of the success, or lack thereof, of the Germans' scheming about their futures can be gotten from the following communication dated 31 October. It was sent from Lieutenant Colonel Calvert, the assistant to the military attaché at the American Embassy in London, as the signature indicates, to Major A. E. Britt in General Groves's office. The pertinent part reads:

> In regard to paragraph 3 of page 1, Farm Hall Report No 12 *[the brief report covering the dates from the 8th to the 14th of November]* wherein Heisenberg and Hahn complained that nothing was being done about their families, you are advised, the following action has been taken: On 30 October 1945, a cable was dispatched from this office to General Sibert advising him that General Montgomery was reluctant to accept the guests under the conditions first laid down. These conditions, as you know, were that the guests would be returned to some location in the British sector, preferably a university town; that, while they would not be physically confined, it would be necessary for them to obtain special permission for leaving such location. General Montgomery stated that if these men were under his custody, the only conditions he would accept them were that they would be confined and under close surveillance. General Sibert was asked, in the above mentioned cable, that until the decision came down on these men,

if the theater would assume responsibility for the protection of dependent members of their immediate families. This is similar to Project Overcast which was described in our cable 65971 of 11 October. *[Project Overcast, an effort to move German scientists and technicians temporarily to the U.S., was succeeded by Project Paperclip, which aimed at the permanent settlement of German scientists and their families in the United States.[9]]* The only two scientists General Sibert would have to provide for are those in the American sector who are Prof. Werner Heisenberg and Prof. W. Gerlach. As of this writing we have received no reply from General Sibert; however, it is believed that the theater will assume responsibility of these two families.

The next and final part of these reports describes one of the most curious episodes in this entire affair—the awarding of the 1944 Nobel Prize for Chemistry to Otto Hahn for the discovery of fission.]

---

[9]Clarence G. Lasby, *Project Paperclip: German Scientists and the Cold War* (Atheneum, New York, 1971).

PART VI

A NOBEL FOR OTTO HAHN
12 November–31 December 1945

[The atomic bomb fell on Hiroshima on August 6, 1945. On November 16 of the same year the Swedish Royal Academy announced that the Nobel Prize in Chemistry for the year 1944—delayed by the war—would be given to Otto Hahn for his discovery of fission. We will not know until the records are opened exactly why the Swedish Royal Academy decided to give Hahn a Nobel Prize at precisely this time for the discovery of nuclear fission. Surely they must have been aware of the fact that it was a uranium fission bomb that had led to the destruction of Hiroshima less than four months earlier. One might well argue that Hahn, along with Meitner, Strassmann and Frisch, deserved the Nobel Prize for one of the great discoveries in nuclear physics, but why the timing? When Alfred Nobel, who had made a fortune by means of his discovery of dynamite, and other "safe" explosives, died a bachelor in San Remo in December 1896, he left in his will money for prizes to be awarded annually to "those who have conferred the greatest benefit on mankind." Did the Swedish Academy really believe in November 1945 that nuclear fission, whose only practical realization had been, up to that time, nuclear weapons, had conferred a great "benefit on mankind"? Or was there an element in this prize, as it sometimes seems to be, of the political? On January 31, 1937 Hitler had issued a decree forbidding Germans to accept Nobel Prizes, a decree that affected in the first instance the German biochemist Adolph Butenandt, who was to be awarded the Nobel Prize in chemistry later that year, only to be forced to decline it. Was Hahn's prize also the Swedish Academy's way of signaling the end of Nazism? If so, why weren't Hahn's Jewish co-workers included in the award?

Of course, Hahn and his colleagues had their own political theories. They surmised that British scientists had lobbied Swedish representatives during a recent visit to England in favor of a Nobel Prize for Hahn. This was seen by the detainees as a way for the British scientists to get back at Welsh and the military authorities for excluding Blackett and other high-ranking scientists from administrative decisions about the release of the German captives. Their theory is expounded by Bagge in his diary entry for 18 November 1945.

From a practical point of view, there were problems with Hahn's prize. To where should one address the traditional congratulatory telegram? Hahn was still being held largely incommunicado at Farm Hall and his whereabouts were a secret. There was no question of his going to Stockholm to receive the prize, to say nothing of holding a press conference. All of this emerges in the final, rather surrealistic part of these reports. There are also flashes of humor surrounding the celebration of Hahn's prize—a very rare commodity in these reports—and the reaction of the Germans to the news that, at long last, they are finally going home.]

317

Report 18
TOP SECRET

To: Mr. M. Perrin and Lt. Comdr. Welsh
From: Major T. H. Rittner

OPERATION "EPSILON"
(12th November–18 November 1945)

I. GENERAL

1. This has been a quiet week with no noticeable signs of discontent.

2. The announcement of an award of a Nobel Prize to Hahn in the <u>Daily Telegraph</u> for Friday 16th November was the highlight of the week.

II. HEALTH

3. On Monday, 12th November, von Laue, Heisenberg and Gerlach visited the doctor, who considered that their various troubles were principally nervous. The subsequent improvement tends to confirm this.

III. HEISENBERG'S FINANCIAL AFFAIRS

4. At the request of Colonel Calvert, I *[Capt. Brodie]* took to London on Saturday 17th November forms of power of attorney for Mrs. Heisenberg, one in English and one in French; the former being in the normal English form, the latter homemade. These were handed to Lt. Warner. *[First Lt. W.L. Warner was assistant to the military attaché in the American Embassy, London.]*

IV. COMING MEN

5. On the 13th November I delivered a list of promising young German physicists, compiled by Heisenberg, to Lt. Comdr. Welsh. *[The purpose for this list of names is uncertain. Heisenberg may have hoped they would receive special financial support; Welsh may have wanted the names for Project Paperclip.]*

6. Wirtz expressed disapproval of the compilation of the list in a conversation with Diebner:

7. **WIRTZ:** To be quite honest, I would have nothing to do with that business. It's wrong, I wouldn't give any names. I should have time enough to see that these people did not suffer when I got back to Germany. I do not mind dealing with the Commander, but I don't trust him. I have another reason for not doing it: After the coming war with the Russians [!], if Germany is occupied by Russia, they will say: "Who gave the lists to the English?" They will find the lists somewhere in Germany and then one would be in a fearful hole.

DIEBNER: Have you discussed this with Heisenberg?

WIRTZ: No. It makes me uncomfortable when our fellows give them such lists.

---

8. Both Hahn and Heisenberg had scruples, but readily believed that no harm was intended.

V. NOBEL PRIZE

---

9. The Daily Telegraph's announcement of the award to Hahn of the Nobel Prize for Chemistry caused general pleasure and also deep misgivings as no official confirmation was forthcoming. It was even thought that some unaccountable malice was responsible for our withholding the news. However, great efforts were made in London [*especially by Capt. Brodie, who telephoned numerous sources*] to try to verify the report and, as the source seemed reasonably reliable, the award was duly celebrated with songs, speeches, baked meats and some alcohol. Proceedings started very badly with an unfortunate speech by von Laue, at the end of which both he and Hahn were in tears to everybody's great discomfort, particularly mine, as I was sitting between them. However, the united efforts of the rest of the party restored our normal good spirits.

10. I hope to obtain copies of the better songs and speeches and to publish them later in the form of an appendix to this report. They will, of course, be of no operational interest.

11. Laue told Hahn that there was good reason for the award of the prize.

---

12. **LAUE:** You have not got the Nobel Prize as a consolation for we *[sic]* ten German scientists who are shut up here, but I think that is their reason for giving it to you now instead of waiting till next year, which was probably their original intention.

---

13. Hahn said that if he were allowed to go to Sweden to receive the prize, he would not be able to give his word to say nothing about his detention here.

---

14. **HARTECK:** They (Allies) cannot make you give your word not to say where you have been and with whom.

HAHN: Out of the question!

HARTECK: They won't make you give your word, but they will say: "Of course we are delighted to send you to Sweden, but please don't say with whom you are."

HAHN: I should tell them: "I have not for years been in a country at peace. I used to like my glass of wine. I have friends in Sweden, such as Professor Quenzel (?), who has a very good cellar. I cannot guarantee, you know what old German students are, not to get a bit tight in a friendly way. I obviously can't give you my word for what might happen then.

VI. THE FUTURE

15. Gerlach told Hahn that he would on no account go to America.

16. **GERLACH:** I would not go to America for all the tea in China. I considered it thoroughly, because it is so often said that might be a possibility.

HAHN: As soon as one can do anything in Germany, of course, it is our duty to be there. Personally, I shall do no more work, but I will perhaps nevertheless be able to help or advise someone or other now and then. *[He became the president of the Max Planck Society, the successor to the Kaiser-Wilhelm Society.]*

GERLACH: Conditions in Germany make no difference whatsoever. To be there is the most important thing in the world.

17. Gerlach has, for the past week or two, been in a particularly nervy state, but in the last few days has been a little quieter.

VII. TECHNICAL

18. There were colloquia on Tuesday and Friday, both of which were continuations of that begun last week on "Molecular structure of various chemical compounds."

19. There was nothing else of technical interest during the week.

FARM HALL	(signed) P.L.c.Brodie
GODMANCHESTER	Captain,
for Major T. H. Rittner	20th November 1945

APPENDIX

[The following is Hahn's Nobel Prize celebration dinner, which was attached as an appendix to Report 18. As before, no corrections have been made to the originals, but we have provided translations.]

TOP SECRET

Copy No. 1
Ref: App/F. H. 18

To: Mr. M. Perrin and Lt. Comdr. Welsh
From: Major T. H. Rittner

OPERATION "EPSILON"
(Appendix to F. H. 18.)

I. SPEECHES IN HONOR OF HAHN

1. Attached are copies of various speeches, jokes, songs, etc., composed by the guests to celebrate the news of the award to Hahn of the 1944 Nobel Prize for chemistry.

2. These have not been translated as they would lose too much of their character in process. *[Translations are provided below by Richard Beyler and myself.]*

3. They are not of operational value but are passed on for interest's sake only.

FARM HALL   (signed) P.L.c. Brodie
GODMANCHESTER   Captain,
                                              for Major T. H. Rittner
                                                        26 Nov 45

[Some of the following will refer to Hahn's "cocktails." This appears to be a bilingual play on words. "Hahn" in German means "cock" or "rooster," and Hahn was always fond of telling "tales."]

"Tischrede, gehalten in Farmhall, Godmanchester am 16/11/1945 zur Feier der Verleihung des Nobelpreises an Otto Hahn,

VON M. v. LAUE

Lieber Otto Hahn!

Je länger sich unsere Detainung hinzeiht, um so schlechter werden unsere Sitten; jetzt gibt es sogar schon Tischreden. Aber ich muss Dir *[von Laue permits himself the familiar "Du"]* heute ein kleines Geheimnis verraten.

Vor zehn oder mehr Jahren schenktest Du mir Dein Bild. Ich liess es rahmen und hänge *[sic]* es in mein *[sic]* Instituts–Arbeitszimmer; dort in Hechingen hängt es heute noch—hoffentlich. Auf seine Rückseite schrieb ich: Otto Hahn, geb. 8. März 1879, aufgenommen 1933 (was wenigstens eingermassen stimmen dürfte.) Solche biographische Notizen schreibe ich naemlich auf alle Bilder von Bekannten, damit diese auch über mein Leben hinaus einen gewissen Wert behalten, und damit sich nicht die Goettinger Geschichte wiederholt, bei der Bilder von Gauss und Bessel verwechselt wurden. Aber hinter <u>Deinem</u> Bild steht ausserdem noch ein Distichon:

Gaben, wer hätte sie nicht? Talente, Spielzeug für Kinder! Erst der Ernst macht den Mann, erst der Fleiss das Genie.

Dies dichtete einst Theodor Fontane auf Adolf v. Menzel zu dessen 70-ten Geburstag. Wenn ich Gelehrten überblicke, deren Lebensweg ich einigermassen zu kennen glaube, so finde ich keinen, auf den es so gut passte, wie auf Dich. Denn—um nur einen Punkt zu erwähnen—zu Schnellanalysen von rasch zerfallenden radioaktiven Stoffen, die Du so oft ausgeführt hast, reichen Gaben und Talente nicht aus; vielmehr muss noch eine Ausbildung der angeborenen Fähigkeiten hinzutreten, die tiefen Arbeitsernst und ungeheuren, lebenslänglichen Fleiss erfordert. Aber weil Du Beides hast, so lässt sich die Reihe Deiner Entdeckungen auch einer Kurve vergleichen, die auf hohem Niveau—mit der Entdeckung des Radiothor, die Du in dieser Gegend machtest—beginnend über die Entdeckung des Mesothoriums (alias Megatheriums) dauernd ansteigt, um in der Entdeckung der Uran-Spaltung ein Maximum, aber kein Ende, zu finden. Und als äussere Krönung Deines Lebenswerkes hast Du nun heute die schönste Ehrung erfahren, die dem naturwissenschaftlichen Forscher zu Teil werden kann, den Nobel Preis. Ich glaube, man kann Dir in keiner besseren Form dazu gratulieren, als mit jenem Verslein.

Aber meine Rede wäre arg unvollständig, wollte ich nicht noch einer anderen Persönlichkeit gedenken: Deiner Frau. Auch sie muss ja die Nachricht erhalten haben; wie widerstreitende Empfindungen mögen da heute Abend auf sie einstürmen! Aber ich hoffe doch, überwiegen wird bei ihr schliesslich die Freude, die stolze Freude, die Gattin eines solchen Mannes zu sein.

Meine Herren! Wir erheben unsere Gläser und trinken auf das Wohl von Otto und Edith Hahn.

Sie leben hoch!

TRANSLATION

Dear Otto Hahn!

The longer our detainment goes on, the worse our manners become; now, already, there are even after-dinner speeches. But today I must tell you a little secret.

Ten or more years ago you gave me your picture. I had it framed and hung it in my office in the Institute; there in Hechingen it is hanging still today—let us hope. On the back I wrote: "Otto Hahn, born 8 March 1879, taken 1933" (which ought to have been at least approximately correct). I write such biographical notes on all my pictures of people I know, so that these can keep a certain value beyond my own life, and so that the Göttingen story in which pictures of Gauss and Bessel got mixed up, does not repeat itself. But behind <u>your</u> picture is, in addition, a distich:

> Gifts, who does not have them? Talents, toys for children!
>
> Only seriousness makes the man, diligence the genius.

Theodor Fontane wrote this for Adolf v. Menzel on his 70th birthday. When I survey the scholars whose journey through life I believe to know to some degree, I find none for whom this fits so well as you. For—to mention only one point—rich gifts and talents do not suffice for the rapid analysis of quickly decaying radioactive materials which you have so often carried out; rather, a cultivation of one's inborn abilities must be added, which calls for deep earnestness in work and enormous, lifelong, diligence. But because you have both, the series of your discoveries can be compared to a curve which, beginning at a high level—the discovery of radiothorium which you made in this vicinity—continually increases, over the discovery of mesothorium (alias megatherium), to find a maximum, but no end, in the discovery of uranium fission. And as the external crowning of your life's work you have today experienced the most beautiful honor that can be bestowed upon a natural-science researcher, the Nobel Prize. I believe that one can congratulate you in no better form than with that little verse.

But my speech would be grossly incomplete if I did not also come to mention yet another person: your wife. She must have received the news also; what conflicting feelings must be assailing her this evening! But I hope, indeed, that joy will finally predominate with her, the proud joy to be the wife of such a man.

Gentlemen! We lift our glasses and drink to the health of Otto and Edith Hahn.

Three cheers for them!

[It is little wonder the assembly was reduced to tears. Fortunately the mood lightens with the parodies that follow. The presenters, who apparently also invented the

parodies, are listed in Bagge's diary entry for 18 November 1945.[1] See the Epilogue for another account of all of this.]

Auszug aus der <u>Times</u> vom 17. November 1945

[Read by Heisenberg.]

Prof. Dr. Otto Hahn, German radiologist, has been awarded the 1944 Nobel prize for chemistry. It has been stated in official circles that Otto Hahn has been detained since the end of the war. No further comment was available.

Uebersetzung aus <u>Sunday Pictorial</u> vom 18. November 1945

[Read by Heisenberg.]

NOBEL ATOM ACE MYSTERY. WHERE IS OTTO HAHN?

Die neueste Atombombe ist die Nachricht aus Stockholm, dass Hitler's Atomexpert, Prof. Otto Hahn aus Berlin, den Nobelpreis für Chemie erhalten hat. Wie wir aus zuverlässiger Quelle erfahren, hat die schwedische Akademie gleichzeitig mit der Preisverleihung einen Preis augeschrieben fuer diejenigen Person, die zweckdienliche Angaben über den gegenwärtigen Aufenthaltsort Otto Hahns machen kann. Zahlreiche Lösungen sind eingegangen und harren der Bearbeitung. Die naechstliegende Annahme war, dass Otto Hahn vom U-Boot 530 gleichzeitig mit Hitler und Eva Braun in Patagonien abgesetzt worden ist und dort an der Herstellung neuer und besserer Atombomben arbeitet. Diese Vermutungen haben sich jedoch bisher nicht bestätigen lassen; eine andere Quelle bringt jetzt die aufsehnerregende Mitteilung, dass Otto Hahn vor wenigen Tagen in Tel Aviv gesehen worden ist, wo er offenbar mit anderen dort lebenden Frankfurtern und Dahlemern über die Weiterführung seiner Arbeiten beraten will. Der Bedarf an Fachleuten für Spaltung scheint dort aber nicht mehr gross zu sein, und eine sichere Bestätigung seiner Answesenheit in Tel Aviv liegt bisher nicht vor.

Um zuverlässige Nachrichten über den Aufenthaltsort O. Hahns zu erhalten, haben wir unseren Sonderkorrespondenten nach Deutschland entsandt; dieser hat zunächst das kleine württembergerische Städtchen Tailfingen besucht, in dem Otto Hahn in letzten Kriegsjahren seine Atomspaltungen durchgeführt hat. Da die Familie des Professors offenbar in der letzten Zeit mehrfach die Wohnung gewechselt hat, gelang es unserem Korrespondenten erst nach langer Mühe, bis zu einer kleinen, bescheidenen Wohnung vorzudringen, in der ihn zwar nicht Prof. Hahn wohl eben seine reizende Schwiegertochter empfing und freundlich bewirtete. Leider konnte aber auch diese junge Dame keine weiteren Angaben machen, als dass der Professor im April von amerikanischen Truppen weggeführt worden sei und sich wahrscheinlich in England oder Amerika aufhalte. Nach längeren erfolglosen Reisen,

---

[1]*Ibid.*, entry of 18 November 1945, pp. 67–68.

die unseren Korrespondenten nach Heidelberg, Versailles und ins Maastal bei Lüttich führten, stiess er auf ein Gerücht, dass Otto Hahn in England in einem kleinen Stätchen Godmanchester zusammen mit anderen Warcriminals unter schärfstem Arrest gehalte würde.

Ein Besuch in Godmanchester zeigte denn auch, dass dort ein roter Backsteinbau mit schwer vergitterten Fenstern durch Geheimpolizisten in Civil und Soldaten in Uniform so scharf bewacht war, dass jede Annäherung während des Tages völlig unmöglich schien. Unser Korrespondent versuchte daher, während der Nacht sich über die benachbarten Wiesen an den rückwärts gelegenen Gefängnishof anzuschleichen und es gelang ihm, in der ersten Morgendaemmerung einen mit Stacheldraht umwundenen eisernen Zaun zu erreichen, von dem er einen Rasenplatz hinter dem Gefängnis ürberschauen konnte. Hier bot sich ihm ein merkwürdiger Anblick: Eine nackte Gestalt mit müdem Gesichtsausdruck lief ununterbrochen an einem Rosenbett auf und ab, auf und ab, dem Eisbär im zoologischen Garten vergleichbar. Auf einen leisen Anruf unseres Korrespondenten zuckte die Gestalt zusammen und rannte mit einem Schrei des Entsetzens in wilder Flucht in das Haus. Wer diese bemitleidenswerte Gestalt war, hat sich bisher nicht mit sicherheit ermitteln lassen. Ein Schappschuss, den unser Korrespondent, noch eben nehmen konnte, führte zu einer schlechten Aufnahme, auf der einige Wissenschaftler, um Rat gefragt, tatsächlich die Züge Otto Hans erkennen wollten. Sic transit gloria mundi. Aber auch diese Feststellungen haben keine Sicherheit über den Aufenthalt Otto Hans gebracht.

Wir sind daher noch anderen Gerüchten nachgegangen, die behaupten, dass Otto Hahn in England gut untergebracht sei und dort an seinen Memoiren schreibe, die unter dem Titel: "Von Oxford Street nach Farm Hall" in Buchform herauszugeben gedenkt. Dieser Hinweis auf Oxford Steet hat uns zu einer Umfrage in den Kaufhäusern und Geschäften dieses Viertels veranlasst. Dabei stiessen wir auf eine ältere, würdig aussehende Matrone, Leiterin der Verkaufsabteilung eines Bekleidungshauses, die sich an Prof. Hahn gut erinnern konnte. Sie erzählte mit einem glücklichen Lächeln (happy smile) über die Zeit ihrer Bekanntschaft mit Otto Hahn, aber sie war nicht in der Lage, nähere Einzelheiten aus dieser Zeit mitzuteilen (she was not in a position, to tell more intimate details of this time). Irgendein Anhaltspunkt für den gegenwärtigen Aufenthaltsort Otto Hahn liess sich also auch hier nicht gewinnen. WHEN THE MYSTERY OF OTTO HAHN WILL BE SOLVED, NOBODY KNOWS.

TRANSLATION

Translation from the <u>Sunday Pictorial</u> of 18 November 1945

NOBEL ATOM ACE MYSTERY: WHERE IS OTTO HAHN?

The latest atom bomb is the news from Stockholm that Hitler's atom expert, Prof. Otto Hahn of Berlin, has received the Nobel Prize for Chemistry. As we have learned from a reliable source, the Swedish Academy has simultaneously offered a reward for any person who can give useful information as to Otto Hahn's present location. Numerous answers have been received and are awaiting processing. The supposition nearest at hand was that Otto Hahn was put off from Submarine 530 in Patagonia, at the same time as Hitler and Eva Braun, and is working there on the production of newer and better atom bombs. These conjectures, however, have not been confirmed; another source now brings the sensational communication that Otto Hahn was seen in Tel Aviv a few days ago, where he was evidently wanted to consult other Frankfurters and Dahlemers about the continuation of his work. However, the demand there for experts on fission does not appear to be large at the moment, and a definite confirmation of his presence in Tel Aviv is not yet at hand.

In order to obtain reliable reports about O. Hahn's location, we sent our special correspondent to Germany; he first visited the small Württemburgian town of Tailfingen, in which Otto Hahn carried out his atomic fissions in the final years of the war. Since the family of the professor has evidently changed its address frequently in the recent past, our correspondent was, only after a long effort, able to press forward to a small, modest home, in which not Professor Hahn but rather his attractive daughter-in-law received him and played hostess. Unfortunately, this young lady could not furnish any further information either, other than that the professor was taken away in April by American troops and was probably staying in England or America. After lengthy, fruitless travels, which led our correspondent to Heidelberg, Versailles, and into the Maas valley near Liège, he came upon a rumor that Otto Hahn was being held, together with other war criminals, under close arrest in England in the small town of Godmanchester.

A visit to Godmanchester then revealed that a red brick house there, with heavily barred windows, was being so strongly guarded by secret police in mufti and soldiers in uniform that any approach during the day seemed totally impossible. Therefore, during the night our correspondent attempted to sneak up to the prison courtyard, located in back, through the adjoining fields, and in the first light of dawn he was able to reach an iron fence wrapped with barbed wire, from which he could see the lawn behind the prison. Here a remarkable sight presented itself: a naked figure with a weary facial expression ran continuously back and forth, back and forth, by a bed of roses, like a polar bear in the zoo. Upon a soft call from our correspondent the figure gave a start, and with a cry of fright ran headlong into the house. Who this pitiable figure was has not yet been ascertained with certainty. A snapshot, which our correspondent was just barely able to take, led to a poor photograph in which some scientists, asked for advice, seemed to recognize Otto Hahn's features. Sic transit gloria mundi. But these determinations also have brought no certainty about Otto Hahn's location.

Therefore we pursued other rumors which assert that Otto Hahn is well-housed in England and is writing his memoirs, which he is thinking of publishing in book form under the title: "From Oxford Steet to Farm Hall." This reference to Oxford Street induced us to make an inquiry among the shops and businesses of this quarter. There we ran into an older matron with a dignified appearance, the director of the sales department of a clothing establishment, who could remember Prof. Hahn well. With a happy smile she told about the times of her acquaintance with Otto Hahn, but she was not in a position to tell the more intimate details. Any reference point for Otto Hahn's present location was not to be found here either. WHEN THE MYSTERY OF OTTO HAHN WILL BE SOLVED, NOBODY KNOWS.

Frankfurter Zeitung

Vereinigt mit dem Frankfurter Generalanzeiger

Von Goethe bis Hahn

[Read by von Weizsäcker.]

In unserer Reihe "Grosse Frankfurter" umspannen wir heute zwei Jahrhunderte Frankfurter Geschichte mit einem erlauchten Zwillingspaar: unsere Stadt darf einerseits Goethe, den Spalter des Herzen, andererseits zugleich, um der Sache eine neue Wendung zu geben, Hahn, den Spalter der Atome, zu Ihren rechnen. Gehen wir über die Lebensschicksale des Älteren der beiden, die den meisten unserer Leser bekannt sein dürften, rasch hinweg, und richten wir unsere Blicke auf die neue Säule im deutschen Chemikerwalde, Otto Hahn. 1879 in unserer Stadt geboren, verehren wir in ihm den Entdecker des Mesozoikums, den Erfinder der Hahnenkammeinheit und des Cocktails, den Gründer mehrer Sportklubs und langjährigen unermüdlichen Leser unserer Zeitung. Er ist Ehrenversitzender des Vereins für Sparsamkeit und Gewerbefleiss und Inhaber verschiedener Patente für die Erhöhung der Lebensdauer von Rasierklingen, Zigaretten und Anekdoten. Dem Fass seiner Verdienste hat er aber erst unlängst die Krone der Uranspaltung ins Gesicht geschlagen. Wie wir der Sekretärin der Liga für Körperkultur erfahren, soll er dabei ein neues Verfahren zur Fällung strahlender Körper angewandt haben. Er stand sozusagen gewissermassen mit dem einen Bein fest zwischen den Stühlen der Tatsachen, mit dem anderen aber griff er nach der goldenen Leiter des Ruhms. Mit ihm sonnt sich seine Vaterstadt im bunten Abglanz der verdienten Ehrung, die ihn soeben erleit hat, und möchten wir wie ein Vogel an mehren Orten zugleich sein, um sowohl dem Jubilar unsere aufrichtig gemeinten Glückwünsche zu Füssen legen als auch unsern Lesern einen Augenzeugenbericht von dem jüngsten und groessten Weltereignis geben zu können.

Wir verweisen darauf, dass im Feuilleton dieses Blattes von der berufenen Hand von Wilhelm Westphal die wissenschaftliche Verdienste Otto Hahns gewürdigt werden, während wir im Wirtschaftsteil einen Beitrag aus der geschätzten Feder unseres Sonderkorrespondenten P.H. über die finanzielle Bedeutung des Nobelpreises bringen. (Red.)

Wirtschaftsteil der Frankfurter Zeitung

Nobelpreis und Atomkernenergie

Otto Hahn, der Entdecker der Uranspaltung, hat den Nobelpreis für Chemie erhalten. Die erste Frage, die sich dem unbefangenen Beobachter aufdrängt, lautet: Steht die Geldsumme, die er erhält, in einem angemessen Verhältniss zu der Summe, die er der Menschheit durch seine Entdeckung geschenkt hat?

Der Nobelpreis beträgt etwa 6.000 Pfund Sterling. Das wären unter der Vorraussetzung des Goldstandards RM 120.000. Die Unsicherheit aller Währungsverhältnise legt es nahe, einen anderen Wertmasstab zu wählen, der auf den elementaren menschlichen Bedürfnissen basiert. Setzen wir den Preis eines Pfundes Zucker zu 40 Pfennigen an, so erhielte Prof. Hahn den Gegenwert 150.000 kg Zucker. Diese Zahl ist mit der Energieausbeute, die seine Entdeckung zur Verfügung stellt, deshalb noch schwer zu vergleichen, weil man das Uran nicht essen kann. Wir führen deshalb den Zucker und das Uran auf das gemeinsame Mass der Kalorie zurück. Ein kg Zucker enthält etwa 4000 Kcal; der Nobelpreis beträgt demnach rund 600 Millionen Kilokalorien.

Andererseits können aus einer Tonne Uran 235 nach Hahn etwa 10^{13} Kcal freigemacht werden. Die Gesamtmenge das Urans auf der Erde ist nur schätzungsweise bekannt. Wir nehmen an, dass der hundert-millionste Teil der Materie der Erdoberfläche aus Uran besteht.

Setzen wir voraus, dass das Uran bis eine Tiefe von 1km ausgebeutet wuerde, so erhalten wir, da die trockne Erdoberfläche rund 100 Millionen Quadratkilometer betraegt, 100 Kubikkilometer ausbeutbare Materiel, von der ein Kubikkilometer Uran ist. Das sind, da das spezifische Gewicht von Uran rund 20 ist, 20 Milliarden Tonnen Uran. Etwa der hundertste Teil des Urans ist Uran 235, so dass wir 200 Millionen Tonnen Uran 235 hätten. 2.10^{18} to Uran 235 zu je 10^{13} Kcal geben 2.10^{21} Kcal. Die 6.10^{18} Kcal des Nobelpreises sind davon der dreibillionste Teil oder der Bruchteil 3.10^{-13}. Diese Zahl hat man vermutlich gewählt, weil sie gerade der Radius eines Atomkerns ist.

TRANSLATION

Frankfurt News

United with the Frankfurt General Advertiser

From Goethe to Hahn

In our series "Great Frankfurters," today we encompass two centuries of Frankurt history with a pair of illustrious twins that our city may count as hers: on the one hand, Goethe, the splitter of the heart, along with, on the other hand, Hahn, the splitter of the atom—to put the matter in a new way. We quickly pass over the fortunes of life of the older of the two, which ought to be well known to most of our readers, and direct our sights to the new pillar in the forest of German chemists, Otto Hahn. Born in our city in 1879, we honor him as the discoverer of mezoicum, the inventor of the cockscomb unit and the cocktail *[see above]*, the founder of many sport clubs, and tireless long-time reader of our newspaper. He is the honorary chair of the Union for Thriftiness and Industry and the holder of various patents for the enhancement of the life span of razor blades, cigarettes and anecdotes. Not long ago, however, he completely re-scaled the measure of his accomplishments with the crowning achievement of uranium fission. Here, as we learn from the secretary of the League for Physical Culture, he applied a new procedure for the precipitation of radiating bodies. He stood, so to speak, with one leg firmly between the chairs of the facts; with the other, however, he reached for the golden ladder of fame. With him basks his father city in the bright reflection of the deserved token of honor which has just now been bestowed upon him, and we would like to be like a bird in many places at once, in order to proffer our sincerely meant best wishes to him who is celebrating, as well as to be able to give our readers an eyewitness report of this newest and greatest world event.

We note that in the cultural section of this paper Otto Hahn's scientific accomplishments will receive an appreciation from the able hand of Wilhelm Westphal *[a Berlin physicist]*, while in the business section we publish a contribution from the valued pen of our special correspondent P. H. *[Harteck]* about the financial significance of the Nobel Prize. (Ed.)

Business section of the Frankfurter News

Nobel Prize and Nuclear Energy

Otto Hahn, the discoverer of uranium fission, has received the Nobel Prize for Chemistry. The first question that presses itself upon an impartial observer is: Does the amount of money which it comprises stand in a suitable relation to the amount which he has given to humanity through his discovery?

Today the Nobel Prize amounts to about 6,000 pounds sterling. That would be, under the presupposition of a gold standard, RM 120,000. The uncertainty of all currency exchange rates suggests choosing another measure of value which is based on elementary human needs. If we set the price of a pound of sugar at 40 pfennig, Prof. Hahn would receive the equivalent of 150,000 kg of sugar. This quantity is still hard to compare with the yield of energy which his discovery places at our disposal, since uranium cannot be eaten. Therefore we reduce the sugar and uranium to the common measure of calories. One kg sugar contains about 4,000 kcal; consequently, the Nobel Prize amounts to around 600 million kilocalories.

On the other hand, from one ton of uranium-235, according to Hahn, about 10^{13} kcal can be set free. The total amount of uranium on earth is only known roughly. We assume that a hundred-millionth of the material of the earth's crust consists of uranium. If we assume that the uranium up to a depth of 1 km could be exploited, we obtain, since the dry area of the earth's surface amounts to around 100 million square kilometers, 100 cubic kilometers of exploitable material of which one cubic kilometer is uranium. That is, since the specific weight of uranium is around 20, 20 billion tons of uranium. Perhaps one hundredth of the uranium is uranium-235, so that we would have 200 million tons of uranium-235. 2×10^8 tons uranium-235 at 10^{13} kcal per ton gives 2×10^{21} kcal. The 6×10^8 kcal of the Nobel Prize is the three-trillionth *[Note: 1 billion in German = 1 trillion in American English]* part thereof, or the fraction 3×10^{-13}. This quantity has presumably been chosen because it is exactly the radius of the atomic nucleus.

Moose Jaw Herald, 16/11/45

[Read by Wirtz. "Moose Jaw" was the name Hahn gave to a "cocktail" he often drank. He had apparently visited Moose Jaw, Saskatchewan, in 1905 when he came to Canada to work with Rutherford in Montreal for nine months.]

Recent Nobelpreisträger for chemistry ist famous Dr. Otto Hahn. His name is nicht unbekannt in Moose Jaw, wie wir erfahren. In the remarkable year 1905, aus offiziell nicht bekannten reasons, unterbrach er hier eine seiner importanten Welt-voyages für einige days *[not exactly known how many]*, und, first of all, besuchte einen hiesigen Friseurladen. Der Friseur erinnert sich lebhaft, dass Hahn gemäss der Landessitte eine Kopfwäsche unter Verwendung von 14 fresh eggs verlangte. Er erinnert sich ferner very well, dass der Kopf von Professor Hahn was very geeignet für die Spaltung der Eier und er findet es sehr einleuchtend, dass er spaeter sich auch der Spaltung von Atomkernen zugewendet hat. One of the most important problems für die Mitbürger von Moose Jaw ist die question, why Dr. Hahn seine voyage hier interruptete. Der Friseur hat eine dunkele Erinnerung, dass nicht ein wissenschaftlicher, sondern mehr ein privater Anlass vorlag, und dass der Verbrauch von 14 Eiern mehr eine Vorbereitung war for that purpose.

TRANSLATION

Moose Jaw Herald, 11/16/45

The recent Nobel Prize winner for Chemistry is the famous Dr. Otto Hahn. His name is not unknown in Moose Jaw, as we have learned. In the remarkable year 1905, for officially unknown reasons, he interrupted one of his important world voyages here for a few days (not exactly known how many), and, first of all visited a local barber shop. The barber remembers vividly that Hahn, according to the national customs, asked for a shampooing using 14 fresh eggs. He further remembers very well that the head of Professor Hahn was very suitable for the splitting of eggs, and he finds it very illuminating that he later turned to the splitting of atomic nuclei. One of the most important problems for the citizens of Moose Jaw is the question of why Dr. Hahn interrupted his voyage here. The barber has a dim memory that it was not a scientific, but a private occasion that was at hand, and that the use of 14 eggs was more a preparation for that purpose. (Note of the editor: Already at that time Canada and especially Moose Jaw were famous for pin-ups and other beautiful girls.)

Zusammenfassung und Schlussansprache auf der Nobelfeier

In der Tat und so war es denn auch. Der alte Mann bekam seinen Hut wieder, die Feuerwehr holt das Grammophon vom Dach. "Heijoho!" riefen die Matrosen, und der Kapitän schwang sich jubelnd von Mast zu Mast. Im Hintergrund sah man einen Einjährigen mühsam sein Jahr abdienen. Der kleine Scheich von Nubien aber warf den Käse zum Fenster hinaus, hob die Duzbrüderschaft mit seiner Schwiegermutter auf und reiste plötzlich ab, nicht wissend, war dies nun Zufall oder Absicht, kluge Üeberlegung oder Heuchelei.

TRANSLATION

Summary and closing speech of the Nobel celebration

And, in fact, so it was. The old man received his hat again, the fire brigade fetched the gramophone from the roof. "Yo-ho-ho!" called the sailors, and the captain swung himself, shouting with joy, from mast to mast. In the background one saw a one-year-old painstakingly serving out his year. The little sheik of Nubia, however, threw the cheese out of the window and suddenly set out on a journey, not knowing if this was then chance or intention, shrewd deliberation or dissimulation.

[The following was presented by Bagge.]

In der hier mitgeteilen Geschichte wurden die unterstrichenen Adjektive in der von Festteilnehmern zugerufenen Reihenfolge an für sie freigelassen Plätzen eingesetz. Den Zurufern war dabei Inhalt und Anordnung des Stoffes unbekannt. Für den Inhalt verantwortlich: Seine Majestät der Zufall!

Die einwandfreie Geschichte der unbrauchbaren Kernphysiker seit ihrer überflüssigen Detainung.

[The underlining is in the original. This was a kind of game in which the story was told and the audience supplied the underlined words.]

Am 27. April starten die <u>unwiderstehlichen</u> Vertreter des <u>durchwachsenen</u> KWI. f. Chemie in Tailfingen und des <u>masslos traurigen</u> KWI. f. Physik in Hechingen zu

einer süssen Autofahrt in die saeure Detainung. Durch krumme Städte, vorbei an
unendlichen Mengen von groben Panzern, zog die düstere Reisegesellschaft
westwärts, bis sie am Nachmittag im übertriebenen Heidelberg eintraf. Sie wähnte
sich schon am Ziele ihrer stummen Fahrt, aber sie sollte erste im Laufe der schnieken
Zeit bemerken, dass dies nur die erste Haltstelle auf einer langen Reise war, die sie
damit antrat. Das nächste Ziel was Reims, wo sie wenige Tage später eintraf und
zunächst mal das Ende des Krieges abwartete. Aber dann gings smart weiter. In
einem blauen Flug von Reims nach Versailles zog sie hinweg über Nordfrankreich,
um nur für einige Tage in einem himmlischen Chateau zu hausen, das ganz darauf
eingerichtet war, die idiotischen Atomphysiker überheizt zu empfangen. Hier
geschah etwas Unerwartetes. Nachdem sie die erste Nacht und den ersten Tag auf
eisigkalten Britschen und Feldbetten verbracht haben, kam Verstärkung. Der
jammervolle Herr Heisenberg und der ebenso fabelhafte Herr Diebner trafen ein.
Trotzdem jedoch missfiel es den Detainen, so lange in Chesney zu bleiben und so
beschlossen sie aufgeregt von da nach Vesinet zu übersiedeln, zumal sich ihnen am
neuen Aufenthaltsort gewisse kümmerliche Chancen boten, mit ihren tobsüchtigen
Familien in Verbindung zu treten. Inzwischen war es Ende Mai geworden und weil
man ja doch die rätselhafte Abwechslung liebte und weil man in vielen 100-Runden
Läufen um die dumme Villa Argentina diese gefrässige auch schon gut kannte,
packte man abermals die souveränen Koffer und reiste nach Faqueval. Man kam
damit den rüksichtsvollen Wünschen unserer alkoholischen Detainer auch sehr
entgegen, zumal man inzwischen auch den schamlosen Herrn freundlichst und
angebrannt eingeladen hatte sich in dieser scheinheiligen Fahrt zu beteiligen, was
er bereitwilligst und mit geistvollem Gesicht auch tat. Im lüsternen Faqueval
schliesslich erfuhr der inzwischen schon auf neun übelriechende Personen
angewachsene wohlschmeckende Kreis der Atomisten seine letzte und endgültige
Erweiterung, als sich ihm auch noch der boshafte Herr Gerlach zugesellte.—
Reisfreudig wie man war, hielt man es in Faqueval aber nicht lange aus. Man
wollte weiter. Ja, und nach einigem schauerlichen Zögern begab man sich—stets
im besten und schrecklichen Einvernehmen mit den uns eigentümlichen Behörden
wie im trichinösen Fluge in das nun historische gewordene mieselsüchtige
Godmanchester.—Hier verbringen nun alle in ehrenwerter Stimmung seit ihrem
lächerlichen Eintreffen am 3.Juli 1945 ihre o-beinigen Tage. Die Zehn Detainen
sind seitdem eifrig bemüht, sich diesen blumigen Aufenthalt so verwegen wie
möglich zu gestalten und weil die Charaktaere der Beteiligten nicht gerade in allen
Punkten übereinstimmen, erfolgt die Freizeitsgestaltung auf verschiedene Weise.
Da ist zunächst der kühne Senior unseres Kreises, der bescheidene Herr Prof. Hahn.
Er bearbeitet—wenn man hier aus der Schule plaudern darf—seine von ihm so
getauften Memoroiden [sic] sofern er nicht gerade in einem gleisnerischen 10 km
Lauf die verschlafene Bewunderung seiner haarsträubenden Genossen von Farm
Hall erregt. Aber nicht nur das ist's was alle Leute seiner Umgebung von ihm zu
erzählen wissen. Wenn er nicht noch ganz andere Dinge auf dem Kerbholz hätte—
von denen wir noch reden müssen—so muss doch berichtet werden von seinem
gefrässigen Cocktails, die er in seiner zarten Güte zum besten gibt, von den sieben

gespalten Eiern auf seinem <u>lauen</u> Haupt in Mossejaw von der <u>zutiefst empfundenen</u> Lady in der Oxford Street, von den Berliner <u>Fangkuchen</u> *[sic]* und von den verlorenen 300 Talern bei einer Bahnfahrt, und von der präsidialen Wendung, die Tischgespräche nehmen können, aber nicht müssen, wenn er zur Unterhaltung beiträgt. Man könnte vieles von anderen <u>mittelprächtigen</u> Herren dieses Kreises erzählen, was für spätere Generation von Detainten als <u>grundlose</u> Anleitung zum wildromantischen Zeitvertreib beitragen könnte. Wir müssen uns aber kurz fassen. Immerhin sind die molerten Verdienste des <u>übermütigen</u> Herrn v. Laue ganz unbestritten der es verstanden hat, für das von ihm geleitete <u>trockene</u> Kolloquium seit einem halben Jahre wöchentlich zwei <u>eiförmige</u> Vortragende zu bekommen und so zur schleimigen *[sic]* unseres <u>gewürzten</u> Aufenhaltes ganz wesentlich beizutragen. Unser <u>anmutiger</u> Herr Gerlach hingegen vertreibt sich die Zeit mit der ganz <u>heldenhaften</u> Beschäftigung mit den <u>humoristischen</u> Erscheinungen des Magnetismus, ausserdem trägt er zur <u>dunstigen</u> Verschönerung unserer Zimmer bei, indem er sich zum <u>verzuckerten</u> Vorsatz gemacht hat, pro Tag etwa 20 Blumenvasen zu betreuen. Wieder anders sieht die <u>sentimentale</u> Freizeitgestaltung bei unserem <u>froschähnlichen</u> Herr Heisenberg aus. Von der <u>lächerigen</u> Quantentheorie und der Kernphysik kam er zur <u>dickbäuchingen</u> Supraleitung. Die ist aber jetzt schonfertig. Es war im ersten Augenblick ganz <u>bekümmert</u>, weil es nichts mehr zu tun hatte, aber seitdem er den <u>gewürzten</u> Trollop liest, leidet er nicht mehr supra, sondern nur noch ein ganz klein wenig, aber auch dies wird überwunden, weil der immer freundliche und <u>zweideutige</u> Herr Harteck, ihm da stets mit einem <u>gemischten</u> Wort in <u>sportfreudige</u> Laune versetzt. Und wenn das nichts hilft, versteht es Herr Harteck, die <u>atemlose</u> Stimmung dadurch zu heben, dass er uns vorrechnet wie langhaxert es uns geht, indem er den Kaloriengehalt unserer <u>vertrauenseligen</u> Speisen bestimmt. So könnte man noch von vielen Leidensgenossen reden, von unseren <u>feuchtfröhlichen</u> Detainern selbst, an ihrer Spitze unser <u>unrasierter</u> Capt. Brodie, vom <u>lüsternen</u> Weizsäcker mit seinen schnippischen Schüttelreimen, vom <u>erhabenen</u> Wirtz und seinen <u>erhebenden</u> Eiweissen, vom <u>launischen</u> Diebner und seinen gutmütigen Witzen und vom hochmütigen Korsching mit seinem pathetischen Barte. Aber wir müssen damit schliessen. Denn wenn auch das Leben allein schon durch diese Dinge bei den <u>hohlen</u> Detainten sehr interessant ist, wirklich aufregend ist es geworden, seit Herr Heisenberg heute im <u>Daily Telegraph</u> entdeckte, dass unser <u>grünschnaebliger</u> Prof. Hahn zum <u>gottwollten</u> Nobelpreisträger bestimmt wurde. Wir suchen <u>katastrophac</u> nach den richtigen Adjektiven, um diesen genialen Sachierhalt <u>kolossal</u> zu beschreiben. Unsere sonst so <u>allübertreffende</u> Stimmung hat plötzlich unerreicht <u>strenge</u> Höhen erklommen und wir können wieder <u>unglaublich</u> in die <u>unerschütterliche</u> Zukunft blicken und in diesem Sinne beglückwünschen wir unseren <u>nichtendenwollenden</u> Meister zu dieser <u>nebligen</u> Ehre!

Farm Hall, Godmanchester,
am 16 November 1945
Die Detainten

TRANSLATION

In the story passed on here, the underlined adjectives were inserted into the spaces left blank for them, in the order in which they were called out by the celebration participants. The content and arrangement of the subject matter were unknown to the participants when they called out the adjectives. Responsible for the content: His Majesty, Chance!

The unobjectionable story of the useless nuclear physicists since their superfluous detention.

On 17 April, the irresistible representatives of the interpenetrated K*[aiser]* W*[ilhelm]* I*[nstitute]* f*[or]* Chemistry in Tailfingen and the masslessly sad KWI for Physics in Hechingen started on a sweet trip into a sour detention. Through crooked cities, past endless numbers of rough tanks, the gloomy traveling company moved westward, until in the afternoon they arrived in exaggerated Heidelberg. They thought themselves to be already at the destination of their mute drive, but they should have noticed already in the course of this chic time that this was only the first stop on a long journey which they had thereby set out on. The next destination was Rheims, where they arrived a few days later and waited awhile for the end of the war. But then they left right away. In a blue flight from Rheims to Versailles they passed over northern France in order to lodge for several days in a heavenly chateau which was completely arranged to receive the idiotic atomic scientists overheated. Here something unexpected happened. After they spent the first night and the first day on ice-cold Britishers *[possibly some type of sleeping accomodation]* and camp beds, there came refreshments. The lamentable Mr. Heisenberg and the likewise fabulous Mr. Diebner arrived. Nevertheless, it displeased the detained to stay so long in Chesnay, and so they decided excitedly to move from there to Vesinet, especially since at the new location certain wretched chances to make contact with their maniacal families offered themselves. In the meanwhile May had come to an end, and because they loved the puzzling changes and because they already knew this voracious place well, through many 100-lap runs around the stupid Villa Argentina, they packed their sovereign suitcases once again and traveled to Faqueval. Thereby the considerate wishes of our alcoholic detainer were also greatly obliged, especially since the shameless gentlemen in the meanwhile had been most amiably and searingly invited to take part in this sanctimonious trip, which he also then did most readily and with ingenious countenance. In lustrous Fraqueval, finally, the savory group of atomists, meanwhile grown to nine foul-smelling persons, experienced its last and definitive expansion, as the evil Mr. Gerlach was yet delivered to them. Travel-happy as they were, they did not long remain in Faqueval, however. They wanted to go further. And indeed, after some horrid hesitation one set out—always in best and most frightful agreement with the authorities proper to us, as in the trichinous flight to the now historic, morose Godmanchester. Here all pass their bow-legged days in an honorable mood since their <u>laughable</u> arrival on 3 July 1945. Since then the ten detainees have been eagerly concerned to structure this <u>flowery</u> stay as <u>audaciously</u> as possible for themselves, and because the characters of the parties concerned do not exactly agree on all points, the structuring of free time occurs in various ways. There is first of all the <u>clever</u> elder of our group, the <u>modest</u> Mr. Prof. Hahn. He works—if one may here tell tales out of school—on what he has christened his memoiroids, insofar as he is not exciting the <u>sleepy</u> admiration of his <u>hair-raising</u> Farm Hall colleagues by a <u>hypocritical</u> 10-kilometer run. But it's not only that which people in his vicinity know what to tell about him. If he does not yet have entirely other things to answer for—about which we must yet speak—there still must be a report of his <u>voracious</u> cocktails, which he gives to the best in his <u>tender</u> goodness, of the seven broken eggs on his <u>tepid</u> head in Moose Jaw, of the <u>deeply sensitive</u> lady of Oxford Street, of the Berliner doughnuts and of the 300 lost thalers *[a silver coin that once circulated in North Germany]* on a rail trip and of the presidential turn of phrase which dinner addresses could, but did not have to, take if he contributed to the conversation. One could tell much about the <u>middling splendid</u> gentlemen of this group which, for later generations of detainees, could contribute to very romantic pastimes as <u>groundless</u> introduction. But we must bring ourselves together concisely. In any case the plump of the <u>high-spirited</u> Mr. v. Laue are quite undisputed, who has understood how to get two <u>egg-shaped</u> speakers each week for a half a year for the <u>dry</u> colloquium led by him, and thus contribute quite essentially to the <u>slimy</u> aspects of our <u>spiced</u> stay. Our <u>graceful</u> Mr. Gerlach, on the contrary, passes the time with a completely <u>heroic</u> occupation with the <u>humoristic</u> phenomena of magnetism; besides he contributes to the <u>vaporous</u> beautification of our rooms, in that he set himself the <u>sweetened</u> project to care for about 20 vases of flowers per day. Different again appears the <u>sentimental</u> structuring of free time by our <u>froglike</u> Mr. Heisenberg. From <u>porous</u> quantum theory and nuclear physics he came to <u>pot-bellied</u> superconductivity. This, however, is now quite finished. In the first moment he was quite worried because he had no more to do, but since he had been reading the <u>spiced</u> Trollop *[sic]* he does not suffer in a big way any more, but rather still only a very little bit; however, also this will be overcome, because the always friendly and <u>ambiguous</u> Mr. Harteck then puts him into a <u>sporting</u> humor with a <u>mixed</u> word. And when that does not help, Mr. Harteck knows how to lift the <u>breathless</u> mood through calculating for us how <u>long-shanked</u> it is going, by determining the calorie content of our <u>gullible</u> food. One could yet speak of many companions in misfortune, of our <u>hilarious</u> detainers themselves, at their head our <u>unshaved</u> Capt. Brodie, of the <u>lustrous</u> Weizsäcker with his impertinent spoonerisms, of the <u>elevated</u> Wirtz and his elevating proteins, of the <u>ill-humored</u> Diebner and his good-natured jokes and of the proud Korsching with his pathetic beard. But we must close with this. For if life among the <u>hollow</u> detainees already just through these things is very interesting, it has really become exciting since Mr. Heisenberg discovered in the *Daily Telegraph* today that our <u>greenhorn</u> Prof. Hahn was selected as a <u>divinely willed</u> Nobel Prize winner. We are seeking <u>catastrophically</u> for the right adjectives to describe this <u>ingenious</u> state of affairs <u>colossally</u>. Our otherwise all-surpassing mood has suddenly climbed to unparalleled strict heights, and we can unbelievably look into the unshakable future and in this sense we congratulate our never-wanting-it-to-end master this foggy honor!

Farm Hall, Godmanchester,
16 November 1945.
The Detainees

TOP SECRET

To: Mr. M. Perrin and Lt. Comdr. Welsh
From: Major T. H. Rittner

OPERATION "EPSILON"
(19th–25th Nov. 45)

I. GENERAL

1. A rather more interesting week, the lack of confirmation of Hahn's Nobel Prize and general impatience with their present condition are making the guests querulous and, on past form, should lead to another minor crisis within the next week or so.

II. NOBEL PRIZE

2. On Wednesday morning, 21st November, Hahn asked me if it were not possible to get confirmation of the award to him of the 1944 Nobel Prize for chemistry and I told him, which was true, that I was doing what I could. Hahn felt that, at the least, the Swedes would think his silence discourteous.

3. In the evening he discussed the matter with Heisenberg in the following terms:

4. **HAHN:** If a letter from Sweden has arrived for me, which they won't give me until the Commander's return, it must seem rude if I don't reply to it.

HEISENBERG: It is really nonsense that the Captain relies on the papers for confirmation of the award. It is not his business to contact the Swedish correspondent of the Times or someone like that, but what he should do is to approach his superiors in order to get them to make enquiries with some higher authorities.

HAHN: Well, he did say he would make some further enquiries, but I can't tell him very well where to go for them.

HEISENBERG: I think you could mention some of the higher-placed people whom we know, such as Blackett, who is bound to know the facts.

HAHN: Yes, I could do that. I suppose Sir John Anderson has not returned from Canada yet?

HEISENBERG: Well, he is really on too high a level for the Captain to approach him. In any case, I would mention some of those names or he should ask that American Colonel.

(Pause)

After all, a whole week has already gone.

HAHN: There must eventually be a communication from Sweden as well. It would just not do for them to keep that from me.

HEISENBERG: Well, it might be that these people have said that for the time being, nothing should be done until an official decision has been made on a high level. It could be that they have waited for the return of Attlee and Sir John Anderson.

HAHN: In any case, I could have another talk with the Captain before he goes to town again. On the other hand, I don't want to trouble him too much after I have talked to him only this morning. I know he is doing his best.

---

5. On Thursday Hahn discussed the matter further with Heisenberg and Wirtz, who tried to egg him on to take a strong line with me. Wirtz in particular likes to run with the hare and hunt with the hounds.

---

6. **WIRTZ:** The Captain is lying to you. He knows perfectly well that letters for us are in London and everything else. Only nothing is being done about it as the Commander is still away.

HAHN: He told me that. He does not know whether the letters are already in London. *[The two prior sentences should probably be one sentence.]* The day before yesterday, he told me he thought the letters had not yet arrived, but he said, in any case, they would have to remain there until the Commander's return, which will be some time in the middle of next week.

WIRTZ: I do think we should compile a statement about this whole case.

HAHN: I could tell him that I am of the opinion that, in a matter which concerns me so directly, they should give me permission to write to Sir Lawrence Bragg if they have no means of finding out for themselves.

HEISENBERG: I would even ask whether you could not write to Sir John Anderson.

HAHN: That is out of the question.

WIRTZ: I think we should clearly show our resentment and a deterioration of morale. That depresses the Captain more than <u>anything</u> else.

HAHN: I shall tell him: "We are most surprised that, in a matter such as this, we cannot get definite news although anybody should easily be able to understand that we are most curious about it." I want to write that to Bragg as well. It is possible that they won't allow me to send that letter, but then we would know for sure that we are considered as war criminals after all.

WIRTZ: I would be even more to the point. The only thing that has ever impressed the Commander and the Captain was that occasionally we have shown our resentment.

---

7. In Friday, 23rd November, Hahn came to see me in the afternoon, having obviously worked himself into a state of courageous fury. He was red in the face and was shaking all over even when he first came into the room. He said that he wanted to write to Sir Lawrence Bragg for confirmation of the award, that it was monstrous to keep him in doubt and that, in fact, our guests here are treated worse than war criminals in that they had no proper communication with their families and are detained without even a charge being brought against them. *[In fact there was a British wartime law which allowed anyone to be detained for six months at the "pleasure" of the Monarch. The six months were not yet over.]* I tried to say that I had no objections to his writing such a letter, but that I did not think the chances of it being delivered were particularly bright. Hahn, however, was hardly in a mood to consider my replies and left the room abruptly.

8. Allowing himself half an hour to cool off, he discussed the interview with Heisenberg who produced his usual theory about the withdrawal of parole. They also seemed to think a firm line with me would best serve their purpose:

---

9. **HEISENBERG:** That would be quite useful. Do go for him for a change. After all, he could approach some other people in this matter. There must be someone to take the Commander's place when he is away, that is obvious.

HAHN: Well, I can't do a thing at the moment.

HEISENBERG: I don't agree, but, in any case, it is perfectly right that you have gone for him. He must be made to realize that things can't go on in this way.

HAHN: Let us not talk about this to the others. I shall just be frigidly polite to the Captain.

HEISENBERG: I feel that we should not put up with just everything from these chaps. This constant reference to the Commander is perfectly ridiculous. There must be someone to take his place, that is obvious. When Captain Brodie goes to London, he goes to see somebody! He also has been able to arrange everything about the power of attorney for my wife. Probably the Commander, before leaving, has specially impressed on him not to do a thing in his absence.

HAHN: But I have said quite a lot.

HEISENBERG: That is good. And he hasn't said anything in particular at all, not even what is going to happen to you?

HAHN: No, nothing at all.

HEISENBERG: I always think the first thing to do would be for all of us to withdraw our parole. In that case he could not wait for the Commander either, he would <u>have</u> to act.

HAHN: I don't think that will serve any purpose, Mr. Heisenberg, since these people are so very set on their plans. That would only make matters worse. In any case, he knows my opinion now and perhaps he will think it over and, when he is at his office next time, he might talk to somebody sort of semi-officially, or at least when the Commander does return <u>that</u> rogue will tell us something.

HEISENBERG: (bitterly) By that time it will be Christmas and besides, the celebration in Stockholm will be over. I think we must apply pressure.

HAHN: Well, let us see first whether he hits on an idea.

---

10. I, after a further half hour, sent for Hahn and discussed everything with him rather more calmly and was able to satisfy him for the time being that I really was trying to get him the information he required but that there were certain difficulties in my way and so on. After this he decided apparently to exercise a little more patience.

11. I think Hahn is prepared to wait for about a week before "going for" me again.

III. GENERAL IMPATIENCE

---

12. On Sunday morning, 25th November, Wirtz and Heisenberg had conversations expressing their dissatisfaction. To begin with, Wirtz said we were making enemies of them and suggested a written protest as follows:

---

13. **WIRTZ:** The result of our long detention may well be that we shall be filled with a desire for revenge. I mean, if they kept us another two years, I might well say: "My sole object in life is to drop an atomic bomb on London." I think that round about Christmas we should make some sort of demarche with the object of reuniting us with our families. Otherwise we shan't get it done in the next ten years. We should have to say: "We admit, there are arguments which justify the detention of German nuclear physicists, firstly because they are nuclear physicists and secondly because Germany has to some extent justified such measures." But it must be said on the other hand that we were neither Nazis nor particularly for the war and that we are civilians... (int.)

HEISENBERG: The American militarists who are already at loggerheads with scientific opinion would get this letter. They would not accept any argument of ours but would merely say something like this: "There you are, the usual Nazi arrogance. They pretend to have some rights. They have none, we'll show them!"

WIRTZ: It could hardly be called arrogance, when we say: "We have been shut up for seven months without trial although we are not war criminals or prisoners of war and it is particularly hard in that our families are left helpless."

HEISENBERG: I agree.

---

14. Discussing the best tactics to use in order to put an end to their detention, Heisenberg and Wirtz complained that they don't know enough about what is being done about them. Wirtz has frequently said that they would all be very much happier if they knew what was going on. This conversation suggests that something more than happiness was what he was after.

---

15. **HEISENBERG:** We must find some dodge to alter our position.

WIRTZ: Yes, the most important thing for us would be to find out what is being done about us. If we only knew, we could settle everything to our own advantage in three weeks. We have had plenty of experience of that sort of thing in Hitler's Germany. All our contacts with our detainers so far have been failures. This Nobel Prize business is not our cue. Our cue is that your mother has died or your children are starving.

HEISENBERG: All my fights were on that score. Hahn's Nobel Prize is really also a personal problem which is certainly very important. If he gets it, his whole future life is changed, but I agree one's family is really more important. The whole trouble in this business between us and the militarists is that they are able to arrange that we know nothing of what is going on so that every move we make is a mistake. The worst of it is that we have nobody on hand, neither Captain Brodie, nor Major Rittner nor Commander Welsh, to give us the tip when to do what.

---

16. Their appreciation of their situation seems somewhat misguided in that they think the big decisions lie with them and they feel they should stress the family problem as being the most likely to influence us.

---

17. **WIRTZ:** The only chink in the Commander's armour is the difficulty in which our families are placed, because these things, in the long run, will make him unpopular with the rest of the scientific world. So I should say: "Let us keep stabbing at it."

HEISENBERG: I quite agree.

WIRTZ: That is the sort of headline we want to see: "Poor little anti-Nazi toddlers," or something like that. That would finish them.

IV. THE FUTURE

---

18. The guests are inclined to see themselves as exerting great political influence in the future. They fairly frequently come back to the idea that in the future, government will be by scientists and not by politicians. Apparently the programme is not yet defined:

---

19. **WIRTZ:** Scientists should be able to form a political organization but there is much more to it than being an expert in one line. It is not only a matter of

organisation, but there must be a definite programme. Even our own political ambitions are more than vague. We are always saying, just as Hitler used to: "First power and then the details," but clear concrete plans we just haven't got.

V. TECHNICAL

20. Heisenberg gave a lecture of Thursday, 22nd November on "The Structure of organic compounds, their symmetry, etc."

21. There was nothing of technical interest during the week except the above colloquium.

FARM HALL   (signed) P.L.c.Brodie
GODMANCHESTER   Captain,
                                          for Major T. H. Rittner
                                                     26 Nov 45

Copy No. 1
Ref. F. H. 20

To: Mr. M. Perrin and Lt. Comdr. Welsh
From. Major T. H. Rittner

OPERATION "EPSILON"
(26th Nov.–2nd Dec. 1945)

I. GENERAL

1. This week started badly with a disappointment over the last lot of letters sent home and ended more cheerfully with a further mail and a successful visit from Lt. Comdr. Welsh.

II. LETTERS

2. On Wednesday, 28th November, I informed the guests that the American authorities in Frankfurt had not been able personally to deliver the letters to their families which had been sent from here on Tuesday, 23rd October, and that, therefore, no answers could be expected.

3. This caused general gloom and annoyance.

4. Hahn, in conversation with Heisenberg and von Laue, expressed his disappointment as follows:

5. **HAHN:** I am so disgusted about this letter business. Perhaps it is not Brodie's fault; it may be a dirty trick of the Commander. Now suddenly we are calmly informed that there is no courier. It is such a dirty trick to lie to us. If I went to the Captain now, I would—(very agitated)—no, I must not!

6. Colonel Calvert *[of the American army]*, however, agreed to arrange a two-way mail in time for Christmas. This somewhat lightened the gloom, the guests reacting characteristically; for instance, the following conversation between Hahn, Wirtz and Bagge:

7. **HAHN:** Brodie made efforts to have the letters delivered by the Americans via Paris.

WIRTZ: Brodie does not take any trouble; the American Colonel proposed that to him. They are a dirty lot of scoundrels.

HAHN: I would not say that it is the Captain's fault.

WIRTZ: All these fellows, including Brodie, behave badly. That is the crux of the matter.

HAHN: Captain Brodie cannot help that.

BAGGE: He reports regularly about us to the Commander.

HAHN: I am sure of that; therefore it is no use abusing him in the Captain's presence. That only makes the Commander more furious.

WIRTZ: Unfortunately, we don't abuse him at all.

8. Letters were duly written and taken to London on Thursday, 29th November.

III. HEISENBERG'S FAMILY

9. I was able to tell Heisenberg on Tuesday 27th November that Colonel Calvert had met his wife and to reassure him about her welfare, since when Heisenberg has been much relieved and more cheerful.

IV. LT. COMDR. WELSH'S VISIT

10. Lt. Comdr. Welsh came down on Saturday, 1st December, for the night and cheered everybody considerably. The crisis forecast last week now seems much more remote.

11. Von Laue was particularly pleased to get a letter from his son in the U.S.A., which he carried about proudly.

12. The results of the visit were thought satisfactory as the following conversations show:

13. **HAHN:** He did give us a lot of useful information after all.

HEISENBERG: The remarkable thing is that he really does know all these people like Bohr and so on.

14. **HEISENBERG:** The conversation at breakfast this morning with the Commander was extremely pleasant.

GERLACH: I thought he was more friendly than usual last night.

HEISENBERG: I think he was quite satisfied himself. The visit may not have been 100% valuable, but, nevertheless I should say 50%. He really did say a lot that was useful.

15. There were no adverse comments.

V. TECHNICAL

16. On 27th and 30th November Heisenberg gave a lecture on the subject of "Molecular structure from a mathematical point of view."

17. There was nothing else of technical interest during the week.

FARM HALL

(signed) P.L.c. Brodie
Captain
for Major T. H. Rittner
3rd December 1945

Report 21
TOP SECRET

Copy No. 1
Ref. F. H. 21

To: Mr. M. Perrin and Lt. Comdr. Welsh
From: Captain P.L.c. Brodie

OPERATION "EPSILON"
(3rd–9th Dec. 1945)

[Capt. Brodie has now taken over sole responsibility for filing these reports.]

I. GENERAL

1. In spite of the visit from Lt. Col. Calvert and Lt. Comdr. Welsh on 4th December, this has been a very quiet week without difficulties or happenings of interest.

II. THE VISIT

2. Lt. Col. Calvert and Lt. Comdr. Welsh *[accompanied by Lt. Warner, see note at end of this report]* came down on Tuesday, 4th December to persuade Hahn to write a letter to Sweden accepting the Nobel Prize awarded to him but regretting that he did not think that it would be possible to go to Stockholm himself. Hahn was not at all keen to write without saying he was prevented from visiting Stockholm by his detention at the hands of the Anglo-Americans. However, he was eventually persuaded to write as required. *[Bagge quoted the bottom line of Welsh's argument: "You are Germans, you have lost the war."[2]]*

III. THE FUTURE

3. In the early morning of 5th December Wirtz, in conversation with von Weizsäcker, gave vent to his now usual anti-British spleen, and von Weizsäcker expressed a more definite opinion than usual:

4. **WIRTZ:** From what I have seen in England during these months, I should not like to settle down here on my own free will or to volunteer for work here, no matter what conditions in Germany may be. It might be different, of course, if they were to offer me some terrific position in Manchester, or somewhere, but I would never actually apply for it.

[2]Bagge, *Diary*, in Bagge, Diebner, and Joy, entry of 5 December 1945, p. 69.

347

WEIZSÄCKER: No, for that sort of thing one could only consider America or Russia.

---

5. There is at present a fairly general tendency to regard the British as the authors of all their discomforts and the Americans as their one hope of salvation.

IV. TECHNICAL

---

6. Diebner, on 7th December, used the work of Baldwin and Koch of the University of Illinois to hold a lecture on <u>Kern-Photoeffekte</u> *[nuclear photoeffects].*

7. There was nothing else of technical interest during the week.

FARM HALL   (signed) P.L.c. Brodie
GODMANCHESTER   Captain
                                                          10th December 1945

[On the seventh of December Lieutenant W. L. Warner, who was assistant to the military attaché in London, wrote a letter to Colonel W. R. Shuler of General Groves's office in Washington which, if the Germans had seen it, would really have relieved their gloom. The pertinent part read:

> ...2. On 4 December 1945 Colonel Calvert and myself visited the guests at Farm Hall and spent the evening with them. Their morale seemed considerably improved over the last time either of us saw them. Professor Hahn had requested previously permission to go to Stockholm to receive the Nobel Prize award. This permission was denied him, but in lieu thereof he was permitted to write a letter stating that he would be unable to receive this award, at least for the present time. This letter, of course, was in full compliance with all security measures.

> 3. The guests will probably be returned in a group by the first of next year to the British Army of the Rhine Headquarters and then be discharged individually.*]*

Report 22
TOP SECRET

Copy No. 1
Ref. F. H. 22

To: Mr. M. Perrin and Lt. Comdr. Welsh
From: Captain P.L.c. Brodie

OPERATION "EPSILON"
(10th–16th Dec. 45)

I. GENERAL

1. Nothing of interest has happened this week, either in direct contact with the guests or in the monitoring service, although they are entering upon one of their periodic fits of gloom.

II. LETTERS

2. The promised courier from Germany is eagerly though rather skeptically awaited. The effect, if the letters from the guests' wives do not arrive before Christmas, will be extremely disagreeable.

III. DR. ING. HANSEN

3. At the request of Lt. Col. Calvert, I asked Hahn and finally everybody else whether they knew of anyone of this name. Nobody did.

IV. TECHNICAL

4. Heisenberg, on 11th December, gave a lecture on the absorption of light by molecules.

FARM HALL
GODMANCHESTER

(signed) P.L.c. Brodie
Captain
17th December 1945

TOP SECRET

Copy No. 2.
Ref. F. H. 23/24

To: Mr. M. Perrin and Lt. Comdr. Welsh
From: Captain P.L.c. Brodie

OPERATION "EPSILON"
(17th–30th Dec. 45)

I. GENERAL

1. This report covers two weeks, including the Christmas period 22nd–27th December, when Lt. Comdr. Welsh nobly relieved me.

2. There was nothing to report before the arrival of Lt. Comdr. Welsh; the guests, however, were considerably cheered by the news of their impending return to Germany, which the Commander conveyed to them, and this, together with Christmas celebrations, produced a general feeling of good will.

II. CHRISTMAS

3. Lt. Comdr. Welsh brought Lt. Col. Dean *[not further identified]* and Lt. Warner down for the night on 22nd December. Our guests were gracious enough to speak well of the Colonel:

4. **WIRTZ:** His quiet thoughtfulness made a very deep impression on me. Compared to him we are a lot of hysterical children.

HEISENBERG: A fine type!

5. Lt. Comdr. Welsh brought the gratifying news of our guests' impending departure to Germany. Wirtz, however, made a last and not very earnest attempt to keep his querulous colours flying:

6. **WIRTZ:** Who knows, he may have just made this up so that he will have a pleasant Christmas here.

The Company: Rubbish!

7. The news of the return had a good effect on the guests' opinion of us all:

8. **WEIZSÄCKER:** To be quite honest, I would not have minded being here another six months. They have looked after us marvelously.

HEISENBERG: If one had only known that we were to go back after a certain time, there would have been absolutely nothing to complain about.

(And a ragged broadside from:)

WIRTZ: There is one solid comfort, the Commander and Brodie are going to fly with us, so at least they don't intend to have us crash.

---

9. About their eventual dispersal in Germany they have the following ideas:

---

10. **WEIZSÄCKER:** I am convinced that you (Heisenberg) and Hahn will get away at once and most of us not too long thereafter.

HEISENBERG: I am not yet sure.

WIRTZ: I think von Weizsäcker is right and I should add Harteck. The problem is what is going to happen to people like Diebner. We know what sort of man he is, but I don't think we should just drop him.

HEISENBERG: I agree. He has behaved himself very well recently.

WEIZSÄCKER: It ought to be possible to do something for him. He is not a physicist in the real sense of the word, but as it seems that we shall be able to work again, we shall need somebody to get hold of apparatus, to look after it and so forth. We could very well use him for something like that.

HEISENBERG: That is roughly my idea.

---

11. Werewolves still lurk in the background and the guests are anxious to avoid giving an impression in Germany that they have done anything for us.

---

12. **WIRTZ:** It would be a mistake, when we get back to Germany, to say how <u>marvelous</u> everything has been.

HEISENBERG: Yes, but, of course, there is a danger of that happening with people like von Laue. That should be avoided at all costs, but, on the other hand, we must do justice to the British who really have treated us extremely well.

WIRTZ: We should say that we were physically very well treated and mentally wretchedly.

III. LETTERS

---

13. Letters arrived in time for Christmas Day which gave very great pleasure to everybody.

IV. WIRTZ HAULS DOWN HIS COLOURS

OR

HE WHO FIGHTS AND RUNS AWAY, LIVES TO FIGHT ANOTHER DAY

14. **WIRTZ:** There is a lot to be said for the Commander after all, no matter how much we may have cursed him. In any case, it may be wise to be in his good books. We never know when we may have another use for him.

FARM HALL   (signed) P.L.c. Brodie
GODMANCHESTER   Captain
                                          31st December 1945

[On January 3, 1946, exactly six months after arriving at Farm Hall, the ten German scientists (and presumably their prisoner-of-war servants) were flown to Lübeck in the British occupation zone in northern Germany. Farm Hall was over.]

EPILOGUE

Erich Bagge and His Diary

In May of 1957, Diebner, Bagge, and the British physicist Kenneth Jay published a monographic history of nuclear energy in Germany and Britain from 1918 to 1955 (see Bibliography). Included in this history was Bagge's diary covering the period from the 22nd of April 1945 until the 12th of March of 1946.[1] This diary, which we have drawn upon throughout our commentaries on the Farm Hall reports, gives a unique insight into the events at Farm Hall as seen from the point of view of one of the interned "guests." The reports, in contrast, with their intelligence nature and laconic British commentary, provide a view from the outside looking in.

Before turning to more of the entries in Bagge's diary, a little background on Bagge: Born in 1912, he was one of the youngest of the detainees, and, as of this writing, is still alive. It will be recalled from the reports that Bagge claimed that, without his knowledge, he was enrolled by his mother in the Nazi Party in May 1935. He and Diebner were the only two acknowledged party members in the Farm Hall group. In the 1930s, Bagge had worked on heavy hydrogen (deuterium), and because of that, it seems, he was offered a job in 1938 with German Army Ordnance. He refused it so that he could join Heisenberg's institute at the University of Leipzig. But, when fission was discovered and seemed to have important military applications, Diebner remembered Bagge and recruited him for the newly formed nuclear research branch of German Army Ordnance. Bagge, in turn, brought Heisenberg into the project.

The most important thing that Bagge did in the development of nuclear technology during the war was to invent a method for separating isotopes, an "isotope sluice" (or "lock"). The idea was that a beam of molecules was sent through a set of rotating blades. In principle, the blades would select the molecules of a certain speed—the others would be stopped by the blades—and hence a certain mass. This work, which at the end of the war was being carried out in Hechingen, came to the attention of the Alsos Mission; on April 26th of 1945 Bagge and his sluice were collected by a commando team from the mission, and he eventually found himself at Farm Hall. Hechingen, where he was taken prisoner, was occupied by the French— in particular, by French–Moroccan soldiers who terrified Bagge. He was obsessed about them while at Farm Hall.

---

[1] Bagge, Diebner, and Jay, see Bibliography. The page numbers of the quotes from this work are as in the original.

The Bagge that emerges from his diary is somewhat more sympathetic than the Bagge of the Farm Hall reports. A comparison of the published version with the purported original diary, available on microfilm (see Bibliography), indicates no substantial alteration from the original. In the meantime, Goudsmit's book, *Alsos*, had been published—the first edition was in 1947—and it is cited in the Bagge–Diebner article. It contained several unattributed quotations from the still-secret Farm Hall reports. There is no indication in the Bagge–Diebner–Jay book that they had put two and two together and realized that, for Goudsmit to have been able to produce such quotes the Germans must have been overheard at Farm Hall. The characters, as we have gotten to know them from the Farm Hall reports, ring true. At the same time, Bagge's diary adds a new dimension by dealing with things that were not "operational," just the sorts of things that the British intelligence officers left out: what the detainees ate; how they passed their days, as well as some of the things their captors said to them. It also helps us to understand how the detainees got their information and what sort of information it was. It is, for anyone interested in this saga, a fascinating document.

Arrival at Farm Hall

After describing his capture and transfer to Belgium, Bagge wrote a long entry in his diary for the fourth of July, 1945, describing the trip to England. The group flies from Liège to a military airport near Huntington. Bagge states that this airport is about 20 kilometers from Cambridge, although how he knows this at this time is unclear. (This is one of the few places in the diary that makes one wonder if Bagge added things retrospectively.) Bagge gives his first impressions of the Farm Hall manor house, which he notes is 250 years old. He notes that their prisoner of war chef is told that he can use the gas stove for now, but that coal is better for the winter. The chef and the waiter have now been complemented by some additional war prisoners who have been taken on to serve as valets and batmen. Bagge especially likes the "old, old" pictures on the wall depicting the English upper class and the small library with its English books. (One wonders whether some of the concealed microphones were behind the pictures or in among the library books.) He is especially pleased by the fact that the guards with their machine pistols seem to have disappeared. The British captors probably figured that there was no place for men with conspicuous German accents to run. (By Churchill's order, even the German and Austrian refugees in England had been interned since June 1940.)

Soon their daily life falls into a routine that Bagge describes a little later in the diary, hour by hour. At 8 A.M. they are awakened. At 8:30 they perform their morning toilette. At 9:00 they have breakfast—porridge and bacon. From 9:45 until 11:00 they work in their rooms. From 11:00 to 12:30 they play fistball, followed by a half-hour wash-up. At 1:00 P.M. they have a meal that Bagge refers to as "dinner," which he says can consist of meat, vegetables, potatoes, desert, cheese and tea. (The detainees appear to have gained weight at Farm Hall. In fact, at one point Harteck is inspired to make a sort of calorie chart. He decides that a pound of

From left to right: Werner Heisenberg, Felix Bloch, Niels Bohr, Carl Friedrich von Weizsäcker; Easter, 1932. (Max Planck Institute, courtesy of AIP Emilio Segrè Visual Archives.)

The Kaiser-Wilhelm Institute for Physics soon after it was built in 1936. The tower dominating the picture housed a Van de Graaff generator. (AIP Emilio Segrè Visual Archives.)

Otto Hahn's work table displaying the apparatus used to produce the first fission reaction now on display at the Deutsches Museum. (AIP Emilio Segrè Visual Archives.)

The radiation laboratory building at Gottow, near Berlin circa 1942, where Dr. Kurt Diebner's research team worked to develop a nuclear reactor. (Photo by Samuel Goudsmit, AIP Emilio Segrè Visual Archives.)

Abraham Esau, plenipotentiary for German nuclear physics, circa 1942. (AIP Emilio Segrè Visual Archives, Goudsmit Collection.)

The Alsos Mission with British agents reviewing operations at Hechingen. Back row (from left to right): Maj. David C. Gattiner (UK), Lt. Cmdr. Eric Welch (UK), Dave Griggs, Capt. Reginald C. Augustine, Wing Cmdr. Rupert G. Cecil (UK). Seated around the table (from left to right): Lt. Col. Percy Rothwell (UK), Sir Charles Hambro (UK), Dr. Carl Bauman, Fred A. Wardenburg, Lt. Col. John Landsdale, Sir Michael Perrin (UK), James A. Lane, Col. Boris T. Pash. (AIP Emilio Segrè Visual Archives, Goudsmit Collection; courtesy of Brookhaven National Laboratory.)

The Farm Hall listening team. From left to right: Brodie, Heilbron, Rittner, Ganz, unknown, unknown, Pulay, Lehmann. (Courtesy of Peter Ganz.)

The Trinity test, the world's first detonation of a nuclear device on July 16, 1945, 5:29 a.m. near Alamogordo, New Mexico. (Los Alamos Photo Laboratory; courtesy of AIP Emilio Segrè Visual Archives.)

From left to right: Werner Heisenberg, Max von Laue, and Otto Hahn, circa 1947. (Max Planck Institute; courtesy of AIP Emilio Segrè Visual Archives.)

Farm Hall as it looked in March 1987. (Courtesy of M. Louisa de Echenique.)

apples contains some 450 calories and that they should all eat more fat in the winter.) From 2:00 to 4:00 they return to their rooms to work. From 4:00 to 4:45 there is coffee and pastry. From 4:45 to 7:45 there are either the colloquia, the radio, or something that Bagge calls "Konzert," which from other entries in the diary seems to mean a communal listening to a radio concert performance. From 7:45 to 8:30 there is supper. This meal is apparently less memorable than the others since Bagge does not describe its ingredients. Then from 8:30 to midnight there are card games and occasional piano recitals, especially by Heisenberg.

This pleasant-sounding idyll is occasionally ruffled by communications from the outside world. In his entry for July 31 Bagge quotes from an item that appeared in the previous day's *Evening Standard*. It is headlined "V-weapon experts are threat," and reads:[2]

> Some of Germany's best warmaking [sic] plans are still at large because of a loophole in SHARE's plan for arresting dangerous Germans. [Bagge identifies SHARE as an entity put together by the Allies for arresting German war criminals.] There is no provision for the arrest of research workers who made possible the terror weapons of this war. Many of these workers were held briefly but practically all of them have since been allowed to go. There is nothing to prevent them continuing the experiments they started under the Nazis except perhaps lack of laboratory facilities. Hundreds of people familiar with one or more of the V-weapons are at large. A former executive of the IG-Farben Industry declares: "The occupation authorities can take our administrative leaders but they cannot take our brains." [Needless to say, this is just what the Allies and the Russians did do—witness Werner von Braun, to say nothing of the German uranium scientists who went East.] The Allied view is that lack of facilities would prevent the researchman [sic] from carrying out experiments. A close watch is being kept on the German borders to prevent scientists fleeing to neutral countries where they might be able to continue the experiments. Our instructions called for the arrest of non-Nazi scientists and for the holding for a time those assistants we know had desirable information, an intelligence officer declared. But research workers who were not members of the Nazi party have in many cases been released. They may be potentially dangerous but we never let that potential develop.

Bagge bemoans the fact that the "harmless" scientists from the Kaiser-Wilhelm Institute, like himself, are apparently being punished for being "dangerous" along with the rest.

---

[2] "Some of Germany's..." *Ibid.*, pp. 55–56.

Aftermath of Hiroshima

One of the high points of Bagge's diary is his long entry of the 7th of August, the day after Hiroshima. It is such an excellent counterpoint to the Farm Hall transcripts of the evening of Hiroshima that I quote it in full. The reader may find it instructive to re-read the corresponding section of the Farm Hall reports. Bagge writes:[3]

> Tuesday, 7 August 1945
>
> Morning. That was an exciting evening yesterday. English radio announced that an atom bomb was dropped on a site in Japan. We were at supper when this news shocks our circle. At once, there is an extremely animated discussion as to whether such a thing is possible or rather a misunderstanding. Heisenberg strongly takes the viewpoint that "perhaps they have a new explosive with atomic hydrogen or oxygen or something similar!" Didn't Goudsmit ask us again and again, how we Germans could do that kind of [nuclear] science at all, while in America physicists were devoting themselves to "true" war physics? Mr. Hahn is at first very shaken, hoping that Heisenberg is right, because he dreads the thought that his discovery might have military consequences. Harteck estimates that even under the most favorable conditions an explosive with atomic hydrogen or oxygen could only have 10 times the explosive power of conventional explosives, while the announcement says that one bomb alone is supposed to have the effect of 20,000 tons of [conventional] explosives. That leaves only the uranium bomb! Mr. von Laue and Mr. Gerlach are very shaken, Gerlach finds it hardly credible, but will wait for the 9 P.M. news. Mr. Weizsäcker asks Mr. Heisenberg once again what his opinion really is, and Heisenberg re-affirms that for the moment he doesn't believe it, although after Harteck's remarks, which Hahn also supported, he was less certain and said that they had to listen again at 9 o'clock. Mr. Diebner, on the other hand, thinks that it might have been a real atomic bomb, a position supported by Korsching, who thinks that the Americans had probably produced the explosive by separating isotopes. It seemed clear that the explosive must have been produced by isotope separation; mass spectrometers might have been employed. The time passed with these discussions until at 9 o'clock we were all once again in the drawing room, and the skeptics learned that the Americans and the English really do possess the atom bomb. An accomplishment whose development cost 500 million pounds Sterling. Good heavens, what are our 15

---

[3] "Tuesday..." *Ibid.*, pp. 56–58.

million *Reichmarks* in comparison? And now the bomb has already been used on Japan. Allegedly the bombed city is still invisible, after many hours, because of all the smoke and dust. The talk is of 300,000 Japanese dead. Poor Prof. Hahn!! He told us that when he first realized what frightful effects uranium fission might have, he had not slept for many nights and had thought of taking his own life. For a while he thought that to prevent this catastrophe all the uranium should be sunk in the ocean. But should one also do away with the potential beneficial effects of uranium for humanity? And now there it is, this frightful bomb. The Americans and English, undisturbed, ceaselessly labored to produce pure uranium-235 in immense factories. In Germany we had to fight enormous battles for a couple of thousand marks, and, in addition, we looked on as our activities were bombed out over and over again. Also some of our leaders looked down on the matter of isotope separation and only tolerated it on the margins. Now instantly everything has become clear; why we are detained, why we are so ultrasecretly hidden away from the entire world, why no mail can go to our families, and why everything suspicious was hauled off from Hechingen and blown up at Haigerloch. At this moment I have to think of the three nuclear physicists who are trophies of Stalin. [This is presumably a reference to some of the German nuclear physicists who went East.] Certainly in the East billions will be spent and physicists, along with their wives and children, lodged in barracks, like the Americans did. [At Los Alamos, and elsewhere in the Manhattan project, the housing was pretty basic.] Now it also becomes understandable why the major came to us precisely on Saturday night, August 5th, and informed us that soon a fundamental change in our status would take place and it would become clear what had been planned for us. He was, indeed, very well informed. Is it not ironic that on the morning of the 6th of August we were allowed to deliver the first letters to our families—we, among whom is the discoverer of fission Prof. Hahn, could do this on exactly the day on which the first uranium bomb lays waste to a Japanese city and in which the world learns of the kind of epochal discovery that occurs very rarely in human history. Certainly, the uranium bomb will cause developments of world significance; to be sure it can bring much unhappiness to humanity, but we hope that it will, on the other hand, contribute to making the life of mankind more agreeable, more beautiful and perhaps more happy than before. No doubt that is possible. It is only necessary that men show that they have grown morally because of this development. And we believe in that. What did Prof. von Laue say tonight as he went to bed at 1 o'clock after long discussions? "When I was young, I wanted to do physics and experience world history. I have done physics, and I have witnessed world history. I can really now say that, in my old age." But he was unable to get to sleep. At 2 there was a knock on our door and Mr. von Laue entered: "We must do something; I am very worried about Otto Hahn. This news has shaken him horribly, and I fear the worst." We stayed awake a long time, and only when we were able to tell from the next room that Mr. Hahn had finally fallen asleep did we all go to bed."

Of course Bagge's memory, even assuming he wrote this entry contemporaneously, is selective, as a re-reading of the reports makes clear. He has chosen, for example, to leave out his argument with von Weizsäcker about their decision to try to make an atomic bomb in September of 1939. In the transcript he remembers Bothe as saying "Gentlemen, it must be done."[4] The bomb must be made if possible. In his diary, he alternates between shock and pious sentimentality. But, at least, among the reasons he gives for their not having done it—lack of money, constant air raids and the rest—he does not include not wishing to give it to Hitler for moral reasons, nor does he indicate that the only thing they worked on were "peaceful" reactors. Whatever his faults, Bagge appears to have been too honest for this sort of historical revisionism.

On Friday the 10th of August there is a somewhat enigmatical but important entry describing the scientists' preparation of the memorandum on German atomic research (see Report 5). The reader will recall that in preparing this memorandum the leading members of the Farm Hall scientists formulated the so-called *Lesart*, or "version," of their participation in wartime nuclear research for Germany. Bagge's laconic entry reads:

> The last days were for us under the spell of the press and radio announcements about the atom bomb. After we had learned enough, the idea took hold with our older gentlemen here that it was very important to compose, and deliver to the Major, a statement to the effect that in Germany work was not done on the atom bomb, but rather on a stabilised reactor. The plan found widespread, though not complete, approval. [It is a pity that Bagge does not tell us what the disagreements were over.] So an appropriate statement was written by Heisenberg and Gerlach which then, after some difficulties [again, no explanation] was signed.

If we only had the full German transcript so that we could follow this debate. We will see below that von Laue later had some vivid recollections of it.

There is a long entry in Bagge's diary for August 14, the day of Heisenberg's bomb lecture. Surprisingly, very little of this entry deals with the lecture, which does not seem to have made much of an impression on Bagge. There is no specific mention of Nagasaki. In the transcripts of their conversations, at least, the Germans

---

[4] "Gentlemen..." Farm Hall transcript Report 4.

do not seem to exhibit much interest in the second atomic bomb. Most of this diary entry deals with their daily routine and Harteck's calorie counting.

In his entry of August 20th Bagge ruminates on Roosevelt's death and Churchill's defeat at the polls and how this has perhaps brought in a new era. After that, the diary entries become more sparse—weekly rather than daily. On the 12th of September, Captain Brodie takes them for an automobile ride in the English countryside, which Bagge finds wonderful. As indicated in the commentary, on the 19th of September Bagge alludes to an illness that has caused Major Rittner to retire to his house. It must have been serious because Rittner never reappears as author of the reports.

Bagge Reports on Hahn's Nobel Prize

On Sunday the 19th of November Bagge provided a long report on the news of Hahn's Nobel Prize, which I present in its entirety.[5]

> Sunday, 18 November 1945
>
> Today I can report an interesting event, one without peer. Friday morning, shortly after breakfast, most of us were sitting in the drawing room in order to listen to "this week's composer"— it was Rimsky-Korsakov—and naturally also to study the "latest news" when Heisenberg said to Hahn: "Mr. Hahn, take a look at this!" Therewith he handed him the *Daily Telegraph*. Mr. Hahn, who was then himself reading busily in another paper, said: "I don't have the time." "But it is very important for you; it says that you are supposed to receive the Nobel Prize for 1944." The excitement that struck the ten detainees at this moment is hard to describe in a few words. Hahn did not believe it at first. In the beginning he turned away all the offers of congratulations. But gradually we broke through, with Heisenberg in the lead, who congratulated him heartily on the 6200 pounds [the value of the Prize at the time]. Then the rest of us succeeded in turn. Heisenberg immediately went to the Captain, who was completely surprised by the news, and was still totally stunned a half hour later. He immediately called the London Office. Apparently nothing was known there as yet, but the telephone was kept buzzing. The Information Ministry, *Times* correspondents and all sorts of other newspaper people were called. It gradually became apparent that we were not dealing with a false report.
>
> The Swedish Academy had evidently decided on this step only recently, probably in part influenced by our situation. A few weeks ago the Swedish Prof. Westgren informed Mr. Hahn that

---

[5] "Sunday, 18..." Bagge Diary pp. 66–68.

unfortunately one could not welcome him in Stockholm this year. Because of the global feeling about the atomic bomb they had shunned away from this option. [The sense of this seems to be that somehow Westgren had informed Hahn that this would not be an auspicious year to give him a Nobel Prize.] But perhaps the English physicists helped out a little. There is no doubt that in the small war between the Commander and Blackett, the Commander was ahead for the time being. But now the counter-offensive of the scientists was coming. [It is again not clear what "war" Bagge is talking about.]

The Swedish physicists Siegbahn and Svedberg seem to have come to the Röntgen celebration in London on the 9th of November and saw the English scientists there. A few days later the Nobel Prize was awarded to Hahn. That does not seem to be chance. However, we don't know that for certain. It is only a guess since none of us is in a position to be properly informed. Whether it is a good thing for us that the award is being given now as a political action is not yet clear; for now the "commanders" will again return the fire and they own the good powder. We must wait and see.

The Captain went to London and back today. Nothing new. But, at least, the Nobel Prize report was not denied. In the meanwhile we had prepared a little celebration. The Captain donated a bottle of gin and two bottles of red wine, and already during supper the affair began with an address by Mr. von Laue.

He celebrated our doyen fittingly [actually Hahn and von Laue had been born the same year—1879], spoke of genius and diligence, and at the end touched upon what he thought would probably move Hahn in Germany. Thereafter [see the Appendix to Report 6] Heisenberg read a very funny collection of newspaper statements [which presumably he made up] which referred to Otto Hahn. Weizsäcker followed with an article [which presumably he also made up] from the *Frnkfurter Zeitung* with the remarkable headline "From Goethe to Hahn—two great Frankfurters." Mr. Wirtz read an article from the "Moose Jaw Herald." "Moose Jaw" was one of Hahn's "cocktails," the one with seven eggs broken on the head of someone who has just had his hair washed. [The word "Hahn" in German means "cock" or "rooster." Hahn seemed to like the odd tipple, and this appears to have been one of his concoctions.] Then Diebner and Wirtz sang a song with the refrain, "And if one asks who's to blame—the answer is Otto Hahn." To close, I read a story about the detainees in which the adjectives had to be provided by the participants who inserted them afterwards in the blank spaces which had been provided. [This is the odd bit of prose in the Appendix to Report VI with all the underlinings given as one of Hahn's party offerings.]

Even the title came out well. The "unobjectionable" story of the "unusable" nuclear physicists from the time of their "superfluous" detainment. There were other wonderful jokes, such as that of the "interpenetrated" Kaiser-Wilhelm Institute for Chemistry in Tailfingen and that of the "alcoholized" detainees. In any case, there was much laughter this evening. For the first time, it was forgotten that we were imprisoned here.

The Captain did not refer to the Nobel Prize in the days that followed. There was not a single word about the award in the English newspapers, and slowly we grasped why our guardian had to go to London so quickly on Friday. Dead silence is evidently the order of the day. But what will the scientists in the rest of the world do?

By the first week in December, the Nobel Prize award to Hahn was confirmed. Bagge reports that, on the 4th, the Commander and two American officers appeared at Farm Hall to get Hahn to write a letter of acceptance without disclosing the reasons why he could not make the trip to Stockholm. A heated argument followed, in which Bagge reports that the Commander said to Hahn, "You are Germans, you have lost the war."[6] This is the conversation that Captain Brodie summarized in the transcripts by noting, laconically, "However, he [Hahn] was eventually persuaded to write as required."

On Sunday, the 23rd of December, Bagge was able to begin his entry with "*Hura, wir kommen nach Deutschland! In unser altes, liebes Deutschland! Wie soll man diese Freude beschreiben ...*" "Hurrah, we are going back to Germany! To our old, beloved Germany! How can one describe such joy ..."[7] He learns that the group will be flying back on the third of January. Bagge also reports that, in the light of this news, he has decided to step up his mastery of quantum mechanics in preparation for his return to his normal scientific activities. By Monday, the 31st of December, the travel plans are complete. Of the group, only the Commander will stay behind. To celebrate their imminent return, Bagge reports, that on New Year's Eve they gathered around the piano and sang "Silent Night," while Heisenberg played. Afterwards, Heisenberg addressed a brief thank-you speech to the Commander.

Bagge and the Others Return to Germany

Fortunately, Bagge kept up his diary after leaving Farm Hall, so that we can get a glimpse of what happened to the ten Germans immediately upon their return. They landed in Lübeck and were bused to the nearby town of Alswede. Here they were given living quarters in a confiscated clothier emporium—a

---

[6] "You are Germans..." *Ibid.*, p. 69.

[7] "Hurra..." *Ibid.*, p. 70.

Konfektionsgeschäft—which had been cleaned out and prepared for them. They were free, but only within limits. They were required to report to quarters every evening. In addition, they were at all times to remain within the English occupation zone, and they were separated from their families. By sheer determination, Elisabeth Heisenberg did succeed, a month later, in making the very hazardous trip across a divided Germany to find her husband.

One by one, the group began to separate. In his entry for the 3rd of February, Bagge reports that Harteck and Diebner had left for Hamburg on the 28th of January. Harteck returned to his institute in Hamburg where he reclaimed his professorship. He became rector of the university in 1948 and then emigrated to the United States in 1951, becoming a professor at the Rensselaer Polytechnic Institute in Troy, New York, where he remained until his death in 1985. Diebner joined what Bagge describes as a "private" (that is, not state-supported) research institute in Hamburg that dealt with measuring instruments. He died in 1964. Gerlach went to Bonn as a "guest professor," since the Allies refused initially to allow him to take up his old professorship in Munich. But in 1948 he was allowed to return to Munich where he became rector of the university. He died in 1979 at age 90.

At the end of February 1946, Hahn and Heisenberg returned to Göttingen. The British allowed them to reestablish their old institutes in some empty rooms of what had been Ludwig Prandtl's institute for aeronautical engineering. Here they were soon joined by the rest of the detainees—von Weizsäcker, Wirtz, Korsching, Bagge and von Laue. Shortly thereafter, the Kaiser-Wilhelm Society was abolished by the Allies but resurrected as the "Max Planck Society," named after the aged Max Planck who, at the end of the war, had sought refuge in Göttingen and had remained there until his death in 1947.

Origins of the Heisenberg–Goudsmit Debate

No sooner had Heisenberg returned to Germany than he launched a series of attempts, which had begun with the August 7, 1945 Memorandum from Farm Hall, to present the German wartime nuclear program in the most favorable light possible. Part of his motivation was certainly the impression left after the declarations of Truman and Churchill that the Germans had been engaged in a "feverish race"—Truman's phrase—to build a bomb. But he was further motivated by several popular articles that Goudsmit had written in 1946 that were critical of Heisenberg and the German nuclear effort. These articles may have awakened a lingering animosity deriving from Heisenberg's interrogation by Goudsmit at the end of the war. I would like to speculate a little on how this began and offer some critical remarks on the assertions later made by Heisenberg's widow.

We have seen, both in the reports and in Bagge's diary, the claim made that Goudsmit misled—"led us up the garden path"—the Germans during their interrogations. In the quotation above from the August 7th entry in Bagge's diary, we see Goudsmit allegedly asking why the Germans would spend their time on uranium research when in "America the physicists were doing 'real' wartime physics." In her book *Inner Exile*, first published in 1980, four years after Heisenberg's death, Elisabeth Heisenberg, Heisenberg's widow, raised the same issue.

After describing the "amicable" character of Goudsmit's interrogation of Heisenberg, she writes: "So, during the course of the long discussion he [Heisenberg] asked Goudsmit what was going on with the atomic bomb in America, whether work was being done on it. With a smile, Goudsmit answered that there had been more important things to do during the war."[8] After observing that this seemed to confirm the German intelligence reports that Heisenberg had seen, she concludes, "So what could have been more natural than to believe Goudsmit's statement? And Heisenberg believed him without reservations." Then she goes on, "Perhaps there was also a deeper psychological reason for Heisenberg's credulity: in Copenhagen [a reference to Heisenberg's 1941 visit with Bohr], he had made such great efforts to achieve just what Goudsmit was telling him now and he was all too willing to believe it; it was such a pleasing thought, that his mission might have made a small contribution to preventing the disaster of this development. [This, of course, requires accepting the notion that Heisenberg had come to Copenhagen on a mission of world peace. That was certainly not Bohr's impression.] On the other hand, Heisenberg was naturally aware that Goudsmit was sworn to deepest secrecy and not permitted to say anything about the bomb. But for Heisenberg, the war was over; he was a prisoner of the Americans and he was now irrelevant in the further course of events. Had Goudsmit said that he could and would not answer these questions—after all, the war was still going on—Heisenberg would have accepted this and it would have been different. But he had quite decisively said: 'We made no efforts in that direction; we had more important things to do.' It made sense to Heisenberg. Thus he felt betrayed by Goudsmit, and when, after the bomb had been dropped, his [Heisenberg's] demeanor was interpreted as arrogance and absolute ignorance, he once said with some bitterness: 'How was I to know that Goudsmit was lying right in my face?'" Goudsmit is conveniently turned into the villain of the piece and, indeed, Mrs. Heisenberg makes the absurd and false claim that Goudsmit came to "regret" having written the book and apologized to Heisenberg for having done so.

The proposition I want now to examine is the last sentence of the above quotation: "Goudsmit was lying right in my face." Even Mrs. Heisenberg admits to the possibility that Goudsmit was not actually "lying." Whether he "lied" or not—

---

[8] "So during..." Elisabeth Heisenberg, *Inner Exile* (Birkhäuser, Boston, 1984), pp. 108–109.

and I will shortly argue that as far as I am concerned this is not the real issue—depends on what Goudsmit knew at the time. To do his mission, Goudsmit needed to know next to nothing about the Allied project, and was selected in part for that reason. His job was to find out about the German project. He would have to have been alerted to look for installations which the Germans might have used to separate isotopes or manufacture plutonium. He would not have needed to know about Oak Ridge or Hanford. In his book, Goudsmit does say that he knew in a general way about the test at Trinity, but this was on July 16th. Goudsmit's interview with Heisenberg took place in early May, at which time the final design of the plutonium bomb had not yet even been fixed at Los Alamos. In addition, Goudsmit's background was in radar. There were people working on radar, such as I. I. Rabi, who knew everything about Los Alamos and the bomb project, but who were nonetheless convinced that, while the Allies might win the war with a nuclear weapon, they had a good chance of losing it without radar. Rabi might well have given the same answer as Goudsmit to Heisenberg's question. In fact, when I once asked Rabi, who was one of the prime movers in the development of radar, why he had not actively worked on the bomb, he told me that he had been "serious about winning the war."

To understand why I think that all of this is secondary to what Heisenberg's feelings really were, let us imagine the following scenario. Suppose that when asked the same question, under the same circumstances, Goudsmit had been able to tell Heisenberg all about the Manhattan project—Fermi's reactor, Los Alamos, Oak Ridge and the rest, bearing in mind that at this time no actual nuclear device had been successfully tested—what would this have changed? Why was it so important to Heisenberg that he know this in May as opposed to August when it became general knowledge? The answer seems clear to me; then he would not have made a fool of himself in front of his colleagues at Farm Hall on the night of August 6. Bagge does not comment in the diary, but what could he have thought after Heisenberg's far-fetched speculations about the bomb's being hydrogen or oxygen were revealed for what they were? If Heisenberg had been briefed by Goudsmit, his "omniscience" would have been left intact. He could at least have had the satisfaction of knowing more than the others. Instead, he was reduced to being like them in their mutual ignorance and confusion. This, it seems to me, is why 4 years after his death, and 40 years after the fact, Heisenberg and his widow were still so angry—and it is one of the motivations behind Heisenberg's early postwar debate with Goudsmit.

Goudsmit's Mistakes

Goudsmit's critical articles in 1946 also drove the debate with Heisenberg. These articles, which a year later became the basis of Goudsmit's book *Alsos*, were, as was to become clear in the ensuing years, somewhat unfortunate. They were unfortunate because by misstating a few of the relevant facts about the

Germans' knowledge of nuclear weapons—plutonium being the most notorious example—Goudsmit let Heisenberg avoid the real issues raised by the book. Heisenberg could, and did, react to these errors, but he left largely untouched the underlying issues.

It took Goudmsit some years before he acknowledged that the Germans had thought of using plutonium as an explosive. He also made the incorrect statement that they did not understand the use of fast neutrons produced in uranium-235 fission, as opposed to the moderated neutrons needed to fission uranium-238, to make an explosive chain reaction. The Farm Hall reports make it clear that Heisenberg understood this difference. But the reports also make it clear that Heisenberg understood very little else about bomb physics. To me, an apt comparison would be between someone who knew, in a general way, why heavier-than-air machines can be made to fly, and someone who had tried, and succeeded, in designing a passenger jet.

By confusing these issues and not reading the reports with enough care and technical expertise—it is a pity that he was not allowed to go over the reports with one of the Los Alamos physicists—and by not having access to other important documents, Goudsmit could not effectively oppose the attempts by others to muddy the waters. If he had been more informed about bomb physics, he would have held Heisenberg accountable for his constant attempts to characterize his wartime activities on reactors as "peaceful." Once one knows about plutonium there is, in a certain sense, no such thing as a "peaceful" reactor, as we have found out, all too painfully, in this era of nuclear proliferation. For example, Goudsmit could have focused on the telltale sentence in Heisenberg's September 18, 1945 letter to Blackett in which he wrote, "In wartime, naturally these results would have been followed by technical developments which would have aimed at a practical use of the energy."[9] Goudsmit should have insisted that Heisenberg explain the significance of this statement.

Heisenberg Blames Bothe

In 1946, Heisenberg obtained permission from the British occupation authorities to write an account of the German wartime nuclear program. As Mark Walker has pointed out, this account exists in two versions, a draft and a published article that appeared in *Die Naturwissenschaften* (a slightly abridged translation of which appeared in the British journal *Nature* in 1947). The two German versions are substantially different. The most significant difference, perhaps, has to do with what Heisenberg began referring to as Bothe's "error."

---

[9] "In war time.." Farm Hall transcript Report 8.

It will be recalled that in 1941 Bothe had made a measurement of neutron absorption in graphite, which was published as an Army Ordnance report. The report claimed that too many neutrons were absorbed by graphite for it to be employed as a useful moderator in reactors. This forced the Germans to the use of heavy water and all that that entailed. However, by 1946 Heisenberg had seen the Smyth report in which Fermi's reactor, which had used a graphite moderator, is described. Also described were the efforts, largely by Szilard, to obtain graphite that was free from neutron-absorbing impurities such as boron and cadmium. Heisenberg then, at least in the draft of his 1946 article, blamed Bothe for not understanding this impurity problem and thus preventing graphite from being used by the Germans in their reactor program. The draft was shown to Bothe, who objected strongly, and so this argument does not appear in the published article.

Nonetheless, the proposition that it was somehow Bothe's fault for the German failure continued to be part of Heisenberg's postwar litany. Witness this sentence from Elisabeth Heisenberg's book: "Naturally, he [Heisenberg] would have been glad to see the reactor operating before the end of the war, and he was always a little hurt by the fact that he had not followed the easier path of using carbon instead of heavy water, because he had relied on the incorrect calculations [Bothe's work involved experiments, not "calculations."] of another institute."[10] But as Walker points out, Bothe's measurements were repeated at the time by a German physicist named Wilhelm Hanle who used a differently prepared graphite sample and got more promising results, and, indeed, understood the impurity problem.

These results were communicated to German Army Ordnance and the decision was made that the graphite impurity problem was too costly to solve—hence the use of heavy water. Walker feels that this decision by Army Ordnance was at the time "reasonable and justifiable."[11] I would like to examine this issue a little more closely. It seems clear to me that the graphite matter is symptomatic of the deeper problem that plagued the entire German nuclear program: lack of effective leadership and coordination. I do not know the details of what went into this evaluation by German Army Ordnance, but, in retrospect, it seems difficult to understand why the purification of a common substance like graphite would be more costly than the separation of a rare isotope like deuterium which, furthermore, had to be done in a hostile, occupied country (Norway). In any event, the decision was made by people like Schumann and Diebner, who may have been competent on some level but were certainly not at the very top of their professions.

That aside, from what he writes, Heisenberg does not seem to have been aware of the work by Hanle. All he comments on is Bothe's "mistake." Why was he not alerted to the other work? Still worse, as Harteck remarked in the postwar interview

---

[10]"Naturally..." Heisenberg, *op. cit.* pp. 94–95.
[11]"...reasonable and justifiable..." Walker, *op. cit.*, p. 207.

I quoted from in the Introduction, he did not even know the details of Bothe's experiment. He went so far as to claim, incorrectly, that it had never been published. Not knowing any of this, but realizing that carbon might be a very good moderator, Harteck proceeded, independently of everyone else, to design a reactor that would function with dry ice—frozen carbon dioxide—which could be purified easily. He then ran into the same problem of disorganization and lack of authority. He was not able to requisition enough dry ice and metallic uranium in one place, and at one time, to do a decent experiment. What the German enterprise lacked was a General Groves or a Wernher von Braun. Speer might have done it, but by the time he had a chance to get into the act, the physicists had lost their nerve. They did not want to commit themselves to producing a "wonder weapon" in six months when they knew they could not.

It is clear to me that if Harteck had been able to build his reactor in 1940, when he tried to, the whole situation would have been totally different. The German military, like our own, was exceedingly sceptical about the use of nuclear power. Diebner, in his 1957 monograph with Bagge and Jay, quotes an unnamed German Army official who said to him in 1939, "*Ach, hören Sie mir doch mit Ihrer Atomkakerei auf!*"—roughly "Leave me alone with your atomic 'kakerei.'"[12] In his interview, Harteck reports a high official coming to him about that time and saying, "Look here—if you could make a reactor and get a temperature increase of one degree or a tenth of a degree [indicating that a chain reaction was taking place] you would be able to get all the money in the world."[13] With a working reactor, the Army, in my opinion, would have taken over and pushed the project with the highest priority. There would have been no turning back.

Jungk's Book

The Goudsmit–Heisenberg debate continued publicly and privately for the next few years until the two men agreed to cut it off. Never again, it appears, did they discuss politics. During the few years I spent at the Brookhaven National Laboratory in the early 1960s I saw Goudsmit on a daily basis. By this time Robert Jungk's book *Brighter Than a Thousand Suns* had appeared in English translation. It was published in 1958, and it infuriated Goudsmit. It provoked a widespread controversy that has continued to the present day. Jungk's position turned around the statement: "It seems paradoxical that German nuclear physicists, living under a saber-rattling dictatorship, obeyed the voice of conscience and attempted to prevent the construction of atomic bombs, while their professional colleagues in the democracies, who had no fear, with very few exceptions concentrated their whole energies on the production of the new weapon."[14]

---

[12] "Ach, hören..." Diebner, *op. cit.*, p. 21.

[13] "Look here..." Harteck interview, *op. cit.*, p. 110.

[14] "It seems paradoxical..." Jungk, *op. cit.*, p. 105.

As I have pointed out, Jungk's caricaturial evaluation agrees almost verbatim with the comments made by von Weizsäcker and Wirtz in the Farm Hall reports. There is no doubt that von Weizsäcker contributed actively to the creation of Jungk's book. Heisenberg's role was, as usual, somewhat more murky. He was apparently asked by Jungk to help with the book but declined to meet with him. Later, when sent a copy, he gave a detailed criticism of many points, but never commented on Jungk's characterization of the German nuclear physicists' wartime activities.

I know of Goudsmit's infuriated reaction to Jungk's book because I spoke with him about it often. His feelings about von Weizsäcker and Heisenberg differed greatly. Heisenberg was of his generation. They had grown up in physics together and had remained friends until the war. In one of the last lectures I ever heard Goudsmit give, he spoke with regret of his angry exchanges with Heisenberg and expressed his wish that Heisenberg had been as great a man as he had been a physicist.

Towards von Weizsäcker Goudsmit's feelings were nothing short of contempt. He despised von Weizsäcker. This resulted in a very personal exchange that the two men had in the Dutch newspapers. Von Weizsäcker claimed that Goudsmit's judgment had been compromised by the loss of his parents at the hands of the Nazis. Goudsmit, in turn, claimed that von Weizsäcker's judgment had been compromised because his father had been convicted at the Nuremburg trial. "At least," he concluded, "my parents were innocent."[15]

Jungk, for his part, has apparently changed his tune recently.[16] In his preface to the German edition of Mark Walker's book he writes, "That I have contributed to the spreading of the myth of passive resistance by the most important German physicists is due above all to my esteem for these impressive personalities, which I have since realized to be out of place."[17]

Max von Laue and the Lesart

Goudsmit was, of course, not alone in his negative reaction to Jungk's book. One of the people who at the time of the original publication of Jungk's book had no delusions about it was Paul Rosbaud. Rosbaud, it may be remembered, was the Austrian-born chemist who had remained in Germany during the war and had

---

[15]"At least..." There exists a tape recording of a lecture given by Goudsmit at Harvard on the 8th of April 1975 in which he quotes this exchange.

[16]For a discussion of Heisenberg's role in relation to Jungk's book see Mark Walker, "Legends surrounding the German atomic bomb," in *Science, Medicine, and Cultural Imperialism*, edited by Teresa Meade and Walker, (New York, 1991), pp. 178–204. I thank Professor Walker for sending me a reprint of this article.

[17]"That I have..." Siedler, Preface to *Die Uranmaschine* (Siedler, Berlin), 1990.

functioned as one of the major sources for British intelligence. He had later moved to Britain.

Rosbaud wrote a negative review of Jungk's book in the British magazine *Discovery*. His review prompted two remarkable letters from Max von Laue. As we have seen, during Farm Hall von Laue had, for whatever reasons, supported the position arrived at by Heisenberg and others and expressed in the August 8 Memorandum: namely, that the Germans had, after a preliminary feasibility study, given up all notions of making nuclear weapons in favor of the construction of a "peaceful" reactor. Jungk's claim over a decade later that, for moral reasons, the German scientists had prevented the construction of nuclear weapons in their country was too much for von Laue to stomach. Hence his letters to Rosbaud. They are remarkable. They are given in full in the original German and in English translation in Appendix 2. I cite some relevant extracts here.

In his letter of 4 April 1959, von Laue writes:[18]

> ...I never had the ambition to be a nuclear physicist, as you know. Only the Western Allies called me one, in 1945. Only once—I do not remember whether it was in 1941 or 1942—was I invited to a meeting of the Uranium Club in Berlin, where I got the impression of a somewhat comical secret affair. (In the discussion, uranium was mentioned only as "metal.") It seemed to be a rather muddled business, without a real purpose. Much was changed after the Kaiser-Wilhelm Institute was moved to Hechingen. Once I visited a cave in the rocks in Haigerloch, where the experimental pile of uranium was supposed to be protected from the bombs. But my previous impression was not changed by what I saw there ...

> After that day [August 6, 1945], we talked much about the conditions of an atomic explosion. Heisenberg gave a lecture on the subject in one of the colloquia which we prisoners had arranged for ourselves. Later, during the table conversation, the version [*Lesart*] was developed that the German atomic physicists really had not wanted the atomic bomb, either because it was impossible to achieve it during the expected duration of the war or because they simply did not want to have it at all. The leader in these discussions was Weizsäcker; I not did hear the mention of any ethical point of view. Heisenberg was mostly silent.

---

[18]"Prof. Dr. Max von Laue ..." The photocopies of these letters were supplied to me by Arnold Kramish. In his book, *The Griffin* (Houghton Mifflin, Boston, 1986). Kramish gives a translation of these letters. He leaves a part of the second letter out and I have somewhat modified his translations.

Rosbaud answered this letter on the 12th of April, which prompted a second letter from von Laue (see Appendix 2). This letter gives a very disturbing picture of von Laue's life at Farm Hall, in which he recounts several personality conflicts with his fellow detainees, as well as his apprehensions about postwar Germany.

It is difficult to sort out from this second letter how much of von Laue's revelations and complaints about his fellow detainees and of his fear of being spied on in Berlin were legitimate and how much was the furniture of the imagination of a 78-year-old man—von Laue's age when he wrote these letters. But it is clear that at Farm Hall, and afterwards, von Laue was alienated from his fellow detainees. In a sense, he and Diebner, although occupying opposite ends of the spectrum, posed similar problems for the others. Diebner never entered into a compromise with the regime. Instead, as a member of the Nazi Party and an official in German Army Ordnance, he was part of it. The fact that his fellow detainees—von Laue excepted— had all been part of the enterprise, of which Diebner was a prime mover, compromised them. On the other hand, von Laue was a constant reminder to the rest of them that it was possible for a courageous individual to have survived in Germany without having compromised; something that they had done over and over again.

In any event, one thing about von Laue's letters—the first one especially— which seems undeniable, is von Laue's account of the "version" of the Germans' wartime nuclear effort that was clearly invented at Farm Hall. We have already seen its genesis and, finally, its fruition in the remark that von Weizsäcker made to von Laue the night of August 6: "History will record that the Americans and the English made a bomb, and that at the same time the Germans, under the Hitler regime, produced a workable engine. In other words, the peaceful development of the uranium engine was made in Germany under the Hitler regime, whereas the Americans and English developed this ghastly weapon of war." This is what von Laue called the *Lesart* in his letter.

But these Germans, especially von Weizsäcker and Heisenberg, were not satisfied with this. A subtle escalation was introduced. Not only did they work only on the "peaceful" reactor, but they actually "prevented" the atomic bomb from falling into Hitler's hands. This, of course, assumes that they knew how to make an atomic bomb. However, what the Farm Hall reports make transparently clear is that, while they knew a few general principles—the use of fast fission from separated ^{235}U and the possibility of plutonium—they had not seriously investigated any of the details. All of the really hard problems were left untackled and unsolved. They had gotten far enough to realize that the separation of uranium isotopes would require a major industrial effort. They also realized that the use of plutonium required a successful reactor project on a very large scale. Since they never produced any plutonium, they had not yet confronted the implosion question. All their Farm Hall speculations on how to design an actual weapon were based on using some kind of cannon barrel to assemble the subcritical pieces. In fact, they had decided that making a bomb in wartime Germany was unfeasible on technical and economic grounds. It was simply too big and too costly. Morality had nothing to do with it. But if it was unfeasible, what was there to "prevent"? If these scientists had simply pointed out that they had made these studies, found the bomb unfeasible, and gone on to trying to build a reactor, one might have felt differently about them. But to claim some high moral ground for what they did or did not do is what so many people found so distasteful.

Will the publication of the Farm Hall reports settle these matters? Perhaps not for everyone. Even before they were released in their entirety, some of the people affected were already working to diminish their importance. Here is Elisabeth Heisenberg: "Since these tapes [of which she had seen only the tiniest excerpts of the transcribed conversations] are quoted so frequently in the United States and are used as proof for the presumptuousness and lack of knowledge of the German scientists, the objection should be made that the interpretation of such documents as these tapes must be wrong of necessity, if the originals are not examined by experts familiar with the nuances of the German language; they must also be capable of including correctly the psychology of the various individuals in their analysis, especially the complicated relationships among them."[19]

While one might have cautionary thoughts about snippets of the recorded conversations, taken as a whole, the message of these reports seems absolutely clear, especially since significant parts of them are in their original languages—English for the conversation with Blackett and German for Heisenberg's lecture and the August 8th Memorandum. The "presumptuousness and lack of knowledge of the German scientists" comes through on every page. In the end, the Farm Hall reports speak for themselves.

---

[19]"Since these tapes..." Elisabeth Heisenberg, *op. cit.*, p. 115.

APPENDIX 1

THE THEORETICAL FOUNDATIONS FOR OBTAINING ENERGY FROM FISSION OF URANIUM
by Werner Heisenberg
Translation by William Sweet

(Manuscript of the lecture delivered February 26, 1942 at the House of German Research.[1])

At the beginning of the work on the uranium problem, done in the framework of the Army Weapons Bureau task force, the following experimental facts became known:

1) Normal uranium is a mixture of three isotopes: $^{238}_{92}U$, $^{235}_{92}U$, and $^{234}_{92}U$, which are found in natural minerals approximately in the relationship 1:1/140:1/17,000.

2) The uranium nuclei can, as *[Otto]* Hahn and *[Fritz]* Strassmann discovered, be split by means of neutron irradiation; specifically, the nucleus of $^{235}_{92}U$ by neutrons of all (including low) energies (Bohr), and the nuclei of $^{238}_{92}U$ and $^{234}_{92}U$ only by means of fast neutrons.

3) Each fission releases, per atomic nucleus, an energy of about 150 to 200 million electron volts. This energy is about 100 million times greater, per atom, than the energies released in chemical reactions. Furthermore, in each fission reaction a few neutrons are ejected from the atomic nucleus.

From these facts can be concluded: If one managed, for example, to split all the nuclei of 1 ton of uranium, an enormous energy of about 15 trillion kilocalories would be released. It had been known for a long time that such high amounts of energy are released in nuclear transmutations. Before the discovery of fission, however, there was no prospect of inducing nuclear reactions in large quantities of material. For in artificially induced reactions in high-voltage facilities, cyclotrons and so on, the expenditure of energy is always much greater than the energy produced.

The fact that in the fission process several neutrons are ejected opens the prospect, on the other hand, that the transformation of large quantities of material could be effected in a chain reaction. The neutrons ejected in fission would, for their part, split other uranium nuclei, more neutrons would be produced, and so on; by repeating this process many times one obtains an ever greater increase in the number of neutrons, which only stops when a large proportion of the substance has been transformed.

---

[1]The parenthetical description is a handwritten note by Heisenberg.

Before addressing the question of whether this program can be carried out in practice, it will be necessary to study more closely the various processes that can generate a neutron from uranium. A neutron liberated in fission can either, if it has enough energy, after traveling a short distance, collide with another uranium nucleus, split it and generate another neutron, or it can—and unfortunately this is much more likely—just give up energy in the collision to the nucleus, without splitting it, whereupon the neutron continues on its way with less energy. In this case the energy of the neutron will be so small after a few collisions that only the following possibilities exist for its destiny: In the course of colliding with an atom it can get stuck in the nucleus, in which case further propagation is impossible; or—and this unfortunately is rather improbable—it can collide with a nucleus of $^{235}_{92}$U and split it. Then further neutrons are generated in the process, and the events just described can begin again. Some of the neutrons can escape from the surface of the uranium bulk and thereby be lost.

The exact description of the probabilities of each process taking place was an important programmatic point in the work of the task force, and Mr. *[Walther]* Bothe will report on the results.

For our purposes it is sufficient to state that in natural uranium, neutron absorption (in which a neutron is captured by $^{238}_{92}$U, yielding the new isotope $^{239}_{92}$U) is much more common than fission or propagation. Therefore the chain reaction we are looking for cannot take place in natural uranium, and one has to sniff out new ways and means of effecting initiation of the chain reaction.

The behavior of the neutrons in uranium can be compared to the behavior of a population, such that the fission process has an analog in marriage and neutron capture in death. In normal uranium the death toll greatly outweighs the number of births, so that the existing population always will have to die out after a short time.

An improvement in the fundamentals obviously is possible only if one succeeds in (1) raising the number of births per marriage, (2) boosting the number of marriages or (3) reducing the probability of death.

Possibility (1) does not exist in the neutron population, because the number of neutrons per fission is established by natural laws and constants that cannot be influenced. (For the determination of these important constants, take note of the talk by Mr. Bothe.)

There remain therefore only paths (2) and (3). An increase in the number of fissions can be reached if one enriches the uranium in the fissionable but much rarer isotope $^{235}_{92}$U. If in fact one succeeded in producing pure $^{235}_{92}$U, then the conditions would come into play that are portrayed on the right side of the first figure. Every neutron would, after one or more collisions, cause another fission, provided it did not escape from the surface. The probability of death by neutron capture is vanishingly small compared with the probability of propagation. So if one just assembles a certain amount of $^{235}_{92}$U, so that neutron loss through the surface stays small compared with internal multiplication, then the number of neutrons will increase enormously in a very short time and the whole fission energy of 15 trillion kilocalories per ton is released in a fraction of a second. The pure isotope $^{235}_{92}$U undoubtedly represents, then, an explosive material of unimaginable force. Granted, this explosive is very hard to obtain.

A big part of the work of the Army Weapons Bureau task force has been devoted to the problem of enrichment, that is, the production of pure $^{235}_{92}$U. American research also appears to be oriented in this direction, with considerable emphasis. In the course of this session Mr. *[Klaus]* Clusius will report on the status of this question, and so I will not have to go into it any further.

There remains to be discussed now only the third possibility for initiating the chain reaction: reduction of the death toll, that is, the probability of neutron capture. According to general principles of nuclear physics it can be assumed that the probability of capture becomes large only at very specific neutron energy levels. (The investigations of the past year have yielded valuable results on just this point.) If one succeeded in quickly slowing the neutrons, without too many collisions, to the region of lowest possible energies (that is, the energy region given by thermal motion), then one could reduce the death toll substantially. In practice one can effect a rapid diminution of neutron speed by adding suitable braking substances *[or moderators]*, that is, substances whose nuclei—when hit by a neutron—take away part of the neutron's energy. If one adds enough braking substance, then one can bring the neutrons without danger into the region of lowest energies. But unfortunately most braking substances have the property of also capturing neutrons, so that too much braking substance will increase the probability of capture, that is, the death toll. These relations are portrayed schematically on the other *[left]* side of the first figure.

It is a question, accordingly, of finding a moderator that quickly removes energy from a neutron without, as far as possible, absorbing it.

The one substance that does not absorb at all, helium, unfortunately cannot be used because of its low density. The most suitable material almost certainly is deuterium, which is available in its simplest combination—and also in sufficient proportion—in water. Admittedly, heavy water is not easy to obtain in large quantities. The task force has initiated thorough investigations into the production of heavy water and other substances that are possibilities, such as beryllium and carbon.

Pursuant to an idea of *[Paul]* Harteck, it has proved advisable to separate the uranium and the moderator *[in a reactor]*, so that the kind of arrangements result that are seen in the layered ball shown in the second and third figures, which was built as a small-scale experiment at the Kaiser-Wilhelm Institute *[for Physics at Berlin–Dahlem]*.

Whether this kind of layering of natural uranium and moderator can lead to a chain reaction and therewith to the liberation of large energies, that is, whether the "death rate" can be reduced enough for the "birth rate" to outweigh it, so that an increase in the population begins, has to be regarded as a completely open question, since the properties of the few substances that can be used as moderators are given and cannot be changed.

To illuminate this point was again one of the most important assignments of the task force.

Let us now assume for a moment that this question has been resolved in a positive sense; then it still has to be investigated how this particular arrangement behaves with greater multiplication of the neutron population. It turned out that multiplication does not stop only when a greater part of the uranium is transformed, but much sooner. The ever greater propagation leads in fact to a strong warming, and with the warming—since the neutrons move faster and therefore spend less time in the neighborhood of a uranium nucleus—the probability of fission gets smaller. The warming has as a consequence, then, a diminution in the number of "marriages" and hence in the multiplication; because of that, at a certain temperature the neutron multiplication will be exactly balanced by absorption.

So the layered arrangement as described will stabilize itself at a certain temperature. As soon as energy is drawn from the machine, cooling and a renewed multiplication set in, and the drawn energy in turn is replaced by fission energies; the machine stays for all practical purposes at the same temperature.

One arrives with this at a machine that is suitable for heating a steam turbine and that can put its very large energies over a period of time at the disposal of such a thermal power machine. One can therefore think of practical applications for such machines in transportation, especially in ships, which would acquire enormous range from the huge energy reserve contained in a relatively small quantity of uranium. That such a machine does not burn any oxygen would be a particular advantage if used in submarines.

As soon as such a machine is in operation, the question of how to obtain explosive material, according to an idea of *[Carl Friedrich]* von Weizsäcker, takes a new turn. In the transmutation of the uranium in the machine, a new substance comes into existence, element 94, which very probably—just like $^{235}_{92}U$—is an explosive of equally unimaginable force. This substance is much easier to obtain from uranium than $^{235}_{92}U$, however, since it can be separated from uranium by chemical means.

Whether a mixture of uranium and moderator can be found in which the chain reaction can take its course has still—as stated—to be determined by experiment.

But also, when such a mixture is found, a large quantity of this mixture must still be amassed to allow the chain reaction really to run, since with smaller quantities the loss of neutrons through the surface always will be greater than the internal multiplication. Experiments with very small quantities of substance are therefore from the outset insufficient for deciding the suitability of the mixtures for the chain reaction. Without generous support of the research work—with materials, radioactive sources, funds—as obtained from the Army Weapons Bureau, it would not have been possible to progress. But even with the larger quantities—for example, of heavy water—that have been made available, the chain reaction still cannot take place. Therefore we must still touch on the question of how one can recognize in a small-scale experiment whether in the chosen mixture the "birth rate" is outweighing the "death rate."

To resolve this question effectively, one introduces into the mixture a neutron source about which it is known how many neutrons per second it emits. If the number of neutrons escaping from the mixture is greater than the number introduced with the source, then one can conclude that multiplication is outweighing absorption and that a suitable mixture has been found.

Experiments conducted in Leipzig in the last few years have shown that a certain mixture of heavy water and uranium actually has the desired properties. To be sure, the surplus of the "birth rate" over the "death rate" was so small in these experiments that it was canceled by additional absorption in the container material. But the container material can be dispensed with later or can be replaced by something else.

To the extent one can extrapolate from laboratory-scale experiments to large-scale experiments, the experiments unequivocally support the possibility that with a layering of uranium and moderator a machine can be built as indicated.

The results to date can be summarized as follows:

1) Obtaining energy from uranium fission is undoubtedly possible if enrichment in the $^{235}_{92}$U isotope is successful. Production of pure ^{235}U would lead to an explosive of unimaginable force.

2) Natural uranium also can be used for energy production in a layered arrangement with heavy water. A layered arrangement of these substances can transfer its great energy reserve over a period of time to a thermal power machine. Such a reactor provides a means of liberating very large, usable quantities of energy from relatively small quantities of substance. An operational machine can also be used to obtain a hugely powerful explosive; over and above that, it promises a number of other scientifically and technically important applications, which go beyond the scope of this talk.

[A concluding sentence refers to the three figures, shown here on page 384.]

DIE THEORETISCHEN GRUNDLAGEN FÜR DIE ENERGIEGEWINNUNG AUS DER URANSPALTUNG

Werner Heisenberg

(Manuskript zum Vortrag am 26/2/1942 im Haus der Deutschen Forschung[2])

Zu Beginn der Arbeiten über das Uranproblem im Rahmen der Arbeitsgemeinschaft des Heereswaffenamtes waren die folgenden experimentellen Tatsachen bekannt:

(1) Gewöhnliches Uran ist ein Gemisch aus drei Isotopen: $^{238}_{92}U$, $^{235}_{92}U$, $^{234}_{92}U$, die in natürlichen Mineralien etwa in dem Verhältnis 1:1/140:1/17000 vorkommen.

(2) Durch Neutronenbestrahlung können nach *Hahn* and *Strassmann* die Urankerne gespalten werden, und zwar der Kern $^{235}_{92}U$ durch Neutronen *aller* (auch geringer) Geschwindigkeiten (*Bohr*), die Kerne $^{238}_{92}U$ and $^{234}_{92}U$ nur durch energiereiche Neutronen.

(3) Bei der Spaltung wird pro Atomkern eine Energie von etwa 150 bis 200 Millionnen Elektron-Volt frei. Diese Energie ist etwa 100 Millionen mal größer als die Energien, die bei chemischen Umsetzungen pro Atom gewöhnlich freigemacht werden. Ferner werden bei jeder Spaltung einige Neutronen aus dem Atomkern herausgeschleudert.

Aus diesen Tatsachen kann man schließen: Wenn es gelingen würde, sämtliche Atomkerne von z. B. 1 to Uran durch Spaltung umzuwandeln, so würde dabei die ungeheure Energiemenge von etwa 15 Billionen Kilokalorien frei. Daß bei Atomkern-Umwandlungen so hohe Energiebeträge umgesetzt werden, war seit langem bekannt. Vor der Entdeckung der Spaltung bestand jedoch keine Aussicht, Kernumwandlungen an größeren Substanzmengen durchzuführen. Denn bei künstlichen Umwandlungen mit Hochspannungslagen, Cyclotrons, usw. ist der Energieaufwand stets viel größer als der erreichte Energiegewinn.

Die Tatsache, daß beim Spaltungsprozeß mehrere Neutronen ausgeschleudert werden, eröffnet dagegen die Aussicht, die Umwandlung großer Substanzmengen durch eine Kettenreaktion zu erzwingen: Die bei der Spaltung ausgeschleuderten Neutronen sollen ihrerseits wieder andere Urankerne spalten, hierdurch entstehen wieder neue Neutronen usw.; durch mehrfache Wiederholung dieses Prozesses setzt eine sich immer weiter steigernde Vermehrung der Neutronenzahl ein, die erst aufhört, wenn ein großer Teil der Substanz umgewandelt ist.

Vor der Untersuchung der Frage, ob dieses Programm durchgeführt werden kann, mußten die verschiedenen Prozesse näher studiert werden, die ein Neutron in Uran hervorrufen kann. Die Abb. 1 gibt eine schematische Übersicht über diese

---

[2]Handwritten additional note by Heisenberg. Based on the text published in Heisenberg, "Papers" (see Bibliography), pp. 517–521. Reprinted with permission.

Prozesse. Ein etwa durch Spaltung freigewordenes Neutron kann entweder, wenn es genügend Energie besitzt, nach kurzer Wegstrecke mit einem Urankern zusammenstoßen, ihn spalten und dabei neue Neutronen erzeugen. Oder es kann, was leider viel wahrscheinlicher ist, bei einem solchen Zusammestoß nur Energie an den Atomkern abgeben, ohne ihn zu zerlegen, worauf das Neutron mit geringerer Energie weiterfliegt. In diesem Fall wird nach einigen Zusammenstößen die Energie des Neutrons so gering geworden sein, daß für sein weiteres Schicksal nur folgende beiden Möglichkeiten bestehen: Es kann einmal beim Zusammenstoß mit einem Urankern in diesem steckenbleiben. Dann ist jede weitere "Vermehrung" unmöglich. Oder es kann—was leider relativ unwahrscheinlich ist—mit einem Kern $^{235}_{92}$U zusammenstoßen und diesen spalten. Dann entstehen bei diesem Prozeß wieder neue Neutronen und die geschilderten Vorgänge können von Neuem beginnen. Ein Teil der Neutronen kann durch die Oberfläche aus dem Uran austreten und dadurch für die weitere Vermehrung verloren gehen.

Die genauere Untersuchung der Wahrscheinlichkeiten, mit der die verschiedenen Prozesse stattfinden, war ein wichtiger Programmpunkt für die Arbeit der Arbeitsgemeinschaft, über deren Ergebnisse Herr Bothe berichten wird.

Für das Folgende genügt die Feststellung, daß im gewöhnlichen Uran der Prozeß der Neutronenabsorption (Einfang eines Neutrons im $^{238}_{92}$U unter Bildung eines neuen Isotops $^{239}_{92}$U) sehr viel häufiger geschieht als der der Spaltung und Vermehrung. Im gewöhnlichen Uran kann also die gewünschte Kettenreaktion nicht ablaufen, und man muß auf neue Mittel und Wege sinnen, um den Ablauf der Kettenreaktion doch zu erzwingen.

Das Verhalten der Neutronen im Uran kann ja mit dem Verhalten einer Bevölkerungsdichte verglichen werden, wobei der Spaltungsprozeß das Analogon zur Eheschließung und der Einfangprozeß die Analogie zum Tode darstellt. Im gewöhnlichen Uran überwiegt die Sterbeziffer bei weitem bei Geburtenzahl, so daß eine vorhandene Bevölkerung stets nach kurzer Zeit aussterben muß.

Eine Verbesserung dieser Sachlage is offenbar nur möglich, wenn es gelingt, entweder: (1) die Zahl der Beburten pro Eheschließung zu erhöhen; oder (2) die Zahl der Eheschließungen zu steigern; oder (3) die Sterbewahrscheinlichkeit herabzusetzen.

Die Möglichkeit (1) besteht bei der Neutronenbevölkerung nicht, da die mittlere Anzahl der Neutronen pro Spaltung eine durch die Naturgesetze festgelegte und nicht weiter zu beeinflussende Konstante ist. (Über die Bestimmung dieser wichtigen Konstanten vgl. den Vortrag von Herrn Bothe.)

Daher bleiben nur die Wege (2) and (3). Eine Erhöhung der Anzahl der Spaltungen (2) läßt sich erreichen, wenn man das auch bei kleineren Energien spaltbare aber seltenere Isotop $^{235}_{92}$U anreichert; wenn es etwa gelänge, das Isotop $^{235}_{92}$U sogar rein darzustellen, so bestünden die Verhältnisse, die auf der rechten Seite der Abb. 1 dargestellt sind. Jedes Neutron würde nach einem oder mehreren

Zusammenstößen eine weitere Spaltung bewirken, wenn es nicht vorher etwa durch die Oberfläche austritt. Die Sterbewahrscheinlichkeit durch Einfang ist hier gegenüber der Vermehrungswahrscheinlichkeit verschwindend gering. Wenn man also nur eine so große Menge von $^{235}_{92}$U aufhäuft, daß der Neutronenverlust durch die Oberfläche klein bleibt gegen die Vermehrung im Inneren, so wird sich die Neutronenzahl in kürzester Zeit ungeheuer vermehren und die ganze Spaltungsenergie von 15 Bill. Kalorien pro to wird in einem kleinen Bruchteil einer Sekunde frei. Das rein Isotop $^{235}_{92}$U stellt also zweifellos einen Sprengstoff von ganz unvorstellbarer Wirkung dar. Allerdings ist dieser Sprengstoff sehr schwer zu gewinnen.

Ein großer Teil der Arbeit der Arbeitsgemeinschaft des Heereswaffenamtes ist dem Problem der Anreicherung bzw. der Reindarstellung des Isotops $^{235}_{92}$U gewidmet. Auch die amerikanische Forschung scheint diese Arbeitsrichtung mit besonderem Nachdruck zu betreiben. Im Rahmen der Sitzung wird Herr Clusius über den Stand dieser Frage berichten, ich habe daher hierauf nicht weiter einzugehen.

Es bleibt jetzt nur noch die dritte Möglichkeit zur Herbeiführung der Kettenreaktion zu erörtern: Die Herabsetzung der Sterbeziffer, d. h. der Einfangswahrscheinlichkeit der Neutronen.

Nach allgemeinen kernphysikalischen Erfahrungen konnte angenommen werden, daß die Einfangswahrscheinlichkeit nur bei ganz bestimmten Energien der Neutronen große Werte annimmt. (Die Untersuchungen des letzten Jahres haben gerade über diesen Punkt neues wertvolles Material ergeben.) Wenn es also gelingt, die Neutronen rasch, ohne viel Zusammenstöße mit Urankernen, in das Gebiet der kleinsten möglichen Energien (d. h. der durch die Wärmebewegung gegebenen Energien) zu befördern, so kann man dadurch die Sterbeziffer erheblich herabsetzen. In der Praxis kann man die rasche Verminderung der Neutronengeschwindigkeit bewirken durch den Zusatz geeigneter Bremssubstanzen: d. h. Substanzen, deren Atomkerne dann, wenn sie von einem Neutron getroffen werden, dem Neutron einen Teil seiner Energie entziehen. Wenn man nur hinreichend viel Bremssubstanz zusetzt, kann man also die Neutronen gefahrlos in das Gebiet der niedrigsten Energien bringen. Aber leider haben die meisten Bremssubstanzen wieder die Eigenschaft, auch gelegentlich Neutronen einzufangen, so daß eine allzugroße Menge Bremssubstanz die Einfangswahrscheinlichkeit, d. h. die Sterbeziffer wieder heraufsetzt. Schematisch sind diese Verhältnisse auf der einen Seite der Abb. 1 dargestellt.

Es kommt also darauf an, eine Bremssubstanz zu finden, die den Neutronen schnell Energie entzieht, aber sie so wenig wie möglich absorbiert.

Die einzige Substanz, die überhaupt nicht absorbiert, das Helium, kommt leider wegen seiner geringen Dichte praktisch kaum in Frage. Als die dann am meisten geeignete Substanz muß Deuterium betrachtet werden, das in seiner einfachsten

Verbindung, in schwerem Wasser, auch in hinreichender Dichte verfügbar ist. Allerdings ist auch schweres Wasser nicht leicht in großen Mengen zu gewinnen. Die Arbeitsgemeinschaft hat über die Eignung von schwerem Wasser und anderen noch in Betracht kommenden Substanzen (Beryllium, Kohle) ausführliche Untersuchengen angestellt.

Es hat sich nach einem Gedanken von *Harteck* als zweckmäßig erwiesen, Uran and Bremssubstanz räumlich zu trennen, so daß dann Anordnungen entstehen, wie die in Abb. 2 und 3 dargestellte Schichtenkugel, die für einen Modellversuch im Kaiser-Wilhelm Institut gebaut worden ist.

Ob eine solche Schichtung aus gewöhnlichem Uran und Bremssubstanz zur Kettenreaktion und damit zur Freimachung der großen Energien führen kann, d. h. ob die "Sterbeziffer" soweit gesenkt werden kann, daß die "Geburtenzahl" überwiegt und eine Vermehrung der "Bevölkerung" eintritt, mußte zunächst als völlig offe betrachtet werden, da die Eigenschaften der wenigen Substanzen, die zur Bremsung überhaupt benützt werden können, ja gegeben sind und nicht verändert werden können.

Diesen Punkt zu klären, war wieder eine der wichtigsten Aufgaben des Arbeitskreises.

Nehmen wir nun für einen Augenblick an, diese Frage sei im positiven Sinne gelöst, dann muß untersucht werden, wie sich diese gewählte Anordnung bei weiterer Vermehrung der Neutronenbevölkerung verhält. Dabei stellte sich heraus, daß der Prozeß der Vermehrung hier nicht erst aufhört, wenn ein großer Teil des Urans umgewandelt ist, sondern schon viel früher. Die immer weiter steigende Vermehrung hat nämlich eine starke Erwärmung zur Folge und mit der Erwärmung wird—da die Neutronen sich schneller bewegen und daher küzere Zeit in der Nähe eines Urankernes zubringen—die Wahrscheinlichkeit zur Spaltung geringer. Die Erwämung hat also eine Verringerung der Anzahl der "Eheschließungen" und damit der Vermehrung zur Folge; daher wird bei einer bestimmten Temperatur gerade die Neutronenvermehrung die Absorption kompensieren.

Die geschilderte Schichtenanordnung wird sich also auf einer bestimmten Temperatur von selbst stabilisieren. Sobald der Maschine von außen Energie entzogen wird, so tritt Abkühlung und damit erneute Vermehrung ein, die entzogene Energie wird auch durch die Spaltungsenergien wieder ersetzt; die Maschine bleibt praktisch stets auf der gleichen Temperatur.

Man kommt damit zu einer Maschine, die etwa zum Heizen einer Dampfturbine geeignet ist und die einer solchen Wärmekraftmaschine ihre ganzen großen Energien im Laufe der Zeit zur Verfügung stellen kann. Man kann daher an die praktische Verwendung solcher Maschinen in Fahrzeugen, besonders in Schiffen, denken, die durch den großen Energievorrat einer relativ kleinen Uranmenge einen riesigen

Aktionsradius bekommen würden. Daß die Maschine keinen Sauerstoff verbrennt, wäre bei der Verwendung in U-Booten ein besonderer Vorteil.

Sobald eine solche Maschine einmal in Betrieb ist, erhält auch, nach eine Gedanken von *v. Weizsäcker*, die Frage nach der Gewinnung des Sprengstoffs eine neue Wendung. Bei der Umwandlung des Urans in der Maschine entsteht nämlich eine neue Substanz (Element der Ordnungszahl 94), die höchstwahrscheinlich ebenso wie reines $^{235}_{92}U$ ein Sprengstoff der gleichen unvorstellbaren Wirkung ist. Diese Substanz läßt sich aber viel leichter als $^{235}_{92}U$ aus dem Uran gewinnen, da sie chemisch von Uran getrennt werden kann.

Ob eine Mischung von Uran and Bremssubstanz gefunden werden kann, in der die Kettenreaktion ablaufenkann, mußte, wie gegsagt, erst durch die Experimente entschieden werden. Aber auch, wenn eine solche Mischung gefunden ist, muß eine große Menge dieser Mischung angehäuft werden, um die Kettenreaktion wirklich ablaufen zu lassen, da bei kleineren Mengen der Neutronenverlust durch Abwanderung der Neutronen nach außen stets größer sein wird als die Vermehrung im Inneren. Versuche mit sehr kleinen Substanzmengen sind daher von vornherein unzureichend für die Entscheidung über die Eignung von Mischungen zur Kettenrektion. Ohne die großzügige Unterstützung der Forschungsarbeit durch Material, radioaktive Präparate und Geldmittel, wie sie vom Heereswaffenamt erfolgt ist, wäre hier also überhaupt nicht weiterzukommen gewesen. Aber selbst mit den größeren Mengen z. B. an schwerem Wasser, die bisher zur Verfügung stehen, kann die Kettenreaktion noch nicht ablaufen. Daher muß noch kurz die Frage gestreift werden, wie man im Modellversuch erkennen kann, ob in der gewählten Mischung schon die "Geburtenziffer" die "Sterbeziffer" überwiegt.

Man bringt zu Entscheidung dieser Frage zweckmäßig ein Neutronenpräparat in die Mischung, von dem man weiß, wieviele Neutronen *[es]* pro sec aussendet. Wenn die Neutronenmenge, die dann außen aus der Mischung herauskommt, größer ist als die, die durch das Präparat hereingesteckt wird, so kann man schließen, daß die Vermehrung die Absorption überwiegt, daß also eine geeignete Mischung gefunden ist.

Die im letzten Jahre in Leipzig durchgeführten Versuche haben gezeigt, daß eine bestimmte Mischung aus schwerem Wasser and Uran tatsächlich die gewünschten Eigenschaften hat. Allerdings ist der Überschuß der "Geburtenziffer" über die "Sterbeziffer" bei diesen Versuchen noch so gering, daß schon die geringe zusatzliche Absorption durch das dort verwendete Halterungsmaterial den Überschuß wieder aufhebt. Aber das Halterungsmaterial ist später nicht notwendig oder kann durch anderes ersetzt werden.

Mit dem Grad von Sicherheit, mit dem überhaupt aus Laboratoriumsversuchen auf Großversuche geschlossen werden kann, sprechen die Versuche daher eindeutig für die Möglichkeit, mit einer Schichtung aus Uran und Bremssubstanz eine Maschine der bezeichneten Art zu bauen.

Die bisherigen Ergebnisse lassen sich in folgender Weise zusammenfassen:

(1) Die Energiegewinnung aus der Uranspaltung ist zweifellos möglich, wenn die Anreicherung des Isotops $^{235}_{92}$U gelingt. Die *Reindarstellung* von $^{235}_{92}$U würde zu einem Sprengstoff von unvorstellbarer Wirkung führen.

(2) Auch gewöhnliches Uran kann in einer Schichtung mit schwerem Wasser zur Energiegewinnung ausgenützt werden. Eine Schichtenanordnung aus diesen Stoffen kann ihren großen Energievorrat im Lauf der Zeit auf eine Wärmekraftmaschine übertragen. Sie gibt also ein Mittel in die Hand, sehr große technisch verwertbare Energiemengen in relativ kleinen Substanzmengen aufzubewahren. Auch die Maschine im Betrieb kann zur Gewinnung eines ungeheuer starken Sprengstoffs führen; sie verspricht daüberhinaus eine Menge von anderen wissenschaftlich and technisch wichtigen Anwendungen, über die jedoch hier nicht berichtet werden sollte.

Hierzu Abb. 1–3 nah den Diapositiven, die wohl bereits in Händen des H[eeres]W[affen]A[mtes]sind.[3]

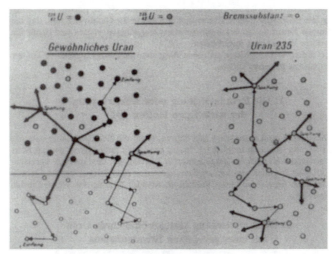

Fission reactions in pure uranium-235 (right) and unenriched uranium above a layer of moderator (left) are depicted in this first figure from Heisenberg's talk. Spaltung means "fission" and Einfang "capture."

---

[3]Handwritten note by Heisenberg referring to the three figures.

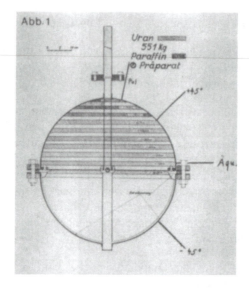

Layered reactor built at the Kaiser-Wilhelm Institute for Physics in Berlin–Dahlem. Top: In the design for the reactor, sheets of uranium metal are seen to alternate with sheets of paraffin. Bottom: The actual reactor, seen externally in a container of water.

APPENDIX 2

The following letters appear to have been typed by von Laue himself. There are words crossed out and the typewriter seems to have had some defective keys. There does not seem, for example, to have been a character for "w," which was given as "u." English translations follow the original German. Translations are provided by Richard Beyler and myself.

1. Max von Laue to Paul Rosbaud, Berlin-Dahlem, April 4, 1959

PROF. DR. MAX VON LAUE
Berlin-Dahlem den 4.4.59
Faradayweg
Tel: 76 45 86

An Herrn Dr. Paul Rosbaud
7 Ashley Garden Westminster
London SW 1 (England)

Lieber Rosbaud!

Gestern kam mir der Neusletter der Society for Social Responsibility in Science vom Dezember 1958 (No. 80) in die Hand. Ich habe ihn mit grösstem Interesse gelesen und möchte Einiges selbst dazu sagen; zwar nicht öffentlich, wohl aber Ihnen mit der Bitte, diese Äusserungen bis zu gegebener Zeit aufzubewahren. Zu meinen Lebzeiten dürfen sie jedenfalls nicht weiteren Kreisen zugänglich gemacht werden.

In den Kritiken an Jungk's Buch *Heller als tausend Sonnen*, die jener Newsletter enthält, fällt mir nämlich auf dass sie alle die Gruppe der deutschen Kernphysiker, die im zweiten Weltkriege wirkten, wie eine Einheit betrachten; nur einmal wird eine versuchte Sonderaktion Heisenbergs erwähnt (von Edward Condon) [Condon was an American physicist who had been at Los Alamos.] Tatsächlich waren doch aber die Meinungen individuel verschieden, wie sich das ja von selbst versteht. Aus diesem Grund möchte ich Ihnen hier berichten, was aus der Zeit des Zweiten Weltkrieges und darauf folgenden Gefangenschaft mir in Erinnerung geblieben ist. Ich bin überzeugt, dass mein Gedächtnis noch recht gut ist. Ausserdem habe ich nicht allzuviel zu berichten.

Wie Sie wissen, habe ich nie den Ehrgeiz gehabt, Kernphysiker zu sein; erst die West-Alliierten haben mich 1945 dazu ernannt. Einmal wurde ich—ich weiss nicht mehr ob 1941 oder 1942—zu einer Sitzung des "Uranvereins" in Berlin zugezogen und hatte da nur den Eindruck einer etwas komischen Geheimhaltung (Uran wurde nur als "Metall" in den Diskussionen bezeichnet) sonst den einer ziemlich planlos verfahrenen Sache. Daran änderte sich nicht viel nach der

385

Verlagerung des Kaiser-Wilhelm Institutes für Physik nach Hechingen. Allerdings war ich einmal in dem Felsenkeller in Haigerloch, der den versuchten Uranpile vor den Bomben schützen sollte. Aber was ich dort erfuhr, änderte nichts an dem geschilderten Eindruck.

Nach der Besetzung Hechingens durch die Franzosen und des Kaiser-Wilhelm Institutes durch das Unternehmen Groves (Alsos) untersuchten Mitglieder des Letzeren das Institut nach Unterlagen für die vermutete Entwicklung unserer Deutschen in Richtung auf die Atombombe, fanden aber nicht viel. Nur die Vorräte schweren Wassers die in Haigerloch versteckt worden waren fanden sie bald. Sie teilten unseren Institutsmitgliedern dies aber nicht mit sondern sie veranstalten ein Verhör über den Verbleib dieses Wassers, an dem Otto Hahn, Weizsäcker, Wirtz sicher aber Bagge und ich teilnehmen mussten. Nur Wirtz und Weizsäcker waren von Heisenberg (der vorher an den Walchensee gegangen war) in das Geheimnis des Verstecks eingeweiht worden, sodass das ganze Gespräch sich zwischen zwei Alliierten Offizieren und diesen Beiden abspielte. Und nun geschah etwas sehr Unerfreuliches. Beide Weizsäcker und Wirtz leugneten etwas darüber zu wissen. Erst nach stundenlangem Ausweichen auf alle möglichen Vorwände gabe[n] sie endlich zu, wo der Versteck sich befand. Worauf die Alliierten erwiderten: "Das stimmt, wir haben es nämlich schon seit einigen Tagen gefunden."

In der darauf folgenden Gefangenschaft wurde von Kerphysik und Atombomben kaum gesprochen, wenigstens nichts, was mir in Erinnerung gebleiben wäre. Wir glaubten alle die Herstellung der Bombe wäre an anderen Stellen ebensowenig gelungen, wie bei uns. Als am 6. August 1945 mittags die British Broadcasting Corporation in London verkündete, dass eine Atombombe über Hiroshima abgeworfen wäre, hielten wir es für einen Propaganda Trick. Allerdings versammelten wir uns Alle des Abends um den Rundfunkapparat und hörten dort die Ansprache Attlees, der eine noch von Winston Churchill aufgesetze Erklärung verlas, aus der zweifelsfrei hervorging, dass es sich um eine wirkliche Uran-Bombe handelte. Der Eindruck war natürlich bei uns Allen ein ungeheurer.

Aber er war doch individuell sehr verschieden. Otto Hahn sagte tief erschüttert: "Damit habe *ich* nichts zu tun." Der englische Major Rittner der uns mit Captain Brodie zusammen buachte [sic] und betreute, rief mich zu einem Gespräch unter 4 Augen beiseite und bat mich dafür zu sorgen, dass sich Hahn kein Leid antäte. Ich erwiderte, dass ich in der Beziehung gar keine Besorgnis habe, ich aber bei Gerlach für nötig hielte, ihn in dieser Nacht etwas zu überwachen. Ich sprach in demselben Sinne mit Heisenberg und Weizsäcker, die gemeinsam ein dem Gerlachschen benachbartes Schlafzimmer bewohnten. Sie dachten über Gerlachs Gemütszustand ruhiger, obwohl dieser einen richtigen Nervenzusammenbruch mit vielen Tränen gehabt hatte. Sie behielten zum Glück recht.

Nach diesem Tage war viel, von den Bedingungen für eine Atomexplosion bei uns die Rede. Heisenberg trug darüber in einem der physikalischen Kolloquien vor, die wir Gefangen uns eingerichtet hatten. Allmählich entwickelte sich dann auch, in Tisch-Gesprächen, die Lesart, die deutschen Kernphysiker hatten die Atombombe gar nicht haben wollen, sei es, weil sie es während der zu erwartenden Kriegsdauer für unmöglich hielten, sei es, weil sie überhaupt nicht wollten. Führend war bei diesen Diskussionen war [sic] Weizsäcker. Ethische Gesichtspunke habe ich dabei nicht gehört. Heisenberg sass zumeist stumm dabei.

Soweit mein Bericht. Das zitierte Buch von Jungk habe ich nur stückweise gelesen und dann mit dem Bemerken fortgelegt, dass ich in ihm viel nachweislich Unrichtiges gefunden habe und mich daher auch auf das Andere nicht verliesse. Ich wundere mich jetzt, dass es bei Amerikanern vielfach eine so milde Kritik gefunden hat, wie es jener Newsletter erkennen lässt.

Mit recht herzlichem Gruss
Ihr
M. v Laue

TRANSLATION

PROF. DR. MAX VON LAUE
Berlin-Dahlem April 4, 1959
Faradayweg 8
Tel:76 45 86

To: Dr. Paul Rosbaud
7 Ashley Garden, Westminster
London SW 1 (England)

Dear Rosbaud!

Yesterday it happened that I read the newsletter of the Society for Social Responsibility in Science of December 19 (No. 80). I read it with the greatest of interest, and I should like to say something in connection with it, not for the public but to you with the request that you keep this letter private until the appropriate time. It should not be read by wider circles as long as I live. [*Von Laue died in 1960 in an automobile accident.*]

In the reviews of Jungk's book *Brighter Than a Thousand Suns* which appear in this newsletter, it strikes me that all the reviewers treat the German nuclear physicists who were active during the Second World War as a unified group. Only once is an attempted individual action by Heisenberg mentioned (by Edward Condon). In fact, each individual opinion was different, which is natural, of course. For this reason I wish to report here what I remember about the time of the Second World War and the captivity which followed. I am convinced that my memory is still pretty good.

Anyhow, I do not have much to report. I never had the ambition to be a nuclear physicist, as you know. Only the Western Allies made me one, in 1945. Only once— I do not remember whether it was in 1941 or 1942—was I invited to a meeting of the Uranium Club in Berlin, where my impression was of a somewhat comically kept secret—and otherwise of a rather aimlessly muddled affair. (In the discussion, uranium was mentioned only as "metal.") Much was changed after the Kaiser-Wilhelm Institute was moved to Hechingen. Once I visited the cave in Haigerloch, where the experimental pile of uranium was supposed to be protected from the bombs. But my previous impression was not changed by what I saw there.

After the occupation of Hechingen by the French and of the Kaiser-Wilhelm Institute by the action group Alsos, members of the latter searched the institute for the assumed German development of the atomic bomb. But they did not find much: they only found the supply of heavy water that had been hidden in Haigerloch. But they did not tell that to us members of the institute and commenced an interrogation, about the water, in which Otto Hahn, Weizsäcker and, I believe, also Bagge had to participate. Heisenberg (who had previously gone to the Walchen Lake) had initiated only Wirtz and Weizsäcker into the secret of the hiding place, so the entire conversation was conducted between two Allied officers and those two. Then something very unpleasant happened. Both Weizsäcker and Wirtz pretended to know nothing about it. After an hour-long fencing and all sorts of subterfuges, they finally admitted to knowing where the hiding place was, whereupon the Allies responded, "That's correct; we found it several days ago."

Atomic physics and atomic bombs were hardly mentioned during the time of our captivity, at least not as far as I remember. We all believed that, as with us, nowhere had the production of the bomb been successfully achieved. We thought it was a propaganda trick when the BBC in London reported on August 6, 1945 that an atomic bomb had been dropped on Hiroshima. But in the evening we all assembled around the radio and heard Attlee's speech, who read a declaration that was composed by Winston Churchill, and then there was no doubt that there was a true uranium bomb. Of course, our reaction was tremendous.

But it was very different with each person. Otto Hahn said, deeply shaken, "I had nothing to do with that." The English Major Rittner, who together with Captain Brodie guarded us and took care of us, called me in for a talk tête-à-tête and asked me to make sure that Hahn did not do any harm to himself. I responded that I had no fear in this respect at all, but that I thought it necessary to keep a check on Gerlach during the night. In the same sense I spoke with Heisenberg and Weizsäcker, who shared a bedroom next to Gerlach. They judged Gerlach's mental condition more benign, though he seemed to have a real nervous breakdown, with many tears. Fortunately, they were correct.

After that day we talked much about the conditions of an atomic explosion. Heisenberg gave a lecture on the subject in one of the colloquia which we prisoners had arranged for ourselves. Later, during the table conversation, the version was developed that the German atomic physicists really had not wanted the atomic bomb, either because it was impossible to achieve it during the expected duration of the war or because they simply did not want to have it at all. [*The German word being translated here for "version" is* <u>*Lesart*</u>. *The dictionary definition of Lesart is "version" or "reading." The sense of von Laue's statement seems clear. He is explaining the circumstances in which the "spin" that the Germans gave their version of the history of their wartime activities in nuclear physics arose.*] The leader in these discussions was Weizsäcker. I not did hear the mention of any ethical point of view. Heisenberg was mostly silent.

That's my report. I read the book by Jungk only in parts and put it away because I found so much that could be proven incorrect, and thus could not rely on the rest. I am surprised that the criticism by the Americans is so mild, as can be gathered from the newsletter.

Very cordial greetings,
Yours
M. v. Laue

2. Max von Laue to Paul Rosbaud, Berlin-Dahlem, 17 April 1959

PROF.DR.MAX VON LAUE
Berlin-Dahlem, den 17.4.59
Faradayweg 8
Tel:76 45 86

Lieber Rosbaud!

Haben Sie allerherzlichsten Dank für Ihre freundliche Antwort vom 12.4.59. Ich möchte meinen vorhergehenden Brief heute etwas ergänzen. Während ich diesen, um ihn vor unbefugten Lesern zu sicheren, in Charlottenburg 2 aufgab, nehme ich den heutigen morgen [sic] mit auf eine Reise nach der Bundesrepublik. Dort ist er jedenfalls sehr sicher; denn viel mehr als den Postbestellbezirk Steglitz, zu dem Dahlem gehört, können jene Leser denn doch nicht überwachen, um auf meine Briefe Jagd zu machen. Das war schon unter Hitler so. Nun, Sie kennen das ja.

In der von Ende April 1945 bis Anfang Januar 1946 dauernden Gefangenschaft hatte ich am Meisten zu leiden unter meinen Mitgefangenen, inbesondere unter Weizsäcker. Der kam schon mit einem Vorurteil gegen mich in jene Zeit hinein, sie verstärkte sich bei dem Verhör wegen des schweren Wassers, von dem ich das letzte Mal schrieb, und brach in offene Feindschaft aus, als ich in den ersten Tagen, die uns der Englische Major Rittner bewachte, in Hinblick auf die Röhm-Affäre und den "Sieg" Hitlers den Busch-Vers zitierte: "Der grösste Lump bleibt obenauf." Darauf wurde Weizsäcker sogleich ausfallend, sagte u.A. einen solchen Ausdruck nehme man überhaupt nicht in den Mund u.s.w.

Seinen Einfluss, den er ja auf Jeden auszudehenen versteht, der gerade die Macht hat, schreibe ich es zu, dass Rittner, sonst ein ganz freundlicher Mann, ein paar Tag später vom Militarismus der Deutschen zu sprechen anfing, wobei ich ihm, wie Ihnen schon bekannt, erwiderte, der Satz "Right or wrong, my Country" stamme jedenfalls nicht aus Deutschland. Ich sagte das etwas erregt und mit lauter Stimme, und dies hat mir Rittner nie verziehen. So hatte Weizsäcker sein Ziel erreicht und Unfrieden zwischen Rittner und mir hervorgerufen. Auch Andere wendeten sich gegen mich. Dr. Horst Korsching nannte mich einmal einen "Verräter." (Korsching war als Assistent Heisenbergs mit in die Gefangenschaft gekommen). Aber recht schlimm würde die Lage erst, als der stimmgewaltige Kollege Gerlach zu uns stiess-das geschah est im Juni, in Faqueval (Belgien). Der hatte anscheinend geheimes Material aus deutschen Heeresbeständen gegen mich mitgebracht, sodass nun der erboste Rittner auch darauf zurückgreifen konnte. Gerlach hatte schon in der Kriegszeit eine Wut auf mich gefasst, weil ich ihm auf seinen Ausruf: "Wir *müssen* siegen" die Antwort verweigert hatte. Gerlach hetzte auch unsere Burschen, deutsche Kriegsgefangene, gegen mich auf. Einmal gab ich eine Hose dem einen Burschen zum Bügeln und erhielt sie mit zwei grossen Brandflecken zurück, sodass ich sie nie wieder tragen konnte; das war angeblich "aus Versehen" geschehen.

Nun das Alles ist nun vergeben und vergessen, auch, dass Gerlach mir die ganze Zeit nach der Gefangenschaft Schwierigkeiten innerhalb des Verbandes Deutscher Physikalischer Gesellschaften machte. Namentlich hetzte er die Süddeutschen Kollegen mir auf, weil ich angeblich ein Vorurteil gegen sie habe. Die Wahrheit ist, dass er selbst sich manchmal recht abfällig über "die Preussen" geäussert hat. Wie es unter seinem (und Karl Wolfs) Einfluss mit den von Westphal und mir entworfenen Satzungen des Verbandes gegangen ist, muss ich Ihnen einmal mündlich erzählen. Die Hauptsache ist: Sie wurden nach jahrelangen Mühen schliesslich von der Mitgliederversammlung angenommen.

Entschuldigen Sie bitte diesen Herzenserguss. Ich muss dabei denken an Einsteins Antwort an eine ihm Unbekannte, die ihm ihr Herzleid aus Schulzeit berichtete. Er riet ihr dringend von der beabsichtigten Veröffentlichung ab, weil Jeder, der sich über vergangene Leiden beklagt, in ein schiefes Licht geriete. Aber Sie werden die Sache schon richtig auffassen.

Mit herzlichem Gruss
Ihr
M v. Laue

TRANSLATION

PROF. DR. MAX VON LAUE
Berlin-Dahlem, April 17, 1959
Faradayweg 8
Tel.: 76 45 86

Dear Rosbaud!

My heartfelt thanks for your friendly response of the 12th of April 1959. I have something that I want to add today to my earlier letter. In order to secure it from unauthorized readers, I mailed that one in Charlottenburg 2 [*in West Berlin*]. I am going to take this one on a trip to the Federal Republic tomorrow. There, it is in any case much more secure than in the Steglitz Postal District to which Dahlem belongs, and where anyone, authorized or not, can read my letters. That is the way it was under Hitler. Now you know it all.

In the captivity from the end of 1945 to the beginning of January 1946, I suffered most from my co-prisoners, particularly from Weizsäcker. At that time he was already prejudiced against me. The prejudice became stronger during the [*Alsos*] interrogation about the heavy water and became open hostility when I quoted the Busch verse [*a reference to the humorist Wilhelm Busch*], "The biggest scoundrel always comes out on top" in reference to the Röhm affair [*Ernst Röhm, head of Hitler's Storm Troopers (SA), was assassinated in the so-called Röhm Putsch, Hitler's 1934 liquidation of the SA.*] and Hitler's victory [*in it*]. It happened in the first days that British Major Rittner guarded us. Right away, Weizsäcker became aggressive and said, among other things, that one does not even use such expressions, and so on.

I attribute it to his influence, which he [*Weizsäcker*] knows how to use with everybody who happens to be in power. Rittner, basically quite a friendly man, started to talk about German militarism. As you already know, I responded, using the original English "Right or wrong, my country" was not formulated in Germany. I said it rather excitedly and in a loud voice. Rittner never forgave me for that. Dr. Horst Korsching called me "traitor" once. As Heisenberg's assistant Korsching had become a prisoner. The situation became really bad when the loud-mouthed Gerlach joined us. That happened at Faqueval (Belgium).

It seems he had brought some materials against me from German army files so that Rittner could use them. Gerlach was already furious with me because during wartime I had properly not responded to his statement "We must be victorious." [*This was presumably a reference to von Laue's lack of enthusiasm for Hitler's war.*]

Gerlach also incited our batmen against me. Once I gave a pair of trousers to one of them for ironing and received them back with large burned spots so that I could not wear them anymore. It happened by "mistake."

Now all of that is forgiven and forgotten. The whole time after our internment Gerlach made difficulties for me within the Association of German Physical Societies. Namely he stirred up the animosity of our south-German colleagues against me, because I allegedly had a prejudice against them. The truth is that he himself sometimes expressed himself quite conspicuously about "the Prussians" [*a term Bavarians used contemptuously to refer to all north Germans*]. I'll have to tell you verbally sometime how it went under his (and Karl Wolf's) influence with the statutes of the Association drawn up by Westphal and me. The main thing is: After a year-long effort the statutes were finally adopted by the members' meeting.

Please excuse this emotional outburst. I must think of what Einstein replied to an unknown person who told him of her difficulties during her school years. He strongly advised her against publishing, saying that everybody who complains about past sufferings is cast personally in a poor light. But you will understand me correctly.

With heartfelt greetings
Yours
M v. Laue

APPENDIX 3

[Following is the transcript from the August 6, 1945 BBC report announcing the use of the bomb, supplied courtesy of the BBC Written Archives Centre.]

Monday,
August 6th 1945
9:00 P.M.

Here is the News:

It's dominated by a tremendous achievement of Allied scientists—the production of the atomic bomb. One has already been dropped on a Japanese army base. It alone contained as much explosive power as two-thousand of our great ten-tonners. President Truman has told how the bombs were made in secret American factories, and has foreshadowed the enormous peace-time value of this harnessing of atomic energy. A statement by Mr. Churchill (written before the change of Government) has described the early work on the project in this country, and told the story of its development.

Field Marshal Montgomery and General Eisenhower have told the German people of coming relaxations in the second stage of Military Government and have called on them to help to get their country on its feet again.

A Prince and five Generals have given evidence for the Defense in the Petain trial.

At home, it's been a Bank Holiday of sunshine and thunderstorms; a record crowd at Lord's has seen Australia make 273 for 5 wickets. The news ends with a sound picture of London on holiday.

The greatest destructive power devised by man went into action this morning—the atomic bomb. British, American, and Canadian scientists have succeeded, where Germans failed, in harnessing the basic power of the universe; at present it's being used for war purposes, but it's expected that further research may make this atomic energy available as a source of power to supplement coal, oil, and hydroelectric plants.

The bomb, dropped today on the Japanese war base of Hiroshima, was designed for a detonation equal to twenty-thousand tons of high explosive—that's two-thousand times the power of the R.A.F.'s ten-ton bomb. There's no news yet of what devastation was caused—reconnaissance aircraft couldn't see anything hours later because of the tremendous pall of smoke and dust that was still obscuring the city of once over three-hundred-thousand inhabitants.

President Truman made the announcement about the new bomb from Washington this afternoon. He said that it would help shorten the war. The Potsdam ultimatum was issued on July 26th to spare the Japanese people from utter destruction. The Japanese leader rejected the ultimatum promptly. "Now," he said, "if the Japanese don't accept our terms they may expect a rain of ruin from the air the like of which has never been seen on this earth."

The Allies have spent five-hundred-million pounds on what President Truman calls the greatest scientific gamble in history—and they've won. British, Canadian, and American scientists worked together on it; on the decision of Mr. Churchill and the late President Roosevelt, the factories to make the bombs were built in the United States because Britain was still under air attack and threat of invasion at the time, in 1942.

Up to a hundred-and-twenty-five-thousand people helped to build the factories, and sixty-five-thousand people are running them now. Few of them knew what they were producing; they could see huge quantities of materials going in, and nothing coming out—for the size of the explosive charge is very small. In some factories the workers went into a sort of voluntary internment for the sake of secrecy; and their families lived with them in barracks.

In the past few hours many stories have been coming out about the scientific work allied with the release of atomic energy. Mr. Stimson, American Secretary for War, announces that *uranium* is used in making the bomb, and steps have been taken to make sure of an adequate supply of it. Mr. Stimson says scientists are confident that the atomic bomb can be developed still further. The fact that atomic energy can be released on a large scale will mean that it will ultimately be used in peace-time industry; but this will mean a lot of research in building the machines to use this power.

A statement by the Prime Minister from 10 Downing Street tonight deals with the part *this* country has played in the new discovery. Mr. Attlee says: "Before the change of Government Mr. Churchill had prepared this statement which follows, and I am now issuing it in the form in which he wrote it."

(Here it is:)

By the year 1939 it had become widely recognized among scientists of many nations that the release of energy by atomic fission was a possibility. The problems which remained to be solved before this possibility could be turned into practical achievement were, however, manifold and immense; and few scientists would at that time have ventured to predict that an atomic bomb could be ready for use by 1945. Nevertheless, the potentialities of the project were so great that His Majesty's Government thought it right that research should be carried on in spite of the many competing claims on our scientific man-power. At this stage the research was carried out mainly in our universities, principally Oxford, Cambridge, London (Imperial College), Liverpool, and Birmingham. At the time of the formation of the Coalition Government, responsibility for coordinating the work and pressing it forward lay in the Ministry of Aircraft Production, advised by a Committee of leading scientists presided over by Sir George Thomson.

At the same time, under the general arrangements then in force for the pooling of scientific information, there was a full interchange of ideas between the scientists carrying out this work in the United Kingdom and those in the United States.

Such progress was made that by the summer of 1941 Sir George Thomson's Committee was able to report that, in their view, there was a reasonable chance that an atomic bomb could be produced before the end of the war. At the end of August 1941 Lord Cherwell, whose duty it was to keep me informed on all these and other technical developments, reported the substantial progress which was being made. The general responsibility for the scientific research carried on under the various technical committees lay with the then Lord President of the Council, Sir John Anderson. In these circumstances (having in mind also the effect of ordinary high-explosive which we had recently experienced), I referred the matter on August 30th, 1941, to the Chiefs of Staff Committee in the following minute:

"General Ismay for Chiefs of Staff Committee. Although personally I am quite content with the existing explosives, I feel we must not stand in the path of improvement, and I therefore think that action should be taken in the sense proposed by Lord Cherwell, and that the Cabinet Minister responsible should be Sir John Anderson. I shall be glad to know what the Chiefs of Staff Committee think."

The Chiefs of Staff recommended immediate action with the maximum priority.

It was then decided to set up within the Department of Scientific and Industrial Research a special division to direct the work, and Imperial Chemical Industries, Ltd. agreed to release Mr. W. A. Akers to take charge of this Directorate, which we called, for the purposes of secrecy, the Directorate of "Tube Alloys." After Sir John Anderson had ceased to be Lord President and became Chancellor of the Exchequer, I asked him to continue to supervise this work, for which he has special qualifications. To advise him, there was set up under his chairmanship a consultative council composed of the President of the Royal Society, the Chairman of the Scientific Advisory Committee of the Cabinet, the Secretary of the Department of Scientific and Industrial Research, and Lord Cherwell. The Minister of Aircraft Production at that time, Lord Brabazon, also served on this committee.

Under the chairmanship of Mr. Akers, there was also a technical committee on which sat the scientists who were directing the different sections of the work and some others. This committee was originally composed of Sir James Chadwick, Professor Peierls, and Drs. Halban, Simon, and Slade. Later it was joined by Sir

Charles Darwin and Professors Cockcroft, Oliphant, and Feather. Full use was also made of university and industrial laboratories.

On Oct. 11th, 1941, President Roosevelt sent me a letter suggesting that any extended efforts on this important matter might usefully be coordinated or even jointly conducted. Accordingly all British and American efforts were joined and a number of British scientists concerned proceeded to the United States. Apart from these contacts, complete secrecy guarded all these activities and no single person was informed whose work was not indispensable to progress.

By the summer of 1942 this expanded program of research had confirmed with surer and broader foundations the promising forecasts which had been made a year earlier, and the time had come when a decision must be made whether or not to proceed with the construction of large-scale production plants. Meanwhile it had become apparent from the preliminary experiments that these plants would have to be on something like the vast scale described in the American statements which have been published today.

Great Britain, at this period, was fully extended in war production and we could not afford such grave interference with the current munitions programs on which our war-like operations depended. Moreover, Great Britain was within easy range of German bombers and the risk of raiders from the sea or air could not be ignored. The United States, however, where parallel or similar progress had been made, was free from these dangers. The decision was therefore taken to build the full-scale production plants in America. In the United States the erection of the immense plants was placed under the responsibility of Mr. Stimson, United States Secretary of War, and the American Army administration, whose wonderful work and marvelous secrecy cannot be sufficiently admired. The main practical effort and virtually the whole of its prodigious cost now fell upon the United States authorities, who were assisted by a number of British scientists. The relationship of the British and American contributions was regulated by discussions between the late President Roosevelt and myself, and a combined policy committee was set up.

The Canadian Government, whose contribution was most valuable, provided both indispensable raw material for the project as a whole and also necessary facilities for the work on one section of the project which has been carried out in Canada by the three Governments in partnership.

The smoothness with which the arrangements for a cooperation which were made in 1943 have been carried into effect is a happy augury for our future relations and reflects great credit on all concerned—on the members on the Combined Policy Committee which we set up; on the enthusiasm which our scientists and technicians gave of their best—particularly Sir James Chadwick who gave up his work at Liverpool to serve as technical adviser to the United Kingdom members of the Policy Committee and spared no effort; and not least on the generous spirit with which the whole United States organization welcomed our men and made it possible for them to make their contribution.

By God's mercy British and American science out paced all German efforts. These were on a considerable scale, but far behind. The possession of these powers by the Germans at any time might have altered the result of the war, and profound anxiety was felt by those who were informed. Every effort was made by our Intelligence Service and by the Air Force to locate in Germany anything resembling the plants which were being created in the United States. In the winter of 1942/43 most gallant attacks were made in Norway on two occasions by small parties of volunteers from the British Commandoes and Norwegian forces, at very heavy loss of life, upon stores of what is called "heavy water," an element in one of the possible processes. The second of these two attacks was completely successful.

The whole burden of execution including the setting-up of the plants and many technical processes connected therewith in the practical sphere, constitutes one of the greatest triumphs of American—or indeed human—genius of which there is a record. Moreover the decision to make these enormous expenditures upon a project which however hopefully established by American and British research remained nevertheless a heart-shaking risk, stands to the everlasting honor of President Roosevelt and his advisers.

It is now for Japan to realize in the glare of the first atomic bomb which has smitten her what the consequences will be of an indefinite continuance of this terrible means of maintaining a rule of law in the world.

This revelation of the secrets of Nature, long mercifully withheld from man, should arouse the most solemn reflections in the minds and conscience of every human being capable of comprehension. We must indeed pray that these awful agencies will be made to conduce to peace among nations, and that instead of wreaking measureless havoc upon the entire globe they may become a perennial fountain of world prosperity.

That is the end of Mr. Churchill's statement on the atomic bomb.

APPENDIX 4

Biographical Sketches of the Ten Detainees

ERICH BAGGE (1912–). Studied physics in Munich, Berlin and Leipzig, where he obtained his doctorate in nuclear physics with Werner Heisenberg in 1938. He continued to work with Heisenberg on nuclear theory as a postdoctoral researcher and an assistant until the outbreak of war, when he began work with Kurt Diebner for the research office of the Army Ordnance Bureau (*Heereswaffenamt*). In 1941, he joined the Kaiser-Wilhelm Institute (KWI) for Physics under Heisenberg, where he worked on isotope separation. 1946–1948, assistant at the Max Planck Institute (MPI) for Physics directed by Heisenberg in Göttingen; 1948–1957, associate professor of physics at the University of Hamburg; 1957 until retirement, professor of pure and applied nuclear physics at the University of Kiel and collaborator with Diebner on the construction of nuclear-powered ships.

KURT DIEBNER (1905–1964). Studied experimental physics in Innsbruck and in Halle with Heisenberg's future Leipzig colleague, experimental physicist Gerhard Hoffmann, receiving his doctorate in 1931. 1931–1934, assistant professor in physics at the University of Halle. In 1934 he became a staff member of the German Bureau of Standards (*Physikalisch-Technische Reichsanstalt* in Berlin and joined the Army Weapons Bureau where he headed the research section for nuclear physics and explosives. 1939–1942, administered German uranium research at the KWI for Physics, when he was replaced by Heisenberg after the Army relinquished command of the institute. 1942–1945, performed reactor research at the Army's research station in Berlin-Gottow and in Stadtilm, Thuringia. 1946–1948, private work on electrical instruments. 1948–1964, active in private industry in Hamburg, especially in the development of nuclear-powered commerical ships.

WALTHER GERLACH (1889–1979). Studied physics at the University of Tübingen, where he received his doctorate in 1911. After serving in the German Army during World War I, he taught at the University of Frankfurt am Main, 1920–1924, where he performed a series of famous experiments in quantum physics with Otto Stern. 1924–1929, professor at Tübingen; 1929–1957, professor at the University of Munich. In 1944–1945, he served as the "plenipotentiary," or administrative head, of German nuclear research under the Reich Research Council, overseeing both Heisenberg's and Diebner's reactor experiments.

OTTO HAHN (1879–1968). Studied chemistry at the universities of Marburg and Munich, receiving his doctorate from Marburg in 1901. 1901–1904, lecturer at the University of Marburg; 1904–1906, postdoctoral researcher with Sir William Ramsey, University College London, and with Ernest Rutherford, McGill University, Montréal. 1906–1911, assistant professor at the University of Berlin; 1911–1928, head of the radiochemistry section at the KWI for Chemistry in Berlin; 1928–1945, director of the institute. Served at the front during World War I as a German Army chemical warfare specialist. 1947–1960, president of the Max Planck Society and leading figure in West German science policy. In 1945 he was awarded the Nobel Prize for Chemistry for the year 1944 for his work on the discovery of nuclear fission.

PAUL HARTECK (1902–1985). Studied chemistry and physics in Vienna and Berlin, obtaining his doctorate in 1926. 1926–1933, member of the KWI for Physical Chemistry in Berlin; 1934–1951, professor of physical chemistry at the University of Hamburg. 1951–1968, professor at the Rensselaer Polytechnic Institute in Troy, New York. During the war he worked on heavy-water production and reactor construction.

WERNER HEISENBERG (1901–1976). Studied physics in Munich and Göttingen, receiving his doctorate in theoretical physics with Arnold Sommerfeld in 1923. 1924–1927, postdoctoral researcher in Göttingen (with Max Born) and Copenhagen (with Niels Bohr), where he helped found and establish quantum mechanics. Received the Nobel Prize for Physics in 1933 (for 1932). 1927–1942, professor of theoretical physics at the University of Leipzig; 1942–1945, head of the KWI for Physics in Berlin and Hechingen and professor at the University of Berlin, during which time he directed Germany's main fission-research effort. 1946–1970, director of the MPI for Physics in Göttingen and (after 1958) in Munich, and a leading figure in West German science policy.

HORST KORSCHING (1912–). Received his doctorate at the University of Berlin in 1938. Worked with Peter Debye at the KWI for Physics in Berlin. During the war, he researched isotope separation techniques under Diebner and Heisenberg at the KWI in Berlin and Hechingen. After the war, he was a scientific co-worker at the MPI for Physics directed by Heisenberg in Göttingen and later Munich.

MAX VON LAUE (1879–1960). Studied physics in Strasbourg, Munich, and Berlin, receiving his doctorate with Max Planck in 1903. 1903–1912, assistant and postdoctoral researcher in Göttingen, Berlin and Munich, where he inaugurated the research on x rays that led to his Nobel Prize for Physics in 1914. 1912–1914, professor of physics in Zurich; 1914–1919, professor in Frankfurt am Main, and 1919–1943, professor at the University of Berlin and Vice Director of the KWI for Physics (until 1945). Von Laue did not actually engage in any war-related research during World War II.

CARL FRIEDRICH VON WEIZSÄCKER (1912–). Studied physics in Berlin, Copenhagen and Leipzig, where he received his doctorate in theoretical physics with Heisenberg in 1933. 1933–1936, assistant with Heisenberg; 1936–1942, member of the KWI for Physics in Berlin. 1942–1944, professor at the University of Strasbourg in Nazi-occupied France, then associated with the KWI for Physics in Hechingen. 1946–1957, scientific co-worker of the MPI for Physics headed by Heisenberg in Göttingen. 1957–1970, professor of philosophy at the University of Hamburg; 1970–1980, director of the MPI for Research on Living Conditions of the Scientific-Technological World.

KARL WIRTZ (1910–). Studied physics in Bonn, Freiburg and Breslau, receiving his doctorate in 1934. 1935–1937, assistant in physical chemistry to Karl Friedrich Bonhoeffer in Leipzig and, 1937–1945, at the KWI for Physics in Berlin and Hechingen. 1948–1957, professor of physics in Göttingen; 1957 until retirement, professor in Karlsruhe and head of the Nuclear Research Center in Karlsruhe. An expert on heavy water and isotope separation.

SELECTED BIBLIOGRAPHY

This is by no means a complete listing. Items have been selected for their general interest or historical significance, with preference given to English-language sources and translations, where available. The emphasis is on the German nuclear program with secondary emphasis on the Manhattan Project for comparison. Comments are descriptive only.

Books and Document Collections

Badash, Lawrence, *Scientists and the Development of Nuclear Weapons: From Fission to the Limited Test Ban Treaty 1939–1963* (Humanities Press, Atlantic Highlands, N.J., 1995).

Bagge, Erich, Kurt Diebner, and Kenneth Jay, *Von der Uranspaltung bis Calder Hall* (Rowohlt, Hamburg, 1957). Contains excerpts from Bagge's diary while at Farm Hall.

Beyerchen, Alan D., *Scientists under Hitler: Politics and the Physics Community in the Third Reich* (Yale University, New Haven, 1977).

Bothe, Walther and Siegfried Flügge, editors, "Kerntechnik," in *Naturforschung und Medizin in Deutschland 1939–1946*, FIAT Review of German Science (Verlag Chemie, Weinheim, 1953), pp. 142–193. Summary technical articles on German wartime reactor research by Werner Heisenberg and Karl Wirtz; Otto Haxel; K.H. Höcker; and Paul Harteck.

Cassidy, David. *Uncertainty: The Life and Science of Werner Heisenberg* (W. H. Freeman, New York, 1992).

Ermenc, Joseph J., editor, *Atomic Bomb Scientists—Memoirs, 1939–1945* (Meckler, Westport, Conn., 1967). Interviews conducted by Ermenc.

Frank, Sir Charles, *Operation Epsilon: The Farm Hall Transcripts* (University of California Press, Berkeley, Calif. and Institute of Physics, Bristol, 1993). The unedited Farm Hall reports.

Gimbel, John, *Science, Technology, and Reparations: Exploitation and Plunder in Postwar Germany* (Stanford University Press, Stanford, 1990).

Goudsmit, Samuel A., *Alsos* (Henry Schuman, New York, 1947). Reissued with an introduction by R. V. Jones (Tomash, Los Angeles 1983); and with a new introduction by D. Cassidy (American Institute of Physics, New York, 1995).

Groves, Leslie R., *Now It Can be Told: The Story of the Manhattan Project*. 1962. Reissued with an introduction by Edward Teller (DaCapo, New York, 1983).

Heisenberg, Elisabeth, *Inner Exile: Recollections of a Life with Werner Heisenberg*, translated by S. Cappellari and C. Morris (Birkhäuser, Boston, 1984).

Heisenberg, Werner, *Physics and Beyond: Encounters and Conversations*, translated by Arnold J. Pomerans (Harper, New York, 1971). Not always reliable translation of Heisenberg's memoirs of conversations, originally published as *Der Teil und das Ganze* (Piper, Munich, 1969).

Heisenberg, Werner, "Papers on the Uranium Project," in *Heisenberg: Gesammelte Werke/Collected Works*, edited by W. Blum *et al.* (Springer, Berlin, 1989), Vol. A2, pp. 365–601. Publication in German of all of the extant declassified wartime research reports authored or co-authored by Heisenberg.

Heisenberg, Werner, "Die Physik im Dritten Reich und das Uranprojekt." in *Heisenberg: Gesammelte Werke/ Collected Works*, edited by W. Blum *et al.* (Piper, Munich, 1989), Vol. C5, pp. 1–52. Republication of 14 public statements, articles, and interviews on physics and uranium research during the Third Reich, 1936–67.

Hoddeson, Lillian, *et al.*, *Critical Assembly: A Technical History of Los Alamos during the Oppenheimer Years, 1943–1945* (Cambridge University Press, Cambridge, 1993).

Hoffmann, Dieter, editor, *Operation Epsilon: Die Farm Hall–Protokolle oder Die Angst der Allierten vor der deutschen Atombombe*, translated by Wilfried Sczepan (Rowohlt, Berlin, 1993). German retranslation of the English translations constituting the Farm Hall reports. Does not contain Heisenberg's important fission lecture of 14 August 1945.

Irving, David, *The Virus House* (Simon and Schuster, New York, 1967). Reissued as *The German Atomic Bomb: The History of Nuclear Research in Nazi Germany* [DaCapo, New York, n.d. (1982)].

Irving, David, editor, *Third Reich Documents*, Group 11: *German Atomic Research* (Microform Academic, Wakefield, England, 1966). Microfilms of numerous published and unpublished documents on German nuclear research assembled by Irving for his book, above.

Jones, Vincent C., *Manhattan, the Army and the Atomic Bomb* (Center of Military History, U.S. Army, Government Printing Office, Washington, D.C., 1985).

Jungk, Robert, *Brighter than a Thousand Suns: A Personal History of the Atomic Scientists*, translated by James Cleugh (Harcourt Brace Jovanovich, New York, 1958). Originally published as *Heller als tausend Sonnen* (Alfred Scherz, Bern,

Verlag, 1956). Promotes view that German scientists prevented a German atom bomb.

Kramish, Arnold, *The Griffin: The Greatest Untold Espionage Story of World War II* (Houghton Mifflin, Boston, 1986). The story of Paul Rosbaud.

Macrakis, Kristie, *Surviving the Swastika: Scientific Research in Nazi Germany* (Oxford University Press, New York, 1993).

Pais, Abraham, *Niels Bohr's Times* (Oxford University Press, Oxford, 1991).

Powers, Thomas, *Heisenberg's War: The Secret History of the German Atomic Bomb* (Jonathan Cape, London, 1993). Revives the Jungk thesis.

Rhodes, Richard, *The Making of the Atomic Bomb* (Simon and Schuster, New York, 1986). An authoritative account of the Manhattan Project.

Serber, Robert, *The Los Alamos Primer* (University of California Press, Berkeley, 1992). The basic primer on bomb physics for workers at Los Alamos in 1943.

Smyth, Henry DeWolf, *Atomic Energy for Military Purposes: The Official Report on the Development of the Atomic Bomb under the Auspices of the United States Government, 1940–1945* (Princeton University Press, Princeton, 1946). The first official account of bomb physics and the Manhattan Project.

Walker, Mark, *German National Socialism and the Quest for Nuclear Power, 1939–1949* (Cambridge University Press, New York, 1989).

Walker, Mark, *Nazi Science: Myth, Truth and the German Atomic Bomb* (Plenum, New York, 1995).

Williams, Robert C., and Philip L. Cantelon, editors, *The American Atom: A Documentary History of Nuclear Policies from the Discovery of Fission to the Present, 1939–1984* (University of Pennsylvania, Philadelphia, 1984).

Selected Essays, Reviews, and Commentary

Bernstein, Jeremy, "The Farm Hall Transcripts: The German Scientists and the Bomb," *The New York Review of Books* **39** (49) (13 August), 47–53 (1992).

Bernstein, Jeremy, "Revelations from Farm Hall," *Science* **259** (26 March), 1923–1926 (1993). Essay-review of Powers.

Cassidy, David, "Germany and the Bomb: New Evidence," *Scientific American* **268** (February) 120 (1993).

Cassidy, David, "Atomic Conspiracies," *Nature* (London) **363** (27 May), 311–312 (1993). Review of Powers.

Frank-Steiner, Vincent C. (nephew of Paul Rosbaud), "Legendenbildung begann in Farm Hall," *Physikalische Blätter* **49**, 268–269 (1993). Review of Hoffmann, with response by H. Rechenberg.

Goldberg, Stanley, "Inventing a Climate of Opinion: Vannevar Bush and the Decision to Build the Bomb," *Isis* **83**, 429–452 (1992).

Goudsmit, Samuel, "Heisenberg on the German nuclear power project," *Bulletin of the Atomic Scientists* **3**, 343 (1947). Response to Heisenberg, *Nature* article below.

Goudsmit, Samuel, "Werner Heisenberg (1901–1976)," *Yearbook of the American Philosophical Society* **1976**, 74–80.

Heisenberg, Werner, "Research in Germany on the Technical Application of Atomic Energy," *Nature* **160**, 211–215 (1947). Abridged translation of "Über die Arbeiten zur technischen Ausnutzung der Atomkernenergie in Deutschland," *Die Naturwissenschaften* **33**, 325–329 (1946). Facsimile reprint in *Heisenberg: Gesammelte Werke/Collected Works*, edited by W. Blum *et al.* (Springer, Berlin, 1984), Vol. B, pp. 414–418.

Himmelheber, Max, "Die deutschen Physiker und die Bombe," *Frankfurter Allgemeine Zeitung*, No. 155 (7 July 1990), p. 8. Letter to the editor.

Kaempffert, Waldemar (science editor), "Nazis spurned idea of an atomic bomb," *The New York Times*, December 28, 1948, p. 10. Interview with Heisenberg.

Klotz, Irving, "Germans at Farm Hall Knew Little of A-Bombs." *Physics Today* **46** (October), 11 (1993). Comment on discussion of critical mass at Farm Hall.

Kramish, Arnold, "Powers on Heisenberg: Embellishments on the *Lesart*," *American Scientist* **81**, 479–480 (1993).

Laue, Max von, "Die Kriegstätigkeit der deutschen Physiker," *Physikalische Blätter* **3**, 424–425 (1947). Response to Morrison essay, below.

Logan, Jonothan L., "Bomb maker or bomb breaker?," *The Boston Globe*, March 7, 1993, pp. B43–B45. Review of Powers.

Logan, Jonothan L., Helmut Rechenberg, Max Dresden, and A. van der Ziel, "Heisenberg, Goudsmit and the German 'A-Bomb,'" *Physics Today* **44** (5) (May), 13, 15, 90–96 (1991). Letters to the Editor in response to Walker, below, with a reply by Walker.

Logan, Jonothan L. and Robert Serber, "Heisenberg and the bomb," *Nature* **362** (11 March), 117 (1993).

Lurçat, François, "La bombe nucléaire allemande et la révision de l'histoire," *Les Temps Modernes* **50**, 118–143 (1995).

Morrison, Philip, "Alsos: The story of German scientists," *Bulletin of the Atomic Scientists* **3**, 354, 365 (1947). Essay-review of Goudsmit, *Alsos*.

Rose, Paul Lawrence, "Did Heisenberg Misconceive A-Bomb?," *Physics Today* **45** (2) (February), 126 (1992).

Sweet, William, "Uncertainties," *Bulletin of the Atomic Scientists* **49** (7) (September), 50–52 (1993). Review of Powers and Cassidy.

Walker, Mark, "Heisenberg, Goudsmit and the German Atomic Bomb," *Physics Today* **43** (1) (January), 52–60 (1990).

SUBJECT INDEX